Encyclopedia
of the Holy Grail

ALSO BY JEFFREY JOHN DIXON
AND FROM MCFARLAND

Goddess and Grail: The Battle for King Arthur's Promised Land (2017)

The Glory of Arthur: The Legendary King in Epic Poems of Layamon, Spenser and Blake (2014)

Encyclopedia of the Holy Grail

JEFFREY JOHN DIXON

McFarland & Company, Inc., Publishers
Jefferson, North Carolina

ISBN (print) 978-1-4766-8794-0
ISBN (ebook) 978-1-4766-4809-5

LIBRARY OF CONGRESS AND BRITISH LIBRARY
CATALOGUING DATA ARE AVAILABLE

Library of Congress Control Number 2022056418

© 2023 Jeffrey Dixon. All rights reserved

No part of this book may be reproduced or transmitted in any form or by any means, electronic or mechanical, including photocopying or recording, or by any information storage and retrieval system, without permission in writing from the publisher.

Front cover: Old chalice on stone (Shutterstock/F.J. CARNEROS), shafts of sunlight streaming through stained glass (Shutterstock/SueC)

Printed in the United States of America

*McFarland & Company, Inc., Publishers
Box 611, Jefferson, North Carolina 28640
www.mcfarlandpub.com*

In memory of my friends
Jill Dibling
(1946–2019)
and
Steven Harris
(1955–2022)

Here in our chamber of glass
Paved with marble, tinted rose
We will await the aeon's close
And watch the age of darkness pass.

Acknowledgments

Through five years of writing, I have been sustained by the support of my family and friends. Special thanks must go to Andy, Ben, Jon, Simon and Steve, for thoughtful and inspirational walks; to Jenny and Skye, for blessedness; to Del and Sum, for reminding me to be here now; and to Sharrisimo, for having been here with me for so many years, now faded into light.

Table of Contents

Acknowledgments	vi
Preface	1
Introduction: THE ABSENT PATH	3
The Encyclopedia	13
Afterword: Higher Mysteries: Grail Initiation as Twentieth Century Mythology	277
Appendix I: The Grail Chronology	309
Appendix II: The Medieval Grail Literature	312
Appendix III: The Company of the Grail: Some Twentieth Century Writers	319
Bibliography	321
Index	327

Preface

It was while I was researching and writing my two previously published books on the Grail legend—*Gawain and the Grail Quest* (2012) and *Goddess and Grail* (2017)—that I became aware of what I could only consider to be a scholarly anomaly: Although there exist useful A–Zs of the Arthurian legends and literature, there is no equivalent for the serious student of the Grail stories. In the absence of a *miglior fabbro* ("a better craftsman"), I set out to make one myself.

I use the term *miglior fabbro* advisedly, since the Anglo-American poet T.S. Eliot, borrowing it from Dante, used it as a dedication to his friend Ezra Pound, in tribute to the latter's inestimable help in editing Eliot's *The Waste Land* into the modernist masterpiece it would become. As Eliot explains in the Notes to his poem, *The Waste Land* borrows its title and much of its symbolism from the Grail legend. Moreover, Eliot draws explicitly on the theories of Grail origins put forward by the Arthurian scholar Jessie Laidlay Weston in her key work, *From Ritual to Romance*, which was published in 1920, two years before the publication of *The Waste Land*.

In an earlier work, *The Quest of the Holy Grail* (1913), Weston had set out clearly what she saw as the three principal theories of Grail origins, which she calls the Christian, the Folklore and the Ritual Theory. As I discuss in the Introduction, I think her threefold distinction is still useful, although the Folklore Theory would be better called the Celtic Background Theory; and the term Ritual Theory is too narrow to cover the plethora of alternative approaches which have flourished in the century since Weston wrote. I therefore speak of the Enchantment Theory, for it seems to be that just as a spell was believed to have fallen on King Arthur's Britain, so Grail scholarship itself has become enchanted.

It is for this reason that the reader will find, in addition to predictable entries on Galahad, the Fisher King and the Grail Castle, more unexpected headings such as "Adonis" and "Hyperborea." Scattered references throughout to pagan mysteries, Gnosticism, Christian mysticism and Nazi occultism are synthesized in an Afterword, which gives an overview of what I call the "twentieth century mythology" of Grail Initiation.

The main body of each entry, a retelling of the principal adventures attached to a character, a place or an object (including major variants), is designed to present the stories in a way that is accessible to everyone. Several of the longer entries are divided into subsections. The commentaries which follow some of the entries are intended to give a useful context and help to clarify some of the many mysterious and confusing aspects of the legend. The footnotes are intended for those who wish to check sources or follow up leads and, in many instances, they include quotations from the original texts. It is hoped that the encyclopedia will therefore be both a handbook for beginners and a useful reference for scholars.

And something more: The French philosopher Henry Corbin urged the importance of the "true" creative imagination for unearthing the secret of the Holy Vessel. He lamented that we have not yet undertaken what he calls a "hermeneutic" of the Grail—a coordinated and systematized interpretation of the legendary literature as a whole, similar to biblical exegesis. It is the sincere hope of this author that, by making the principal elements of the Book of the Grail easily accessible, this encyclopedia can be used as part of this undertaking.

Introduction

THE ABSENT PATH

> "Then they rode out from the castle and separated as they had decided amongst themselves, striking out into the forest one here, one there, wherever they saw it thickest and wherever path or track was absent."[1]

In the first episode of the BBC television series *Detectorists*, the viewer discovers what is perhaps the most important secret of the mysterious Grail legend, in an exchange between two metal detectorists: One, Andy (played by the writer/director of the series, Mackenzie Crook), believes that he knows the location of a Saxon treasure hoard; which his friend Lance (played by the actor Toby Jones, no relation to Indiana) claims is the Holy Grail of treasure hunting. No, replies Andy, *the Holy Grail* is the Holy Grail of treasure hunting.[2]

In this exchange we learn something very important: which is that the Holy Grail is not a specific *material object*, but a *symbol* of whatever is most sacred or, in the profane world, most desired.[3]

Nevertheless, in popular culture (as seen in modern retellings, often filtered through the lens of Hollywood), the Grail has become indelibly associated with the cup from which Jesus drank at the Last Supper, containing the wine that, by a miracle, becomes changed into blood—although, once again, the widespread belief that the Grail is a cup owes more to Spielberg's *Indiana Jones and the Last Crusade* than to the medieval texts, where it is more likely to be described as a serving dish or even a stone.

The name of the hero who successfully achieves the Grail Quest is likely to be remembered as Sir Galahad, thanks to modern versions inspired by Sir Thomas Malory and Tennyson, although older versions give us Perceval and even, in a German poem, the womanizing Gawain. But it is the virginal Galahad who has become a symbol of the purity required to achieve the most spiritual of knightly quests. The example of Galahad, like that of Christ, is hard for most of us to emulate—hence Raymond Chandler's honorable private eye Philip Marlowe describes himself as a "shop-soiled Galahad" as he pursues the Holy Grail of truth and justice down the mean streets of the modern metropolis; but he is "the best man in his world" as Galahad is the Best Knight in his.[4]

The Romance of Perceval

The exalted figure of Galahad is very unlike that of the naïve, sometimes foolish Perceval, who is the hero of the first literary version of the Grail Quest that has come down to us: the last romance written by a poet from the Champagne region, Chrétien de Troyes, whose work represents the high point of the first great flowering of Arthurian literature.

King Arthur, if in fact he ever had a historical existence, is presented in early chronicles as a Romano-British warlord leading the indigenous resistance to the encroachments of the Saxons, who would have to wait until his death (or passing) before creating the first English kingdoms in post-Roman Celtic Britain. Arthur features in Welsh poems and chronicles written in the centuries after he is believed to have lived, but his opponents are often supernatural rather than human, as exemplified by the first prose Arthurian tale, *Culhwch and Olwen*, usually dated from the eleventh century. Here we also find figures borrowed from medieval Irish literature; the extent of Irish influence on the development of the Grail legend will come to be an important object of scholarly enquiry and dispute from the nineteenth century onwards.

In the twelfth century a Welsh cleric, Geoffrey of Monmouth, writing in Latin, gave us the first complete account of the conception, birth, life and doubtful death of King Arthur, as part of a wider history of the Kings of Britain from the settlement of the island by Trojan refugees to the English conquest; it is Geoffrey who develops the prophetic figure of Merlin from the Welsh seer Myrddin.

Around the middle of the century, the Anglo-Norman Jerseyman Wace reworked Geoffrey's history into French verse, along the way introducing Arthur's Round Table and its fellowships of knights. With their help he brings the whole of the island of Britain and much of northwest Europe under his rule; it is in the great peace which follows that the wondrous adventures associated with Arthur's reign take place.

Writing around 1160–90, Chrétien produced five of the greatest medieval verse romances featuring the Knights of the Round Table, the last of which is the Romance of Perceval or the Story of the Grail (*Conte del Graal*). Here we are introduced to a rustic boy brought up by his widowed mother in a forest, who sets out to join King Arthur's court but ends up in a mysterious castle, whose king has been maimed by a wound through the thighs and spends his days fishing. In the hall of the Fisher King, he is presented with a sword which is destined to break, before witnessing a strange procession of objects illuminated by candle-light: a lance which bleeds; a golden, bejeweled serving dish (a *graal*) carried by a maiden; and a silver trencher or carving dish (a *tailleoir*). The procession passes into a back chamber; but, as dinner is served, the *graal* passes before them between each course.

Perceval is of course extremely curious about all this but says nothing because the man who knighted him taught him not to ask too many questions. He leaves the castle but later learns that, had he but asked about what he saw, the king (whom he has discovered is his cousin) would have been healed; because he did not do so, lands will be laid waste. Perceval is determined to find the castle again to put right his mistake. But, in the meantime, he learns that the *graal* is such a holy thing that the life of the Fisher King's aged father is sustained by a single Host (or consecrated wafer) served from it each day.

Chrétien died before finishing his poem, so that it had to be completed by others. But he had already set up the principal themes which would dominate the literature to come—the Broken Sword, the Bleeding Lance, the maimed Fisher King, the Waste Land, the Quest—and had hinted at the transformation of the *graal* into the Holy Grail.

But in Chrétien's poem there is no connection made between the mysterious objects seen in the Grail Procession and the Passion of Christ. It would be the Burgundian poet

Robert de Boron, writing in the last decade of the twelfth century, who would provide a back-story for the Grail: He identified it as the Vessel with which Christ made the sacrament of the Last Supper and in which Christ's disciple Joseph of Arimathea collected the Holy Blood.

But Robert de Boron for his part makes no attempt to explain the Bleeding Lance. That story is provided by the first of four poets who continued Chrétien's narrative where it breaks off: It is, we learn, the Lance with which the centurion Longinus pierced the side of Christ on the Cross. Moreover, as we discover from another continuator called Manessier, the blood that flowed from His side was collected in the Vessel, which was in turn covered by the silver trencher as it was transported to Britain by Joseph and Philosofine, Perceval's mother.

As for the sword with which Perceval was presented in the castle, it does break as predicted and is repaired by he who forged it. Perceval does indeed return to the castle, more than once in fact; and he does eventually remember to ask about what he sees there. The maimed Fisher King is healed and, when he dies soon afterward, Perceval succeeds him as ruler of the Grail Kingdom. The Romance of Perceval, it would seem, has been brought to a satisfactory conclusion.

If only things were that simple.

Anyone reading Chrétien's poem and the four continuations (which can now easily be done thanks to a superb English translation by Nigel Bryant) will soon notice that the anomalies start to pile up. No explanation is given, for example, as to why asking who was being served from the Grail in the back chamber would have brought about the healing of the maimed Fisher King; in fact, Manessier tells us that the healing comes about when the murder of the Fisher King's brother is avenged. The sword that killed the brother is also broken and has to be mended but, when another Knight of the Round Table (King Arthur's nephew Gawain) attempts but fails to do so at the request of the Grail King, the latter appears to be hale and whole; while there is now no mention of an aged father in a back chamber.

To make matters even more confusing, the Romance of Perceval is only one story of the Grail and not by any means the best known. The Welsh prose Romance of Peredur, whose relationship with Chrétien's poem is uncertain, has a Broken Sword and a Bleeding Spear and, as in Manessier, is a tale of vengeance; but instead of a wafer in a dish, it has a head on a bloody platter. However, the most important prose developments of the Grail legend would undoubtedly continue to be in French and would be roughly concurrent with the verse continuations.

The Prose Cycles

Robert de Boron's poem, which first introduced Joseph of Arimathea and explained the Grail as a relic of the Passion, was redacted into prose and continued by his or another's hand, in order to form a trilogy of romances which I refer to as the De Boron Cycle.

Here the story of the Grail's coming from the Holy Land to Britain is interwoven with the story of Merlin and the coming of Arthur, familiar from Geoffrey of Monmouth and Wace. A novel (and miraculous) explanation is given for the title of the Fisher King, who is presented as aged but not maimed. Merlin is deemed to have created the Round Table; it has an empty place where only the knight who is destined to achieve the Grail Quest can sit. Moreover, that knight, through Merlin's guidance, will bring an end to the enchantments which plague Logres (King Arthur's Britain).

The first two parts of the De Boron Cycle are also continued by another, highly martial and frequently allegorical, prose romance, which is so original that it is difficult to reconcile much of it with other Grail stories: The name of the hero is even given as Perlesvaus rather than the more familiar Perceval, although the same character is clearly intended. Perlesvaus' mother is the niece of Joseph of Arimathea so that, as is the case with de Boron, only one generation of the Grail family separates the Passion from the reign of King Arthur, several hundred years later. The Grail itself has five changes of form, the last of which is a chalice.

Equally original, but much more influential, is the *Queste del Saint Graal*, a story as full of allegory as the Romance of Perlesvaus but replacing that text's crusading spirit with Christian mysticism. Here, the Grail itself is both a relic of the Passion (the dish containing the Paschal lamb at the Last Supper) and a metaphor (it symbolizes the grace of the Holy Spirit). Although Perceval remains an important figure, it is Sir Lancelot's son Galahad who is destined to achieve the Quest. The *Queste* provokes a rewriting and continuation of an earlier prose Romance of Lancelot, in order to reveal the story of Galahad's begetting on the Grail Bearer, the daughter of the Fisher King. The Prose *Lancelot* and the *Queste*, when combined with an account of the final wars and death of King Arthur, provide the basis for a new cycle of romances, known, because of their popularity, as the Vulgate.

In order to complete the Vulgate Cycle, two further "histories" were written to act as prequels. The *Queste* contains numerous allusions to the prehistory of the Grail. These are now fleshed out and combined with the first part of the De Boron Cycle to form the Vulgate History of the Holy Grail (*Estoire del Saint Graal*), which traces the story of the sacred Vessel from the Passion to just before the birth of Merlin. It provides us with a detailed account of how Joseph of Arimathea and his companions brought the Grail from the Holy Land to Britain. It further explains the gap of several hundred years between the Passion and the reign of Arthur by positing a dynasty of Fisher Kings who guard the Vessel in a castle near the Welsh border, awaiting the Destined Knight.

The tale is continued in the Story of Merlin (*Estoire de Merlin*), retelling the account in the second part of the De Boron Cycle of Merlin's role as the Prophet of the Grail, including the creation of the Round Table with its Perilous Seat and the begetting of King Arthur, whom he assists in the wars to establish the sovereignty of Britain. The Lady of the Lake famously beguiles Merlin and brings about his magical disappearance from the world. But she then goes on to abduct and raise the infant Lancelot, thus linking the end of the *Estoire de Merlin* with the beginning of the Prose *Lancelot*.

The five parts of the Vulgate Cycle now eclipse the three parts of the De Boron Cycle; although Robert will continue to be invoked as an authority in order to justify the production of yet another prose cycle, usually known as the Post-Vulgate Romance of the Grail (*Roman du Graal*). This adopts the Vulgate *Estoire del Saint Graal* and the first part of the *Estoire de Merlin*, taking off in its own direction after the marriage of Arthur and Guenevere.

In the Post-Vulgate *Merlin* Continuation (published as *La Suite du Roman de Merlin*), there is a bold attempt to clear up the considerable confusion that still remained around the identity of the Maimed King, the cause of his injury and his family relationship to Perceval. Briefly, the Maimed King is called Pellehan and he is struck by the

Lance which wounded Christ, now wielded by Balin the Savage (the Dolorous Blow). One of Pellehan's sons is Pellinor, the (murdered) father of Perceval; another is Pelles, the grandfather of Galahad.

The Post-Vulgate account of the Grail Quest is greatly expanded from the Vulgate version in order to accommodate it to the adventures of the knight Tristan, as the Vulgate *Queste* had accommodated the adventures of Lancelot. It largely eschews the allegorical mysticism of the Vulgate *Queste* in favor of recounting the adventures and misadventures of several Knights of the Round Table.

Much of the Post-Vulgate Cycle was translated into Spanish and Portuguese, which is fortunate because a lot of the French original has been lost. The very nature of the cycle had to be established by the scholarly detective work of Fanni Bogdanow (1927–2013) over decades.

When, in the fifteenth century, Sir Thomas Malory came to write his *Hoole Book*, usually known as *Le Morte Darthur*, he drew on both the Post-Vulgate *Merlin* Continuation (for his Tale of Balin) and on the Vulgate *Queste* (for his Noble Tale of the Sangreal). Malory was an enormous influence on later English writers and artists such as the pre-Raphaelites, Swinburne and Tennyson, but it would be from Germany that would come the most important original contribution to the legend outside of France.

What Ails You?

In the first decade of the thirteenth century, the Bavarian poet Wolfram von Eschenbach set about completing Chrétien's unfinished romance, being unaware of the French continuations, except possibly the first. Although much of his *Parzival* follows Chrétien quite closely, he made some important changes: Thus, the maimed Fisher King is the eponymous hero's uncle rather than his cousin; the spear that wounds him is not a relic of the Passion, as it is in the First Continuation; while the Grail itself is a stone rather than a dish.

For these and other changes Wolfram made, he called on the authority of a Provençal called Kyot, whose existence many have disputed; what is indisputable is that he made a satisfactory whole out of an incomplete original. In doing so, he fashioned two intriguing characters (the Grail Messenger Cundrie and the enchanter Clinschor) out of a mysterious Ugly Maiden and an unnamed astrologer in Chrétien. These characters would also play an important role in Wagner's music drama *Parsifal* at the end of the nineteenth century.

Like Chrétien and the First Continuator, Wolfram gave a lot of space to the adventures of Gawain. Unlike those authors, the poet Heinrich von dem Türlin makes Gawain the Grail Winner; but the Grail is once more a reliquary fashioned from gold and a single jewel, containing bread.

Other poets say that the jewel fell from the crown of Lucifer during the War in Heaven and was fashioned into the dish used by Christ at the first Eucharist. These "strange transformations," as they have been called,[5] influenced the esoteric interpretation of the Grail legend developed in the early twentieth century by the French metaphysician René Guénon (1886–1951), for whom the jewel fell, not from the crown, but from the forehead of Lucifer: It is the Third Eye, with which we see Eternity.[6]

Guénon was an important influence on the Italian esoteric philosopher and sometime practicing magician Julius Evola (1898–1974), for whom the Grail is a symbol of sacred kingship. In his writings on the Grail mysteries, Evola emphasizes the importance of two questions which Wolfram's Parzival asks on his triumphant return to the Grail Castle. The first is: Where is the Grail? The second, to his maimed uncle: What ails you?

For Evola, these questions demonstrate Parzival's hard-won suitability to be the next Grail King. The first he elaborates as meaning: What has happened to the sacred regal power symbolized by the Grail? The second demonstrates Parzival's compassion for human suffering, for a true king can never be indifferent.

Evola was in turn an influence on the young Romanian writer Mircea Eliade (1907–86), who would go on to become the leading western historian of religion after the Second World War. In the first of his Eranos lectures, given in 1950 to a select audience of provocatively "spiritual" thinkers,[7] Eliade revisits these two questions but gives them a wider significance: Where, today, is the spiritual center of our being? And he concludes that the world is perishing from a lack of imagination, exemplified by our indifference to Eternity.

For Eliade, that is what ails us.

The Enchantment Theory

Both Evola and Eliade give, as a scholarly source for their speculations, the work of the leading English Arthurianist of the first decades of the twentieth century, Jessie L. Weston (1850–1928). Initially influenced by her friend Alfred Nutt's hypothesis that the origin of the Grail legend could be found in Celtic mythology, Weston came to believe that what she called the Folklore Theory could not account for the exalted Christian mysticism of its later developments.

Between 1906 and 1920, Weston published a series of books in which she gradually pieced together the Ritual Theory, for which she is today best known: The stories preserve fragments of a forgotten faith, a prehistoric fertility cult which developed into a Mystery Religion. According to Weston, an account of an initiation ritual going fatally wrong is found in the Romance of Perlesvaus; while a record of the suppression of the cult is found in a little-known prologue to the Romance of Perceval.[8]

This was startling stuff, as Weston herself admitted, especially when she confessed her belief in a spiritual rather than material origin for humankind, as well as in the reality of the Otherworld. No one could accuse her of lack of imagination. But, while I believe that we should celebrate what Mimi Winick has called her "scholarly enchantment,"[9] we should also beware of taking any such theories too literally: Mythic, symbolic stories like those of the Grail cannot be pinned down to historical events in known geography without destroying their power to open us up to new horizons.

Writing in 1913, Weston identified what she considered to be the three principal theories of Grail origins: the Christian, the Folklore and her own Ritual Theory. This threefold model I consider to be still useful as a starting point.

The Grail is clearly a Christian relic in most medieval Arthurian stories; its association with the Last Supper and Joseph of Arimathea has become part of popular culture. Nevertheless, the image of a Vessel containing the Holy Blood (or consecrated wafer of the Mass) carried by a maiden is difficult to reconcile with Roman Catholicism. In some stories there is even the suggestion that there is an alternative apostolic succession, which is certainly heterodox.[10] Weston's contemporary, the Christian mystic A.E. Waite (1857–1942), argued that whatever folklore elements may have survived in the stories, they were transmuted into the symbols of a "hidden church" of Johannine Christianity. Others have found Byzantine influences, or even the shadow of Cathar heresy.

What Weston refers to as the Folklore Theory would perhaps better be named the Celtic Background Theory. Scholars have been arguing, since the middle of the nineteenth century, for a provenance of the legends in Celtic tradition, whether oral or written, such as in Breton storytelling or in Irish and Welsh medieval literature, with their surviving traces of pagan mythology. It has been suggested that the Grail was originally one of the magical cauldrons of indigenous gods and heroes; that, along with the Sword and Lance, it formed one of the Treasures of Britain or of the Irish "god-peoples"[11]; or that it was the Vessel of Sovereignty, bestowed on the hero worthy to rule the land.[12] In addition, several Grail Kings and questing knights have been speculatively identified with Celtic gods and heroes. Into the twenty-first century, more cautious scholars such as John Carey continue to make a strong case for the transmission of key elements of the legend from Ireland to the continent via Wales.

If the Christian and Folklore or Celtic origin theories continue to have their champions, the same cannot be said for Weston's Ritual Theory, at least within mainstream Arthurian scholarship; it has fared better among Wiccans and Pagans.[13] Moreover, in her last published Grail study, *From Ritual to Romance*, Weston opened her theory up to occult and esoteric explorations of alchemy, Mithraism and Gnosticism, touching on the fate of the Albigensians and the Knights Templars. Further, she broadened and deepened her search for origins by invoking Indo-European mythology, embracing the burgeoning field of comparative religion.

As a result, the Ritual Theory needs to be included in a wider category: Here I think it is useful to recall the phrase "scholarly enchantment" which Mimi Winick has used for the pioneering work of women writers such as Weston and the classicist Jane Ellen Harrison, to whom Weston dedicated *From Ritual to Romance*.

In the decades since Weston's death in 1928, the "strange currents" that she saw stirring in the Middle Ages[14] have continued to make ripples in the literature, both popular and scholarly, inspired by the image of the Grail. It has been sought from Scotland to Georgia and Iran, from India and the Kingdom of Prester John to Hyperborea, in Hermetic Gnosis and in the depths of the psyche.

Several Grail stories talk of the enchantment which has fallen upon the land and which can only be lifted by the Grail winner; it appears that an enchantment has also fallen upon Grail scholarship. If we allow the Enchantment Theory to join the Christian and Celtic or Folklore origins theories, we can maintain the threefold symbolism which was so important to poets such as Robert de Boron and scholars such as Weston.

The three theories can be seen to correspond with the three worlds of Being, according to traditional cosmology: the material world, which we can perceive with our physical senses; the intermediate world, which we can perceive with the creative imagination; and the archetypal world, which we can perceive with the intuitive intellect. These three worlds in turn correspond with the three aspects of the human being, according to traditional anthropology: body, soul and spirit.

The Grail itself can be seen to exist on all three levels: In the material realm, it is the bountiful Earth, ever-giving; in the spiritual realm, it is divine grace, ever-flowing; and in the middle realm of the soul, it is the true imagination, ever-changing.[15] These three levels give us the three principal symbolic images of the Grail and the three corresponding theories of interpretation: a cauldron of plenty or Vessel of Sovereignty (the Celtic or Folklore Theory); the grace of the Holy Spirit incarnate in a relic of the Last Supper (the Christian Theory); a mysterious, many-formed Vessel of Light (the Enchantment Theory).

Strange Adventures

In the pages that follow, I have attempted to summarize the most important stories associated with the key characters, places and talismans or hallows (sacred objects) of the Grail legend. Inevitably there will be some repetition; but I have tried to keep the entries as varied as possible.

In doing so, I have followed the precept set by the Romance of Perlesvaus, in a little-known episode: King Arthur is on a pilgrimage to the Grail Castle, accompanied by the two leading Knights of the Round Table, Gawain and Lancelot. They pass by Tintagel, where Arthur was conceived and where the knights hear for the first time about the mysterious events which brought about the king's birth. They also see there the (empty) tomb of Merlin, whose "art" enabled Arthur's conception.

The king is mortified to have the circumstances of his conception exposed to his favorite knights; but in the morning a greater mystery confronts them. As they ride into the surrounding forest, with which Gawain and Lancelot are usually only too familiar, they are somewhat taken aback to discover that they no longer know where they are. The landscape they are used to, is completely transformed.

The knights never learn the reason for this, but the narrator of the story explains that it has come about by the will of God,[16] who wants to ensure that the adventures the knights encounter as they travel around the country, bringing Christ's New Law to pagans, are as diverse as possible. They might otherwise find their sacred mission wearisome. But when they come to forests or islands which they have already visited, only to find different fortresses and castles there, and encounter new adventures, then the hardship they must undergo seems easier to take. The stranger the adventures on the Grail Quest, the better.

For the knights, the mysterious transformations of the landscape during the Grail Quest replace and overtake the earlier mysteries associated with the conception of Arthur and the disappearance of Merlin, which are found in the Arthurian chronicles, the De Boron Cycle and the Prose *Lancelot*. If we find in these latter texts the development and growth of a legend out of pseudo-history, what we encounter in the Grail stories is nothing less than the creation of a new mythology[17]: The Myth of the Absent Path is the story of all those seeking to leave the Waste Land; and, insofar as the modern West has lost its sacred center, are we not all Grail Seekers now?

Notes

1. *QHG* 53.
2. "The Holy Grail," episode of *Detectorists*, British Comedy Guide (website), https://www.comedy.co.uk/tv/detectorists/videos/8013/the_holy_grail/.
3. Thus, typing the keywords into an Internet search engine on a random date produced over forty-eight million results, including the revelation that it is the name of a heavy metal band from Pasadena, of a strain of marijuana, and of a bottled beer from Yorkshire, originally brewed to celebrate the thirtieth anniversary of Monty Python (who went on their own Grail Quest).

4. O'Reilly, 47–8: Chandler's chivalric hero was originally to be called Mallory; in the course of his adventures, he champions women called Quest and Grayle.

5. Barber 2005, 190-1, 195.

6. See the entry for THE GRAIL CHALICE.

7. For the history of the Eranos Conferences, see Hakl (2013).

8. See CAHUS and AMANGON: Weston's choice of apparently marginal incidents to become the cornerstone of a grand theory, precisely illustrates what Mimi Winick calls an alchemical transformation: "Scholarly enchantment is created when one finds in a conventionally insignificant phenomenon some meaning that transforms the phenomenon into a significant or valuable one…. The transformation of the apparent trifle into a phenomenon of significance suggests a further transformation of our understanding of the order of reality in which we find the phenomenon" (Winick, 189). It is the stone the builders rejected….

9. Winick, 188.

10. See JOSEPHUS.

11. See CORBENIC and THE GRAIL PROCESSION.

12. See PEREDUR.

13. Winick, 221–2.

14. Weston 1913, 138: "we know, and every student of mediæval literature will bear the same witness, that there were strange currents stirring in those days, that more was believed, more was known, than the official guardians of faith and morals cared to admit." Many conspiracy theorists in today's Internet world seem to feel the same way about the official guardians of knowledge.

15. Dixon 2012, 156.

16. See JOSEPHUS THE CLERK.

17. Poiron, 88.

The Encyclopedia

> One could wish that, like the Bible, the entire cycle of the Grail poems could be read by "believers" not as a *corpus* but as the "Bible of the Holy Grail"—a hermeneutic of the Grail which would coordinate and systematize the data of the *corpus* from beginning to end is a task which has yet to be undertaken.
> —Henry Corbin, *Temple and Contemplation* (1986), 356

A

ADONIS

The lover of Aphrodite (Venus), Adonis is gored in the thighs by a wild boar and bleeds to death; whereupon the goddess of love declares that every year his death will be re-enacted to the accompaniment of wailing cries.[1] Furthermore, due to Aphrodite's tearful entreaties, the supreme god, the Sky Father Zeus (Jupiter) grants that Adonis is freed from the Underworld for the summer months of every year.[2]

* * *

Jessie L. Weston saw this story as a myth of the god who embodies "the vivifying principle of vegetation" and whose wounding or killing causes the fertility of the natural world to be suspended. His annual rites involve weeping women mourning him while casting his effigy into the sea, followed by their hailing his restoration to life. It is the Rites of Adonis which, she argued, though "misunderstood and imperfectly remembered," provide us with "the most characteristic features" of the Grail story[3]; especially if, "at a certain stage of development," the nature cult "assumed the character of a mystery."

A Mystery Religion with Adonis as its central mythic figure (the Dying-and-Resurrected God) would have had two grades of initiation: the lesser mystery, concerned with "the origin of physical life"; and the higher, with "regeneration and spiritual life."[4] This cult could have been brought to Britain by Phoenician traders. In a short story entitled "The Ruined Temple," Weston dramatizes what she imagines a successful initiation would be like:

> A traveler finds the ruins of a Phoenician temple on a headland looking out to the western sea. When he falls asleep to the sound of the waves, he has a dream in which he encounters various initiatory tests. First, he must overcome his fear of death, exemplified by a dead body on a slab. Then, after a priest-king invites him to sit down to table in a great hall, he feels *something* pass through, leaving the tables piled high with wondrous food. He asks: "What passed but

now?" and, although he is not yet ready to know the answer, he is rewarded by partaking of the Food of Life. He is next tempted by seductive women offering sex, but he realizes that he must sublimate his desire in order to move on to the next level of experience. *I live indeed by the Flesh*, he cries, *yet not by the Flesh alone*. Finally, he is vouchsafed a vision of the Lance and Cup and hears a voice saying: *Behold the Flesh transformed by Spirit*.[5]

While it seems unlikely that this account bears too close a resemblance to temple incubations ever carried out in Britain, it does at least have the merit of restoring the Grail Hallows to the realm where they originally appeared—the realm, that is, of imaginative fiction.

Notes

1. *MO* 244.
2. Graves 1960, 70: According to Carl Kerényi, women brought the living Adonis little "gardens," symbolizing their feminine sexuality: "In eastern shrines they gave themselves to strangers. Whoever did not do this must at least sacrifice her hair to Adonis" (1951, 76). Weston (1920, 51) suggests that "the curious detail" in the Romance of Perlesvaus where the Grail Bearer loses her hair when Perceval fails to ask the Question, may be explained by the hair sacrifice to Adonis. In the Vulgate Cycle, Perceval's virginal sister cuts off her hair on the day that Galahad is knighted, but this was commonly required of women becoming a nun, a bride of Christ: In this context, it suggests that she has become the spiritual bride of the equally virginal Galahad.
3. Weston 1907, 66.
4. Weston 1913, 86–90.
5. Weston 1916, 78–80.

AGLOVAL

A Knight of the Round Table, Agloval fathers a son on a Moorish princess, promising to return to her when he is able. He brings to Arthur's court his younger brother Perceval, who lives with their mother in the Waste Forest. Joining the Round Table, Perceval takes his place next to the Perilous Seat. Together the brothers avenge their father's wrongs, reclaiming his lands from their enemies; but Agloval is badly injured in battle.

At this time, he has a dream that he emerges from a shelter-less wilderness to find a tower with a stairway leading up to a door from which streams healing light. He starts walking up to the light, but sees the stairs disappearing beneath his feet as he climbs; serpents and wild bears wait below to devour him. As fear possesses him, the stairs give way ... and he wakes up in fright!

A learned clerk interprets the dream for him: The wilderness symbolizes the struggles that the brothers have in this life, but the door at the top of the tower represents the Kingdom of Heaven. The stairway is the Holy Grail, which is the bridge between the worlds; while the beasts represent Agloval's sins, which threaten to devour him. Perceval, by contrast, will aid in the winning of the Grail and will die in its service. But for now, his quest is hindered by his sin of abandoning his mother in the Waste Forest.

As a result of this dream the brothers go to stay with their hermit uncle, with whom they both seek healing, though of different kinds—Agloval for physical, Perceval for emotional wounds—and both seek forgiveness for their sins. While they are at the hermitage, they are found by Agloval's son Morien, now grown up, who wants his father to honor his commitment to his mother. Consequently, they travel to the land of the Moors, where Agloval marries his princess and rules with her as his queen.[1] He dies seven years after the healing of the Fisher King.[2]

Notes

1. This story of Agloval is told in the thirteenth century Dutch Romance of Morien, which gives us an interesting variation on the more familiar account of the Grail family as found in French and German sources. The romance has been translated by Jessie L. Weston (*MW*).
2. *CSG* 555: According to the Post-Vulgate *Roman du Graal* however, he is killed by Gawain (who has already killed his father and two older brothers) during the Grail Quest: *Et Agloval ochist il en la queste del Saint Graal* (*SRM* 115). Perceval would have avenged his death if he had known at the time what had happened, because of his love for Agloval. This will all be recounted directly by

Robert de Boron, we are assured (*LG* IV, 199). But, in fact, it is only referred to obliquely during the Grail Quest, when Perceval asks a hermit if he will ever see his brother again. No, says the hermit, for Agloval will die at the hands of the man who has already killed so many of Perceval's companions, a man whom the hermit refuses to name because no good would come of it (V, 168).

AGRESTES

When Joseph of Arimathea and the Company of the Grail, who have brought the sacred Vessel from the Holy Land to Britain, arrive at Camelot on a missionary expedition, they find that its ruler is a wicked and cruel pagan king called Agrestes. He is a follower of the astral cult centered at Sarras, which the Company has already destroyed in its heartland.

Treacherous to the core, Agrestes goes through the motions of baptism and presides over the mass conversion of his people. But, as soon as Joseph departs, leaving just twelve of the Company to care for the spiritual needs of the city, the king shows his true colors, executing all those who refuse to return to their ancient forms of worship.[1] Many return to polytheism out of fear, but the twelve Companions of the Grail are dragged naked through the streets by horses and tied to a cross that Joseph had erected at the edge of the forest. There, their brains are beaten out!

For his crimes, Agrestes is punished with madness: he strangles his brother, his wife and their small son and tries to eat his own hands, before throwing himself alive into an oven. The blood on the cross of martyrs turns black and can never be washed clean. The Black Cross remains as a memento of the wickedness of Agrestes.[2]

Notes

1. Confusingly, the Vulgate *Lancelot* refers to this as *mahomerie* (*LM* II, 323), thereby mixing the strictly monotheistic faith of Islam up with the worship of many gods, as the medieval writers frequently do.
2. *LG* I, 136–7; III, 86–7.

ALAN of the Isle

Alan of the Isle is the eldest son of King Pellehan of Listenois (the sixth Fisher King) and, when his father is maimed by the Dolorous Blow, he succeeds him[1] to become King of the Land Beyond and guardian of the Holy Grail in the Castle of Corbenic.

King Alan, however, like his father before him, is sick; and is destined to remain so unless the best knight in the world comes to him and asks him both the cause of his sickness and the nature of the Grail from which he is served.[2] Unfortunately Alan does not live to see the coming of the Best Knight and his role as Fisher King is taken over by his younger brother Pelles, the eighth and last Fisher King.[3]

Notes

1. There is only one reference to Alan of the Isle of Listenois as one (presumably the seventh) of the Fisher Kings (*LG* I, 254). His presence is somewhat shadowy and I have reconstructed his story from brief mentions in the Vulgate *Estoire de Merlin*—where he is called the *le riche roi Pescheour* (*LDG* I, 939) and *roi Helain de la Terre Foraine* (1410, 1472)—and the little-known *Livre d'Artus* (*VS* VII).
2. *LG* I, 235: *devant ce que li mieudres chevaliers del monde viegne a lui et li demande ce dont cele maladie li vient et quel chose li graaus est que on sert* (*LDG* I, 861). According to the *Livre d'Artus*, neither Alan nor his brother Pellinor, who are both Maimed Kings, can be healed unless a knight comes to their dwelling and asks who is served by the Grail: *ne garront de lor plaies tant que li chevaliers gise en lor ostel et ait demandé cui l'en sert du Saint Graal* (*VS* VII, 147).
3. I have here reconstructed the most likely sequence of succession between Pellehan and Pelles.

ALAN the Fat

After the Deposition of Christ and the liberation of His disciple Joseph of Arimathea from prison, Enigeus (Joseph's sister) and her husband Bron go into exile with Joseph, because of their Christian beliefs.

Bron and Enigeus have twelve sons, of whom the youngest is Alan the Fat. When Alan is grown, he alone of all the brothers says that he will not take a wife. Joseph thereupon prays to God to reveal the truth

ALAN the Fat

about his nephew's future life and, in response, he hears a voice saying that Alan will be granted grace and fulfillment of heart. Alan is to lead his brothers into the farthest West where, despite his vow of chastity, he will father a son who will sit in the empty place at the Table of the Grail.[1] He will in turn be a keeper of the Holy Vessel.

With his father's blessing, Alan leads his brothers into distant lands, where they spread the good news of Christ.[2] Many years later the prophet Merlin tells King Arthur that Alan and his people have arrived in these western isles. Equally, the renown of King Arthur's court reaches the land where Alan is living and he tells his young son Perceval that, when he is grown up, he will take him there. However, Alan dies before he can do so.[3]

Lord of the Vales

It is also said that Alan is the grandson of Nicodemus, the companion of Joseph of Arimathea.[4]

Neither he nor any of his eleven brothers lives more than twelve years as knights, before dying in battle with the pagan Red Giant while trying to advance the New Law of Jesus Christ. Alan himself comes to the giant's island to avenge his brothers' deaths but, although he kills the giant, he later dies of his wounds. Rich and beautiful tombs are then set up on the island for each of the brothers, watched over by twelve hermits, but the finest tomb is that of Alan.[5]

During his life, Alan was the Lord of the Vales of Kamaalot in Wales but, before his death, he had lost most of his lands to the Lord of the Fens. Only the castle of Kamaalot itself remains to his widow, Yglais. For this reason, his son is christened Perlesvaus, meaning He Who Has Lost the Vales.[6] But his son will avenge his father's honor and restore to his mother her lands.

The Rich Fisherman

Yet others say that Alan becomes known as the Rich Fisherman after performing a miracle in which he feeds many sinful followers of Josephus, the son of Joseph of Arimathea. They had been denied the nourishment of the Grail but, at the command of Josephus, Alan feeds them with a single fish that he catches in a pond, which is henceforth known as Alan's Pond.[7]

When Josephus is dying, he comforts the weeping Alan by telling him that God will watch over him like a Good Shepherd. He then hands to him the Holy Vessel and bids him entrust it to whoever he wishes when Alan, in turn, passes from this world. As soon as Josephus dies, Alan and his brothers take the Grail to the Land Beyond, where Alan converts its king to Christianity by showing him the Grail and instantly curing him of leprosy.

At the king's request, Alan agrees that the Grail should stay in the Land Beyond in a fortress that was specially built to house it: the castle of Corbenic. The Grail is brought to a high room next to the main palace and, the following Sunday, Alan's brother Joshua is married to the daughter of the King of Corbenic. Alan entrusts Joshua with the guardianship of the Holy Vessel after his death and, as it transpires, he and the king both die ten days after the marriage. They are buried next to each other in the Church of Our Lady in Corbenic.[8]

Joshua and his descendants all bear the title of Rich Fisherman and they all rule in Corbenic, hence they are known as the Fisher Kings.[9]

Notes

1. Corresponding to the place of Judas at the Table of the Last Supper, this seat seems originally to be destined for Alan himself: *Icil lius wiz si senefie/ Le liu Judas...// Cil lius estre empliz ne pourra/ Devant qu'Enygeus avera/ Un enfant de Bron sen mari,// Et quant li enfes sera nez/ La sera ses lius assenez* (EG ll. 2527–8, 2531–3, 2535–6). But the voice of the Holy Spirit later explains to Joseph, to comfort him, that it will never be filled but by the *son* of Alan, the "third man" of Joseph's lineage: *Meis le te di pour ton confort,/ Que cist lius empliz ne sera/ Devant que li tierz hons venra/ Qui descendra de ten lignage/ Et istera de ten parage,/ Et Hebruns le doit*

engenrer/ Et Enygeus ta suer porter;/ Et cil qui de sen fil istra/ Cest liu meïsmes emplira (ll. 2788-96). He who will be born to the son of Hebrun (Bron) and Enygeus is Perceval (see THE FEARED SEAT).
  2. *MG* 40-42.
  3. *MG* 113-5.
  4. *HBG* 20.
  5. *HBG* 257.
  6. *HBG* 30.
  7. *LG* I, 139-40.
  8. *LG* I, 157-9.
  9. The genealogies found in the De Boron Cycle and the Romance of Perlesvaus, above, make Alan's life span the centuries between the time the Grail leaves the Holy Land and the time of King Arthur. The Vulgate and Post-Vulgate Cycles attempt to make more sense of the chronology by placing several generations between Alan the Fat and Perceval.

AMANGON

Before the coming of Arthur and his revival of the Round Table, Logres was destroyed by the evil actions of Amangon, King of Morain.[1]

Once upon a time it was the custom for visitors to the court of the Fisher King to be offered hospitality by the Maidens of the Wells, with all the food and drink one might wish brought on a gold-and-silver dish[2] and a golden cup. But Amangon rapes one of the Maidens of the Wells and seizes her golden cup, which is henceforth reserved for his exclusive use; his followers do likewise.

As a result, the voices of the wells and the maidens who dwell in them are lost,[3] the kingdom becomes a Waste Land and the Fisher King's castle disappears. King Amangon himself meets an unspecified but fittingly bad end. His descendants—and those of his knights who followed his example—people the Waste Land, until they are destroyed by the Knights of the Round Table who are searching for the Fisher King, a sorcerer and shape-shifter. When they find him, the land is restored.[4]

* * *

The story of King Amangon is found only in the so-called *Elucidation* to the Story of the Grail which, unfortunately, elucidates very little, if anything merely adding another layer of confusion to the verse tradition. But scholars have been drawn to it "by a sense of something archaic in its very strangeness,"[5] some being tantalized by its suggestion of pagan vestiges. Thus, R.S. Loomis suspects that it may indicate the survival of Celtic belief in the nymphs of the springs, who cause drought if offended.[6] John Carey identifies Amangon with King Mangon of Morain, who sends a magical drinking-horn to Arthur's court. He also follows Lucy Paton in identifying Mangon in turn with the Irish enchanter and shape-shifter Mongán (the son of the sea god Manannán mac Lir), who was carried away by his father to the Land of Promise when only three nights old.[7] Mongán would "very properly" inherit Manannán's marvelous drinking vessel, "a touchstone for truthfulness."[8]

J.L. Weston, finding the attempts to explain the story in terms of Celtic folklore "interesting, but hardly illuminating" sees it rather as an account of an outrage done to the priestess and temple maidens of a fertility cult which was, as a result, driven underground.[9] This cult Weston relates to a pagan mystery religion influenced by Gnostic Christianity. The suppression of the outward rituals (the exoteric aspect of the cult), its acolytes believe, causes the wasting of the land. But the "higher, esoteric" aspect of the cult continued to be observed in secret, probably by "the descendants of the outraged maidens."[10]

Notes

1. The thirteenth century verse romance *Le Chevalier as Deus Espees* makes him King of Granlande (*CDE* l.89: Greenland?), the Land of No Return (ll.12129-30).
2. The word used in Old French is *escüele* (*EB* l.50), this being the word that is used in the Vulgate *Estoire del Saint Graal* for the Holy Vessel itself.
3. *...il pierdirent des puis les vois/ Et les puceles k'ens istoient* (*EB* ll.32-3). Hélène Bouget, in her edition of the *Elucidation*, understands *puis* as *caverne* (*P* 19-20). The sixteenth century prose rendering of this poem tells us that the maidens *se tenoient en caves que l'ancienne hystoire appelle aultrement puys* (154). Jessie L. Weston refers to them as "maidens dwelling in the hills" (1920, 172&n17). For Caitlín and John Matthews they are fays or "faery women" (2019, 112) and the story refers to the

breaking of the Faery Accord between humans and the Otherworld: "a fracture whose environmental consequences can be easily appreciated, for the faery kind uphold the world of nature" (120).
    4. *CSG* 557–60.
    5. Carey 2007, 182.
    6. Loomis 1963, 281.
    7. Carey 2007, 192–3.
    8. Paton, 112.
    9. Weston 1913, 110–5.
    10. Weston 1920, 170–4: The Maidens of the Wells are, according to Caitlín Matthews (2001, 215), the voices of Sophia, the personification of Divine Wisdom who plays a central role in Gnostic mythology, "in her aspect of World Soul."

AMFORTAS

The son of Titurel, to whom the sacred relics of the Passion of Christ (the Cup of the Last Supper and the Spear that pierced the side of Jesus on the Cross) were first entrusted, Amfortas now rules the mountainous castle of Montsalvat in which the relics are guarded by the Order of Grail Knights. But he is opposed by the sorcerer Klingsor, whose admittance to the Order was refused. Moreover, he has been wounded by the Spear in a struggle with Kundry, his seductress, which results in Klingsor's gaining possession of the Spear. No known remedy can heal Amfortas' wound[1]; but the oracular Grail has declared that healing will come through a pure fool who will learn wisdom through compassion.

At the Grail feast, despite the fact that its miraculous powers to sustain life only enhance his agony, Amfortas blesses bread and wine with the Cup. But when Parsifal arrives at Montsalvat and joins the feast, he appears foolishly oblivious to what he is witnessing. It is only after overcoming Klingsor and gaining the Spear that Parsifal, now wiser, is able to return to Montsalvat, where Amfortas has despaired of health, to use the very Spear which wounded the king, to cure him.[2] Parsifal now takes the place of Amfortas as Grail King.[3]

Notes

    1. Amfortas is the Maimed King of Wagner's music drama *Parsifal*, corresponding to Wolfram's Anfortas (q.v.). The Kahanes (93–5) follow earlier scholars in deriving his name from Latin *infirmitas*, but they see this as a symbolic description of his moral "incontinence" as much as of his physical wounding.
    2. Weston argues that by placing the hero's quest for the Spear and the healing of the Maimed King center-stage, Wagner "is probably reproducing with fidelity original features of the story" (1896, 189).
    3. Weston 1896, 176–8.

AMINADAP

Son of Joshua (the first Fisher King) and the daughter of King Alphasan of the Land Beyond, Aminadap is conceived in Corbenic Castle on the day that his parents are married. He is, therefore, the first of the Fisher Kings to be born in Britain. Aminadap cements the relationship of the Grail family with the royalty of his native country by marrying the daughter of Lucius, King of Britain.[1] Their descendants are the line of Fisher Kings that reaches down to Pelles and his daughter, the mother of Galahad.

Note

    1. *LG* I, 159.

AMITE

The daughter of King Pelles of Corbenic is baptized Helizabel but her nickname is Amite. A girl of incomparable beauty, she is entrusted with the great honor of bearing the Holy Vessel.[1] But her father has a destiny in mind for her which will make her no longer worthy to do so: She is to bear a son who will witness the wonders of the Grail, pass the test of the Perilous Seat and bring to an end the adventures of the dangerous realm that is the Kingdom of Logres.[2]

In order to accomplish this, Pelles tricks Lancelot into sleeping with his daughter when the hero comes to Corbenic. The king accomplishes this with the aid of Amite's tutor Brisane, who uses herbal potions to so befuddle Lancelot that he believes he is sleeping with his only true love, Guenevere. Unlike Lancelot, Amite has acted, not out of physical lust, but because she knows that she will conceive a hero who will restore to its original beauty the Waste Land. Because God does not wish the two kingdoms destroyed by the Sword with the Strange Straps to remain waste forever, He looks on their coupling as conferring benefit on the land. He therefore allows Amite's sacrifice of her maidenhead to be atoned for by the lifelong virginity of her son, Galahad, who is conceived that night.[3]

Notes

1. *Icele pucele garda le saintisme Graal jusqu'à tant que Galaas fu engendrés* (LDG I, 940).
2. LG II, 16: *fille au roi Pellés de Listenois qui fu aiouls a Galaad, a celui qui vit apertement les merveilles del Saint Graal et acompli le Siege Perillous de la Table Reonde; et cil mena a point les aventures del roiaume de Logres* (LDG II, 61–2). Other manuscripts of the Prose *Lancelot* make Amide/Heliabel the sister of Perceval (*Perlesvax*); their father is the Maimed King Pelles (LDL I, 122).
3. LG III, 164–5: In his more famous version of the conception of Galahad, Malory calls this princess Elaine (q.v.).

ANFORTAS

A richly dressed nobleman known as the Man of Sorrows is fishing on a lake when the young knight Parzival rides up and asks him where he can find shelter for the night. The nobleman directs Parzival to an unassailable stronghold on Mount Savage, in an unknown region, where he is made welcome. Parzival now discovers that his host, the ailing lord of the castle, is that same man whom he mistook for a mere fisherman.[1]

After witnessing the Grail Procession, Parzival is presented by the king with the very sword that he had wielded in battle when he was fit. This is meant to prompt him to ask a question about the lord's health, but he fails to ask it.[2] He later learns from his cousin that the Maimed King is his uncle Anfortas[3]; he would have been healed if Parzival had asked the Question.[4] The monstrous Grail Messenger Cundrie likewise criticizes Parzival for not having compassion for Anfortas' sorrows.[5]

Parzival eventually learns the whole sorry tale from his other uncle, Anfortas' brother the hermit Trevrizent: Having inherited guardianship of the Grail Stone from his late father King Frimutel,[6] Anfortas ignored the commandment (in the form of an inscription on the Stone) that its chosen ones must only give their hearts to the one that the Grail instructs them they can marry. But Anfortas chose his own ladylove, the Proud Lady of Logres, winning renown under the battle cry of "Amor!" One day, riding to adventure, he was struck through the genitals by a poisoned spear, engraved with the name of the Grail, wielded by a pagan warrior.[7] The warrior was born at the source of the Tigris, one of the four rivers of Paradise; when the wound from the spear festered, it is from these rivers that the Company of the Grail sought herbs to cure Anfortas. When these failed, the companions turned to other mythical sources of healing, such as the heart of the unicorn, but to no avail.

Anfortas has never recovered: The proximity of the Grail only makes his agony worse, since the virtue of the Stone is that none can die in its presence.[8] However, the companions find writing on the Stone, warning them that a knight is destined to arrive who will cure the king and inherit his kingdom, if he asks the right question; it further warns that any attempt to alert the visitor would invalidate the process.[9]

Having failed Anfortas on his first visit to Mount Savage, Parzival returns several years later. But, by this time, Anfortas wishes only that he be removed from the presence of the Grail long enough to die of his wounds and thus end his agony. Nevertheless, this time Parzival speaks the magic words: He asks his uncle what ails him; whereupon Anfortas is restored to the bloom of health.[10] Henceforth he will fight only in the service of the Grail, the lordship of which he has lost through his arrogance, but nevermore for the love of woman.[11]

Notes

1. *WP* 120–3, 249–50; *PT* 95–7, 206–7.
2. *WP* 127; *PT* 101.
3. According to Weston (1896, 187), the name Anfortas is derived from the French *enfertez*, "the sick man"; while the *-as* ending indicates a Provençal derivation, in keeping with Wolfram's ascription to the Provençal Kyot of the Grail story.
4. *WP* 133–5; *PT* 106–8.
5. *WP* 165; *PT* 133.
6. Anfortas is the third of the Grail Lords, who have been entrusted with the Grail Stone by the angels who were neutral during the War in Heaven.
7. In Wagner's operatic version, the Grail Lord is wounded by the Spear that shed Christ's blood, wielded by the evil sorcerer Klingsor; he is healed by the same Spear, wielded by the Holy Fool Parsifal.
8. In the Romance of Perlesvaus, a hermit tells Gawain that in the most holy place (*saintisme repaire*) where the Grail is housed, a year seems like a month, and those who serve the Grail do not age (*HLG* 210)—much like those who spend time in Faerie, in British folklore.
9. *WP* 243–6; *PT* 201–4.
10. *WP* 391–5; *PT* 329–333.
11. *WP* 407–8; *PT* 343–5.

ANGELS

It is said that the angels who remain neutral in the War in Heaven bring the Grail down to Earth and leave it in the care of the Christian Titurel, before re-ascending beyond the stars.[1] Others say that Perceval's mother Philosofine brings the Grail to the Castle of Maidens and that angels carry it thence to the house of the Fisher King,[2] where it will be seen by Perceval and others.

An angel also brings the Lance of Longinus to the city of Orcaut, where it wounds Josephus who is attempting to prevent the demon Selaphas from killing unrepentant pagans. The angel—its face, feet and hands red as a thunderbolt, its clothes black as pitch—says that Josephus must be reproached for attempting to rescue those who scorn the true faith.

Josephus takes the Avenging Lance to Sarras, but his wound continues to bleed for twenty-two days. At the end of this time the angel who wounded him emerges from the ark in which the Grail is kept, announcing that its great vengeance will be followed by an equally great remedy, its fury by calm. Taking the blood that drips from the Lance, the angel uses it to anoint Josephus' wound and thereby heal it.[3]

The angel then prophesies the beginning of the adventures of the Kingdom of Logres, which will commence when the Lance starts bleeding again; they will only end when the marvels of the Holy Grail are revealed to the last man in the lineage of Duke Nascien.[4] The angel's words come true when Galahad, the last of Nascien's descendants, comes to Corbenic. Galahad there witnesses an angel who is bearing the Bleeding Lance place it against the Grail, so that the Holy Vessel catches the blood that flows down the shaft. Galahad uses the blood from the Lance to anoint and heal the wounds of the Maimed King. When Galahad himself, now King of Sarras, dies, angels—such as have already appeared to him in vision—carry his soul away amid great rejoicing.[5]

Notes

1. *WP* 232, 240; *PT* 192, 199: "It is therefore those angels who were opposed to the rending apart of the divine inner opposites and who sought to maintain a state of balance and to hold fast to the original unity of the God-image who now watch over the Grail." Baphomet, whom the Templars were accused of worshipping, is a figure which appears to have represented a "light-dark unity of the divine opposites" (Jung & Franz, 150–1).
2. *CSG* 364: For Rudolf Steiner (2001b, 32), the angelic transmission is of the suppressed gnosis of the Mysteries.
3. Thus foreshadowing the healing of King Pellehan by the blood from the same Lance with which Balin has stricken him, at the end of the Post-Vulgate Grail Quest (*LG* V, 279).
4. *LG* I, 49–51
5. *LG* IV, 84, 86–7; V, 286–8; *QHG* 275, 279–80, 283; *MD* 782, 787–8.

ANSCHAU

The famous Master Kyot, having found the original version of the Grail story written in heathenish letters in Toledo, embarks on a search for the Grail Lords. He reads the

Latin chronicles of Britain, France and Ireland, but it is in Anschau that he finds the tale.¹

* * *

Anschau is usually translated as Anjou, which Wolfram considers to be the kingdom ruled by Parzival's family (and it was the Angevin dynasty who first promoted the spread of Arthurian literature in the English court). But for Trevor Ravenscroft, Anschau is not a kingdom that can be found on earthly maps; rather it is "the name given to spiritual realms which can only be experienced through initiation."² The Chronicle of Anschau in which Kyot learns of the family who keep the Grail Stone is a "cosmic chronicle" which can only be read by one who has reached the seventh degree of initiation, in which past, present and future are one. Anschau symbolizes intuition; it is "the transcendent kingdom of the Grail" which can only be ruled by one who has gained "the capacity for spiritual hearing—the faculty of true inspiration."³

Notes

1. *WP* 232–3; *PT* 192: *ze Anschouwe er diu mære vant* (*PKL* 455.12).
2. Ravenscroft 1982b, 50–1.
3. Ravenscroft 1982b, 75.

APOLLO

When the Company of the Grail first arrives at Sarras, the city of the Saracens, they find that its inhabitants are devotees of an astral cult. One of the idols to whom they make offerings is an image of Apollo, their god of wisdom. Invoking the power of his God, the Christian Josephus binds the statue of Apollo so that it can no longer speak. Taking a golden eagle from the altar of the Sun god, he uses it to break the idol, then proceeds to treat the others in similar fashion.¹ It is the first blow in the forced conversion of the city.

However, when they travel on to Western Europe, Josephus, his father Joseph of Arimathea and their followers discover that the Saracenic cult is already well-established there. Travelling in the Forest of Broceliande, Joseph encounters a Saracen who tells him that they worship not one but four gods, including Apollo.² Thanks to the efforts of Joseph and the Grail missionaries, the Saracens of Broceliande are converted to Christianity; as, eventually, is the whole of Britain, in the reign of the good King Lucius.

Notes

1. *LG* I, 30–1.
2. *LG* I, 140–1; III, 88–9: The other three are Jupiter, Tervagant (in whom we can recognize the goddess Diana) and a certain "Mahomet," indicating that the medieval author could not differentiate between an indigenous pagan deity and the Prophet of Islam.

ARGON the Saracen

One of the indigenous worshippers of a pre–Christian Quaternity,¹ Argon encounters the missionary Joseph of Arimathea in the Forest of Broceliande. Argon is looking for someone who can heal his brother Matagran of a head wound. But he is incredulous when Joseph claims that he will be able to do so without the help of those four powerful gods whose reign will endure as long as the world itself—gods whose grace infuses the images that the Saracens worship. Argon explains to Joseph that the power of the images lies not in themselves, but in the gods in whose image they are made. Joseph in contrast trusts in the One God who created the Sun, the Moon and the four elements.

Argon brings Joseph to his mountainous home in the Castle of the Rock, where he is killed by an escaped lion. As a result, Joseph, who is unfairly blamed for the accident, is stabbed in the thigh by the seneschal of the castle.² Nevertheless, Joseph proves the power of his Triune Deity by bringing Argon back to life and healing Matagran's wound. Everyone in the castle is forthwith baptized.

Argon lives for eight more years. The

sword with which Joseph was stabbed is kept in the Castle of the Rock as its most prized possession, until it is claimed by Eliezer, the son of the last Fisher King.[3]

Notes

1. In contrast to the Christian Trinity, the Quaternity of the Saracens consists of Apollo, Diana (Tervagant), Jupiter and (astonishingly) a certain "Mahomet"—in whom we can only see a distorted reflection of the Prophet of Islam, transformed by medieval Christian misunderstanding into a pre–Christian pagan deity.
2. See THE BLEEDING SWORD.
3. *LG* I, 140–2; III, 88–91.

ARNANTES

It is in the forest of Arnantes that Moses, son of Simeon, is buried in the Perilous Palace. His tomb has burnt constantly since he dared to sit in the Perilous Seat at the Table of the Grail. The punishing flames are only put out with the arrival of Galahad, who delivers Moses' spirit as he did his father's.[1]

Notes

1. *LG* V, 276: This forest, which is also called Darnant, stretches along the south coast of Wales. It is the place where Merlin, the Prophet of the Grail, ends his days: trapped in a pit by the Lady of the Lake, the fay who steals not just his heart, but also his spell-craft.

ARTHUR

When Arthur becomes King of Britain, he is approached by the prophet Merlin, who was his father Uther's chief soothsayer. Merlin tells Arthur that it was he who had instructed Uther to have built the Round Table, modelling it on the table that Joseph of Arimathea had constructed in the desert when his people were starving (and which was itself modelled on the Table of the Last Supper).

Joseph's table was established for the Grail, the Vessel which Our Lord had given to him when Joseph was in prison and which can tell the good from the wicked. The keeper of the Grail, the Fisher King, lives in a beautiful island in the West but he is old and sick, being unable to die until the world's most renowned knight comes to his court and asks what purpose the Grail serves. Only when this happens will the Fisher King be healed. Moreover, when he has passed on to that knight the Secret Words that Our Lord spoke to Joseph in prison, he will die, leaving the knight with the blood of Christ in his keeping. At that moment the enchantments of Britain will vanish and Arthur will go on to conquer the Romans.

The king's role in all this, Merlin continues, is already fixed, having been prophesied two hundred years before Arthur was born: He is to exalt the Round Table by making it the assembly point for a fine chivalry, so that one of its knights will become the Grail Hero in fulfillment of the prophecy. And so it proves: Arthur is such a valiant king and his renown so universal that knights from all over the world make their way to his court.[1]

Shortly after Arthur has re-established the fellowship of the Round Table, rumors reach his knights about a Most Holy Vessel which has come down from Heaven: This is the Grail in which Joseph of Arimathea had caught the blood that flowed from the side of Jesus on the Cross and which can only be found by the best knight in the world.[2] Later the king hears from Merlin that the Questing Beast is one of the adventures of the Grail[3] and that, on the same day that the prophet himself dies, the Dolorous Blow will be struck; as a result of this the adventures will begin in Logres, lasting twenty-two years. Arthur will know the time is here because on that day there will be darkness at noon.[4] The adventures when they come will be cruel and ugly; hence Arthur will become known as the King of Adventures.[5]

The Chapel in the White Forest

All transpires as Merlin has predicted: The Dolorous Blow is struck and the Fisher

King maimed as a result. When, only ten years after Arthur's coronation, Perceval fails to ask the Grail Question that would have cured the Maimed King, debility spreads to the heart of Logres and its king. It is as though Arthur himself were wounded spiritually as the Fisher King is maimed physically. As he loses his passion for great deeds, Arthur's knights start to leave and adventures no longer befall his court.[6]

The queen, grieving for his spiritual weakness, suggests that he could regain his former eagerness to excel by going to the White Forest and searching for the Chapel of St. Augustine,[7] which can only be found by chance. She insists he takes a squire with him but the lad, Cahus, is found dying on the morning they are due to depart. Cahus tells the king that during the night he dreamed that he had gone alone to the chapel, stolen a golden candlestick from the bier of a dead knight and been stabbed by a dark, ugly giant. Now he has awoken, only to find that the dream has come horribly true. The king sees the dagger, still stuck in the squire's side, while Cahus presents him with the candlestick which he has brought back with him from the dream world. After the squire's death, Arthur presents the candlestick to St. Paul's Church in London, which has just been built.

In the forest, unaccompanied, Arthur witnesses angels and demons arguing for the soul of a dying hermit. He is warned by a maiden he encounters of its perils and, when he finally reaches the chapel, he is unable to enter within. Standing outside, he sees the hermit celebrating Mass and has a vision of the Madonna and child. He then sees a man crowned with thorns, bleeding from his side, head and hands—a man who turns into that child.

After the Mass, the hermit tells Arthur that war and fighting are rending the land because the knight who was lodged at the house of the Fisher King failed to ask about the Grail and the Bleeding Lance[8]; the king himself will soon be obliged to take up arms. Indeed, as he leaves the chapel, Arthur is attacked by the Black Knight who killed Cahus, angry that the king took possession of the candlestick from the bier of his dead brother. The Black Knight is defeated, despite wielding a demonic burning lance, whose flames can only be extinguished by the king's blood.[9] Finally, he is hacked to pieces by over twenty other knights who turn up at this point.

Arthur makes off with the Black Knight's head, at the request of the maiden who had warned him earlier of the dangers he would face. She uses the blood dripping from the head to heal the wounds the king had sustained in the course of the fight.

On his way back to the court, penetrating the densest part of the forest, Arthur hears a dreadful voice shouting that he should hold court as soon as possible, for he has renewed his eagerness to excel. The Knights of the Round Table, who have been scattered throughout the lands and forests, hear the joyful news and return to the court at once.

Accordingly, Arthur holds a great court on St. John's Day, to which come three maidens from the realm of the Fisher King. The first maiden, who is bald, tells Arthur that his own waning valor can be attributed to the failure of the knight to ask the Question. Her own hair will not grow back until a knight conquers the Grail.[10]

Various knights set out to find the Knight of the Question (who is in fact Perceval, known as Perlesvaus, the son of the Widow Lady). Eventually, after seeing a vision of two Suns in the sky, Arthur is summoned by a voice to make a pilgrimage to the Grail Castle, which is now ruled by Perceval.[11] There he is shown the sepulcher of the Fisher King and attends Mass, during which he sees the five changes of the Grail. The last of these transmutations is the form of a chalice.[12] Arthur will later be responsible for introducing the chalice into the service of the Mass in Britain.[13]

Notes

1. *MG* 112–5.
2. *LG* I, 352: *li saintismes vaissaus qui vint del ciel ... et la saintisme lance de coi Jhesu Crist ot tresperchié le costé ... ne ja ne sera trouvee ne veüe ... tant que li miudres chevaliers del monde venist. Et par celui seroient descouvertes les merveilles del Saint Graal et oies et veües* (*LDG* I, 1350–1).
3. *LG* IV, 171.
4. *LG* IV, 199–200.
5. *LG* IV, 232–3.
6. In the most familiar versions of the Grail Quest, King Arthur is merely upset by the departure of his knights, fearing the breaking up of the Fellowship of the Round Table. But, in the Romance of Perlesvaus, of which this adventure forms the opening episode, his suffering parallels that of the Fisher King and, as a consequence, he is goaded into playing a far more active role in the healing Quest.
7. St. Augustine of Canterbury is post–Arthurian, so this chapel would have to be dedicated to St. Augustine of Hippo, who died in 430 CE.
8. *Mes une granz doleurs est avenue novelement par un chevalier qui fu herbergiez en l'ostel au riche roi Pescheeur, si s'aparut a lui li sainz Graauz e la lance de coi la pointe de fer saine, ne ne demanda de coi ce servoit, ne cui on en servoit* (*HLG* 156).
9. Armand Strubel sees the origin of this image in Irish mythology (*HLG* 160n1).
10. *HBG* 20–35.
11. *HBG* 173–5.
12. *HBG* 195–6: *Li Graaus s'aparut el secret de la messe en .V. manieres que l'on ne doit mie dire, kar les secrés choses del sacrement ne doit nus dire en apert, se cil non a qui Dieus en a grace donee. Li rois Artus vi totes les muances* (*HLG* 790), which Bryant translates as "transubstantiations."
13. *HBG* 210: According to the fourteenth century Glastonbury Tablets (*MTG* 142), Lambor, the fifth Fisher King, is the grandfather of Arthur's mother Igerna. Thus, Arthur is descended from the Fisher Kings and, through them, from Lucius, the first Christian King of Britain. Grail Christianity is literally in his blood.

ARTHUR the Less

The illegitimate son of King Arthur and a woman he mistakes for a fay, the lesser Arthur only discovers his true identity when he first arrives at his father's court: He finds that there is an empty seat at the Round Table with the name Arthur the Less on it.[1] There is also a place reserved for him at another table, the one on which the Round Table was modelled: This is the Table of the Grail at Corbenic, where Arthur the Less arrives on the day that Galahad heals the Maimed King. He is one of twelve chosen knights who receive the sacrament from Christ and is filled with the grace of the Grail.[2]

Notes

1. *LG* V, 214–6.
2. *LG* V, 278–80.

AVALON

While he is still in the Holy Land, Joseph of Arimathea is given a mysterious letter that appears in a blaze of light. He is then instructed by a heavenly voice to give the letter to his relative Peter, one of his most faithful followers. When Joseph asks Peter where his heart bids him take it, Peter replies that he will go to the Vales of Avalon, a solitary place in the West.[1] There he must await the son of Alan the Fat (Perceval), for he cannot die until he meets the one who will read him the contents of the letter and teach him the power of the Holy Vessel, the Grail.[2]

The Isle of Avalon is also where the original Latin version of the Grail story, set down by a certain Josephus at the behest of angels,[3] is found: in a holy house of religion which is situated at the edge of the Adventurous Lands, where King Arthur and his queen lie.[4]

* * *

The mythical Fortunate Isle, renowned as the place where King Arthur goes for the healing of his wounds after the Last Battle and whence it is prophesied he will return at the hour of his country's greatest need, is first associated with the Grail by the poet Robert de Boron, who tells us that the Vales of Avalon (*Avaron*) are in the wild West.[5] Unfortunately, Peter's mysterious celestial message is never explained, in what remain to us of Robert's poems; nor is it taken up by the prose continuation that has survived. So, we would be obliged to leave Peter himself in Avalon, like Arthur, deathlessly awaiting a call to fulfill his destiny, were it not that the

Vulgate Cycle sends him to Orkney to found a Christian dynasty.

Notes

1. *...es Vaus de Avaron en un soltain liu vers Occidant* (RG 67); *Ces terres trestout vraiement/ Se treient devers Occident* (EG ll. 3125–6); *En la terre vers Occident/ Ki est sauvage durement* (ll.3219–21).
2. *MG* 41; *RG* 65–7; *EG* ll.3107–34.
3. *HBG* 19: An alternative tradition, found in the Vulgate *Estoire del Saint Graal*, is that the story is transcribed into Latin from the language of Heaven by the hermit Nascien in the eighth century (Pickens, 101–3).
4. *HBG* 265: The Glastonbury monks claimed to have found the joint grave of Arthur and Guenevere, thus establishing a persistent identification of the region with the fabled Avalon.
5. Despite punning references in the prose version to Avalon as the Land of the Setting Sun—*ensi com il mondes vait avalant ... vers Occidant* (RG 69); *ceste partie la u li solaus avaloit* (226)—it is never clearly stated by Robert de Boron that any member of the Grail Company apart from Peter is sent to Avalon. On the contrary, it is specified that the Fisher King's westward journey has brought him to the *illes d'Irlande* (194).

The AVENGING LANCE

When Perceval first sees the Bleeding Lance in the Grail Procession at the court of the Fisher King, no explanation is given of this mysterious object. It is rather his friend Gawain who learns, firstly, that it is destined to destroy Logres and, secondly, that it is the Lance which pierced the side of Christ on the Cross.

After the crucifixion, when he took the body of Jesus down from the Cross and laid it to rest in the Holy Sepulcher, Joseph of Arimathea keeps the Lance which had pierced the side of Christ, as well as the Holy Vessel in which His blood had been collected.[1]

We next hear of the Lance during the evangelizing mission of the Company of the Grail to Sarras. Josephus, the son of Joseph, is struck through the left thigh by a Lance wielded by an angel: His sin is having interrupted his baptizing of the citizens of a pagan city in order to save the unbaptized from being killed by a devil, which claims it is acting on the orders of Christ. The angel later heals Josephus' wound with the same Lance, explaining that the True Crucified One had prophesied that the vengeance of His Adventurous Lance would be inflicted on the first and last of the new ministers anointed and consecrated at His pleasure, so that they can witness to the Lance blow that brought about His death on the Cross.[2]

When Alphasan, the King of the Land Beyond, has the stronghold of Corbenic built to house the Holy Vessel, it is placed in a room next to the main palace. Alphasan has his bed made up in the palace. But when, around midnight, the Grail appears in the palace, a man enveloped in flames and bearing a Lance tells him that he is very foolhardy to sleep there, for Our Lord seeks vengeance. At that he strikes the king through both thighs with the Lance.[3]

King Pellinor is also wounded through the thighs by the Avenging Lance,[4] which Joseph has brought to Logres[5]; as is Pellinor's father Pellehan, who is struck by Balin the Savage with the Lance in the palace of Corbenic. When the Dolorous Blow is struck, a voice is heard announcing the beginning of the marvels of the Adventurous Kingdom, for the vengeance of the High Master will fall on those who have not deserved it.[6]

At the end of the Grail Quest, the Lance will become an agent of healing when Galahad uses the blood that drips from it to anoint the thighs of the Maimed King, who is thereby restored to health. At that moment the Avenging Lance is taken up to the heavens so that no-one in Great Britain would ever again be bold enough to say that he had seen it.[7]

* * *

Contributors to the twentieth century mythology of Grail Initiation (see AFTERWORD: HIGHER MYSTERIES) have claimed that the Avenging Lance was originally wielded by the Biblical Phineas, the third High Priest of Israel, who used it to kill an Israelite woman and the indigenous pagan man she was consorting with, *pour encourager les autres* to avoid doing the same (Numbers 25.6–8). It is said that Phineas caused the Lance to be forged "to symbolize the magical powers inherent in the blood of God's Chosen People"[8] but that it was later seized by Adolf Hitler for whom the divinely chosen ones were not the Jews but the Aryans. For Hitler, the Avenging Lance was the Spear of Destiny which would enable him to rule the world.

Notes

1. *HBG* 19.
2. *LG* I, 49–51: The first minister anointed by Christ to feel the Lance's vengeance is Josephus himself; the last must presumably be Pellehan, who is struck by Balin the Savage with the Lance, which he keeps in his castle of Corbenic (IV, 212).
3. *LG* I, 159.
4. *LG* I, 254: *Icil estoit malades et plaïés de la lanche vengeresse* (*LDG* I, 939).
5. *LG* I, 352.
6. *LG* IV, 212: *Ore comenchent les aventurez e lez mervaillez du roialme aventurus…. Si en prendra li Haus Maistrez sa venjanche sor cheus qui ne l'ont pas deservi* (*SRM* 161–2).
7. *LG* V, 279: *…la Lance s'en ala sus vers le ciel et s'esvanoï en tel maniere qu'il n'ot puis si hardi en toute la Grant Bertaigne qui osast dire qu'il veist la Lance Vencherresse* (*PV* III, 320).
8. Ravenscroft & Wallace-Murphy, 22.

B

BADEMAGU

When Galahad initiates the Grail Quest, King Bademagu is one of the hundred and fifty knights who set off to seek the Holy Vessel in the hope of seeing it uncovered.[1] Arriving at an abbey of white monks, he decides to try on a shield which is kept there, despite being warned that all who do so suffer death or injury soon after. Determined to try the adventure for himself, Bademagu sets off wearing the shield, which bears a red cross on a white background. But he has not ridden very far when he is attacked by a knight wearing white armor who overthrows him, declaring that only the finest knight in Christendom should dare to bear the Red Cross Shield. The White Knight sends the shield to Galahad.[2]

Bademagu recovers, but his quest has not started well. It ends even more badly, for in the course of it he is killed by Gawain.[3]

Notes

1. Malory's Sir Bagdemagus has already seen a sign of the Sangreal, in the form of *a braunche of holy herbe*, a token that can only be found by *a good lyver and a man of prouesse* (*MD* 106). But here Malory may have confused his source, the Post-Vulgate *Merlin Continuation*, in which *une des brankes del Graal* (*SRM* 311) refers to part of the true history of the Grail translated by Helyas.
2. *MD* 678–9; *QHG* 53–57; *LG* IV, 11–12; V, 126–7.
3. *MD* 777; *QHG* 268; *LG* IV, 82; V, 193–6.

BALIN

A poor but virtuous knight of Northumberland whose family has long been involved in a feud with the Maiden of the Lake of Fays (whom he will eventually kill), Balin is destined to strike the Dolorous Blow which will maim the Grail King.

Balin has been disinherited and imprisoned for killing a relative of the King of Northumberland; he is only freed through the intervention of the king's daughter. On that same day a maiden comes to the court (sent by the Lady of the Isle of Avalon) carrying a sword forged there, which can only be drawn from its sheath by the best knight in the land. The king and all his nobles try to draw the sword but it is only Balin who, despite being despised for his poverty, is successful.

The maiden now utters a dire prophecy: If he takes the Ill-Fated Sword away, the first man he kills with it will be the one he loves most in the world; and that man will kill him with the same sword. As it turns out, however, the first person he kills with it will be a woman.

The Maiden of the Lake of Fays, who had given Arthur his sword Excalibur, chooses this moment to enter the court, asking, as her reward for the gift, the head of either Balin or of the maiden from whom he had gained the sword. The Lake Maiden and Balin both accuse each other of murdering members of their family; but the argument is cut short when Balin strikes off her head.[1]

Banished from the royal court, the Knight with Two Swords, as Balin is now known, tries to redeem himself in the king's eyes by capturing Arthur's enemy Rion; but bad luck and tragedy seem to follow him everywhere he goes. It truly seems that the sword is ill-fated, as the maiden who brought it to the court claimed, and that its weird has fallen on Balin for claiming it. This becomes evident to him when he meets Merlin, who tells him that he will strike a blow that will waste three kingdoms for twenty-two years.[2]

Later, when Balin is pursuing a murderous knight who has the power to make himself invisible, Merlin appears to him again and tells him that the felon he is pursuing is none other than Garlon, the brother of King Pellehan of Listenois. Unless Balin gives up his pursuit, he will end up using the Avenging Lance to strike a blow that will devastate the Kingdom of Logres. It will be worse even than the blow struck by the Sword of David, which killed King Lambor and turned Listenois and parts of Wales into a Waste Land; Balin himself will die miserably as a result.[3]

One of the victims of Garlon was accompanied by a maiden, whom Balin now takes under his protection. But, in fact, he is unable to prevent her from being forced to give so much blood, according to the custom of a castle they come to, that she nearly dies as a result.[4] This evil custom will only be brought to an end when Perceval's sister dies from giving her blood but, in doing so, cures the lady of the castle of leprosy.[5]

Doggedly continuing his pursuit of Garlon, Balin, with the maiden in tow, arrives at the court of Pellehan in Corbenic, where a feast is in progress, at which all the guests are required to disarm. Balin insists on keeping one of his two swords, invoking the custom of his country, but he leaves the Ill-Fated Sword in a chamber with the rest of his armor.[6]

Seeing the king's brother serving at table, Balin joins the feast. He is contemplating how to take his revenge and get away with it, when Garlon takes offence at the fact that he does not seem to be tucking in with gusto. Slapping Balin round the face for being so discourteous as to be sat thinking (instead of eating) at the royal table, Garlon is rewarded by a blow from Balin's sword that splits his head all the way down to his chest. Balin then takes the lance with which Garlon had killed one of his victims and strikes his dead body through with it. The court is in uproar and the king himself grabs hold of a wooden rod with which to avenge his brother, bringing it down on Balin's sword so hard that it shatters.

Running from room to room in search of something to defend himself with, Balin eventually looks into a chamber where he sees a Lance standing point upwards in a basin on a silver table.

Ignoring a voice that warns him he is not worthy to enter the chamber, and another which pronounces it sinful for him to touch the Lance, Balin takes it in both hands and strikes King Pellehan with it, piercing both his thighs.[7] At once the castle walls start to shake and fall and its inhabitants drop to the floor in fear. A voice loud enough to be heard throughout the castle proclaims that the marvels of the Kingdom of Adventures will now begin, because soiled hands have befouled the Holy Lance and maimed the most honored of princes. More than a hundred people die of fear at hearing this voice and others—including the maiden Balin brought with him—are crushed by the collapse of the castle walls and of other buildings in the nearby village.

For two days and nights Balin lies unconscious in the ruins, until finally Merlin, who had prophesied the Dolorous Blow, arrives and wakes him. Finding him a horse, Merlin leads Balin out of the castle precincts lest any survivors take their vengeance on him. Balin rides off, but in five days he sees nothing but devastated lands and mourners who wish him nothing but ill.[8] Nor are his troubles over: His destiny has not yet run its course, for he still bears the Ill-Fated Sword, which he has retrieved along with his armor from the chamber where he left it.[9]

In fact, he does not draw the Ill-Fated Sword until, once more ignoring warning signs, he comes to an island guarded, unbeknownst to him, by his brother Balan. Both knights are in disguise and do not recognize each other. After a joust with spears, it is Balan who first draws his sword and strikes his brother. At this, Balin finally draws the cursed sword and thereby kills the man he loves most in the world, but not before they have accidentally exchanged swords after dropping them to the ground.[10] Thus it transpires that both brothers die, after recognizing each other at last, from blows dealt by the Sword of Avalon. As they were born from the same womb, so they are buried in the same tomb.

Merlin, who had earlier warned the Knight with Two Swords that the maiming of King Pellehan would incur divine retribution, arrives later that day and writes on the tomb that Balin was the knight who struck the Dolorous Blow with the Avenging Lance, thus destroying the Kingdom of Listenois. The enchanter stays on the island for more than a month, creating various marvels and prophesying that the Ill-Fated Sword will later be used by Lancelot to kill Gawain. He takes another sword[11] and fixes it by magic in a block of marble so that only the best knight in the world can draw it out, prophesying that ill fortune will befall anyone else who tries to do so. He then pushes the stone into the water so that it floats away. Many years later it will arrive at Camelot on the day that Galahad comes to the court; for he of course is now the Best Knight and so he will draw the Sword in the Floating Stone.[12]

* * *

The tragic fate of Balin is inextricably tied up with the Dolorous Blow which maims the Grail King and extends the Waste Land. It appears to be an inevitable consequence of his pursuing vengeance despite warnings from the Beyond.

He first ignores the warning of the maiden sent by the Lady of the Isle of Avalon, who advises him not to take away with him the sword she has brought to court; he then uses it to behead the Lady of the Lake, in revenge for her murder of his brother.[13] Secondly, he ignores Merlin's warning that, if he pursues his quest to avenge the crimes of Garlon, he will end up using the Avenging Lance to strike a blow against the man (Garlon's brother) who is most valiant in the sight of Our Lord, thus breaking a divine commandment.[14] Thirdly, he ignores a voice that warns him that he is not worthy to enter the room where the Lance is kept, a voice which further warns him not to touch the Lance.[15] Fourthly, he ignores a warning written on a cross in a castle cemetery not to go any further, another from an old man to turn back, and yet another warning from a young girl speaking on behalf of Merlin, about the danger of changing his shield.[16] Inevitably, when he does so, he ends up killing his brother and being killed himself, because unrecognized. This is God's vengeance for the maiming of the Grail King or, as Heinrich Zimmer sees it, for not acquiescing to "the requirements of the mysterious presences from the transcendental realm."[17]

Notes

1. *LG* IV, 186–7; *MD* 46–52.
2. *LG* IV, 190–1: In Malory's version, Merlin

prophesies that *thorow that stroke thre kyngdomys shall be brought into grete poverté, miseri and wrecchednesse twelve yere* (*MD* 57). But twenty-two is the number of years that the marvelous adventures of Logres will last, as predicted by the Angel of the Avenging Lance (*LG* I, 51).

3. *LG* IV, 206.

4. The maiden is required to fill a silver *escuiiele* with her blood (*SRM* 148), recalling the *escüele* in which Joseph of Arimathea caught the blood of the crucified Jesus (*ESG* 25) and which Josephus will later see, in a vision, filled with the Holy Blood (74). We later learn that Garlon's victims can only be truly avenged with the very lance with which he killed the first unknown knight in the presence of Balin (*LG* IV, 206), just as Pellehan can only be healed by Galahad with the weapon with which Balin maimed him. This suggests that Garlon's weapon is an anti–Grail Lance, just as the silver basin of blood which the knight's maiden must fill is an anti–Grail Vessel, and Balin is an anti–Galahad.

5. *LG* IV, 208–9; *MD* 65.

6. This detail is only provided in the Spanish translation of this story, added presumably to explain why the Knight with Two Swords is defenseless when one of his swords breaks in combat with Pellehan (Bogdanow 1966, 48–9).

7. According to the Angel of the Avenging Lance, this is the moment when the Lance will start to bleed, for the first time since it wounded Josephus, signaling the start of the adventures (*LG* I, 51).

8. *LG* IV, 211–14; *MD* 66–8.

9. This clarification is provided by the Spanish version (Bogdanow 1966, 49–50).

10. This detail is only given in the Spanish version of the tale (Bogdanow 1966, 51; *SRM* 648–9).

11. In Malory's version it is the same sword that Balin received from the Maiden of the Isle of Avalon that is claimed by Galahad (*MD* 74) who, therefore, in a sense redeems it. This reinforces the salvific circularity whereby the great-grandson of King Pellehan will heal the Maimed King with the blood from the very Lance that Balin used to strike him and thus, bring to an end the tragic chain of events.

12. *LG* IV, 217–22; *MD* 70–5.

13. *LG* IV, 187.

14. *LG* IV, 191.

15. *LG* IV, 212.

16. *LG* IV, 217–8.

17. Zimmer, 144.

The BLACK HAND

One of the many perilous places which those on the Grail Quest must survive, the Chapel of the Black Hand is first encountered by Gawain, while he is searching for his lost son. A knight on an urgent mission, Silimac, has been killed in his company by an invisible hand. Now, Gawain is led by the knight's horse to complete the dead man's mysterious quest.

Allowing the horse to lead him, Gawain rides through a terrible storm until he comes to a chapel at a crossroads. Taking shelter there, he sees nothing inside, save an altar with a single gold candlestick on top of it and a tall candle giving off a brilliant light. Suddenly a ghastly Black Hand comes straight through a window behind the altar, grasps the candle and snuffs it out. Hearing a voice groaning horribly, Gawain crosses himself and the storm abates. He rides away in the clear night, not stopping until daybreak when he realizes, to his astonishment, that he has crossed from one side of Britain to the other.[1]

The horse now leads him to the court of the Fisher King, on the White Island, where Gawain experiences his second sight of the Grail Procession.

The Chapel of Queen Branguemeure

Perceval also has a close encounter with the Black Hand while searching for the Grail Castle in the hope of making up for his unfortunate reticence on his first visit there. It is while riding through a forest one stormy night that Perceval sees, firstly, the Tree of Candles, with its mysterious fairy lights. Then, just beyond it, he catches sight of a chapel, through the open door of which he can see a candle burning.

He dismounts and enters the chapel, where he finds a slain knight on the altar, his body covered with an embroidered cloth of samite. Before him burns a single candle. Finding it very strange, Perceval waits, hoping to hear someone approach, until he sees a brilliant light, coming from he knows not where: But this light vanishes as inexplicably as it appeared, followed by a thunderous noise so loud that it threatens to shake the chapel to its foundations.

At the stroke of midnight, a Black Hand emerges from behind the altar and snuffs out the single burning candle, leaving Perceval in total darkness. Full of wonder, but undaunted because of his faith in God, he leaves the chapel and rides away in the moonlight.

The next day he meets some hunters in the forest who are in the service of the Fisher King and who show him the way to the Grail Castle. First, however, he meets a girl who tells him that his vision of the Tree and his experience at the chapel are signs of the holy secret[2] about which he will soon hear the truth.

When he comes to the castle, Perceval asks the king about his experiences, including his sighting of the Black Hand in the chapel, but the king replies that he will tell him nothing until he has eaten.[3] Because he is only partially successful when he attempts, like Gawain before him, the test of the sword,[4] Perceval must wait until he comes to the castle for a third time before he learns the holy secrets.

After dinner the Grail Procession passes before them and the king explains that the Lance is the one that pierced the side of Jesus on the Cross. The Vessel is the one in which His blood was caught. The Tree is one where fays gather to lead the faithful astray.

As for the chapel, it was built at the command of Branguemore, the mother of Espinogris, a cruel and violent king who killed her on the day she became a nun and buried her beneath the altar. Since that day, no less than four thousand knights have been killed, either by the Black Hand itself or by the tumult which attends its snuffing out of the candle!

In amazement, Perceval asks whether anyone can rid the chapel of this blight. The king replies that it can only be accomplished if someone were to take from the cupboard in the chapel a white veil which has been placed there, plunge it in holy water and sprinkle it all over the altar, the dead body and the rest of the chapel.

But this would require doing battle with the accursed demon which guards it. Only a man of the utmost prowess would even dare attempt it.[5]

After winning new armor made of gold and silver, forged in Egypt, Perceval returns to the chapel during a terrible thunderstorm and uses his sword, not as a physical weapon, but as a spiritual one: He makes the sign of the Cross with it over his face and the demon of the chapel is driven away, although not before a fearsome thunderbolt burns the chapel, the body and all the countryside thereabouts. Finding the white veil in the cupboard as the Fisher King had predicted, he cleanses everything with holy water. The next day he calls the local priest to bury the badly-burnt body.

A marble tomb has appeared next to a tree, with the name of the dead knight written on it. The priest says that this has happened every day since the death of Queen Branguemore: Whenever a knight died fighting the Black Hand, a made-to-measure tomb appeared in the graveyard beneath the tree where he was to lie. But the knight they bury that day will be the last, thanks to Perceval.[6]

* * *

The First Continuation of the Story of the Grail has a nightmarish, *film noir* quality that continues to puzzle and intrigue the reader. One of the most striking images its author creates is that of the Black Hand. But, as with Chrétien's presentation of the Grail Hallows, the anonymous poet never gets the chance to explain its mysteries. This is left to a later versifier, Manessier, whose "elucidations," no doubt influenced by the prose romances, too often reduce every threat to demonic possession.

Thus later, in episodes which also form part of the Vulgate *Queste*, when the Devil in the shape of a black horse attempts to throw Perceval from a cliff into a raging torrent, or to seduce him in the form of his beloved Blancheflor, this is, or so a hermit explains, an attempt at revenge for his defeat in the Chapel of the Black Hand. For, when he overcame the demon there, the Devil was enraged.⁷

Notes

1. *CSG* 214.
2. *Senefie lou saint secré* (*CP* IV, l.32254).
3. *CSG* 333–5.
4. See THE SWORD OF PARTINAL.
5. *CSG* 480.
6. *CSG* 513–6.
7. *CSG* 521: *Et quant an la chapelle fustes,/ Et vos illuec vaincu eüstes/ Et l'anemi et la main noire// Molt correciez li anemis* (*MTC* ll. 38287–9, 38294).

The BLACK MAIDEN of Proud Castle

King Arthur is holding court at Caerleon-on-Usk when he sees a black woman with hideously misshapen face and body enter, riding a yellow mule. She greets the king and his retinue, with the exception of Peredur Long Spear, whom she sharply criticizes for failing to ask the cause and meaning of the marvels that he saw in the court of his uncle the Lame King¹: These included two squires carrying an enormous spear with three streams of blood running from it, as well as two girls carrying a large platter on which was a man's disembodied, blood-covered head.² Had Peredur but asked, the king would have been made well and the kingdom peaceful.

The Black Maiden dwells in Proud Castle,³ one of the fortresses built by the Knights of the Waste Land.⁴ She later explains that she was one of the girls who carried the platter with the bleeding head (which belonged to his late cousin) and also one of the squires who carried the bleeding spear (which lamed his uncle).

Peredur's cousin had been killed and his uncle lamed by the hags of Gloucester, the Black Maiden (who is also Peredur's cousin) explains: It was prophesied that Peredur would take revenge, which indeed, is precisely what he does.⁵ She gives no explanation, however, for her shape-shifting abilities.

* * *

For R.S. Loomis, the Welsh figure of the Black Maiden is derived, not from Chrétien's Ugly Maiden (q.v.), but from the Irish mythic figure of Lady Sovereignty, one of whose most notable traits is "her transformation from extreme ugliness to radiant beauty."⁶

More recently, Caitlín Matthews sees her as the ugly, reproachful form of that divinely mutable Lady, from whom Peredur has become estranged: "The Black Maiden is the Goddess in her guise as the Dark Woman of Knowledge."⁷ For both writers she represents the angry face of the Grail Bearer,⁸ turned ugly by the hero's failure at the court of the Maimed King.

Notes

1. *M* 248–9.
2. *M* 226.
3. *M* 249.
4. *CSG* 561.
5. *M* 256–7: Revenge—in this case for the death of the lame Fisher King's brother—is also what motivates Perceval in Manessier's Continuation to the Story of the Grail.
6. Loomis 1926, 50.
7. Matthews 2002, 194.
8. For Glenys Goetinck (1975, 6): "She brings with her a breath of the Other World at its most fearsome."

BLAISE

The Master Blaise is the confessor of Merlin's mother and, as a consequence, the first person to discover the secret of the half-human, half-demonic prophet. He is also the first person to whom Merlin reveals the secret history of the Grail. As a result, Blaise becomes the first person to write the story of the Holy Vessel, thus inaugurating a literary tradition that continues to the present day.

Merlin is in fact no more than two-and-a-half years old when he convinces a skeptical Blaise that his knowledge of the future is divinely inspired and asks him to set down certain revelations in a book. He then tells

Blaise about the love between Christ and Joseph of Arimathea and how Joseph suffered imprisonment because of his role at the Deposition. Merlin continues with the history of the Holy Grail from the time Joseph, before his death, passed it on. He then tells Blaise about Joseph's brother-in-law Bron, Bron's son Alan the Fat and the Company of the Grail, including their relative Peter, who had all set out on a journey to the West. Merlin concludes with an account of how the demons agreed to create a man who would counteract the harm done to their cause by the prophets of God. This man is, of course, Merlin himself who, through his mother's repentance, is lost to the demons.

Blaise writes everything down. Merlin tells him that Blaise will finish his book among the Company of the Grail, when he at last meets the people whose lives he has been chronicling. At that time, his book will be combined with that of Joseph of Arimathea to produce one book of great beauty, which will contain the entire sacred history—with the exception of those words that were uttered in private between Joseph and Christ, words which Merlin will keep secret.[1]

As we should expect, all transpires as Merlin has prophesied: When Perceval finds the court of the Fisher King and asks the purpose of the Grail Procession, the king is cured of his sickness and three days later dies, after entrusting to Perceval the Secret Words of Christ. When Blaise, who has been living in Northumberland, is told of this, he asks Merlin to fulfill his promise. He is accordingly brought to the court of the new Fisher King, Perceval, where the scribe joins the Company of the Grail as soon as he has finished his writing. He leads such a saintly life that he is often visited by the Holy Spirit.[2]

* * *

This is the story of Blaise as it has come down to us in the trilogy of prose romances attributed to Robert de Boron. However, in the Vulgate Cycle, where the work of Robert de Boron was rewritten, significant changes were introduced, putting at risk our trust either in the reliability of Blaise's narrative or in the infallibility of Merlin.

So many details in the earlier writings—that, for example, Joseph of Arimathea dies in the Holy Land, rather than bringing the Grail to Britain; that Joseph's disciple Peter washes up in Avalon rather than Orkney; that Perceval is the son of Alan the Fat and the grandson of Bron, the Fisher King; and that it is Perceval, rather than Galahad, who successfully heals the Grail King—are all contradicted in the Vulgate texts. These claim a higher authority than that of Blaise and Merlin, since they have allegedly been written by Christ Himself and translated into Latin by Nascien the Hermit in the middle of the eighth century (some three hundred years after the death of Arthur) before eventually being translated into French by de Boron.

Nascien, in fact, having been entrusted with the Holy Story by Christ, writes it down at the behest of the Holy Master until he fits it to Blaise's book,[3] which we might feel has now become redundant. As Rupert T. Pickens has pointed out, Christ and His Incarnation are at the center of early Grail history, so that the Grail Book He gives to Nascien is His autobiography, just as Merlin dictates *his* autobiography to Blaise.

When Nascien joins his book to Blaise's the story, begun by one who is half demon, half man is completed by one who is both God and Man; one whose story it essentially is. Just as the poem and prose redaction of Robert de Boron are superseded by the later Vulgate Cycle, so the revelations of Merlin to Blaise are superseded by those of Christ to Nascien: The Son of the Devil is outranked by the Son of Man when it comes to the writing of the divine autobiography.

Insofar as the De Boron Cycle was subsumed into, and replaced by, the Vulgate, which became the popular reading of the thirteenth century and beyond, discrepancies between the two accounts would not have been of concern. But for the modern reader, the question that must be posed is whether the incorrect information that Merlin gives Blaise is deliberately faulty, in order to greater glorify Christ as what Pickens calls the "mediator of divine text"[4]; or whether we should simply accept that, since it does not come naked into the world, something of the truth is always lost in translation.

Notes

1. MG 61–3; LG I, 176: ...*tu t'en iras en celes parties ou celes genz sont qui le vaissel dou Graal ont.... Lors si assembleras ton livre au lor.... Et quant li dui seront assemblé, s'en i avra .I. biau, et li dui seront une meisme chose, fors tant que je ne puis dire ne retraire, ne droiz n'est, les privees paroles de Joseph et de Jhesu Crist* (RBM 75–6).
2. MG 155–6: *Quant Blaise sot fait sen escrit, si l'en aporta chiés Perceval qui le Graal gardoit, et estoit de si sainte vie que li sains Esperis descendoit a lui sovent* (RG 301; MG 171). However, the Book of Blaise is not combined with the Book of Joseph (a text transmitted by Christ to the hermit Nascien) until the eighth century.
3. LG I, 288–9.
4. Pickens, 106.

The BLEEDING LANCE

When Perceval first arrives at the castle of the Fisher King, he witnesses several wondrous things, including a Lance from whose tip fall three drops of blood. Gawain later learns that it is destined to destroy Logres, but it is only after much tribulation and testing that the heroes discover that the Lance is the one with which Jesus was struck in the side on the Cross by the centurion Longinus. What they are not told is the secret history of the Holy Lance, which has, since the crucifixion, played a pivotal role in the peregrinations of the Company of the Grail.

The Adventurous Lance

When Joseph of Arimathea, his eldest son Josephus, and the rest of his family and followers leave Jerusalem, they are carrying with them an ark, containing the Vessel in which Joseph had collected the Holy Blood of Christ. After several days, the Company of the Grail, as they will come to be known, reaches the pagan city of Sarras, where they are received by its king, Evalach the Unknown.

Here Josephus is invested as a priest of Christ in the Spiritual Palace and, as he and his followers pray before the ark, the Holy Spirit descends on them in a flash of fire. A voice tells Josephus to open the door of the ark and he sees therein a man in a robe redder than fiery lightning. The man is escorted by five angels who each have six wings and carry, in their left hand, a bloody sword and, in their right hand, the bloody emblems of the Passion of Jesus. The third angel holds in his right hand a Lance whose iron tip and wooden shaft are covered with blood.[1]

Josephus then has a vision of the crucifixion, in which he sees the angel's Lance embedded in the side of the crucified Man. A stream of blood mixed with water runs down from the wound into the Holy Vessel that his father Joseph has placed in the ark. It seems to Josephus that the Vessel is nearly full and the blood is about to spill.[2]

But the first blood that the Lance will spill in fact turns out to be that of Josephus himself, in accordance with a prophecy of the crucified Jesus that He will spread the vengeance of His Adventurous Lance on the first and last of His new ministers, who have been anointed and consecrated at His pleasure.[3]

The first of these ministers is Josephus, who is maimed by the Angel of the Bleeding Lance when he disobeys a divine decree: Josephus has been baptizing the citizens of Orcaut, the richest city in the domains of King Evelach, but stops in order to try to prevent the demon Selaphas from killing those who would rather leave the country than abandon their pagan faith. When Josephus attempts to restrain the demon, he is confronted by the angel, with a face like a blazing thunderbolt, who pierces him through the left thigh with the Lance.

Josephus pulls the Lance out easily, but the metal tip remains in the wound.

Joseph takes the Lance back with him to Sarras and leans it against the wall, next to the ark that holds the Holy Grail, in the Spiritual Palace. Later the angel emerges from the ark, holding a white box. He removes the tip of the Lance from Josephus' thigh and places it on the box, which starts to fill with blood.

The angel washes the eyes of Evalach's brother-in-law Nascien (who has been blinded by looking at the Grail) with the blood and restores his sight.[4] With the same blood the angel heals the wound of Josephus, although he will always henceforth walk with a limp. The Lance now stops bleeding. But the angel tells Josephus that, when the Lance starts bleeding again, it will symbolize the beginning of the marvelous adventures which will take place in the land where God intends to lead him (Britain).

Just as Josephus is the first of Christ's ministers to be struck by the Lance, so the last will be a king of his family, who will not be healed until the marvels of the Holy Grail are revealed to the last man in Nascien's lineage. The angel further prophesies that the adventures, which will take place in the land where Josephus' family and their descendants will settle under divine guidance, will last as many years as the number of days he carried the tip of the Lance embedded in his thigh (that is, twenty-two).[5]

Misery and Destruction

It will be hundreds of years later before the second half of Christ's prophecy is fulfilled and the last of the good, an anointed king and consecrated minister, experiences the vengeance of His Adventurous Lance.

When the Company of the Grail eventually make it to Britain, the role of Josephus as guardian of the Grail passes to his cousin Alan the Fat, then to Alan's brother Joshua, who is made King of the Land Beyond. From Joshua the guardianship passes to his descendants, who keep the Grail in the castle of Corbenic in Listenois. The fifth of Joshua's lineage is King Pellehan, whose fate is to fulfill the angel's prophecy[6]: He has a brother, Garlon, who is as evil and treacherous as Pellehan is holy and noble, and who is able to make himself invisible.

The evil Garlon makes use of his invisibility to strike down knights, apparently at random, but he comes unstuck when he kills those under the protection of Balin the Savage. Balin pursues Garlon to the court of Listenois (despite Merlin's warning that, if he does so, he will strike a blow with the Avenging Lance which will cause misery and destruction to many kingdoms[7]) and slays him during a feast.

Balin, chased by King Pellehan through the castle, enters a room containing a silver table, despite hearing a mysterious voice which tells him that he is not worthy to do so. Standing with its blade pointing down, in a vase of silver and gold in the middle of the table, is a Lance which, astonishingly, stands upright, though apparently unsupported.[8]

Again, ignoring a voice warning him not to touch it, Balin seizes the Lance and strikes the king with it through both his thighs. He then puts the Lance back into the vase, where it stands as upright as before. But Pellehan falls wounded to the ground and his castle starts to collapse around him. His kingdom is devastated.

Thus, is struck the Dolorous Blow. Thus is the Grail King maimed. Thus, does divine vengeance fall, on innocent and guilty alike, because sinful hands have been laid on the Most Holy Lance.[9]

Tears of Blood

The hero Perceval is the first to arrive at the castle that houses the Bleeding Lance. After being given a sword by the maimed lord of the castle, the Fisher King, Perceval observes a ritualistic procession led by a youth holding a white Lance, from whose iron tip blood runs down to his hand.[10]

Perceval, who has been taught not to ask too many questions, refrains from asking how this marvel comes about and continues to remain silent in the presence of the Grail itself.

He stays the night at the castle and gets up the next morning, intending to ask one of the page boys about what he has seen, but he finds the castle deserted. Riding out into the forest, he comes upon his cousin, who questions him about his visit to the Grail Castle. She upbraids him for not asking why the Lance bled, despite being without flesh and veins,[11] or where the Grail Procession was going. Had he done so, the Maimed King would have regained the use of his limbs and been able to govern his land.[12]

Sometime later, when Perceval is at Arthur's court, he is similarly criticized by the Ugly Maiden. She says that when he was in the house of the Fisher King it was too much effort for him to open his mouth to speak, so that he couldn't ask why blood fell from the Lance head.[13] As a result of Perceval's failure to ask the appropriate questions, the king will now never hold any part of his lands, which will be laid waste. As a result, many knights will perish, ladies will be widowed and maidens made orphans. Perceval swears that he will not rest until he discovers who is served from the Grail or until he has found the Lance and been told the truth about why it bleeds.[14]

At that moment there enters the court a knight who accuses Arthur's nephew Gawain of treacherously killing his lord, the King of Escavalon. Gawain is summonsed to appear at the court of the new king to answer the charges in hand-to-hand combat. When he arrives there, Gawain finds himself besieged in the keep by the angry townsfolk, who recognize him as the killer of the old king. The young king's vavasor offers him an escape route: The duel will be postponed for a year while Gawain searches for the Lance whose head weeps blood. Gawain must give his oath that he will return in a year and hand over the Lance, or be subjected once more to captivity. The vavasor adds, alarmingly, that it is written that the realm of Logres will one day be destroyed by the Lance[15]; but Gawain nevertheless swears to do all in his power to find it.[16]

After many adventures, Gawain arrives at the Grail Castle, where he is invited to dine in the hall. While he is there, he sees a handsome boy enter carrying the Bleeding Lance,[17] followed in a procession by the Holy Grail and a Broken Sword on a bier. Gawain, realizing that this is the Lance he has sworn to find, asks the king about the meaning of these things. He is told that he can only discover the truth about the Grail and the Lance if he can make the sword whole again. Gawain is only partially successful, falling asleep while the king is talking to him. When he awakes, he is no longer in the castle, but in a marsh.[18]

Further distractions intervene until, fearing that he is in danger of missing his appointment at Escavalon, he sets out once more and eventually confesses to the king that he has been unable to bring him the Lance. The situation is only resolved by the arrival of King Arthur, who makes peace between the parties.[19]

Later Gawain comes to the White Island, which is joined to the mainland by a causeway, where in a great hall he sees the Grail feeding everyone there. Once again, he sees the Lance, which this time is standing upright, bleeding into a silver vase. The blood flows from the vase through a golden pipe into an emerald channel and thence out of the hall and out of sight.[20]

Gawain is astonished that a lance can bleed and asks the Grail King where all the blood comes from. The king explains that the Lance represents both healing and salvation, for it is the one with which Jesus was smitten in the side when He was crucified.[21] Ever since that day the Lance, which has always been kept in the house of the Grail Kings, has bled constantly and will continue to do so until the Last Judgment.[22]

Once again, however, Gawain falls

asleep, waking to find himself on a towering cliff beside the sea. Vowing to find the court again, so that he can also ask about the Grail, he sets off across the once-ruined country, which had been devastated when an evil blow was struck by a sword—evil in contrast to the joy brought about when the Lance pierced Christ's side, since His blood is our ransom. Yet now the Waste Land is, once more, green and flourishing: God restored the waters to their courses as soon as Gawain asked why the Lance bleeds. All the people who pass him, bless him for what he has achieved, but also berate him for not staying awake long enough to hear what the Grail is for. Had he done so, Gawain would have repopulated the kingdom.[23]

The Well-Struck Blow

Meanwhile, Perceval has also been searching for the court which houses the Bleeding Lance.[24] When at last he arrives for the second time at the Grail Castle, he sees as before the Holy Vessel. He also sees a sword which is broken in two,[25] although now it is not a boy but a girl, dressed in white silk, who carries the Lance.[26] He asks the king to tell him the truth about these wonders, but the king says that only if Perceval can fully repair the Sword will he tell him about the Grail and the Lance with the "royal" head.

Perceval succeeds in joining the two halves of the sword together, but just by the join there remains a small notch. The king tells Perceval that he cannot know the secret of the Lance and the Grail until the notch in the sword has been repaired. If he can do this, he should return to the Grail Castle, for only then will he learn all the truth concerning the secrets of God's work.[27]

When, after many trials and tribulations, Perceval makes his way once more to the Grail Castle, he sees again the Bleeding Lance carried by a girl in white silk.[28] When Perceval this time succeeds in perfectly joining the sword, the king tells him what he has already explained to Gawain: The Lance is the one with which Longinus struck Christ on the Cross. What flows from it is what flowed from God's side when He was pierced: the Holy Blood of Jesus who, mortally wounded, harried Hell.[29] The blow was well struck, for Christ's death delivers us from Hell and reverses the evils of the Fall.[30]

When, following the death of his uncle, Perceval becomes the new Grail King, the Lance is among the hallows that appear to everyone at his coronation.[31] It later follows him to a hermitage, when he retires from this world. Perceval dies on Candlemas Eve and the Lance accompanies his soul to Heaven.[32]

Anointing with Blood

However, others say that Lancelot's cousin, Sir Bors, is the first of the Knights of the Round Table to see the Avenging Lance, on his second visit to Corbenic, after surviving the perils of the Adventurous Palace. The Lance is carried by an old man and Bors is astonished to see drops of blood running from the iron head adown the shaft, ending up he knows not where.[33] But, recognizing that the Lance is a holy thing, the knight bows before it.

The old man who brought it in acclaims him as the purest and worthiest of all the knights whom adventure has brought to the castle. When he returns to his own country, Bors can say that he has seen the Avenging Lance; yet he cannot know the truth about the Lance until the Perilous Seat has found its master. It is only through him who is destined to sit there that Bors will find out where the Lance came from and who brought it to the Land Beyond.[34] The old man then carries the Lance back into the Grail chamber.[35]

The knight of whom the old man speaks is Galahad and he, along with Bors and Perceval, are the principle three of the twelve blessed knights who arrive at Corbenic to witness the achieving of the Grail Quest. They see four angels carrying Josephus, the first Christian bishop, on a throne, which they place next to the Table of the Grail. One of the angels is bearing a Lance which bleeds so profusely that he has to catch the drops in a container held in his other hand. The angel then holds the Lance against the Holy Vessel so that the blood runs into it.[36]

The knights now watch the Mass of the Holy Grail performed by the spirit of Josephus and receive the Eucharist from the hands of Christ at the Table of the Grail. But it is Galahad, the great-grandson of King Pellehan, who is instructed by the Savior to anoint the legs of the Maimed King with the blood dripping from the Lance.[37] When the chosen knight does so,[38] Pellehan is immediately restored to health.[39]

Galahad, Perceval and Bors, two life-long virgins and one chaste knight, take the hallows to the city of Sarras, where Galahad is made king for a year. On the day of his death, a hand comes down from Heaven and carries both the Grail and the Lance away, never to be seen again.[40]

Notes

1. *Et li tiers angeles tenoit en la main destre une grant lanche, dont li fiers estoit tous sanglens et la hanste estoit toute sanglente ausi jusque par la ou li angeles le tenoit empoignie* (ESG 73).
2. *LG* I, 24: This divine spilt blood becomes, in the medieval legend, something that must be avenged; and it is this obsession with vengeance, if not the Lance itself, that is indeed to bring about the destruction of the Kingdom of Logres. In the First Continuation the Holy Lance brings great joy to humankind, for the spilt blood is our ransom; but in the Vulgate Cycle, the Lance becomes the agent of divinely sanctioned vengeance (see THE AVENGING LANCE).
3. *LG* I, 51: Jesus adds: "I want these two to be loyal witnesses to Me, for it was through the blow of My lance that My death on the cross was sought and approved by the evil Jews." This antisemitic "blood libel" is characteristic of some of the Grail legends: The belief that the Jews were collectively and indefinitely responsible for murdering Jesus fed the inspiration for the Holocaust.
4. The Vulgate author may have been familiar with the hagiographical story, incorporated into the thirteenth century *Golden Legend* (and printed in the fifteenth century by Caxton) that the blood of Jesus restored the sight of Longinus, who once was blind.
5. *LG* I, 49-51.
6. The *Estoire de Merlin* confuses matters by telling us that Pellinor, one of Pellehan's sons, is ill, having been wounded by the Avenging Lance through both his thighs (*LG* I, 254): *Icil estoit malades et plaïes de la lanche vengeresse dont il estoit plaïes et apelés Mehaigniés et estoit navrés par ambes .II. les quisses, et fu apelés par son droit non li rois Pellinor de Lystenois* (LDG I, 939). According to the *Livre d'Artus*, also, Pellinor is *mahaignié de la cuisse de la lance vencheresse* (VS VII, 146). Since Pellinor is here the father of Perceval, the original Grail Hero, this detail may be an attempt to link with Chrétien's poem, in which Perceval's father is struck through the thighs.
7. *LG* IV, 206.
8. *En un lieu de la chamber avoit un tabel d'argent.... E desus la tabel, droit en mi lieu, avoit un orçuel d'argent et d'or, e dedenz cele orçuel estoit une lance drescie, la point desoz e le haut desuz* (SRM 160); *and upon the table stoode a mervaylous spere strangely wrought* (MD 68). The Lance is not bleeding, because the Adventures of the Grail have not yet begun. But when Galahad comes to Corbenic for the final time and sees *La Lance Aventureuse, celle meemes dont li filz Deu soufri mort* (PV III, 320), it has been dripping blood for twenty-two years, in accordance with the angelic prophecy.
9. *LG* IV, 212-3.
10. *Uns vaslez d'une chambre vint,/ Qui une blanche lance tint/ Anpoigniee par le milieu,// S'issoit une gote de sanc/ Del fer de la lance an somet* (PCG ll.3191-3, 98-9); *Aprés vint un vallés qui aporta une lance, et sannoit par le fer trois goutes de sanc* (RG 245). In the Welsh Romance of Peredur, two lads enter the hall carrying "a spear of incalculable size with three streams of blood running from the socket to the floor" (M 226).
11. *La lance don la pointe sainne,/ Et si n'i a ne char ne vainne* (PCG ll.3549-50).
12. *CSG* 28-32.
13. *Por quoi cele gote de sanc/ Saute par la pointe del fer blanc!* (PCG ll.4657-8).
14. *CSG* 41-2: Perceval will eventually find out who is served from the Grail when he visits his hermit uncle, who also tells him that it is his sinfulness which prevented him from asking about the iron lance which never stops bleeding: *le fer qui ainz n'estancha/ De seignier* (PCG ll.6410-1).
15. *La lance don la pointe lerme/ Del sanc tot cler que ele plore,/ Et s'est escrit qu'il iert une ore/ Que toz li reaumes de Logres,// Sera destruiz par cele lance* (PCG ll.6166-9, 6171).
16. *CSG* 53-4.
17. *Une blanche lance roonde/ Tint li vallés dedens sa main.// Et de la lance li fers saine/ Et point a saignier ne laissa* (CP I, ll.1334-5, 1338-9; PSG 111).
18. *CSG* 108-9.
19. *CSG* 115-20.

20. *Et une lance tote entiere/ Qui sist en un orcel d'argent,/ Enficie i ert droitement./ Icele lance si sainot,/ Si que li sans vermeus colot/ Dedens cel vaisel a fuison./ Tot entor la lance environ/ Paroient les traces des gotes/ Qui en l'orcel caoient totes./ Si tos con cil sans i estoit,/ Par un tüel d'or s'en issoit,/ S'entroit en un conduit errant/ D'une esmeraude verdoiant./ Hors de la sale s'en aloit* (PCP ll.7324-37).

21. *Quar c'est cele veraiement/ Donc li filz Dieu omnipotent/ Fu le jor el costé feruz,/ Quant en la croiz fu estanduz* (CP II, ll.17515-8): In the German version of Wolfram von Eschenbach, the Lance has no Christian connotations, being merely a poisoned weapon wielded by a pagan warrior from Ethnise—"where the Tigris flows out of Paradise"—who seeks to win the Grail by force of arms. Jousting with Anfortas, he pierces the king in the scrotum but is himself killed. The lance-head is removed from Anfortas' body but the wound continues to fester (WP 244-5), being only alleviated by the weapon that caused it, during the right astrological configuration (249). It is because the Lance has to be thrust into the wound that it is covered with blood when Parzival sees it (250).

22. *Puis a esté toz jorz ici,/ Et si sainne toz jorz einsi/ Et saingnera durablement/ Desi au jor du jugement* (CP II, ll.17519-22): This explanation is contradicted by the Vulgate which, as we saw above, says that the Lance bled when Josephus, who had been wounded by it, was healed by the blood, stopped bleeding afterwards, but would start bleeding again to signal the beginning of the adventures of Britain.

23. CSG 216-20.
24. CSG 237.
25. See THE SWORD OF PARTINAL.
26. Following the girl carrying the Grail, *une autre pucelle est venue,/ Ainz plus belle ne fu veüe,/ Vestue d'un dyapre blanc./ La lance portoit qui lou sanc/ Par ansonc le fer degoutoit* (CP IV, ll.32403-7). In the Prose *Perceval*, in what is the hero's second and final visit to the court of the Fisher King, we are not told who carries the Bleeding Lance, only that it is the Lance of Longinus with which Christ was struck on the Cross (MG 155).

27. CSG 336-9: *Et lors si porriez demander/ Et del Graal et de la Lance,/ Et sachiez bien tout affiance/ Qu'adont savrez la verté fine,/ Les secrez et l'oevre devine* (GCP ll.38-42).

28. GCP ll.17027-31: In the *Elucidation*, Perceval sees the Lance bleeding into a basin, from which the blood streams along a silver channel: *Et li russiaus de sanc couroit/ D'un orçuel ou la lance estoit,/ Par le rice tuiel d'argent* (EB ll.273-5). In this version, although he asks about the Grail and the dead body on the bier, he fails to ask about the Lance and the Sword (CSG 558-9).

29. *Li sans precïeus qui se lance/ Dou fer qui est desus la lance,/ Qui si est tres bel et tres blanc,/ Ce est li sains precïeus senc/ Qui dou costé Dieu descendi/ Quant Longis dou fer lou feri./ Ce est la lance, c'est li fer/ Dont celui qui brisa anfer/ Fu a mort feru et plaié* (MTC ll.32663-71). In the Prose *Perceval* the Fisher King simply says: *saciés que ce est ci li lance dont Longis feri Jhesucrist en le crois* (RG 270). This is expanded in the alternative ending to the Second Continuation found in one manuscript: *C'est la lance tot vraiement/ Dont li fix Deu soffri torment/ Quant en la crois fu estendus./ Ens el costé en fu ferus,/ Li sans contreval en glaça,/ Longis s'en terst et raluma* (CP IV, 591).

30. CSG 474-7: The lance is in the Third Continuation a symbol of redemption rather than, as in the Vulgate, the agent of divine vengeance: a role which Manessier reserves for the Sword of Partinal.

31. This time it is once more, as in Chrétien's original poem, carried by a boy rather than a girl, following the Grail Bearer (MTC ll.42493-6).

32. CSG 554-5.

33. *Et de tant com Boorz le voit plus, d'itant est il plus esbahiz, car il voit que dou fer issoient goutes de sanc, l'unne aprés l'autre degoutant aval le fust, mais il ne set qu'eles devienent* (LM V, 268).

34. *Or porrez dire, quant vos serez en vostre païs, que vos avez veu la lance vengerresce; si ne savez que ce est a dire ne ne savroiz devant que li perileux sieges de la Table Reonde avra trouvé son mestre, mais par celui qui s'i aserra savrez vos de la verité de ceste lance et qui l'aporta en cest païs et dom ele vint* (LM V, 268). One manuscript describes the Lance, not as *vengerresce*, but as *virginesse* (LDG III, 626), which, given the Vulgate's obsession with virginity and chastity, may count as a medieval example of a Freudian slip *avant la lettre*.

35. LG III, 270; *and that speare was called the Speare of Vengeaunce* (MD 629).

36. In the Post-Vulgate version, Galahad is led alone into a chamber where the Maimed King lies next to the Table of the Grail, on which he sees a Lance which he thinks must be the one with which the holy flesh of Christ was wounded. The Lance stands upright, "point down and shaft up," in a silver basin. From the point it sheds drops of blood which fall thickly into the basin, only to disappear from sight (LG V, 279). Here the ability of the Lance to stand without support—*et celle estoit mise en l'air, la pointe desouz et li fust desus, et pendoit si merveilleussement que mortex hom ne peust pas veoir qui la sostenoit* (PV III, 320)—is as astonishing as when Balin first saw it: *Et qui regardast mult la lanche, il merveillaist coment el tenist droite, car ele n'estoit apoié ne d'un part ne d'autre* (SRM 160-1).

37. Christ says *por ce que ge ne voil pas que tu t'en ailles de cest païs sanz la garison au Roi Mehaignié, voil je que tu pregnes del sanc de ceste lance et li en ong les jambes: car ce est la chose par quoi il sera gariz, ne autre chose nel puet garir* (QP 271).

38. *Et Galaad vient a la lance qui ert couchiee sus la table et toucha au sanc, puis vient au Roi Mehaignié et li en oinst les jambes par la ou il avoit esté feruz* (QP 271-2).

39. MD 782-4; LG IV, 84-5: It is at this point, in the Post-Vulgate version, that the Lance and the basin in which the blood was caught rise up, skywards. The author comments that, though we cannot know for sure whether the Holy Lance and basin

went to Heaven, it was nevertheless God's will that nobody in Britain from then on could claim to have seen them (*LG* V, 279).

40. *LG* IV, 87; *MD* 788: However, in the later Romance of Sone, the eponymous hero is shown (along with other sacred relics such as the Holy Grail, a fragment of the True Cross and the tomb of Joseph of Arimathea) the holy iron tip—*saint fier* (*MGL* 316, l.4913)—of the Bleeding Lance, in the Abbey of the Isle of Galoche: *Li fiers mout biaus et blans estoit./ A la pointe devant pendoit/ Une goute de sanc viermeille,/ Dont mout de gent vient a mierveille* (318, ll.4917-20). If many people marvel at the site of the Bleeding Lance, it may be that its function is precisely to make us wonder: *La lance qui saigne invite à s'interroger sur la merveille* (Dubost, 170).

The BLEEDING SWORD

Joseph of Arimathea, after bringing the Grail vessel to Britain and converting the pagans of Camelot to Christianity, is wounded through the thighs by the seneschal of the Castle of the Rock in Broceliande. The sword with which the blow is struck breaks in half, leaving the point in Joseph's thigh.

Though wounded himself, Joseph heals the pagan lord of the castle of a head wound and brings his dead brother back to life, causing all the people of the castle to convert to Joseph's God. He then draws the metal tip of the sword out of his thigh, cleanly, without shedding any blood. But he declares that from then on it would bleed, until such time as the two halves of the sword can be joined together by him who is to accomplish the adventures of the Holy Grail.[1]

After Joseph leaves the castle, the sword is kept there until it is eventually won from its guardians by Eliezer, the son of the rich Fisher King Pelles, keeper of the Holy Grail. Eliezer carries with him at all times the two halves of the sword, in the hope of meeting the man who can join them together. When he meets Gawain, whose noble reputation precedes him, Eliezer believes he has found the man he is looking for, the man who will bring to an end the adventures of the Grail.[2]

Drawing from its scabbard the broken sword, Eliezer keels before it and kisses its pommel. Gawain and his nine companions are astonished to see drops of blood, one after the other, flowing from the tip of the sword.[3] But, though they are the pinnacle of earthly chivalry, the Knights of the Round Table have not yet been joined by him who is to be the pinnacle of spiritual chivalry. One after the other, they fail, much to Eliezer's distress.

Weeping bitterly, he explains that he kissed it because he can never die on the day that he does so; that he kneels before it, because it is holy; that through it, the adventures of the Grail will be accomplished; and that it has produced many miracles since he has been carrying it.[4] Eliezer then returns to Corbenic, to await the coming of the best knight in the world.[5]

When, finally, the three companions on the Quest (Galahad, Perceval and Bors) arrive at the Grail Castle, Eliezer immediately presents them with the sword.[6] They all try to mend it, but only Galahad succeeds.[7] The two halves are now joined so perfectly together that no one could tell that it had ever been broken.[8]

The people of Corbenic, delighted that the adventure has been brought to a satisfactory close, give the sword to Bors, saying it could have no better owner.[9]

Notes

1. *LG* I, 141-2; III, 89-90: *Ha! espee, jamés resoudee ne seras devant ce que cil te tendra a ses mains qui les hautes aventures del Graal doit assomer, mais, si tost come il te tendra, si rejoindras a force; et cele partie qui en ma char entra ne sera jamais nule foiz veüe que sans n'en isse, tant qe cil qui la soudera la tiengne* (*ESG* 501).

2. *...cil qui doit les hautes aventures del Graal asomer et mener a chief* (*LM* II, 328). In fact, in another prose romance, *Perlesvaus*, Gawain wins another Bleeding Sword, the one with which John the Baptist was beheaded, thus gaining entry to the Grail Castle.

3. *...trop s'esmiervellent tout cil ki le regardent, car il voient ke de le pointe de l'espee chieent goutes de sanc l'une avant l'autre menuement* (*LDL* V, 630).

4. *...je sai bien qu'ele est sainte, kar par li seront achevees les aventures del saint Graal, et maint miracle en ai je veu, puis que je la portai premierement* (*LM* II, 339).

5. *LG* III, 87–91.

6. ...*l'Espee Brisiee* ... *cele dont Joseph ot esté feruz parmi la quisse* (*QP* 266).

7. Perceval's failure to mend the sword marks a definitive break with the earlier, verse tradition (see THE BROKEN SWORD and THE SWORD OF PARTINAL): Galahad has taken his place, in the prose cycle, as the Best Knight. In some manuscripts of the Prose *Tristan*, it is Galahad alone who tries the "marvelous test" of the sword, joining the two halves together so that it is better than before. It would later perform other miracles (Barber 2005, 202): *Et li rois le mainne en une cambre et li moustre l'espee qui ert brisie, qui se brisa en la quisse de Joseph de Barimachie. Galaad le prent et le joint ensamble, et ele se saude ausi com ele fu onques miex. Et fist mout autres beles miracles* (*TPM* IX, 253–4).

8. *Et maintenant reprennent les pieces si merveilleusement qu'il n'a pas home ou monde qui la briseure qui devant i estoit poïst reconoistre, ne que ele eust onques esté brisiee* (*QP* 266).

9. *LG* IV, 83–4; *QHG* 272–3: Presumably this is the sword that Bors bears when he, alone of the three companions, returns to Logres, a sword "which now may have symbolized the coming destruction of the Round Table," as A.E. Waite (1933, 215) suggests.

BLIHOS the Storyteller

When the Knights of the Round Table enter the Waste Land for the first time, they find beautiful maidens escorted by heavily armed knights, who take on Arthur's knights in battle. Sir Gawain succeeds in capturing one of them, whose name is Blihos Bliheris. An accomplished storyteller, Blihos tells such entertaining stories that no one ever tires of listening to him.

In answer to the questions of his listeners, Blihos explains that the knights who guard the maidens of the Waste Land, himself included, are descended from the Maidens of the Wells, who once upon a time served visitors to the court of the Fisher King. When the maidens were raped by Amangon (a tyrannical king) and his knights, the country was laid waste and the castle of the Fisher King disappeared.

The descendants of Amangon and his followers now people the Waste Land and fight against any who enter the perilous realm. This has inevitably brought them into conflict with the Knights of the Round Table, who have vowed to restore the wells and make the country, once more, safe for travelers. But, Blihos adds, they will encounter many adventures before they find the court of the Fisher King.

So thrilled are those knights who hear Blihos' story that they set out to find the court of the Fisher King and so restore the Waste Land.[1]

* * *

In the prologue to the Story of the Grail known as the *Elucidation*, Blihos Bleheris is introduced shortly after a certain Master Blihis is invoked as a truthful authority; and this "good master" turns out to be he who revealed to the author of the *Elucidation* what purpose the Grail serves.

It seems likely that the Welsh storyteller known variously as Bledri, Bréri, Bleheris or Bledhericus the Interpreter, who is credited with being the first to translate Celtic stories for the Anglo-Norman conquerors (and with thereby kick-starting the twelfth century explosion of Arthurian and Grail literature), here makes an appearance himself as a character in his own narrative.[2]

Notes

1. *CSG* 557–61.
2. Weston 1920, 192–4, 196–7, 201: Also, in the First Continuation a certain Bliobliheri is invoked as an authority (*PCP* l.6552)—marking the beginning perhaps of his transformation into the knight Blioberis (Plihopliheri in *Parzival*), who plays a minor role in the Grail Quest.

BLIOCADRAN of Wales

Despite the fact that his eleven brothers have all been killed in tournaments, Bliocadran cannot resist attending one called by the King of Wales, setting the Cornish knights against those of the Waste Spring. But Bliocadran is mortally wounded and dies two days later. At the same time as he dies, Bliocadran's wife gives birth to a baby boy, christened Perceval (although he is never told his name). When the child is seven months old, she carries him to the

Waste Forest, where she hopes to spare him the same fate that befell his father and uncles.[1] But the son of the Widow Lady has a different destiny, which will be inextricably bound up with the story of the Grail.

Note

1. *CSG*, 562–8.

The BOOK OF THE GRAIL

When the young Merlin learns that he is to be seized by the agents of the usurper to the throne of Britain, Vortigern, so that his blood can be used to cement the foundations of a defensive tower, he begins to dictate to Blaise, his mother's confessor, a story that only he, with his demonic knowledge of the past and his prophetic knowledge of the future, can truly know—unless God Himself chooses to reveal it.

Merlin then recounts the love that Jesus and Joseph of Arimathea felt for each other. He tells of the departure of the Grail Company[1] from the Holy Land; of the death of Joseph and the passing on of the Holy Vessel; and of Merlin's own diabolical conception, thwarted by his mother's goodness. Blaise will have the great responsibility of writing this all down, just as the apostles wrote about the life of Jesus. But whereas they wrote down what they both saw and heard, Blaise will only be able to write down what Merlin tells him.

Blaise's book will therefore lack apostolic authority and, although his work and writings will be known about forever afterwards, it will remain mysterious. Few will recognize its wonders, which will be a cause of suffering for Blaise. But, when he has completed his great task and has shown himself worthy to join the Grail Company, his book will be combined with that of Joseph.[2] Out of the two books will be produced one, beautiful work, the truth of which will be revealed to all.[3] This is the Book of the Grail, which will be listened to, told and retold until the end of the world, thanks to the grace bestowed by Our Lord upon Joseph of Arimathea at the Deposition.[4]

The Holy Story

Two hundred years pass; and a hermit called Nascien,[5] living in a remote part of Britain, has a vision of Christ in which the Great Master gives him a book, written in His own hand. This astonishing book, which can fit into the palm of the hermit's hand, belies its size, for it contains divine secrets which can be named by no mortal tongue, lest the balance of the four elements be disturbed. Anyone who looks at it regularly will win joy of both body and soul. As Nascien reads, astonished that such a small book can contain so many words, he discovers that the contents are divided into four sections, each with its own title.[6]

After celebrating Good Friday Mass, the hermit locks the Book up in a chest in his chapel, but is dismayed to find it vanished when he returns there on Easter Sunday. Nevertheless, he hears a voice telling him that he should not be surprised if the Book has been removed from a locked chest. After all, did Jesus not leave His sepulcher without moving the stone which covered the entrance?[7]

The voice now sends him off to the far north of Britain, where he discovers the Book again in the chapel of another hermit, who is possessed by the Devil; Nascien uses it to perform an exorcism. Nine days later, Nascien returns to his home, taking care to bring the Book with him. On the second Monday after Easter, following the Voice's instructions, he begins copying the contents of the Book, for it will nevermore be seen on Earth after the Feast of the Ascension.[8]

The hermit will then add the Holy Story, the text transmitted by Christ, to the Book of Blaise, transmitted by Merlin.[9] The whole beautiful book will eventually be translated into French by Robert de Boron.[10]

* * *

The reference to a Book of Joseph which will be combined with the Book of Blaise throws wide open the vexed question of the authorship of the Book of the Grail. The Book of Joseph, we would at first assume, must be the prose text adapting the verse *Estoire dou Graal* of Robert de Boron.[11] The Book of Blaise would then be the prose text adapting or completing a fragmentary verse *Merlin*, also by de Boron. These two texts—the Prose *Joseph* and the Prose *Merlin*—constitute the first two parts of a trilogy attributed to de Boron; a trilogy which is completed by a Prose *Perceval*, which may or may not ever have had a verse equivalent.[12]

A curious aside found in some manuscripts, although difficult to interpret, may suggest that Robert de Boron, unlike Merlin, did not know the Story of the Grail.[13] The passage in question would thus support the view of some scholars that de Boron was not in fact the author of the Prose *Perceval*. It is indeed the case that it was only the first two parts of the trilogy which were reworked into the Vulgate Cycle to form part of the *Estoire del Saint Graal* and the *Estoire de Merlin*. These *estoires* also became the starting point for the Post-Vulgate Cycle, in which Robert de Boron's authority is frequently invoked.

But in these later prose cycles, neither Robert de Boron nor Blaise, nor even Merlin himself, can claim to be the original author of the Book of the Grail. According to the *Estoire del Saint Graal*, which constitutes the first section of both the Vulgate and the Post-Vulgate Cycles, the "high history" is contained in a book written by the Great Master Christ Himself and given to the hermit Nascien in the middle of the eighth century CE. Nascien copies it down in Latin (we are not told the language of the celestial original) and combines it with the Book of Blaise. We can now see that Nascien's Latin text is the one also referred to as the Book of Joseph, so that the long-lived Blaise must wait until the eighth century to see his life's work completed.

Notes

1. The details given in one manuscript of the Prose *Merlin*—about *celes genz qui le vaissel dou Graal avoient ... et d'Alein et de sa compaignie si com il estoit partiz de chiés son pere, et coment Petrus s'en estoit alez, et coment Joseph se dessaisi de son vaissel et coment il fina* (RBM 73–4)—are slightly altered in a later one: Mentions of Alan the Fat, his father (Bron) and Peter (all important characters in the De Boron Cycle) are replaced by a reference to Duke Nascien, an important character only in the Vulgate Cycle (RMP 21–2).

2. *Et quant tu auras ta paine achievee, et tu sera tels con tu dois estre en la conpaignie del Graal, lors sera tes livres ajoins al livre Joseph* (RMP 192). It is possible that this *livre Joseph* refers to a book written by the Arimathean himself (193n89), which would presumably finish before Joseph's death—so that Blaise's book, at Merlin's dictation, would continue the story up to the present (and beyond?). However, an earlier manuscript tells us that *si sera le Joseph et le Bron* (RBM 75), suggesting that it is the story of Joseph and Bron which will be completed by the story of Merlin. In other words, the Prose *Merlin* will complement the Prose *Joseph* (itself a redaction of Robert de Boron's verse *Estoire dou Graal*).

3. *LG* I, 176; *MG* 61–2: *Et quant li dui livre seront assamblé, s'en i avra .I. biau, et li dui seront une meisme chose* (RBM 76).

4. *LG* I, 181; *MG* 70–1: Joseph's reward for protecting the body of Christ was the sight of the Grail (*le glorious vaissel*) and Blaise will also see it, as a reward for recounting the story of Joseph and his lineage (RMP 216–7&n103). He will live long enough to recount the life of King Arthur, in whose time the Book will first gain the attention it deserves (RG 120). It is only after telling the story of Arthur and his knights that Blaise will have earnt the right to share in the joy of those who live in the presence of the Holy Grail: *Et quant tu auras tot aconpli et lor vies retraites, si auras deservie la joie que cil ont qui sont en la conpaignie del saint vaissel qui a a non Graaus. Et tes livres que tu as fet, si aura a non li Livres dou Graal tant con li mondes duerra et sera molt volentiers oïs* (RMP 218).

5. It is only in the *Estoire de Merlin* that Nascien is finally named as the recipient of the sacred book (*LG* I, 288–9). Throughout the *Estoire del Saint Graal* he remains anonymous, describing himself as *Chil ki la hauteche et la signourie de si haute estoire com est chele du Graal met en escrit par le commandement du grant Maistre* (ESG 1).

6. The first section describes his illustrious ancestors (the *Estoire de Merlin* will reveal that he is the son of Bron, the brother-in-law of Joseph of Arimathea). The second is entitled, Here Begins the Book of the Holy Grail: *Chi commenche* Li Livres du saint Graal (ESG 6); the third, Here Begin the Great Fears; the fourth, Here Begin the Marvels.

7. The analogy takes on added significance when we recall that Jesus Himself has compared

the sepulcher with "the vessel of the sacrament" and its stone lid with the paten that covers the vessel (*MG* 22). The Fisher King tells Perceval that the Grail is the vessel containing the Holy Blood: The silver trencher which he sees in the procession originally covered the vessel so that the blood would not be exposed as it was being brought to Britain (*CSG* 478). There is thus established a symbolic identity between the sepulcher, the Grail and the chalice of the Mass; as well as between the stone, the silver trencher and the paten which covers the chalice.

8. *LG* I, 1–9.

9. *LG* I, 288–9: *Icil ot puis la Sainte Estoire en sa baillie et escrit de sa main propre par le conmandement del Saint Maistre, et tant en escrit qu'il ajousta au livre Blayse qui par Merlin en fist ce qu'il en fist* (*LDG* I, 1086).

10. *LG* I, 112: This is done "by order of Holy Church" (136), although Henry Corbin will see the lost original as a symbol of an esoteric, initiatory tradition associated with the Gospel of John—*le johannisme de la chevalerie du Graal* (Corbin 1983, 204–5)—whose disappearance from mainstream Christianity leaves the exoteric Word as empty as Christ's tomb. He compares it with the Secret Words which Christ spoke to Joseph of Arimathea and which not even Blaise can hear (*MG* 62–3), words which are therefore not included in the translation authorized by Holy Church.

11. Edited by W.A. Nitze and published as *Roman de l'Estoire dou Graal* in 1927.

12. The three texts together constitute the first prose Grail Cycle, which has been edited by Bernard Cerquiglini (as *Le Roman du Graal*, 1981) and translated into English by Nigel Bryant as *Merlin and the Grail*.

13. *Einsi dist mes sires Roberz de Borron qui cest conte retrait que il se redouble, et einsi le dita Mellins, que il ne pot savoir le conte dou Graal* (*RBM* 76). Alexandre Micha, in his modern French translation, reads it as meaning that it was Merlin who did not know the story (*MM* 54). But this would fly in the face of the traditional presentation of Merlin as omniscient, his God-given knowledge of the future ensuring that he would know all about the Grail Quest to come. The passage would more plausibly be read as meaning that it was Robert de Boron who did not know the story. Corinne Füg-Pierreville delights in the modernist implications of a text in which the author, the narrative voice and the central character are one and the same person, Merlin (*RMP* 40–6).

BORS of Ganis

Sir Bors is one of the three knights who achieve the Quest of the Holy Grail, but the only one to return to Logres afterwards. The lineage of Bors is an illustrious one: Like his cousin Lancelot,[1] he is a direct descendant of King David (through his mother Evaine) and, through his father, of Celidoine (the second minister of Christ in Britain and first Christian King of North Wales). Like Lancelot also, he is brought up by the Lady of the Lake.

Encouraged by his cousin to seek adventure, Bors is triumphant at a tournament held to celebrate the anniversary of the coronation of King Brandegorre, who is hoping that the winner will marry his daughter. Bors, however, is dedicated to chastity, so the beautiful princess is only able to get into his bed with the aid of a magic ring. This is much to the chagrin of the Lady of the Lake, who understood that Bors would always conserve his virginity. But the product of their union is the noble knight, Helain the White,[2] who will be one of the chosen twelve who witness the accomplishing of the Grail Quest in Corbenic.

In the Castle Adventurous

One day, shortly after the Feast of St. John, a maiden arrives at King Arthur's court on behalf of the Lady of Galway, who is seeking a knight to champion her in a land dispute: The case is to be held at the court of King Pelles, in the castle of Corbenic.

Bors takes up the challenge and defeats the noble who has wronged the lady. He is then invited to eat with the king. It is now that he sees for the first time the Holy Grail, about which he has heard so much, carried by the king's niece, who is virginal both physically and mentally. When Bors sees the Holy Vessel, he is profoundly moved.[3] After the Grail has been carried through the hall, the tables are miraculously filled with the finest of foods. All sorrow turns to joy—except in the case of the king's daughter, who was once the Grail Bearer, but who can no longer fulfill that high function since she is no longer a virgin.[4]

Bors stays the night at the castle, but not in the main hall, because so many dangerous adventures take place there. This is a caution for which he will shortly thereafter be upbraided by a maiden on a black palfrey, who accuses him of cowardice: Since everyone knows that the trials of the Fisher King can only be brought to an end by a worthy Knight of the Round Table, he should at least have stayed in the Palace of Adventures to see how he fared. Bors insists, however, that he knew nothing about it.[5]

Bors will make up for this omission on his next visit, when he sees for the first time King Pelles' grandson and discovers that the child, who is not yet two years old, is the son of his cousin Lancelot. As soon as he sees the child, Bors is convinced that he has seen the future hero who will sit on the Perilous Seat (which kills everyone else) and who will bring the adventures of the Holy Grail to an end.[6] Once more he sees the sacred vessel and, this time, he spends a night in the Palace of Adventures, but only after making a full confession to ensure that his soul is purified before the ordeal to come.

And this precaution turns out to be necessary for, when he sits down on his bed, a burning spear strikes him in the shoulder and a knight attacks him. Having defeated the knight, Bors is beset by arrows and obliged to behead a hideous lion. He then sees a battle between a dragon and a leopard (symbolizing King Arthur and Lancelot) which ends when the dragon is torn apart by its own progeny: This we can recognize as a prophecy of the civil war between the houses of Pendragon and Benoic, which will end with Arthur's destruction by his son and the people of Logres, his "children." But Bors is completely mystified.

While he is pondering the significance of what he has seen, an old man with twin adders round his neck and carrying a harp sings a lay about how Joseph of Arimathea came into this land.[7] He assures the knight that it will not be Bors himself but the Good Knight (he who is destined to accomplish the adventures of the Holy Grail) who will deliver the old man from his suffering. Another old man bearing the Avenging Lance tells Bors that he who is to sit in the Perilous Seat will explain to Bors both where the Lance came from and who brought it to this land. He adds that, although Lancelot surpasses all men in worldly adventures, he has many betters in spiritual matters.

After seeing twelve weeping maidens,[8] Bors tries to enter the room where the Grail rests on its silver table, but is prevented from doing so by a shining sword. However, he sees a bishop (who we will later discover is the spirit of Josephus, the first minister of Christ in Britain) kneeling before it. When the bishop removes the samite that is covering the Holy Vessel, Bors is struck blind and a voice tells him that he is unworthy of seeing any more.

Bors spends a wretched night alone but, when day breaks, his sight is restored and his wounds are healed. King Pelles and his daughter arrive to congratulate the hero, who has survived the experience better than any knight before him; they also explain some of its mysteries. Pelles reveals that his father was maimed by a sword which he attempted to draw from its scabbard when it was not meant for him, but that he will be healed by the blood of the Lance. However, when Bors asks him the meaning of the Lance, the king replies that he will only discover *that*, when the last Grail Quest is undertaken.[9]

The Last Quest

When Lancelot's son is fifteen years of age he comes to Camelot, takes his place at the Round Table (sitting in the Perilous Seat, with Perceval at his right-hand side and Bors at his left[10]) and wins the Sword in the Floating Stone. The Grail appears to the assembled knights, but then disappears. They vow to search for it.

In the course of his quest, during which he vows to live on nothing but bread and water until he comes to sit at the Table of the Grail,[11] Sir Bors dismisses as a fool's errand the chase for the Questing Beast which has diverted so many of his fellows from the true path. However, this does not prevent him from getting caught up in it for a while.[12] A hermit explains to him that he is involving himself in something very important by seeking Heaven's hidden things and the Earth's greatest wonders. The prize is the grace of the Holy Grail, which is the holy food foretold by the prophets.[13]

Shortly thereafter Bors is faced with an excruciating dilemma when he sees his brother Lionel being carried off by brigands, at the same time as a maiden is being attacked by knights who would violate her. Bors decides to put the maiden's honor first and is tricked into believing that his brother has died as a result. He overcomes the temptations of a false priest and a demon disguised as a beautiful woman,[14] only to be attacked by his real brother, angry that Bors did nothing to help him. Bors is saved by another Round Table Knight, Calogrenant, who dies for his pains. A ball of fire prevents further conflict between the brothers, scorching the ground and leaving them stunned.[15]

Bors then hears a voice telling him to make his way to the sea, where he embarks on a ship. There, already on board, he finds Perceval.[16] Later, they pick up Perceval's sister and Lancelot's son Galahad. In the course of their adventures the maiden dies and the three companions separate, only to be reunited at the Grail Castle. Here they are presented with the sword which broke when it pierced the thigh of Joseph of Arimathea[17] and asked if they can mend it. Both Bors and Perceval fail to do so, but Galahad succeeds, although the sword is given to Bors, because of his valor.[18]

The three companions celebrate the Mass of the Holy Grail before travelling together to Sarras, where they see the Grail for the last time. Galahad and Perceval die there and Bors buries them in the Spiritual Palace, before taking ship for Logres.

Back at the royal court of Camelot, Bors relates the adventures he has witnessed and Arthur's clerks write them down. The records are kept at Salisbury library.[19]

Notes

1. The *Livre d'Artus* says of Bors that he is the best knight of his lineage apart from Lancelot, but that he is more successful when it comes to heavenly chivalry such as the adventures of the Grail, of which he will see more than his cousin: *mais il fu plus aventureus des chevaleries celestials cest as aventures du Graal dont il vit plus que Lanceloz* (VS VII, 141).
2. *LG* III, 55–6: While this is not explicit in the text, this emphasis on virginity might indicate that the Lady of the Lake was grooming Bors to be the Grail Winner and that his unexpected loss was Galahad's gain.
3. *Et quant Boorz vit le Saint Vessel, si l'aoura moult doucement et l'anclina o plors et o lermes, car bien pensoit que c'estoit li Sainz Graal dont il avoit mainte foiz oï parler* (LM IV, 271).
4. *LG* III, 178–9: Elaine was the Grail Bearer until she lost her maidenhead. King Pelles takes full responsibility for this sad state of affairs, since he deceived Lancelot into sleeping with his daughter, but the fruit of this union will be Galahad.
5. *LG* III, 181.
6. When Bors hears how his cousin was so cleverly ensnared (*sagement deceuz*) by the daughter of King Pelles he thanks God for permitting such a ruse (*angin*) since it is from the lineage of the King of Corbenic that will issue *li verais chevaliers par cui les aventures dou Saint Graal seront menees a chief et qui serra el siege perilleus de la Table Reonde: onques nus ne s'i asist qu'il n'i moreust* (LM V, 256).
7. The Lay of Tears (*li lays de plours*) relates a dispute that took place, in the early days of the conversion of Great Britain, between Joseph of Arimathea and the enchanter Orpheus, who founded the *chastel d'Enchantement* in the Scottish marches (LDG III, 624–5). The old man with the snakes round his neck can be seen as Orpheus himself living on, if only in spirit, as a symbol of the old pagan religion (1546). In the Prose *Tristan* he is called Manibel (q.v.), an apostate like Simeon, Moses and the twelve weeping women.
8. These weeping maidens are explained in the Prose *Tristan* (TPM IX, 256–8) as apostates, like Manibel (above), forced to suffer until the coming of their savior Galahad.
9. *MD* 626–30; *LG* III, 268–72: Here the Vulgate Cycle breaks decisively with the earlier poetic tradition, where asking about the Lance and the Grail is itself a source of healing (see THE GRAIL QUESTION). It will itself be contradicted by the Post-Vulgate Cycle, where Pelles' father is maimed by the Lance rather than by a sword.
10. *LG* III, 325; V, 86.
11. *MD* 731; *LG* IV, 53; *QHG* 179.
12. *LG* V, 145–7.
13. *LG* V, 158–9.

14. *MD* 736–40; *LG* IV, 56–8; *QHG* 187–194: The devil woman has twelve handmaids, a demonic counterpart to the twelve weeping maidens Bors saw in the Grail Castle. They appear to kill themselves when Bors refuses to sleep with their mistress, in a diabolical foreshadowing of the genuine self-sacrifice of Perceval's sister later. Alfred Nutt sees this episode as exemplifying the "unhuman realm" in which the Vulgate Quest is pursued: Bors is sorry for the apparently dead maidens, "but unmoved, thinking it better 'they lose their souls than he his.' So little had the Christian writer apprehended the signification of Christ's most profound saying" (239).
15. *CSG* 536–42.
16. *LG* V, 160–5, 188; IV, 60–2; *QHG* 200–7; *MD* 743–8.
17. See THE BLEEDING SWORD.
18. *LG* IV, 83–4: *QHG* 271–3; *MD* 781.
19. *LG* V, 287–8; IV, 87: *QHG* 283–4; *MD* 788–9. Gareth Knight considers it significant that Bors returns to Logres but cannot bring the Grail back with him (1983, 194): "He represents the initiate, achieved in and rooted in the world, who can maintain the responsibilities of a man in the world, and yet still achieve the Vision Splendid. It is not insignificant that it is upon him that earthly knowledge of the achievement of the Grail Quest relies" (268).

BRÂN the Blessed

The giant Brân the Blessed is King of the Island of the Mighty and possessor of a cauldron of regeneration, which comes originally from a lake in Ireland. Brân sends the cauldron back to Ireland as part of the dowry for his sister, who has married the Irish king.[1] But he is obliged to go there himself at the head of a British army when he discovers that his sister is being ill-treated.

Although Brân wins the ensuing battle against the Irish, it is a pyrrhic victory since both Britain and Ireland are devastated. Brân himself is wounded in the foot with a poisoned spear, although the true nature of the wound is revealed by the fact that Brân is now known as Pierced Thighs.[2] The wounded Brân commands his surviving followers to decapitate him and bury his head in the White Hill in London. But, until they do so, the Wondrous Head continues to entertain them and they forget all earthly sorrow.[3]

* * *

The Welsh hero *Bendigeidvran* is a giant whose father Llŷr may originally have been a sea god.[4] Brân himself is almost certainly a euhemerized deity, which makes it all the more ironic that in later tradition he should be credited with the introduction of Christianity to Britain.[5]

Moreover, despite his pagan origins, many scholars have argued that he has metamorphosed into Bron the Fisher King,[6] the guardian of that most sacred relic of medieval Christianity, the Holy Grail—possibly through a medieval conflation of his name with that of the Biblical Hebron, one of the servants of the Ark of the Covenant.[7]

His epithet Pierced Thighs and his wounding by a spear give credence to those who see in Brân the mythic antecedent of the Maimed King of the Grail romances. The connections between the stories are certainly striking: In the De Boron Cycle, Bron takes the Holy Vessel to Ireland; while, in the Vulgate and Post-Vulgate Cycles, the guardian of the vessel is maimed when struck by a lance through his thighs and a Dolorous Blow destroys two kingdoms.

Another character suspected of being derived from the Welsh Brân is King Brandegorre.[8] It is therefore perhaps fitting that the only speech attributed to him in the Vulgate Cycle is one in which he describes the maiming, ailing and sickness of various members of the Grail family.[9] Brandegorre's daughter will later use magic to seduce Sir Bors, despite his dedication to chastity, which means that Bors must yield first place in the Grail Quest to the ever-virginal Galahad.

Notes

1. *M* 71–3.
2. *M* 78–9.
3. *M* 79–81: Nor do they age, a characteristic also of those who are in the company of the Grail. In the Welsh Romance of Peredur, the hero encounters a talismanic severed head along with a Lame King, a Broken Sword and a Bleeding Lance.
4. *TYP* 419.
5. *TYP* 290–1.
6. *TYP* 292.

7. Carey 2007, 147–9.
8. Graves 1997, 55.
9. *LG* I, 235.

BRISANE

The tutor of the Princess of Corbenic, the elderly Brisane acts on behalf of King Pelles to bring about the conception of Galahad, the knight who is destined to sit in the Perilous Seat and achieve the Quest of the Holy Grail. Knowing that Lancelot loves only Guenevere, Brisane drugs the hero with an herbal potion and takes him to the bed of the princess, where he imagines, in his befuddled state, that he is making love to the queen ... and the rest is legend.[1]

* * *

It is perhaps surprising that we are told so very little in the Vulgate about this pivotal figure. Malory calls her *one of the grettyst enchaunters that was that tyme in the worlde*, while his Sir Launcelot accuses her of deceiving him with *her wycchecrauftys*.[2] Philippe Walter sees in her an avatar of the goddess Brigit, one of whose domains is medicine.[3]

Notes

1. *LG* III, 163–4; *MD* 622–5.
2. *MD* 623–4.
3. Walter 2004a, 88; 2014, 82.

The BROKEN SWORD

When Perceval first comes to the court of his cousin, the maimed Fisher King, the king's niece sends to her uncle a sword with its provenance engraved on the blade. It is made of such strong steel that it can only be broken in a situation of exceptional peril, one known only to the man who forged and tempered it[1]: This man made only three like it and will die before making any more.[2] The niece tells the king that he can give it to whomever he likes, but she hopes that the recipient will use it well. The Fisher King gives it to Perceval, saying that the sword was destined for him.[3]

The Sword of Destiny

When Perceval leaves the Grail Castle the next day, having failed to ask the question that would have healed the Fisher King, he encounters another cousin, weeping over the dead body of her slain lover, who tells him that she knows about the sword he bears: It has never been drawn and therefore has never killed anyone. He should not trust it, for it will fly into pieces when he is relying on it in combat.

It was made, she tells him, by the smith Trebuchet, who dwells by a lake below Cothoatre[4]; he alone can repair it. If the sword should break, Perceval must take it there.[5]

Perceval sets off to avenge his cousin on the man who killed her lover and, in the course of their battle, the sword[6] does, indeed, break as predicted. Placing the fragments back in their sheath, Perceval defeats his opponent with a sword he had won earlier.[7]

Meanwhile, a valet arrives from the Grail Castle and takes the broken Sword of Destiny back to the court of the Fisher King[8]: It is this sword that is displayed, lying on royal silk covering a body in a bier, when Gawain arrives at the castle some years after Perceval's first visit. The bier, carried by four boys, forms the tail of the Grail Procession, which is led by a handsome boy carrying the Bleeding Lance and which includes a girl, grieving bitterly, who holds aloft the Grail.

This procession passes three times in front of Gawain and, when he asks the Fisher King its significance, the noble lord calls for his sword, the pieces of which are placed in his hand. If he can make the sword whole again, the king says to Gawain, he will be able to know the significance of the bier and the weeping girl, as well as the truth about the Grail and the Lance.

Gawain attempts to do so and the pieces join together as though they are one but, when the king instructs Gawain to tug on the blade, the pieces separate again. The Fisher King says that the truth he seeks can only be made known to the greatest knight in the world. Gawain's failure indicates he has not yet reached that position, but he may do so in the future and then the truth will be revealed to him.

Gawain responds by falling asleep. When he wakes up, he finds himself in a marsh.[9]

The House on the Lake

However, others say that the sword given to Perceval by the Fisher King does not break in battle, but only when struck against the gates of the Earthly Paradise.

Thus, we hear that it is many years before Perceval returns to the Grail Castle and, when he does so, he partially repairs another sword—that which originally belonged to Partinal the Wild. Having done so, Perceval sleeps at the castle but, when he awakens, it has vanished and he finds himself in a beautiful meadow with a river running through it. He sees a circular wall, half-red, half-white, with a gate in it. But, when he calls out for the gate to be unlocked, he gets no response, although he can hear the sounds of rejoicing inside. He hammers three times on the gate with the pommel of his sword but, at the third stroke, thunder cracks and lightning falls. The sword breaks in half.

A white-haired man now comes to the gate and tells him that as a result of breaking the sword he has added seven and a half years to the time it will take him to see once more the Bleeding Lance or learn the secrets of the Grail, but that he has seen quite openly the Earthly Paradise. When he asks the old man whether his sword will ever be made whole, Perceval is told that he who forged it knows what has caused it to break; the forger alone can repair it.[10]

Gathering up the pieces of the Broken Sword and sliding them into the scabbard, Perceval sets off for Cothoatre, where the smith who forged the sword lives. As he approaches his destination, Perceval sees first of all a castle atop a cliff, but then notices down below a lake with a great house in the middle of it.

The lady of the castle tells him that an ancient smith lives in the house, which he was given as his reward for forging three swords. Of one of them, which took him a year to make, he has said that it will only break in special circumstances and that it can only be repaired by he who made it.[11] Moreover, never will the aged smith forge another sword; he knows that he will not live long after he repairs the one that breaks. It is for this reason that he has two chained serpents guarding the bridge leading to his lake house, to prevent anyone reaching him with the pieces of his third sword.

Girding on his Broken Sword, Perceval ignores the laments of the crowd who have come out to watch him and dispatches the serpents with an axe he has borrowed from the lady of the castle. The smith curses Perceval for killing them but, nevertheless, he recognizes the sword he made many years previously: Trebuchet tells Perceval that he sinned greatly when he broke it on the gate of the Earthly Paradise, but agrees to join the pieces together so that it will never break again.[12]

Perceval hands the sword to him and the smith blows his bellows on the strange, ever-burning deep-blue flame in his forge. He restores the sword so perfectly that there is no sign that it has ever been broken. Trebuchet then tells Perceval that he does not have much longer to live and, indeed, as Perceval rides away from the castle, he hears the church bells tolling for the man who has repaired his sword.[13]

* * *

From ancient Nordic mythology, through Wagner, to Tolkien, the Broken Sword remains one of the most numinous of symbols in literature. It has an important status in the Arthurian legends, because the sword that Arthur draws from a stone to prove his divine right to rule breaks in battle and has to be replaced by Excalibur.

There are other broken swords, however, which are explicitly associated with the Grail Quest. Specifically, there are two quite distinct traditions, the first of which centers on the heroes of poetic romance (Perceval and Gawain): It involves two swords, which risk getting confused in the Continuations. The first is the sword given to Perceval by the Fisher King; the second is the sword used by Partinal the Wild to kill the Fisher King's brother. The second tradition centers on the hero of the later prose Vulgate version, Galahad, as the knight who is destined to repair it.[14]

The sword that is destined to break is first introduced by Chrétien de Troyes as one of the mysteries of the court of the maimed Fisher King. But the account of its shattering on the gates of the Earthly Paradise and its repairing by the smith who forged it, is provided by Chrétien's continuator, Gerbert de Montreuil.

In yet another variation, Chrétien's last continuator, Manessier, tells us that the Sword of Destiny breaks when Perceval is fighting against ten knights,[15] thus fulfilling his cousin's prophecy; consequently, he is anxious to find a smith who can re-solder it.[16] While Perceval is on his way to rescue his ladylove Blancheflor from a siege, his horse gets a nail stuck in his hoof. Perceval heads for the nearest forge where the smith removes the nail and then tells Perceval that he is the man who made the sword hanging at his side. In response Perceval announces that he has carried it from afar, that it failed him in his greatest need, but that he has now encountered the one who can repair it.[17] This the smith does easily, telling Perceval to look after it, only drawing it when necessary, for he will never again have so fine a sword.[18]

Manessier appears to have been unaware of the Continuation of Gerbert, whose account of the finding of the smith and the repairing of the sword is far more otherworldly. However, there is one manuscript in which the scribe attempts to combine the versions of Gerbert and Manessier, by making the smith who repairs the sword the son of the Smith of Cothoatre.[19] But this makes nonsense of his father's claim that the sword would never break again once he had repaired it! It seems more likely that Gerbert was aware of Manessier's Continuation, felt (rightly) that it was somewhat lacking in its treatment of the Broken Sword and provided an alternative (and much more satisfactory) resolution to the themes inaugurated by Chrétien.[20]

Notes

1. *...ele estoit de si bon achier/ Que ja ne porroit depechier,/ Fors que par un tot seul peril/ Que nus ne savoit fors que cil/ Qui l'avoit forgie et temperee* (RP ll.3139–43).

2. *Onques cil qui forga l'espee/ N'en fist que trois, et si morra/ Que jamais plus n'en forgera/ Espee nule enprés cesti* (RP ll.3154–7).

3. CSG 28: *ceste espee/ Vos fu voëe et destinee* (RP ll.3167–8).

4. Cothoatre may be derived from the Middle English Scottewatre, meaning the Firth of the Forth (CTO 523).

5. CSG 32-3: In the German version, Parzival's cousin tells him that the sword will break with the second blow. As long as all the pieces are gathered together, the sword can be made whole by reciting a magic spell while wetting it in the waters of the Spring of Lac in the realm of Karnant, before the first rays of dawn strike the source (PT 107; WP 134). But neither Wolfram nor any other writer follows this up.

6. *Le bon brant al Roi Pescheor* (RP l.3926g).

7. CSG 35.

8. This detail is only found in two manuscripts and appears to be a later interpolation designed to explain the presence of the Broken Sword in the Grail Castle when Gawain first visits, as recounted in the longer version of the First Continuation (Weston 1906, 137–140).

9. CSG 108-9.

10. *Cil qui le fist set le peril/ Par coi ele est brisie et fraite;/ Portez li, si serai refaite/ Nus autres n'en venroit a chief* (GCP ll.226–9).

11. *Et dist que ja ne seroit fraite/ Fors par un peril qu'il savoit,/ Ke nus fors que il ne savoit:/ Par ce peril seroit brisie L'espee qui tant est prisie/, Ne ja refaite ne seroit/ Devant que il le referoit* (GCP ll.554–60). The smith's knowledge of the Earthly Paradise remains mysterious.

12. *Vassal, fait il, par grant pechié/ Avez vostre brant pechoié,/ Que je fis passé a mains dis:/ A le porte de Paradis/ Le brisastes, tres bien le voi;/ Mais sachiés refaire le doi/ Ou ja refaite ne sera.// Si rajoindrai chascune piece,/ N'avra mais garde que depieche/ Por cop c'on en doie ferir* (GCP ll.851-7, 861-3).

13. CSG 340-6.

14. See THE BLEEDING SWORD.
15. *CSG* 484; *an deus brisa/ L'espee, don molt s'angoissa* (*MTC* ll.33493–4).
16. *CSG* 513.
17. *Molt l'ai aportee de loing/ Et si m'est faillie au besoing,/ Fait Percevaux, mais je sai bien,/ De çou n'estuet douter de rien,/ Que par vos sodee sera/ Ou ja nus ne la refera* (*MTC* ll.38985–90).
18. *MTC* 438–45; *PSG* 291.
19. *CSG* 527&n33.
20. Stephens, 55–6, 58–9.

BRON

Joseph of Arimathea, when he takes the body of Jesus for burial, uses the vessel of the Last Supper to collect the blood from His wounds. When Christ rises from the tomb, the angry Jews imprison Joseph, believing he has stolen the body. But the risen Christ comes to His disciple in the prison, bringing the vessel of the Holy Blood, and tells Joseph he is to be the first of its three keepers. Certain words Christ speaks to Joseph can never be revealed except to the Keepers of the Vessel.

When Joseph is eventually released from prison, it is his sister Enigeus and her husband Bron[1] who first believe what he tells them, become Christians and gather around him a company of believers. It is Bron who is divinely chosen to perform a miracle when he feeds Joseph's company, with one fish he has caught, at the table Joseph has made to commemorate the Table of the Last Supper.[2] This is the Table of the Grail (their name for the sacred vessel), which has an empty place between where Joseph and Bron sit, a place that can only be filled by Bron's grandson.[3]

Bron and Enigeus, in fact, have twelve sons, who all marry, apart from the youngest, Alan the Fat, who wishes to remain a virgin and serve the Grail. Concerned about Alan's future, Bron takes him to see Joseph, who prays to God to reveal Alan's destiny. In response, he hears a voice saying that Alan must not remain a virgin but rather will father a son to whom His vessel will come. Moreover, he is to lead his brothers and their companions into the West.

While Alan does so, an angel tells Joseph to entrust the Grail into the keeping of Bron, saying that he and his people must move towards the setting sun in the West, as the world moves towards night. Wherever he comes to rest, there Bron must await his grandson and, when the time is right, pass on to him the Holy Vessel and the grace that Bron has received from Joseph, just as Joseph received it from Christ.

Joseph also entrusts to Bron privately, in writing, the words given to him by the risen Christ when he was imprisoned beneath the tower in Jerusalem, which are the holy words of the Grail sacrament.[4] Three days later, Bron sets off on his journey to the West.[5]

The Fisher King's Castle

When Arthur becomes King of Logres, Merlin tells him about the three tables that signify the Trinity: the Table of the Last Supper, the Table of the Grail and the Round Table, which he had made for Uther Pendragon.

He then tells him the story of Joseph, who was entrusted with the Grail: Joseph, before dying, passed it on to his brother-in-law Bron who, having fathered twelve sons,[6] now lives in Ireland,[7] but has fallen gravely ill. Despite his age and infirmity, Bron cannot die until one of the Knights of the Round Table, one who has proved himself to be the world's most renowned knight, comes to the court of the Fisher King and asks the purpose of the Grail. Only then will the king be healed and he will, at last, be able to pass on Christ's Secret Words before he himself passes on.[8]

Consequently, it is Perceval the Welshman, the son of Alan and the grandson of Bron, who hears from his relatives that he is the one destined to fulfill the prophecy. He immediately sets off to find the Grail Castle and, with the help of Merlin,[9] comes to a river where he sees an old fisherman in a boat.

This worthy man, who is none other

than his grandfather (although Perceval does not know this), sends him upriver to his castle, which is obviously a more fitting abode for a king than a fisherman. When Perceval arrives, the fisherman, who is now known as the Fisher King, is there to greet him, although he is old and ill. They sit down to dine. Perceval witnesses the Grail Procession but, due to excessive politeness and exhaustion, he refrains from asking the necessary question, despite attempts by the Fisher King to prompt him. Even when the procession returns, he says nothing, much to Bron's distress.[10]

It will be seven years before Perceval gets another chance. Once again it is Merlin who sets him on the right path to find his grandfather's castle. This time, when the procession passes in front of him, Perceval asks Bron to tell him the purpose of the things he sees. The old man is instantly healed.

Perceval tells Bron that he is his grandson and, in return, the king explains that the Lance is the one with which Longinus struck Christ on the Cross and that the Grail contains the blood which Joseph gathered as it flowed from His wounds to the Earth. Bron kneels down before the Vessel that contains the Holy Blood and asks for a sign. In response, the voice of the Holy Spirit tells him to pass on to Perceval the sacred words that Christ taught Joseph in prison, thus fulfilling the prophecy. Perceval is filled with the grace of the Holy Spirit and the aged Bron places the Grail in his grandson's hands.

Three days later Bron dies, lying before the Grail with his arms spread wide to form a cross. Perceval has a vision of a host of angels waiting to receive the old king's soul.[11]

Notes

1. The name may represent a fusion of the Biblical Hebron, one of the keepers of the Ark of the Covenant, with the Welsh Brân in order to create a "transitional" character who will convey the Grail from Jerusalem to the Celtic West (Carey 2007, 147–8).

2. It is because of this miracle that Bron is called the Rich Fisherman (*EG* ll.3343–8), a title that is reserved for his son Alan in the Vulgate Cycle. In the prose version he is even called the Fisher King at this stage (*MG* 42–3), despite his not having a kingdom to rule; whereas, in the Vulgate, the first Fisher King is Alan's brother Joshua.

3. *MG* 34–5.

4. *Et les paroles que il t'aprist quant il parla a toi en le tor, ce sont iceles saintimes paroles que on tient au sacre dou Graal* (*RG* 68). In the original metrical version of this passage, the *seintes paroles* are called the *Secrez dou Graal* (*EG* ll.3332–6).

5. *MG* 41–3.

6. *Or si sacés que li Graaus fu bailliés a Joseph, et aprés se fin le laissa a son serorge, qui avoit non Bron. Et cil Bron si a douze fils* (*RG* 194).

7. The association of Bron with Ireland recalls that of the Welsh Brân the Blessed (q.v.), who invades Ireland to defend the honor of his sister after giving her in marriage to the Irish king. Her dowry is a cauldron of regeneration, which can be seen as one of the Celtic prototypes of the Grail vessel (Carey 2007, 146).

8. *MG* 113.

9. Perceval first encounters two children from the Earthly Paradise who have been sent by the Holy Spirit to guide him, for he has entered into the quest for the Grail which is looked after by his grandfather Bron, who is known in many parts as the Fisher King: *Tu es entrés en le queste del Graal que Bron tes taions a en garde, que on apele en mainte contrée le Roi Pescheor* (*RG* 242). But he is still prevaricating until the voice of Merlin speaks to him from the shadows and insists that he follow the route indicated by the children (*MG* 140).

10. *MG* 140–1.

11. *MG* 154–6.

BRUMAND the Proud

Shortly after the birth of his son Galahad, Lancelot is attending court at Camelot on the Feast of Pentecost when he sees that the Perilous Seat, the place next to his own at the Round Table, bears a new inscription declaring that, unless Merlin lied in his prophecies, Brumand the Proud must die there on that very day.

After the lords have all eaten, a knight clad in white armor enters the hall: It is Brumand, the nephew of King Claudas. Hearing the knights at his uncle's court sing Lancelot's praises, the proud knight determines to do something that even Lancelot himself has never achieved: He will sit in the Perilous Seat, which is reserved for the best knight in the world. When he comes to the Round Table, however, Brumand starts weeping, believing he has come to his death. Indeed, when he nevertheless sits in the forbidden place, a fire from above burns him to a crisp. His pride has brought him nothing but shame. The ashes on the Perilous Seat smell so foul that the other knights feel ill.[1]

Note

1. *LG* III, 283–4.

C

CAHUS

The grandson of King Urien of Gorre, Cahus is given the great honor of being chosen to be Arthur's squire when the king decides to assay the adventure of the Chapel of St. Augustine in the White Forest.

Arthur is at first reluctant to take anyone at all with him, because of the perils associated with the place, which are more harrowing the more people are involved. Nevertheless, he is persuaded by his wife to take a squire, despite his feeling that ill would come of it—a feeling which turns out to be only too accurate.

Cahus sleeps fully-dressed in the great hall at Carduel, wanting to be ready first thing. But as soon as he falls asleep, he dreams that the king has gone to the Perilous Chapel without him.

Plunging into the forest, he follows what he thinks are the king's tracks to the chapel, where he sees a knight lying dead on a litter, a golden candlestick at each corner. Impulsively, Cahus takes one of the candlesticks and rides off into the forest in search of the king, only to be confronted by a dark, ugly giant brandishing a huge, double-edged knife. The Black Knight, the brother of the dead man, demands the return of the candle-stick and, when Cahus attempts to ride past him, stabs him in the side … and at that moment, as we would expect, Cahus wakes up.

But what we would not expect is that he still has the knife sticking in his side. He also still has the candle-stick, which he presents to the king, who comes running into the hall, alarmed by his cries. Cahus knows that he is dying and asks to be confessed before Arthur pulls out the knife. As soon as the king does so, the squire's soul leaves his body.[1]

* * *

Dreaming you are late for an important commitment is a not uncommon type of anxiety dream. What follows for Cahus, however, is far from common, even in dreams.

We might think that Cahus' soul had already left his body, having gone astral travelling to Dreamland: Indeed, something similar was suggested by Jessie L. Weston, as part of her argument for the Grail stories containing fragmentary recollections of a forgotten mystery religion, with its attendant initiation rituals. More specifically, she suggests that the story of Cahus is the record of an aspirant undergoing "the test preceding, and qualifying for, initiation into the secrets of physical life"—a test which, in this case, ended disastrously.[2] For the test was *carried out on the astral plane*; and the failure of the aspirant produced a reaction *with fatal results upon the physical.*

Weston's is however a singularly literal interpretation of a story which can equally be read as a comment on the dangers of literalism, of confusing the planes—taking the psychic (astral) for the material (physical), as Cahus does, making his dreams come only too true. Whether or not there were ancient Mysteries enacted on the Welsh/English border in Shropshire, in Glastonbury or in (Weston's preferred location) Northumberland[3] in post–Roman Britain, the story of Cahus, one of the most exciting and mysterious in the baffling Romance of Perlesvaus, continues to test our ability to be initiated into wonder.

Notes

1. *HBG* 21–3.
2. Weston 1913, 90.
3. Weston 1920, 181–3.

CAIAPHAS

As punishment for giving Jesus a proper burial, Joseph of Arimathea's Jewish enemies capture him and imprison him in a stronghold belonging to the High Priest Caiaphas, who instructs the jailor to give him nothing to eat or drink, but to let him die of hunger and thirst.[1]

Joseph, however, is sustained by the Holy Grail. Forty-two years after his imprisonment, he is rescued by the Roman general Vespasian, who has been cured of leprosy by the image of Christ on the Veil of Veronica. Vespasian persuades the aged Caiaphas to reveal Joseph's location by promising not to kill the priest by fire or sword: Instead, at the suggestion of Joseph, Vespasian has him set adrift on a rowboat, so that his ultimate fate rests in God's hands.[2]

Hundreds of years later, Galahad and his companions on the Grail Quest, Perceval and Bors, come across Caiaphas on a narrow spit of land where he has become marooned. Bemoaning his plight, Caiaphas complains that he is without food, but cannot die,[3] and that he cannot even find anyone to put him out of his misery. The companions leave him there, for they believe they are witnessing God's vengeance.[4]

Notes

1. *LG* I, 10.
2. *LG* I, 12–4.
3. The fate of Caiaphas mirrors that of Joseph in prison, who also lived without food indefinitely. But, where Joseph was nourished by the grace of the Grail, Caiaphas is sustained only by self-pity.
4. *LG* V, 233: According to one manuscript, Caiaphas was killed in the course of a dispute with other Jews at the gates of Jerusalem. It is therefore his spirit (*l'esperit de Cayphas*), rather than his miraculously-preserved living self, that the three companions encounter (*PV* IV.2, 60).

CALOGRENANT

The first Arthurian knight to attempt (unsuccessfully) the adventure of the fountain in the Forest of Broceliande,[1] Calogrenant dies, tragically, at the hands of Lancelot's cousin Lionel, during the Grail Quest.

Calogrenant has gone to the rescue of Bors, whom Lionel has attacked, but ends up being killed instead: Lionel gives him a fatal head wound.[2] Calogrenant falls down in the shape of a cross and milk flows from the wound instead of blood. Flowers appear on the soaked ground and thereafter bloom every summer. They are called *calogres* and have the property of staunching the flow of blood, but are fatal to animals.[3]

Notes

1. As recounted in Chrétien de Troyes' Romance of Yvain.
2. *LG* IV, 61; *QHG* 202–4; *CSG* 536–42; *MD* 745–6.
3. *LG* V, 164–5: In Heinrich von dem Türlin's *The Crown*, Calogrenant arrives with Lancelot to witness the achieving of the Grail Quest, but they fall asleep at the crucial moment (*HTC* 325–31).

CAMELOT

Before it becomes the capital city of that most Christian king, Arthur, Camelot is one of the most important cities of pagan Britain, where its kings are crowned.[1] It is inevitable therefore that the Company of the Grail should come there in the course of their evangelical mission during the reign of good King Lucius.

Faced with the missionary zeal of Joseph of Arimathea and his son Josephus, Agrestes, the pagan King of Camelot, pretends to convert to Christianity. But, as soon as Josephus and his father have left, Agrestes crucifies the leading Christians, before himself going mad and committing suicide. At the request of the people, Josephus returns to Camelot and buries the murdered men at the site known as the Black Cross. He then has the pagan temples knocked down and the idols burnt, thus completely destroying the edifices of the old religion. As if to symbolize his conquest, he has the Church of Saint Stephen the Martyr built in the middle of the city.[2]

It is sometimes said that there is a western Camelot, which is not to be confused with the city where King Arthur so often holds court: The latter is situated on the edge of the Kingdom of Logres, from where he can control the lands that border his.[3] Arthur's Camelot is besieged by King Mark during the Grail Quest,[4] but Arthur himself is rescued by Galahad.[5] Nevertheless, the city is finally destroyed by King Mark after Arthur's death, along with the Round Table and Galahad's place at it, the Perilous Seat.[6] No-one now knows where Camelot once stood.

Notes

1. The *Estoire del Saint Graal* adds the somewhat surprising detail that the mosque in Camelot was the tallest in the country (*LG* I, 136). Unfortunately, the author was not alone in being unable to differentiate between pagans and Moslems: Elsewhere, the Prophet Mohammed is described as a god called Mahom! Confusion abounds because the pagans are called Saracens—meaning, of course, not Moslems but *Sarrasins*, followers of the religion of Sarras, an astral cult originating in the Near East. The pagans of Sarras are converted to Christianity by Joseph before he comes to Britain, but will later convert in turn to Islam. The pre–Christian spiritual center of Camelot may have been, as in Sarras itself, not a mosque but a Temple of the Sun.
2. *LG* I, 136–7.
3. *HBG* 197: See KAMAALOT.
4. *LG* V, 240.
5. *LG* V, 246.
6. *LG* V, 311.

CASE CASTLE

In order to engender the hero who will achieve the Grail Quest and bring to an end the adventures of Britain, a great deception is engineered by King Pelles, the last Fisher King, one involving his daughter and utilizing the skills of her tutor Brisane. Pretending that Guenevere is at Case Castle, Brisane leads Lancelot there for an illicit rendezvous with his queen. Once there, she gives him drugged wine and, in his befuddled state, he entertains and delights King Pelles' daughter in bed as well as he normally did Arthur's wife. As a result, Galahad is conceived.[1]

Note

1. *LG* III, 164–5; *MD* 623–5.

The CASTLE OF ENQUIRY

It is after Perceval has failed to ask the Grail question that Gawain wins the Sword of John the Baptist, the price of his entry to the Grail Kingdom, then sets off for the castle of the Fisher King. But he first comes to the Castle of Enquiry, whose entrance is guarded by a lion and copper figures shooting crossbows.[1] Here he is told that he can learn the significance of anything he asks about. The priests of the castle have been instructed by the clerk and hermit Josephus, who had himself received an angelic revelation from the Holy Spirit.[2]

The head priest goes on to explain the allegorical significance of many of the adventures he has had up till then, with one notable exception, when Gawain tells him about his adventure at a fountain which he came upon in a forest: There was a statue which came to life and plunged into the spring water as soon as Gawain appeared; there was a golden vessel attached to a marble pillar, from which a priest filled his own container with healing liquid; and there were three maidens, who brought offerings of bread, wine and meat which they placed in the golden vessel. The three then miraculously appeared as one.[3]

But when Gawain recounts this strange experience to the priests, he is told that he will hear no more about it, because no-one to whom the secrets of the Savior have been entrusted should reveal them.[4] The priest does however direct Gawain to the Fisher King's castle, telling him to worship at the holy chapel there.[5]

Notes

1. *HBG*, 61, 73.
2. *...la signefiance, par la tesmoignage Josephes le bon clerc et le bon hermite, par qui nos le savons; et il le seit par l'anunchement del saint esperit et del angle* (*HLG* 322, 4).
3. *HBG* 67–8.
4. *...ne doit on pas descovrir les secrés al Sauveor, ains les doivent cil garder secreement a cui eles sont comandees* (*HLG* 334). For Caitlín and John Matthews (1992, 197), the phrase "the secrets of the Savior" conjures up the ancient Gnosis; while the three appearing to be one reveals that "the source of the mystery" is the Goddess of the Grail and that its guardians are priestesses.
5. *HBG* 75.

The CASTLE OF MAIDENS

A fortress inhabited only by women, the Castle of Maidens was originally built by the Knights of the Waste Land, descendants of the Maidens of the Wells and the followers of King Amangon.[1]

When the Company of the Grail first comes to Britain, it houses the Grail Hallows there but, due to the sinfulness of the local people, the land is derelict. God Most High commands that the sacred relics are taken away by angels and brought to the court of the Fisher King.[2] The holy lady Ysabel, cousin to Perceval's mother Philosofine, had carried the Lance of Longinus from Jerusalem to Britain.[3] Although hundreds of years have passed, she still dwells in the castle, where she gives shelter to Perceval's sister.[4]

Later the castle (which is situated on the banks of the River Severn, a few days' ride from the Waste Forest) is captured by seven villainous knights, but the knights are killed by Gawain, Gaheriet and Yvain. The maidens there are liberated by Galahad.[5]

Note

1. *CSG* 561.
2. *CSG* 364: *Le Graal cha oltre aportames,// Qui tant par est chose saintisme;/ Par le comant au roi altisme/ Le ravirent li angle puis,/ Car li païs estoit destruis/ Et plains de gent trop pecheor./ Et chiés le bon Roi Pescheor,/...fu portez* (*GCP* ll.3185, 3187–93).
3. *CSG* 422.
4. *CSG* 409.
5. *LG* IV, 17–19; *QHG* 72–80; *MD* 687–92.

The CAULDRON OF ANNWFN

Also known as the Island of the Strong Door, Annwfn is the object of a raiding expedition by King Arthur in his ship Pridwen. He passes through several fairy castles, accompanied by the bard Taliesin.[1] The poet sings of the pearl-encrusted cauldron of the King of Annwfn and the virgins who warm it. It will only feed the brave.[2]

* * *

The purpose of the expedition—like much of the medieval Welsh poem ("The Spoils of Annwfn") which describes it—is obscure, but may involve the seizure of treasures such as the Cauldron belonging to the Head or King of Annwfn, which cannot boil the food of a coward. As a "testing talisman,"[3] the Otherworld cauldron can be seen as a pagan equivalent to the Christian Grail, which (in Robert de Boron's poem) will also not feed the unworthy. It is also described as bejeweled and can only be carried by a virgin. This reading led early scholars such as John Rhŷs to argue that the Grail Quest has its origins in Arthur's search for this Celtic treasure.[4] More recently this view has been championed by some contemporary writers,[5] but it is not widely accepted by mainstream scholars.

Others have detected an Irish provenance. Indeed, when we read in the Vulgate

Estoire del Saint Graal that everyone who was filled with the grace of the Holy Vessel had whatever he could desire to eat,[6] the Grail can be seen to have inherited the characteristics of the Cauldron of Muirias in Irish mythology, from which no company ever went away unsatisfied.[7]

Notes

1. Or one castle with several evocative names, such as Caer Sidi (the Fairy Fortress), Caer Vedwit (the Castle of Carousal) and Caer Wydyr (the Glass Fortress). Taliesin possibly acts as Arthur's guide since he is familiar with the locality, having gained his poetic chair in Caer Sidi (Loomis 1956, 148–9).
2. "The cauldron of Annwfn's king, what's its nature—/ The black-rimmed cauldron with its trim of pearls?/ It was never designed to boil food for a coward" (*BT* 98).
3. Loomis 1956, 157.
4. Rhŷs, 305–6.
5. See John and Caitlín Matthews (2008).
6. *LG* I, 159.
7. Loomis 1956, 156.

CELIDOINE

The child who will grow up to be the first Christian King of North Wales is born in the Middle East, in the city of Orberica, where his father Seraph is duke. His parents call him "he who is given to heaven," ostensibly because of the extraordinary celestial phenomena that occurred at his birth. But, after his parents convert to Christianity, the name would indicate a higher calling, for he is destined to become the second minister of Christ in Britain, while retaining a life-long love of astronomy.

On the day of his birth,[1] the sun at noon appears as it does at dawn, while the moon and stars are clearly visible: These portents indicate that he will explore and learn all about the heavens.

However, when he is only seven years and five months[2] old, he is imprisoned, along with his father, who has now been baptized as Nascien, after converting to Christianity: Nascien is suspected of complicity in the disappearance of his brother-in-law Mordrain, the first Christian King of Sarras.

Mordrain has, in fact, been carried off by the Holy Spirit after having a vision in which he sees his nephew Celidoine carried over the sea by an eagle. When Celidoine alights, all the people of the land kneel before him. A lake comes forth from his stomach and, from the lake, spring nine rivers.[3]

Later the ghost of St. Salustes, in whose name the king had founded a church in Sarras, appears to Mordrain. He explains that the lake, which sprang from Celidoine, symbolizes a son who will be born to him, while the nine rivers are the nine generations of holy men that will follow. The ninth is the one prophesied by the Angel of the Bleeding Lance (on the day when he struck Josephus through the thighs), saying that the wonders of the Grail would only be revealed to one mortal man, through whom great miracles will happen on Earth.

Nascien and Celidoine spend seventeen days in prison before they are rescued. After Nascien is carried away in a cloud by a burning hand, Celidoine's gaolers throw him off the battlements of the tower, but nine hands catch him and carry him far away.[4] He is deposited soon thereafter on a rock six days' travel from the Turning Isle and two days' travel from Sarras but, during this time out of time, he has aged more than two and a half years, being now ten years old.[5] Here he encounters Label, King of Persia, whom he converts to Christianity by interpreting his dreams and telling him things about his life that no one else knows. In this (and in predicting the king's imminent death) Celidoine is inspired by the Holy Spirit.

After Label dies, Celidoine encounters the Ship of Solomon, which brings him to his father Nascien on the Turning Isle.[6] After their reunion, another ship arrives to take him to Britain, where, after spending four months in a forest with a hermit, he finds his way to the city of Galafort. Here he is once more reunited with his father, who finds him debating with the pagan masters of philosophy, and he joins the Company of the Grail.

He travels with his father to North Wales to rescue Joseph and Josephus from the treacherous pagan King Crudel and there he is reunited with his mother Flegetine, who has travelled from Sarras with his uncle Mordrain. It is now that he meets for the first time the Princess Sarrasinte, daughter of the late King of Persia, who is also in their company. After Crudel is killed and the Grail Keepers rescued, the company returns to Galafort, where Celidoine and the Persian Princess are betrothed and invested with the Kingdom of North Wales.

A week later the wedding is celebrated and the happy couple conceive a son.[7] This child, Narpus, is a tall and handsome man by the time Josephus dies. When Nascien and Flegetine die, on the same day, Celidoine leaves Galafort and takes Narpus with him to North Wales.

There he rules in peace for twelve years, his knowledge of the stars enabling him to foresee and prevent wars with his neighbors. He uses this same knowledge to mitigate the effects of a famine by stockpiling food and to defeat a Saxon invasion by preparing an ambush.[8]

Thus, Celidoine's wisdom enables him to protect his land from internal as well as external threats. He will also sire an illustrious dynasty: For nine kings will reign after him, all holy men, but the ninth will be the most holy of all, the perfect spiritual knight.

A Man Surrounded by Stars

When Celidoine dies,[9] his son Narpus is crowned King of North Wales. King Narpus has a son whom he baptizes Nascien, in honor of the Duke of Orberica. Nascien reigns after his father; from King Nascien is born a son who later reigns as King Helain the Large.[10] Helain is succeeded by his son, Isaiah, then Isaiah by his son Jonah.

Jonah gives up his kingdom, abdicating in favor of one of his brothers and making his way to Gaul, where he marries the king's daughter and inherits his kingdom. He has a son who is christened Lancelot, who inherits the Kingdom of Gaul and who marries the Princess of Ireland. Their children are Ban and Bors, two brothers who inherit kingdoms of their own: Ban becomes King of Benoic and Bors, King of Ganis.

Allies of the young King Arthur, the brother kings will sire heroes who will be even more famous than their illustrious ancestors: King Bors has a son, also called Bors, who will be one of the three knights who achieve the Quest of the Holy Grail; while Ban is the father of Lancelot of the Lake.[11] Lancelot's son Galahad will lead the Grail Quest and eventually will be crowned King of Sarras (the city where Celidoine's uncle once reigned), thus making him the ninth (and last) king to issue from Celidoine.

This is all made clear to Sir Lancelot during his own, unsuccessful Grail Quest, after he has a vision of a man surrounded by stars and accompanied by seven kings and two knights. Arriving (as knights in search of the Holy Grail always do, before long) at a hermitage, Lancelot tells the holy man about his vision. The hermit exclaims that Lancelot has witnessed the glory of his lineage.

The worthy man proceeds to explain to Lancelot that the Holy Grail was brought by Joseph of Arimathea to Sarras, whose king was converted to Christianity and baptized Mordrain. This Mordrain later had a vision of his nephew as a lake from which issued nine rivers. The hermit explains that the man from whom the lake gushed out was Lancelot's ancestor Celidoine, who had been sent by God to Britain to eradicate paganism. He appeared surrounded by stars because of his knowledge of the heavens.[12]

The nine rivers of Mordrain's vision are the seven kings and two knights of Lancelot's: The seven are the kings descended from Celidoine, from Narpus to Ban of Benoic, while the two knights are Lancelot himself and his son Galahad.[13]

Notes

1. Unusually, we are given enough detail to work out that Celidoine was born in the summer of 62 CE. This and other calculations of dates in the Grail story are based on information provided in the Vulgate Cycle matched against the historical record, such as it is. See Appendix I: The Grail Chronology.
2. If, as I suggest (see Appendix I), Joseph of Arimathea came to Sarras in 69 CE, this would mean that Nascien and Mordrain were converted in that same year, while Nascien and Celidoine were imprisoned in the autumn.
3. *LG* I, 54.
4. *LG* I, 68–71.
5. Following the above chronology, we are now in the year 72 CE.
6. *LG* I, 87–97.
7. *LG* I, 133–5: According to the Vulgate *Queste*, Celidoine is the first Christian King of Scotland, rather than North Wales—there may be an attempt here at providing an etymology for Caledonia.
8. *LG* I, 160–1.
9. Celidoine, we are told, is buried at Camelot but, by this, we should perhaps understand not the later Arthurian capital but the western Camelot (see KAMAALOT) situated in Wales.
10. This Helain the Large should not be confused with Alan the Fat, the son of Bron, who was never a king.
11. *LG* I, 161–2.
12. "He was a very lake of learning and of science in which the fisher after truth might find the principles and moving force of the divine ordinance" (*QHG* 152).
13. *LG* IV, 42–4; *QHG* 147–53.

The CHESSBOARD CASTLE

While trying to find again the court of the Fisher King, after his disastrous first visit, Perceval comes to a river that he recognizes as the one where he first saw the Maimed King fishing. A young lady in a little castle offers to ferry him across but Perceval's horse shies away from her; another ferryman warns him that she would have drowned him. The ferryman offers to take him to the castle of the Fisher King, but Perceval's attention is attracted by a beautiful castle that he sees across the river.[1]

There he finds a magnificent chessboard with the pieces all set up: Whenever he moves one, the pieces play against him, moving of their own accord, and successfully checkmate him three times. In exasperation he sweeps up the pieces and is about to throw them out of the window into the river below when a beautiful girl calls upon him to stop. Perceval is instantly smitten. She says that she will give him her love if he brings her the head of a white stag that lives in the nearby forest. Perceval instantly agrees.

After staying the night, he sets off with the hunting dog she lends him, promising to bring it back safely. However, things do not go to plan. Although he quickly hunts down the stag and cuts off its head, the dog is stolen by a girl[2] who explains that she hates the Lady of the Chessboard Castle and will keep the dog in return for his killing her stag. If Perceval wants the dog back, he must go to a nearby tomb and ask a knight he will meet what he is doing there.

But as Perceval is calling through a window he sees in the side of the tomb, a black-clad knight appears behind him and forces Perceval to fight him. While they are doing so the Black Knight's brother Garsallas carries off both the dog and the stag's head. Forcing the Black Knight back into the tomb, Perceval is unable to get any information from him about the whereabouts of the dog, which he must return to the Lady of the Chessboard Castle if he is to win her love. He sees the Lady of the Stag, but she too keeps her counsel and rides off swiftly.[3]

Perceval eventually catches up with Garsallas and, after defeating him in battle, learns that the Black Knight of the Vaulted Tomb had fallen in love with a beautiful fay,[4] Criseuz the Fair, whom he met by a spring in the Forest of the White Stone in the Isle of Avalon. She agreed to return his love if he did everything she asked. But while he slept, she built an invisible castle around him and, next to it, a tomb, from which he issues forth to combat passing knights.[5]

Torn between his quest to find the castle of the Fisher King again and his desire for the Lady of the Chessboard Castle, Perceval hears a voice in a tree which tells him to allow the dog (which, along with the stag's head, he has retrieved from Garsallas) to lead him. It accordingly takes him to a familiar castle by a river, but it is the Castle of the Magic Chessboard, not that of the Grail. Explaining that the chessboard had been given to her by Morgan the Fay (who had in turn received it from a girl skilled in magic and astrology), its lady reproaches him for his delay in returning, but is now ready to bestow on him her love.

Some say that they lie together all night and the Lady fulfils her promise to him.[6] Others say that, despite the almost supernatural beauty of the lady, resembling that of a fay, Perceval remembers that he has vowed to keep his virginity. The next day he sets off for the Grail Castle, promising to return after finding it. The Lady of the Chessboard Castle sets him on the right path,[7] but many adventures will ensue before he once more finds the Maimed King. He never returns to his fairy-like temptress.

Notes

1. In the later verse continuations, as in the prose Grail romances, the Otherworld is set in opposition to the spiritual Grail Kingdom; its fays are seen as a distraction from, if not directly inimical to, the Quest. This is illustrated in this episode from the Second Continuation to the Story of the Grail, reprised in the Prose *Perceval* attributed to Robert de Boron (*MG* 125–8, 143–6).
2. The thief appears as an old woman in the prose version (*MG* 127), but she is in reality a shape-shifting fay who appears to the Black Knight as a beautiful young maiden (144). The theft has been instigated by the Grail Bearer, the Fisher King's daughter, who wants to punish Perceval for his failure to ask the Grail Question (*CSG* 248): *el voloit travaillier / Un molt alosé chevalier/ Qui a la cort avoit esté,/ Et si n'avoit riens demandé/ De ce don demander devoit:/Dou Graal cui l'an an servoit* (*CP* IV, ll.20967–72).
3. *CSG* 240–5.
4. It is only in the prose version that Criseuz is identified as *une fée qui molt estoit bele* (*RG* 250). Her lover only agreed to live with her as long as he could still perform deeds of chivalry but, instead, she took him to "one of the most beautiful meadows in the world" where they ate together—always a dangerous pastime when your hostess is from the Otherworld. After eating, the Black Knight lay down to sleep but, when he awoke, he found himself in a magnificent castle, waited on hand-and-foot. The castle is situated next to a tomb, which was placed there by the fay, but it is invisible; it is from there that the Black Knight appears to do battle.

The shape-shifting fay, who can also take the form of an old woman, is really the sister of the Lady of the Chessboard Castle, who asked Perceval to hunt the stag in order that he might confront and defeat the Knight of the Tomb: For this latter, at the instigation of her despised sister Criseuz the Fair, has brought so many knights to grief (*MG* 144–5).
5. *CSG* 281–2.
6. *CSG* 300–4.
7. *PSG* 176–7: Similarly, in the Prose *Perceval*, the hero preserves his virginity when he brings the stag's head and the dog back to the Lady of the Chessboard Castle. She offers to make him her lord if he will stay, but Perceval says that he has vowed never to stay more than one night in any one place until he has fulfilled his quest. He promises to return once he has achieved his goal but, of course, he never does (*MG* 145–6).

CLAUDIN

The son of King Claudas of the Land Laid Waste, Claudin comes to Britain in order to take part in the Quest of the Holy Grail.[1] Arriving at King Arthur's court, he discovers that the seat at the Round Table that had once belonged to the late King Bademagu (who has been killed by Sir Gawain), now bears his name.[2]

Claudin is one of the twelve knights who arrive at Corbenic to witness the accomplishing of the adventure of the Holy Grail.[3] After Galahad heals the Maimed King with blood from the Lance that wounded him, the twelve go into the chamber and are given Holy Eucharist from the Grail Chalice. Afterwards Claudin says that he feels full of celestial nourishment and spiritual grace.

He then returns to Camelot, taking with him Galahad's greetings.[4]

Notes

1. *LG* V, 186.
2. *LG* V, 214.
3. *LG* IV, 85; *QHG* 278; *MD* 784.
4. *LG* V, 278–80.

CLINSCHOR the Sorcerer

Despite being a cleric, the Italian duke Clinschor is caught in bed with the wife of the King of Sicily and is punished with castration: As a result, he now seeks the ruin of noble men and women. He goes to the city of Persida, where magic was first invented. There he learns the cunning skills he needs to achieve his goal of wielding power over all those who do not have divine protection.[1]

In order to placate Clinschor, the King of the Sabins Rock gives him a mountain and eight miles of territory around it, known as the Land of Marvels. On the mountain he builds a mysterious edifice, an enchanted castle where he holds many ladies prisoner, including King Arthur's mother, sister and two nieces. In the castle's great hall, Clinschor has constructed through his magical lore a Wondrous Bed: Gawain alone is able to withstand its dangers,[2] thus disenchanting the castle and becoming its lord. Clinschor's power is broken, but Gawain has been deflected from the Grail Quest.

* * *

Klingsor, the evil enchanter of Wagner's opera *Parsifal*, has his origins in Wolfram's Clinschor. But Wolfram himself seems to have developed the character from certain hints in Chrétien de Troyes' Romance of Perceval, where we find *Uns clers sages d'astronomie* (*RP* l.7548), who is brought by Queen Igerna to a remote land to escape the civil war that followed the death of her husband Uther Pendragon. Here, on behalf of the queen, the scholar uses his starry wisdom to construct a wondrous palace full of strange marvels.

Hither come women widowed and young girls orphaned as a result of the failure of Perceval to ask the Grail Question, as well as boys and men who have not been initiated into knighthood. They await a hero who will survive the magical tests he will encounter there and thus free them to return to the outer world. They are not imprisoned by the scholar, but by their own *grant folie*: their belief that a savior will come, who will find the women husbands and make knights of the boys and men.

Chrétien's benign astrologer is replaced by Wolfram with a malign, twisted sorcerer who suffers a terrible price for illicit love and who inflicts a savage vengeance on the world. It is this image that appealed to Wagner.[3]

Notes

1. *WP* 328–30; *PT* 276.
2. *WP* 286–9; *PT* 238–41.
3. For Caitlín and John Matthews (2019, 176), the Castle of Marvels is an anti–Grail Castle, Klingsor an anti–Grail King whose wound parodies that of Amfortas and who "enacts a kind of perverse Grail magic, drawing upon dark powers to recreate a sacred mystery that he cannot grasp."

The COMPANY OF THE GRAIL

When Joseph of Arimathea first leaves the Holy Land, to escape persecution as a Christian, he takes with him the Grail Hallows[1]: the Holy Lance that had pierced the side of Jesus on the Cross; the Vessel in which Joseph had collected the blood that He shed; and the silver trencher that covers the Vessel to prevent the Holy Blood from being exposed to the gaze of the vulgar. Accompanying him is a group of relatives and disciples including his sister and her husband Bron (their son Joshua will be the first Fisher King) and Peter (who will found a Christian dynasty in Orkney). Joseph himself carries the beautiful Holy Grail, his niece Philosofine brings the trencher, which shines brighter than the moon, while her cousin Ysabel brings the Bleeding Lance.[2]

The companions reach the city of Sarras in the Middle East, where they convert the people to Christianity. They then travel on to Britain, where they find the astral cult of Sarras has long been established. They then begin the long and arduous process of converting the star-worshipping Sarrasins to the worship of Christ. In this, they are aided by two of those they converted in the Middle East, Duke Nascien and King Mordrain.

The base for their mission is Camelot,

the capital city of Logres, but the hallows are housed initially at the Castle of Maidens in the Waste Land. From there, angels carry them to the court of the Fisher King,[3] the title of a dynasty of Grail Keepers founded by Joshua during the reign of good King Lucius (who is converted to Christianity by Peter of Orkney).

It is nearly three hundred years after the death of Lucius, during the reign of the treacherous King Vortigern, that Merlin promises his clerk, the Master Blaise, who has been writing down all that Merlin has told him about the Company of the Grail, that he will one day join them and experience the joy that is theirs.[4]

It is also said that the Grail itself chooses those who are to serve it.[5]

Notes

1. For A.E. Waite, these "sacred objects" are the Cup, Lance, Sword and Dish (1909, 90).
2. *CSG* 422: According to Gerbert's Continuation, Joseph comes to Britain with a company of sixty persons including the two cousins: *Philosofine ot a non l'une,/ Un tailleoir plus cler que lune/ Aporta, et l'autre une lance/ Qui onques de sainier n'estance./ Et Joseph ot un tel vaissel,/ Onques nus hom ne vit si bel* (*GCP* ll.10411–16).
3. *CSG* 364.
4. *LG* I, 181; *MG* 62: Blaise joins the Company of the Grail after King Arthur's passing to Avalon (171): *Et atant pris Merlins Blaise et l'en aporta ciés le maison le rice Roi Pescheor qui avoit non Percevaus, et demoura en la compagnie del Graal* (*RG* 272); *la compaingnie del saint vaissel qui est apeles Graaus* (*LDG* I, 631).
5. *PT* 353.

CORBENIC

Following the deaths of both Joseph of Arimathea and his son Josephus, the leadership of the Company of the Grail (who have brought the sacred Vessel from the Holy Land to Britain) passes to Alan the Fat, Joseph's nephew. He leads a hundred of his followers into a pagan kingdom called the Land Beyond,[1] ruled by the leprous King Calafes. Alan tells the king that if he destroys his pagan idols and converts to Christianity, he will show him a Holy Vessel that will cure him completely. This is precisely what happens.

The king, who now takes the baptismal name Alphasan, declares that the vessel is truly holy and begs Alan to keep it in his country, promising that in return he will not only give his only daughter and the succession of the kingdom to Alan's brother Joshua, but he will also build a splendid stronghold for the Grail. Accordingly, he has sumptuous palaces with a great manor and large houses built on a site above rapid-running water.

It is only when the building is completed that there is found on one of the gates a miraculous inscription in the Chaldean language which reads that the castle should be called Corbenic—a word meaning "the place of the holy vessel."[2] On the following Sunday, Joshua is married to King Alphasan's daughter and crowned in Corbenic Castle. That night their son Aminadap is conceived.

But the child's grandfather is not so fortunate: Alphasan decides to sleep in the main palace of Corbenic, where he sees a vision of the Holy Vessel surrounded by disembodied voices singing praise to God. But his dream quickly turns into a nightmare: A man enveloped in flames and bearing a lance accuses the king of presumption for sleeping in the place where the Grail is honored. Declaring that Our Lord wants vengeance, the angel strikes the king through both thighs with the lance and warns anyone else against staying in the Palace of Adventures. Alphasan dies ten days later and is buried in the Church of Our Lady. This is the first appearance of the Avenging Lance in Corbenic.[3]

The Castle of the Perilous Palace

For centuries, the Grail remains in Corbenic.[4] King Joshua's descendants rule there until the time of King Lambor, who is killed by his neighbor King Varlan, wielding the Sword of King David, as a result of which the Land Beyond becomes waste. Further disaster befalls when Lambor's son, King Pellehan, is wounded through both thighs, so that henceforth he is called the Maimed King.

Because of these adventures, many knights make their way to the castle[5] and stay the night in the palace where greater marvels happen than anywhere else in the world. But all are found dead in the morning, until the arrival of Arthur's nephew Gawain. Although he survives the experience, he is badly injured and his honor is shamed when, as a result of his failure to recognize the significance of what he sees there, he is summarily ejected from the castle.[6]

The most important visitor to Corbenic, however, is Lancelot, who arrives there apparently by chance during the reign of Pellehan's son Pelles, the last of the Fisher Kings. While there, Lancelot sees the Grail borne by Elaine, Pelles' daughter. Little does Lancelot know that his host, who has prophetic powers, has determined his visitor is destined to father a knight who will end the devastation of the realm and bring the strange adventures that occur there to an end. The mother of this child is to be the Princess Elaine, but there is a seemingly insuperable obstacle to Pelles' plan: Lancelot is in love with Guenevere, the Queen of Logres, and has vowed to have no other woman if he cannot have her. Pelles has to resort to sorcery in order to trick Lancelot into spending the night with a woman whom he thinks is the queen—but who is really, thanks to the magic of Brisane the Enchantress, the Grail Bearer.

The Princess Elaine conceives a son that night and names him Galahad, which was his father's baptismal name. She acts not out of physical desire but purely in order to restore to its original beauty a land which had become waste because of the blow struck by the Sword of David. Our Lord permits this sinful coupling because of its value to the kingdom, which He does not wish to remain a wasteland forever.[7]

The next visitor to Corbenic is Lancelot's cousin Bors, who is defending a lady's cause at King Pelles' court. While there he sees the Grail, born by the king's niece and not by the Princess Elaine (who cannot now bear the Holy Vessel, since she is no longer a virgin). But he does not sleep in the Palace of Adventures, because the king does not want him to be endangered.[8] For this, he will later be mocked and accused of cowardice, so that he is determined to try the adventure the next time he comes to the castle.[9]

When adventure brings him to Corbenic once more, Bors is presented with the child Galahad and thus becomes the first of Arthur's court to meet the boy who will grow up to be the True Knight. When he hears about the ruse by which his cousin was so cleverly tricked at the castle, he is not, as we might imagine, indignant, but rather thanks God for all the good that will result: For the boy is destined to exceed his father in chivalry.[10]

This time, Bors tries and survives the perils of the Palace of Adventures. He is rewarded with a vision of the Grail uncovered. He also learns that Pelles' father, the Maimed King, was struck by a sword, one which was only to be drawn from its scabbard by him who is to achieve the Grail Quest, the Good Knight who will heal the king with the blood from the Avenging Lance. But he will learn no more about the Lance until the last quest is undertaken,[11] a quest on which Bors will accompany the grown-up Galahad and Galahad's mother's cousin, Perceval.

Marvels There Are

If Corbenic is a castle of testing, it is also a place of healing. When Lancelot is caught in flagrante with Pelles' daughter and banished from the queen's sight, he is driven mad and becomes demonically possessed. Arriving by chance at Corbenic

Castle on Midsummer Eve, he starts throwing sticks and stones at the people, who respond by beating him. But the king, not recognizing him in his disheveled, unshaven state, has him looked after in the main palace; although he is unable to stay there when the Grail is brought in, since the demon that possesses him cannot abide such a holy object.

Eventually Lancelot is recognized by Pelles' nephew Lamorat, bound and carried into the Palace of Adventures where angels frequently go to honor and exalt the Grail. At night, when the Holy Vessel appears in the palace, the Devil is driven out of Lancelot so ferociously that it takes a section of the roof with it as it flies away. But the hero is cured and is reunited with his son and the boy's mother.[12]

His next visit to Corbenic will not be so fortuitous: The same vessel that cures can also harm those who are unworthy. Thus, Lancelot is injured when attempting to approach the Grail. He is struck senseless for twenty-four days, exactly equivalent to the number of years of his service to the Devil (that is, his adulterous affair). When he recovers, he learns that Galahad's mother has died and that his half-brother Hector is not worthy even to gain admission to the castle.[13]

When Galahad and his two companions arrive at Corbenic for the final time,[14] he cries out in joy as soon as he recognizes the castle.[15] They are greeted by the villagers with great rejoicing, for those who live in Corbenic know that the three will bring to an end the adventures that have dominated their castle for so long.

First of all, Galahad mends a sword which has been broken since it wounded Joseph of Arimathea in the early days of the conversion of Britain. The three are then joined in the Palace of Adventures by nine other knights who have arrived there by chance. They take part in the Grail Mass (performed by the spirit of the long-dead Josephus), receive the blessed Host from the hands of Christ Himself, and witness the healing of the Maimed King, who is anointed by Galahad with the blood from the Avenging Lance.[16]

At the Table of the Grail, the twelve knights took the place of the twelve apostles at the Last Supper, with Christ as the thirteenth; now they must disperse, as the apostles did. The three companions must travel to the Spiritual Palace in Sarras. They will be accompanied by the Holy Vessel, which will nevermore be seen in the Kingdom of Logres, because its people neither respect nor rightfully serve it, having turned away from the spiritual path despite having once been nourished by its grace.[17]

Others say, however, that the Grail Hallows (the Holy Vessel, the Avenging Lance and the silver trencher which the Fisher King's niece carries in procession) remain at Corbenic after the healing of the Maimed King and that, when he dies, the king names Perceval as his heir. Perceval goes therefore to Corbenic to be crowned and holds the guardianship of the kingdom for seven years. After this he abdicates, bequeathing the kingdom to the Fisher King's son-in-law. He passes the remaining years of his life in a hermitage with the hallows. After Perceval is buried in the Palace of Adventures,[18] we hear of no more about Corbenic.

Notes

1. According to the Post-Vulgate Cycle, the land is called Listenois and only becomes known as the Land Beyond after Balin strikes the Dolorous Blow.

2. *CIST CHASTIAUS DOIT ESTRE APELÉS CORBENYC. Et ces letres estoient escrites en caldieu, et Corbenyc valt autant en cestui language come: le Saintisme Vaissel* (LDG I, 551); *et Corbenic en celui langage vaut autretant conme en françois "liu a seintisme vessel"* (ESG 562). Loomis (1926, 234–5) has suggested that the original name was *li Chastel del Cor Benit*, the Castle of the Blessed Horn. He thus relates the Grail to the mythical cornucopia, which appears in Welsh tradition as the Horn of Brân, one of the Thirteen Treasures of the Isle of Britain. He further suggests that this horn (*cors* in Old French) may have become confused with the body (also *cors*) of Christ, which is fed to the Grail Questers in Corbenic (1949, 173–4).

3. *LG* I, 158–9: The first appearance of the Grail Castle in literature occurs in Chrétien de Troyes' seminal but unfinished *conte* and it reappears in each of the verse continuations that followed. But it is only in the third of these continuations that the Grail Castle is named Corbenic (*CSG* 554): This name is borrowed from the prose Grail romances that gradually replaced the poetic versions in the thirteenth century, providing a coherent back-story for the Grail Castle, its kings and its sacred objects (the Grail Hallows).

4. The Holy Vessel cannot, in fact, be carried outside of the castle by human hands—*li Saint Vaisel si n'estoit nulle foiz porté hors de Corbenic par main d'ome mortel* (*PV* II, 524)—although it sometimes appears elsewhere without support or carried by angels. When Perceval is told that the Fisher King has the Grail carried with him when he goes into the forest surrounding his castle (*CP* IV, ll.25783–805), we do not know who does the carrying.

5. It is difficult to locate for, in the troubled times before the reign of Uther Pendragon, Tanabos the Enchanter put a spell on it so that it could only be found by chance (*LG* V, 266). The Kingdom of Listenois, the Land Beyond, shares a border with Wales, Gorre and Logres. But Corbenic, as Henry Corbin has said, "must be sought elsewhere" (1986, 352), for it is a castle of the imagination whose true home is the *mundus imaginalis*, the realm of archetypal images.

6. *LG* III, 99–103.
7. *LG* III, 164; *MD* 620–5.
8. *LG* III, 179.
9. *LG* III, 181.
10. In Malory's version, it is on Bors' first visit to the castle that he sees the child Galahad and a maiden bearing the Sangreal, after which he says to King Pelles that *this castell may be named the Castell Adventures, for here be many straunge adventures* (*MD* 627).
11. *LG* III, 268–72; *MD* 626–30.
12. *LG* V, 75–8; III, 332–5; *MD* 648–51.
13. *LG* IV, 79–82; *QHG* 260–7; *MD* 772–7: In the Post-Vulgate version of this episode, Gawain and his brother Gaheriet are also refused entry to the Palace of Adventures, for its doors and windows close of their own accord and start shaking whenever anyone unworthy tries to get in. Gawain is so annoyed at being refused admission that he hopes the castle will be knocked down by lightning. In fact, it will stand until the coming of Charlemagne, who will have it pulled down (*LG* V, 266–8).
14. Galahad is brought up away from Corbenic. The first time he returns there, he drives out the demon Dagon from a possessed man posing as a magician (*LG* V, 224–5).
15. "Oh, Corbenic, how long have I been seeking you, and how much have I labored to find you, and how many days and nights have I ridden in order to see the marvels there are in you!" (*LG* V, 278).
16. In the Post-Vulgate version, Galahad goes alone into the room where the Grail and Lance are kept and sees there the Maimed King, who recognizes in him the one who will heal him. Galahad accordingly takes the blood from the Lance with which Christ was wounded and uses it to heal the king's wounds. He is then joined by the other knights for the sacrament of the Grail (*LG* V, 279–80).
17. *LG* IV, 83–5; *QHG* 272–8; *MD* 781–4.
18. *CSG* 554–5.

CRUDEL

The last pagan King of North Wales, whose very name betrays the fact that he is cruel and treacherous,[1] Crudel is determined to halt the missionary activities of the Company of the Grail on his lands. He is, furthermore, determined to give the lie to their claim that they possess a Vessel which gives them nearly all they need to survive.[2] Consequently, he has Joseph and his son Josephus captured and thrown into prison, insisting that he will give them nothing to eat for forty days in order to test their belief in the grace of the Grail.[3]

Their belief is not found wanting: For Joseph displays the Holy Vessel to his fellow prisoners, whereupon its radiance surrounds them and they are provided in abundance with all their needs.[4] Far from abandoning their faith, moreover, the Christians are rewarded with a vision of Our Lord who promises to send someone to avenge their ill-treatment. That same night He appears in a dream to Mordrain, the Christian King of Sarras, telling him that He is being crucified again in North Wales. Mordrain, He commands, should raise an army and cross the seas to Britain to avenge Him against His torturer, King Crudel.

And this is just what the king does.[5] While Crudel himself is killed by a British duke who has recently converted to Christianity, Mordrain pursues the fleeing pagans into a nearby town and slaughters them to a man, cleansing the town of unbelievers. The crown of North Wales passes to Mordrain's nephew Celidoine.[6]

Notes

1. We can only speculate as to whether Crudel's parents gave him this name (presumably from Latin *crudelis*, "cruel") because they had foreknowledge of the type of king he would turn out to be, or whether it is an instance of nominative determinism.
2. *...un vaissel repleni de si grant grasce que il s'en vivoient presque tuit* (ESG 454).
3. *Car je voel ... qu'il vivent de la grasse lor signour et de lor saint vaissel tant com il seront en ma prison* (LDG I, 454).
4. CSG 422: *Car Josep qui molt fu sains hon/ Et qui molt fu de grant renon/ Le saint Graal en garde avoit./ Et quant chascuns veü l'avoit,/ Si avoit entr'aus tel clarté/ Et de toz biens si grant plenté/ Qu'il estoient tout raempli,/ Et tout lor voloir acompli* (GCP ll.10439–46).
5. *LG* I, 130–1; IV, 28; *QHG* 105–6.
6. *LG* I, 134–5.

CUNDRIE the Sorceress

The Grail Messenger Cundrie comes from the land of Tribalibot by the river Ganges (that is, India), where the women are intemperate in their use of herbs. Adam had been advised by God as to which herbs were safe for women to use during pregnancy, but the women of Tribalibot ignored the sacred lore that had been handed down from our first ancestor, just as Eve ignored God's command in the Garden of Eden. As a result, many children were born with deformities. One such is Cundrie, whose learning and culture belies her bestial appearance.

The Queen of Tribalibot sent Cundrie as a gift to Anfortas, the Grail King. It is on his behalf that she comes to King Arthur's court to curse Parzival for his failure to ask the Question. She says to him that she is the less monstrous, for he failed to free the sorrowful Fisher King from his grief! Parzival turned out to be a heartless guest, who should have had compassion on the king's suffering.

Cundrie claims that, as a result of his inaction, Parzival is condemned to Hell[1]—but later she returns to the court, wearing a white wimple wrought with golden doves, to apologize: For an inscription has appeared on the Grail Stone, announcing that Parzival is to be the next Grail Lord.[2]

Notes

1. *WP* 163–6; *PT* 132–5: She also announces the marvelous adventure of the Castle of Wonders, which will divert Gawain from the Grail Quest.
2. *WP* 387–8; *PT* 327–8: Wolfram's Cundrie is the original figure on which Wagner's Kundry (q.v.) is based. For Caitlín Matthews she "appears as the Dark Woman of Knowledge in northern mythology, a figure of skillful wisdom." Here she is "a delivering goddess" for the doves she wears are "the Sophianic sign of the Grail's achievement" (Matthews 2001, 208), doves being the insignia of the Grail as well as symbol of the Goddess of Wisdom (Sophia) as female Holy Spirit (42).

D

DAGON

When Sir Galahad travels through Britain seeking adventure, he comes by chance to the city of Corbenic, where he was raised as a child by his mother, the king's daughter. He has arrived during the spring celebrations[1] for his grandfather King Pelles, who was crowned in April, and who is being entertained by the magic tricks of an enchanter.

The king asks the magician to perform for their guest, but the enchanter can do nothing. The king is taken aback by this but, although he admits that it is the presence of Galahad that prevents him performing his magic, the enchanter refuses to explain why—until Pelles threatens to have him beheaded.

At this point the magician confesses that he is of North African origin and was a pagan[2] until he washed up on these shores by chance, being converted to Christianity by Nascien the Hermit. But the good news of Christ does not bring with it earthly riches. While he is lamenting his physical poverty, he falls prey to the temptation of a demon called Dagon (one of Hell's favorite devils[3]), who appears to him as a rich and powerful man. In return for denying Christ and agreeing to serve the Devil, the African is given magical powers, which enable him to impress the last of the Fisher Kings. But, when the Good Knight comes to Corbenic, the magician loses all his knowledge and power, because Dagon cannot stay in the same place as anyone as holy as Galahad, who is always accompanied by angels.

To prove his point, the magician moves some distance away from Galahad, so that he is no longer under the angelic influence. At this point he starts to burn up and is carried off into the clouds. It is only now that the king recognizes his grandson.[4]

* * *

Dagon was worshipped as a god in the form of a sea monster by the ancient Palestinians. According to William Blake, he is one of the twelve false gods worshipped in this island[5] after the primordial revelation (the Eternal Gospel) degenerated and before it could be restored by Jesus, who inspires the true Imagination.

We should therefore perhaps view Dagon as one of the gods brought to this island by the pagan Saracens, whose astral cult was centered on the holy city of Sarras. Although the old pagan gods were all overthrown in the time of the good King Lucius, it appears that some of their power still survives as demonic possession.

Notes

1. A feast is laid out in pavilions on fields outside the city walls. But the food does not come from the grace of the Grail (*la grace del Saint Vaisel*), for the Holy Vessel is never carried outside the city by human hands (*PV* II, 524).
2. ...*uns hom nez de Barbarie* ... *et estraiz de toutes pars de Sarrazins* (*PV* II, 526).
3. ...*uns ennemi qui est apellez Dagon et est des plus mestres desciples d'enfer* (*PV* II, 527).
4. *LG* V, 224–5.
5. *These twelve gods are the Twelve Spectre Sons of the Druid Albion*. According to Blake's editor W.H. Stevenson: "Britain (Albion) worships this kind of divinity, a perversion of the truth once known in the ancient, supposedly prepatriarchal druid tradition" (*BCP* 588).

DANDRANE

Although some say that Perceval's mother dies when her youngest son goes off to search for knightly adventure, others claim that she survives the shock of his leaving home: She and her daughter Dandrane lose all but one of their fifteen castles when, with no hero to protect them, their land is invaded by the Lord of the Fens. Dandrane searches for her brother for many years[1] and, when at last she finds him, informs him that he will not be able to defeat their enemy unless she goes alone to the Perilous Cemetery and takes from there a piece of the cloth that covers the altar.

This cloth is, in fact, the Shroud of Jesus.[2] The entrance to the cemetery is haunted by the ghosts of damned knights, who attack each other with flaming red swords and burning lances. Nevertheless, they cannot enter the cemetery, which has been blest by St. Andrew the Apostle. When Dandrane enters the chapel, she finds it filled with light. Her prayers enable her to take the cloth, but the tumult continues outside until, around midnight, she hears a voice saying that the Fisher King, her uncle, is dead, and that his wicked brother, the King of Castle Mortal, has seized the Grail Castle.

At daybreak, Dandrane leaves the Perilous Cemetery and returns to her mother's castle in the Vales of Kamaalot, their ancestral home, in time to witness her brother's victory over the Lord of the Fens.[3] While her brother goes on to conquer the Grail Castle, however, Dandrane is abducted by Aristor of Amorave, the Lord of the Fens' cousin. One of her servants, who has been wounded while trying to protect her, sends a message to Perceval to say that Aristor intends to marry Dandrane by force and seize the Vales of Kamaalot. He adds that Aristor maintains the cruel custom of beheading his wife at the end of each year before seeking a new maiden to wed. His only saving grace is that he never rapes the maiden before marrying her![4]

Despite this small mercy, Dandrane is understandably in great distress while being held in the castle of one of Aristor's vassals, until her brother arrives. He throws the severed head of Aristor at her feet, announcing that her marriage is hereby cancelled. She has the head thrown into the great river that runs around the castle.[5]

At the behest of the Grail Bearer, Dandrane goes with her mother to live in the Grail Castle, bringing with her the cloth from the Shroud of Jesus, which she places in the Chapel of the Grail.[6]

Notes

1. *HBG* 119–20.
2. This "most holy cloth," Dandrane tells Perceval, is the same sheet which once shrouded Christ in the tomb; He wore it at the Resurrection (*HBG* 143).
3. *HBG* 142–52.
4. *HBG* 196–7.
5. *HBG* 234–5.
6. *HBG* 263–4.

The DOLOROUS BLOW

The Grail Kingdom is devastated by two blows struck against the Fisher Kings who rule it: The first Dolorous Blow is the killing of Lambor with the Sword of David (also known as the Sword with the Strange Straps). The second is the maiming of King Pellehan with the Avenging Lance.

Lambor, the fifth Fisher King, is at war with his neighbor, the Welsh King Varlan, when the Ship of Solomon, on which the King of Israel had placed his father's sword, arrives at the shore. King Varlan boards the ship and seizes the sword, using it to kill Lambor, but he is struck dead for his presumption. As a result of this blow, both their kingdoms are destroyed; they are, in fact, henceforth known together as the Wasteland.[1]

But a second blow, as dolorous as the blow of the sword, will be struck against Pellehan, Lambor's son and successor as Fisher King.

Whereof Shall Fall Great Vengeance

It is the tragic hero called Balin the Savage, known as the Knight with Two Swords, who is destined to deliver the Dolorous Blow that maims the Fisher King and lays waste three kingdoms. The weapon with which he strikes that blow will be one of the most holy relics of Christendom, the same Holy Lance that is otherwise described as the source of great joy, but which is also a tool of divine vengeance.

All this, of course, is prophesied by Merlin, who first meets Balin shortly after the ill-fated warrior has killed a knight of King Arthur's court in front of the woman who loves him. Witnessing the death of her lover, the woman snatches Balin's sword and stabs herself to death with it before he can stop her. He will not be so slow, announces Merlin, when he strikes the Dolorous Blow, which will devastate three kingdoms for twenty-two years and cause much misery.[2]

Merlin goes on to compare the impoverishment and devastation that the people of the three kingdoms will experience, with the suffering and misery inflicted on the world by the sin of Eve. He further compares the prohibition on eating the fruit of the Tree of Knowledge[3] with the prohibition against the deed that Balin is fated to commit, for Our Lord has commanded that no one should wound the man most valiant in His sight at this time. Balin will break this commandment, although he will later wish he had died before doing so.[4]

Merlin also prophesies these events to Arthur following his victory over twelve rebel kings. To commemorate the victory, Merlin sets up statues of the defeated kings, each of which holds a lighted candle in its hand. He says that they will only go out on the day that the Knight with Two Swords strikes the Dolorous Blow. Because of this flouting of Our Lord's prohibition, the troublesome and astonishing adventures of the Holy Grail will occur throughout the Kingdom of Logres.[5]

In the course of his adventures, Balin has the further misfortune to have a knight who was under his protection killed by an unknown assailant. Merlin arrives and tells Balin that the killer is called Garlon the Red and that he is the brother of King Pellehan of Listenois: This is none other than the man who, it turns out, is him whom Merlin earlier referred to as a man valiant in the eyes of Our Lord. Against his wounding there is accordingly a divine prohibition.[6] Balin has no ill intention towards Pellehan, but is determined to find the king's murderous brother.

Merlin counsels him to abandon his quest for vengeance for, if he follows it through to the end, he will strike a blow with the Avenging Lance as a result of which, not only will he himself die in misery, but even more misfortune will befall the Kingdom of Logres than that which came from the blow struck with the Sword of David.

Undeterred, Balin doggedly makes his way to the Kingdom of Listenois, where Pellehan is holding a magnificent court in the Castle of the Perilous Palace. There he confronts and kills Garlon before fleeing for his life, the king in hot pursuit.

Balin runs through various rooms of the palace until he reaches a room smelling sweetly of spices. Ignoring a voice that warns him he is not worthy to enter such a noble place, he runs into the room where he sees a Lance standing upright, though unsupported, point down in a vessel of silver and gold. Realizing that the king is close behind him, Balin grabs the Lance, ignoring the Voice that tells him what he is doing is sinful, and strikes Pellehan through both his thighs. Balin just has time to replace the Lance in the vessel when the walls start to shake and everyone in the palace falls down as if dead, believing that the end of the world has come. At this moment the voice is heard again, declaring that the marvels of the Kingdom of Adventures are now beginning; a high price will be paid by innocent and guilty alike for the befouling of the Holy Lance and the wounding of the most honored of princes.

More than a hundred are killed, many more crushed and injured when the castle comes crashing down. The survivors lie unconscious for two days and two nights until Merlin, knowing that the blow struck by the Avenging Lance would be accompanied by great marvels, arrives to assess the damage. Finding the Holy Lance and the Grail amid the ruins, Merlin laments the outrage done to them, bemoaning how dearly it will be paid for and how many perilous adventures are yet to happen because of the striking of this Dolorous Blow.[7]

The Unhappy Blow of the Holy Lance

Twenty-two years later, as prophesied, Galahad arrives at the court of his great-grandfather King Pellehan, who is now known as the Maimed King: For he was so badly hurt by the Dolorous Blow that he cannot stand up and remains lying down, unable to leave his room, his life sustained by the grace of the Holy Grail.[8]

Galahad sees the Lance which wounded the holy flesh of Jesus standing upright, with its shaft up and its point down, but now, unlike when Balin saw it, it is dropping blood thickly into a silver basin. At Pellehan's request, Galahad fetches the basin and the king uncovers his thighs, exclaiming that his grievous wounds are the result of the Dolorous Blow struck by the Knight with Two Swords, from which much harm came.⁹

Galahad, seeing that the king's wounds are as fresh as the day the Blow was struck, empties the bowl over Pellehan's thighs. Three drops of blood fall on the wounds, instantly healing them.¹⁰

* * *

There has long been an understanding within Christian theology that the sin of Adam and Eve can be considered to be a "happy fault," since it enabled God to become incarnate in a human being and, by dying on the Cross, to take away the sins of the world.

Thus, from the Vulgate Cycle we learn that the Virgin Mary has brought to humankind "joy greater than the misery has been"; for, by conceiving the Son of God "in her blessed vessel," she repaired "woman's misdeed" (the sin of Eve which led to the expulsion of "our first mother" from the Garden of Delight).¹¹ Furthermore, the death of the Savior "confounded our death and restored eternal life to us."¹² He even descended to Hell to free Adam and Eve.¹³

It is in this context that the blow of the Lance of Longinus, which struck Jesus Christ when he was on the Cross, can be considered to be a "happy blow," insofar as it redeems us from Hell and heals our pain.¹⁴ Moreover, the blood that Our Lord shed as a result is our ransom.¹⁵ But the great honor that this blow confers on us must be contrasted with two "unhappy blows": The first, struck by the Sword of David, creates the Waste Land. The second is struck by the very Lance with which the Son of God was pierced to the heart on the day He was crucified; a blow which, in the First Continuation, is described as the source of so much joy.¹⁶

That which saves can also harm: The blow struck can be happy or dolorous and the blood that flows can heal the stricken, just as the blood of the Crucified One heals us all.

Notes

1. *LG* I, 160; IV, 160; *QHG* 215–6; *MD* 754: The Grail Bearer will later justify her tricking Lancelot into sleeping with her because the fruit of their union is destined to restore to its former beauty the Grail Kingdom, which was devastated by the Dolorous Blow of the Sword with the Strange Straps: *qui par le doloreux cop de l'espee as estranges ranges avoit esté desertez et essiliez* (*LM* IV, 210; *LG* III, 164).

2. *Tu ne seras mie si liens, fait Merlins, comme tu fus chi quant tu ferras le Dolereus Cop par coi .III. roiame en seront a povreté et en essil .XXII. ans. Et saces que onques si dolereus ne si lais ne fu fais par un homme ne n'iert comme chi cops sera, car toutes dolours et toutes miseres en averront* (*SRM* 85): "Know that there never was nor will be so dolorous or odious a blow struck by a man as this one will be, for all misery will result from it" (*LG* IV, 190).

3. The eating of *le dolereus fruit* in defiance of God's prohibition (*SRM* 86) foreshadows *le Dolereus Caup encontre le desfence Nostre Signour* (118). Malory's Merlin explicitly links the maiming of the Fisher King with the wounding of the Crucified One, by the same Lance, when he tells Balin: *Because of the dethe of that lady thou shalt stryke a stroke moste dolerous that ever man stroke, excepte the stroke of Oure Lorde Jesu Cryste* (*MD* 57). He later tells Arthur: *Balyn, the worshipfull knyght, shall gyff the Dolerouse Stroke, whereof shall falle grete vengeaunce* (62).

4. *LG* IV, 190–1.

5. *LG* IV, 199: *pour coi les aventures dou Saint Graal averront, especiaument ou roiaume de Logres. Et lors commenceront les dolours et les tempestes par toute la Grant Bretaigne, et averront si souvent que tout cil qui les verront avenir en seront tout esbahi* (*SRM* 118).

6. *LG* IV, 191.

7. *LG* IV, 212–3: *tantez mervaillez e tantez aventurez perillousez en avendront encore por cest dolerouz colp qui a esté fais!* (*SRM* 164).

8. This description of Pellehan matches well that of the (un-named) old king confined in the back chamber, sustained by a single Host from the Grail, as described by Perceval's hermit uncle in the original poem by Chrétien de Troyes (*PCG* ll.6415–31).

9. *Veez ci li Cop Doloreus que li Chevalier as Deus Espees me fist. Par cestui cop sunt maint mal avenu. Ce poise moi* (*PV* III, 321).

10. *LG* V, 279.

11. *LG* I, 82.

12. *LG* I, 9.

13. *LG* I, 167.

14. Thus, in the First Continuation, Gawain is told that the blow of the Lance brings *grant angoise* and *dolor* but also confers *grant onor* (*PCP* ll.7435–8) for, through it, we are *racatés/ D'enfer et de paine getés* (ll.7461–2).

15. *Ses sans iert nostre raençons* (*PCP* l.7459).

16. *CSG* 217: The First Continuation specifically contrasts the "happy blow" of the Lance with a sword-blow which kills the Grail King's brother and destroys Logres (see THE SWORD OF PARTINAL). But although this blow is *damages et peciés* (*PCP* l.7700), it is never described as "dolorous."

E

The EARTHLY PARADISE

The sin of Eve, our first mother—her disobedience to the divine command—causes her to be cast out of the Paradise of Delight and bring sorrow and misery to her descendants.[1] But Eve carries with her a little branch from the Tree of Knowledge in the Garden of Eden, which she plants in the Earth where it takes root and grows into a tree of aid and comfort, a new Tree of Life which will be a sign to all mankind that Paradise is not lost forever, but that we can enter it one day.[2]

Perceval finds out for himself that Paradise can be regained, in an adventure that befalls him after his second visit to the Fisher King's Castle, at which he makes up for his failure the first time to ask about the Grail and the Lance, but is unable to mend the Sword of Partinal. In the course of this second visit, Perceval will experience the shattering of his own sword (the one given him by the Fisher King himself on his first visit): an event predicted by his cousin, who warned him not to trust it.

Searching for his mother's house, Perceval comes across an enclosure protected by battlement walls, half red, half white. From within he hears joyous sounds and melodies so sweet that he forgets all his troubles. Wishing to join the merry-making within, Perceval is heartened to find a gate, but it is shut fast.

Perceval starts hammering on the gate, calling for it to be unlocked but, when no one responds, he draws his sword and strikes the gate with the pommel. Three times he strikes, but at the third blow there is an eruption of thunder and lightning so violent that it seems like it could be the end of the world. His sword shatters.[3]

A moment later a white-haired old man appears at a wicket-gate and, through the crack, Perceval can see joyful people bathed in radiant light. But the old man tells him he will see no more until he has washed away all his sins; moreover, his impatience has lengthened his quest by seven-and-a-half years. Only at the end of that period will he learn the truth about the Grail and Lance.[4] Only then will he be worthy to witness the joy of the Earthly Paradise, if he is able to return there, and uncover the secrets for which he has for so long striven.[5]

The old man tells Perceval to find the man who forged his sword, since that man alone can mend it. He then gives Perceval a rolled-up letter, which will protect him from diabolical tricks and restore to sanity anyone who has lost his mind. Perceval has seen the Earthly Paradise quite openly, but we must all await the Last Judgment in order to enjoy the supreme glory of Eternity in the heavenly Paradise.[6]

We also learn that the river that encircles the Grail Castle, one of whose names is Eden, flows from the Earthly Paradise; the soul of anyone who dies in that blessed place goes straight there.[7]

Notes

1. *LG* I, 126.
2. *LG* I, 79.

3. *Mais al tierc cop que il i done/ Si durement esclistre et tone/ Qu'il samble que li siecles fine;/ L'espee qui fu d'acier fine /Li brise en deus pieces par mi* (GCP ll.171–5).

4. *Set ans entirs et un demi/ En avez alongié vo paine/ De veoir la Lance qui saine;/ Ne del Graal sachiez de voir/ Ne porrez les secrez savoir/ Devant que tant averez fait/ Que tout pechié et tot mesfait/ Vous esteront tout pardoné* (GCP ll.194–201).

5. *Mais tres bien porroit avenir,/ Se vous cha poez revenir,/ Que nostre joie verrez toute,/ Et du Graal sanz nule doute/ Sarez la verité certaine/ Et de la Lance por coi saine,/ Dont tant avez eü travaus* (GCP ll.215–21).

6. CSG 340-1: Perceval will travel to Cothoatre to have the Broken Sword mended by the smith who forged it (see TREBUCHET) and he will also have an opportunity to use the healing letter (see MOUNT DOLOROUS).

7. HBG 195.

* * *

For Joscelyn Godwin, the archetypal image of the Earthly Paradise symbolizes a "warmer" feeling towards Nature than that evinced by some of the more anti-cosmic sayings of Jesus, which contrast Heaven with *this* world: "Esoteric traditions such as that of the Grail envisage the salvation and sanctification of the entire natural world without requiring it to be translated to Heaven."[1]

Similarly, Joseph Campbell sees the various paradisiacal other worlds of Celtic and Arthurian mythology as representing not a geographical place but rather a "condition of the experienced world." The Earthly Paradise is "everywhere and nowhere" for it is actually "where the transcendent radiance of that which is beyond form is made visible through, and from within, the forms of all things. This is not a revelation for which one has to wait until the end of time." Campbell relates this experience to the words of Jesus in the non-canonical Gospel of Thomas, in which He describes the Kingdom of the Father as spread out around us, here, now, though we do not see it.[2]

From this perspective, the promise made to Perceval that he can one day return to the Earthly Paradise and see all its joys in *this* life makes him a spiritual heir of Seth who, in medieval legend, also returns to the Garden of Eden, in order to bring back the seeds from which will grow the three trees whose wood will be used to make the Cross of Christ.[3] The symbolism comes full circle when we learn from the Romance of Perlesvaus that Eden is one of the names of the Grail Castle, so that the triumphal entry of Perceval into the Grail Castle as its conqueror[4] represents his joyful return to the Earthly Paradise.

Notes

1. Godwin 1993b, 196.
2. Campbell 2015, 19–20.
3. QHG 298n60.
4. HBG 172.

ELAINE of Corbenic

The daughter of King Pelles of the Land Beyond, Elaine has two uncles—Alan of the Isle and Pellinor of Listenois, her father's brothers—and a brother, Eliezer. Her beauty is reputedly a match for Guenevere's,[1] and she will indeed take the place of Guenevere as Lancelot's lover on two significant occasions, the first of which leads to the conception of Galahad.

Until that day, Elaine keeps the Most Holy Grail,[2] carrying it in procession to the feast in the hall of the Fisher King. But the Grail Bearer, like the Grail Winner, must be a virgin in thought and deed, and this blessed condition does not survive the arrival at Corbenic of Lancelot of the Lake. Unbeknownst to the latter, it is prophesied that he will father the best knight of the world on the king's daughter. Pelles and Brisane, the princess' governess, are determined to bring the prophecy to fruition.

Pretending that the queen is staying at nearby Case Castle, Brisane leads him to Elaine, whom he mistakes for his royal mistress after being given drugged wine. Elaine is happy to welcome to her bed the paragon of earthly chivalry, but only because she knows their child will restore the Waste Land[3]: She is willing to sacrifice her own virginity in order to conceive the ever-virginal

Galahad, the paragon of spiritual chivalry. In the face of Lancelot's fury when he realizes the deception that has been played on him, Elaine begs him to forgive her as Jesus forgave Mary Magdalen. He takes pity on her because of her amazing beauty.[4]

With the loss of her virginity, Elaine also loses the right to bear the Grail.[5] After giving birth to Galahad, she contrives to sleep with Lancelot once more, though this time her motives are more earthy than spiritual. Once again, Brisane manages to deceive Lancelot when Elaine and Galahad come to a Pentecostal court at Camelot. Guenevere and Elaine are sleeping in the same room when Brisane once more leads Lancelot to her mistress' bed, when he thinks that he is going to Guenevere's. Once more, despite the absence of drugs and alcohol, he manages to let himself be fooled again.

Guenevere is not in a forgiving mood when she discovers that Lancelot has been having sex in the very same room where she spent a lonely night; he goes mad when she banishes him from her presence. Elaine returns to her father's kingdom, weeping bitterly,[6] but she has a chance to redeem herself when a bedraggled madman turns up at her castle. She realizes that the down-and-out, who is being chased by dogs and children, is none other than her handsome former lover, the father of her child.

After he has been healed by the presence of the Holy Grail, Lancelot dwells chastely with Elaine and her maidens on the Isle of Joy, part of the Kingdom of Listenois. But he returns to Logres when he hears that Guenevere has forgiven him.[7] He never sees Elaine again for, when he returns to Corbenic on the Grail Quest, he learns that she has died.[8]

Notes

1. *LG* I, 254.
2. *...la fille au roi Pellès ... garda le saintisme Graal jusqu'à tant que Galaas fu engendrés* (*LDG* I, 940). The daughter of King Pelles of Corbenic is sometimes called Amite or Helizabel, but is best-known by the name adopted by Malory: Elaine.
3. *...si se desirrent par diverses entancions, car ele ne le fait mie tant por la biauté de celui ne por luxure ne por eschaufement de char com ele fait por le fruit recevoir dont toz li païs doit venir a sa premiere biauté, qui par le doloreux cop de l'espee as estranges ranges avoit esté desertez et essiliez* (*LM* IV, 210).
4. *LG* III, 164–5; *MD* 622–5: In Malory's version, Elaine is acting purely in obedience to her father, who commands her to fulfill the prophecy whereby Lancelot *shulde gete a pusyll uppon his doughtir, whyche shulde be called Sir Galahad, the good knyght by whom all the forayne cuntrey shulde be brought oute of daunger; and by hym the Holy Grayle sholde be encheved* (623).
5. *LG* III, 179: *ne ele ne portoit mie le Saint Graal par devant les tables, por ce que ele estoit desfloree de sa virginité, car par ce ne pooit ele avenir au servise ou ele estoit devant, car il couvenoit que tuit li menistre qui devant le Saint Graal servoient fussent virge et net* (*LM* IV, 270–1).
6. *LG* III, 320–1; V, 60; *MD* 630–5.
7. *LG* III, 332–8; V, 76–9; *MD* 649–56.
8. *LG* IV, 81; *QHG* 266; *MD* 776: By contrast, the Prose *Tristan* gives us a cringe-worthy farewell scene between Galahad and his mother, in which the son refuses to let Elaine kiss and cuddle him, since her touch would bar him from bearing the Grail: *Dame, pour Dieu merci, ne me touciés mie, que je ne vauroie en nule maniere que feme me touchast, pour ce que je doi porter le Saint Vaissel!* (*TPM* IX, 258). Not only has Elaine's loss of virginity debarred her from carrying the Holy Vessel ever again, she risks contaminating her son with her unworthiness merely by cuddling him!

ELIEZER

The son of the Fisher King Pelles[1] and the brother of Elaine of Corbenic, Eliezer's uncles are Alan of the Isle and Pellinor, who is known as the Maimed King because he was pierced through the thighs by the Avenging Lance.[2] It is Eliezer's destiny to be born into a spiritual dynasty whose role as keepers of the Grail will come to an end in his lifetime and before he can inherit the sacred guardianship.

At the time of the Saxon Wars, in the early years of King Arthur's reign, Eliezer tells his father that he will never accept knighthood until the best knight in the world gives him arms: He will show the knight the way to Corbenic so that he can fulfill the adventures of Logres and heal Eliezer's uncle Pellinor of his thigh wound.[3]

He then tells his father that he wishes to

go to King Arthur's court and, with Pelles' blessing, sets off. On the way he is beset by Saxons, who have taken advantage of the rebellion of eleven kings to invade Britain, but is rescued by Gawain, who makes him a knight.[4]

Later, Eliezer conquers the Castle of the Rock in Broceliande and wins the Bleeding Sword of Joseph of Arimathea from its guardians. The sword broke when it pierced Joseph through the thighs and, although the wound healed, the point of the sword drips blood slowly. It will continue to do so until the two halves can be joined together by the best knight in the world. Eliezer carries the sword with him at all times, hoping to meet that knight.

When he is once more rescued by Gawain, after being attacked by ten knights, Eliezer explains that he was not in mortal danger for the sword protects him as long as he kisses it each day. He asks Gawain to attempt to join the sword, but he cannot do so, proving that he is not the one who will bring to an end the high adventures of the Holy Grail. Gawain asks Eliezer to join him in his quest for Lancelot of the Lake, who has gone mad, but Eliezer says he is not authorized to do so; he must return to the court of the rich Fisher King.[5]

What Eliezer does not realize is that, at this time, the Best Knight is yet to be born, and that it is Eliezer's own sister who will mother him. Galahad is brought up in Corbenic but goes to live with an aunt in the Forest of Camelot until he is knighted. When he turns up at Corbenic seeking adventure, Eliezer does not recognize his nephew now that he is grown up. Galahad insists on keeping his anonymity and Eliezer equally insists on fighting him but, of course, is roundly defeated.[6]

When Galahad returns to Corbenic, it is to repair the sword that Gawain failed to mend, which Eliezer presents to him.[7] But neither Eliezer nor his father Pelles are permitted to witness the last performance of the Grail Liturgy in Corbenic, nor the healing of the Maimed King (Eliezer's grandfather), for they are not companions on the Quest.[8]

Notes

1. ... *fiz al Riche Roi Pescheor qui tient le saint Graal en sa maison* (*LM* II, 339).
2. *LG* I, 254.
3. *LG* I, 359.
4. *LG* I, 382: Here Gawain is seen, prior to Lancelot, as the epitome of earthly chivalry; as Galahad, who alone can heal the Maimed King, is the epitome of spiritual chivalry. In the event, Gawain kills Pellinor before the conception of Galahad and it is Pellehan (Eliezer's grandfather, rather than his uncle) whom *li miudres chevaliers del monde* (*LDG* I, 1378) eventually heals.
5. *LG* III, 87–91.
6. *LG* V, 225–6.
7. *Elyezer, li filz lo roi Pellés, lor aporta devant els l'Espee Brisie ... cele dont Joseph avoit esté feru parmi la cuisse* (*QSG* 628): Than Elyazar, Kynge Pelles sonne, brought tofore them the brokyn swerde wherewith Joseph was stryken thorow the thyghe (*MD* 781).
8. *LG* IV, 83–4; *QHG* 272–4; *MD* 781–2: We are not told whether Eliezer succeeds his father as King of Listenois. But he presumably never claims the title of Fisher King, since that is reserved for the Guardians of the Grail and, after the repairing of the Bleeding Sword, the Holy Vessel is carried from Corbenic to Sarras and thence to Heaven, nevermore to be seen on Earth.

EREC

Along with Helain the White, Erec is made a Knight of the Round Table on the very day that Galahad takes his place on the Perilous Seat.[1] But he will not survive the Quest, being killed by Gawain,[2] a fate shared by several of his companions.

Notes

1. *LG* V, 116.
2. *LG* V, 209–13.

ESCAVALON

When the Ugly Maiden comes to King Arthur's court at Caerleon to upbraid Perceval for his failure to ask the Grail Question, she also dares the knights to take up the adventure of the Sword of the Strange

Belt. Gawain readily assents to try out this adventure but, before he can start, a knight called Guigambresil arrives and accuses Gawain of having treacherously slain his lord, the King of Escavalon.[1]

Gawain determines to prove his innocence through trial-by-combat.[2] But, when he arrives at Escavalon, he swears an oath to bring to the young king the Bleeding Lance which will one day destroy Logres, or else to deliver himself up for judgment.[3]

Nevertheless, although he finds the Grail Castle and sees the Lance, Gawain falls asleep and awakes in a marsh far away. He is forced to turn up at Escavalon empty-handed. Fortunately, his uncle intervenes at the last minute. Arthur marries one of his nieces to Guigambresil, in exchange for freeing Gawain from his oath.[4] We never discover to what purpose the King of Escavalon would have put the Lance.

Notes

1. Although we learn nothing more about this king, Chrétien de Troyes tells us that one of Perceval's older brothers died in his service (*CSG* 5). We also learn from the Romance of Perlesvaus that Perceval has an uncle called Elinant of Escavalon who dies in battle in the service of Christ (*HBG* 20), as well as a cousin called Alain, the son of Elinant, who is killed by the Knight of the Dragon (158). Escavalon is in Wales (*CSG* 306).
2. *CSG* 41–2.
3. *CSG* 53–4.
4. *CSG* 117–20.

EVALACH the Unknown

Eleven days after he is released from prison in Jerusalem by Vespasian, Joseph of Arimathea comes to the city of Sarras, bringing with him the Grail Dish containing the blood of Jesus. This city is an important religious center in its own right, since it gave its name to the Saracens, this being the first city where they developed the astral cult that would eventually spread from the Middle East to Britain.

Evalach, the lord of the city of Sarras, is a pagan conqueror, who has a very mysterious origin,[1] unknown even to his own people—hence his strange epithet—but he is so valiant that he has extended his kingdom to the borders of Egypt.[2]

Through the miracles Joseph and his son Josephus perform, including saving the king from his enemies through the power of the Red Cross Shield, Evalach is converted to Christianity, taking the baptismal name Mordrain (a Chaldean word meaning "late to believe").[3] He goes to Britain with his wife where he lives for hundreds of years, sustained by the Grail, until the coming of Galahad, the ninth descendant of his sister and her husband Nascien.

Notes

1. The origin of the name Evalach is equally mysterious. John Rhŷs (335–7) derives it from the Welsh Avallach, the eponymous king of Avalon, whose daughter Modron he identifies with Morgen the Healer (Morgan the Fay). Rachel Bromwich points out that, as son of Beli, Avallach is the divine ancestor of King Urien (*TYP* 451), although the Grail romances make Urien the descendant of Joseph of Arimathea, rather than of the pagan he converts.
2. *LG* I, 16.
3. *CSG* 421–2; *LG* I, 47–8; IV, 12–3; V, 127–8; *QHG* 58–60; *MD* 680–2.

EVE

After plucking the fruit from the forbidden Tree of Knowledge, Eve keeps hold of the small branch that she breaks off in order to share it with her husband. She carries it with her out of Eden when they are expelled from Paradise.

This branch, Eve plants in the earth. From it grows a white tree that turns green when Adam and Eve have sex beneath it, then red when their first child Cain kills his brother Abel. But since saplings have grown from the tree at each stage of its transformations, three differently colored pieces of wood—one white, one red and one green—are used to create spindles for a bed that King Solomon, on the instructions of his wife, has built. The bed is placed on a ship which will, over a thousand years later, test the faith of the Company of the Grail.

Meanwhile the original tree that Eve planted survives the Deluge, although it can no longer bear fruit. It becomes known as the Tree of Life, because it gives help and comfort to all who are in sorrow and despair. The Tree exists as a sign that the human race (who have been created as a replacement for the tenth legion of angels, thrown out of Heaven for their pride) has not lost its heritage forever, but will enter Paradise at another time. For the eternal life that was lost through a woman (Eve) will be regained by a woman (the Blessed Virgin Mary). Through Mary—who Solomon, learning about her in a vision, believes should be considered our true spiritual mother, with Eve as our stepmother—will come about joy greater than the misery caused by Eve.[1] This joy includes the freeing from Hell of Adam and the prophets by Christ, who comes to Earth to save the sinful descendants of Eve.[2]

The sinfulness of Eve is invoked by Merlin to make clear to Balin the Savage the awful consequences of his actions: For, just as Eve ignored God's prohibition by eating the dolorous fruit, so Balin will flout the divine prohibition on harming the Fisher King, the man most valiant in the sight of Our Lord at that time, by striking the Dolorous Blow.[3]

* * *

The wife of Adam, who, in Christian story, is responsible for the Fall of Man, also has a redemptive role in the Grail romances, in what is an apparently unique variant on the medieval legend of the Tree of Life. In the more familiar version, it is Adam and Eve's son Seth who carries three seeds from the Tree of Knowledge, from which will grow the three trees which will provide the wood for the Cross. As Pauline Matarasso points out, by making Eve the carrier of a sign from Paradise, the Grail version means that "she who had been responsible for sin entering the world unknowingly prepares the world's redemption."[4]

Notes

1. *LG* I, 79–82, 84; IV, 67–71; *QHG* 222–30, 233–4; *MD* 757–9.
2. *LG* I, 167.
3. *LG* IV, 190–1.
4. *QHG* 298n60.

F

The FAIRY'S SEAT

In the course of the Grail Quest, the Fay of Roche Menor sends Arthur an enchanted seat which must be displayed at every high feast, but which only the Grail Winner can sit on safely.[1] No less than six of Arthur's knights nevertheless take their seats there—and are swallowed up by the Earth!

But when Perceval arrives at the court at Caerleon, amid much rejoicing, he determines that he will sit there straight away; and does so, despite the king's tears and the queen's fainting. But as soon as he sits down, the seat gives out a terrifying groan and the ground beneath it splits open, leaving the Fairy's Seat suspended in air over the void.

Unlike everyone else who witnesses this, Perceval feels no fear. To the delight of the court, the six knights who had previously been swallowed up emerged alive, but not unscathed; they had, they say, suffered greatly.[2] But the fay was aware that the true-hearted Grail winner would free them from the abyss: It is he who will learn why the Lance sheds blood from its iron tip.³

Notes

1. The chair of *La fee de Roche Menor* (*GCP* l.1438) is an otherworldly variant of the Feared Seat at the Table of the Grail and the Perilous Seat of the Round Table.
2. But their suffering, they add, was nothing compared to the fate that awaits those who are so unworthy (*desloial*) that they prefer young men to girls: At the Last Judgment, they will be deep in the blackest pit of Hell! The fay who sent the seat wanted everyone to know what the punishment for that "vice" (*tel vische*) would be (*GCP* ll.1556–70); the modern reader might prefer to suspend judgment.
3. *CSG* 350-1: *cil qui le Graal devoit/ Assomer et savoir la fin// C'est chil qui sara de la Lance,/ Por coi la pointe del fer saine* (*GCP* ll.1572–3, 1578–9).

The FEARED SEAT

At the Last Supper with His disciples, Jesus declares that one of those seated at the table with them will betray Him. At that, Judas gets up and walks away from His companions, leaving an empty seat at the table: It will not be filled until the Last Judgment.¹

Similarly, there will be an empty seat at the table which Joseph of Arimathea is divinely instructed to create for the feast of the Holy Grail. Joseph is told that he should sit at the place corresponding to that of Christ at the Table of the Last Supper. When he invites his brother-in-law Bron to sit at his right hand, Bron moves one seat away, leaving an empty place next to that of Joseph, a seat which is reserved for the family of Joseph and Bron.² So it is that, when a member of the company called Moses, who is one of many previously excluded from sitting at the Table of the Grail because of his sinful lusts, ignores all Joseph's warnings and dares to sit there, he is immediately swallowed up into the abyss and is never heard of again.

The voice of the Holy Spirit also declares that a third table will be created in the future, a table which will also have an empty seat corresponding to the place abandoned by Judas, and that this seat can only be filled by one of Bron's lineage.³

However, others say that the empty seat at the Table of the Grail corresponds symbolically⁴ to the place of Jesus Himself at the Table of the Last Supper, and that it will remain empty until Christ either returns or sends someone to take His place at the Grail Table. Josephus, the son of Joseph of Arimathea, sits on one side of it and his uncle Bron on the other. When Moses presumes to occupy the empty seat, seven flaming hands come down from the heavens and carry him off, burning fiercely,⁵ to the nearby Forest of Darnant, beyond the river Celise. Here, in a ruined castle, he must burn, awaiting the coming of Galahad, the Good Knight, who will bring to an end the adventures of Logres.⁶

Yet others say that the empty seat has been blessed and hallowed by Christ and is reserved for Josephus as head of all the Christians. When one of his relatives attempts to usurp Josephus' place, the earth swallows him up. From then on, the place is known as the Feared Seat⁷; no one dares to sit there unless he has been chosen by Our Lord.⁸

Notes

1. *EG* ll.2775–84.
2. According to Robert de Boron's verse *Estoire dou Graal*, the voice of the Holy Spirit reveals that the empty seat will initially be used by Joseph himself, when he commemorates Christ's death (*EG* ll.2785–7; *RHG* 56); but that, after Joseph, it will remain empty, awaiting the coming of a member of his family. This appears initially to be the son of Bron and Enygeus (*EG* ll.2527–36)—presumably Alan the Fat, the only one of twelve brothers who chooses virginity. But later the voice of the Holy Spirit declares that it is destined for the *tierz hons* of Joseph's family, the son of Bron's son (ll.2788–96): that is, Perceval the son of Alan.
The prose version seems to confirm this, suggesting at first that the place is reserved for Bron's grandson: *Cil lius ne pora estre aemplis devant ce que li fils qui istra del fil Bron l'emplisse* (*RG* 55). But it later states that the place of Perceval (the third man of Bron's lineage) will be at another table which is created to commemorate the Table of the Grail (that is, the Round Table): *Et li tiers hom qui*

del lignage Bron sera, raemplira le liu u un autre qui el non de cestui sera fondés (61).

3. *MG* 34-9: In the De Boron Cycle it is Perceval who sits prematurely on the empty seat at the third table and is lucky to escape the fate of Moses (119-20). But in the Vulgate Cycle it is Galahad, also a descendant of Bron, who sits there, unscathed. When Galahad comes to Corbenic, he sits at the Table of the Grail, although we are not told which seat he chooses.

4. ...*par grant senefiance* (*ESG* 485).
5. *LG* I, 137-8.
6. *LG* I, 144-5.
7. ...*li Sieges Redoutez* (*QP* 76); Moses calls it a *siege esperitel* which is not suited to mere mortals (*ESG* 509).
8. *LG* IV, 26; "the Seat of Dread" (*QHG* 98-9).

FEIREFIZ

The son of Parzival's father Gahmuret and the pagan queen Belacane, Feirefiz is the mighty, wealthy and renowned monarch of two oriental kingdoms.[1] But no power on Earth will allow him to see the Grail until he is baptized, which he agrees to in order to win the love of the Grail Bearer.[2] Once married, he and his new wife depart for his kingdom of India, where he fathers a son, whom they christen John. He becomes known as Prester John and this name is given to his descendants.[3]

Notes

1. *WP* 170-1; *PT* 138.
2. *WP* 404-6; *PT* 341-3.
3. *WP* 408; *PT* 344.

The FISHER KING

The young hero Perceval comes by chance upon a man fishing in a boat on a deep and rushing river, who offers to put him up for the night. Arriving at the fisherman's home, which turns out to be a castle, he finds his host leaning on his elbow on a couch in front of a great fire in the main hall. The lord, who can only sit up with some difficulty, presents his guest with a sword that, he says, is destined for him.[1] They then watch the Grail Procession, headed by a Bleeding Lance, pass before them.

Though naturally curious, Perceval remains silent, not wishing to be rude, as they sit down to eat. With every course they are served, the Grail passes in front of them and then is carried into a back bedroom. Here it is used to serve a single consecrated wafer to an old man who, we later discover, is Perceval's uncle. Perceval is expected to ask whom the Grail serves, but he fails to do so. The fisherman is carried into his bedroom. Perceval goes to sleep and, when he wakes up, the castle is deserted.

In the nearby woods Perceval encounters his cousin, who tells him that he has just passed the night with the rich Fisher King.[2] The king's infirmity is due to the fact that he was wounded through the thighs by a javelin and, as a result, his only occupation is fishing, hence his title.[3] Had Perceval asked the Grail Question, the Fisher King would have been healed of his wounds and would once again have assumed governance of his realm. Instead, as Perceval will later discover, lands will be laid waste, men will be killed, women widowed and maidens orphaned.[4]

Setting off once more to discover the secrets of the Grail, Perceval meets one of his uncles, a hermit, who informs him that the wondrous fisherman is the son of the old king in the back chamber, who is served by the Grail. The old man is, in fact, Perceval's other uncle, and the Fisher King, his cousin.[5]

Later, Perceval is travelling in a forest when he sees a supernatural light reaching up to the clouds. He then encounters a maiden who explains to him that the fiery light is a sign of the presence of the rich Fisher King, a holy man who lives nearby. The king has carried with him into the woods the Vessel in which the blood of Jesus was gathered at the crucifixion.[6] She will tell Perceval no more, despite his pleas, but agrees to show him the way to the Fisher King's castle again, admonishing him not to stray from the path.[7]

This, however, is exactly what Perceval does. Many adventures intervene before Perceval eventually encounters some huntsmen who direct him to the Fisher King's castle. This time he goes straight there and once more witnesses the Grail Procession. The Fisher King asks Perceval to attempt to mend a sword, which is broken in half.[8] Perceval does so, except that there is a notch left in the blade. The king tells him that he is destined to know all the secrets of the Grail, but that his time has not yet come. Perceval spends the night there but wakes up in a meadow.[9]

During his travels, Perceval learns from one of his uncles that legions of angels bearing the Holy Grail descend frequently on the castle of the Fisher King, to bring the king's father the Host that alone sustains his life.[10] Once more, many adventures intervene before Perceval comes for the third time to the court of the king, who bids him try again to repair the sword. This time, Perceval is successful and the Fisher King delighted—so much so that he confers on his cousin all his lands.[11]

The Fisher King now, finally, explains to Perceval that the Bleeding Lance is the one with which Jesus was struck on the Cross, and that the Holy Grail is the Vessel with which Joseph of Arimathea caught the blood that dripped from His side. Joseph was imprisoned by the Jews for burying Jesus, but liberated by Titus and Vespasian, who brought him to Rome. Joseph brought the Holy Lance with him and the Grail followed after. Joseph eventually settled in Britain, building the very house in which they are now talking. The Grail has also remained there, kept by Joseph's descendants,[12] of whom the Fisher King is one

The sword that Perceval has repaired was used to kill the Fisher King's brother and maim the king himself[13]; he will only be healed when the murder is avenged by the one who proves his worthiness by joining the halves of the sword back together.[14] This has been accomplished by Perceval, who goes on to kill and behead the man, Partinal, who killed the Fisher King's brother. Perceval then returns to the Grail Castle.

When the king sees Perceval approaching, carrying the head of the one who had caused him so much distress, he leaps up from his sick-bed, hale and whole. He goes to meet Perceval without the need of any support, all his grief now forgotten.

The Fisher King places the head of his enemy on a stake at the top of the main tower, and confirms that Perceval is the heir to his kingdom by bestowing upon him the royal arms.[15] Shortly thereafter the Fisher King, who had feared living in pain, dies in great joy. Perceval inherits his throne.[16]

The Second Grail Keeper

Some say that the Fisher King is called Bron, that he is the brother-in-law of Joseph of Arimathea, and that he gains the title after miraculously catching a fish to feed the Company of the Grail in the Judaean desert.[17] It is an angel of the Lord who first announces that, once he becomes the second keeper of the Grail, Bron will be known by all who hear tell of him as the rich Fisher King. He must, the angel commands, journey westwards over land and sea, whither his heart leads him,[18] to await the coming of his grandson Perceval, to whom he will pass on the Holy Vessel and the grace of the Grail. Many words have been spoken of the Fisher King since his departure into the West.[19]

Hundreds of years later, the Fisher King is still alive, though grown old and sick: He is unable to die until the greatest quest ever undertaken by King Arthur's knights is achieved. Before departing this world, Merlin tells Arthur that the Fisher King is living in a beautiful spot on an Irish island,[20] but is in a terrible state physically. He cannot be healed until the most renowned knight in the world comes to his court and asks the purpose of the Grail. When this happens, Merlin continues, the enchantments of Britain will end and the prophecy will be accomplished.[21]

When Perceval first comes to Arthur's

court, he learns that the Fisher King is his grandfather and that he cannot be healed unless the best knight in the world comes to his court and asks what is done with the Grail.[22] Perceval is determined to prove that he is that knight; signs and wonders lead him to the goal of his quest.

Nevertheless, when Perceval encounters the Fisher King lying on a boat in a river, he does not recognize his grandfather. The extremely aged man directs the young knight to his splendid castle. There, Perceval is led to the chamber of the Fisher King, who has the Grail in his keeping,[23] a man who is so old and frail that he cannot move his hands or feet.

Perceval witnesses the Grail Procession, but politeness inhibits him from asking about it. The Fisher King is most distressed when he realizes no question is going to come, for he has presented the Grail to all the knights who have lodged at his castle, knowing (for he has been told by Christ Himself) that he will only be healed if the finest knight in the world asks him what the Grail is for.

They retire for the night but, when Perceval gets up the next day, he finds the castle deserted. When he rides out from the castle, he is accused by a weeping woman of having failed to ask the question that would have restored his grandfather to health. He tries to return to the house of the Fisher King to rectify his mistake, but he cannot find the right path.[24]

Nor will he do so until Merlin guides him there. This time, witnessing once more the wonders of the court, Perceval asks the Grail Question and, as soon as he does so, the Fisher King is cured of all the ills of old age. Having passed on his sacred legacy, he dies three days later. Perceval becomes the third Keeper of the Grail.

Merlin, having promised his scribe Blaise that he would bring him into the company of the Grail when the Quest was achieved, takes him to the house of the Fisher King—who is now Perceval—and tells King Arthur that his reign has seen the fulfilling of the greatest prophecy of all time: that concerning the healing of the Fisher King and the casting out of the enchantments of Britain.[25]

The Guardians of the Grail

Others say that it is not Bron, but his youngest son Alan the Fat, who earns the title of Rich Fisherman after performing a miraculous catch in a pond in Britain. It becomes the hereditary title of a dynasty of Grail Guardians, who are also kings.

After Josephus, the son of Joseph of Arimathea, confers the Grail on him, Alan travels to the Land Beyond with the Holy Vessel. There, the Rich Fisherman converts its pagan king to Christianity along with the king's daughter, who marries Alan's older brother Joshua. The newly baptized Alphasan, the first Christian King of the Land Beyond, has a fortress built to house the Grail: This is the Castle of Corbenic. It is here that the king dies, on the same day as Alan. Joshua therefore inherits not only the realm but also its most precious treasure, as well as the title of Rich Fisherman, which will henceforth be carried by the firstborn of his descendants. At the same time, Joshua is the first of the Rich Fishermen to be a crowned king: He is therefore known as the Fisher King, a title that will be inherited by seven of his descendants.

Joshua is succeeded by his son Aminadap, who marries one of the daughters of Lucius, King of Britain. Their son is Carcelois, who is succeeded by his son, Manuel, who in turn fathers Lambor. They are all kings and are called the Rich Fishermen[26] in honor of Alan, so they constitute a dynasty of Fisher Kings.

King Lambor meets a tragic fate that will also constitute a dynastic pattern. He is killed by a blow from the Sword of David, as a result of which the Land Beyond suffers such devastation that it becomes known as the Waste Land. After the death of Lambor, his son Pellehan inherits the title of Fisher King. He is wounded through the thighs and so becomes also known as the Maimed King.[27]

The title of Fisher King then passes to Pellehan's son Alan of the Isle.[28] He is also stricken with illness, hoping for the arrival of the best knight in the world to heal him.[29] But, by the time that knight comes to Corbenic, the Fisher King is Alan's brother Pelles.

Over the next few years, the knights of King Arthur's court hear tidings of the wondrous adventures that will be encountered by those who come by chance to the court of the Fisher King. Thus, Gawain recounts seeing the Holy Grail carried unveiled by the most beautiful maiden he had ever met. He describes the other marvels of the Palace of Adventures, without concealing his ignominious departure.[30]

By contrast, Lancelot gives the court a slightly censored version of his adventures there: He mentions how the Grail filled the tables with food, but glosses over the fact that he had not only admired the beautiful maiden carrying it, but had actually slept with her, though unintentionally.[31]

Lancelot's cousin Bors, having been scolded for not risking the dangers of the Palace of Adventures on his first visit to the Fisher King's court,[32] makes up for it on his second. He impresses those who hear about it with the way that he (unlike Gawain) escaped unscathed after encountering the marvels of the court, including the Bleeding Lance and the silver Table of the Grail, among other wondrous adventures.[33]

During the Grail Quest undertaken by the entire Round Table, Lancelot comes to a ruined chapel in the Waste Forest where he sees, in a half-awake, half-dreaming state, a sick knight cured by a vessel on a silver table. He recognizes these as the Holy Vessel and the Table of the Grail which he had seen previously in the palace of the Fisher King.[34] A hermit later explains to him that his inability to approach the Grail at this time indicated his sinfulness.

Perceval, on the other hand, is told by a good man that he will reach the house of the Fisher King and share its holy food with eleven companions.[35] This is precisely what comes to pass: While Lancelot accomplishes nothing in the house of the Fisher King,[36] the twelve have a wondrous adventure.[37] But the Grail leaves Logres forever; and it would appear that the role of Fisher King now becomes redundant.

* * *

The figure of the Fisher King is first introduced to western literature in Chrétien de Troyes' Romance of Perceval. But, because Chrétien left the poem unfinished, the mysteries of the character were explored by many subsequent authors who, in the course of writing their continuations, subtly transformed the figure. At last, in the *Elucidation*, he becomes a magical shape-shifter who can assume a hundred different forms. When his court is lost, the Kingdom of Logres falls to ruin.[38]

The Fisher King's ability to change shape continues in early twentieth century scholarship. Thus, William A. Nitze describes him as an Otherworld being, an "intermediary" between the planes of existence: "Through him mortal man gains knowledge of the secrets of existence. But Nature herself is dependent on him; for when his power wanes, the country is laid waste and the soil rendered sterile. In order to restore his strength … certain rites are required, which become efficacious when shared in by a person whose qualifications have been tested. The latter, the Grail Knight, is thereby made immortal and becomes the Fisher King's successor."[39]

For Nitze therefore, "the Fisher King is the central figure of the Grail story,"[40] which "is *au fond* an initiation," whose rites, like those of the mystery religion of Eleusis, "may have been agrarian and mystic from the start."[41] The Fisher King symbolizes "the creative, fructifying force in nature, specifically associated with water"; hence he is first presented as fishing on a river. He is both the guide to the Otherworld (directing Perceval to the Grail Castle in his fisherman guise) and officiates at its rites (presiding over the Grail feast): "And his weakness or infirmity agrees with Nature's declining strength; thus his land lays waste or is under the ban of enchantment."[42] But if the rites are successful the initiate, the Grail Knight, becomes the new Fisher King.

If for Nitze the Fisher King is "probably the crux of the Grail problem,"[43] for Jessie L. Weston he is "the very heart ... of the whole mystery," the "essential center" of a Grail cult, similar to the Mysteries of the Eastern Mediterranean, but influenced by the indigenous pagan religion and, later, by Gnostic Christianity. Like Adonis and Attis the Fisher King is "a being semi-divine, semi-human, standing between his people and land, and the unseen forces which control their destiny."[44]

Agreeing initially with Nitze that the Fisher King is the Priest of the Cult ("It would be his office to preside at the ritual feast, and at the initiation of the neophyte"[45]), Weston went on to develop the theory of a threefold initiation in which the Fisher King presides over the highest, "philosophic" stage as spiritual guardian of the Mystic Vessel, the *Holy* Grail.[46] The fish is a symbol of Divine Life[47] and the Fisher King is therefore at the heart of "a ritual, originally presumed to exercise a life-giving potency," a decayed record of which has survived ("sometimes partially understood, sometimes wholly misinterpreted") in the Grail story.[48]

Notes

1. See THE BROKEN SWORD.
2. *Chiez le riche Roi Pescheor* (*RP* l.3495).
3. *Por che li Rois Peschiere a non* (*RP* l.3520).
4. *CSG* 27–32: In the Romance of Perlesvaus, the Fisher King will die before Perceval returns to the Grail Castle, which falls into the hands of the King of Castle Mortal (*HBG* 146).
5. *CSG* 55–6.
6. *Et li feus qui estoit si hauz/ Senefioit que li Graaux,/ Qui tant est biaux et precïeus,/ An quoi li clers sens glorïeus/ Dou roi des roi fu receüz/ Qant il an la croiz fu panduz,/ Aveques lui ou bois l'avoit* (*CP* IV, ll.25791–7).
7. *CSG* 286.
8. See THE SWORD OF PARTINAL.
9. *CSG* 334–40.
10. *CSG* 409: Ysabel, the Lady of the Castle of Maidens, *Sovent voit mainte legion/ Des angles qui vont sanz desroi/ A l'ostel le Pescheor Roi/ Et entr'aus le saint Graal tienent./ Et l'oiste ens, de coi il soztienent/ La vie al pere celui roi/ Que Perchevaus trova sanz roi/ Peschant ens el petit navel* (*GCP* ll.8792–9).
11. *CSG* 474–5.
12. In the Vulgate Cycle, the Fisher Kings are descended, not from Joseph, but from his brother-in-law Bron.
13. The *Elucidation* gives a somewhat confused variation on this episode: Perceval finds the court of the Fisher King after scouring the land for it. He asks what is done with the Grail and about the identity of the dead man whom he sees on a bier. But he fails to ask about the Bleeding Lance or the broken half of the sword which he sees lying on the dead body. As a result, it will be not be Perceval but Gawain who, when he finds the Fisher King, will engender a joy which restores the whole kingdom (*CSG* 559).
14. *CSG* 477–9.
15. *CSG* 549–51: The Fisher King acknowledges Perceval as his nephew, his sister's son (*MTC* ll.42022–3), as he is in the Romance of Perlesvaus. But we had earlier learnt that the Fisher King was Perceval's cousin (*RP* ll.6415–9). In the Vulgate Cycle, Perceval is the son of Pellinor, the brother of the last Fisher King, Pelles.
16. *CSG* 543.
17. *MG* 35.
18. *...et tout cil qui oront de lui parler le clameront le rice Roi Pescheor por le pisson que il pescha.... Si tost com li Rice Peschiere sera saisis del vaissel et de la grasse, si couverra que il voist vers Occident, la u ses cuers li dira* (*RG* 68–9).
19. *MG* 42–3.
20. *Et li Rois Peschiere si converse en ces illes d'Irlande en un des plus biaus lius del monde* (*RG* 194).
21. *MG* 113: *Et cil, quant il s'ara si essaucié que il pora venir a la cort le rice Roi Pescheor, et que il ara demandé de quoi li Graaus a servi et de quoi il sert, et tant tost sera garis.... Et lors charront li encantement par la terre de Bretagne, et adont si sera la prophesie toute paracomplie* (*RG* 194–5).
22. *MG* 119–20.
23. *...li Rois Pesciere ... qui avoit le Graal en garde* (*RG* 244).
24. *MG* 139–43.
25. *MG* 154–6: *Car li Rois Pesciere est garis, et sont cheü li encantement de le terre de Bretagne* (*RG* 272).
26. *Tuit cil furent rois et tindrent terre et furent apelé en sornon Riche Pescheor* (*ESG* 565).
27. *LG* I, 157–60; III, 272: As his son Pelles says to Bors, *ce est li rois mehaigniez que l'an apela le Roi Pescheor* (*LM* V, 273). When Perceval first meets

Pellehan, the king is "sick and infirm" and fishes to amuse himself, since he cannot ride or fight like other knights (*LG* V, 109): It is of Pellehan that a certain count is speaking when he says to Galahad, with his dying breath, that he must go at all speed to the house of the Fisher King, who has been waiting so long to be healed (236).

28. *LG* I, 254: *la fille au roi Pellés de Listenois del chastel de Cornebic* [sic]... *qui fu niece le riche roi Pescheour et le roi malades des plaies dont li uns ot non Alain de l'ille en Listenois* (*LDG* I, 939). The third brother (*le roi malades des plaies*) is Pellinor, the father of Perceval, who is sometimes called the Maimed King but never (apart from in the confused *Livre d'Artus*) the Fisher King.

29. *LG* I, 235: We must assume that it is this unknown malady which obliges Alan to send his seneschal to (rather than attend in person) the great meeting on Salisbury Plain that establishes peace between Arthur and a group of kings who have rebelled against him (*LG* I, 380). We are not told of Alan's ultimate fate, but it appears that the world's best knight did not arrive in time, for we hear no more about Alan. His title presumably passes to his brother Pelles, who becomes the eighth Fisher King.

30. *LG* III, 206: *Aprés lor conte ... comment il vint chiés le Roi Pescheor et conment il vit le Saint Graal tout apertement porter devant lui a la plus bele pucele qu'il onques veist et les merveilles qu'il vit el Palais Aventureux* (*LM* IV, 397). Later, when the Grail appears at King Arthur's court, Gawain will declare that this is the only court where the Holy Vessel has ever been seen, apart from that of the Fisher King, who is called the Maimed King: *Et ce n'avint onques mes en nule cort, se ne fu chiés lo Roi Pescheor que l'en apele lo Roi Mehaignié* (*QSG* 114).

31. *Lors conmance Lanceloz a conter conment il vint chiés le Roi Pescheor ... et conment li Sainz Vaisiax raempli les tables de toutes les beles viandes; mais il ne lor conte pas conment il avoit esté deceuz de la bele damoisele, la fille au Roi Pescheor* (*LM* IV, 395).

32. "Did you not sleep two straight nights at the home of the Fisher King and never dare stay in the Palace of Adventures for fear of its trials?" (*LG* III, 181).

33. ...*et des merveilles qu'il avoit veues chiés le roi Pescheor et de la lance qui saignoit et de la table d'argent et des autres aventures de leanz* (*LM* VI, 60).

34. *LG* IV, 20-1; *QHG* 82-3: *Et aprés voit venir sor une table d'argent le Saint Vessel que il ot jadis veu chiés le Roi Pescheor, celui meismes que len apeloit le Saint Graal* (*QP* 59); Also there cam a table of sylver, and the holy vessell of the Sankgreall which Sir Launcelot had sene toforetyme in Kynge Pescheours house (*MD* 693).

35. *LG* V, 168.
36. *LG* V, 274.
37. *LG* V, 281.
38. *CSG* 558-9: *on ne peut puis trover jor/ Le cort au rice Pescheour/ Qui resplendissoit le païs* (*EB* ll.99-101); *rice Pesceour/ Qui mout savoit de ningremance/ Qu'il muast .C. fois sa samblance* (220-2).
39. Nitze 1909, 379-80.
40. Nitze 1909, 381.
41. Nitze 1909, 394: For the modern mythology of Grail Initiation, see AFTERWORD: HIGHER MYSTERIES.
42. Nitze 1909, 395-6.
43. Nitze 1909, 381.
44. Weston 1920, 136.
45. Weston 1907, 67.
46. Weston 1909, 259-61; 1913, 94.
47. Weston 1920, 127.
48. Weston 1920, 113: "If the Grail story be based upon a Life ritual the character of the Fisher King is of the very essence of the tale, and his title, so far from being meaningless, expresses, for those who are at pains to seek, the intention and object of the perplexing whole" (136).

The FISHER KING'S NIECE

When Perceval first comes to the Grail Castle he is welcomed by its lord, the Fisher King. While they are talking, a messenger enters with a sword hanging from his neck. The sword is a present from the king's niece, the beautiful Fair-Haired Girl,[1] who would be very pleased if the king gave it to someone who would use it well. It is the last of three that were made by a smith who will die before he can make another. The king gives it to Perceval, saying that the knight was destined to have it.[2]

* * *

Perceval doesn't actually see the Fair-Haired Girl who sends the sword but, when he leaves the castle, having failed to ask the Grail Question, he meets for the first time his long-lost cousin. She knows so much about the sword he was given, that she might even be the sister of the Fisher King, possibly even the mother of the girl who sent the sword in the first place.

The Fair-Haired Girl of the Grail Castle may be identical to the sister of Silimac, Lord of the Rock, who asks Gawain to avenge her brother's death, for she also calls herself the Fair-Haired Girl.[3] It seems likely that Silimac and his sister are the children of Gon of the Land Laid Waste,[4] who was treacherously killed by Partinal of the Red Tower. This act is eventually avenged by

Perceval with the sword that the Fair-Haired Girl sent to the Fisher King.

Notes

1. *la sore pucele* (*RP* l.3145).
2. *CSG* 28.
3. *Je ai non la Sore Pucelle;/ Et mon frere ot Silimac non,// Sire iert dou Chastel de la Roiche* (*MTC* ll.36562–3, 36566).
4. The Maiden of the Silver Trencher is also described as Gon's daughter and therefore the Fisher King's niece (*MTC* 295n91). But if she is also the *Sore Pucelle* who asks Gawain's aid to avenge her brother then it is surprising that a knight with such an eye for a beautiful lady did not recognize her: For he had already seen the Maiden of the Silver Trencher in the Grail Castle on his first visit, when he was struck by her beauty (*CSG* 108).

FLEGETANIS

The scholar Flegetanis is a descendant of Solomon but, although he has a Jewish mother, his father is a pagan who brings his son up to worship the divine calf.[1] As the hermit Trevrizent explains to Parzival, the heathen Flegetanis knew how to read what was hidden in the constellations and saw in them the secret name of the Grail.[2] The account of the Grail that Flegetanis writes in a heathen language is translated into French by Kyot of Provence.[3]

Notes

1. This form of idolatry presumably corresponds to the worship of the Golden Calf condemned in the Book of Exodus.
2. *WP* 232; *PT* 192: For the Kahanes, this indicates that the word Grail is derived from the Greek Krater, which also gives us the name of one of the constellations; and that Wolfram's version has been influenced by the Hermetic Mysteries (Kahane, Henry and Renée, 2).
3. This is the principal source, Wolfram von Eschenbach tells us, of his German version of the Grail legend, thus explaining why it contradicts Chrétien's story in several crucial details (*WP* 213–4; *PT* 176).

FRIMUTEL

King Frimutel is entrusted with the Grail when his father Titurel, the Lord of Mount Savage, grows weak through age and sickness.[1] Frimutel, however, abandons his role for the call of adventure and later dies in a joust for the love of a woman; he is replaced as Grail Lord by his son Anfortas. He has another son called Trevrizent, a hermit, a daughter who acts as Grail Bearer, and another called Herzeloyde, who is the widowed mother of Parzival.[2]

It is his father Frimutel's sword, fashioned by Trebuchet, which Anfortas gives to Parzival; When it is broken in a duel, Parzival takes it to a spring near Karnant where it is made whole by taking water before dawn from a spring, then strengthened through a magic spell.[3]

Notes

1. "...the Grail, which was perfection surpassing all earthly realms" (*PT* 350).
2. *WP* 133; *PT* 106.
3. *WP* 134, 223; *PT* 107, 183: This is Wolfram's brief nod to the theme of the Broken Sword, which runs throughout the verse continuations to Chrétien and is further reworked in the prose romances.

G

GALAFORT

A half-day's travel from Caleph Castle, on the border of the Kingdom of North Wales, stands the city of Galafort, the first target of the mission of the Company of the Grail to bring Christianity to Britain; its pagan duke, Ganor, is the first of the local nobility to be baptized. Neighboring Saracen rulers believe he has dishonored himself by abandoning his pagan faith. They tell the King of Northumberland, whose liegeman the duke is, that he deserves to lose his land. The king summons Ganor to account for himself, and besieges Galafort when the duke replies that he now acknowledges no other authority than Christ.[1]

In the ensuing battle, the king, who says that he prefers to die a pagan than to live as a Christian, is killed, whereupon his men flee across the Humber. Thus, the Christians win an honorable victory in their first battle against the pagans in this land.

When the Christian King Mordrain helps to secure victory against the pagans of North Wales in the Battle of Caleph Castle, he is blinded during a celebration Mass when he tries to come too close to the Grail—ironically, in order to see it clearly! Having also lost the strength of his limbs, he is carried in a litter to Galafort Castle, where he asks for the marriage of his nephew Celidoine and the Persian Princess Sarrasinte to be celebrated; they are also to be invested with the rulership of North Wales.

Mordrain retires to a hermitage in the forest near Galafort, where an abbey will later be established.[2]

Notes

1. *LG* I, 128
2. *LG* I, 135–6.

GALAHAD, King of Hoselice

Since leaving the Holy Land at the express request of Christ, whenever Joseph of Arimathea and his wife Elyab lie together, they are filled with religion rather than with lust. But Our Lord wants them to conceive a child from whom will issue the sacred lineage which will honor Britain, the land to which He wishes to lead them.[1] Galahad is, accordingly, conceived one winter's night in a wood, after Joseph hears the voice of the High Master, at whose command he had left his native country in search of the Promised Land of the Grail. The voice tells him to have sex with his wife and prophesies that there will be born to them a son whose descendants will maintain in faith the land they seek.[2]

It is after Joseph and his followers have arrived in Britain that Galahad is born, in the castle of Galafort, whose duke, Ganor, they have converted to Christianity. Fifteen years later, when Galahad is a grown man, news comes to Galafort, from the people of the Kingdom of Hoselice, that they have no lord, for their king has recently died. They beseech Josephus, Galahad's older brother, to send them someone worthy of ruling over the land, to prevent its devastation.

Duke Ganor tells Josephus that Galahad is undoubtedly the most worthy to rule a kingdom, so they accompany the young knight to Hoselice, in the west of Britain, where Josephus crowns, anoints and consecrates his brother in the city of Palagre.[3] King Galahad marries the daughter of the King of the Distant Isles and fathers a dynasty from which will issue King Urien and his son Yvain.[4] In honor of their first Christian king, the people of Hoselice rename it Wales after his death; this is the name by which it is known today.[5]

One day, while out hunting, King Galahad loses his way and comes by chance upon a fiery pit in a wasteland where his relative Simeon has been condemned to torment. Simeon must expiate a crime he committed against Peter, the founder of the Christian House of Orkney, but he asks Galahad to lighten his burden by establishing a religious community there.

Galahad promises to build an abbey where people will pray for Simeon's soul every day, saying that he will arrange to be buried there himself when he dies. Simeon thanks him profusely, adding that his pain will end when King Galahad's namesake arrives there: Only he can extinguish the fire, because in him alone will never dwell the fires of lust. At that time will be brought to an end the adventures that will occur throughout the land, the wonders of the Holy Grail.[6]

True to his word, King Galahad has an abbey founded there in honor of the Holy Trinity. When he dies, Galahad is buried there, his body prepared against decay. He is placed in a golden casket covered over by a tombstone so heavy that no one can ever lift it until Lancelot of the Lake comes there and raises it without any difficulty. Once the tomb has been opened, the body is transferred to Wales, the country named in Galahad's honor, in fulfillment of one of Merlin's prophecies. While there, Lancelot also tries to raise the tomb of Simeon, but is unable to do so, thus learning that he will not always be the best knight in the world; for that role is reserved for his son, the second Galahad.[7]

Notes

1. *LG* I, 23.
2. *LG* I, 119.
3. *LG* I, 155: According to the Vulgate *Lancelot*, Galahad is conceived in Hoselice (III, 12); but, according to the *Estoire del Saint Graal*, his conception occurs before Joseph and his wife arrive in Britain.
4. It is noticeable that Yvain and his father, neither of whom play a significant role in the Grail Quest, are the only Knights of the Round Table descended directly from Joseph of Arimathea (though Perceval, Bors, Lancelot and his son Galahad, descended from Joseph's brother-in-law Bron, are part of Joseph's extended family). King Urien's grandson (via an illegitimate son), Cahus, will also play a memorable role in the Romance of Perlesvaus.
5. *LG* I, 155–6: *de Galaaz, Gales* (*ESG* 551), Wales being *Gales* in Old French. Although this story is usually dismissed as one of many examples of the medieval penchant for false etymology, John Darrah (1994, 234–5) considers it to be more acceptable if we see Galahad as embodying a Bronze Age Celtic religious system spreading across Wales, Gaul, Galicia in Spain and Galatia in Asia Minor.
6. *...et en celui tens faudront auques les aventures qui en cest païs avendront par les merveilles del saint Greal* (*ESG* 553).
7. *LG* I, 156; III, 12–14.

GALAHAD, the True Knight

On his way to Gorre, the Kingdom of No Return, to rescue the many prisoners (including the woman he loves, Queen Guenevere) who are being held captive there, Sir Lancelot comes to a monastery where are to be found two wondrous tombs: One in a meadow, contains the body of Joseph of Arimathea's youngest son Galahad, the first Christian King of Wales; the other, in a crypt, contains the burning-but-still-living Simeon, Joseph's sinful nephew.

Both tombs have inscriptions detailing the subsequent achievements of whoever can raise their lids. The inscription on the tomb in the crypt prophesies that he who lifts it will dispel the enchantments of the Adventurous Kingdom, taking his place in the Perilous Seat at the Round Table. But, although Lancelot succeeds in opening King Galahad's sepulcher, he is unable to do the same to the tomb of Simeon, which proves that he is not the one who will take the empty seat and achieve the high Quest of the Holy Grail. The Good Knight who will deliver Simeon and bring to an end the adventures of Britain[1] is, however, of Lancelot's lineage[2]; he will in fact be another Galahad, Lancelot's own son.

The Knight of the Prophecy

The inscription that Lancelot reads in the Holy Cemetery where the first Galahad is buried is but one of many prophecies relating to the coming of the perfect knight, who will achieve the Grail Quest; prophecies which date back to the Old Testament epoch of the Kings of Israel.

The coming of the second Galahad is originally prophesied to King Solomon by a mysterious voice that comes to him in the night when he is pondering the deceitfulness of women. The voice tells him that the misdeed of our first mother, Eve, will be repaired by a woman of his lineage. By studying the secrets of Scripture, Solomon learns that this woman will be the Virgin Mary who will conceive the Son of God in her blessed vessel.[3] The same nocturnal voice later tells him that this woman will not be the end of his lineage; rather, that distinction will be reserved for a knight who will surpass all others as the sun's brightness surpasses that of the moon.[4]

Wishing to leave a message for his descendant that he had foreknowledge of his coming, Solomon consults his wife, who advises him to build a ship that will last four thousand years. In it, he should place the sword of his father, King David—the most marvelous sword ever forged, which should be prepared for the coming of the knight who will be marvelous beyond all others. Solomon, who knows all the properties of precious stones, removes the pommel and replaces it with a single stone containing every color imaginable. He then makes an equally wondrous scabbard for it, at which the voice speaks to him again, saying that only the one for whom he has prepared it will ever draw the sword, without repenting of doing so.

When the ship has been finished and rigged out, Solomon has a wooden bed made in it and leaves on it his father's crown, which he believes only the prophesied knight will be worthy of wearing. Solomon now writes a letter to that knight. He places it underneath the crown, then has the ship placed in the sea. In a waking dream he hears a voice say that his desire will be fulfilled, for the knight who will be the end of his line will enter the ship and discover the truth about him.

A wind rises up, and takes the ship out to sea.[5]

The Ship of Solomon

A thousand years later, the ship appears to a descendant of Solomon, Duke Nascien (the brother-in-law of the King of Sarras), who is travelling westwards to the land promised to the followers of Joseph of Arimathea. Falling asleep on board the ship, the travel-weary Nascien has a dream in which a man in a red robe appears before him. Since the man appears to know the future, Nascien asks him if he will ever return to his own country. The man replies that Nascien will remain in the western Promised Land and that the ship will also remain close to that country, until the last man in his lineage travels in it to Sarras with the Holy Vessel called the Grail.

The man in red gives him a letter, which, he says, contains the names of his noble descendants. As soon as the man leaves, Nascien's son Celidoine appears before him, accompanied by nine kings. One by one, the first eight kings fall at Celidoine's feet. But the ninth takes the form of an uncrowned lion and, when the lion passes away, the whole world mourns him.

When he awakens, Nascien finds that the letter he dreamed about is really in his hand. He reads it and discovers the names of the nine kings. The last bears the name Galahad: It is he who will bring an end to the adventures that befall, wherever chance or divine will leads him.

Later, the man in the red robe returns, to tell Nascien that Galahad's end will be more wondrous than that of any mortal knight of his time, but that he will die before his father.[6] And so indeed it comes to pass.

The Coming of the Red Knight

Hundreds of years pass and Lancelot, the eighth knight of Nascien's lineage, comes by adventure to the castle of Corbenic where the descendants of Bron, Joseph of Arimathea's brother-in-law, rule. These are the Fisher Kings who are entrusted with the custodianship of the Grail.

As he approaches the castle, Lancelot is told of a tombstone in a nearby cemetery, which can only be lifted by the "leopard" who will father the "great lion" on the daughter of the King of the Land Beyond.[7] When he succeeds in lifting the lid of the tombstone and slaying the dragon which lurks beneath, Lancelot is approached by King Pelles, the last Fisher King, who tells him that he is convinced that either Lancelot himself—or someone begotten by him—will deliver the land from the strange adventures which beset it day and night.

While he is in Corbenic, Elaine, who is the Grail Bearer and the daughter of Pelles, seduces Lancelot with the aid of her governess and in accordance with her father's wishes.[8] She gives birth to a child whom she calls Galahad.[9] It is he who will survive sitting in that place where all before him have died; who will bring to an end the adventures of the Holy Grail; and whose life-long virginity will make up for the loss of hers.[10]

When he is not yet a year old, Galahad is seen and admired by his father's cousin Bors, who is brought by adventure to Corbenic. When Bors hears of the trickery used to conceive the child, Bors thanks God for the ruse, for he is convinced that this boy will grow up to be the True Knight who takes his place in the Perilous Seat at the Round Table and accomplishes the adventures of the Holy Grail,[11] a Vessel which Bors himself sees in the Palace of Adventures.[12]

The first time that Lancelot sees his son, however, is when Elaine brings Galahad to Camelot, where he is introduced discreetly to his relatives, including Lancelot's half-brother Hector.[13] The latter sees his nephew again when he travels himself to Corbenic, where Lancelot is recovering from one of his recurring spells of insanity. Hector brings Lancelot back to King Arthur's court. But Galahad, who is now ten years old, is sent to live in an abbey run by King Pelles' sister in the Forest of Camelot. There he also receives instruction from Nascien the Hermit,[14] who understands the young man's significance.

And there he stays until he is fifteen, when Nascien suggests that he goes to the court at the feast of Pentecost to be knighted. The hermit then goes to see King Arthur, to warn him that great wonders will occur at the feast[15] and that he should therefore ensure that all his nobles are there to witness them.[16]

On the eve of Pentecost, a maiden leads Lancelot to the abbey in the forest where he sees his son, now grown into a child of wondrous beauty.[17] Galahad is knighted by his father but refuses to accompany him to the court, for it is not yet time. Moreover, when he does so, the following day, his arrival is heralded by two mysterious events: On the empty place at the Round Table known as the Perilous Seat, an inscription appears proclaiming that the seat will find its master on the day of Pentecost, four hundred and fifty-four years after the Passion of Christ; while, on the river that flows past Camelot, there is found floating a stone of red marble with a sword fixed in it. The sword is inscribed with letters stating that only the best knight in the world could draw it out.

After some knights have tried but failed to draw the sword from the stone, they all return to the great hall to eat, but have barely finished the first course when all the doors and windows close by themselves. Mysteriously, an old man in a white cloak appears in the room, leading by the hand a young knight in red armor, who is introduced as a descendant of King David and kin to Joseph of Arimathea. It is he, the old man says, who will put an end to the wondrous happenings in this and other lands.[18] Everyone there is convinced that this must be true, when Galahad's name appears on the Perilous Seat and he sits there without danger.[19] Realizing the adventure of the Sword in the Floating Stone is also Galahad's, Arthur leads him to the river. There, the knight draws the sword out with ease, announcing that he was so sure of obtaining it that he didn't bother bringing any other sword with him. He exclaims that he now lacks nothing but a shield.

After a tournament at which, despite being shield-less, Galahad excels, the company sit down to eat their evening meal. But they are fed instead by the Holy Grail, covered by a cloth of white silk; everyone receives what he most desires through the grace of the Holy Spirit. The next day,

Galahad swears that he will go on a quest to see the Grail more clearly and that he will not return to court until he has learnt the truth about the Holy Vessel, if he is able to do so. The rest of the company vow to do the same.[20]

So begins the Quest of the Holy Grail.

The Adventurous Shield

On the fifth day after he is made a knight, Galahad, still without a shield, comes to a white abbey[21] where, behind the altar, hangs the Adventurous Shield, snow white with a red cross. Galahad is told by Bademagu, King of Gorre, who is also staying in the abbey, that no man may bear it unscathed. But this does not stop Bademagu himself trying it out, with disastrous consequences: He is overthrown in a joust with a mysterious White Knight on a white horse and injured so badly that he is lucky to escape with his life. The knight gives the Red Cross Shield to Bademagu's squire and bids him take it to Galahad, who alone can bear it without mishap.

The squire leads Galahad to meet the White Knight in the forest, where they discover the history of the Shield: Forty-two years after the Passion of Jesus, the White Knight tells him, Joseph of Arimathea and his son Josephus came to the city of Sarras, only to find its king, Evalach, at war with his neighbor Tholomer. Josephus promised Evalach victory if he would believe in the New Law of Christ and Evalach agreed to do so. As a token of his faith, he was given a white shield marked with a red cross, which brought him victory[22] and led to his conversion. When he is dying, Josephus tells Evalach to leave the shield at the abbey where his brother-in-law Nascien will die. There it must await the coming of the Good Knight who is the last in Nascien's line and who alone can bear the Shield without regretting it.

The White Knight finishes his tale and vanishes and the squire (Meliagant, the son of the King of Denmark), hearing all this, asks Galahad to make him a knight. This he does, back at the abbey, after removing a demonically possessed body from the cemetery, an act that leads to Galahad's coming being explicitly compared to that of Christ.[23] Just as the prophets predicted that Christ would deliver us from the bonds of Hell, so holy men have for more than twenty years been announcing that Galahad will deliver the Kingdom of Logres from the perilous adventures that beset it.[24]

Beautiful Marvels

Galahad begins his mission of deliverance with maidens imprisoned in a castle on the Severn[25] but is soon to receive more miraculous signs that he is the prophesied knight. As if to divert him from his true task, a bizarre creature known as the Questing Beast appears in his path. But, although acknowledging it as a wondrous adventure, Galahad is instead drawn to follow a white stag guarded by four lions, which he recognizes as one of the adventures of the Holy Grail.[26]

But another temptation soon arises: Lodged at Castle Brutus, Galahad awakens in the night to find that his host's lovesick daughter has climbed into bed with him. She is distressed to find that he sleeps in a hair shirt, revealing that he is one of the true knights of the Grail Quest, while he is horrified at her advances. When she grabs his sword, he prepares to die rather than lose his honor. But, when she threatens to kill herself, he relents, agreeing to do all her pleasure—too late, for she runs herself through[27] with the very weapon that Galahad claimed as proof of his spiritual election.

On a day in April, Galahad finds himself once more at Corbenic where he was born, although he is so stained by his armor that no one recognizes him. Pelles and his courtiers are all in the gardens, celebrating the anniversary of the king's accession with a magician providing their entertainment. But what they do not know is that the performer is really a lapsed Christian who has sold his soul to the Devil in the form of the pagan god Dagon. As soon as Galahad comes near him, however, the magician loses his powers for, as he admits, the knight is always accompanied by angels who neutralize demonic powers. Once Galahad puts sufficient distances between them once more, the magician is carried off by the infernal powers he serves.

Galahad resists all entreaties to stay at the castle, even having to fight his uncle Eliezer to get away,[28] presumably because he wants to continue having adventures rather than bring them to an end prematurely. He will soon get another opportunity to cast out demons.

After taking part in a tournament where he wounds Gawain with the sword that he drew from the Floating Stone (thus effectively ending that knight's Grail Quest), Galahad is staying at a hermitage near Corbenic when a maiden arrives who summons him to a lofty adventure.[29] She takes him to her cousin's castle, where he discovers a lady of consequence who has had to be chained up since she went mad. But she is cured as soon as she lays eyes on Galahad, whose mere presence frees her from the Devil who has been possessing her. He later cures a lady of leprosy by giving to her his hair shirt to wear.[30]

Galahad now follows the maiden to the seashore where they find a ship containing two of their relatives: his father's cousin Bors and her brother Perceval. This ship takes them to a secluded island where awaits them yet another ship.

Despite the fact that the second ship bears a warning that only those steadfast in their Christian faith should enter therein, Galahad crosses himself and is the first to enter, the others following his lead. On the ship is a bed and, on the bed, a wondrously powerful sword.[31] The maiden explains that it can only be drawn by the very good knight who will bring to an end the adventures of Logres.[32] Galahad draws it from its sheath without meeting any harm, whereupon Perceval's sister attaches a belt made out of her own hair to the sword, which she girds on Sir Galahad.[33]

The Good Knight goes to sleep on the bed that Solomon had long ago prepared in the ship. While his companions wonder at the marvels God has shown them, Perceval's sister promises more to come. Accordingly, it is not long before they come upon an impossibly aged man marooned on a spit of land. He turns out to be Caiaphas, whom Vespasian set adrift on the sea hundreds of years earlier as a punishment for his part in the execution of Jesus. But Caiaphas is unable to set foot on the Ship of Faith, so Galahad decides they should leave his fate to divine providence.[34]

Travelling onwards, Galahad has the chance to try out his new sword when they come to a castle ruled by three brothers who raped their sister and imprisoned their father, the count. The brothers are soon dispatched, much to Galahad's regret, for he avoids killing his enemies whenever possible. But the dying count, to whom it was revealed that his redeemer would one day come, considers that they were enacting God's vengeance. The count dies happily in Galahad's arms, urging the knight, with his last breath, to make all speed to the house of the Fisher King, who has long awaited him.[35]

But more adventures first await the companions: The mysterious stag and lions that Galahad earlier encountered re-appear and lead them to a hermitage. As the holy hermit celebrates the Mass of the Holy Spirit, the companions see the stag turn into a Man who is seated on the altar, while the lions also transform: One becomes more beautiful than ever while another takes the figure of an angel, a third the figure of an eagle and the fourth, the figure of an ox. All four sprout wings which bear them up as they carry the seated Man right through a window in the apse of the chapel, without breaking the glass. Recognizing Galahad and his companions as those who will achieve the Grail Quest and can therefore be entrusted with divine secrets,[36] the hermit explains that the Man and the four creatures are Christ and the evangelists; they passed through the glass without breaking it, just as the Blessed Virgin gave birth without breaking her maidenhead.

Later Perceval's sister sacrifices herself to heal a leper. As she lies dying, she bids the three companions to separate and urges Galahad to return to Camelot, for his help is needed by King Arthur, who is in great danger.[37]

On the way, Galahad comes to the abbey where Simeon, an early Christian from the Holy Land who plotted the murder of his more worthy companions, lies buried. In the crypt beneath the church, Galahad finds a burning tombstone, beneath which Simeon is buried alive as punishment for his sin. Galahad's mere presence causes the fire to die down and the soul of Simeon to find forgiveness.[38]

Galahad has thus succeeded where his father failed, for Lancelot had already been there but had been driven back by the fire. This was when Lancelot first realized that, although he was the greatest of earthly knights, his son would surpass him in spiritual chivalry.

Arriving at last at Camelot, Galahad and a small group of knights succeed in driving back King Mark, who is besieging the city in alliance with the pagan Saxons. Galahad sees the conflict as a battle to save Christian Britain, to the extent that he is reluctant to accept the help of the pagan Palamedes.

After the battle, Galahad goes to a house of white brethren to recuperate. But while he is there, the fugitive King Mark comes upon him by chance and attempts to poison him; Galahad is saved by a miracle.[39] Yet another miracle occurs when he is imprisoned in the Castle of Treachery, a pagan stronghold which has survived since the Trojan conquest of Albion, resisting all attempts to convert its people to Christianity. Lightning strikes the tower where Galahad is imprisoned and he is able to free many maidens who have been held captive there.[40]

After a meeting with his father, during which Galahad shows Lancelot the sword he has won,[41] he travels on to an abbey where King Mordrain (who was converted to Christianity by Josephus) has lain, sick and blind, for hundreds of years. When he realizes his redeemer has finally come, Mordrain asks Galahad to hold him so that he can die in his embrace. Later, Galahad quenches the heat in a boiling fountain in the Perilous Forest, a sign that he has never known lust.[42]

When he next encounters Palamedes, Galahad defeats him in battle and then persuades him to convert to Christianity, something Palamedes had already inwardly done. Further, at Galahad's behest, Palamedes goes to Camelot to be made a Knight of the Round Table, so that he can join in the Grail Quest.[43] Galahad and Perceval are both present when Palamedes finally kills the Questing Beast, and the three knights travel on to Corbenic together.[44]

The Grail Liturgy

As soon as he returns to the castle where he was brought up,[45] Galahad once more meets his uncle Eliezer bearing a sword. But this time it is not to fight, but to ask Galahad to try to mend a weapon which was broken in the days of Joseph of Arimathea.[46] As soon as Galahad joins the two halves together, they meld so seamlessly that no one would ever know they had been parted.

The three companions are now joined by nine other Round Table Knights in the great hall, and the Maimed King is carried in. A voice commands everyone else to leave. Those who remain are amazed to see Josephus, the first Christian bishop (who died hundreds of years earlier), descend from the sky, accompanied by angels, one of whom carries a Lance which bleeds into the Holy Grail.[47] Josephus begins celebrating the Mass but disappears after elevating the

Host, which they clearly see takes on human form. Christ Himself then issues from the Grail Vessel to give, first to Galahad, then to each of the twelve knights, heavenly food.[48]

Christ explains to Galahad that the Holy Vessel is the serving dish from which He ate the paschal lamb at the Last Supper, the sacred platter that no faithless man can behold without suffering; Galahad will see it even more fully in the Spiritual Palace in the city of Sarras.[49] Thither the Grail will now go, for the people of Logres have proved unworthy of its presence.

But before following the Grail eastwards, Galahad must achieve the last great spiritual adventure: the healing of the Maimed King. Touching the blood from the Holy Lance, he anoints the wounds on the king's legs,[50] whereupon Pellehan arises from his bed, strong and healthy once more, as he was before he was struck by the Dolorous Blow.

The twelve knights who have been fed at the Table of the Grail must now go their separate ways, as the apostles did after the Last Supper, while King Pellehan goes to live in a hermitage.[51] It is there that Galahad, Bors and Perceval find him shortly thereafter; he explains to them the origins of the Questing Beast and other marvels that they have encountered on the way.[52]

Hidden Marvels

In the morning, the companions leave the hermit king and travel to the seashore where they find the Ship of Faith. In it they discover the silver Table of the Grail and the Holy Vessel itself, covered in silk cloth. A wind sends the ship into the sea.

On the voyage, Galahad prays to be allowed to pass out of this world whenever he requests it for, having seen the wonders of the Grail, he has known unearthly joy. He longs to be forever in the presence of the hidden marvels that are not disclosed to everyone, but only to those who serve Christ in their hearts.[53] A voice replies that, whenever he asks, he will be granted the death of the body and the life of the soul. Later, he learns in a dream that neither he nor Perceval will ever return to Logres.

The ship takes them to Sarras, where they also find the boat containing the body of Perceval's sister. They bury her in the Spiritual Palace, as she had requested. Galahad heals a disabled man so that he can help them carry the Table of the Grail into the city. But when the king of the city, who is a pagan tyrant,[54] hears of their arrival, he casts them into prison.

The knights, fortunately, are fed by the Grail, as Joseph of Arimathea before them had been fed, when he was in prison in Jerusalem. Providentially, at the end of the year the king dies and the people of the city are commanded by a supernatural voice to make Galahad their king. His first act is to have a curved vault of gold and precious stones made over the Table of the Grail, where they make their daily prayers before the Holy Vessel.

On the anniversary of his coronation, Galahad encounters Josephus once more, performing the Mass of the Glorious Lady in the Spiritual Palace, surrounded by angels. At the consecration of the Mass, Josephus removes the paten that covers the Grail, allowing Galahad to look into the Holy Vessel. Here he sees openly, for the first time, what tongue cannot tell nor heart imagine: the beginnings of high endeavor, the source of great prowess, the marvel that surpasses all other marvels.[55]

Josephus gives Galahad the Host, the Body of Our Lord, telling him that he has been sent to bear him fellowship, for they are both virgins. Galahad kisses goodbye his companions, bidding Bors greet his father Lancelot for him. Angels carry his soul away and a hand comes down from the sky to bear off the Holy Vessel, which is nevermore seen on Earth.

Galahad is buried in the Spiritual Palace next to Perceval's sister. Perceval himself joins them fourteen months later, at which point Bors returns to Camelot.[56] But Galahad has at last fulfilled Solomon's prophecy, and the spiritual adventures of Logres are at an end.

* * *

The name Galahad (*Galaad*) appears for the first time in the Vulgate Cycle, probably written by clerks in the early thirteenth century. It is almost certainly derived from the Biblical name Gilead, meaning "a heap of testimony,"[57] suggesting that Galahad is a rock on which can be built a Grail martyrology. Under the influence of the Cistercians, who were dedicated to combating the purism of the "good Christians" or Cathars in the Languedoc,[58] Galahad came to epitomize a world-renouncing Grail Quest which pits Heaven against Earth in a conflict that can only lead to death.

The late Victorian scholar Alfred Nutt, a proponent of the pagan Celtic origins of the legends, denounced the "unhuman realm"[59] of the Galahad Quest with its "nauseating disquisitions upon chastity"[60] which he finds ethically false and aesthetically lifeless.[61] The character of Galahad himself he considers "wholly remote from the life of man on earth." He is "a shadowy perfection throughout, a bloodless and unreal creature,[62] as fit when he first appears upon the scene as when he quits it, to accomplish a quest, purposeless, inasmuch as it only removes him from a world in which he has neither part nor share."[63]

But although it is true that, as Nutt points out, the Vulgate Quest can be achieved "only by renouncing every human desire, only by passing into a land intermediary between this earth and heaven,"[64] the nature of this intermediary world has been more positively evaluated by Henry Corbin, who sees it as what he calls the *mundus imaginalis* or "imaginal" world. This phrase of his own coinage describes a world of spiritual images which can only be perceived by the "true" or visionary Imagination—a faculty of perception intermediate between sensory perception and intellectual intuition. For Corbin, Galahad's journey to the East, from Corbenic to Sarras, is a journey into the spiritual source of the Imagination, which alone can enable us to mend the Broken Sword of the Word of God.[65]

The sword that Galahad is called upon to mend is one wielded by a pagan to wound Joseph of Arimathea. It can thus be seen to symbolize the fracturing of the indigenous spiritual tradition by the Christian conquest (a violent one, as it is presented in the Vulgate Cycle). Esoteric writers such as Caitlín and John Matthews therefore stress the need for paganism and Christianity to find a new harmony (just as Corbin always spoke of the importance of the *harmonia Abrahamica*, the harmonizing of the three monotheistic, "Abrahamic" faiths).

For the occultist Gareth Knight, this re-harmonizing can be visualized in sexual terms: Galahad should have a female partner in order to balance the polar forces in the aura.[66] This, of course, would have been anathema to the ubiquitous hermits of the Vulgate Cycle, for whom woman, unless she were both chaste and virginal (like Mother Mary or Perceval's sister), could only be the cause of sin.

Curiously, in a little-known late poem by William Wordsworth ("The Egyptian Maid," 1830), Sir Galahad wins a wife, whom he first sees in "noontide vision," in "a waking dream" inspired by the Lady of the Lake. When he sees the maiden in the flesh, at King Arthur's court in Caerleon, Galahad is clad in the same mantle that he wore "on a day of glory,/ The day when he achieved that matchless feat,/ The marvel of the Perilous Seat." He touches the hand of the "insensate" Egyptian Lady, who lies in a death-like sleep; and she stirs to life, signifying that he is the bridegroom who "was for her ordained by Heaven." Their nuptials follow soon after.[67]

Notes

1. ...*abatroit les enchantemens del Roialme Aventureus et metroit fin as aventures et acompliroit le*

siege de la Table Reonde (*LM* II, 32); *acomplira le siege perillos et les aventures de Bretaigne metra a fin* (36); *achievera le Siege Perillous de la Table reonde et metera a fin la haute queste del saint Graal* (*LDG* II, 1351).

2. *LG* III, 12-13.

3. *...son beneüré vaissel* (*ESG* 282): If the Blessed Virgin Mary is the sacred vessel that bears Jesus, then apocryphal tales make Mary Magdalen the sacred vessel that bears His child. As the mother of the Holy Bloodline, she is the archetypal Grail Bearer in modern mythology. Philippe Walter (2004a, 98-9) points out that Galahad will be conceived on the night of the feast of Mary Magdalen, with whom Elaine his mother will compare herself.

4. In Malory's version, Solomon learns from the Holy Spirit that *there shall com a man which shall be a mayde, and laste of youre bloode*; and from his wife *that thys knyght oughte to passe all knyghtes of chevalry whych hath bene tofore hym and shall com afftir hym* (*MD* 758).

5. *LG* I, 82-5; IV, 69-71; *QHG* 230-5.

6. *LG* I, 116-18.

7. *ET CIL GRANS LYONS ERT ENGENDRÉS DEL LIEPART EN LA BELE FILLE LE ROI DE LA TERRE FORAINNE* (*LDG* III, 230): *And this lybarde shall engendir a lyon in this forayne contrey whyche lyon shall passe all other knyghtes* (*MD* 622). The coming of the lion son of the leopard has already been prophesied to Lancelot's friend Galehaut (*LG* II, 251-3) who, nevertheless, keeps it to himself.

8. *...the kynge knew well that Sir Launcelot shulde get a pusyll uppon his doughtir* (*MD* 622-3).

9. Galahad was also the name Lancelot's mother gave to him when he was born, although Elaine cannot know this (unless she has heard it from Brisane, whom Malory considers to be a great enchantress). It was the Lady of the Lake who gave her handsome foundling the name Lancelot in honor of his grandfather. She may well have known he would not be worthy of the name Galahad, because of the flames of carnal desire—*par escaufement de luxure* (*LDG* III, 239)—which would burn in him as an adult. By contrast, the son of Lancelot and Elaine would remain a virgin, in thought and deed, his entire life.

10. *LG* III, 162-5: *Galaad, li virges, li tres bons chevaliers, cil qui les aventures del saint Graal mist a fin et s'asist el perilleus siege de la Table Reonde ou onques chevaliers ne s'estoit assis qui ne fust morz* (*LM* IV, 210-11).

11. *...li verais chevaliers par cui les aventures dou Saint Graal seront menees a chief et qui serra el siege perilleus de la Table Reonde* (*LM* V, 256). In Malory's version, the Grail Bearer (not Galahad's mother, since only a virgin can carry the Holy Vessel) tells Bors that *thys chylde is Galahad that shall sytte in the Syege Perelous and enchyve the Sankgreall, and he shall be muche bettir than ever was Sir Launcelot, that ys hys owne fadir* (*MD* 626).

12. *LG* III, 268.

13. *LG* III, 320.

14. *VS* VII, 261.

15. *...au jor de Pentecoste qui vient sera noviaux chevaliers cil qui les aventures del Saint Graal metra a fin et venra celui jor a ta cort et acomplira sanz faille le siege perilleus* (*LM* VI, 244): *And men sey that he shall do many mervaylouse thyngys* (*MD* 657).

16. *LG* III, 337-8.

17. Malory describes Galahad as *semely and demure as a dove* (*MD* 666), recalling the bird whose entrance into the palace of the Grail Castle so often heralds the appearance of the Holy Vessel.

18. *...le Chevalier Desirré, celui qui est estraiz dou haut lignage le Roi David et del parenté Joseph d'Arimacie, celui par cui les merveilles de cest païs et des estranges terres remaindront* (*QP* 7); *a yonge knyght the whych ys of kynges lynage and of the kynrede of Joseph of Aramathy, whereby the mervayles of this courte and of straunge realmys shall be fully complevysshed* (*MD* 669). Galahad is descended from King David through his grandmother, Elaine of Benoic, and from Bron, the brother-in-law of Joseph of Arimathea, through his mother, Elaine of Corbenic. In the Post-Vulgate version, the knights are struck dumb by the appearance of Galahad and only regain the power of speech after he takes his place in the Perilous Seat (*PV* II, 27-9).

19. Arthur and the Knights of the Round Table recognize Galahad as the long-awaited knight who will fulfill the Adventures of the Holy Grail—*cil que nos atendions a achever les aventures del Saint Graal* (*QP* 7)—and the wonders of Logres—*cil par cui les merveilles del roiaume de Logres doivent faillir* (*QSG* 98); *Thys ys he by whom the Sankgreall shall be encheved, for there sate never none but he there but he were myscheved* (*MD* 670). When the ladies of the court hear of his achievement, they proclaim that he is the one who will bring to an end the adventures of Great Britain and heal the Maimed King: *cil qui metra a fin les aventures de la Grant Bretaigne, et par cui li Rois Mehaigniez recevra garrison* (*QP* 10).

20. *LG* IV, 3-10; V, 113-23; *QHG* 32-50; *MD* 665-76.

21. The (anachronistic) reference is to the Cistercians, whose influence on the Vulgate Grail is much in evidence (Barber 2005, 153-5).

22. In the Post-Vulgate version, the White Knight tells Galahad that He Himself came to Evalach's aid at a moment of great danger (*PV* IV.1, 124).

23. The comparison is qualified: Galahad's coming resembles that of Christ's, but not on such an elevated level: *de semblance ne mie de hautece* (*QP* 38).

24. *LG* IV, 11-15; V, 126-30; *QHG* 53-66; *MD* 678-84.

25. *LG* IV, 17-19; *QHG* 71-6; *MD* 687-9: A hermit later explains to Gawain that the *Chastel as Puceles* represents Hell and the maidens, the souls of the just wrongly detained there (*les bones ames qui a tort i estoient enserrees*) who could only be redeemed by Christ's Passion (*QP* 55): *Also I may sey you that the Castell of Maydyns betokenyth the good soulys that were in prison before the Incarnacion of*

Oure Lorde Jesu Cryste. Thus, Galahad can be likened to the Son of the High Father *that bought all the soules oute of thralle: so ded Sir Galahad delyver all the maydyns oute of the woofull castell (MD 691).*
   26. *LG* V, 136.
   27. *LG* V, 142-4.
   28. *LG* V, 224-6.
   29. *LG* IV, 62-3; *QHG* 207-10; *MD* 749-50.
   30. *LG* V, 226-9.
   31. *LG* IV, 63-5; V, 230-1; *QHG* 211-18; *MD* 751-53.
   32. *...li tres bons chevaliers qui doit mener a fin les aventures du roiaume de Logres (PV III, 39).*
   33. *LG* IV, 72; V, 232; *QHG* 237; *MD* 760-1: See THE SWORD WITH THE STRANGE STRAPS.
   34. *LG* V, 233.
   35. *Sir Galahad, well hast thou ben avenged on Goddis enemyes. Now behovith the to go to the Maymed Kynge as sone as thou mayste, for he shall ressayve by the helth whych he hath abyddyn so longe (MD 764).*
   36. *...ye beth the good knyghtes whych shall brynge the Sankgreall to an ende; for ye bene they unto whom Oure Lorde shall shew grete secretis (MD 764-5).*
   37. *LG* IV, 72-5; V, 234-9; *QHG* 238-49; *MD* 761-9.
   38. *LG* IV, 83; V, 243-4; *QHG* 270-1; *MD* 780.
   39. *LG* V, 244-9.
   40. *LG* V, 254-6.
   41. *LG* IV, 79; *QHG* 258; *MD* 771.
   42. *LG* IV, 82-3; *QHG* 269-70; And so thys was takyn in the contrey for a miracle, and so ever afftir was hit called Galahaddis Welle (MD 779).*
   43. *LG* V, 273-4.
   44. *LG* V, 278.
   45. *So there was grete joy, for they wyste well by her commynge that they had fulfylled the queste of the Sankgreall (MD 781).* In the Post-Vulgate version, Galahad declares that, if they are truly *chevaliers del Saint Grahal*, the doors of the Palace of Adventures will swing open for them; which, of course, they do (*PV* III, 316-7).
   46. See THE BLEEDING SWORD.
   47. See THE BLEEDING LANCE: Although as far as we know Galahad has never seen the Lance before, the Post-Vulgate version has him immediately recognize its sacred character: It is the Adventurous Lance, which gave the Son of God his death-blow: *Quant Galahaz voit ceste merveille, il pense bien maintenant que ce est, sanz faille, la Lance Aventureuse, celle meemes dont li filz Deu soufri mort (PV III, 320).*
   48. *Than toke He Hymselff the holy vessell and cam to Sir Galahad. And he kneled adowne and resseyved hys Saveoure (MD 783).*
   49. *And now hast thou sene that thou moste desired to se, but yet hast thou nat sene hit so opynly as thou shalt se hit in the cité of Sarras, in the spirituall paleyse. Therefore thou must go hense and beare with the thys holy vessell (MD 783).*
   50. *And Sir Galahad wente anone to the speare which lay upon the table, and towched the bloode with hys fyngirs, and cam aftir to the Maymed Kynge and anoynted his legges and hys body (MD 784).*
   51. *LG* IV, 83-5; V, 278-80; *QHG* 272-7; *MD* 781-4.
   52. *LG* V, 283-6.
   53. *...les repostes choses qui ne sont pas descovertes a chascun (QP 274); les merveilles del Saint Graal et les repostailles et les secrez que Nostre Sires demostre a ses amis qui de cuer le servent (QSG 644).*
   54. Joseph of Arimathea had converted the city to Christianity, but it has presumably lapsed in the interim.
   55. *Ici voi je la començaille des granz hardemenz et l'acheson des granz proeces; ci voi je la merveille de totes les autres merveilles! (QSG 650).*
   56. *LG* IV, 86-7; V, 286-8; *QHG* 279-84; *MD* 785-8.
   57. Walter 2004a, 191-4.
   58. Barber 2000, 6.
   59. Nutt, 239.
   60. Nutt, 244n.
   61. Nutt, 236.
   62. Jessie L. Weston, who was mentored and encouraged by Nutt, echoed his language a few years later, in a book celebrating Wagner's *Parsifal* and other music dramas, dismissing Galahad as a "shadowy ascetic ... standing apart from man's hopes and needs" (1896, 212). Moreover, in the second volume of her Perceval Studies, Weston sees Galahad as replacing Perceval in his role of fulfilling the trinitarian symbolism which is such an important aspect of the De Boron Cycle (in which Perceval is the third Grail Keeper), and which is absorbed into the Vulgate Cycle (in which there are three Grail winners). What was originally the holiest symbol of her supposed Grail Mystery Cult is replaced by the miracle of transubstantiation, which is what she believes Galahad witnesses fully in his final vision in Sarras: "he beholds with mortal eye the stupendous and ineffable Mystery of the conversion of material elements into Spiritual Food—and forthwith departs this life" (1909, 275-6).
   63. Nutt, 239.
   64. Nutt, 238.
   65. Corbin 1995, 107: For Corbin, as for René Guénon, the shattering of the mystic Sword of the Word is caused by the sundering of exoteric religion from the esoteric, initiatory aspect of a spiritual tradition (see AFTERWORD: HIGHER MYSTERIES).
   66. Knight 1983, 193-4: "Therefore the Grail, when it was won, instead of being a Cauldron of Plenty in tune with the fruits of the Earth, became a Cup of Spiritual Illumination divorced from the Earth."
   67. *WPW* 294-5.

GARLON the Red

The brother of Pellehan, King of Listenois, Garlon is the very opposite of the good Fisher King: an evil knight[1] who uses his powers of invisibility to kill or wound.² Those injured by him will not recover unless they are given Garlon's blood.

When a knight who is under the protection of Balin the Savage is killed by a lance thrown by an unknown hand, Balin vows to avenge him and fulfill the mission that the knight was on. He is joined in this by another knight who becomes Garlon's next victim. But Balin persists in his quest, despite Merlin's warning that, if he does so, he will bring about more destruction to the Kingdom of Logres than was caused by the killing of Garlon's father Lambor, which produced the Waste Land.³ It is Merlin, nevertheless, who reveals to Balin the identity of the silent killer.⁴

Ignoring Merlin's prophecy (something that anyone does at their peril), Balin pursues the wondrous murderer to Garlon's brother's court at Listenois and there kills him with a blow of his sword. He takes the truncheon with which Garlon had killed a knight (and which, he has been told, is the only weapon which can truly avenge his victim⁵), smites him through the body with it, and gives the blood that flows from the dead man to the father of one of his victims, so that the man's son can be healed.

This act foreshadows the events that are to come. In attempting to avenge the death of his brother, Pellehan is maimed by Balin with the Avenging Lance⁶; years later, Galahad will heal Pellehan with the blood that now drips from the Lance.

* * *

The story of Garlon the Red is full of oppositions and dualities: Thus Garlon, like the King of Castle Mortal, is as bad as his brother the Fisher King is good.⁷ Balin seeks vengeance on Garlon, whose crimes can only truly be avenged by the lance with which he has killed one of his victims; the unintended consequence is that Balin uses the Avenging Lance (the Lance of divine vengeance, which falls even on those who have not deserved it) to maim the good brother of the evil man he kills. Garlon maims a knight, who can only be healed with the blood of the man who wounded him; Galahad heals Garlon's maimed brother with the blood from the weapon that Balin used to wound him. Only Garlon's blood can heal his victim; only Christ's blood can heal the victim of divine vengeance.

The themes of invisibility and the healing power of blood suggest that Garlon is the vampiric, inverted mirror image or shadow of his brother; just as the vampire, for whom "the blood is the life"—who dies and is reborn to wreak, not save us from, death—is the shadow of Christ, offering a hell-on-earth version of eternal life.⁸ Garlon's maiming lance is the shadow of the Lance that maims the Fisher King; Garlon's blood is the shadow of Christ's.

Notes

1. In the Romance of Perlesvaus, the good Fisher King also has an evil brother, the King of Castle Mortal.
2. Interestingly, Balin does not see Garlon's powers of invisibility as a form of enchantment, telling the father of one of Garlon's victims (who knows only that his son was wounded by someone who struck without being seen, though in broad daylight and with no place to hide) that magic is not involved: The killer is someone who has the power to prevent anyone else seeing him for as long as he wants: *che n'est pas enchantemens, ains est uns chevaliers qui a tel pooir que nus ne le voit tant comme il voelle* (*SRM* 153). Where this power derives from, if not from magic, we are never told.
3. The first indication of the destruction to come is the appearance, on the tombstone of the second of Garlon's victims, of an inscription announcing that, in the very cemetery where the knight is buried, Garlon's nephew Pellinor will be killed by Gawain (*SRM* 144).
4. *LG* IV, 203–7.
5. *Et saichiés bien que li chevaliers ne puet estre vengiés fors dou tronchon meismes dont il fu ferus* (*SRM* 139).
6. *LG* IV, 211–12; *MD* 63–8.
7. Garlon, or *the knyght with the blacke face*, as Malory calls him, *ys the mervaylyste knyght that ys now lyvynge. And he destroyeth many good knyghtes, for he goth invisible* (*MD* 66). His brother, by contrast, is *the trewyst knyght and the man of moste worship that now lyvith* (57).
8. As the psychologist Stan Gooch once observed, the vampire has no reflection in a mirror

because it *is* a reflection; we might add that it casts no shadow because it *is* a shadow.

GAWAIN

It is said that Sir Gawain, King Arthur's nephew, first hears about the Grail when he befriends the young Perceval at his uncle's court in Caerleon. An Ugly Maiden on a mule enters and upbraids Perceval for his failure to ask the Grail Question when he was earlier at the house of the Fisher King, as a result of which lands will be laid waste. She goes on to throw down various challenges for Arthur's knights, including the announcement that, if anyone wants to gain the world's esteem, he should go to the castle of Montesclaire. Whoever can raise the siege there and free its mistress would win great praise, and would prove himself to be worthy to gird on the Sword of the Strange Belt.

With that the Ugly Maiden leaves, and Gawain vows to do all in his power to rescue the girl at Montesclaire. However, barely has he done so when fate intervenes: He is accused of having treacherously killed the King of Escavalon[1] and can only escape imprisonment by finding, within the year, the Bleeding Lance which, it is written, will bring about the destruction of the Kingdom of Logres.[2] This quest is itself derailed by a close encounter with an enigmatic woman, the Proud Lady of Logres, and a sojourn in a magical castle, where he meets three generations of his family: his sister, their mother and their grandmother.[3]

Gawain succeeds in casting out the enchantments of the castle and is later exonerated of the murder of which he stood accused. Nevertheless, he will eventually find the Lance that he has been tasked with claiming, when he arrives at another mysterious castle, one ruled not by an aged queen but by a grey-haired and wounded king.

At the Castle of the Grail

After restoring a magic horn to a maiden from whom it had been stolen, Gawain is rewarded with a ring which enables the bearer to overcome at least five opponents. This will come in handy when he eventually reaches Montesclaire which, as a hideously ugly dwarf reminds him, is still under siege, its lady eagerly awaiting his arrival.[4] Meanwhile, he is also very aware that he has long delayed finding the Lance; but also that he is completely lost, having no idea what country he is in, since he can find no landmarks to guide him.

After riding aimlessly for a fortnight, feeling utterly thwarted in both his quests, his frustration turns to elation when he glimpses a tower at the edge of the forest. Entering, he sees the Maimed King reclining on his bed. The king forgets his troubles in chatting with Gawain. The tables have just been laid for dinner when they see a handsome boy coming out of a chamber, holding the very Lance that Gawain has been seeking, followed by a girl carrying a silver trencher; she is so beautiful and delightful that he cannot take his eyes off her.[5] Behind her walk two boys carrying candlesticks and, after them, a grieving girl holding aloft the Holy Grail. She disappears into another room and, to complete the procession, four servants carry a bier containing a dead body covered with silk and with a sword broken in half across it.[6]

This procession passes three times in front of Gawain who, unlike Perceval, does not hold back from asking the significance of the Grail and the Lance; why the girl was crying so bitterly; and why the sword was lying on the top of the bier. The king replies that he will be worthy to know the answers to all these questions if he can mend the Broken Sword.

Gawain discovers that, though he is able to fit the two halves together perfectly, they come apart again at the first tug. He is not yet worthy; and, to make matters worse, he falls asleep[7] on the table!

When he awakes the next day, Gawain is astonished to find himself alone in a marsh; his arms have been returned to him and his horse is tied to a tree. But he is furious with himself for having failed to learn the truth about the mysteries[8]; furthermore, he still hasn't got the dangerously destructive Lance.

The Sword of Montesclaire

Nevertheless, the pragmatic Gawain soon focuses on his other quest: to lift the siege of Montesclaire and gain the Sword of the Strange Belt. Emerging from a dark forest, he has the good fortune to encounter the uncle of the Lady of Montesclaire, who puts him up for the night and guides him there the next day. Overcoming the three knights who have been guarding the narrow approach to the lady's castle, atop a lofty and imposing crag, Gawain finds himself greeted as a savior.

He is taken to a grotto beneath a walled garden in the castle keep. An iron door, which had not been opened for more than a hundred years, swings wide as the hero approaches; much to the delight of the lady and her people, who believe that the deliverance they have long hoped for is at hand. Descending deep underground, Gawain uncovers a chamber walled with gold, with a ceiling of silver, lit by precious jewels. In the middle of the room is a golden pillar, from which a knight seeking renown may take the sword without hindrance.

In the Grail Castle, Gawain had not yet achieved enough as a knight to mend the Broken Sword and had fallen asleep before he could learn its provenance; but he will not make the same mistake here. Thrusting out his right hand, he grasps the sword and hangs it at his left side. Then, apologizing for his long delay in arriving at Montesclaire, he asks its lady to reveal the truth about the Sword of the Strange Belt.

The sword, she explains, was once wielded by Judas Maccabeus, but had been brought to Britain by Joseph of Arimathea. He, on his deathbed, gave instructions that the sword should be brought to Montesclaire and hidden beneath the secret grotto where only the most valorous of knights could find it. The iron doors had never swung open before, no matter how many men of high renown came seeking the sword. It confers invincibility on anyone who wields it in a just cause; but will make a coward of anyone who tries to use it unjustly.

The lady wants Gawain to wed her and become the Lord of Montesclaire but, once his wounds are healed, he finds himself thinking about the Bleeding Lance. Much to the lady's disappointment, he decides he must leave to complete his mission. He departs with the Sword of Judas Maccabeus strapped to his side.[9]

To the White Island

One day, when Queen Guenevere is waiting with her knights at some crossroads, she sees a knight riding by so fast that he does not greet her. Offended, she sends after him Sir Kay, who accosts the knight with his customary tactlessness and is unhorsed for his pains.

The queen now sends Gawain who, through his courtesy, elicits the information that the knight (who we later learn is called Silimac) is on a most urgent mission. Returning with Gawain to see the queen might cause him to fail; therefore, he will only do so if Gawain agrees to complete the mission in his stead. This Gawain is willing to do but, as they approach the queen's tent, Silimac is struck through the body by a javelin, thrown by an unknown hand—although Gawain is convinced Kay is responsible. As Silimac dies, he reminds Gawain of his promise: Gawain must take Silimac's sword, put on the knight's armor and allow Silimac's horse to lead him wherever he wants to go. Swearing to avenge Silimac's death on his return, Gawain sets off.

After a frightening encounter with a demonic force at the Chapel of the Black Hand, Gawain rides all night and discovers to his astonishment, when the sun rises, that he has crossed from one side of Britain to the other! He is now by the sea and, after riding all day through a vast forest, he sees a covered causeway, at the end of which shines a light like that of a fire.

Gawain wants to wait until the morning to risk the narrow, wind-swept path, but Silimac's horse has a mind of its own and races along the causeway until, around midnight, it brings the knight to a great hall full of people. At first, they rejoice to see him whose arrival they have long been awaiting but, after they have disarmed him in front of the fire, they start to grumble that he is not the one they expected. At that, the crowd leaves him alone in the hall. In the middle of it he sees an enormous bier and, stretched out on it, a corpse covered in silk, with the blade of a sword lying across its chest. He hears the sound of lamentation and watches the celebration of a requiem Mass, after which the crowd returns with their king. They are served with food and drink by the rich Grail, which moves of its own accord, taking away the old course and bringing the next one. When the meal is finished, everything vanishes in the wink of an eye and Gawain is alone again. He inspects the hall and finds, next to the bier, the Bleeding Lance, the object of his quest.

At that moment the king returns, carrying the sword that Silimac had given Gawain. Drawing the sword, which turns out to be only the top half of a broken weapon, the king matches it to the blade on the corpse, lamenting the death that had ravaged a kingdom. The king asks Gawain if he can join the two halves together again, for whoever can do this, can accomplish the task that Silimac had undertaken: to avenge the dead man on the bier. Sadly, Gawain cannot manage it, but the king suggests that the knight may be able to do so in future, if he grows in merit. Gawain then asks him: Whence comes the blood that runs down the Lance and what is the truth about the sword and the bier?

The king explains that the Lance is the one with which Jesus was pierced on the cross; this was a joyous stroke, since it delivers us from hell. The sword, however, is responsible for the unhappy stroke that ravaged Logres. As for the Grail, it was made by Joseph of Arimathea, who used it to catch the blood that was running from the wound caused by the Lance and who, to avoid persecution by the Jews, took it with him to the White Island,[10] the land promised him by God. The king is about to tell him the story of the warrior who struck the blow that caused the sword to break in two but Gawain, exhausted from his journey, has fallen asleep.

When he awakens the next morning, he finds himself in a field by the sea. He is angry with himself for having fallen asleep when the wise king had been so kind as to talk to him about the wonders of the Grail. But he determines to make himself worthy of rejoining the sword and finishing the quest that he has undertaken on Silimac's behalf.

As he travels across the country, he notices that it is now covered in green woods and meadowlands and running with streams, though still sparsely populated. The inhabitants bless him for asking about the Lance, since that is why God has partially restored the Waste Land; but they hate him for not finding out why the Grail serves, since this would have completed the process.[11]

Gawain returns to Arthur's court, where he recounts his adventures on the White Island to a thrilled Round Table.[12]

The Knight of the Green Sword

Gawain never discovers the connection between the mission he undertook on behalf of Silimac and the bodies he sees in the Chapel of the Black Hand and the hall of the King of the White Island; although he will later avenge Silimac's murder. These mysteries will, to a large extent, be cleared up when Perceval returns to the scene of his former failure and finally asks the Grail Question.[13] But there is another account of Gawain's visit to the Grail Castle, in which new mysteries await him.

Gawain is in search of the court of the Fisher King when he encounters the Grail Bearer, who has lost her hair, as a result of Perceval's failure to ask the Question. She is accompanied by two maidens, one of whom is forced to travel on foot as a penance. When Gawain asks the reason for this, the Bald Maiden replies that, if he reaches the castle of the Fisher King, he must ask who is served from the Holy Grail; only then will be lifted their afflictions and those of the lands that have fallen into war while the Fisher languishes.

The Bald Maiden asks him to escort her past the Castle of the Black Hermit, where Gawain wins the Shield of Judas Maccabeus, a red shield emblazoned with a golden eagle, which he hands over to the maidens.[14] As he wanders on, Gawain comes by chance to the rich and fertile land where stands the magnificent Castle of Enquiry, at the edge of the Kingdom of the Grail; but it is guarded by a lion and two copper figures armed with crossbows. Gawain is told that he cannot enter the castle or get any nearer to the Grail, unless he is bearing the sword with which John the Baptist was beheaded. It is, he discovers, in the possession of Gurgaran, the pagan[15] King of Albany; and it has been offered as a reward to whosoever can bring back the king's son, who has been abducted by a giant.

Accordingly, Gawain travels to the Kingdom of Albany, where Gurgaran tells him that if he will risk his life to save the prince's, he will win the sword that bleeds each day at noon. This is the very time when John the Baptist was decapitated; but the sword turns the bright green color of emeralds as soon as that hour is past. Gawain succeeds in killing the giant, but not in saving the prince's life: Nevertheless, the king, after cooking the flesh of his dead son and feeding it to his people (!), presents Gawain with the sword, has himself baptized[16] and forcibly converts his land to Christianity.[17]

Bearing the sword, Gawain finds that the Castle of Enquiry is now open to him and, after hearing allegorical explanations of many of the adventures that have befallen him, he continues on into the beautiful land of the Fisher King. Stopping only to worship at the holy chapel at the entrance to the Grail Castle, the chapel where the flame of the Holy Spirit descends each day, Gawain crosses three perilous bridges before he at last reaches the hall of the Fisher King, to whom he presents the holy sword. They sit down to eat, served by twelve knights who appear much younger than they are; whereupon they see two maidens emerge from a chapel, bearing the Grail and the Holy Lance.

The maidens pass three times before the company. Gawain sees, inside the Grail, a chalice into which the blood from the Lance is falling. He then beholds the shape of a child,[18] before witnessing three drops of blood fall onto the ivory table; whereupon he goes into a trance.[19] He then has a vision of Jesus as a crowned king nailed to the Cross, with a Lance thrust in his side. Gawain is unable to speak, despite being prompted by those present. He is left alone and, after being defeated three times in a game of chess, playing against gold pieces that move of their own volition, he goes to sleep.

The next day he finds that the interior of the castle is barred to him, for he neglected to ask the question that could have brought joy to the court.[20]

In the Palace of Adventures

Others say that Gawain's first visit to the Grail Castle is even less successful; in fact, frankly ignominious. Once again, the hero is stupefied by what he sees, but here it is not the mystic vision of the Grail Chalice that astounds him, but the beauty of the Grail Bearer herself.

Gawain arrives as if by chance at Corbenic, but his first encounter with the Grail Mysteries is heralded by two incidents in which we discover something of the prehistory of the Company of the Grail in Logres.

The first, is when he comes to the site of the Black Cross, where the pagan King of Camelot, Agrestes, had murdered twelve companions of Joseph of Arimathea, who was leading the conversion of Britain to Christianity. Joseph had placed the cross at the entrance to the forest of Camelot, but it had been turned black by the blood of the martyrs whom Agrestes battered to death there. Gawain appears to know nothing of this, but shortly thereafter he encounters Eliezer, the Prince of Listenois, who asks him to attempt to rejoin the shattered Sword of Broceliande.[21] This sword has been bleeding ever since Joseph was wounded by it in the thigh, in the course of his missionary activities. Gawain's failure to do so is the first indication that there is a spiritual chivalry, the chosen ones of the Grail, which is of greater worth than even the mightiest of the Knights of the Round Table. Eliezer tells Gawain that the sword is holy and that, with it, will be accomplished the adventures of the Grail.[22]

Gawain is very sad and thoughtful after his failure; but his feelings of inadequacy are only increased when, in the company of Lancelot's half-brother Hector, he comes to the Cemetery of the Burning Tomb. The knights have been travelling for half-a-league across a barren heath when they come to an old, decrepit chapel, whose walls are crumbling and whose altar is wrecked. Beyond the altar is a huge cemetery; before it is a red marble tomb upon which white letters have been inscribed. These announce that no knight errant should attempt to accomplish the adventures of the cemetery unless he is that miserable creature whose lust will prevent him from achieving the Grail Quest.

Such is Gawain's reputation in the lust department that he could be forgiven for thinking that the inscription refers to himself; so, he determines to try this marvelous adventure. As he approaches, he sees a tomb flaming with intense fire, surrounded by twelve others with erect swords above them, suspended in mid-air. These floating swords belabor him as soon as he gets close, and he is knocked unconscious. When he recovers, he tries again, but fares even worse.

Sir Hector is no more successful, but Gawain is ashamed of his defeat, for he is used to succeeding in everything. Salt is rubbed in his wounds when he sees an inscription on the cemetery gate, announcing that only the son of the Sorrowful Queen will ever leave the cemetery without shame. Gawain does not understand the reference but, to the reader, it is a clear indication that Lancelot (whose mother became the Queen of Sorrows after the death of her husband and the abduction of her son) has replaced him as the greatest knight of Logres.

After the two knights separate, Gawain comes upon a tent where men are eating and tries to join them, for he is ravenous; but they attack him when he does so. Gawain fends them off and continues on his way, but we have perhaps been warned that his physical appetites stand in the way of his spiritual progress, for, in his next adventure, he will be denied something more than purely material nourishment.

Arriving at the head of a long valley, he sees at the end of it a small castle, surrounded by water.[23] The castle is approached by a wooden bridge; and Gawain will experience another failure as soon as he crosses it. He sees a maiden in a marble bath of boiling water, but is unable to pull her out, despite her pleas. She says that this indicates that he will not leave the castle without dishonor; and this proves to be the case.

He goes into the main hall, where he is greeted by the king, Eliezer's father Pelles, who welcomes him, bids him disarm and invites him to sit at table with him. A white dove enters the hall, bearing an incense burner that fills the room with perfume. Everyone apart from Gawain falls to their knees, while the dove disappears into an adjoining chamber. Gawain smiles to hear all the prayers and orisons spoken by the king's company. The only thing that astounds him is the sight of the beautiful Grail Bearer, the daughter of King Pelles, who emerges from the same chamber that the dove entered. She carries above her head a chalice made of no known material, but he admires the beauty of the Vessel less than that of its bearer, before whom he falls into a trance.

Everyone apart from Gawain falls to their knees before the Holy Vessel and, as they do so, their places at table are filled with sumptuous foods. Only Gawain's place remains empty, as he discovers when he can finally drag his eyes away from the sight of the princess, who returns to her chamber. Realizing he has done something wrong, Gawain sits, quiet and hungry, until the meal is over and all the others have left. When he tries to follow them down to the lower court, however, he finds the doors are barred to him; a dwarf threatens him with dishonor if he stays. Notwithstanding, Gawain sees a bed in a corner of the hall and, warned by a female voice, puts his armor back on before lying on it. This is just as well for, the moment he does so, he hears a demonic cry and a fiery lance[24] strikes him (passing straight through his shield and hauberk) in the shoulder, causing him to faint.

When he comes to, it is night and, in the light of the moon penetrating the forty windows of the hall, Gawain sees a serpent battling a leopard to a standstill. The moonlight blinds him temporarily, then, when his sight is restored, he sees the serpent give up the battle with the leopard, only to kill and be killed by its own children. Although he does not know it, this is a vision of the future: The leopard is a symbol of Lancelot who will battle against the "serpent," Arthur Pendragon. Gawain himself will not live to see this battle: Just as the moonlight blinds him, so the light of his own prowess will be extinguished by death. Afterwards, Arthur will be killed by his "children," the people of Logres, led by his natural son, Mordred.

A violent wind sweeps the hall, the windows crash against each other and, when everything is calm once more, Gawain sees twelve maidens emerge from a chamber, lamenting and asking God when He will free them from their torment.[25] The maidens kneel before the entrance to the chamber whence the dove appeared that evening, then return to their own chamber. An armed knight now enters, demanding that Gawain go into one of the adjoining chambers; when Gawain refuses, they fight to a standstill. A violent storm erupts in the hall, followed by angelic voices singing praises to the King of Heaven. The Grail Bearer once more enters the hall, placing the Holy Vessel on a silver table. When she returns with it to her chamber, the voices fade away and Gawain realizes that his wounded shoulder is completely healed.[26]

Gawain looks for the knight he has fought, but now the hall becomes so dark he can see nothing. He feels himself being grabbed by many hands and is carried out of the hall and tied to a cart in the courtyard. An old lady drives it out of the castle, while the shopkeepers chase them and throw ordure and rubbish at him; in this ignoble fashion, Gawain is evicted from Corbenic. He later meets a hermit who tells him that his misfortune was to see the Grail, but not recognize it as the Holy Vessel in which Our Lord's blood was poured and collected.[27] The hermit then goes on to explain the meaning of the vision of the leopard and the serpent to him, including the prophecy of his own death, but swearing him to secrecy.[28]

The Knight of the Bloody Sword

Lancelot comes to Corbenic after Gawain's visit and is not only unable to see the Grail, but is tricked into sleeping with the king's daughter in order to conceive a son. When, fifteen years later, that son comes to court, his arrival is heralded by the appearance of a sword, stuck in a stone and floating down the river towards Camelot. The king prevails upon Gawain, despite Lancelot's dire warning of the consequences, to attempt to draw the sword from the stone, but he is unsuccessful. Lancelot prophesies that the sword will one day cut Gawain to the quick.[29]

It is indeed Lancelot's son Galahad who succeeds in sitting in the Perilous Seat at the Round Table, leading Gawain to acknowledge him as the knight sent by God to free Logres from the great marvels and strange adventures that have beset it for so long.[30] It is also Galahad who draws the Sword in the Floating Stone. This event is followed by an appearance of the Grail, covered by a cloth of white silk and borne by no mortal hand.[31] When it departs, after feeding the company, the king gives thanks to God for this vision, in which He gave a sign of His love in feeding them with His grace.

The divine favor went so far as to feed every man with the food he most desired, adds Gawain, something that has never happened before except at the court of the Maimed King[32]; but here as there, it cannot be seen clearly; its true form remains hidden. He vows he will pursue the Grail for a year and a day until he looks openly upon it.[33]

Most of the Knights of the Round Table make the same vow, much to the distress of the king, who believes that he is witnessing the dissolution of the fellowship; he blames his nephew for bringing sadness to his heart. Gawain has no answer, for he knows his uncle speaks the truth, but it is too late to take back his words.[34]

It is thus into a troubled court that there enters an Ugly Maiden bearing a beautiful sword with a richly-worked scabbard, who tells the king to stop brooding and instead try an amazing adventure: When the knight who will kill more than any other in the Quest draws the sword, he will be identified by it turning a bloody red. The king and several of his leading knights draw the sword, but return it clean to its scabbard. However, when Gawain draws it, it looks like he has pulled it from a bloody wound.

Gawain tries to dismiss this as deceitful enchantment,[35] like the magic tricks of Morgan the Fay. But Arthur believes that evil will come of his participation in the Quest and tries to prevent him from taking part.[36] To avoid this Gawain, concerned for his honor, sneaks out early the next morning. Arriving with the other questers at a nearby castle, he is once more confronted by the Ugly Maiden, who says that he will end up by killing eighteen of his fellows. These include King Bademagu and his nephew Patrides, his cousin Yvain the Bastard, and Erec, son of Lac. Gawain confesses that if he thought any of this would really come to pass, he would turn back; but he doesn't believe her. She in turn insists that, like his brother Mordred, he was born to do bad deeds.[37]

Indeed, he has already killed two of his fellows (Patrides and Yvain the Bastard) by the time he arrives at the hermitage of the elderly Nascien, troubled by a powerful dream he has had about a hundred and fifty bulls. The hermit explains to him that his dream is telling him that most of the Knights of the Round Table (symbolized by the bulls) have the wrong attitude to the Quest, imagining that it will bring them worldly honors; many will in fact die on the Quest. Of the three who achieve it, only one (a reference to Bors) will return: The other two (meaning Galahad and Perceval) will find such delight in the food of the Grail that they will never be parted from it once they find it.

But the last part of Gawain's dream, Nascien refuses to interpret, for no good would come from doing so. In fact, this part of Gawain's dream refers to the internecine strife which will destroy Arthur's kingdom after the Quest, culminating in his own demise.

Gawain now asks the hermit why he no longer meets with as many adventures as he used to. Nascien explains that the adventures of the Quest are of a spiritual order, signs of the Holy Grail, and will not befall treacherous killers of men such as himself, caught up in dissolute pleasures.[38] Realizing that he will accomplish nothing of any value on the Quest, Gawain promises to return one day to hear more from the hermit[39]; but of course, he never does.

In fact, his life is nearly brought to an ignominious end when he is severely wounded at a tournament by Galahad, who is wielding the Sword of the Floating Stone. This leads Gawain to ponder the truth of the words that were spoken to him on the feast of Pentecost, that he would learn to rue ever having set a hand to it.[40]

Gawain will have much cause for regret soon enough, when he comes upon his brother Mordred, badly wounded, and sets out to avenge him on his attacker. He has already delivered a fatal blow when he discovers, too late, that it was King Bademagu who had injured Mordred, after intervening to stop a rape; Gawain is deeply upset to be the cause of the king's death.[41]

But if he kills Bademagu before he realizes that his victim is a fellow Knight of the Round Table, the same cannot be said of Gawain's next, Erec, whom he targets deliberately because Erec beat him in a competition. Furthermore, Erec is already severely wounded from a previous battle, when Gawain catches up with him and takes his revenge for what he perceives as his earlier humiliation.[42]

When news of the deaths he has caused—and in particular the fact that he killed both Patrides and Erec knowing that they were companions of the Round Table—King Arthur considers stripping Gawain of his place in that august assembly.[43]

Meanwhile, Gawain and his brother Gaheriet arrive at Corbenic, where they are refused entry to the Palace of Adventures. For Gawain, this rejection only confirms the animosity he feels towards a castle where he has already experienced dishonor; he wishes a bolt of lightning would strike it and cast it into the abyss.[44]

To add to their humiliation, the brothers are then defeated in battle by the Knight of the Spring of Healing, who imprisons them in the Giant's Tower. They are only freed when Palamedes defeats the knight,[45] but this good deed is badly rewarded. Encountering Palamedes badly wounded after an encounter with Lancelot, Gawain takes advantage of his weakness by attacking him; but he still requires the assistance of his brother Agravain to kill him.[46]

Hearing of the death of Palamedes as well as of so many other good men at his nephew's hands, King Arthur asks God to never again bring Gawain to his court.[47] Indeed, when Gawain does return, he soon gets embroiled in the internecine strife which will destroy the Kingdom of Logres—precisely as he saw in a vision in the Grail Castle and as foreseen by Nascien, without Gawain's knowing it.

The Crowning Adventure

But others say that, although his first visit to the Grail Castle is a failure, Gawain will have the opportunity to return and successfully complete the adventure.

Gawain is travelling in the Forest Adventurous when he encounters a weeping maiden cradling a dead knight. She laments the fact that Perceval, when he met the fisherman, failed to ask any questions about the Grail and the Lance. Had he done so, he would have freed her and many other women from sorrow.

Shortly thereafter, Gawain witnesses a bloody sword and spear, which appear to float in the air unaided.[48] It is while he is on the trail of these mysterious weapons that Gawain comes at evening to a four-towered castle where the gatekeeper, who knows him, lets him into the hall. Here Gawain encounters a gray-haired, ancient lord, whose great age afflicts him so much that he cannot move from the bed he is sitting on.[49]

Gawain continues his exploration of the castle until he comes to the chapel. Darkness falls and the chapel is lit up by candles, enabling him to observe a shrine containing a broadsword, which is lowered from the ceiling but then, mysteriously, vanishes. Equally mysterious are the two gloved hands holding the shaft of a Lance that streams blood, which Gawain sees reaching through the wall. He hears a mighty crash of thunder resound through the chapel, knocking down the candles.

All light is now extinguished and, in the darkness, Gawain hears a voice cry out three times in distress, followed by a much louder cry of grief. Gawain falls to the ground like one dead, not getting up until the sun shines through the chapel windows.[50]

Returning to the hall where he met the old king, he finds it full of worthy knights; a feast is being prepared, to which Gawain is invited. As he sits down to eat, he sees four maidens carrying four candle-sticks enter the hall, followed by another carrying a crystal vessel filled with fresh blood. She carries it over to the old king, who drinks from it through a tube.

Gawain notices that no matter how much the king drinks, the contents of the crystal vessel never seem to diminish. But he is too polite to interrupt the feasters with questions, preferring to wait instead till everyone has finished. However, they all leave the room as soon as they finish eating and, although Gawain sits there waiting patiently for them to return for half the night, he never sees them again.

Gawain's only hope now is to talk to the old man himself, so he lights the candles around the king's bed ... and sees at once that he is dead! Gawain makes his way to the stables, where he finds his horse. He beds down there for the night, but in the morning, when he wakes up, he is alone in a field.[51] Gawain, like Perceval before him, has failed to ask the redemptive question in the Grail Castle. Indeed, he does not even appear to be aware that *that* is where he has been.[52]

After a visit to the Land of Maidens, whose lady gives him the gift of eternal youth in the form of bath-salts,[53] Gawain is compelled by a knight he has wronged to fetch for him the Lance and the splendid Grail. He must achieve this within a year and a day or be imprisoned.[54]

After many other adventures, with the appointed date fast approaching, Gawain sets off with Kay, Lancelot and Calogrenant as companions, to find the Grail Castle. They temporarily separate at a junction of four roads, and Gawain travels on alone to a castle of maidens, ruled by a fay.[55] She instructs him carefully in what to do when he reaches the Grail Castle: She herself will be there to prompt him, but he must not drink anything in case he falls asleep. Moreover, she gives him a magic hauberk, which alone will protect his companion Kay from great danger.

Gawain now rides on, passing through a wasteland[56] and a realm resembling an Earthly Paradise, as well as other mysterious terrains, until he meets up again with Lancelot and Calogrenant. But Sir Kay has met with potential disaster: Arriving alone at a castle, he went straight to the chapel where he was told he could learn all about the Grail. Unfortunately, seeing a statue of an old knight pierced through the knees by a spear, Kay could not resist breaking it open to find out if there was blood inside. As a result, he has been condemned to spend the rest of his life in prison, unless he can overcome in battle nine knights who are protected by magic.[57]

Meanwhile, Gawain and his companions arrive at the Grail Castle, where they are warmly welcomed. They see the lord of the castle presented with a beautiful broadsword and they are offered drink; but Gawain refrains, thus avoiding the slumber that seizes his companions. Food is served but, before the last course is offered, Gawain witnesses a procession in which youths carry a Lance and a beautiful lady wearing a crown carries a golden, bejeweled reliquary. Gawain recognizes her as the fay who had instructed him about the Grail; she is followed by a weeping maiden.

The Lance is placed over a bowl and three drops of blood fall from it, which the lord of the castle drinks. The Grail Bearer and the weeping maiden open the reliquary and the lord takes from it bread, which he eats. It is at this point that Gawain remembers his instructions and asks the meaning of the miracle he has witnessed, at which all the company are delighted.

The Grail Lord now explains that Perceval's failure to ask the same question caused great distress, especially since it was the murder of Perceval's father by his own brother that cause all the trouble: God's punishment drove the living from the land and kept the dead unable to rest, going about as if still alive, but suffering terribly. The Grail Lord himself is one of the dead, sustained by the Lance and by the hope that a member of the Grail family would seek to find out the truth. For having done so, Gawain has won the world's praise and the gratitude of both the living and the dead, who can now be released from their sorrow.

Finally, the Grail Lord presents Gawain with the broadsword, which will never fail him. At that he vanishes, along with all his companions and the Grail itself, which will never again be seen openly. Only the Grail Bearer and her maidens remain, for they were not among the living dead of the castle: They had been chosen to fulfill the sacred mystery whereby the Grail Lord was nourished once a year, in the land ruled by the fay.

Before returning to King Arthur's court, Gawain goes to the chapel where Sir Kay languishes and gives him a magical hauberk, earlier bestowed on Gawain by the Grail Bearer.[58] This allows Kay to overcome the magical resistance of his nine opponents and thus to free himself. When the four Grail questers arrive safely back at Carduel, the joy of the court is unbounded.[59]

* * *

In the earliest Arthurian poems, Gawain, the king's oldest nephew, is presented as the first of the Knights of the Round Table, the paragon of chivalry, a mentor to younger knights and someone irresistible to women, whom he loves abundantly. This latter characteristic may be one of the reasons why the later prose romances, with their "ecclesiasticized" morality, not only disapprove of him but remove from him nearly all the positive traits with which he was originally endowed, presenting him as a treacherous murderer unworthy of a spiritual quest like that of the Grail. But another reason may be that he has suspiciously close links with the Otherworld and cannot wholly conceal his pagan origins.

For Jessie L. Weston, the earliest traditions connected with Gawain made of him the lover of the Queen of the Otherworld and therefore the champion of all fairy women.[60] As the "purely mythical hero" of a pagan mystery religion, he was increasingly "out of place" as the Grail story evolved from "the vague traditions of an ancient, and mystical, cult," into a "distinctively Christian legend."[61] Thus we see the role and character of Gawain change as the Grail literature itself develops from the early poems into the prose romances, and as the events the knights encounter change from mysteries to allegorical miracles, explicated at wearisome length by hermits. Gawain's mythology is drowned by theology.

But Heinrich von dem Türlin's poem *The Crown* both presents (or restores) Gawain as Grail Hero and gives an unprecedented importance to the Grail Bearer who, as fay or goddess, presides over the Grail Castle and its mysteries; she guides the hero to their achievement. At roughly the same time that the Vulgate *Queste* was denying women any agency in the search for the highest of spiritual symbols—allowing only Perceval's virginal and self-sacrificing sister to even accompany the divinely destined knights—Heinrich makes a woman of supernatural power magical director of the blood mysteries of Grail and Lance. Who better, then, than Gawain, as if reconnecting to his pagan roots, to be her champion?

Notes

1. *CSG* 41-2.
2. *CSG* 53-4.
3. Gawain's encounter with his lost family echoes in a more complete way that of Perceval in the Grail Castle: Perceval encounters his cousin and hears about his cousin's niece, but fails to discover the presence of his uncle in a back room. For Pierre Gallais (1998b, 54–5), Gawain's diversion by otherworldly adventures reveals his unworthiness for the spiritual Grail Quest.
4. *CSG* 98-100.
5. If he is here entranced by the beauty of the Maiden of the Silver Trencher, the Vulgate Cycle will make it even clearer that it is lust for women rather than desire for spiritual enlightenment that prevents him from uncovering the mysteries of the Grail Castle.
6. The Broken Sword which Gawain first encounters can only be the one that the Fisher King conferred on Perceval and which broke, as it was destined to do, when he first used it; and the pieces of which, a valet brought back to the Grail Castle (Weston 1906, 137–8).
7. This drowsiness might go some way to explaining his slightly garbled memory of this visit to a "desolate castle" across a ford (as Gawain recalls it in Book One of *The Crown*), where he remembers finding the "treasures" for which Perceval had been cursed: "the spear and the mighty Grail that once a day let fall three drops of blood" (*HTC* 100). Gawain later discovers the secret of the death of Perceval's father, which would also give us the identity of the body on the bier (328).
8. *CSG* 107-109.
9. *CSG* 110-115.
10. It is this island, presumably, which lies at the end of the covered causeway and on which was built the hall of the Grail Kings. Jessie Weston considered that Gawain's experiences on the White Island come closest to revealing details of the Mystery Religion in which she believes the Grail stories originated, and that the hero is "the original protagonist of the Quest, in its primitive, pre–Christian form" (1913, 118–9).
11. It appears as if knowledge of the Lance restores the fertility of the land, knowledge of the Grail the fertility of the people.
12. *CSG* 211-20: *Lors leur conta molt doucement/ Mesire Gauvains et moustra/ Les merveilles que il trouva./ Quant de la lance lor a dit,/ Trestoz merveillier les en fist;/ Et du Graal qui si servoit/ Par lui que nus nu soustenoit;/ Et de l'espee et de la biere/ Lor conta toute la maniere;/ Com il perdi par son dormir/ Les granz merveilles a oïr* (*CP* II, ll.18338–48).
13. It is only in the Third Continuation that we discover that the body on the bier is that of Gon of the Land Laid Waste, the brother of the Maimed King, and that Silimac's broken sword is the one with which Gon was treacherously slain (see THE SWORD OF PARTINAL). Although the texts do not make it clear, scholars have conjectured that Silimac was the son of Gon who was seeking to prove his worthiness to avenge his father's murder, a feat that will ultimately be achieved by Perceval.
14. *HBG* 36-40.
15. *HBG* 61-2.
16. Arguably, in gaining possession of the sword, Gawain becomes a type of John the Baptist, the precursor of Perceval as the Messiah; while the eating of the flesh of the Son echoes the mystery of transubstantiation in a gruesome parody. Jessie L. Weston (1988, 61-2) sees Gurgaran as a werewolf.
17. *HBG* 67-70.
18. *Atant es vos .II. damoiseles ou issent d'une chapele, et tient l'une en ses .II. mains le saintisme Greal et l'autre la lance de coi la pointe saine dedens.... Mesire Gauvain esgarde le Greal et si samble qu'il voit un calice dedens ... et voit la pointe de la lance dont li sans vermaus en chiet dedens ... et li samble qu'il voit en mi le Greal la forme d'un enfant* (*HLG* 348–50).
19. This image echoes a famous scene in Chrétien's poem in which Perceval goes into a trance when he sees three drops of blood fall on the snow, reminding him of his ladylove Blancheflor.
20. *HBG* 72-80.
21. *LG* III, 87-8: see THE BLEEDING SWORD.
22. *LG* III, 91.
23. This location is only too familiar to readers of the Grail literature, but it is unfamiliar to Arthur's knights since, in the Vulgate version, Gawain (rather than Perceval) is the first of them to arrive there.
24. A burning spear features in Irish late medieval literature where it is associated with one of the mythical Immortals, Lugh, who arguably appears in Arthurian romance as Loth, Gawain's father (Walter 2014, 249).
25. Weston points out that this lamentation has no discernable cause in the context of the Vulgate *Lancelot*, where this episode occurs: "there is no dead knight to be mourned, no spell to be broken. The inhabitants of the Grail castle, so far from being in torment have all that heart can desire, and the special honor of being guardians of the sacred vessel" (*GGC* 84). This later leads her to believe that the origin of the Weeping Women is to be found in the ritual mourning for Adonis, which she identifies as the origin of the Grail legend (Weston 1913, 81–3). The Prose *Tristan*, however, identifies the Weeping Women as followers of Joseph of Arimathea, who refused to believe in the Grail and who are therefore condemned to suffer until the coming of Galahad, hundreds of years later (*PV* III, 707–8; *TPM* 258).
26. Later, Perceval and Hector of the Fens will both be healed of their wounds by a vision of the Grail.

27. ...*ce fu li Sains Graas ou li sains sancs Nostre Seignor fu espandus et recueillis* (*LM* II, 387).
28. *LG* III, 97–103.
29. *LG* IV, 4; V, 116; *QHG* 35–6; *MD* 668–9.
30. *QHG* 40: *celui que Diex nos a envoié por delivrer nostre païs des granz merveilles et des estranges aventures qui tant sovent i sont avenues par si lonc tens* (*QP* 11).
31. When Gawain first saw the Grail it was borne by the Fisher King's daughter; now that she has lost her virginity, she can no longer fulfill the office of Grail Bearer.
32. *...il n'a ceanz home qui n'ait esté serviz de quan qu'il demandoit et pensoit. Et ce n'avint onques mes en nule cort, se ne fu chiés le Roi Mehaignié* (*QP* 16).
33. *But one thyng begyled us, that we myght nat se the Holy Grayle: hit was so preciously coverde. Wherefore I woll make here avow that to-morne, withoute longer abydynge, I shall laboure in the queste of the Sankgreall ... and never shall I returne unto the court agayne tylle I have sene hit more opynly than hit hath bene shewed here* (*MD* 674).
34. *LG* IV, 6–8; *QHG* 44–6; *MD* 673–6.
35. *Sabede que todo he encantamento e chuffa* (*PV* II, 44).
36. *LG* V, 119–22.
37. *LG* V, 123–5: In the Vulgate *Queste*, Gawain leaves with the other knights, but only after Bademagu insists that it should not be Gawain but Galahad, the lord of the Round Table, who first takes the oath. Galahad's oath is repeated by Lancelot, then by Gawain, followed by the others (*LG* IV, 9–10; *QHG* 48–50).
38. *Les aventures qui ore avienent sont les senefiances et les demostrances dou Saint Graal, ne li signe dou Saint Graal n'aparront ja a pecheor ne a home envelopé de pechié* (*QP* 160–1): *The adventures of the Sankgreall whych be in shewynge now ye fynde not, for hit apperith nat to no synners* (*MD* 729). Nor is Nascien the only holy man who takes it upon himself to point out the errors of Gawain's ways: one monk describes him as *wycked and synfull*; while another, learning that he has not been to Confession for four years, denounces him for having *lyved myschevously many wyntir*s (*MD* 690–1; *LG* IV, 18–9; *QHG* 76–80).
39. *LG* IV, 47–52; V, 154–8; *QHG* 162–75; *MD* 723–30.
40. *LG* IV, 62–3; V, 189; *QHG* 207–9; *MD* 749–50.
41. *LG* V, 193–6.
42. *LG* V, 209–10.
43. *LG* V, 212–3.
44. *LG* V, 268.
45. *LG* V, 276.
46. *LG* V, 281–2.
47. *LG* V, 283.
48. *HTC* 159–60.
49. The fact that both the old king and his gatekeeper know who Gawain is, even though he does not appear to have been there before, suggests that he is the predestined knight whose arrival they have been awaiting.
50. This scene recalls the visit of Cahus to the Perilous Chapel, which Weston, apparently on the advice of occultists, described as a failed initiation (1913, 96–7). By contrast, Gawain's experience in the chapel suggests that he has passed the test for worthiness: He has, at least symbolically and vicariously, experienced death and rebirth; he has passed from darkness into light, but he does not yet know the meaning of these strange events.
51. *HTC* 165–9.
52. The whole episode, like the Welsh Romance of Peredur, has an oneiric quality, as though Gawain encounters dreamlike versions of the Grail Castle and its dead king in advance of his waking visit; or, as if he sees the death of the king in a dream before meeting the "undead" reality.
53. *HTC* 197–8: Although both Bron and Mordrain are described as living for hundreds of years, agelessness *without infirmities* is a different matter: For alchemists it is the gift of the Philosopher's Stone, which has sometimes been compared with Wolfram's Grail Stone.
54. *HTC* 213–4: "He also demanded that I swear to discover the manifold wonder of the mysterious Grail" (256). In Wolfram's *Parzival*, Gawain is obliged on behalf of the elven King Vergulaht to seek the Grail but, although he rides off to meet fantastic perils on a horse from the Savage Land, Gawain is distracted by the magic of the Castle of Wonders and never actually finds the Grail.
55. The medieval German word is *gotinne*, literally "goddess," but the term is used interchangeably with *fei* (= French *fée*) elsewhere in Middle High German literature, according to Neil Thomas (2002, 69). He adds that the term should be understood "in the sense of a woman of power, of course, rather than in the sense of one of Shakespeare's gossamer-winged diminutives." The idea that the old pagan goddesses became the "fairies" of medieval Christendom is a persistent one.
56. *HTC* 317–9.
57. *HTC* 323–4: Like Cahus in the Perilous Chapel, for whom the dreamworld and waking reality fatally cross over, Sir Kay has mistaken an image for a material reality: a form of literalism which can be literally deadly.
58. Uniquely, this version of the Grail Quest, written by Heinrich von dem Türlin in the first half of the thirteenth century, makes the Grail Bearer not only "a woman of power" but a supernatural being who rules over the realm of the Grail and, alone among the living, knows its secrets. It is she who presides over the annual ritual in the Grail Castle; she who instructs Gawain in what to do when he gets there; and she who gives him the magical means of rescuing Sir Kay from prison. For Heinrich, she is indeed the Grail Goddess.
59. *HTC* 325–33: The *Elucidation* tells us that Gawain finds the lost court of the Fisher King, and promises to describe the joy that he will gain by restoring the whole kingdom: *La joie qu'il i gaengna,/ Dont tous li regné amenda* (*EB* ll.229–30).
60. Weston 1897, 45.
61. Weston 1906, 335.

GLASTONBURY

It is said that Mary Magdalen and Joseph of Arimathea, two of the principal witnesses to the death and resurrection of Jesus, travel, after the Passion, to Gaul, bringing with them the Holy Grail. From there Joseph is sent by Saint Philip to evangelize Britain.[1] An angel, appearing to Joseph in a dream, tells him to take with him twelve disciples and to found a church in the shadow of a hill that resembles Mount Tabor in the Holy Land.

Joseph travels westwards carrying the Grail until he and his companions glimpse the Tor, whose likeness to their sacred mountain they immediately recognise.[2] Following an old straight track (what is now popularly known as a "ley"), Joseph, at one point, places the Grail on a standing stone atop a prehistoric barrow: Its light blazes out, illuminating its surroundings.[3]

In the church that Joseph builds, the Vessel stands upon the altar, until, after Joseph's death, the wickedness of the times leads his successor as Grail guardian, the Fisher King, to place it in his treasury, an underground chamber within Chalice Hill. There it is watched day and night by three pure maidens and only brought out at high festivals.

Rumors of this miraculous Vessel reach King Arthur's knights: Those who are successful in their search are welcomed by the Fisher King and drink from the same Vessel as Our Lord.[4] Not all who partake of this "love-feast" live to tell the tale: some are rapt up to Heaven. As the times grow yet more evil, the Fisher King conceals the holy cup in a spring which was once sacred to the Druids, a spring whose red waters give it the name: Blood Well.[5]

But the hidden Vessel only represents the microcosmic form of the Holy Grail, which also manifests itself macrocosmically, in the form of a vast circle of effigies created by the Earth itself and only later reworked by humans to form a Zodiac.[6] At the northern edge of the Zodiac is the Celtic Christian foundation at Glastonbury, whose dimensions correspond to those of the New Jerusalem described by St. John of Patmos in the Book of Revelation; while the town itself is at a confluence of leys forming an even greater model of the same pattern.[7]

* * *

The Glastonbury Zodiac, which had been hiding in plain sight, was discovered by the artist Katharine Maltwood (1878–1961) when she was commissioned to draw a map for the 1929 reprinting of the Everyman's Library edition of *The High History of the Holy Graal*, a translation by the poet Sebastian Evans of the Romance of Perlesvaus. At the end of the romance, we read: "The Latin from whence this history was drawn into Romance was taken in the Isle of Avalon, in a holy house of religion that standeth at the head of the Moors Adventurous, there where King Arthur and Queen Guenievre lie, according to the witness of the good men religious that are therein, that have the whole history thereof, true from the beginning even to the end."[8] In addition to being the first text in which Glastonbury is clearly identified with Avalon, following the apparent discovery of the tomb of the royal couple by the monks of the Abbey, this little-known romance inspired Maltwood to find Arthurian sites all over South Wales and Somerset; as well as discovering the Zodiac, which she called the Temple of the Stars and identified with King Arthur's Round Table.

Although later researchers have attributed the human reshaping of the Glastonbury Zodiac to the Atlantean era, some twelve thousand years ago, Maltwood herself proposed a more modest date of 2700 BCE,[9] which would place it within the currently accepted chronological framework for the building of Stonehenge, between four and five thousand years ago. More recently, John Darrah has argued that, since the Vulgate Cycle has the Grail mission to Britain preceding the erection of the bluestones of Stonehenge[10]—which he also suggests could be identified with the Round Table[11]—the legends could originally refer to a religious transformation marking the transition to the Bronze Age, rather than to the arrival of Christianity on these shores.[12]

Notes

1. Baigent *at al.*, 344.
2. Fortune, 14: Contrary to popular belief, the identification of the Grail with Glastonbury can only be definitively dated to the nineteenth century: When Tennyson published *The Holy Grail and Other Poems* in 1869. "he remedied the omission of the Holy Grail from Glastonbury's own medieval legendary accounts of itself, and, perhaps for the first time, had Joseph bring the Cup ... itself hither" (Ashdown, 238): "Probably as a reflection of Tennyson's *The Holy Grail*, there arose at Glastonbury a local belief that Joseph had hidden the Grail at Glastonbury's Chalice Well or on nearby Chalice Hill" (241).
3. Roberts, 38: "The Holy Grail is the Sacred Centre: the generative flux of the matrix of reality" (19).
4. "Whosoever drank of it, never thirsted again, for it was to him a well-spring of the Waters of Life within his soul" (Fortune, 16).
5. Fortune, 15–16.
6. Guénon 1962, 93–5.
7. Roberts, 173–6: "The Grail is the beckoning beacon of Spirit.... It is a glimpse into the immortal heart of God" (19).
8. *HH* 379.
9. Roberts, 28.
10. Darrah 1994, 210.
11. Darrah 1994, 207n70.
12. Darrah 1994, 10–11.

GON, King of the Land Laid Waste

The brother of the Fisher King, Gon[1] is killed treacherously by Partinal of the Red Tower, whose sword breaks on impact. The shards of the broken sword are then carried by Gon's daughter, the Maiden of the Silver Trencher, to Gon's brother, the Fisher King, who maims himself with them.[2] The quest to mend the sword and avenge Gon's death (and thereby heal the maimed Fisher King) is taken up first by Silimac; then by Gawain, on Silimac's death; but only achieved by Perceval. There is much rejoicing at the avenging of Gon's death.[3]

Notes

1. The name of the brother of the Fisher King is given at first as *Goondesert* by Manessier (*MTC* l.32804), later as *Gondebert/ Qui fu sire et rois du Desert* (ll.42059–60). Nigel Bryant translates the name as Gon of Sert (*PSG* 273), but *deserte* can also be translated as Land Laid Waste (*LG* V, 415). This has the advantage of resonating with the image of the Waste Land, which is elsewhere created by the killing (see LAMBOR) or maiming (see THE FISHER KING) of its lord.
2. *CSG* 478–9.
3. *CSG* 551.

GORNEMANT of Gohort

The failure of Perceval to ask the Grail Question means that the Maimed King cannot be healed nor the Waste Land restored. But the hero's disastrous reticence is due to his taking too literally some advice about courteous behavior he receives from his first chivalric mentor.

It is a Knight of the Round Table called Gornemant who initiates Perceval into knighthood and trains him in warfare.[1] Intending to teach the uncouth lad some manners, Gornemant also gives him the advice against speaking too freely[2] that will later cause Perceval to keep silent about the wonders he sees in the Grail Castle[3]—a silence that will have disastrous consequences.

Later, Gornemant finds himself under attack from an army of the living dead, sent by the pagan King of the Waste City, who has been inspired to do so by the Devil. This is both because of Gornemant's role in knighting Perceval and because, through Gornemant's guidance, Perceval will restore to joy those friends of God, whose destruction the Devil has been seeking.[4] In the event, Perceval defeats the army of the undead and marries Blancheflor, Gornemant's niece. He then entrusts his bride and her lands to her uncle while he sets off on the Grail Quest.[5]

Notes

1. For Philippe Walter (2004, 143–4), Gornemant's name recalls that of the Irish mythical

Gorias, which he considers to be one of the druidical initiation centers in the north of the world (see HYPERBOREA). Gornemant's role is therefore to initiate Perceval into the mythic dimension of the Round Table.
2. *CSG* 16.
3. *CSG* 29.
4. *CSG* 384.
5. *CSG* 394.

The GRAIL BEARER

When Perceval first witnesses the Grail Procession in the house of his cousin the maimed Fisher King, the Holy Vessel is borne by a beautiful girl, the king's daughter, who is accompanied by a light so brilliant that it outshines the many candles in the room.[1] It is not altogether clear whether the light comes from the Grail or its bearer.

When he fails to ask who is served from the Grail (and thereby heal the king), Perceval angers the king's daughter; and she later decides to cause trouble for him by trying to prevent him from completing a quest for the Lady of the Chessboard Castle.[2] But it is only on his third visit to the Grail Castle that Perceval finally learns that the daughter of the Fisher King is she who bears the Holy Vessel.[3]

Gawain also sees the Grail Bearer on his first visit to the Grail Castle, but this time she is weeping bitterly.[4] On his second sighting of the Grail, on the White Island, he cannot understand who, if anybody, is carrying the Holy Vessel.[5] We later learn about the tragic events which led to the killing of the Grail Bearer's uncle and the maiming of her father, which would explain her tears.[6] Perceval sees the Grail Bearer again after he has avenged his family's wrongs.[7] Following the death of the Fisher King, after she has borne the Grail quite openly before King Arthur and his vassals, Perceval arranges a marriage for her to the king of a land that borders Wales.[8]

* * *

The French prose cycles make the Grail Bearer the daughter of King Pelles and give her a name—Amite, nicknamed Helizabel, or Elaine—and we also learn that she ceases to be worthy when she loses her virginity, being replaced in that role by her cousin.[9]

A very different account of the Grail Bearer is given by Wolfram von Eschenbach, who made the first German translation of the Story of the Grail, but who also made significant changes to the story, which he claimed to have got, not from Chrétien, but from one Kyot of Provence, who has never been convincingly identified. Wolfram tells us that "she by whom the Grail permitted itself to be carried" had to guard her chastity and renounce falseness.[10] The first person whom the Grail permits to be its bearer is Schoysiane, the daughter of Frimutel, the second Grail Lord. When she dies in childbirth,[11] the honor passes to her sister Repanse de Schoye. It is she who brings the Grail before Parzival and his pagan[12] brother Feirefiz, whom she later marries when he is baptized for her sake.[13] Their son is Prester John.

Notes

1. *CSG* 29; *Un graal entre ses deus mains/ Une damoisele tenoit,// Bele et gente et bien acesmee./ Quant ele fu laiens entree/ Atot le graal qu'ele tint,/ Une si grans clartez i vint/ Qu'ausi perdirent les chandoiles/ Lor clarté come les estoiles/ Font quant solaus lieve ou la lune* (*RP* ll.3220–1, 3223–9). In the German version of Wolfram von Eschenbach, the countenance of the Grail Bearer is likened to daybreak (*PT* 99; *WP* 125).
2. *CSG* 248: *Por ce qu'el voloit travaillier/ Un molt alosé chevalier/ Qui a la cort avoit esté,/ Et si n'avoit riens demandé/ De ce don demander devoit:/ Dou Graal cui l'an an servoit* (*CP* IV, ll.20967–72). In Heinrich von dem Türlin's *The Crown*, by contrast, the Grail Bearer responds to Gawain's initial failure to ask the Grail Question by instructing him what to do when he returns and prompting him when he gets there!
3. *CSG* 478: The Grail Bearer is "whiter than snow on a branch" (*CSG* 336), reflecting her purity: For, were she not a virgin of royal descent, she would never be able to hold the Vessel in her hands: *Celle qui porte lou Graal/ Si est de lignie roial,/ Pucelle virge, n'autremant// Ja entre ses mains nou tenist/ Por riens nule qui avenist* (*MTC* ll.32793–5, 32797–8). In the Prose *Perceval* the Grail (*le vaissel que nostre Sire douna a Joseph en le prison*) is carried by *uns vallés* (*RG* 245), but we are not told whether or not he is also a royal virgin.

the great hall and in front of the hall are the galleries.¹

Inside the castle, Perceval is given a sword that he is told is destined for him. He then witnesses a mysterious procession of talismanic objects, including a Lance that bleeds, a golden bejeweled serving dish or Grail and a silver trencher, or carving dish, all amid the splendid light of candles shining brighter than the heavenly bodies.² Perceval is astonished at this, but is too polite to ask what is going on and, after dining, stays the night. In the morning he finds the castle deserted and, when he goes out into the forest, the drawbridge is raised so that he cannot return.

The mystery is only partly resolved when he meets his cousin who tells him that, had he asked about what he saw there, the Lord of the Grail Castle—who has been injured so that his only relaxation is fishing—would have been healed and much conflict averted. The castle is the only decent lodging for forty leagues³; but it does not appear to everyone.⁴

Perceval later learns that the castle was built expressly to house the Grail (a relic of Christ's Passion) and other sacred objects, or hallows, in the time of Joseph of Arimathea's evangelizing mission to Britain.⁵ The Fisher King, as the maimed Grail Lord is known, tells him that the Holy Vessel remained in the castle after Joseph's death and expresses the wish that it will never make its home elsewhere.⁶

Some call the castle Corbenic, a Chaldean word meaning "holy vessel"⁷; others call it Eden, the Castle of Joy and the Castle of Souls. No one ever dies there without his soul going to Paradise, for it is surrounded by a river which has its source in the Earthly Paradise and from which emanate all things necessary for the life of the body. The river thrice encircles the castle⁸ before entering a nearby forest, where it disappears into the earth by the dwelling of a pious hermit, leaving the soil rich and fertile.⁹

Outside the castle is a chapel where, every day, the flame of the Holy Spirit

4. *CSG* 108: According to the Romance of Perlesvaus, Gawain first meets the Grail Bearer, who has lost her hair and travels in a cart, when he is in search of the court of the Fisher King after Perceval's failure to ask the Question. She tells him that, if he reaches the Grail Castle, he must ask who is served from the Holy Vessel; only then will be lifted both her afflictions and those of the lands that have fallen into war while the king languishes (*HBG* 37). She also wears her arm in a sling while away from the Grail Castle because she does not wish to hold anything else with the hand with which she bears the "precious vessel" into which falls the blood that drips from the Lance (54): *le precious vassel en quoi li glorious sans en degote de la pointe de la lance* (*HLG* 254). When she meets Perceval for the last time, after his conquest of the Grail Castle, she no longer wears her arm in a sling (*HBG* 259).
5. *CSG* 216.
6. *CSG* 479.
7. *CSG* 550.
8. *CSG* 554–5.
9. *LG* III, 179: Her compensation is that she will mother the ever-virginal Galahad.
10. *PT* 100; *WP* 125.
11. *PT* 351.
12. For some scholars it is the Grail Bearer herself who is originally pagan: For Glenys Goetinck, the Grail Bearer is "Sovereignty, the goddess who represented the kingdom" (1975, 296); the Black or Ugly Maiden is Sovereignty "in her hideous guise" (257). Proinsias Mac Cana makes interesting connections with goddesses of abundance such as the Celtic Rosmerta, who also personifies Sovereignty (23–5). John Carey follows this up, without going so far as to "imagine that the true origin of the Grail is revealed by the cult of Rosmerta" (2007, 357); but Philippe Walter identifies the Grail Bearer with Lady Abundance (2004b, 161–3).
13. For John Matthews, this marriage represents the conjunction of the opposites, re-uniting the esoteric and the exoteric "in a primal unity." The Grail is Divine Wisdom (Sophia), who can help mankind to regain Paradise (1990b, 57). If the Grail can be seen as a symbol of Sophia, it is also "the objective receptacle of the fullness of divine Wisdom" (D'Arcy, 313).

The GRAIL CASTLE

When the young hero Perceval is offered shelter for the night in the house of a fisherman, it turns out to be a castle.

The first thing he sees is the top of a tower emerging from a valley below. As beautiful and well situated as any that can be found between here and Beirut, it is square, of dark gray stone, with two smaller towers flanking it. In front of the keep is descends in honor of the Holy Grail and the Bleeding Lance.[10] There also is the tomb of Joseph of Arimathea.[11]

When the Fisher King dies, the castle is conquered by his evil brother, the King of Castle Mortal; the Grail and its servitors disappear.[12] The Maiden of the Cart, who was once the Grail Bearer, summons Perceval to regain the land which was once ruled by his good uncle and which risks reverting to paganism.[13]

The evil king has nine bridges built, each guarded by three knights, over the deep and swift river that encircles the castle; two lions guard the gateway. As Perceval approaches the castle he comes upon the tomb by the chapel, which opens at his approach: This, along with the fact that he bears the Red Cross Shield of Joseph of Arimathea, proves that he is the chaste and holy knight who is destined to reconquer the castle.

Seeing his nephew overcome all the obstacles in his path, the King of Castle Mortal commits suicide. Perceval takes control of the castle. The Grail, the Bleeding Lance and other holy relics, including the sword with which John the Baptist was beheaded (brought there by Gawain), reappear in the chapel, which God loves so greatly.[14]

Perceval lives there with his mother and sister until their deaths. One day he hears a voice telling him that he should divide the holy relics in the castle among the local hermits. A ship bearing a white sail with a red cross arrives to take him away, none know whither. Perceval's cousin Joseus stays there until he in turn dies; but the Grail appears there no more.

Although the Grail Chapel remains untouched by the ravages of time, the castle itself falls into ruin. Strange stories circulate about it; but of all those who venture there to find out for themselves, only two ever return. Formerly knights, they become hermits wearing hair shirts and living on roots. But, when asked what caused them to change their lives, they can only respond that if anyone goes where they went, they in turn will know.[15]

* * *

The first appearance of the Grail Castle in literature occurs in Chrétien de Troyes' Romance of Perceval, written towards the end of the twelfth century. Because Chrétien died without finishing his poem, it was left to four other poets to continue the story, to provide explanations for the mysterious events and attempt to tie up the loose ends. It is only in the third of these continuations that the Grail Castle is given a name, Corbenic[16]; and this name is borrowed from the prose Grail romances that gradually replaced the poetic versions in the thirteenth century.

It is uniquely in another prose romance, the *Perlesvaus*, that the Grail Castle has three names: *Edem*, the *Chastel de Joie* and the *Chastel des Ames*,[17] whose ruler is called Messios.[18] It is also here that we learn that King Arthur gives to Perceval, after the latter's conquest of the Grail Castle, the crown which once belonged to his deceased wife Guenevere.[19] The symbolism of this unprecedented gift points to the uniting of the Kingdoms of Logres and the Grail in a sacred marriage, the wedding of earthly and spiritual sovereignty. It is as if the Grail Castle is now the spiritual center of the realm, a secondary manifestation of the Earthly Paradise from which the river that encircles the castle flows. We can imagine that the souls who die there travel upstream from the secondary to the primary sacred center, as Galahad travels from Corbenic to Sarras to die in the Vulgate *Queste*.

Notes

1. *Lors vit devant lui an un val/ Le chief d'une tor qui parut;/ L'an ne trovast jusqu'a Barut/ Si bele ne si bien assise./ Quarree fu, de pierre bise,/ S'avoit deus torneles antor./ La sale fu devant la tor,/ Et les loges devant la sale* (PCG ll.3050–7).
2. When Gawain goes there at night the hall is filled with light though no candles are lit; the king

explains to him that the light is sent by God to show His love to any knight who lodges there (*HBG* 77–8).

3. *CSG* 27–32.

4. It will not appear to those who seek it; they must chance upon it unwittingly (*PT* 106; *WP* 132): "This is," according to A.C.L. Brown (196), "a well-known characteristic of the castle of fairyland." The castle is destroyed when Balin maims its lord (see THE DOLOROUS BLOW), but is apparently restored when visited by first Gawain, then Lancelot and Bors; perhaps testifying to its "fairy" nature. For Loomis (1926, 176), the Castle of the Grail is a composite of Celtic conceptions of the dwelling of the gods.

5. According to the *Estoire del Saint Graal*, the *chastel fort et bien seant* is constructed by Alphasan, King of the Land Beyond, in return for a promise that the Holy Vessel will remain there forever (*ESG* 561). The part of the castle where the Grail is housed becomes known as the Palace of Adventures (*LG* I, 158–9).

6. *CSG* 478: According to the Vulgate and Post-Vulgate Cycles, the Grail in fact leaves Corbenic for Sarras because of the wickedness of the people of Logres.

7. *LG* I, 159.

8. When Gawain first comes to the Grail Castle, he sees what appear to be three great rivers surrounding it, each with its own "long and terrible" bridge. But appearances can be deceptive: The first bridge is not as narrow as it at first seems, nor the second bridge so fragile; while the third bridge is guarded by a lion, but as soon as it sees Gawain it lies down and lets him pass (*HBG* 76–7). In the description of Perlesvaus' attack on the nine new bridges, it is evident that there is only one river, swift and deep: *qui rade et parfonde estoit* (*HLG* 690). This is later confirmed: Behind the castle there is a river which flows from the Earthly Paradise and surrounds the castle, bringing with it many blessings: *Il avoit deriere le chastel un flum … par coi tos li biens venoit el chastel; icis flums estoit molt biaus et molt plentieus … il venoit de Paradis terrestre et avironoit tot le chastel* (788).

9. *HBG* 195.

10. *…la ou la flamme del saint esperit descent chascon jor por le saintisme Greal et por la lance dont la pointe saine, que l'on i sert* (*HLG* 336).

11. *HBG* 75–6, 169.

12. *HBG* 146.

13. *HBG* 152.

14. *HBG* 168–73: *Li sains Graaus se representa la dedens en la chapele et la lance de coi la pointe saine et l'espee de coi saint Jehan fu decoleis, que mesire Gauvain conquist, et les autres saintes reliques dont il ot a grant plenté kar Damnedieus amoit molt le leu* (*HLG* 694).

15. *HBG* 263–5.

16. *MTC* l.42455.

17. *HLG* 788: Commenting on the argument between scholars as to whether the castle is earthly or Otherworldly, Pierre Gallais suggests that we see it as a *lieu intermédiaire* where the two worlds meet (1998b, 56): Perceval imagines it into being, but that does not mean that it is merely *imaginary*. Archetypal images have their own, *imaginal* reality; which is why Perceval is able to carry away from the castle the sword that the Fisher King gave him (1998a, 56–7).

18. *HBG* 88.

19. *HBG* 194–5.

The GRAIL CHALICE

When Jesus is dying on the Cross, one of the Jews responsible for His crucifixion takes a Lance and pierces His side with it, so that three drops of blood touch and remain on the point.[1] At the same time a lady, carrying a vessel in the shape of a chalice, approaches the Cross and collects the blood of the Creator in it.[2] When the chalice is full, she takes it to her house for safe-keeping. But later, when He is risen from the dead, Christ takes it and the Lance to His disciples, where they are gathered for the feast of Pentecost on Mount Zion.[3] From this chalice, the Holy Grail, the disciples are filled with the Holy Spirit.

Christ entrusts the Grail Chalice to Joseph of Arimathea,[4] who brings it to Britain and, on one occasion, uses it to feed two thousand people. After Joseph's death it is passed to one of his nephews[5] and on down through the generations. Now it is King Pelles and his household who are fed by its grace.[6]

The Vessel of the Sacrament

Some say that the Grail is the Vessel in which Jesus made the sacrament at the Last Supper[7] and that it was Joseph of Arimathea who used it to collect the blood that was dripping from His wounds on the Cross.[8] Later, the risen Christ tells Joseph that, when he performs the sacrament of the Mass at the Table of the Grail, the Vessel that contains the blood gathered from His body will be called the chalice.[9]

And so it is that, when Joseph's son Josephus celebrates his first sacrament as the minister of Christ in the Spiritual Palace in

Sarras, where the bread and wine become the flesh and blood of Our Lord, there is a golden chalice in the middle of the altar.[10] It is filled with wine and covered with a paten, on which bread is prepared. As he repeats the words that Jesus spoke to his disciples at the Last Supper, Josephus sees the bread become the body of a child whose blood is falling into the chalice. But despite his resistance to the idea, he obeys Our Lord's command to eat the consecrated bread and partake of the holy drink from the chalice. Filled with sweetness and delight, Josephus watches as angels carry away the chalice, the paten and the holy dish[11] from which Jesus and his disciples ate the paschal lamb at the Last Supper.

Chalice and Child

When Arthur becomes King of Britain, there are no chalices to be found anywhere in the realm,[12] but this will change as a result of the king's experiences in the Grail Castle. It is Arthur's nephew Gawain, though, who first sees a chalice there.

Gawain has won entry to the Grail Castle by bringing as a gift to the Fisher King the sword with which John the Baptist was beheaded. Everyone sits down to eat and two maidens enter the hall from the chapel: one carrying the Holy Grail, the other the Bleeding Lance. As he gazes at the Grail, Gawain seems to see inside it a chalice, which was then a rare sight.[13] But, when it is brought before him again, he thinks he can see the shape of a child within it.[14] He then sees the Grail high in the air with the image above it of a crucified king thrust through his side by a Lance.[15]

Later, when Perceval conquers the Grail Castle after the death of the Fisher King, Arthur himself comes there. He sees the Holy Vessel go through all five of its transformations, shapes whose nature cannot be revealed except by him to whom God has granted the grace to do so.[16] We know only that the last of the changes was into a chalice, a form that Arthur treasures and which he is keen to introduce into worship in his own kingdom, in accordance with God's wishes.[17] This he does when he returns to his court at Carduel.[18]

In the Semblance of a Chalice

Others say that on his first visit to the Grail Castle, Gawain does not see a chalice inside the Grail, but that the Holy Vessel itself takes that form. He sees a beautiful maiden bearing a splendid Vessel which amazingly, though it is in the semblance of a chalice, does not seem to be made of any known substance: neither wood, metal, stone, horn nor bone.[19] Gawain is later healed of wounds sustained in the Palace of Adventures by the presence of the Holy Vessel.[20]

When Lancelot also arrives at the Grail Castle, the second of Arthur's knights to do so, he too sees the beautiful maiden carrying a precious vessel in the shape of a chalice, which he recognizes as something holy and worthy, and before which everyone in the hall kneels.[21] When Lancelot's brother Hector and another Round Table Knight, Perceval of Wales, later encounter the Grail, when they are dying of the wounds that they have inflicted on each other through mistaken combat, it is made like a chalice covered with white samite. It seems to be a holy thing, though they cannot see who, if anyone, is carrying it.[22] The Holy Vessel heals their wounds,[23] as it did those of Gawain before them.

But if the Grail brings physical healing, it can also confer the eternal joy of the soul, though at the expense of the death of the body: And so it will prove, when Lancelot's son Galahad, after healing the Maimed King in Corbenic, is sent by Christ to Sarras, the city where Joseph of Arimathea and his son Josephus first converted a pagan kingdom to Christianity. Here, in the Spiritual Palace, the spirit of the long-dead

Josephus performs the Mass of the mother of God. When he reaches the solemn part of the Mass that follows the consecration, he lifts the paten from the Holy Vessel and bids Galahad gaze into it, to see what neither tongue can describe, nor heart conceive. Galahad is rapt up to Heaven by angels and the Holy Vessel follows him.[24]

* * *

The Holy Grail is today perhaps primarily thought of as the cup from which Jesus drank at the Last Supper, thanks to its portrayal as such in the poetry of Tennyson, the music drama of Wagner and, more recently, in the film *Indiana Jones and the Last Crusade*. Yet when the Grail first appears in literature in the late twelfth century, it is described as a golden, jewel-encrusted Vessel radiant with light from which, we later learn, the Fisher King's aged father is fed with a single Host, or consecrated wafer, each day; the Grail is "such a holy thing" that the "spiritual" old man needs nothing else to sustain life. We also learn that the Grail is big enough to contain pike, lamprey or salmon, suggesting a feeding vessel, perhaps like the magical cauldrons of early medieval Celtic tales; but the reference to the Host, or communion bread, connects the Grail to the sacrament of the Eucharist.

Both these approaches to the true nature of the Grail have been followed up by scholars eager to prove that the Holy Vessel has its origins in pagan mythology, or insisting on it as a purely Christian relic, albeit somewhat heterodox (if not actually heretical). This ambiguity is fostered by the early Grail poems, which make little attempt to clarify the mystery of the Holy Vessel, left unresolved by the unfinished nature of Chrétien de Troyes' original Grail poem. But Robert de Boron follows up Chrétien's eucharistic reference by identifying the Grail with the Vessel in which Christ made the sacrament at the Last Supper, and by making a chalice the form of the Vessel containing His blood collected at the crucifixion.[25]

In the prose texts, beginning with the prose redaction of de Boron's poem, the Grail's Christian nature is stressed. When de Boron's text is reworked into the Vulgate Cycle, it is made clear that the Vessel in question is not a cup but the platter or dish (*escuele*) from which Jesus ate the paschal lamb at the Last Supper; but successive Round Table knights see it in the "semblance" of a chalice.

The Grail's identity as a "holy dish" seems to be confirmed in the Vulgate *Queste*, when the spirit of Josephus takes a consecrated wafer from the Grail and gives it to Galahad, explaining that the Vessel is indeed the *escuele* from which Jesus ate the lamb (and not the cup from which He drank the wine). Although when, just before Galahad dies, Josephus appears to him once more and lifts the paten from off the Holy Vessel so that the knight can look inside and die happy, the image of a chalice is once more evoked.

It seems to be these associations— sometimes symbolic, sometimes literal— between the Grail and the chalice (if only as one of its five metamorphoses) that led to the increasing identification of the Holy Vessel with the cup of the Last Supper. For this cup is the archetype of the communion chalice and, in the Latin translation of the New Testament, it is called a *calix*.[26]

From the medieval period onwards, the legend develops until it reaches its Victorian form in Tennyson's poem "The Holy Grail" where the Vessel is identified as: "The cup, the cup itself, from which our Lord/ Drank at the last sad supper with his own." After the crucifixion, "the good saint/ Arimathæan Joseph," brings it to Glastonbury: "And there awhile it bode; and if a man/ Could touch or see it, he was heal'd at once,/ By faith, of all his ills. But then the times/ Grew to such evil that the holy cup/ Was caught away to Heaven, and disappear'd."[27]

In the twentieth century, René Guénon,

the founder of the Traditionalist school of metaphysics, gave the cup a pre-Christian origin in esoteric legend: Fashioned by angels from an emerald that falls from the forehead of Lucifer when he is thrown down from Heaven, it is entrusted to Adam in the Earthly Paradise, but is left behind when he is cast out. Recovered by Adam's son Seth,[28] it appears as the oracular silver cup of another Joseph, son of Israel (in Genesis 44.5), where it confers the "sense of eternity"—the vision of all things as present realities—which, before the Fall, all mankind had through the Third Eye.[29]

Beginning with Seth, the Grail Keepers (who include the Druids) establish a spiritual center on Earth which is the image of the lost Paradise, where the primordial Tradition is preserved. To achieve the Grail Quest is to find that center and "rejoin that unique place in which all things are contemplated from the standpoint of eternity."[30]

Notes

1. This is the Bleeding Lance that will be seen by Perceval in the house of the Fisher King.
2. *...uns Juis vint a la crois et prist une lance ... et la ficha u flanc Jhesucrist. Et tantost en issi sanc, et deseur la lance remesent trois goutes de sanc.... Et ensi conme li sans couroit par les flancs Nostre Signeur, avint que une dame vint cele part, qui ne veoit goute, et portoit un vaissel en sa main en samblance de galice.... Et ele mist tantost le galice desous la crois et acueilloit le sanc del vrai Crucefis* (TPM IX, 255). This lady is partially-sighted but, when she gets too close to the Cross and some of the Holy Blood touches her eyes, the clarity of her vision is restored, in an echo of the legend of Longinus.
3. The author of the Prose *Tristan*, which uniquely contains this account, is reflecting a tradition that the "upper room" used for the Pentecostal feast (Acts 1.13) is the Cenacle, the room of the Last Supper on Mount Zion, a hill to the west of Jerusalem.
4. *Quant Jhesu Crist fu resuscité ... il vint le jour de la Pentecouste entre ses deciples et aporta avec soi le Saint Graal ... et la lance dont il estoit feruz en sa passion. Et de celui galice raemplist le filz Dieu ses deciples du Saint Esperit a Monte Syon, et puis bailla celui galice Nostre Sires a Joseph de Abarimacie* (PV III, 705).
5. In the *Estoire del Saint Graal*, the Holy Vessel is passed from Joseph to his son Josephus; and from Josephus to his cousins (Joseph's nephews) Alan the Fat and Joshua; then to Joshua's descendants, down to King Pelles, the last Fisher King.
6. TPM IX, 255-6.
7. *...un veissel mout gent/ Ou Criz feisoit son sacrement* (EG ll.395-6).
8. MG 18-19.
9. *Cist veissiaus ou men sanc meïs,/ Quant de men cors le requeillis,/ Calices apelez sera* (EG ll.907-9). In the prose version, the sacramental Vessel commemorates the stone tomb in which He was placed; in both versions, the paten (which covers the chalice in the Mass) will commemorate the lid of the tomb (EG ll.910-13; RG 30).
10. LG I, 25: This chalice is quite distinct from the "holy dish"—*la sainte escüele* (ESG 76)—which Joseph of Arimathea has brought from the Holy Land and placed in an ark, where the consecration of Josephus is taking place; the dish which will later be identified as the Holy Grail.
11. LG I, 28: Although they are distinct objects, there is a symbolic association between the chalice that contains the Child's blood and the holy dish in which was collected the blood of the crucified Man, so that they are eventually conflated in the symbolism of the Grail vessel: *see* THE GRAIL DISH.
12. *Li estores nos tesmoigne c'a icel tans n'avoit en la terre le roi Artu nul galice* (HLG 790).
13. *Mesire Gauvain esgarde le Greal et si samble qu'il voit un calice dedens, dont il n'iert gaires a icel tans* (HLG 348).
14. *...li samble qu'il voit en mi le Greal la forme d'un enfant* (HLG 350).
15. HBG 79: The Grail itself is the Holy Vessel in which the faithful gather the blood which flows from the wound made by the Lance at the crucifixion (19).
16. This caveat does not prevent John Matthews and Marian Green, in *The Grail Seeker's Companion* (171) from revealing that their own researches ("through meditation or inner communication") indicate that the five forms—*manieres* (HLG 790)—are Spear, Dish, Stone, Child and Cup.
17. HBG 195-6: *Li rois Artus vi totes les muances: le daerraine si fu en galice*; and the hermit who conducts Mass in the Grail Chapel finds letters written on the corporal, the cloth on which the chalice is placed, stating that God wants His sacrifice to be commemorated in such a vessel (*en itel vaissel*) henceforward (HLG 790).
18. HBG 210: Strubel has the impression that the adoption of the chalice into the liturgy is here seen to constitute the principal benefit of Perceval's conquest of the Grail Castle (HLG 851n1).
19. LG III, 100: *Ele ... porta entre ses .II. mains le plus riche vaissel qui onques par home terrien fust veus, et fu fes en samblance de calice.... Mesire Gauvain esgarde le vaissel, si le prise plus que rien qu'il eust veue, mais il ne puet savoir de quoi il est, kar de fust n'est il pas ne de nul maniere de metal, ne de pierre ne rest il mie ne de cor ne d'os, et de ceu est il tos esbahis* (LM II, 377).
20. LG III, 101-2.
21. LG III, 163: *Il resgarde le vessel que la*

damoisele tenoit entre ses mains qui est li plus riches a son esciant qui onques fust veuz par home mortel et estoit fait en samblant de galice: se li est avis, et bien le croit, que ce soit sainte chose et dingne (*LM* IV, 206).

22. *Il resgardent et voient .I. vessel qui estoit fez en samblance de galice et fu couverz d'un blanc samit ... mais il ne voient mie qui les portoit ne qui le veissel soustenoit; et neporquant li vaissiaux samble sainte chose* (*LM* VI, 204). The *samblance de galice* does not prevent Hector from explaining to his companion that it is the Vessel in which Our Lord ate the paschal lamb: see THE GRAIL DISH.

23. *LG* III, 328.

24. *LG* IV, 87; V, 287–8; *QHG* 282–4: The rapture of the Grail has been compared with an ancient myth of Wisdom, who withdraws from the world when her message is rejected (D'Arcy, 288–9).

25. The paten which covers the chalice is compared to the stone which seals Christ's sepulcher (*EG* ll.910–13)—an interesting connection, given that Wolfram von Eschenbach will make the Grail a stone.

26. Barber 2005, 97. It has been argued that, insofar as it is seen as "the greatest of all communion chalices," the Grail embodies in literature the twelfth century pre-occupation with the doctrine of transubstantiation (Hutton 1991, 319), that is, the process whereby the bread and wine of the Mass become the body and blood of Christ.

27. *HG* 414: In the First Act of his music drama *Parsifal*, first performed at Bayreuth some thirteen years after the publication of Tennyson's Grail poem, Richard Wagner also describes the Holy Vessel as the precious cup from which He drank at the Last Supper and into which His blood flowed from the Cross (*RWP* 4).

28. Guénon 1983, 26.

29. Guénon 2000, 272n3.

30. Guénon 1983, 26–7: There is no doubt, he writes elsewhere, that the origins of the medieval legend must be traced back to the transmission from Druidism to Christianity of the esoteric (initiatory) elements of the primordial Tradition (2000, 36)—which would explain the Celtic mythological strata in the stories. See AFTERWORD: HIGHER MYSTERIES.

The GRAIL DISH

When he sees the Man whom he believes to be the World Savior on the Cross, Joseph of Arimathea, His faithful disciple, decides to avail himself of something that Jesus had touched while alive. So, he goes to the house of the Last Supper and finds there the Dish from which the Son of God had eaten the paschal lamb.[1]

Finding an honored place for the Dish in his home, Joseph goes to his liege lord, Pontius Pilate, to ask him, as a reward for his loyal service, to grant him custody of the body of Jesus. After taking Him down from the Cross and laying Him in the rock tomb reserved for his own death, Joseph returns to his house to find the Dish of the Last Supper. This he uses to collect as much as possible of the blood which was still dripping from the body of Jesus, before taking the Dish back home. This Dish has been the means for God to perform miracles in the Promised Land and elsewhere.[2]

The first of these miracles occurs when Joseph is imprisoned by those Jews angered by his taking the body of Jesus down from the Cross; they intend to let him die of hunger. But the resurrected Christ comes to Joseph in prison, bringing with Him the Dish containing His blood; and this is all he needs to sustain his life for forty-two years, until he is released by the Roman general Vespasian.[3]

Christ in a vision now instructs Joseph to leave the Holy Land with his friends and family, taking with him nothing of value except the Dish. Later, when Joseph and his followers have reached a wood beyond Bethany, they must create an ark before which the people can pray, sight of the Dish itself being reserved for Joseph and his son Josephus.[4]

Arriving at the pagan city of Sarras, the company are praying before the ark when Josephus is summoned by Christ to become His first minister. Opening the door of the ark, Josephus has a series of intense spiritual visions, including seeing an angel holding a Lance which is thrust into the side of a Crucified Man: blood and water from His wounds drip into the Dish which his father Joseph had placed in the ark.[5]

Joseph himself, outside the ark but looking in, sees a chalice in the middle of an altar, with the bloody tip of a Lance on one side and the Dish he had brought from the Holy Land on the other.[6] He later sees the Holy Dish[7] covered by an emerald green cloth and carried by an angel, writing on whose forehead[8] proclaims him to be the Strength of the Most High Lord.[9] After Josephus is consecrated as a bishop and performs the first sacrament for the Company of the Grail, the angel replaces the Holy Dish on the altar in the ark.[10]

Once the King of Sarras and his brother-in-law Nascien have been baptized by Josephus, they ask to see the Holy Dish and the other sacred objects kept in the ark. Nascien reveals that the true name of the Dish—the Grail—was revealed to him years earlier, although he only knew that it referred to something that would be more *agreeable* to him than anything else.[11] Eager to see more, Nascien raises the paten which covers the Grail[12] and is temporarily blinded: He has seen what no mortal man should see and no mortal tongue can describe, a wonder surpassing all other wonders.[13]

From now on this wondrous Vessel will be known as the Holy Grail. When, in the time of King Arthur, it is seen by Round Table Knights, it is often in the shape of a chalice. Nevertheless, as Hector explains to Perceval, after they have both been healed by its grace of wounds sustained in fighting, the Holy Grail is the Vessel in which Jesus ate the lamb with His disciples, in the house of Simon the Leper.[14] It was brought to Logres by Joseph of Arimathea and it fed him and his descendants. To this day, it feeds King Pelles and his household.[15]

Indeed, when Galahad comes to the castle of his grandfather Pelles and is fed by the Grail, it is Christ Himself who explains that the Holy Vessel is the Dish in which He and His disciples ate the paschal lamb—a Dish which has been most agreeable to His faithful servants and which, for that reason, is called the Holy Grail.[16]

Notes

1. ...*l'escüele en quoi li Fiex Dieu avoit mangié* (*ESG* 24).
2. ...*par qui Diex fist et moustra puis maintes virtus et en Terre de Promission et en maintes autres terres* (*ESG* 25): The Grail Dish will perform miracles both in the Biblical Promised Land (Palestine) and in the western land (Britain) which God will promise to Joseph and his followers.
3. *LG* I, 10–11: This version of the origins of the Grail, taken from the Vulgate *Estoire del Saint Graal*, is a reworking of the prose account attributed to Robert de Boron, which is in turn based on Robert's poem, but with important variations: After performing the sacrament at the Last Supper in the house of Simon the Leper, Jesus is seized by the Jews to whom Judas has betrayed Him and taken before the Roman governor. But one of the Jews takes the Vessel in which He made the sacrament—*ses vaissiaus la u il sacrefioit* (*RG* 22)—and hands it over to Pilate.

After Christ's death, one of Pilate's soldiers, Joseph of Arimathea, asks the governor for the body of Jesus, whom he loved dearly. After granting this request, Pilate also gives Joseph the sacramental Vessel, which the soldier uses to gather the blood from Christ's wounds before wrapping Him in a linen cloth. Later, when the Jews hear that Jesus has come back from the dead, they imprison Joseph. But Christ appears to him there, bearing the Vessel which the soldier had hidden in his house, and declares that Joseph must be its first keeper (*MG* 17–22).

In the prose version the shape or nature of this Vessel is never specified but, in the poetic version, it is symbolically equated with the communion chalice.

4. *LG* I, 14–5.
5. ...*ichele escüele ke Joseph, ses peres, avoit fait aporter en l'arce* (*ESG* 74).
6. ...*un fier de lanche tout sanglant a l'un des chiés de l'autel, et a l'autre chief estoit l'escüele qu'il avoit aportee. Et en milieu de l'autel, si avoit un mout riche vaissiel d'or en samblanche d'un hanap et un couvercle deseure qui estoit d'or autresi* (*ESG* 75): The *hanap*, a golden goblet or drinking cup with its gold covering, is clearly meant to suggest the communion chalice covered with its paten. It is equally clearly distinguished from the Grail Dish (*escüele*) containing the Holy Blood, although elsewhere in the Vulgate Cycle, the Grail itself is described as having the *samblanche* of a chalice (*ESG* 582, 592).
7. ...*la sainte escüele* (*ESG* 76): This is the first time that the Dish is described as holy: It has been sanctified by being used by Christ at the Last Supper and by being used to collect His blood. Similarly, *un graal* (Chrétien's serving dish) becomes *sainte chose* and, eventually, the Holy Grail.
8. *Je sui apielés Forche del tres haut Signour* (*ESG* 76): Ponceau identifies this angel with Gabriel, whose Semitic name means the Strength of God (593). Gabriel is the Angel of Revelation in the Abrahamic faiths.
9. *LG* I, 23–5.
10. *LG* I, 28.
11. *ESG* 163–4: This is a play on words reflecting the kind of folk etymology popular in the Middle Ages, which is also found in Robert de Boron (*EG*

ll.2653–78) and in the prose version: *le Graal, qui tant agree* (*RG* 57).

12. ...*et sousleva une platine dont li glorieus vaissiaus estoit couvers* (*ESG* 164): The mention of the paten once more points us towards the communion chalice.

13. *LG* I, 50–1.

14. *Li sainz Graax est li vaissiaux ou Nostre Sires menga l'aingnel le jor de Pasques o ses deciples en la meson Symon le liepreux* (*LM* VI, 205).

15. *LG* III, 328–9.

16. *LG* IV, 85; *QHG* 276: *Ce est, fet il, l'escuele ou Jhesucriz menja l'aignel le jor de Pasques o ses deciples. Ce est l'escuele qui a servi a gré toz çax que j'ai trovez en mon servise.... Et por ce que ele a si servi a gré toutes genz doit ele estre apelee le Saint Graal* (*QP* 270): "Thys ys," seyde He, "the holy dysshe wherein I ete the lambe on Estir Day" (*MD* 783).

The GRAIL KING

On his first visit to the court of the maimed Fisher King, Perceval sees the Grail Procession pass before the royal bed, then enter another chamber. The boy is curious, but is too polite to ask who is there served from the golden, bejeweled Grail Vessel.[1]

It is only five years later, when he meets his hermit uncle, that he discovers that the one who is served *from* the vessel is another uncle, his mother's brother, the father of the Fisher King; what he is served *with* is the communion Host (the consecrated wafer of the Eucharist), which is carried to him in the Grail. Such a holy thing is the Grail and so spiritual is the king who is served from it that this single Host alone keeps him alive: He needs no other nourishment, nor has he done for all the years that he has lived in the chamber that the Grail was carried into.[2]

When Galahad, accompanied by Perceval, comes to the Grail Castle for the last time, he is taken by an old man into a chamber where he finds the Holy Vessel and the Bleeding Lance. Here also is his great-grandfather King Pellehan, who has not left the room for four years.[3] God has performed many miracles for Pellehan, including sustaining his life all that time with nothing but the grace of the Holy Grail[4]; but the king is so badly hurt that he cannot get out of bed, until Galahad heals him. He then becomes a hermit.[5]

* * *

The old Grail King—brother of Perceval's mother, father of the maimed Fisher King—is he who is served by the Grail, this being the answer to the seemingly all-important Question in Chrétien's poem; but the poet's verse continuators abandon this character. Wolfram (rewriting Chrétien or, as he claims, following a more accurate source) calls the old king Titurel and makes him the great-grandfather of Parzival. Robert de Boron calls Perceval's grandfather the Fisher King Bron. In the prose De Boron Cycle, Bron is presented as a very ancient man who is suffering from the effects of extreme old age, but who cannot die until his destined successor finds him. The prose Post-Vulgate Cycle makes some attempt to reconcile these conflicting versions: Thus Pellehan is confined to his bedchamber and sustained by the Grail; but he is also conflated with the Maimed King, whom his grandson Perceval has earlier encountered fishing.[6]

Notes

1. *CSG* 29.
2. *CSG* 56: *D'une sole oiste li sainz hon,/ Que l'an an cest graal li porte,/ Sa vie sostient et conforte;/ Tant sainte chose est li graaus,/ Et il est si esperitaus/ Qu'a sa vie plus ne covient/ Que l'oiste qui el graal vient* (*PCG* ll.6422–8).
3. This number of years makes little sense either in the context of Chrétien's poem (where Perceval meets his hermit uncle five years after his initial visit to the Grail Castle) or of the Post-Vulgate Cycle (where Pellehan's injuries are sustained twenty-two years before Galahad completes the Quest).
4. *Et li rois Pellianz por cui Dex avoit fait maint beu miracle et qui avoit ja demoré en la chambre, qu'il ne s'en estoit oissuz, plus avoit de quatre anz, ne n'i avoit eu sostenance, se ce n'estoit de la grace de Nostre Seignor ou dou Saint Veissel* (*PV* III, 321).
5. *LG* V, 279.
6. In an episode that reworks Chrétien's account of the first meeting between Perceval and the Fisher King, the young hero encounters his grandfather Pellehan as a crowned king, fishing to amuse himself because he is too "sick and infirm"

to ride or fight. He tells Perceval that he is called both the Rich Fisherman and the Maimed King (*LG* V, 109).

The GRAIL LORDS

The Christian knight Titurel is entrusted by angels with the keeping of the Grail Stone and, when his son Frimutel is killed in battle, the guardianship is taken over by his grandson Anfortas. He in turn is maimed in battle when he fights in the name of a woman who is not his chosen wife.

The dynasty of the Grail Lords is subject to certain conditions imposed by the Stone itself: Thus, an inscription appears on the Grail naming the woman the lord is destined to love. Apart from that, like all those called to the service of the Stone (the Grail Templars and maidens), the Lords must be chaste. As a consequence of his transgression, Anfortas is wounded through the genitals.[1] The son of Anfortas' sister, Parzival, is destined to heal him and succeed to the Kingdom of the Grail, becoming its new Lord.

* * *

In the first known version of the Grail story, by Chrétien de Troyes, the vessel is kept in a castle ruled by an aged king and his son, the maimed Fisher King, who is Perceval's cousin. But, because Chrétien died without completing his poem, we do not know his intentions regarding the Grail Dynasty. In Wolfram von Eschenbach's German language adaptation and completion of Chrétien's story, the Grail triad consisting of the aged king, the Maimed King and Perceval is matched by that of the aged Titurel, the maimed Anfortas and the young Parzival (here Anfortas' nephew). In the prose trilogy attributed to Robert de Boron which also acts as a prequel and completion of Chrétien's story, there are three Grail Keepers: The first is Joseph of Arimathea; the second, his brother-in-law Bron, taking the role of the aged king. The third is Bron's grandson Perceval, who is told that he is one of a line of men devoted to Our Lord, who has exalted them by placing in their keeping His body and blood.[2]

But it is only in the Vulgate Cycle that the concept of the Grail Lords is fully developed into a dynasty bridging the hundreds of years between the Deposition and the reign of King Arthur: Joseph of Arimathea is succeeded as keeper of the Holy Vessel by his son Josephus, who is succeeded in turn by Bron's sons Alan the Fat and Joshua. The Fisher Kings, Joshua's descendants, keep the Grail until Galahad, the grandson of the last Fisher King, comes to Corbenic to heal his great-grandfather, the Maimed King Pellehan.

Notes

1. *WP* 243–4; *PT* 201: "The Lord of the Grail must be chaste and pure" (350).
2. *MG* 131: *vous estes d'une lignie qui molt a nostre Segnor amé, et il les a tant essauciés que il lor a doné sa car et son sanc a garder* (*RG* 226).

The GRAIL PROCESSION

Encountering a fisherman on a river who offers him shelter for the night, the young hero Perceval finds himself in a castle where he is presented with a sword which, he is told, is destined for him.[1] When he is sat down on a bed next to the lord of the castle in a brightly-lit hall, Perceval witnesses a mysterious procession.

Firstly, a boy walks past him holding a gleaming white Lance from whose tip a drop of blood runs down his hand. He is followed by two other boys bearing golden candle-sticks; and by a girl carrying a golden Grail (a serving-dish or platter) inlaid with precious stones. As she enters the hall, a light appears, so bright that it eclipses that of the candles, as the light of the stars is eclipsed by the rising of the sun or moon. After her follows another girl, carrying a silver trencher or carving-dish. Like the boy carrying the Lance, the two girls and the candle-stick holders walk past the bed and go into a back chamber.[2]

A sumptuous feast is now laid out on the tables in the hall. But, as each course is served, the Grail passes before Perceval's eyes, and he longs to know who is served from it, though he is too polite to ask.[3] His failure to do so, however, means that he must leave the castle the next morning, none the wiser.

It is several years before Perceval finds the Grail Castle again. In the meantime, it is visited by his friend Gawain. As he sits down for dinner, Gawain sees a handsome boy carrying the Bleeding Lance[4]; a beautiful girl carrying the silver trencher; two more boys carrying candles burning in holders; and a weeping girl holding aloft for all to see, the Grail.[5] She passes with the Vessel into another room and, as soon as she has done so, there enter four boys carrying a body on a bier, covered with a cloth. On the cloth is Perceval's sword, now broken in the middle, though the break is hardly noticeable.

This procession passes through the hall three times, so that everyone sees the objects perfectly clearly. But, although Gawain asks about what he has seen, he is not yet worthy to know the truth about these things.[6]

Nor will Perceval be, on his next visit to the castle. This time, when he is sat down to dinner, he sees a girl carrying the Holy Vessel, followed by another carrying the Bleeding Lance; and, lastly, a boy carrying a sword broken in two, which Perceval is invited to mend, if he can.[7] He is only partially successful.[8] It is not until his third visit that, after witnessing the identical Procession again, he succeeds in mending perfectly the sword. Once more sat down to eat, Perceval watches as the Lance and Grail process past the royal table, followed by a girl carrying the silver trencher which he had seen on his first visit.

It is only now that Perceval learns that three of the objects in the Procession are relics of Christ's Passion: The Lance is the one that pierced Him in the side on the Cross; the Grail, the Vessel in which was caught the Holy Blood; and the silver trencher, the dish which was used to cover the Vessel so that the blood would not be left exposed. As for the sword, it had been used to kill by treachery the Fisher King's brother; whoever can mend it is destined to avenge him and, as a consequence, heal the Maimed King.[9]

Once Perceval has achieved these tasks, the revitalized Fisher King invites him to a celebratory feast. He sees a girl carrying the Grail, and all those it passes are filled to satiety. She is followed by another girl carrying the Bleeding Lance and a boy carrying the silver trencher. Three times the Grail passes among the tables, and all present see it quite clearly.[10]

When the Fisher King eventually dies, King Arthur and his nobles attend Perceval's coronation in Corbenic. There the whole of the fellowship of the Round Table are soon able to witness the Grail Procession: firstly, the Holy Vessel borne quite openly by the Fisher King's daughter; then a boy carrying the Bleeding Lance; and finally, the Grail Bearer's cousin carrying the silver trencher.[11] But when Perceval retires to a hermitage, the hallows go with him; and when he goes to Heaven, they go too.[12]

* * *

Because Chrétien de Troyes left the original Grail poem incomplete, we cannot know what explanation he would have given for the mysterious objects that Perceval sees in the Procession. The explanation of the Lance and Grail as relics of the Passion is given in the first (of four) verse continuations: We only find out about the silver trencher and what is effectively only one of several broken swords (and distinct from the one presented to Perceval on his first visit) in the Third Continuation, composed by Manessier some fifty years after Chrétien's *conte*.

The Christian mystic A.E. Waite referred to the four principal sacred objects related to the Grail—which he lists as Cup, Lance, Sword and Dish[13]—as the Hallows (an archaic but evocative word surviving mainly in modern usage in the name of Hallowe'en, the eve of the feast of All Hallows,[14] or All Saints Day)—and this term has been adopted by later esoteric authors such as Caitlín and John Matthews. Unlike the Matthews, Waite considered the folkloric, pre-Christian antecedents of the Grail to be "negligible," if "indispensable," compared to their "conversion" into the sacramental presence of the Holy Vessel.

The pagan (and specifically Celtic mythological) "roots of the mystery"[15] had, however, been explored by French and German scholars since the middle of the nineteenth century. In a seminal work published in 1888, the English folklorist Alfred Nutt argued that "a vessel akin to the Grail," along with other sacred objects (which he called "talismans") associated with it, "formed part of the gear of the oldest Celtic divinities." These he lists as a stone of Fate, the sword and spear of Lug the Longhanded,[16] and the cauldron of the Dagda, whom he considered to be an Earth god and head of the Irish pantheon.[17]

The idea that these talismans, sometimes called the Four Treasures of the Tuatha de Danann—"the race of fairies and wizards"[18]—are the originals of the Grail Hallows is a persistent, if controversial, one. It was supported by A.C.L. Brown[19]; whereas Jessie L. Weston argued that there is an "affiliation" and correspondence between the two sets of symbols, bespeaking a "common original, but that they have developed along different lines."[20]

While Weston's theory, that the common original was an initiation ritual connected to a mystery cult, has found few followers since the early twentieth century, the idea that there is something distinctly unorthodox, if not downright heretical, going on in the Grail Castle has nevertheless persisted. Thus, Leonardo Olschki suggests that Perceval meets the wayward, religiously dualist[21] members of his previously unknown family there; he has to be brought back to the true faith by his more orthodox hermit uncle. The key to the mystery of the Grail Procession lies in the "intense light" emanating from the Holy Vessel[22] which, in the absence of orthodox liturgy, leads Olschki to suspect something pagan or heretical about it.[23]

Similarly, the image of a Procession of Light leads Pierre Gallais to consider the events in the Grail Castle as a spiritual initiation, which is often accompanied by an experience of supernatural light.[24] The procession itself, he considers, can be seen to take the form of an arrow (an attribute of the Great Goddess) or a cross, with the Grail itself at the centre.[25] The idea of the procession as forming a "living cross" is taken up by Francis Dubost[26] who, like Olschki, stresses the intense light[27] which emanates either from the Grail *or from her who bears it*; an illumination which eclipses the candle light.

Dubost sees the procession in terms of a silent, choreographed ceremony juxtaposing natural and supernatural light. Here, jeweled splendor and the enigma of a white Lance dropping pearls of blood evoke the visible turning towards the invisible, as the Grail moves from the great square hall towards a secret chamber; earthly becomes spiritual nourishment.[28] For Dubost, the difficulty of interpreting such a ceremony as pagan or Christian, orthodox or heretical, may be precisely the point: The author is after poetic expressivity which cannot easily be slotted into someone else's system or explained away.[29]

Notes

1. See THE BROKEN SWORD.
2. In the Prose *Perceval*, the Procession consists of: a girl carrying two silver platters, followed by a boy carrying the Bleeding Lance and another boy carrying the Grail (*MG* 141).
3. *CSG* 29.
4. *Une blanche lance reonde/ Tenoit li vallez an sa main.// Et li fers de la lance sainne,/ Qui ainz de sainnier ne cessa* (*CP* II, ll.3782–3, 3786–7).
5. *Mais molt pleure et se desconforte;/ Antre ses mains gentement porte/ Un Graal trestot descovert./ Gauvains lou vit tot en apert* (*CP* II, ll.3809–12).

6. *CSG* 108-9.
7. See THE SWORD OF PARTINAL.
8. *CSG* 336-7.
9. *CSG* 477-9.
10. *CSG* 550: *Lors vint la lance et li Graax/ Que les deus puceles portoient,/ Qui gentement se deportoient/ Et passent par devant les tables./ Lors furent de mes deletables/ Repleni tuit conmunement.// Tuit sont replani et refait/ Icil qui as tables seoient,/ Quant le Saint Graal passer voient/ Et la sainte lance au fer blanc/ Ou pandoit la gote de sanc./ Aprés vint uns vaslez molt gent/ Qui tint un tailleor d'argent// Par trois foiees trespassa/ Parmi les tables li Graax/ Si que bien le vit Percevaux/ Et tuit cil qui laienz estoient* (*MTC* ll.41936-41, 41950-6, 41964-7).
11. *CSG* 554: *Mais ne tarda pas longement/ Qu'il virent.../ Le Saint Graal tot descovert/ C'une damoisele portoit,// Aprés cele sanz demorance/ Vint un vallet qui une lance/ Tint en sa main, a un fer blanc/ Dunt ist une goute de sanc./ Aprés, devant toute la gent,/ Oissi un tailleor d'argent/ C'une damoisele tenoit* (*MTC* ll.42488-91, 42493-9). It is unclear why, in Manessier's depictions of the Grail Procession, the Lance is at first carried by a girl and later, the silver trencher is carried by a boy.
12. *CSG* 555.
13. Waite 1909, 90.
14. *All Hallows Eve* is the title of the last published novel by the Grail poet and writer of supernatural shockers Charles Williams (1886-1945)—sometimes known as the Third Inkling because of his association with C.S. Lewis and J.R.R. Tolkien—who had joined Waite's mystical order in 1917. His earlier novels include one, about a battle for the Grail as Christian relic, entitled *War in Heaven* (1930); and another, centering on the Tarot pack, called *The Greater Trumps* (1932).
15. Waite 1909, 138-9.
16. "He was revered by all the Celtic races, and has left his trace in the name of several towns, chief among them Lug-dunum = Lyons" (Nutt, 184*n*).
17. "It is, therefore, no wonder to find him possessor of the magic cauldron, which may be looked upon as a symbol of fertility, and, as such, akin to similar symbols in the mythology of nearly every people" (Nutt, 185*n*).
18. Nutt, 184-5: Contemporary scholars of medieval Irish prefer to talk of the Túatha Dé ("god-peoples") and list their Four Treasures as the Stone of Fál, "which used to cry out beneath every king who used to take control of Ireland"; the Spear of Lug; the Sword of Núadu; and "the Dagda's cauldron: no group of people would go from it unsatisfied." Mark Williams argues that "the balance of probabilities" is that the tradition of the treasures of the god-peoples is the creation of medieval pseudo-historians "rather than an old—let alone pre–Christian—concept" (2016, 148-53).
19. Brown, 228*n*9: "Sword, lance, Grail, and platter doubtless originally belonged together and were the talismans upon which the prosperity of the fairy folk depended" (130*n*29).
20. Weston 1920, 72-4: For Weston, this original is also common to the Tarot, divinatory cards whose four suits (Cup, Lance, Sword and Dish) she compares to the Grail symbols (77-9): see AFTERWORD: HIGHER MYSTERIES. Weston elsewhere points to a "curious" and unique version of the Grail Procession: "here it is composed of a white stag, with a red cross on the forehead and lighted tapers on the horns, carrying on its back a Vessel, beneath a rich silken covering, and followed by a white brachet, and a little maiden leading in a leash two small white beasts, the size of rabbits. The procession is closed by a knight in a litter borne by four little palefrois, while voices in the air above are heard singing: 'Honor, and glory, and power, and everlasting joy to the Destroyer of Death!'" (1913, 154). This episode is found in the *Livre d'Artus* (*VS* VII, 244-5), while the Grail is carried in the horns of a white stag, tied with golden chains held by four men in white vestments, in an Italian romance (*TP* 39).
21. The Bleeding Lance would thus represent the principle of cosmic evil "as a metaphysical necessity" proclaimed by the medieval heirs of the ancient Gnostics and Manichaeans (Olschki 39-40). The "gralophorous" maiden is "one of those mystical women who made their appearance in the heretical movements of the age,"—personifications of Sapientia, replacing the Gnostic Sophia, Divine Wisdom (22-3). The *esperitaus* old Grail King in the back chamber, like the "perfect ones" of the Cathars (19), is fed on supersubstantial bread which nourishes him through its own "mystical power," unlike the *corpus Christi* of the Catholic Church which is "liturgically consecrated" (24-6).
22. *Une si grant clartez i vint/ Qu'ausin perdirent les chandoilles/ Lor clarté comme les estoilles/ Qant li solaux luist o la lune* (*CGM* ll.3164-67). Robert de Boron also speaks of the *grant clarté* which bathes the imprisoned Joseph of Arimathea when Christ brings him the Holy Vessel, illuminating the cell (*EG* ll.717-20)—leading him to ask, whence comes *ceste clartez si granz*? (l.728). For Olschki, this is the Grail Question that Perceval should have asked (31).
23. Olschki 20-2: In the late thirteenth century Romance of Sone, the hero sees the Grail as part of a procession in the Abbey of the Isle of Galoche. When the *saint vaissiel* (*MGL* 316, l.4894) is removed from the ivory reliquary in which the monks keep it, it lights up the whole island— *Et le saint greal en sacha./ Tout li paÿs en raluma* (ll.4905-6).
24. Gallais 1998b, 109-15.
25. Gallais 1998b, 215-6: One aspect of this Goddess is Lady Sovereignty, who can hinder (like Perceval's mother), test (like the Ugly Maiden), or enable: Blancheflor opens him to love, his cousin enables him to discover his true name, while the Grail Bearer shows him the way to the *esperitaus* Old King. She is thus Eternal Woman as mediatrix—Psyche between Physis and Pneuma (body and spirit)—as if her true home were the world of the soul, the *monde intermédiaire* that Corbin has called the *mundus imaginalis* (225-6).
26. Dubost sees the cruciform shape of the Grail

Procession as prefigured by the cross that Perceval traces in the air—but symbolically in space and time—when he practices with his javelins in the Waste Forest: above and below (in space), behind and ahead of him (in time). For Perceval, in fact, Dubost writes, what lies ahead is nothing less than the adventure of the Grail, whose image when it first appears is that of a cross which is formed precisely out of living beings and which brings with it meanings that are impossible to decipher (53–4).

27. As I have argued elsewhere (Dixon 2012, 51–2, 61–3; 2017, 193–5), one of the heretical resonances of the radiant Grail Procession may be the spiritual Cross of Light which, in the apocryphal Acts of John, is opposed to the material cross of wood on which the humanity of Jesus is crucified. The Cross of Light was an important image for Manichaean dualism, so it is not surprising that the Acts of John were condemned as heretical by the Second Nicene Council.

28. Dubost, 163.
29. Dubost, 163–5.

The GRAIL QUESTION

When the young hero Perceval is knighted by Gornemant of Gohort, he is taught several rules of good conduct, of which one in particular will have important ramifications in future: the injunction not to talk too much, lest he say things that make him look foolish.[1]

This apparently unexceptional advice will only become problematic when Perceval comes to the court of the maimed Fisher King, where he sees two remarkable sights. The first is a young man carrying a white Lance with blood running from its tip onto his hand; Perceval politely refrains from asking his host how such a thing could come about.[2] The second marvel is a radiant, jeweled vessel (a "grail") which a girl carries into a back bedroom; once more, Perceval fails to ask a question: Whom does the Grail serve?[3] During the meal that follows, furthermore, Perceval maintains his silence.[4] He determines instead to ask one of the lads at court about it, before he leaves in the morning.

When he awakens, however, there is no one about. The castle is deserted, so he decides to ride out into the forest, thinking he will find some of the youths there, so that he can ask them why the Lance bleeds and where the Grail is carried to.[5] Instead he meets his cousin, who asks him if he saw the Bleeding Lance. When Perceval tells her that he did see it, she wants to know if he asked why it bled[6]; when he replies that he didn't speak, she tells him that he has acted very badly.

Her next question is whether he saw the Grail and, when he replies that he did so, she questions him closely about the details of what he saw, concluding by wanting to know whether he had asked the people in the Grail Procession where they were going. When he replies that he uttered not a word, she exclaims that that is even worse! Had he asked all these questions he would have so improved the condition of the Maimed King that he would have regained both the use of his limbs and the ability to maintain his realm: Great good would have resulted, but Perceval's failure to do so means that, instead, great trouble will come both to himself and to others.

The reason for Perceval's failure to ask the right questions, according to his cousin, lies with the fact that he left his mother alone to die from sorrow when he set off on his adventures. The maiden tells him, however, that she is as upset about his failure to discover what is done with the Grail and whither it is carried,[7] as she is about the death of her aunt.[8]

Later, at King Arthur's court at Caerleon, an Ugly Maiden arrives who upbraids Perceval for failing to ask why the Lance bleeds and what worthy man is served from the Grail.[9] She repeats the assertion of his cousin that, had he spoken when he had the chance, the wounds of the Maimed King would have been healed and he would have been able to govern peacefully his land.

Perceval's response is that he is determined to search for the Grail and Lance until he finds them again[10]; but first he will encounter his hermit uncle who will tell him the answer to the Question that he failed to ask. Having confessed that he was once at the house of the Fisher King, but asked nothing about the blood that hangs from the head of the Lance—and that he still does not know who is served from the Grail[11]—he is told once again that he is being punished for the grief that he caused his mother when he left home; this is the explanation for his unfortunate silence. The hermit is his mother's brother and they have another brother, the Fisher King's father, who was in the back room whither the Grail was carried: He it is who is served from the Holy Vessel.[12]

Although he now knows the answer to one Question, another remains; and so, he continues searching through many kingdoms for the court which houses the Bleeding Lance.[13]

The Waste Kingdom Restored

But it is in fact Gawain who, after riding along a causeway to a mysterious White Island, is the next to witness the Grail Hallows and have the opportunity to ask about what he sees, which now includes a dead body on a bier and a sword which is shattered in two pieces.[14]

Curiously, he does not ask about the Vessel that he has seen floating independently about the hall, serving everyone there with food and drink, without the need of human assistance. Instead, Gawain asks the Grail King where the blood that runs down the Lance comes from, as well as about the sword and the bier.[15]

The king tells him that the Lance is the one which pierced the heart of the Son of God on the day He was crucified; since that day it bleeds continuously, and will carry on doing so until the Last Judgment.[16] As a result of asking this question, Gawain partially restores the country through which he travels the next day: a wasteland which, the evening before, had been completely devoid of life. But God had restored the waters to their rightful courses during the night and all the woods had become green again, as soon as he asked why the Lance bled in that fashion.[17]

If God did not fully restore the Waste Kingdom, it was because Gawain did not ask any more. Moreover, as he rides through the country, the inhabitants bless him for what he has accomplished, but curse him for not asking *why* the Grail serves.[18] Consequently he roams the land, performing many deeds of arms, in order to enhance his worthiness, so that he can one day return to the court and ask directly about the Grail.[19] But he never gets the opportunity to do so.[20]

The Truth about the Grail and Lance

When Perceval eventually finds his way back to the Grail Castle, having sworn to ask the king the truth about the things he saw there, he sees not just the glorious Holy Grail[21] and the Bleeding Lance, as before, but also a naked sword which is broken across the middle. With the king repeatedly exhorting him to eat, Perceval is uncertain as to what he should ask about first. But he eventually asks for the truth about the Lance and the Grail—Who is served *from* it, what is done *with* it?[22]—adding that, after he has explained all that, the king should also tell him whether the sword will ever be repaired and drawn in battle.[23]

The king replies that he will not tell him about the Grail and Lance until he has eaten, but invites him to set the pieces of the sword together so that it becomes whole, apart from a small notch.[24] Now at last Perceval asks the king the questions that he failed to ask on his first, fateful visit: Where the Grail that he's seen was being carried to; who was served from it; and why the Lance was bleeding[25]?

But the king explains that, until he has fully repaired the Sword, Perceval cannot learn the truth about the Grail and the Lance; only then will all the secrets be revealed. Perceval's failure is due to his lack of consideration towards his mother (the

Fisher King's aunt), and he must return to his family home.[26] There Perceval is reunited with his younger sister and, for the first time, prays for forgiveness at his mother's tomb.

It is not until he goes to the Grail Castle for the third time that he can try once again to get the answers he seeks, after fully repairing the Sword (an indication that he has finally expiated his faults). Here Perceval asks the king where the Lance, the Holy Grail and the silver trencher come from and whom they serve[27]; he also asks about the girls who bear the Grail and trencher.

And now, for the first time, Perceval hears the truth he has been seeking for so many years: The Lance is the one with which Longinus struck Jesus on the Cross; the Grail is the vessel in which Joseph of Arimathea caught the Holy Blood, and it was covered with the trencher.[28] Joseph brought the Grail Hallows to Britain and his family, including the Maimed King himself, is its guardian. The girl who bears the Grail is the Maimed King's daughter; the girl who carries the trencher, the daughter of his brother, Gon of the Land Laid Waste, who was killed treacherously by the Sword of Partinal. That sword broke with the force of the blow, and Gon's brother, in his distress, maimed himself with the shards. It is this sword that Perceval has finally succeeded in making whole and, by doing so, he has demonstrated that he alone can avenge the wrong that has been done.[29]

The Grail Question has finally been answered; and the Quest now becomes one for vengeance.

* * *

The mysteries of the Grail raise innumerable questions about its origin and meaning, not least of which is the question that the Grail Hero is supposed to ask, the failure to do so provoking calamity—for the question gradually changes and, with it, the hoped-for answer. When Manessier finally brings the French verse Story of the Grail to its long-drawn-out conclusion, he has reduced it to a vengeance quest, as it is in the Welsh Romance of Peredur. Meanwhile, the French prose Vulgate and Post-Vulgate cycles dispense with the questions altogether, in favor of a quest to be worthy to see inside the Holy Vessel: For Galahad, who alone does so, questions are irrelevant, for he now *knows* what cannot be spoken.

It is left to the German version of Wolfram von Eschenbach to rescue the Grail Question from Manessier's unworthy conclusion by providing an alternative ending: one in which Parzival asks his uncle what ails him, and thus makes the question one of compassion.[30] It is this quality which Wagner put at the heart of his operatic treatment of the subject, seeing it as the essence of both Buddhism and Christianity.

For the esotericist Julius Evola, the problem is the "indifference" which the hero feels, faced with the suffering of the king. What really matters, he writes, is not to uncover the provenance of the talismans in the Procession, but rather to feel the tragedy of the king's situation: "once one achieves that inner realization, the symbol of which is the vision of the Grail, what matters is to assume the initiative of the absolute action that brings about a restoration." The "dignity" that is conferred on the Grail Hero carries with it an obligation: "To ask is the equivalent of stating the problem."[31]

But according to Wolfram, Parzival asks another question when he first returns to the house of the Maimed King: Where is the Grail?[32] "Once this question is asked," writes Evola, "a miracle ensues."[33]

The nature of this miracle is expounded by Mircea Eliade in his first lecture at Eranos, where scholars have for nearly a century continued to meet to explore the archetypal significance of symbols in culture, religion and science.[34] In his 1950 lecture, Eliade relates the Grail Question to the symbolism of the sacred center: The few words of the question suffice "to regenerate the whole of Nature" because they propose "the central question, the one question that can arouse not only the Fisher King but the whole Cosmos: Where is the supreme reality, the sacred, the Center of Life and the source of immortality...? No one had thought, until then, of asking that central question—and the world was perishing...."

Here Eliade combines motifs from French and German verse romances, but then goes beyond the medieval texts to give us what is essentially a Grail Question for the twentieth century: Where is the sacred center of our being in a secular, scientific age? To renew the life of the cosmos, *it is enough only to raise the question of salvation.*[35] And this is what the Eranos scholars have been doing, since the Thirties; it is perhaps too early to judge their success or otherwise.

Notes

1. CSG 16.
2. *Coment ceste chose avenoit* (RP l.3205).
3. *Del graal cui l'en en servoit* (RP l.3245).
4. In the equivalent episode in the Prose *Perceval*, the Fisher King does his best to prompt the youth, but to no avail, much to the king's distress. He has had the Grail presented to all the knights who lodge in his castle, because Christ has told him he would never be healed until the finest knight in the world asks him what it is for: *il ne seroit ja garis devant que uns cevaliers aroit demandé que on en servoit: et cel cevalier covenoit estre le mellor del monde* (RG 246). Perceval is the very knight destined to accomplish the task, and he would have healed the king if he had asked the question (MG 141-2).
5. *De la lance por qu'ele saine,// Et del graal ou l'en le porte* (RP ll.3399, 3401).
6. *Or me dites se vos veïstes/ La lance dont la pointe saine,/ Et si n'i a ne char ne vaine.// Et demandastes vos por coi/ Ele sainoit?* (RP ll.3548-10, 3552-3).
7. *Qu'en en faisoit, n'u on le porte* (RP l.3605).
8. CSG 28-32.
9. *Chiez le Roi Pescheor entras,/ Si veïs la lance qui saine,/Et si te fu si tres grant paine/ D'ovrir ta bouche et de parler/ Que tu ne poïs demander/ Por coi cele goute de sanc/ Saut par la pointe del fer blanc;/ Ne del graal que tu veïs/ Ne demandas ne n'enqueïs/ Quel preudome l'en en servoit* (RP ll.4652-61).
10. CSG 41-2: In the Romance of Perlesvaus, the Grail Bearer tells King Arthur that as a result of Perceval's failure to ask who was served from the Vessel, the Fisher King has fallen into a grievous languor, all lands are engulfed by war (*Ceste langor li est venue por celui qu'il herberja en son osteil, a qui li saintismes Greaus s'aparut; por ço que cil ne volt demander qui on servoit, totes les terres en furent commeües de guerre*), knights do battle without real cause, and Arthur's valor is waning. The Grail Bearer herself has lost her rich golden tresses and her hair will not return until a knight asks the question properly: *mais jou deving chauve por ço qu'il ne fist le demande ne jamais n'iere cavelue dusqu'a icel eure que chevaliers ira qui mieus fera le demande que cil ne fist, ou chevalier qui le Graal conquerra* (HLG 184; HBG 34-5).
11. *Sire, chiez le Roi Pescheor/ Fui une fois et vi la lance/ Dont li fers saine sanz dotance,/ Et de cele goute de sanc/ Que a le pointe del fer blanc/ Vi pendre, rien n'en demandai./ Onques puis, certes, n'amendai./ Et del graal que je i vi/ Ne sai pas cui on en servi* (RP ll.6372-80).
12. CSG 55-6.
13. CSG 237: In some Mss. of the Second Continuation, after leaving his uncle's hermitage, Perceval travels for three days before encountering a hunter. The man refuses to greet him because he recognizes him as the one who caused so much sorrow to so many people by failing to ask why the Lance bled and whither the Grail was going—*Et la lance ...// Por quel ocoison ele saignoit/ Et le graail u il aloit* (DC ll.78, 80-1)—when he saw them at the court of the Fisher King. If only he had asked, those now in distress would instead know joy, but his own sinfulness prevented him from doing so (100-3).
14. This is the Sword of Partinal (q.v.). The longer and later version of the First Continuation tells of an earlier visit by Gawain to the Grail Castle, during which, in addition to the elements of the procession witnessed by Perceval, he sees a body carried on a bier and a Broken Sword, and hears the Grail Bearer weeping uncontrollably. In contrast to Perceval, Gawain asks the Maimed King the significance of the Grail and the Lance, as well as why the girl weeps, why the bier is carried so, and why the sword was placed on it. But when Gawain fails to make whole the Broken Sword, the king tells him that he has not yet achieved enough as a knight to learn the truth about these mysteries (CSG 108-9).
15. *Sire, une lance vi sainier,/ Si m'en puis molt amervellier;/ Si me dites, por Diu amor,/ Dont li sans vient qui cort entor./ Et de l'espee et de la biere* (PCP ll.7421-5). We will learn, although Gawain apparently never does so, that the sword is the one that was used to kill Gon of the Land Laid Waste, the Fisher King's brother, and that it is Gon's body on the bier.
16. CSG 217.
17. *C'estoit li roiames destruis,/ Qui de tos biens ert nus et vuis/ Le soir avant, mais Dex avoit/ Rendu la nuit, si con devoit,/ As aiges leur cors el païs./ Et tot li bois.../ Furent en verdor retorné/ Si tos com il ot demandé/ Por coi seinoit issi la lance* (PCP ll.7757-65).
18. *Del Graal por quoi il servoit* (PCP l.7779). Alternatively, the question is the purpose of the

Grail, what it is for: *Du Graal, de quoi il servoit* (*CP* II, l.17845): "Certes, greatly should we hate thee, in that thou didst not ask concerning the Grail and the service thereof. None may tell the joy that should have followed on thy asking" (*GGC* 29).

19. *CSG* 219-20.

20. This at least is the case in the French Grail romances. But, in *The Crown* of Heinrich von dem Türlin, Gawain, like Perceval, fails to ask about the mysteries in the Grail Castle on his first visit (*HTC* 168). But, on his return, primed by the Grail Bearer, he finally asks the meaning of what he sees and thereby fully completes the Grail Quest (327-30).

21. *Qui tant est gloriëux et sains* (*CP* IV, l.32424).

22. *Cui an an sert et qu'an an fet* (*CP* IV, l.32433). In his edition of the Second Continuation, Francis Gingras prefers the reading of a different base manuscript, changing the first part of the question to a more general one about the service the Grail performs—*Que an an sert* (*DC* l.13044)—rather than a more specific (and redundant) one about the old king who is served from it, which Perceval's hermit uncle has already answered.

23. According to the *Elucidation*, when Perceval returns to the court of the Fisher King, he asks what is done with the Grail, but fails to ask why the Lance that he sees is bleeding, or anything about the sword: *Cil enquist de coi li Grëaus/ Servoit, mais pas ne demanda/ De la lance por coi sainna/ Quant il le vit, ne de l'espee* (*EB* ll.248-51). He also asks who the dead man on the bier is (*CSG* 559).

24. *CSG* 336-7.

25. *Del Graal que il porter voit / Ou va ne qui on en servoit / Et de la Lance por coi saine* (*GCP* ll.7-9): The first two questions have already been answered by Perceval's uncle, but only Gawain so far has learnt the truth about the Lance.

26. *CSG* 339.

27. *Cui l'an an sert et don il vienent* (*MTC* l.32645). In the Prose *Perceval* the Question our hero asks on his second and last visit to the court of the Fisher King is the purpose of the things he sees: *que on sert de ces coses que je voi* (*RG* 269). The Fisher King, who is instantly cured of his sickness, replies that the Lance is the one with which Longinus struck Christ on the Cross: "And this vessel, called the Grail, holds the blood that Joseph gathered as it flowed from His wounds to the earth" (*MG* 154-5).

28. The Grail and trencher thus correspond to the wine-filled chalice and covering paten in the sacrament of the Eucharist (*MTC* 69n12).

29. *CSG* 477-9.

30. This, of course, is quite different to Chrétien's original question, *whom* does the Grail serve? But since Perceval's hermit-uncle has answered this question, it has ceased to be relevant; and, in any case, no-one seems to be quite sure of its significance.

31. Evola 1997, 122.

32. *saget mir wâ der grâl hie lige* (*PKL* 795.21): "Tell me where the Grail lies here?" (*PT* 333; *WP* 394). For Evola (1997, 123), this means: Where is the sacral power of the Hyperborean sacred center, which the king should represent, but with which he has lost contact (see AFTERWORD: HIGHER MYSTERIES).

33. Evola 1997, 123.

34. See Hakl (2013).

35. Eliade 1991, 56: His conclusion will be echoed by Henry Corbin, in a later Eranos lecture (1983, 260).

The GRAIL STONE

Having won the love of the Queen of Belrepaire, the young hero Parzival comes to a castle on Mount Savage where he witnesses an elaborate procession in the court of the Maimed King, Anfortas.

After watching a page carrying a Lance from whose steel blood runs down to his hand, Parzival witnesses a procession of twenty-four ladies, culminating with a princess with a countenance shining like daybreak, carrying the fulfillment of the desire of the heart: something transcendent, more of Paradise than of earth![1] Whatever food or drink one desires in the presence of the Grail, it is found to hand, for the Grail is a cornucopia, providing on Earth what is barely surpassed in Heaven.[2]

Later the hero's uncle, the hermit Trevrizent, tells him that the Grail is a stone called *lapsit exillis*[3]; it restores youth and prevents the person who beholds it from dying for a week afterwards. Every Good Friday a translucent white dove bears a small white wafer to the stone, which enables the Grail to provide its company with all the food and drink that the earth is capable of bringing forth. But the highest power of the Grail is the divine messages that appear on it, naming those who will serve it; when those who are summoned arrive and read their names, the writing disappears.[4]

The pagan astrologer Flegetanis first spoke about the Grail Stone, having read its name in the constellations. He divined that it was abandoned on the Earth by a host of angels,[5] those who were neutral during the War in Heaven, when Lucifer fought against the Trinity; but God sent his loyal angel to one appointed to care for it.[6]

The first man so appointed is Titurel, the Lord of Mount Savage, who, when he grows old, entrusts it to his son Frimutel. When he dies in battle, the Grail passes to Frimutel's son Anfortas. But Anfortas ignores the divine law that the Grail Lords must remain chaste and, as a consequence, is pierced through the genitals by a Lance engraved with the name of the Grail, wielded by a pagan warrior. Moreover, when he is carried into the presence of the Stone, Anfortas experiences a *second* blow: He cannot die, nor can his suffering ever cease, the Grail writes, unless a knight comes and asks a Question unprompted.

Hearing his uncle's account, Parzival knows that he was the knight who came and failed to ask what would have ended Anfortas' suffering.[7] But the Stone will later announce him as its new lord and, on his return to Mount Savage, after asking where the Grail is and genuflecting thrice in its direction, he asks Anfortas what ails him. The Maimed King is forthwith restored to wholeness and wellness.[8] Parzival has inherited the Grail Stone,[9] and his son Loherangrin is also dedicated to its service.[10]

* * *

The legend of the Grail Stone as presented by Wolfram von Eschenbach was elaborated after him by other, lesser German poets, who incorporated popular but apocryphal beliefs so that it underwent "some strange transformations." Thus, in a poem from the late thirteenth century, it is claimed that the Grail was once a jewel which was set in the crown of Lucifer, but which fell to Earth when St. Michael tore the crown from his head and shattered it after his rebellion.[11] According to the late thirteenth century poet Albrecht, the Stone that the neutral angels brought to Earth is later fashioned by human hands into a dish—the very dish that Jesus uses to serve the lamb at the Last Supper and which is preserved thereafter by Joseph of Arimathea.[12] An angel brings it to Titurel so that it can be guarded by his knights in the Grail Kingdom.[13]

As S.R. Wilson points out, Albrecht effectively reconciles two apparently conflicting conceptions of the Grail: that of Robert de Boron, as the Vessel of the Last Supper; and that of Wolfram, as the Stone fallen from Heaven: "Perhaps we can say that Albrecht conceives of a Grail which belongs to an esoteric tradition which is older than Christianity but which also reaches its highest expression in that religion."[14] For Wilson, this tradition is preserved in a "Grail-centered community" which "lives a kind of esoteric, inner Christianity, existing parallel to Church-based religion but in no way in competition with it."[15]

Indeed, Albrecht's account becomes the basis of an esoteric legend, recounted by René Guénon, in which the Grail is fashioned by angels from an emerald that falls from the forehead of Lucifer at the time of his expulsion from Heaven. According to Guénon, the idea that it fell from his crown is due to a confusion resulting from the fact that Lucifer before his fall was known in the Hebrew Kabbalah as the Angel of the Crown.[16]

Lucifer's emerald, Guénon continues, corresponds to the Third Eye, or what in the Hindu Tradition is called the Eye of Shiva (corresponding to the pineal gland). It represents the "sense of eternity" that is characteristic of the prelapsarian "primordial state." The first stage of an authentic initiation into the Hyperborean Tradition restores this sense.[17]

The search for the Grail Stone is thus an initiatory quest to restore the primordial state of humanity, at one with the eternal in the Earthly Paradise. It is fitting, therefore, that Albrecht considers the last resting place of the Grail to be the kingdom of Prester John, whose palace stands near the Earthly Paradise.[18]

Notes

1. *WP* 125: "Upon a green achmardi she carried the perfection of Paradise, both root and branch. This was a thing that was called the Grail, earth's

perfection's transcendence" (*PT* 99–100): *ûf einem grüenen achmardî/ truoc si den wunsch von pardîs,/ bêde wurzeln unde rîs./ daz was ein dinc, daz hiez der Grâl,/ erden wunsches überwal* (*PKL* 235.20–4): "Root and blossom of Paradise garden, that thing which men call *The Grail,/* The crown of all earthly wishes, fair fulness that ne'er shall fail!" (Weston 1913, 146).

2. *WP* 126–7; *PT* 101.
3. This corrupt Latin phrase is sometimes understood to mean "it fell from heaven" (*lapsit ex coelis*). But it has also been read as *lapis exilis* (an "insignificant" stone in the eyes of fools, but cherished by the wise) or *lapis elixir*, alchemical terms denoting the Philosopher's Stone (Jung & Franz, 148–50).
4. *WP* 239–40; *PT* 198.
5. *WP* 232; *PT* 192.
6. *WP* 240; *PT* 198–9.
7. *WP* 242–7; *PT* 200–4.
8. *WP* 394–5; *PT* 333.
9. *WP* 398; *PT* 336.
10. *WP* 407; *PT* 344.
11. Barber 2005, 190–1.
12. Thus we learn from Robert de Boron that it is the Vessel in which Jesus "made the sacrament" at the Last Supper, and which Joseph of Arimathea used to collect the blood that was dripping from His wounds on the Cross (*MG* 18–19). Later the risen Christ tells Joseph that, when he performs the sacrament of the Mass at the Table of the Grail, the "vessel of the sacrament" will commemorate the stone tomb in which Joseph laid Jesus' body (22), but in the poetic version of this scene the Vessel is clearly identified with the communion chalice (see THE GRAIL CHALICE).
13. Barber 2005, 193.
14. Wilson, 149*n*27.
15. Wilson, 149.
16. Guénon 1983, 26*n*5. Kabbalah is a school of Jewish mysticism which has been adopted and adapted by some Christian esotericists.
17. Guénon 1983, 26. See HYPERBOREA and AFTERWORD: HIGHER MYSTERIES.
18. Barber 2005, 196.

The GRAIL TEMPLARS

A martial company of formidable warriors dwells on Mount Savage with the Grail Stone, which provides all their nourishment and keeps them youthful-looking, preserving life indefinitely. From there, wearing the turtle-dove device of Mount Savage on their shields, they ride out on adventure, keeping the sacred Temple safe from intruders; for only those the Grail has summoned may join its company.[1]

Although vowed to chastity, they are sometimes required to marry if requested to take over the rulership of a land that has lost its lord. Their identity as Grail Templars must always be kept a secret, however; whereas the Temple maidens (such as Parzival's mother) are bestowed in marriage openly, in the hope that their children will grow up to serve the Grail in turn.[2]

* * *

According to Wolfram von Eschenbach, the knights who guard the Grail Stone are called *templeisen*—they are an obvious echo of the *templeherren*, the Order of the Knights of the Temple of Solomon (1118–1307), more familiar as the Knights Templar, who guarded, and then lost, the sacred sites of the Holy Land. But unlike the historical order, which was monastic and vowed to celibacy, the Grail Templars may marry if there is an heiress in another land who needs a husband.

It is also striking that the emblem of the Grail Templars (the Order of the Knights of the Temple of the Grail, as we might call them) should be a dove, the conventional symbol of the Holy Spirit, the third person of the Trinity. Less conventionally, the ancient Gnostics, who valued knowledge over faith, identified the Holy Spirit with the figure of Sophia, Divine Wisdom. When the historical Templars were persecuted and their Order destroyed at the beginning of the fourteenth century, they were accused among other crimes of embracing heresy and worshipping a being called Baphomet. The nature of this being remains obscure, but it is at least intriguing that the name has been interpreted as code for Sophia.[3]

The suggestion that the Templars had rediscovered—and been infected by—ancient Gnostic heresy was first widely promulgated by the Austrian Orientalist Joseph von Hammer-Purgstall (1774–1856). He claimed, writes Peter Partner, that the Templars took part in "acts of worship" inspired by the legend of the Grail, which was "the symbol of Gnostic illumination," and that

Baphomet was Achamoth (a variant of Sophia, based on the Hebrew word for "wisdom"). These theories "achieved wide posthumous influence."[4]

The connection of the knights with Wisdom and the Grail was explored at the beginning of the twentieth century by the Austrian philosopher Rudolf Steiner, who called the Templars "messengers of the Grail. They built a center of wisdom on the site of Solomon's Temple and after preparation there they became servants of the Holy Grail, were initiated there by the Grail."[5]

But the first leading Arthurian scholar to acknowledge these connections was Jessie L. Weston, who suggested that, while in the East, the Templars might have come into touch with a surviving Gnostic sect, similar to the one whose rituals she considered to have inspired the Grail legend.[6] Moreover, they might have embraced practices which seemed to offer "a more sensible (not necessarily sensuous) contact with the unseen Spiritual forces of Life" than mainstream Christianity: "If it were so," she concludes, "we could understand at once the puzzling connection of the Order with the Knights of the Grail, and the doom which fell upon them."[7]

Notes

1. *PT* 197–9; *WP* 239–41
2. *PT* 208; *WP* 251.
3. Using the Atbash cypher, whereby the first letter of the Hebrew alphabet is substituted for the last, the second for the second-to-last and so on, Baphomet (תמופב) becomes Sophia (איפוש) (Schonfield, 164).
4. Partner, 141–4.
5. Steiner 2007, 43.
6. "If the Templars had acquired the Secret Tradition of the Sources of Life, and the practices connected with that tradition, it is at once clear how they came into the Grail romances, and how they fell under the ban of the Church" (Weston 1909, 299n1). "Were the Templars idolaters? Were they Gnostics? We cannot tell; but I am strongly inclined to believe that the connection between these knights and the Grail ... has a foundation in fact, and that the same influences which brought about the ruin of the one were responsible for the disappearance of the other" (1913, 136)—that is, of the initiatory cult that Weston believed inspired the Grail romances (see AFTERWORD: HIGHER MYSTERIES).
7. Weston 1920, 187; cf. Partner, 168–9.

The GRAIL TEMPLE

When Titurel, a descendant of the Emperor Vespasian, is entrusted by an angel with the Grail, he sets about constructing a temple for it on Mount Savage,[1] following instructions given him by the Holy Vessel itself; everything the builders require is found ready. When the temple is completed, after thirty years, the Grail hovers in the central sacristy.[2]

It is here, in the Grail Temple, that Parzival's pagan half-brother Feirefiz is baptized with water supplied by the Grail, which had hitherto been invisible to him, but which he can now see.[3]

After the departure of Feirefiz and the Grail Bearer to the East, Parzival and Titurel decide to take the Grail itself there, to prevent it from falling into impious hands.[4] On their journey the Grail Templars leave, at one of the cities they pass through, an image of the Temple, which enables the citizens to construct their own.[5] Once the Grail reaches the Indian Kingdom of Prester John,[6] its devotees pray that the Temple which once housed the Holy Vessel should be re-erected there. The next morning, everyone can see that their prayers have been answered.[7]

Notes

1. Before this the Grail is borne by angels, suspended between Heaven and Earth. As such, it can be seen as a symbol of the world of archetypal images, intermediate between the physical world we perceive with our senses and the abstract world we perceive with the intellect.
2. Barber 2005, 193–5: For Albrecht, the author of this account, "the Grail is the center of an ordered and harmonious state, and its temple not only symbolizes that order and harmony, but also the religious function of the Grail as a mediator of salvation." Thus, Wolfram's Munsalvæsche (Mount Savage) becomes Albrecht's Munt Salvatsch (Mount of Salvation) and, later, Wagner's Montsalvat: which, for Henry Corbin (1986, 360), is "the mountain at the center of the world."
3. *PT* 342–3; *WP* 405–6: This is the only occasion

that Wolfram mentions a Temple of the Grail, but its existence is implied by the presence of Templars guarding it.

4. Barber 2005, 196.

5. Corbin 1986, 389: "This *Image* is also what remains to us ... because this Image is imperishable, to the extent that we see it rise triumphant in the 'waste land,' from an earth that is spiritually more devastated than the domain of the Grail ever was before the coming of Parsifal."

6. "The 'India' to which the knights withdraw ... is not one which we can hope to find on the map. Traditionally, the word designates a distant Orient where the realm of the invisible Paradise begins. It would be futile and absurd to identify the Prester John of the Grail cycle with a ruler of this world" (Corbin 1986, 368).

7. Waite 1933, 286; Matthews & Knight, 227: Corbin considers that the Grail Temple was only ever manifested in that world of spiritual images which Islamic mystics call the "intermediary" Orient: "In a single night, the Temple was transferred from this 'intermediary Orient' to the 'Orient' of the metaphysical world." The soul has returned to its spiritual home (1986, 367–8).

GUENEVERE

When Galahad first comes to King Arthur's court, Queen Guenevere is quick to recognize him as the son of her beloved Lancelot, who had been tricked into fathering a child on the daughter of the Rich Fisher King.[1] It is the queen who reveals to Galahad the truth about his parentage, calling his father the world's best knight. But she is extremely distraught when she realized that Lancelot is going on the Grail Quest, from which she fears he will never return.[2]

* * *

The role of the Queen of Logres in the Grail Quest is essentially a negative one: She is seen as part of the problem, not part of the solution. Her jealousy when Lancelot fathers Galahad on the Grail Bearer drives him mad and, although he is healed by the Holy Vessel, his adulterous love for her means that he can never achieve the summit of spiritual chivalry.[3]

Notes

1. *LG* IV, 6; V, 117–8; *QHG* 39: *Sir Launcelot begate hym on Kynge Pelles doughter, which made hym to lye by her by enchauntemente* (*MD* 670). She later says that Lancelot is of the eighth degree and that *thys Sir Galahad ys of the nyneth degré frome Oure Lorde Jesu Cryst* (673). In Malory's source, the Vulgate *Queste*, Lancelot and Galahad are the eighth and ninth descendants of Celidoine (q.v.), not of Christ!

2. *LG* IV, 9–10; V, 121–2, 124; *MD* 675–7; *QHG* 46–8, 50–1.

3. After a squire tells Lancelot that he has been "bewitched" by the queen—*bien estes enfantosmez* (*QP* 118)—a hermit tells him that the Devil entered into Guenevere and "encouraged her to glance longingly" at him when he was first knighted (*LG* IV, 38, 41; *QHG* 136, 142–3). In the Post-Vulgate version, he dreams that he sees Guenevere in Hell, warning him to repent. His parents then appear to him to say that his adultery with Guenevere will bring him to "eternal death" unless he leaves that sin (*LG* V, 173–4).

H

HECTOR of the Fens

The illegitimate brother of Lancelot of the Lake, Hector is conceived through the magic of Merlin. He is vouchsafed a vision of the Holy Grail when near death, and cured of his wounds by its miraculous powers; but this happens before the inauguration of the Quest, in which he will be dishonored.

He has been travelling with little rest for a couple of years, searching for his lost brother during one of Lancelot's periodic episodes of madness, when he comes across Perceval, who is also engaged in the search. Unfortunately, they do not recognize each other as companions of the Round Table so, as is the way in Arthur's Britain, they immediately start fighting. Their combat only ceases when they are forced to rest at the point of death.

However, at that moment a miracle occurs: They are mystified to see a great brightness like a second sun descend upon them.[1] But they realize it is a chalice covered in white samite, although they cannot see anyone carrying it; so, they recognize it as something holy. Instinctively bowing down before it, they are instantly restored to health; at which point it vanishes away.[2]

Although this is the first time that either knight has seen it, Hector knows what it is. He explains to Perceval that they have witnessed the Vessel in which Jesus and his disciples ate the paschal lamb at the Last Supper—a Vessel which was brought to Logres by Joseph of Arimathea and which continues to feed his descendants and those of his companions including, in the present day, the household of King Pelles.[3] This wondrous truth leads Perceval to swear that he will never rest easy until he has seen it plainly.[4] This is something Perceval will eventually achieve, although Hector himself will not be so lucky.

Later, after the Knights of the Round Table have all set off in search of the Vessel, Hector teams up for a while with Gawain. When they fall asleep in an ancient, deserted chapel, Hector has a dream in which he and his brother Lancelot say to each other that they are seeking what they shall never find. In the dream, they come to a spring whose water recedes from them as they try to drink from it, while Hector is refused entry to the house of a rich man who is holding a wedding feast.

When they awaken, Hector and Gawain both see a hand enter the chapel; it is covered in red silk, holding a candle of great radiance, and from it hangs a bridle. After the hand disappears, they hear a voice proclaiming that they are men of little faith who will gain no honor from the Quest, because they lack the three things they have just seen.[5]

Neither of them understands what this means, so they make their way to the chapel of the hermit Nascien, who explains to Hector that the spring in his dream symbolizes the grace of the Holy Spirit: It will never be exhausted, no matter how deeply one draws from it; rather, the more it gives, the more remains.[6] But this grace will be denied him, as he will discover when he comes to the house of the Fisher King—the rich man of his dream. As for the hand in the chapel, it represents charity; the red silk, the fire of the Holy Spirit; and the bridle, restraint. These three qualities Hector lacks; that is why he will never attain this quest.[7]

As it transpires, Hector arrives at the Grail Castle while his brother Lancelot is there, but is refused entrance. As he leaves Corbenic, mortified by the jeers of the townsfolk, he realizes the truth of the hermit's prediction.[8]

Notes

1. *Au point qu'il erent en tel peril et an tele angoisse qu'il cuidoient vraiement morir virent vers els venir une clarté si grant come se li soulaux descendist sus aux; si se mervillerent moult que ce pooit estre* (LM VI, 204).
2. In Malory's version, Sir Percivale's virginity enables him to see more than Sir Ector: *Ryght so ther cam by the holy vessell ... wyth all maner of swetnesse and savoure, but they cowde nat se redyly who bare the vessell. But Sir Percyvale had a glemerynge of the vessell and of the mayden that bare hit, for he was a perfyte mayden. And furthwithall they were as hole of hyde and lymme as ever they were in theire lyff* (MD 643).
3. *Sachiez vraiement que ce est li sainz Graaux par qui tantes mervilleuses aventures sont avenues el reaume de Logres. Et en maintes autres terres a Nostre Sires monstré por amor de lui mains granz miracles* (LM VI, 205). According to Malory's Sir Ector: *Hit is an holy vessell that is borne by a mayden, and therein ys a parte of the bloode of Oure Lorde Jesu Cryste. But hit may nat be sene ... but yff hit be by a perfyte man* (MD 643). In a version of this episode recounted by Manessier, it is Perceval who has to explain to Hector what they have witnessed.
4. LG III, 327–9.
5. QHG 164–6; LG IV, 48–9; V, 154–5: *et por ce ne poez vos avenir as aventures dou Saint Graal* (QP

151); *and therefore ye may nat com to the aventures of the Sankgreall!* (MD 725).
  6. *ce est li Sainz Graax, les secrees choses Nostre Seignor ... ce est la grace del Saint Esperit ... ce est la grace del Saint Graal ... le Saint Vessel* (QP 158-9); *c'est la grace Nostre Seignor* (QSG 406); *grete prevydence of the Sankgreall* (MD 729).
  7. QHG 171-4; LG IV, 51; V, 157-8.
  8. QHG 266-7; LG IV, 81-2; V, 267-9; MD 776-7.

HELAIN the White

The illegitimate son of Sir Bors and the daughter of King Brandegorre, Helain is made a Knight of the Round Table on the very day that Galahad takes his place unscathed on the Perilous Seat, thus inaugurating the Quest.[1]

Riding on the Quest in the company of Gawain and Hector, Helain, who has received many wounds in battle with the Knight of the Questing Beast, has an astonishing vision when the three knights spend the night in a ruined chapel: Hearing heavenly singing and smelling the fragrance of spices, he witnesses angelic creatures lifting the lid off a stone sepulcher. A naked old woman, clothed only in her white hair which falls to the ground, emerges therefrom, while a radiant man dressed as a bishop descends from Heaven to give her the Host.

When the woman returns to her sepulcher and the bishop to on high, the chapel is dark and silent once more. But Helain realizes that his wounds are healed, indicating that the things he has seen are sacred and of the spirit. When his companions awake, he tells them about these wondrous occurrences. Hector announces that he too has been healed of injuries he sustained earlier. Gawain declares that these are truly signs from God, high wonders of the Holy Grail, pure things of Holy Church.[2] He and Hector agree that Helain is more worthy of the Quest than they.[3] Indeed, so it will prove, since Helain is one of the twelve knights who arrive at Corbenic to witness the accomplishing of the adventure of the Holy Grail.[4]

Notes

1. LG V, 116.
2. *Verdadeiramente sam demostradas de Nosso Senhor e sam altas maravilhas do Santo Graal, e sam as grandes puridades da Santa Egreja* (PV II, 200-1).
3. LG V, 152-3.
4. LG V, 278-9.

HELIZABEL

The daughter of King Pelles of Corbenic is, for reasons that are not at first apparent, baptized with one name (Helizabel) but known by another.[1] She is so beautiful that only two women can compare with her: Guenevere and Elaine the Peerless,[2] the Lady of Gazevilte.[3] It is not therefore surprising that the plan her father and governess hatch to seduce Lancelot is successful.

* * *

Although we have no way of knowing whether the romance authors were aware of it, it is significant that Helizabel is a variant of the Biblical Elizabeth[4]: For this is the name of the mother of John the Baptist in the Gospel of Luke, John being the prophet of the coming of Jesus. The Princess of Corbenic's hidden name therefore hints at the Christ-like nature of her son, Galahad: He is the man who is destined to sit on the Perilous Seat, which corresponds to the place of Jesus at the Table of the Last Supper.

However, in some manuscripts she is described as the sister of Perlesvaus (Perceval) and their father, Pelles, as the Maimed King. There it is her brother rather than her son who is destined to bring to an end the adventures of the perilous Kingdom of Logres.[5]

Notes

1. That is, Amite in the Vulgate or Elaine in the Post-Vulgate and Malory.
2. After the initial discussion of her names, the daughter of King Pelles is never referred to by name in the Vulgate Cycle; her naming as Elaine in the Post-Vulgate may be, therefore, due to confusion with Elaine the Peerless.
3. LG II, 16.

4. Walter 2014, 212.
5. *LDL* I, 122: This suggests an earlier stage in the development of the Prose *Lancelot*, as what has been called a "non-cyclic" romance—that is, before it was expanded into the Vulgate *Lancelot-Grail* Cycle—and which is therefore closer to the romances in verse (in which Perceval is the Grail winner) and to the prose *Perlesvaus*.

HELYAS

The Master Helyas is the author of the Tale of the Cry, a lost "branch" of the Grail story, which he translated from Latin into French at the request of his companion-at-arms Robert de Boron.[1] This is an indispensable section of the story, without which one cannot claim to have grasped the whole.[2]

Notes

1. *LG* IV, 221.
2. *LG* IV, 254.

HYPERBOREA

It is said that, at the beginning of the current cycle of humanity, the supreme spiritual center is a sacred island situated at the North Pole, the White Island,[1] on which stands the mountain of the Earthly Paradise, Montsalvat.[2] From it flow four rivers,[3] one of which encircles the Grail Castle, which is called Eden.[4]

This island is known in the West as Ultima Thule or Hyperborea, "the land beyond the North Wind." The priest-king who rules it, the Lord of the World, combines in his person spiritual authority and temporal power. Here dwell the Golden Race, who do not know death, until a shift in the inclination of Earth's axis[5] causes an endless frozen night to descend on their polar homeland.[6]

Forced to migrate from their ancestral paradise, the Hyperboreans colonize other parts of the world, eventually creating a second spiritual center on an island in the Western Ocean, remembered as Avalon or the Fortunate Isle. It is from there, that there come to Ireland the god-peoples,[7] bringing with them their four treasures: the Stone of Sovereignty; the Spear of Invincibility; the Sword from which none escape; and the Cauldron from which none go unsatisfied.[8] Indeed, it is said that it is in the most beautiful of the isles of Ireland[9] that the Fisher King dwells; it is in his castle that Perceval first sees the Grail Lance and Vessel.[10]

Others tell how Gawain comes to an island where he sees, in the hall of the king, a Vessel that feeds abundantly all who are there; a Lance that bleeds; and a Broken Sword that can only be repaired by the worthiest of knights. He learns that he is on the White Island, a part of what is now England, surrounded by the sea.[11] This island, he is told, had been promised by God to Joseph of Arimathea as a safe refuge for himself, his followers and the Grail, which feeds them when they are in need.[12]

Notes

1. Guénon 1983, 57–8: This cycle, lasting some 64,000 years, is known in Hinduism as a Mahayuga, comprising the four ages of man familiar from Greek mythology as the Ages of Gold, Silver, Bronze and—our current age—that of Iron, also known as the Kali Yuga or Dark Age (Godwin 1993a, 16–8).
2. Guénon 1983, 49–50.
3. The four rivers of Paradise are also found in Hindu mythology (Godwin 1993a, 20).
4. *HBG* 195.
5. "Numerous authorities ... assure us that in primordial times the earth was not tilted, but spun perfectly upright with its equator in the same plane as the ecliptic; or, which comes to the same thing, with its axis perpendicular to the plane of its orbit around the sun." The catastrophe which ended this "geometrical perfection" is expressed by the Myth of the Fall, of which it is the geographical and historical reflection (Godwin 1993a, 13).
6. In the Primordial Tradition, there is no dualistic opposition of the spiritual and the material; the symbolic is real and reality, symbolic; history and meta-history are images of each other: "This is precisely the point at which it is possible to enter into the events conditioned by time." The tilting of the Earth on its axis is both a physical and a metaphysical event, disorder in nature being the reflection of "an event of a spiritual nature" (Evola 1995, 188–9).
7. Evola 1995, 195: Alternatively, the treasures come from "four mysterious cities in the north of the world" (Williams 2016, 148).
8. Williams 2016, 149.
9. *MG* 113.
10. *MG* 141.
11. The discrepancy between our sources as to

I

INDIA

Although he was brought up a pagan, Parzival's half-brother Feirefiz converts to Christianity in order to see the Grail and marry its bearer; the couple then travel to the East. Although the Grail Stone itself remains at first in its temple on Mount Savage, Feirefiz and his bride carry the Christian message to India. Their son, who will found a dynasty of Christian Kings of the East, is Prester John.[1]

Later, Parzival himself and his great-grandfather Titurel also make the journey from Mount Savage to India, bearing with them the Grail[2]; moreover, the Temple in which it is housed is itself transported there, overnight.[3] It is in India, in Prester John's Land, that the Grail will henceforth reside.

* * *

In the Arthurian romances, India is a fantastical realm, found beyond the River of Purgatory, where is situated the Earthly Paradise and the Fountain of Eternal Youth.

For Henry Corbin, the Grail's journey to the East (like its voyage from Corbenic to Sarras in the Vulgate *Queste*) is not a question of the physical transportation of a sacred relic from one geographical location to another. The Temple of the Grail was only ever manifest in what Corbin has called the *imaginal* world, the intermediate realm between the physical and the spiritual, on the threshold of the world of soul: "It was not and could not be 'incarnated' in this world, in the sense that this word is misused today."[4] It could only be incarnated in the *mundus imaginalis*, the Otherworld of the Soul.

For Corbin, the Grail is an image of Christian esotericism: The departure of the Grail from the West to the East, then, symbolizes the triumph of exoteric, legalistic religion in the West and a re-orientation of the western imagination: "The transference of the Temple to India is the return of the soul to its country of origin."[5]

Notes

1. *WP* 408; *PT* 344–5.
2. Barber 2005, 196.
3. Matthews & Knight, 227.
4. Corbin 1986, 367.
5. Corbin 1986, 368.

J

JOSEPH OF ARIMATHEA

A soldier in the service of Pilate when he was Roman governor of Judaea, Joseph is a secret follower of Jesus who only reveals himself after the crucifixion and suffers the wrath of the Jews.

When the news comes of the death of

Jesus, Joseph goes to Pilate and asks for a reward for his long service. When Pilate says he will give him whatever he wishes, Joseph asks for the body of the prophet whom, he believes, the Jews have wrongfully put to death.

Pilate agrees to this and also gives him a Vessel that was handed over to him by one of the Jews who were present at the capture of Jesus.[1] This was the Vessel in which Jesus had made the sacrament at the Last Supper[2]; and this, Joseph uses to collect the blood that drips from the hands and feet of Jesus as he takes Him down from the Cross. He then has Jesus buried; but the stone tomb is guarded by a crowd of Jews who are fearful that Jesus will come back to life again, as predicted by His disciples.

And so it transpires: Jesus descends into Hell on Easter Saturday, harries the demons, and sets free their undeserving prisoners. He then emerges from the tomb, unseen by those who are standing guard, to appear to Mary Magdalen and other of His disciples. When the Jews guarding the tomb realize that the body has vanished, they decide to kill Joseph and then say that they gave the body to him, so that no one could blame them if Jesus comes to life again.

Accordingly, they abduct Joseph from his house, where he has safeguarded the Vessel. Locking him in the dungeon of a tower, they seal it with a stone so that it will become his tomb. However, a wondrous light appears, which fills him with the grace of the Holy Spirit: Jesus Himself stands before him in the dungeon, saying that He will reward Joseph for his fidelity by making him the keeper of the sign of His death.

With these words, Our Lord shows Joseph the Vessel containing the Holy Blood which Joseph had gathered[3] from Jesus' wounds when he washed Him in preparation for burial. When Joseph sees the Vessel, he at once recognizes it as the one he had hidden in his house. But, because no one apart from himself could ever have known it was there, his faith is strengthened.[4]

The First Grail Keeper

Our Lord tells Joseph that the Holy Vessel will have three keepers, corresponding to the three powers that constitute the One God; all who remain in the presence of the Vessel will experience lasting joy and their soul's fulfillment. Jesus goes on to speak other words to Joseph which cannot be repeated, words that are written in the High Book that constitutes the Grail Credo.[5] He then gives the Holy Vessel to Joseph, saying that whenever he seeks counsel, he will hear through it the voice of the Holy Spirit.

Joseph spends a long time in prison,[6] before being released by the Roman Vespasian[7] who, having been cured of leprosy by the Veil of Veronica, is eager to avenge the death of the prophet whose image has such miraculous powers. He forces the Jews to reveal where Joseph was imprisoned, and is delighted to find him still alive; moreover, he converts to Christianity[8] and pardons all those Jews who will do the same.

Leaving Jerusalem with the new converts, including his sister Enigeus and her husband Bron, Joseph sets his followers to work upon the land. But after a while their harvests start to fail them and they are close to starving.[9]

Joseph prays to the Grail, whereupon the Holy Spirit informs him that he must make a table in the name of the Table of the Last Supper. There, Joseph must sit in the place corresponding to that occupied by Christ, leaving an empty seat on his right hand to represent the place of Judas. This empty place will correspond to the Perilous Seat in a third table, to be built by Merlin for Uther Pendragon (the famous Round Table); either seat can only be occupied by the grandson of Bron. The importance of this injunction is brought home to everyone when a convert called Moses insists on sitting in the empty seat and is swallowed up into the abyss.

Joseph is also instructed to send his brother-in-law to fish on the water and bring back the first thing he catches. Joseph then presides over the first Feast of the Grail, from which the lustful are excluded by the power of the Holy Vessel, so that this becomes the first place in which it is tested.

Following the voice of the Holy Spirit, Joseph tells Bron to put Alan the Fat, his youngest son, in charge of all his other children and lead them abroad to spread the gospel of Christ. The Holy Spirit also tells Joseph to send his disciple Peter to the vales of Avalon with a letter explaining the power of the Grail; Joseph should also entrust the Holy Vessel itself to Bron, who is to go into the West, where his line will be exalted forever. Both Peter and Bron must await the coming of Alan's son: he who is destined to be the third guardian of the Grail, thus completing a sign of the Trinity.

The next day Joseph entrusts to Bron privately, in writing, the words given to him by Christ when he was in prison, the holy words of the Grail sacrament.[10] Three days later, the Rich Fisherman, as Bron is now known, departs for the West. He ends his days in a beautiful palace in an Irish island, awaiting the coming of his grandson Perceval, to whom he will pass on the Secret Words of Christ and hand over the Grail. Joseph himself, however, like the Biblical Moses, is destined never to reach the Promised Land of the Grail, for he ends his days in the land where he was born.[11]

The Promised Land

Some say that, after burying Jesus, Joseph keeps the Lance with which His side had been pierced, as well as the Holy Vessel in which those who believe in Him had collected His blood,[12] and that he is imprisoned by Pilate.[13]

It is also said that Joseph is the first person to see the Lord, after His body leaves the sepulcher in which Joseph had deposited Him. The Savior appears to him, bringing the Holy Dish containing the blood which Joseph had gathered, to provide him with both comfort and company.[14] He reassures Joseph that he will neither suffer nor die in prison, but that he will live, so that he and his descendants can carry His name to foreign places.

Joseph spends forty-two years in prison,[15] and is only freed when Vespasian forces the High Priest Caiaphas to reveal his whereabouts. At Joseph's intercession, Vespasian spares the life of Caiaphas, but sets him adrift at sea on a rowboat. Joseph, who has not aged while in prison, is reunited with his wife Elyab, now an old lady, and with his son Josephus, who is now grown up.

The night before Vespasian is obliged to return to Rome, Christ appears again to Joseph, telling him to have himself baptized and to leave Jerusalem, never to return, taking with him nothing of value except the Grail. The next day Joseph is baptized by the Apostle Philip and he also sponsors the secret baptism of Vespasian.

When he first leaves Jerusalem, Joseph takes the road to the Euphrates and comes to a wood near Bethany. Here he is commanded by God the Father to build an ark to contain the sacred Dish, which only he and Josephus should look on directly; after his people have prayed before it, they leave the wood and travel on to the city of Sarras. From this city come the first Saracens, worshippers of the heavenly bodies (whom Joseph will also encounter later in Britain). The Lord commands Joseph to convert them to Christianity. He and his company are received by the King of Sarras, Evalach the Unknown,[16] and, while they are there, Josephus is invested as a priest of Christ.

When Joseph and his company leave Sarras, after converting the king and his people to Christianity, they go where chance takes them, crossing the Euphrates and travelling through many lands. One winter's night, when Joseph and his wife are lying chastely together in a wood, a divine voice commands them to have sex, declaring that the child born from their coupling will maintain the true faith in the land that God has promised them.[17] Thus is conceived their youngest son Galahad, who is destined to be born in Britain and become the first Christian King of Wales.

Every day the company pray before the Grail, asking God to guide them safely to the Promised Land. They wander until, at nightfall on Easter Saturday, God brings them to the sea, but they find neither ship nor galley by which they might cross. In accordance with a divine command, Josephus and the men who carry the Grail start to walk across the water as if it were dry land. Josephus then takes off his under-tunic, stretches it out across the water to the land, and bids first his father, then his uncle Bron and Bron's twelve children, to walk upon it. They are followed by one hundred and fifty of their followers,[18] those who had neither given into lust nor regretted leaving their homeland.

So it is that his eldest son pulls Joseph and his followers across the sea to mainland Britain where, at daybreak, they behold for the first time that country which they must liberate from the unbelieving Saracens who populate it. The first castle they come to is Galafort, whose lord, Duke Ganor, they convert to Christianity. It is here that Joseph's last child, Galahad, is born.[19]

Leaving his wife and newborn son there, Joseph and Josephus now travel to North Wales, taking with them the Grail, but they are thrown into prison by the pagan lord of the land, King Crudel.[20] However the King of Sarras, who is now known by his baptismal name of Mordrain, is warned by Christ in a dream about their fate, and sets sail for Wales to rescue them.

The Maiming of Joseph

After their rescue, Joseph and his son continue their missionary activities. Following the conversion of the pagans of Camelot to Christianity and the investiture of Bron's youngest son Alan as the Rich Fisherman, Joseph tells his son Josephus that he must leave to go where chance leads him.

Joseph accordingly quits his companions and wanders into the Forest of Broceliande, where he encounters a pagan warrior called Argon, who is looking for a doctor to heal his brother Matagran. Argon's brother is ill with a head wound, but Joseph says that he can effect a cure with the aid of his God, who is more powerful than the gods of the pagans.[21]

Argon takes Joseph to his stronghold, the Castle of the Rock, where, without warning, an unchained lion jumps on Argon from above and strangles him. The men of the castle suddenly seize Joseph and tie his hands behind his back. But, as they are taking him to prison, the seneschal from the castle draws his sword and strikes Joseph in the thighs, so that half of the sword remains stuck in his flesh.

Joseph saves himself by promising to heal all the sick people in the castle. He is brought before the wounded Matagran, where he demonstrates the power of his God when lightning strikes and burns the pagan images. Joseph prays to the Cosmocrator who rose from the dead to work the same miracle on Argon. Before long, the dead man rises up, hale and whole.

Matagran, the revived Argon and the other people in the castle are converted and baptized as Christians. Joseph heals Matagran's head wound and then pulls the piece of the sword out of his own thigh, prophesying that the two halves will be rejoined when the one who is to achieve the high adventures of the Holy Grail holds the sword in his hands.[22] He says that his wound will be healed easily, if God wills it. Joseph then leaves the castle and rejoins his companions.[23]

Grave Doubts

It is said that Joseph dies at the same time that his youngest son Galahad, now fifteen, is crowned King of Hoselice; he is buried in Scotland, in the Abbey of the Cross.[24] But others say that Balin the Savage will see the body of Joseph of Arimathea lying in the same chamber of the castle of Corbenic where the Grail and Holy Lance are kept.[25]

For others again, Joseph's final resting place remains a mystery: Sir Gawain is told by a hermit that, at the entrance to the Grail Castle, he will find a holy chapel; between the chapel and the castle is a little cemetery, fenced all around, but containing only one tomb. As he is passing it, a voice calls out to Gawain not to touch the tomb, for he is not the one to whom the identity of he who lies within shall be made known.[26]

The knight, by whom it shall, in fact, be known, is Perlesvaus, who returns to the Grail Castle after the death of the Fisher King to claim his inheritance. He sees, near the bridge over the river, a chapel identical to the one at his mother's castle of Kamaalot, where Nicodemus, who assisted Joseph at the Deposition, is buried—but no one knows who lies within the tomb at this chapel, which remains sealed. Perlesvaus, the new ruler of the Grail Castle, needs only gaze at the tomb, however, for it to burst its seal. The stone lid rises up and a sweet fragrance arises from the body within, which an inscription allows them to identify as that of Joseph of Arimathea.[27]

Perlesvaus has Joseph's body reburied in the same chapel as the body of the Fisher King. Later, when the Widow Lady moves to the Grail Castle, she brings with her the body of Nicodemus, which had been buried in an identical chapel near her castle of Kamaalot. After the death of his mother, Perlesvaus sees a ship with a white sail emblazoned with a red cross arrive to take him to the Island of Plenty. He loads aboard it the tombs of Joseph, Nicodemus, the Fisher King and the Widow Lady, his holy family. The ship sets sail and they are never seen again.[28]

* * *

Joseph of Arimathea (a Judaean village which cannot be conclusively identified) is a figure mentioned only briefly in the Gospels, where he is a disciple of Jesus, who brings His body down from the Cross and buries it in a sepulcher which he had prepared for himself. But Joseph will end up as the unofficial patron saint of Glastonbury, the sacred center of the New Age in Britain, thanks to the legend that he brought the Holy Grail there. But there is little support for these confabulations in the earliest stories.

The connection between Joseph and the Holy Vessel was first made by Robert de Boron in a poem which was also the first to clearly identify the Grail as a Christian relic. Here, drawing on apocryphal sources,[29] de Boron presents the eponymous hero as a soldier in the service of Pilate when he was Roman governor of Judaea. Joseph is a secret follower of Jesus who only reveals himself after the crucifixion and suffers the wrath of the Jews.[30]

De Boron's account of the consequent imprisonment and subsequent liberation of Joseph is followed closely by the Vulgate *Estoire del Saint Graal*, which nevertheless provides some additional details. More importantly, it veers off in a completely new direction before the death of Joseph. This prose "history" provides the saint with a considerable new biography in which he is the leader of a successful proselytizing mission from the Middle East to Britain, accompanied by his son (of whose existence de Boron seems unaware), who will take over the crusade from his father. As the land for which the Grail is destined, Britain will become the new Promised Land: Joseph's lineage will go on to found all the most important dynasties of Arthur's Logres, with the exception of the Pendragon dynasty itself.[31]

In order to justify its deviations from the De Boron Cycle, the Vulgate explains that it is the translation into French of a Latin text which was itself translated from the language of Heaven, for the Book of the Grail was originally confided to the hermit Nascien in the mid-eighth century by Christ Himself. The translator of Nascien's Latin text into French is de Boron himself, which means that the hermit's copy must be the original of "the high book" that de Boron claims to possess. By continually invoking de Boron's authority for its changes, the Vulgate clearly stakes its claim to being the definitive version, trumping all previous texts.

So it is that the Vulgate can retrospectively correct certain aspects of de Boron's earlier account, so that Joseph is wounded in Broceliande and dies in Scotland. But an alternative account of Joseph's maiming and death is given in the late thirteenth century *Romance of Sone*, where we are told that, after leaving the Holy Land, Joseph expels the Saracens from Norway,[32] kills their king and marries his pagan daughter. As a punishment for marrying a heathen, Joseph is wounded through the thighs. He is henceforth known as the Fisher King and his realm of Logres is laid waste. After his death, Joseph's body is preserved as a holy relic in an abbey founded in his honor on the Isle of Galoche,[33] where are also kept the Holy Grail, the Bleeding Lance and a fragment of the True Cross.[34]

With regard to the wasting of Logres as a result of Joseph's maiming, R.S. Loomis suggests that the modern reader would be struck with amazement at the survival in the *Romance of Sone* "of so primitive a superstition as the sympathetic relation between the health of the King and the fertility of his kingdom."[35] But he finds equally amazing the "modern credulity" regarding Joseph's supposed connections with Glastonbury,[36] the earliest testimony for which cannot be dated earlier than twelve hundred years after his alleged arrival there.[37]

Notes

1. According to the Vulgate *Estoire del Saint Graal*, it is Joseph himself who goes to the house of the Last Supper and finds the dish or bowl (*escuele*) from which the Son of God had eaten the paschal lamb (*LG* I, 10). The First Continuation to the Story of the Grail tells us, moreover, that Joseph has had the vessel made—*Voirs est que Josep la fist fere* (*CP* II, l.17574)—and that he brings it to the hill of Calvary, where he collects the blood that is flowing down to Jesus' feet while He is still on the Cross (*CSG* 217).

2. ...*un veissel mout gent/ Ou Criz feisoit son sacrement* (*EG* ll.395–6); *ses vaissiaus la u il sacrefioit* (*RG* 22).

3. ...*Le veissel precïeus et grant,/ Ou li saintimes sans estoit/ Que Joseph requeillu avoit* (*EG* ll.852–4); *le vaissel precieus atout le saintisme sanc que Joseph avoit recuelli* (*RG* 29); *la sainte escüele ... a tout le sanc qu'il avoit recuelli* (*ESG* 27).

4. *MG* 18–22.

5. "...the creed of the great mystery of the Grail" (*MG* 22): Bryant is here translating from the prose version of Robert de Boron's *Joseph of Arimathea*, where Jesus teaches Joseph *paroles* which have only ever been recorded in a *haut livre ... et çou est li creans del grant sacre del Graal*—which Bernard Cerquiglini translates into modern French as *le Credo de la consécration du Graal* (*RG* 31). This enigmatic phrase led A.E. Waite to speculate that these lost words might constitute a secret formula of Eucharistic consecration (1909, 255–6;1933, 153); and Henry Corbin to draw the inference that, since the withdrawal of the Grail from our world, no Mass can ever truly have been celebrated (1983, 203). By contrast, the metrical version says that in this *grant livre* are written *li grant secré.../ Qu'en numme le Graal* (*EG* ll.935–6), which Alexandre Micha translates into modern French as follows: *Là sont consignés les grands secrets qu'on nomme les secrets du Graal* (*RHG* 29–30): "There are recorded the great secrets that are called [the secrets of] the Grail."

6. According to the First Continuation to the Story of the Grail, Joseph is not in fact in prison for very long. In answer to his prayers, he is freed by the hand of God, who lifts up the tower beneath which Joseph is imprisoned (*CSG* 218). This version is close to that of the apocryphal *Gospel of Nicodemus*: see note 26, below.

7. Although he is presented in both the De Boron and the Vulgate cycles as the son of the Emperor Titus, it is clear from the context that Titus' father, the general Vespasian (who in 66 CE was sent to Judaea by the Emperor Nero to crush the Jewish uprising) is meant. Vespasian was proclaimed emperor by his soldiers in July 69 and the following summer returned to Rome, leaving his son Titus to continue the Jewish war. Titus destroyed Jerusalem and enslaved its people in August 70; he succeeded his father as emperor.

8. Vespasian, whom the Romano-Jewish historian Flavius Josephus considered to be a potential Messiah, thus becomes the first Christian Emperor, over two hundred and fifty years before Constantine the Great was baptized on his deathbed.

9. In a reversal of the pagan motif of the Waste Land, where the sexual health of the monarch promotes the fertility of the land and people, the infertility of the land is here attributed to "the sin of unbridled lust" (*MG* 34).

10. *MG* 42: *iceles saintimes paroles que on tient au sacre dou Graal* (*RG* 68); *Les seintes paroles* (*EG* l.3332).

11. *MG* 43: *Joseph fina en le terre et el païs u il fu nes* (*RG* 70).

12. *HBG* 19.

13. *HBG* 98: *Perlesvaus fu del lignage Joseph Abarimatia, que Dieus ama tant, por ço qu'il despendi son cors de la croiz, qu'il le volt geter de la prison la ou Pilate l'avoit mis* (*HLG* 418).

14. *LG* I, 10: *Mais li Sires ... maintenant ke ses cors fu issus du sepulcre, vint il a lui en la chartre ou il estoit et si li porta por compaignie et pour confort la sainte escüele ... a tout le sanc qu'il avoit recuelli.... Ensi aparut li Sauveres du monde a Joseph anchois ke a autrui* (*ESG* 27).

15. *LG* I, 11: In order to square the Vulgate with the historical record, we can therefore tentatively propose a date of 69 CE as the year in which Joseph was liberated by Vespasian; which would in turn mean that the death of Jesus occurred in the year 27. See Appendix I: The Grail Chronology.

16. *LG* I, 12–23.

17. *LG* I, 119.

18. *LG* I, 120: Bron and his twelve sons can be seen as types of Christ and His twelve apostles, but they also foreshadow Arthur and his twelve peers, while the one hundred and fifty faithful disciples foreshadow the Knights of the Round Table.

19. *LG* I, 128.

20. *LG* I, 130: As Joseph was comforted in Caiaphas' prison, so father and eldest son are comforted in Crudel's prison by Our Lord, who promises to send an "earthly avenger" who will destroy all those who seek to torture them.

21. *LG* I, 140–1: They worship the triad of Jupiter, Apollo and Tervagant (Diana), as well as a certain Mahomet (who can only be an anachronistic appearance of the Prophet Mohammed): gods whose images, Argon explains, have power from "those in whose semblance they are made"; that is, "each image through its god."

22. See THE BLEEDING SWORD.

23. *LG* I, 141–2; III, 88–91.

24. *LG* I, 157.

25. Balin is being pursued by King Pellam of Listenois after killing Pellam's brother, in Malory's version, which departs from its known source in the Post-Vulgate Cycle: *And at the last he enterde into a chambir that was mervaylously dyght and ryche, and a bedde arayed with cloth of golde, the rychiste that myght be thought, and one lyying therein.... For in that place was parte of the bloode of Oure Lorde Jesu Cryste, which Joseph off Aramathy brought into thys londe. And there hymselff lay in that ryche bedde.... And Kynge Pellam was nyghe of Joseph his kynne* (*MD* 67–8).

26. *HBG* 75–6.

27. *HBG* 169.

28. *HBG* 263–4.

29. See for example the fifth-century *Gospel of Nicodemus* and the later *Narrative of Joseph of Arimathea*, both available in English translation in *AG* 212–49.

30. According to the apocryphal *Gospel of Nicodemus*, Joseph is seized by the Jews on the Friday and shut up in a windowless building behind a sealed door, with warders in attendance. But on the Sunday, he is gone, although the seals are still intact (*AG* 228–9). Joseph later explains that in the middle of the night he saw a flash of light and experienced the building in which he was imprisoned being picked up; terrified, he fell to the ground. Opening his eyes, he saw Jesus, who grasped his hand, pulled him up, kissed him and told him not to be afraid. Jesus took Joseph to his house and told him to wait there for forty days (234–5).

31. Even this exception must be qualified, if we accept the evidence of the late fourteenth/early fifteenth century Glastonbury Tablets, in which Igerna is the grand-daughter of Lambor, whose great-great-grandfather is Joshua. The Tablets make Joshua the son of Alan the Fat (*MTG* 142) but, in the Vulgate Cycle, Joshua is Alan's brother and the nephew of Joseph of Arimathea.

32. This may in fact be a reference to the area of northwest Scotland and the Isles occupied by the Vikings, where the hermit Nascien goes in search of the Book of the Grail.

33. Loomis 1963, 138–9: Galoche, probably a corruption of *galesche*, meaning "Welsh," may refer to Gwales (now the Isle of Grassholm), where the Assembly of the Wondrous Head spent eighty years before burying the head of the Maimed King of Welsh mythology, Brân the Blessed (140–1). John Darrah (1994, 234) suggests that Gwales may also have been the site of Arthur's expedition to obtain the cauldron of the Head of Annwfn. Joseph's burial there would therefore indicate a powerful continuity between the pagan and Christian religions; as well as suggesting that the Cauldron of the Celtic Otherworld was the prototype for the Holy Grail.

34. *MGL* 316–9.

35. Loomis 1963, 144.

36. "If anyone is so naïve as to hold that the Middle Ages had a monopoly on wild hypotheses, fantastic blunders, and blind credulity, let him contemplate the extraordinary proliferation of local traditions about Glastonbury and their wide acceptance, even in recent times" (Loomis 1963, 265).

37. Loomis 1963, 268–9.

JOSEPHUS

The eldest son of Joseph of Arimathea and Elyab, Josephus is not yet a year and a half old when his father is imprisoned by the Jews for taking the body of Jesus down from the Cross and, as Joseph's enemies believe, hiding it. Having been baptized by James the Less, who becomes the first bishop of Jerusalem after the death of his brother Jesus,

Josephus declares that his only bride will be Holy Church.

His father remains in prison for forty-two years. Towards the end of this period the Roman general Vespasian and his son Titus are sent to Judaea by the Emperor Nero to put down a Jewish rebellion. Taking advantage of the Roman presence, Josephus (who is not just a virgin but eloquent of speech and able to read and write) and his mother approach the general and ask for justice for the man who buried Jesus.[1] Vespasian (who, having been cured of leprosy by the Veil of Veronica, wishes to honor the holy prophet) rescues Joseph (who, having been fed by the Holy Grail, has not aged) from prison and punishes his persecutors.

Josephus accompanies his father when he leaves Jerusalem with a group of Christian disciples[2] and, when Joseph constructs an ark to house the Grail (the dish of the Last Supper in which he collected the blood of Jesus), only he and his son are allowed to look into it.[3] When they come to the pagan city of Sarras, a divine voice comes in the night and tells Joseph that He will give to his son a great honor: Josephus will be a priest, watching over His flesh and blood, and the sole minister empowered to confer holy orders in the lands where He will lead them.

Consequently, at dawn, as Joseph and his people kneel before the Ark of the Grail to worship God in the Spiritual Palace, they feel the ground tremble beneath them. The Holy Spirit descends like a flash of fire and enters into each of their mouths. They hear the voice of God say that His body as well as His spirit will dwell with them, though not in the same form as when He was alive on earth; henceforth, all who are worthy to receive His flesh and blood will receive it from Josephus His minister.

God now instructs Josephus to open the door of the ark. Inside he sees a man as red as fiery lightning, surrounded by five angels, each of whom has six wings and bears a bloody sword in his left hand. They each bear in their right hand one of the relics of the Passion: the Cross, the nails, the Lance, the sponge and the scourge. Josephus has a vision of the crucifixion and sees the blood, which runs from the Lance wound in the side of Jesus, drip into the sacred Vessel. When the Son of Man looks as if He is about to fall to the ground, Josephus runs forward to lift Him up, but the angels restrain him.

Josephus is given the power to cleanse places of evil spirits by sprinkling them with water blest with the sign of the Cross and invoking the Trinity. He is then invested with the robes of a bishop and given a throne to sit on. Next, he is anointed with unction by Christ,[4] who leads him into the ark.

Inside he sees a small altar covered with a red cloth. On one end of the altar is a bloody lance-tip, on the other end the Dish; between them is a gold chalice containing wine with a gold cover, or paten, on top. Josephus sees bread on the paten and speaks the words that Jesus spoke at the Last Supper. Immediately he realizes that he is holding a child's body in his hands and that the wine in the chalice is the child's blood. Our Lord commands him to break what he is holding into three pieces: He snaps off the child's head as if it were overcooked meat and pulls His body apart. Despite his misgivings, Josephus follows the divine injunction to eat the child's flesh and drink from the chalice. One of the angels who guard the ark carries the paten to Joseph and the other disciples, who each receive their Savior in visible form: for, as the bread is put in his mouth, he sees it become a completely formed child.[5]

The Shield of Victory

Once he is anointed and consecrated as the priest of Christ, Josephus is given the power to prophesy and work miracles. Firstly, he exorcises a demon from a statue of Mars and compels it to smash the other pagan idols. Secondly, he reveals to the King of Sarras, Evalach the Unknown, the secret of the king's origin, and tells him that only through faith in Christ will he be saved from defeat by the King of Egypt. Thirdly, he places a cross of red silk on the king's shield, saying that if he believes in this sign, he will escape death and win victory.[6]

When this comes to pass as predicted, both Evalach and his brother-in-law Seraph allow Josephus to baptize them. Evalach thus becomes Mordrain; Seraph takes the Christian name Nascien and also has his son Celidoine baptized.

Josephus then travels throughout the kingdom, baptizing the inhabitants, purifying the pagan temples with holy water and destroying their idols. In the city of Orcaut he exorcises the demon Selaphas, whom the citizens had worshipped as a god. The King of Orcaut gives his permission, to those who do not wish to be baptized, to leave the city. But those who take up his offer are struck down at the gates by the demon with madness or with the sword.

Josephus, who is busy baptizing the willing, interrupts his good work to stop Selaphas, but he is himself struck through the left thigh by the Bleeding Lance. The angel who wielded it vanishes and Josephus succeeds in pulling out the Lance, but the tip remains lodged in his thigh. He will walk with a limp, as a result, for the rest of his days; moreover, the wound cannot be staunched as long as the tip remains embedded.

It is the Angel of the Bleeding Lance (the third of the five angels who guard the Grail) who heals the wound, after twenty-two days, by removing the tip. The angel then tells Josephus about the land whither God will guide him, a land where great marvels will occur and earthly feats of chivalry will become heavenly.[7] Before leaving Sarras, Josephus exposes the king's carnal relationship with a wooden statue in the form of a woman, which he persuades him to burn.[8]

Taking with him the Holy Vessel, Josephus leads the Company of the Grail, including his father, across many lands until they come to the sea that separates Great Britain from the mainland. Having no ship to carry them across, the first Christians enter this island by a miracle, walking over the water on the tunic of Josephus; they will later be joined by another group led by Nascien. The first thing that Joseph does when he sets foot on British soil is to order his followers to plant trees there, symbolizing the cultivation of the Christian faith in the land that God has promised to them and to their descendants. This leads to the uprooting of the pagan faith of the Saracens, followers of the astral cult centered at Sarras which is widespread on the island at that time.

The most faithful of the company are sustained by the grace of the Holy Grail; but the sinners among them require earthly nourishment. When they buy twelve loaves baked by a local woman, they start fighting over them. But Josephus works a miracle: Breaking each loaf into three parts, he has only to bring the Grail near to them to multiply them so that, by the time everyone has had their fill, there is more left over than there was to begin with!

On the seventh day of their arrival in pagan Britain, the company is surprised to see a castle with a red cross above the gate. Entering the city of Galafort, on the river Humber, they discover that its ruler, Duke Ganor, is entertaining Celidoine (the young son of Nascien) who, four months earlier, had been transported to Britain miraculously in a boat and who is, in fact, the first Christian to set foot on British soil. Celidoine introduces Josephus to the duke as the Holy Church's minister, challenging the pagan clerks to dispute theology with him. Josephus reveals to Ganor a secret of his childhood that occurred before Josephus was born, as a result of which the king and his court convert.[9] Josephus' younger brother Galahad is born in Galafort, which becomes the center of the company's missionary activities.

Joseph of Arimathea and Josephus now lead one hundred and fifty of their followers into North Wales to convert the locals, only to be thrown into prison by the king, a cruel pagan. But they are sustained by the Grail[10] until rescued by an army led by Mordrain, who has travelled all the way from Sarras after being warned of their fate in a dream.

Liberated, Josephus sets out for Camelot, where the Saracen kings are crowned; he begins baptizing people in great numbers. The pagan King of Camelot only pretends to convert, however; as soon as Josephus departs, he executes twelve of the leading Christians at the Stone of the Black Cross, just outside the city. But by the time Josephus returns, the king has gone mad. Josephus has all the pagan temples knocked down, the idols burnt, and all traces of the indigenous religion eradicated. In the middle of the city, he has the Church of St. Stephen the Martyr erected.

In keeping with his role as spiritual head of the Grail Christians, it is Josephus who explains the symbolic importance of the empty place at the Table of the Grail. Furthermore, he chooses his cousin Alan the Fat to catch a fish that will feed their sinful followers and inaugurate the line of Rich Fishermen.[11]

Josephus spends the next fifteen years travelling throughout Ireland and what is now Scotland and Wales, preaching the faith of Christ, until he finally returns to Galafort. Here he finds that his youngest brother Galahad is now a grown man. When Josephus is asked to appoint someone to rule the kingdom of Hoselice, to avoid the devastation of the land after the death of its king, he takes the advice of Duke Ganor and Nascien that no one would be more worthy of the honor than Galahad. The four of them travel to Hoselice, where they are greeted with great joy; on the feast of Pentecost, Josephus crowns, anoints and consecrates his brother as king.

After the coronation, Josephus returns to Galafort, where he finds that his father has died. He goes to see King Mordrain in the abbey where he now lives, to tell the king that he has learnt from the Sovereign Master that he, Josephus, will pass away the next day.

Mordrain begs him to leave him some sign of remembrance and comfort. Josephus bids him bring him his shield, the one with which he achieved victory over the King of Egypt. He now paints a cross on it with his own blood. Josephus prophesies that anyone who hangs it around his neck, apart from the Good Knight for whom it is destined, will regret it; It must be kept with the tomb of Nascien until another Galahad (the ninth of Nascien's lineage) comes for it, on the fifth day after he receives knighthood.

Returning to Galafort for the last time, Josephus entrusts the Holy Grail to the keeping of his cousin Alan the Fat. After Alan's death, it passes to his brother Joshua, the first Fisher King, whose descendants guard it at Corbenic until the arrival of the second Galahad. Josephus himself dies as he predicted and is buried in the Abbey of Mordrain. But later, when Scotland is ravaged by famine, the body of Josephus is carried there, to the Abbey of Urglay; its presence restores the fertility of the land.[12]

More than three hundred years have passed since the death of Josephus when the second Galahad, bearing the Red Cross Shield,[13] returns to Corbenic (where he was born and brought up) with his companions Bors and Perceval, to experience the feast of the Grail. They are joined by nine knights: three from Gaul, three from Ireland and three from Denmark.

All those who are not companions on the quest for the Grail depart from the hall where the Holy Vessel is kept. Now the spirit of Josephus appears, wearing the robes of a bishop, seated on a glorious throne borne by four angels. He performs the consecration of the Mass, taking from the Grail a Host that takes human form before he puts it back in the vessel. He then tells those who have striven to share in the wonders of the Holy Vessel that they will shortly receive holy food from their Savior. Josephus vanishes and the twelve companions sit at the Table of the Grail, where no one has sat since the days of Joseph of Arimathea, to receive the consecrated wafer from Christ Himself.[14]

They then follow the Grail to Sarras, whither God has removed it: There, Josephus allows Galahad to look directly into the Holy Vessel, a gift that had hitherto only been awarded to Josephus and his father.[15] Galahad thereupon expires and a hand descends from Heaven to take up the Holy Grail and the Lance, which are never again seen upon Earth.[16]

Notes

1. *LG* I, 11–12.
2. Christ tells Joseph, in a vision, "carnal fruit will never issue from your son Josephus, because he has promised Me eternal chastity" (*LG* I, 14). Josephus' cousin Alan the Fat will also remain chaste; here the Vulgate corrects Robert de Boron, whose Alan also swears eternal chastity but goes on to father Perceval. But it also looks forward to the Grail Quest, the successful accomplishment of which requires chastity as well as virginity.
3. *LG* I, 15.
4. This unction, we learn, would be used to anoint all the Christian kings of Britain until the time of Uther Pendragon, King Arthur's father—*Furent enoint tout li roi, des ce que la crestientés vint en la Grant Bretaingne, jusques a Uterpandragon qui fu peres au roi Artu*—but would be lost before Uther's coronation—*cele onctions fu perdue quant il dut estre premierement coronés* (*LDG* 71). We hear no more about this tantalizing story fragment, but we do know that the daughter of Lucius, the first Christian King of Britain, marries one of the Fisher Kings (Aminadap, the son of Josephus' cousin Joshua) who guard the Grail, thus uniting the royal dynasties of Logres and Corbenic.
5. *LG* I, 22–8.
6. *LG* I, 29–33.
7. The angel says that the Lance will announce the beginning of the wondrous adventures which will take place in the land to which God will lead him: *Che est li commenchemens des mervilleuses aventures qui avenront en la terre ou Diex a proposé qu'il te menra* (*ESG* 167). These marvels (also known as the adventures of Logres, the land whither his lineage will be guided and where they will settle) will last as many years as the days in which the Lance tip was embedded in his thigh: *Et si saches tu bien … ke autrestant de jours com tu as porté le fier de la lanche en ta cuisse, autrestant d'ans durront les mervelleuses aventures en la terre ou Diex te doit mener et conduire por ton lignaige ramanoir* (168).
8. *LG* I, 47–53.
9. *LG* I, 119–27.
10. *LG* I, 130.
11. *LG* I, 136–40.
12. *LG* I, 155–7.
13. The story of the Shield and of how Josephus arranged things so that the Good Knight would one day find it, is summarized for Galahad by a mysterious White Knight, whom we have good reason to suspect is Christ Himself (*LG* IV, 12–13; V, 127–8; *QHG* 58–60; *MD* 680–2).
14. *LG* IV, 84–5; *QHG* 274–5; *MD* 782–3.
15. Josephus tells Galahad that they resemble each other in that they are both virgins and have both witnessed the mysteries of the Holy Grail: *tu as veues les merveilles del Saint Graal ausi come je fis* (*QP* 278); *thou hast sene the merveyles of the Sankgreall* (*MD* 787).
16. *LG* IV, 87; V, 287–8; *QHG* 282–3.

JOSEPHUS the Clerk

An angel dictates to the clerk Josephus the true story of the Grail, the most holy Vessel in which the precious blood of the Savior was collected by those who believed in Him, on the day of the Crucifixion,[1] in order to make known the sufferings that knights and noblemen undertook to exalt the New Law of Christ. Josephus preserves the memory of these events in the High Book of the Grail, which he composes.[2]

It is from Josephus that we learn that the isles to which the knights travel, bringing the New Law, are constantly changing,[3] along with the forests that they penetrate and the castles which they find therein, because God does not want them to find their adventures tiresome.[4] He also tells us that the Grail can appear in five different forms; that the Grail Castle is called the Castle of Souls; and that the river which flows round it comes from the Earthly Paradise.[5]

* * *

According to Nigel Bryant,[6] this Josephus is none other than Flavius Josephus, the first century Romano-Jewish historian. But the *Perlesvaus* itself identifies its author with "the first priest to sacrifice the body of Our Lord,"[7] which is the role played by Joseph of Arimathea's son Josephus in the Vulgate Cycle.

Notes

1. *Li estoires du saintisme vessel que on apele Graal, o quel li precieus sans au Sauveeur fu receüz au jor qu'il fu crucefiez…. Josephes le mist en remenbrance par la mencion de la voiz d'un angle* (*HLG* 126).
2. *HBG* 19.

3. *Josephes nos temoigne que les samblances des illes se muoient* (*HLG* 732): Here Josephus uses a similar word to that which he later uses to describe the transformations of the Grail—*les muances* (790)—suggesting that the *muances* of the landscape are part of the enchantment of the Grail.
4. *HBG* 181.
5. *HBG* 195–6.
6. *HBG* 19n.
7. *HBG* 98: *Cist haut estores nos temoigne et recorde que Josephes qui nos en fait ramenbranche fu li premierains provoires qui sacrefia Nostre Seignor et por tant doit l'on croire les paroles qui de lui vienent* (*HLG* 418).

JOSHUA

One of the twelve sons of Bron and Enygeus, the sister of Joseph of Arimathea, who have come to Britain as part of the Company of the Grail, Joshua accompanies his beloved younger brother Alan, the Rich Fisherman, to the Land Beyond. They have brought with them the Holy Vessel that Alan guards: Through its power, Alan heals the king of the land of leprosy, so that he converts to Christianity and is baptized Alphasan. The king promises Alan that he will build a splendid palace to house the Grail; moreover, he will confer his daughter's hand and his crown on to Joshua, on condition that the Grail stays in the land.

Alan, whose intention it already was to entrust the Grail to Joshua after his death, agrees. As soon as the castle of Corbenic is built to house the sacred Vessel, Joshua marries King Alphasan's daughter and is crowned King of the Land Beyond. At the feast, the Grail fills everyone with its grace and feeds their bodies with whatever they desire[1]; after which, Joshua and his wife fulfill their desire for each other and conceive a son, who is baptized Aminadap.

When Alan dies, Joshua inherits his title of Rich Fisherman. But, because he is also a king, he is henceforth known as the Fisher King. This name is also taken by his descendants, the sacred dynasty that rules Corbenic[2] until the coming of Sir Galahad, the Knight of the Promise.

Notes

1. *Icelui jor furent tuit cil qui el palés maingierent repleni de la grace del saint vaissel en tel maniere qu'il n'i ot celui qui n'eüst totes les viandes que il seüst demander et deviser* (*ESG* 562).
2. *LG* I, 158–9.

JUPITER

The ruler of the Roman pantheon, the Sky Father Jupiter is one of the three gods that Brutus (the founder of Britain) sets up an altar and makes a special offering to, when he arrives at the Mediterranean Island of Leogetia on his way to Albion.[1]

Over a thousand years later, when Joseph of Arimathea brings Grail Christianity to Logres, Jupiter is one of four gods still worshipped by the British Saracens—that is, by the followers of the astral cult whose sacred center is Sarras in the Middle East.[2] This cult has apparently spread southeast as well as northwest of Sarras, for it is Jupiter and his wife the goddess Juno who are invoked by Parzival's pagan half-brother Feirefiz, the King of India, before his baptism.[3]

Notes

1. *HKB* 65.
2. *LG* I, 140; III, 88.
3. *WP* 372–4; *PT* 313–5.

K

KAMAALOT

The castle of Yglais, the Widow Lady of the Waste Forest, Kamaalot stands near the shore of the wildest Welsh island, facing to the West.[1] A river runs round it and there is a forest nearby[2]; the tomb of Nicodemus, Perlesvaus' great-grandfather, is also there.[3]

The Vales of Kamaalot are invaded by the Lord of the Fens when Yglais' husband dies and, of fifteen castles, only one remains in her possession until her son Perlesvaus kills the Lord. After the death of the Fisher King, her brother, Yglais moves to the Grail Castle, taking with her the body of Nicodemus.

Notes

1. Kamaalot in Wales is not to be confused with the Camelot of the story-tellers, where King Arthur so often holds court, and which stands at the entrance to the Kingdom of Logres: In the Old French of the Romance of Perlesvaus, the two castles are both called Kamaalot; but I have retained the traditional spelling of Arthur's capital to avoid confusion.
2. *HBG* 197: This is presumably the Waste Forest where Perceval, as Perlesvaus is usually called, first encounters Arthur's knights.
3. Celidoine, the ancestor of the Grail winners Bors and Galahad, is also described as being buried at *Camahalot* (*ESG* 572). By this, considering that he is the King of North Wales, may be meant the "western" Camelot, the castle of the Widow Lady.

KAY

A Knight of the Round Table and King Arthur's foster-brother, Sir Kay travels with Gawain, Lancelot and Calogrenant to the Grail Castle.

Separating from his companions, Kay hears about a chapel in a castle where he can learn about the Grail and free many prisoners. But, when he gets there, all he sees is a statue of an old knight whose knees are transfixed by a spear. When he breaks the statue to see if there is blood inside, he too is imprisoned.[1] His only way out is to defeat in single combat nine knights protected by magic.[2]

Fortunately for Kay, Gawain, following the instructions of the Grail Bearer,[3] lends him an enchanted hauberk which enables Kay to defeat the nine knights and gain his freedom.[4] But he has missed the sacred and mysterious events which transpire in the Grail Castle.[5]

Notes

1. "No bonds were to be seen on his hands and feet, yet free of restraint as he seemed, he still was bound and could not leave the chapel at will, but only walk back and forth inside" (*HTC* 331).
2. *HTC* 323–4.
3. *HTC* 319.
4. *HTC* 331–3.
5. *HTC* 329: As I have argued in another work (Dixon 2012, 149–50, 164), like the tragic fate of Cahus in the Romance of Perlesvaus, the captivity of Kay can be read as a mental imprisonment caused by literalist thinking: The statue is an image; to break it is an act of iconoclasm, which always misses the sacred mystery.

The KING OF CASTLE MORTAL

Yglais, the mother of Perlesvaus, has three brothers: two (the Fisher King and Pelles, the Hermit King) are virtuous, but the King of Castle Mortal is wicked. He seeks to take control of the Kingdom of the Grail from the Fisher King and thus gain possession of the Holy Vessel and the Bleeding Lance.[1] He attacks the Fisher King's ally, the Queen of Maidens, but is driven off by his nephew Perlesvaus.[2]

Eventually the Fisher King, who has been languishing in ill health ever since Perlesvaus came to his castle and failed to ask the Grail Question, dies; whereupon his evil brother seizes the opportunity to conquer his kingdom. The King of Castle Mortal builds nine bridges over the river that surrounds the Grail Castle, but the Hallows disappear from the chapel and those who serve the Grail also leave, rather than serve a pagan lord.[3] When Perlesvaus, the soldier of Christ, defeats each of the three warriors who guard each of the bridges, the king, in despair, throws himself from the battlements of the castle; whereupon the Grail Hallows reappear and their servants return to the chapel.[4]

* * *

Death haunts the Grail legends: In *The Crown*, the Grail King is dead, though surviving in a state of suspended animation; in the First Continuation to the Story of the Grail, it is his brother who is dead; in the Tale of Balin, the Fisher King's brother is an invisible killer; and, in the Romance of Perlesvaus, it is as if he rules over the realm of death as the King of Castle Mortal.

Jessie L. Weston, in her study of the legend of Sir Perceval, sees this king as one of three guardians of the sacred Vessel in the lost, initiatory Grail cult which she has attempted to reconstruct from the remaining fragments. The King of Castle Mortal presides over the lower, "phallic" initiation, where the Grail is a Cup and is accompanied by the Lance, from which it receives blood (as opposed to the higher, "philosophic" initiation, where the Vessel is rightly called the Holy Grail): "He was the guardian of the Lance and Cup in their primitive aspect"[5]; and Wagner's Klingsor is an equivalent figure.[6]

Notes

1. HBG 46, 116.
2. HBG 117–8.
3. HBG 167–8.
4. HBG 171–2.
5. Weston 1909, 259–60.
6. Weston 1909, 259n1.

KLINGSOR

Unable to join the Grail Brotherhood because of his sinfulness, the evil enchanter Klingsor castrates himself, but is still rejected by its guardian, Titurel. In the valley below Montsalvat, Klingsor turns the wilderness into a garden of earthly delights into which he hopes to lure the Knight of the Grail. Amfortas, Titurel's grandson and successor as Grail Lord, attacks him there; but is in turn wounded by the Lance, which pierced the side of Christ on the Cross.[1] But when Klingsor turns the same Lance against Parsifal, the hero captures it, makes the sign of the Cross with it and thereby destroys Klingsor's magic. His garden becomes a desert.[2]

Notes

1. RWP 4.
2. RWP 17: Jessie L. Weston (1896, 176–7) summarizes Klingsor's story in her essay on Wagner's music drama *Parsifal*: "For the dramatic presentment of Klingsor as an embodiment of evil," she adds, "the sworn foe and opponent of the Grail king and his knights, Wagner is alone responsible" (204); although he derives the name and knowledge of magic from Wolfram's Clinschor, the Lord of the Castle of Wonders.

The KNIGHT OF THE DRAGON

The Lord of the Castle of Giants, the brother of King Maragon,[1] has a city built in the Isles of the Sea that he fills with devil-worshippers. In return for his devotion, his diabolical master gives him a ghastly black shield with a dragon's head set in it, which engulfs in flame any man who challenges him. Moreover, the Devil endows the knight with such power that no-one can withstand him in battle[2]—until he meets Perceval.

The Knight of the Flaming Dragon, as he is now known, invades Arthur's kingdom seeking revenge for the death of the giant Logrin at the hands of Arthur's son Loholt.[3] He now lays siege to Montesclaire, demanding that its lady marry him. The road to Montesclaire is littered with the burnt and dismembered bodies of those who opposed him,[4] including Perceval's cousin Alan of Escavalon.

The Dragon Knight occupies the Isle of the Elephants, in a lake at the foot of Montesclaire. Its lady, the Queen of the Circle of Gold, offers that holy relic as a prize to whoever can vanquish him.[5]

Bearing the Red Cross Shield,[6] Perceval is protected against the diabolical flames and, after a ferocious battle, gives the Dragon Knight a mortal wound. Some say that, realizing the Devil has betrayed him, the knight makes a death-bed confession and dies, facing east, praying to God.[7] Others say that the knight dies unrepentant: Perceval thrusts his sword into the dragon's mouth and the head, turning upon its bearer in rage, burns him to ashes before vanishing.

As a result of this great victory, Perceval wins the Circle of Gold[8] which is, in fact, Christ's Crown of Thorns set in a holy relic,[9] and which is ultimately kept in the Grail Castle.[10]

Notes

1. This King Maragon (*GCP* ll.8979–80) may be the same as King Amangon (Carey 2007, 191–2)— he who, in the *Elucidation*, violates the Maidens of the Wells.
2. *CSG* 410–11.
3. *HBG* 153.
4. *CSG* 411.
5. *HBG* 158–9.
6. The story of *li Chevaliers del Dragon Ardant* is found in verse in the Continuation to the Story of the Grail by Gerbert de Montreuil and, in prose, in the Romance of Perlesvaus. The two versions are roughly contemporary and complement, but sometimes contradict, each other. Thus, according to Gerbert, the shield contains a fragment of the True Cross (*CSG* 406); in *Perlesvaus*, it is the Shield of Joseph of Arimathea in which the Good Knight had sealed some of the blood and clothing of Jesus (*HBG* 162).
7. *CSG* 418–9.
8. *HBG* 161–4.
9. *HBG* 131: It is said that it will only be won by the first knight to behold the Grail.
10. *HBG* 195.

KUNDRY

Having seduced the Grail King Amfortas[1] and caused him to be wounded by the Lance that pierced the side of Christ, the sorceress Kundry attempts to make good her sin by bringing the king healing balsams; but to no avail.[2] She mocks Parsifal when he first arrives at Montsalvat, the Grail Castle in the mountains, as a fool[3]; not realizing that the Grail itself has prophesied that the king will only be healed by a fool made wise through compassion.

Kundry herself was cursed for mocking Christ,[4] and is now in the power of the evil enchanter Klingsor, whom she had also attempted but failed to seduce.[5] She now lures Parsifal to Klingsor's enchanted garden, but it is the Pure Fool who triumphs. Freed of Klingsor's power and absolved of her sins against him by Parsifal, Kundry makes her way to Montsalvat as a penitent, intent on serving the Grail.[6] But, when Parsifal heals Amfortas and replaces him as Grail King, she falls dead at his feet, redeemed.[7]

* * *

Kundry's name, if little else, is derived from that of Wolfram's hideous Grail Messenger Cundrie. Nutt considers her to be "Wagner's great contribution to the legend." She is "tragic in the extreme." She can only be freed from the curse she is under if the hero achieves his task, even though that will doom her. But he sees her importance in the music drama to derive not from Wolfram but from earlier Celtic tales in which a "loathly damsel"[8] is "the real protagonist of the story." The re-emergence of this theme in Wagner, Nutt considers to be "an admirable example of the inevitable, spontaneous character of the growth of certain conceptions, especially of such as have been partly shaped by the folk-mind."[9]

For Caitlín and John Matthews, Kundry speaks with the "deep voice" of the Goddess of Sovereignty[10] as Measurer, Challenger and Protector, Keeper of the Wisdom of the Grail, Dark Woman of Knowledge.[11] But Wagner's reading of Kundry, as cursed for laughing at Christ and needing Parsifal to save her, distorts the archetypal image, turning her into a disempowering temptress rather than an illuminator, a "guardian of tradition" who empowers through her "great knowledge."[12]

Notes

1. *RWP* 10.
2. *RWP* 2.
3. *RWP* 6.
4. *RWP* 15–6.
5. *RWP* 10–1: Klingsor calls her Rose of Hades, Herodias (who had John the Baptist beheaded when he resisted her advances) and Gundrygia (a Valkyrie), thus evoking the three worlds of classical,

Christian and Teutonic mythology. The struggle between Kundry and Parsifal is thereby widened into one between paganism and "the fully developed and mystical Christianity symbolized by the Grail" (Weston 1896, 206-8).

6. *RWP* 17-8: Thus Parsifal "becomes a symbol of the Savior" (Nutt, 255).
7. *RWP* 22: Kundry's story is summarized in Weston 1896, 176-8.
8. See THE UGLY MAIDEN.
9. Nutt, 254&*n*.
10. Matthews 1992, *xxx*.
11. Matthews 1992, *xxxxii-iv*.
12. Matthews 1992, 164-5: The Matthews see Cundrie/Kundry, Chrétien's Ugly Maiden and Peredur's Black Maiden as variants of the same archetypal figure: The blackness is an "essential part" of the image.

KYOT the Provençal

Master Kyot of Provence, a renowned scholar,[1] finds in Toledo the abandoned Tale of Parzival written in a heathen language, and translates it into French. It is Kyot's version (rather than that of Chrétien de Troyes) which Wolfram renders into German.[2]

Notes

1. Also called *laschantiure* (*WP* 213): "This is usually translated as 'singer.' The alternative and correct interpretation is 'magician,' which is altogether unacceptable for the uninitiated" (Ravenscroft 1982b, 12: cf. *PT* 382). For Trevor Ravenscroft, Kyot is an initiate of the seventh (and highest) degree, who knows "the secrets of time" (290) having, in Wolfram's phrase, learnt "the characters' ABC beforehand without the art of necromancy" (*WP* 232; *PT* 191-2).
2. *WP* 213-4, 410; *PT* 176, 346: For Jessie L. Weston, Kyot is not just possessed of "an original and truly remarkable mind" but is an initiate of the Grail cult (1913, 125-7), who knew "that the imagery of the story was founded upon the actual details of a wide-spread and awe-inspiring ritual" (1909, 315-6).

L

LAMBEGUS

Lambegus is the nephew of the seneschal of Ganis, whose liege-lord (King Bors) dies prematurely. When the fay Ninienne takes Lionel and Bors, the young princes of Ganis, to her hidden dwelling in the Lake of Diana, Lambegus is invited to visit them to satisfy himself and his uncle of their welfare.

He tells the Lady of the Lake that she would watch over them with the utmost care if she knew their ancestry as well as he does for, although their father was high-born (being a direct descendant of Nascien and Celidoine, important figures in the evangelization of Britain), the Scriptures tell us that their mother Evaine is descended from King David; it is a member of her family who is destined to bring to an end the adventures of Logres.[1]

And indeed Lambegus, after a distinguished career fighting for Arthur and as one of Tristan's companions, arrives in time to witness, along with Sir Bors, the healing of the Maimed King by Galahad, the grandson of Evaine's sister; although by then Lambegus is an old and holy man.[2]

Notes

1. *...par lo tesmoign des Escriptures* (*LDL* I, 312): "And what greatness they may achieve we can hardly tell, but we know that the people of Great Britain are eager to be delivered from the extraordinary things that have befallen them and that it will be by a man who comes from the lineage of these children's mother" (*LG* II, 45). It is not at all clear which scriptures Lambegus is referring to, unless they are the writings of the Master Blaise who, in his hideaway in Northumberland, has been recording the history and prophecies of the Grail on behalf of Merlin. Be that as it may, Lambegus is correct: The children of Evaine and Elaine, the two sisters of the House of David, will play a vital if indirect role in the achieving of the Grail Quest and the bringing to an end of the adventures of Logres: For Evaine is the mother of Bors, and Elaine, the grandmother of

Galahad, two of the twelve knights who will pursue the Grail to Corbenic and receive its grace.

2. *LG* V, 278–9.

LAMBOR

The son of King Manuel of Corbenic, Lambor, the fifth Fisher King, is also a descendant of good King Lucius, in whose time the Company of the Grail first came to Britain.[1] It is during the reign of Lambor that is struck the blow that creates the Waste Land, the restoration of which will be the great task of the Grail Winner.

Lambor, the worthiest and most God-loving man in Britain, is waging a bloody war against his neighbor King Varlan, even though they are both Christians, at the time that the Ship of Solomon arrives on the shores of Logres. Varlan boards the ship, despite dire warnings. Finding in it the Sword of David, he draws it from its sheath and, thus armed, returns to shore, where he confronts Lambor.

Seeing his enemy, King Varlan brings the sword crashing down on Lambor's head, killing him outright. This is the first blow struck with the sword in the Kingdom of Logres, and it unleashes such devastation on the territories of both kings that no crops grow, trees bear no fruit and the waters support no fish. As a result of this terrible blow, the kingdoms of Varlan and Lambor are together known as the Waste Land.

According to the succession of the Fisher Kings, Lambor's reign is followed by that of his son Pellehan, who is also the victim of a Dolorous Blow[2]: one inflicted this time, not by a sword, but by the Holy Lance, wielded by Balin the Savage.

Notes

1. *LG* I, 159: Lambor's grandfather married one of the daughters of King Lucius.
2. *LG* I, 159–60: The tale is later recounted by Lambor's grand-daughter to her brother Perceval (according to the Vulgate *Queste*, they are the children of Pellehan) and to Lambor's great-great-grandson Galahad (*LG* IV, 65; *QHG* 215–6; *MD* 753–4).

LANCELOT OF THE LAKE

Born in tragedy and raised in the Faerie realm of the Lady of the Lake, Lancelot's adulthood is dominated by his love for Guenevere, the wife of his sovereign. This love will inspire him to his greatest deeds of chivalry, but it will also prevent him from achieving the greatest spiritual quest of his age. It will ultimately cause the destruction of Logres.

The Handsome Foundling

On both his mother's and his father's side, Lancelot is descended from that exalted lineage which came to Britain from the Holy Land to convert the country to Christianity and to make it a suitable dwelling place for the Holy Grail. Lancelot's mother, Elaine, is of the House of David.[1] His father Ban, King of Benoic, is descended from Nascien, a Middle Eastern nobleman who was converted to Christianity by Joseph of Arimathea and who was transported to Britain by the miraculous Ship of Solomon.[2] Nascien's son, Celidoine, the first Christian King of North Wales, who had married into the Persian royal family, had a vision of his descendants, the eighth of whom is Lancelot, of whom it is prophesied that he will endure great suffering.[3] Lancelot, like his friend Tristan, is in fact born to suffering, his father being killed when he is still a baby; his distraught mother loses him to the Lady of the Lake, who abducts him and brings him up in her underwater realm.

When the Handsome Foundling (as Lancelot is known at this time, being ignorant of his true name) is eighteen, he asks to be knighted. The Lady of the Lake responds with a long lecture on the qualities and responsibilities of knighthood, giving as exemplars of chivalry ancient Israelites such as King David and Judas Maccabeus, who fought for the law of God against the unbelievers, along with Christians such as Joseph of Arimathea and his son Galahad, the eponymous founder of the Kingdom of Wales. The descendants of Galahad should also be counted among those who had all the chivalric virtues, along with King Pelles, the noblest of the Fisher Kings.[4]

Although the Handsome Foundling cannot know it at this stage, most of the heroes chosen by the Lady as exemplars will have great importance for his life and that of his progeny: Galahad is his own baptismal name and will be the name of his only son; the daughter of King Pelles will be the mother of that son; and Lancelot's son, Galahad of Corbenic, will win the Sword of King David during the Quest of the Holy Grail, a quest in which Lancelot himself will be unsuccessful.

Across the Sword Bridge

The limits on his chivalric achievements are made known to Lancelot even before he consummates his affair with Guenevere. Discovering that the queen has been abducted by Meleagant, the Prince of Gorre, a knight who specializes in kidnapping those of Logres and keeping them in his father's kingdom, Lancelot sets off to the rescue and reaches the Land Beyond, which is between Logres and the Kingdom of Gorre; This is where the people taken captive are forced to dwell.

Merlin had prophesied that the prisoners would not be liberated until the body of Galahad, the first Christian King of Wales, is brought back to the country he once ruled. It is when Lancelot arrives at the tomb of Galahad, in a cemetery near a monastery, that he learns of the prophecy. The monks take him to the Holy Cemetery, where he raises the tombstone effortlessly, revealing the armored body bathed in the odor of sanctity. At that moment a group of monks arrives from Wales: Eight days earlier, a vision had revealed to them that the tomb would be opened and so they had set out to bring home the body of their first Christian king.

Lancelot is aware of another mystery in the cemetery: This is the Dolorous Tomb, which is buried underground in the Hall of Great Fears, from which a dreadful din and thick black smoke emanate. Determined to resolve this mystery also, Lancelot prevails upon the abbot to lead him through a dark vault to a staircase; but from here on, he must go alone. Moving in the direction of the noise, he walks in pitch blackness until he is suddenly dazzled by a bright light. When his vision clears, he sees another tomb, but one ablaze, from which emanates an over-powering stench.

A braying voice assaults his ears and it is all he can do to stop himself fleeing in terror; but the voice tells him that he has no need to be ashamed. The voice belongs to one of Joseph of Arimathea's nephews, Simeon, who proved unworthy of being one of the Companions of the Grail when he incited his brother to murder. For this crime, Simeon must burn in torment until the coming of the Good Knight. But that perfect one is not Lancelot, although it is from his lineage that will come Simeon's deliverer: The coming of the Good Knight is very near, but has not yet come; it is this Good Knight who will sit in the Perilous Seat and bring to an end the Adventures of Logres.

Simeon advises Lancelot to wet himself all over with the holy water that he will find in a marble stone to the right of his tomb. Lancelot does so; this alone enables him to attempt to raise the tombstone without being burnt. But to no avail: The adventure of the Tomb of the Black Chamber must await one greater than him, the one who will complete the Quest of the Grail.[5]

Lancelot continues his journey across the country, attracting an increasingly messianic group of followers, exiles whom he delivers from what was once known as the Kingdom of No Return, before rescuing (and bedding) the queen and striking off her abductor's head. But it is Lancelot himself who is in danger of losing his head when he first encounters the mysteries of the Grail.

The Beheading Game

When news comes to the court that the Fisher King is languishing and the Kingdom of Logres riven with strife, because Perceval saw the Grail but failed to ask what was done with it or who was served from it, Lancelot sets off to find the Castle of the Grail for himself and set right Perceval's mistake. On the way he meets Gawain who tells him that he too has seen the Grail but failed to ask what was done with it. Lancelot exclaims that there is nothing he desires more than to go to the court of the Fisher King[6]; he becomes angry when a maiden warns him that he will never see the Grail as long as he loves the wife of his lord.[7]

Lancelot rides on until he comes to the Waste City, where he hears all the people lamenting the imminent death of a young knight. However, when the knight appears before them dressed in red, gold and precious stones—and carrying an axe—he confronts Lancelot with a stark choice: Either Lancelot must cut off his head, or he will cut off Lancelot's; furthermore, before striking off the other knight's head, Lancelot must swear to return to the city in a year's time to offer up his own head as willingly.

Preferring to delay death for a year rather than be killed on the spot, Lancelot swears to return. He then takes the axe in both hands and, as the knight kneels down before him with outstretched neck, smites off his head with a single blow. Lancelot throws down the axe and mounts his horse, deeming it unwise to linger. As he leaves, he hears the crowd bewailing the dead knight and saying that he will be avenged at the set time.[8]

One day Lancelot emerges from a great forest to find beautiful meadowland on either side of a wide river, on which he can see a fishing boat with several people in it. Among them is a knight wrapped in an ermine blanket, lying on a silk covered mattress, with his head resting in a maiden's lap. Lancelot greets the people in the boat who tell him that he can take lodging in a castle on the other side of a nearby mountain, at the foot of which he finds a hermitage.

Realizing that he is approaching the Grail Castle, Lancelot decides to make confession to the hermit, but has to admit that there is one sin of which he does not repent: his love for the queen. The hermit warns him that, if he lodges at the house of the rich Fisher King, he will never see the Grail, because his heart is full of sin.

As night is approaching Lancelot sets off for the Grail Castle, crossing three wide bridges and encountering two lions chained at the gates, which he passes without fear. Lancelot is taken in to see the Fisher King, who is lying on his bed in a room filled with light, although it is night-time and Lancelot can see no candles. But even though Lancelot sits down to eat with the company, the Grail does not appear to him, just as he was warned, because of his sinful relationship with the queen. He leaves the next day, later meeting the Fisher King's brother, a hermit who tells him that if he desired the Grail as much as he does the queen, then he would have seen it.[9]

When news comes to the court that Perceval has conquered the Grail Castle, Arthur makes a pilgrimage there, taking with him Gawain and Lancelot. They take shelter at night in a forbidding manor house in a forest and are shocked to discover there a chamber piled high with corpses. They are attacked by a band of demon knights, but Lancelot draws a protective circle with his sword around the house so that they cannot enter. The companions manage to kill some of the knights, whose demonic spirits fly off in the form of crows. But what in the end makes the band gallop away is the sound of a bell, the only one heard in the country at that time.[10]

The time has now arrived for Lancelot to keep his appointment with the axe at the Waste City. When he arrives back there, he hears wailing women lamenting the fact that the knight who beheaded their lord has not returned to meet his fate. But Lancelot, though he wishes he could see the queen just once more before he dies, will not be forsworn. He kneels down before the brother of the man he killed and submits to the axe which he himself had wielded a year earlier.

But as he hears the blow coming, Lancelot ducks and the blade misses; the lord of the city reprimands him for doing so. But just as the lord is raising the axe for the second blow, two maidens appear at the windows of the palace. They recognize Lancelot as the knight who in the past had helped them and their brother, the Poor Knight of the Waste Castle. One of them tells the lord of the city that he will win her eternal love if he spares Lancelot, whom she praises as the only warrior ever brave enough to return there. Lancelot's head is spared but, as a result of his faithfulness, the inhabitants can return. The city is waste no more.[11]

In the Castle Adventurous

Others say that, although Lancelot's first visit to the Grail Castle is unsuccessful, it is not uneventful: For, while there, he conceives a son who will achieve the Quest of the Holy Grail and bring to their conclusion the adventures of Logres.

After winning a tournament, Lancelot is offered overnight accommodation by a lady who promises to show him the most beautiful creature in the world. Accordingly, the next morning, they set off for the castle of Corbenic, where he is taunted by the locals, claiming that he will soon end up in a cart (as, indeed, had Gawain, who was the first of the Knights of the Round Table to assay this adventure). But he who was once obliged to travel in a cart is not fazed. As he approaches the main tower, he sees a maiden trapped in a boiling bath. Gawain had earlier tried unsuccessfully to help her, but Lancelot has no trouble pulling her out of the scalding water.

The people of the castle all gather round to witness the events and, after taking the maiden to the chapel to thank God for her deliverance, they take Lancelot to a cemetery. There he sees a tombstone on which is inscribed letters explaining that it can only be lifted by the Leopard who will, shortly thereafter, beget the Great Lion on the beautiful daughter of the King of the Land Beyond. Lancelot lifts it easily and is then obliged to dispatch a fire-breathing dragon which emerges from the tomb.

The King of Corbenic, Pelles of the Land Beyond, now introduces himself to the visitor. Pelles declares that he is in no doubt that either Lancelot, or someone begotten by him, will deliver the land (which has for so long been laid waste[12] and its people impoverished) from the strange adventures that occur there both day and night. He also secretly arranges with Brisane, his daughter's cunning tutor, to get the knight into bed with the princess.

As Pelles and Lancelot are conversing, a dove flies in through the window, carrying a golden censer which fills the room with sweet scents. Its entrance is followed by that of the beautiful woman whom Lancelot had been brought to Corbenic to see. But it is the vessel she carries, in the shape of a chalice, which most impresses him: He believes it to be both precious and holy.[13] Bowing humbly before it, he notices that the tables have suddenly become covered with the finest foods imaginable.

After the king has eaten, Brisane tells Lancelot that Queen Guenevere is nearby, at Case Castle. The knight sets off to see her immediately, not realizing that a trap has been set for him: Brisane has prepared a potion which will delude his senses so that, when he is led into a bedroom in the castle, he believes that he is in Camelot and that the lady who awaits him is the queen. It is, in fact, the Princess of Corbenic, who was up till then a maiden, but who will, by morning, be a woman!

She is not partaking in the deception out of bodily lust, however, but because she knows that from their union will be born the child who will restore to its original beauty the land that was laid waste by the Dolorous Blow. God Himself does not wish the Land Beyond to remain a wasteland forever; that is why He allows the coming of the virginal Galahad to redeem the sinfulness of his conception, by restoring it to its original beauty.[14]

Sheer Carelessness

The next day Lancelot has recovered his senses and is furious at the deception perpetrated on him. But when the princess begs him to have pity on her as God did on Mary Magdalen, he forgives her. Within three months, it is confirmed that she is pregnant.

Oblivious to the fact that he is soon to become a father,[15] Lancelot returns to Camelot, where news of his failure at Corbenic has preceded him: Gawain had earlier learnt at the Waste Chapel that the son of the Queen of Sorrows (that is, Lancelot) has, through his unfortunate lust, lost the chance to complete the marvelous adventures of the Grail.[16] Now Guenevere expresses regret that his love for her may mean that he will fail to achieve the highest adventure of earthly knighthood: the Quest of the Holy Grail, for which the Round Table itself was founded.[17] But Lancelot insists that it is her love alone that has inspired him to achieve the great deeds of chivalry for which he is renowned.[18]

Nevertheless, there will continue to be many reminders of his unworthiness for the highest spiritual achievement: Thus, after dreaming of his grandfather (King Lancelot of the White Land, after whom he was named), he makes his way, as he has been instructed to do in the dream, to the Perilous Forest. Despite the warnings of a dwarf, who declares that only the Good Knight whose symbol is the lion will free the area of adventures. Lancelot rides on until he comes to a marble tomb guarded by two lions. He sees an ancient cross and, in front of it, a marble block on which it is written that the tomb contains the body of King Lancelot, but that a nearby spring contains his head.

Dispatching the lions, Lancelot sees that blood is running onto the tomb and that the spring water that contains the head in a lead basin is boiling. An inscription on the basin reads that the water will boil until a virgin knight who does not know the fires of lust arrives there. Undeterred, Lancelot pulls the handsome head from the water. At this point he is approached by a hermit from a nearby chapel who suggests he tries to raise the tomb, a feat that can only be achieved by the best knight in the world. Lancelot succeeds in raising the tomb, which is no longer bloody, removes the body, and carries it to the hermit's chapel. There he lays it next to the body of his grandmother, in fulfillment of her dying wish.

The hermit then tells Lancelot about the tragic fate of his grandfather: King Lancelot was of the lineage of Joseph of Arimathea and, during his reign over the White Land, which borders on the Land Beyond, he had driven out the local pagans and spread Christianity throughout the land. But he was treacherously killed by the Duke of the White Fortress, who beheaded him so violently that his head flew into the water. The duke wished to hack the head into pieces, but the spring water started boiling, and he realized that this miracle meant that God was angry with him. The duke tried to get back to his castle before anyone realized what he had done, but a great darkness had engulfed the building and a piece of the wall fell on him. That darkness will remain in the castle, adds the hermit, until the arrival of the Good Knight who will accomplish the adventures of the Holy Grail.[19] Lancelot is not that man, because he has squandered his youth through filthy indulgence. As for the tomb which the Queen of the White Land erected over her husband's body, every day at the hour when the king was killed, it bled. The blood could heal any wounds: The lions which guarded it had fought there and had both been healed.

Before leaving the forest, Lancelot will see more lions—six in all, surrounding a stag with a golden chain around its neck, in defiance of nature—and he will hear news of the "lion" who will accomplish what he has failed to do. A knight tells him that he has recently come from King Arthur's court, where an aged gentleman brought the joyful news of the birth of the one who would accomplish the adventures of the kingdom: He is the son of the best knight and the most beautiful maiden in the world, the Rich Fisherman's daughter.[20]

It is only now that Lancelot, remembering the trick played on him at Case Castle, realizes that he is the child's father.[21] He will soon have the opportunity to meet the boy, when

King Arthur holds the most splendid court of his reign at Camelot on the feast of Pentecost. The daughter of King Pelles is present, much to Lancelot's embarrassment; she brings with her young Galahad and the woman who engineered his conception, her governess Brisane.

The Princess of Corbenic is disappointed that Lancelot has eyes only for the queen, but Brisane is soon up to her old tricks. Hearing Lancelot plan a secret assignation with Guenevere, she leads the hero to the wrong bed where, once again, he makes love with the wrong woman.[22]

Lancelot may have considered being deceived once to be tragic, but twice is sheer carelessness. When Guenevere finds out, she banishes Lancelot from her presence. He goes mad.[23]

The Guilty Knight

For two years, Lancelot runs naked in the woods. But eventually he comes by chance to Corbenic, where the princess recognizes him as he sleeps under a sycamore tree beside a spring in the royal gardens. She calls her father the king, who has the madman bound and carried into the Palace of Adventures, where the Grail was wont to come. Through the grace of the Holy Vessel[24] he is cured and his memory restored.

Remembering how he has lost the love of the queen, Lancelot has no desire to return to Logres; so, the king provides him with a castle on an island from which he can, nevertheless, see the land of his heart's desire. The Guilty Knight, as he now styles himself, asks the princess to keep him company. She brings with her twenty maidens who, every day, dance around the pine tree where Lancelot has hung his shield—one he has specially commissioned, showing a kneeling knight begging for mercy from a silver queen—so that, despite Lancelot's mourning, it becomes known as the Isle of Joy.

In order to regain his chivalric skills, the Guilty Knight challenges all comers; and, for the next six years, he defeats all who venture there. Finally, his half-brother Hector arrives with Perceval—they have been searching for Lancelot to bring him the news that the queen has rescinded her ban and he will be welcome once more at court. Lancelot and Perceval fight to a standstill but, once they discover who each other are, Lancelot declares himself defeated and agrees to leave the island.

Before he returns to Logres, Lancelot bids farewell to his son, who declares his wish to be nearby his father; so, King Pelles sends his grandson to his sister, an abbess in Camelot Forest, where Galahad will be able to see his father often. Once the boy reaches the age of fifteen, a hermit prophesies to the king that he who is to be knighted at the coming feast of Pentecost is he who will take his place on the Perilous Seat and bring to an end the adventures of the Holy Grail.[25] A messenger arrives from King Pelles, bidding Lancelot follow her to a nearby convent, where he is impressed by the sight of his son, now grown. Lancelot is gratified to make the boy a knight, declaring that as soon as Galahad arrives at Camelot, the Grail Quest will begin.[26]

Back at Camelot, Lancelot alone possesses a mysterious knowledge of the events that are transpiring: When he sees an inscription on the Perilous Seat, stating that the seat will find its master on that day, he has it covered up so that no one should see it apart from he who is destined to fulfill the prophecy.[27] Moreover, when a sword stuck in a floating stone appears on the river, bearing an inscription stating that only the best knight in the world can wear it, Lancelot refuses to try to draw it out, warning that any who fail in the attempt to do so will receive a wound. He adds that on this day shall begin the marvelous adventures of the Holy Grail.[28]

It is of course Galahad who, when he arrives, sits in the Perilous Seat and draws the sword without harm.[29] His arrival is followed by an epiphany: The grace of the Holy Spirit in the form of the Grail descends on the assembled Knights of the Round Table, but the sacred Vessel is covered with white samite; Lancelot is among those who swear that they will never rest until they have seen it uncovered.[30]

In the course of his quest, however, Lancelot is led to understand the depth of his sinfulness in loving the queen and the hollowness of his martial victories. In a ruined chapel in the Waste Forest, he comes upon the Holy Vessel, but cannot approach near it.[31] Crestfallen, he confesses his adulterous affair to a hermit and swears to renounce Guenevere. But, at the same time, he cannot but acknowledge that she has made him what he is: It is for her love that he has accomplished the deeds which have made him world-renowned.[32]

But his next encounter with a hermit puts him straight even about that: It is not his love for Guenevere that has enabled him to perform such wondrous deeds, but rather the residue of the virtues with which God imbued him at his birth—virtues which he has been losing since he came to Camelot and was overtaken by lust and pride. If he had managed to keep those virtues intact, he would not have failed in the adventures of the Holy Grail, but would rather have been outdone only by the True Knight[33]—who is, of course, his own son.

Leaving the hermitage, Lancelot travels on until he stops to rest at a wayside cross. Dozing off, he has an extraordinary dream-vision of a man beset by stars, wearing a golden crown and attended by two knights and seven kings. Kneeling before the cross, the nine call on the Heavenly Father, who answers their prayers by coming down among them surrounded by choirs of angels.

God invites the seven kings to enter into His mansion of endless joy. But the eldest of the knights, He rebukes for squandering His treasure; while the youngest knight, He transforms into a winged lion which immediately takes flight, its huge wings enshadowing the whole Earth, before it disappears into the heavens.[34]

Fortunately, it is not long before Lancelot comes across another hermit who is versed in dream interpretation. The seven kings are the ancestors of Lancelot,[35] he learns; by the elder knight is signified himself and, by the younger, his son Galahad.

As if to illustrate his squandering of divine treasure, Lancelot later takes part in a tournament where he supports the black knights against the white, but ends up nearly collapsing from exhaustion and getting captured by his opponents, something that has never happened to him before.[36] Dejected, he comes to the Median River that divides the Waste Forest, where his horse is killed by a black knight who emerges from the water.[37] Praying for guidance, he hears a voice telling him to enter the first ship that he encounters.

This, it turns out, contains the dead body of Perceval's sister. He is joined there by his son Galahad, who was witness to the death of the maiden; he tells his father how he won a sword that had once belonged to King David. Lancelot asks to see it and, not doubting its high provenance, kisses the pommel, the scabbard and the blade, declaring his son's discoveries to constitute the most sublime adventure.[38]

For more than half a year they stay

together in the ship, travelling to lonely islands and triumphing in strange adventures. Eventually Galahad is summoned to depart by a white knight and Lancelot is left to make his way to Corbenic, praying that he might see some tidings of the Holy Vessel. At the gate of the Grail Castle, he sees lions on guard but, when he draws his sword to fight them, a dwarf strikes it out of his hand and a voice from on high tells him to trust in his Maker, not in his armor. He is privileged to witness, through an open chamber door, the Mass of the Holy Grail but, when he tries to enter the room, he is struck blind, deaf and helpless.[39]

For twenty-four days (corresponding to the number of years that he has indulged his sinful love for the queen) he lies between life and death. When at last he recovers, he can only say that he has had a spiritual vision that his tongue cannot describe nor his heart conceive of.[40] But he is brought down to earth when the people of the castle tell him that he will never see more of the Grail,[41] and King Pelles informs him that Elaine, his daughter, is dead. With a heavy heart, Lancelot now returns to Logres.

Stopping at a white abbey on the way, he finds the tomb of Bademagu,[42] the king in whose realm Lancelot had achieved the pinnacle of earthly prowess, the rescue of his queen. He makes his way back to Camelot, to the joy of the court, for few of the Knights of the Round Table have yet returned from the Quest. Lancelot tells the king what he knows of the achievements of his son Galahad, his cousin Bors and their companion Perceval[43]; but his own quest is over.

Notes

1. *LG* II, 8.
2. It is also implied that Ban of Benoic's father, King Lancelot, is descended from Joseph of Arimathea through his mother (*MH* 363n1).
3. *LG* I, 116.
4. *LG* II, 60.
5. *LG* III, 12-4.
6. *HBG* 83.
7. *HBG* 88: *Li Graaus ne s'apert pas a si amoreus chevalier conme vos estes, car vos ameis la roine, la feme nostre seignor le roi Artu et ja tant conme cele amors vos gise el coer, le Greal ne verreis* (*HLG* 384).
8. *HBG* 90-1.
9. *HBG* 109-15.
10. *HBG* 176-9.
11. *HBG* 181-4.
12. The reason the land is *deserté et essillié* and subject to *estranges aventures* (*LM* IV, 204) is because of *le doloreux cop de l'espee as estranges ranges* (210): This is the Dolorous Blow struck with the Sword of David (also known as the Sword with the Strange Straps) during the reign of King Pelles' grandfather, whereby the Land Beyond and part of Wales were turned into the Waste Land.
13. In Malory's version Lancelot asks Pelles what this means, to which the king replies, *this is the rychyst thynge that any man hath lyvynge, and whan this thynge gothe abrode the Rounde Table shall be brokyn for a season ... this is the holy Sankgreall that ye have here seyne* (*MD* 622).
14. *LG* III, 162-5: Loomis (1963, 163-4) probably speaks for "the modern thoughtful reader" when he states that "there can be few passages in Arthurian romance as distasteful and as repellent to reason as the sanctimonious plotting that went into the begetting of Galahad.... King Pelles is nothing short of despicable. If there is morality here it is of the most sophistical sort, and of spirituality there is none."
15. In Malory's version, Elaine reveals to him: *I have in my wombe bygetyn of the that shall be the moste nobelyste knyght of the worlde* (*MD* 624).
16. *LG* III, 97-8: *li chaitis chevaliers qui par sa maleurose luxure a perdu a achever les merveilloses aventures del Graal* (*LM* II, 367); *li maleureux chevaliers ... qui par sa chetive luxure avoit perdu a achever les aventures del Saint Graal* (V, 2).
17. *...il me poise quant vos en avez perdu a mener a chief les hautes aventures del Saint Graal por quoi la Table Reonde fu establie* (*LM* V, 3).
18. *LG* III, 207.
19. *...li bons chevaliers ... par cui les aventures del Saint Graal seront menees a chief* (*LM* V, 127).
20. *...cil estoit nez par qui les hautes aventures del saint Graal seroient menees a fin; si est issuz dou millor chevalier dou monde et de la fille au Riche Pescheor* (*LM* V, 139).
21. *LG* III, 237-42.
22. This, as Loomis (1963, 163) wryly points out, "does not speak well for his intelligence."
23. *LG* III, 320-1: It must be said that, as family reunions go, this one has been singularly traumatic.
24. *...par la vertu dou Saint Graal* (*LM* VI, 224): *and so they bare hym ... into a chambir where was the holy vessell of the Sankgreall. And byfore that holy vessell Sir Launcelot was layde. And there cam an holy man and unhylled that vessell, and so by myracle and by vertu of that holy vessell Sir Launcelot was heled and recoverde* (*MD* 650).
25. *LG* III, 332-8.
26. *PV* II, 15.
27. *Hit semyth me ... that thys syge oughte to be fulfylled thys same day.... I wolde none of thes lettirs

were sene thys day tyll that he be com that ought to enchyve thys adventure (MD 667).

28. ...en cest jor d'ui comenceront les granz aventures et les granz merveilles dou Saint Graal (QP 6): thys same day shall the adventure of the Sankgreall begynne, that ys called the holy vessell (MD 668).

29. In the Post-Vulgate version, a maiden arrives to tell Lancelot that in the course of the day he has ceased to be the greatest knight in the world, as is proven by the adventure of the sword, which he did not dare to touch (PV II, 33; MD 672). When Tristan arrives at court, thus completing the Round Table, Lancelot tells him that Galahad, the Very Good Knight, has also accomplished the adventure of the Perilous Seat (*Seeda Perigosa*), which no other knight has dared (PV II, 36).

30. LG IV, 3–8; V, 113–22; QHG 31–46.

31. *So when the holy vessell had bene there a grete whyle hit went unto the chapell ... so that Sir Launcelot wyst nat where hit was becom; for he was overtakyn with synne, that he had no power to ryse agayne the holy vessell* (MD 694). He acknowledges that his *olde synne* (his adultery with Arthur's wife) has so dishonored him that it rendered him unable to stir or speak when the *Holy Bloode* appeared before him (695).

32. LG IV, 20–4; QHG 82–94.

33. LG IV, 40–1; QHG 141–4.

34. LG IV, 42–3; QHG 147–8; MD 717: In the Post-Vulgate version, the knight who squandered his treasure is delivered over to devils by Morgan the Fay and sees Guenevere burning in a pit. He is then told by the ghosts of his dead parents that his adultery has rendered vain his quest for the Holy Grail. In a subsequent dream he is touched on the thigh by the ghost of Iseut, the adulterous Queen of Cornwall. When he awakens, his thigh feels like it is burning; it is only cured when touched by the virginal Perceval (LG V, 171–4).

35. The seven are descended from Celidoine, the first Christian King of Caledonia (modern Scotland). They are: Narpus; Nascien (named after his great-grandfather, the Duke of Orberica); Helain the Fat; Isaiah; then Jonah, who became King of Gaul; (the first) Lancelot (for whom our hero is named); and lastly, Ban of Benoic.

36. LG IV, 44–6; QHG 151–7; MD 718–20.

37. LG IV, 47; V, 178; QHG 160–1; MD 722: Philippe Walter (2004a, 74–5) suggests that this black knight is, mythologically speaking, the *double sombre* of Lancelot (who was brought up in an underwater realm), *son aspect nocturne et chthonien*.

38. In the Post-Vulgate version, Lancelot is warned by his aged maternal grandfather Galegantin (through whom Lancelot is of the House of David) that he is too sinful to be worthy of achieving the adventure of the Sword with the Strange Straps. Shortly thereafter he is apprised of the "beautiful adventure" whereby Galahad won it (LG V, 258–9).

39. In the Post-Vulgate version, Lancelot sees, on the silver Table of the Grail, the Holy Vessel covered as richly as it had been on the day that Josephus, the first bishop of Christendom, celebrated Mass in the Spiritual Palace in Sarras. Lancelot declares that whoever can see openly the Most Holy Vessel which has brought about the marvels of Logres, would be truly fortunate: *tant fust ore beneureuz qui peust veoir apertement celui saintime veissel ... par cui tantes granz merveilles sunt avenues el roiaume de Logres* (PV III, 244). He approaches the Grail in order to unveil it: *descouvrir le Saint Veissel, por veoir le apertement* (245)

40. ...*grete mervayles of secretnesse ... that no tunge may telle, and more than any herte can thynke* (MD 775).

41. ...*vostre queste est achevee; por noient vos travailleroiz plus por quierre le Saint Graal; car bien sachiez que vos n'en verroiz plus que veu en avez* (QP 259): *the queste of the Sankgreall ys encheved now ryght in you, and never shall ye se of the Sankgreall more than ye have sene* (MD 775).

42. LG IV, 77–82; QHG 253–68.

43. In Malory's version, Arthur expresses the desire to see all three again. Lancelot once more reveals an uncanny knowledge of distant events when he declares that two of them will never return: *But one of them shall com home agayne* (MD 778). This is Sir Bors, who will stand by Lancelot's side in the tragic events that follow.

The LAND BEYOND

A mysterious territory reached by the Company of the Grail in its efforts to convert Britain to Christianity, the Land Beyond[1] is ruled by a pagan king called Calafes.

When Alan the Fat and his followers come to the country's chief city, Malta, the king, Calafes, agrees to be baptized if the Grail can cure him of leprosy.[2] Calafes destroys the pagan idols he worships and gets into a tub of water to be baptized; Alan then shows him the Holy Vessel and the king is instantly healed. He kills all of his subjects who will not also convert,[3] but most of them do so after witnessing the miracle.

Calafes, whose baptismal name is Alphasan, promises to build a citadel to house the Grail on condition that it stays in his land forever. Moreover, he gives his daughter to Alan's older brother, Joshua, whom he decides should rule the land after him. King Alphasan now has a beautiful stronghold including sumptuous palaces built above a rapid running river. When its construction is complete, a miraculous inscription is found on one of the gates, saying that the castle should be called Corbenic.

The night of the wedding of his daughter to Joshua, King Alphasan sleeps in the main palace where, during the night, he witnesses the Mass of the Holy Grail. But a fiery angel warns him that he will be punished for his presumption and strikes him through both thighs with a lance: Thus begins a tradition whereby the Kings of the Land Beyond will often be maimed.

Alphasan himself only lives another ten days: He dies on the same day as Alan and they are buried next to each other in the Church of Our Lady in Corbenic. The place where Alphasan was struck down is henceforth known as the Palace of Adventures[4]; while the Grail remains in the Land Beyond[5] until the arrival of Galahad, the Good Knight.

Notes

1. The Land Beyond is a translation of *el roiaume de Terre Foreine*, a kingdom which borders Wales (*ESG* 566).
2. The name Malta inevitably reminds a Christian audience of the missionary voyages of the Apostle Paul, who was shipwrecked on the Mediterranean Island of Malta, where he received a warm welcome from the pagan king after healing his father through the laying on of hands.
3. While it is sometimes true that recent converts to a cause become its most fanatical adherents, the contemporary Christian may feel that the king has somewhat misinterpreted the teachings of the Savior.
4. *LG* I, 158–9.
5. In the Post-Vulgate Cycle the Grail Kingdom is called Listenois and only becomes known as *li roiames de Terre Forainne* after Balin strikes the Dolorous Blow which wastes the land (*SRM* 167).

LIONEL

The eldest son of King Bors of Ganis and a descendant, through his mother, of the House of David, Lionel is one of the one hundred and fifty Knights of the Round Table who set off on the Grail Quest.

Along the way he is attacked by two knights and, although he manages to escape, he is incensed that his brother Bors, who witnesses the incident, chooses to rescue a damsel in distress instead.[1] Heretofore the best of friends, the brothers engage in deadly warfare when Lionel refuses to forgive Bors for his inaction. A hermit intervenes to pacify the furious Lionel, then a fellow Round Table knight, Calogrenant, also tries to help; Lionel kills them both. Bors would then have killed him, if a bolt of lightning had not separated them.[2]

Notes

1. *LG* IV, 56: *QHG* 187–8; *MD* 736: According to the Post-Vulgate version, Lionel's attackers are struck dead by God in answer to Bors' prayers (*PV* II, 239). This does not mitigate Lionel's homicidal anger towards his brother, which makes him like a man possessed by devils: *como homem que avia diaboos* (243).
2. *LG* IV, 60–2; V, 160–5; *QHG* 200–5; *MD* 742–7.

LISTENOIS

The country bordering Wales in which Corbenic is built, Listenois becomes known as the Land Beyond[1] and the Kingdom of the Waste Land after Balin strikes the Dolorous Blow.[2]

There is in the kingdom an island of giants: King Pelles drives them out and gives the island to Lancelot after he has been cured of madness by the Holy Grail.[3]

Notes

1. In the *Estoire del Saint Graal*, the land where Corbenic will be built and the Grail housed, is already known as *Terre Foreine* when Alan the Fat and his company arrive there (*ESG* 559).
2. ... *le roiame de Listinois* ... *fu puis de tous apielés li roiames de Terre Gastee et li roiames de Terre Forainne* (*SRM* 167).
3. *LG* V, 77–8.

LOGRES

The largest kingdom in the island of Britain, Logres (corresponding to what is now England) is bordered on the west by the realms of Cornwall and North and South Wales; on the north, by the Kingdom of Albany, or Caledonia.

According to the Fisher King, the whole country, which had hitherto been greatly prized, was laid waste by the single blow of a sword[1]—the Sword of Partinal, which killed the king's brother Gon[2]—thus obliging the Company of the Grail to escape to an island off the coast.[3]

Others say that Logres was destroyed by the rape of the Maidens of the Wells and the stealing of their golden vessels, with which they would provide travelers with all the food and drink they required. A direct consequence of this was the disappearance of the court of the Fisher King, which had blessed Logres with the world's riches.[4] Logres would only be restored when the court was found again.[5]

It is also written that Logres, which was once ruled by giants,[6] will one day be destroyed by the Bleeding Lance.[7]

Notes

1. *CSG* 219: *Li roiaumes de Lougres fu/ Destruiz, et toute la contree,/ Par un seul cop de ceste espee* (*CP* II, ll.17546–8); *Ce fu domages et pechiez,/ Quar por ce cop fu essilliee/ La terre qui tant est prisiee/ De Lougres et toz li roiaumes,/ S'en furent puis batues paumes* (ll.17770–4).
2. *CSG* 479.
3. *CSG* 217: This island, where Gawain attempts to mend the broken Sword of Partinal, is described as a part of *Engleterre*, which is the post–Arthurian name for Logres (see THE WHITE ISLAND). Arthur's lost Logres is still remembered in the modern Welsh name for England, *Lloegr*.
4. *CSG* 557–8: *El roiaume de Logres fu/ Toute la rikece del monde* (*EB* ll.114–5).
5. *CSG* 560.
6. According to the chronicler Wace, following Geoffrey of Monmouth, the island of Albion was only inhabited by giants when Brutus and his company of Trojan exiles arrived there. They subdued the giants and settled the land, which was renamed Britain after Brutus. Brutus' eldest son Locrinus was given the rule of the south and east of the island, an area that was named Logres after him.
7. *CSG* 53: *Et s'est escrit qu'il iert une ore/ Que toz li realmes de Logres,/ Qui jadis fu la terre as ogres,/ Sera destruiz por cele lance* (*CGM* ll.6094–97).

LOHENGRIN

When a warrior attempts to compel Elsa, the young Duchess of Brabant to marry him, she appeals to the emperor, who determines that the matter must be settled through trial by combat.

One day Elsa catches a falcon with a golden bell attached to one of its legs; she accidentally rings the bell while praying for divine help. The bell rings so loudly that it is heard on Mount Savage, where the Grail is guarded; whereupon the daughter of Parzival asks the Grail what must be done to quiet it. The oracular Grail reveals to her the peril and sends her brother Lohengrin to Elsa's aid.

Lohengrin is taken to Brabant by a boat drawn by a swan, fed only by a Host, or consecrated wafer, which the angelic bird provides and shares. Arrived in Brabant, Lohengrin defeats the warrior and marries Elsa himself; but she must ask nothing of the country he comes from or the people he is descended from. When she eventually does so, he announces that he is the son of Parzival and that, because his father failed to ask the Grail Question, no question must ever be asked of the Grail Knights. Commending his wife and their two sons to the care of the emperor, Lohengrin departs once more in the swan boat. He is seen no more.[1]

Notes

1. Weston 1896, 233–6: The story summarized here is from a Bavarian poem which, along with references to Parzival's son Loherangrin (q.v.) in Wolfram von Eschenbach's Grail poem, became the basis of Wagner's famous opera (227); in which, however, it is a dove, the Grail's symbolic bird, which leads Lohengrin back to Montsalvat (242).

LOHERANGRIN

The son of Parzival, Loherangrin is destined for the Grail's company and wins fame in its service.[1] Divinely appointed to marry the Duchess of Brabant,[2] he is brought on a skiff drawn by a swan from Mount Savage to Antwerp. But he is obliged to return whence he came when his bride asks him about his origin—a question forbidden to those who marry Grail Templars.[3]

Notes

1. The Grail Stone itself chooses those who are to serve it: Their names appear on it while they are still children, and they are summoned to the Temple of the Grail on Mount Savage. Those who serve the Stone, the Grail Templars, keep all others in ignorance of the Grail Kingdom, Parzival himself being the only person to arrive there unsummoned (*WP* 240-1; *PT* 198-9). They are vowed to chastity unless they are sent to other kingdoms to father an heir in secret (*WP* 251; *PT* 208)—this theme being the basis of the Lohengrin legend, made famous by Wagner's opera.
2. The Kingdom of the Grail is ruled by a dynasty of Grail Lords who can only marry the woman whose name appears inscribed on the Grail Stone. Anyone who seeks any other kind of love will suffer for it, as the hermit Trevrizent tells Parzival (*WP* 243; *PT* 201). This is indeed the fate of the hermit's brother, Anfortas, who is maimed as a punishment for loving the Proud Lady of Logres.
3. *WP* 406-10; *PT* 343-6.

LONGINUS

Both Perceval and Gawain, when they first visit the Grail Castle, see a Lance from the tip of which blood drips. But it is not until his second visit that Gawain hears from his host that the Bleeding Lance is the one with which Jesus was pierced on the Cross: He who struck Him, says the king, was called Longinus[1]; but he would later be granted mercy and his soul is now at peace.[2] Perceval later learns that Longinus was blind but that, when he asked Christ for mercy for killing Him, God the Father gave him his sight and with it, light and clarity.[3]

* * *

Although the French sources describe the Bleeding Lance as being carried off to Heaven towards the end of the Grail Quest, Wolfram von Eschenbach does not recount its ultimate fate, leaving the way open for the modern myth of the Spear of Destiny.

According to Trevor Ravenscroft, the Lance with which the Roman centurion Gaius Cassius (who would later become known simply as the "lancer," *Longinus*) pierced the side of Christ, later came into the possession of St. Maurice (a third century Christian martyr) and of Constantine the Great. After the Arthurian period, it re-emerged as part of the regalia of the Holy Roman Emperors, whose patron saint was Maurice, eventually ending up as part of the imperial treasures of the Hapsburgs displayed in the Hofburg Palace in Vienna. It is there that it was first seen by Adolf Hitler in 1909; although it would be nearly thirty years later before he was able to take possession of it (or perhaps we should say, that *it* took possession of *him*), when he marched into Austria and declared the Anschluss.

Ravenscroft tells us that Hitler was an initiate of the Grail Quest,[4] who became obsessed by the legend that whoever possessed the Lance would be able to rule the world. Hitler began his quest by studying Wolfram's *Parzival* and Wagner's *Parsifal*, but attempted to short-cut the long and arduous process of initiation by taking the psychedelic drug mescaline.[5] But this spiritually illicit path to transcendent consciousness opened him up psychically to the cosmic shadow, personified by the figure of the Anti-Christ!

When Longinus pierced the side of Christ with the Lance, it was an act of compassion for the suffering Jesus—and compassion, for Wolfram, is the very essence of the Grail Quest—so he was rewarded by the restoration of his sight by the Holy Blood that flowed down the shaft. But for those who are blind to the beauty of compassion, such as Hitler, the spirit of the Spear of Destiny is a treacherous ally. And so it was that as, in the ruins of the Third Reich, the Holy Lance passed to the new world-rulers, the Americans, the way was opened for the dropping of the atomic bomb. The Lance that was once believed to be destined to destroy England[6] could now be seen as the harbinger of world destruction.

Although the Lance of St. Maurice is once more on display in the Hofburg Palace, some claim that it is a fake, the real Lance of Longinus having been dispatched by Hitler in a U-boat to Antarctica—whither some believe that the Führer himself escaped—and that, in 1979, a group of neo-Nazis launched an expedition there, to reclaim the Spear of Destiny.[7] The myth lives on....

Notes

1. *Longis ot non qui le feri* (*CP* I, l.13471): According to the *Elucidation*, the seventh branch of the Grail story concerns the Lance with which Longinus struck the side of the King of Holy Majesty: *Dont Longis feri el costé/ Le Roi de sainte Majesté* (*EB* ll.355-6).

2. *PSG* 132: Perceval doesn't learn this until his third visit to the Grail Castle, when the Fisher King also tells him that the blood that flows from the head of the Lance is *li sains prec'ieus senc/ Qui dou costé Dieu descendi/ Quant Longis dou fer lou feri* (*MTC* ll.32666-8): "the precious, holy blood that flowed from God's side when Longinus struck him" (*CSG* 477); "Longinus washed his eyes with it and recovered his sight" (569): *Longis s'en terst et raluma* (*DC* l.13215).

3. *CSG* 397: *Dieus nostre pere Jesu Cris/ A Longis sa mort pardona,/ Quant merchi quist, et li dona/ Veüe, lumiere et clarté* (*GCP* ll.7338-41). Lancelot also learns that, if he truly repents his sinful relationship with the queen, the Savior will forgive him, just as He forgave the one who struck Him in the side with the Lance: *si vraiement com il pardona sa mort a celui qui le feri de la lance el costé* (*HLG* 462).

4. Ravenscroft considers the Grail Quest to be a peculiarly western initiatory "path to self-knowledge" (1982b, 7) which does not require withdrawal from the life of the world (18).

5. Ravenscroft 1982a, 77-88.

6. It is written, Gawain is told, that the Lance will one day destroy the realm of Logres (Welsh *Lloegr*); a realm which, since the Anglo-Saxon conquest, has been called England.

7. Kafton-Minkel, 239-40.

M

MAHOM

When Joseph of Arimathea comes to Britain on an evangelizing mission with the Company of the Grail, he learns that Mahom is the name of one of the four pagan deities (along with Tervagant, Jupiter and Apollo) who are worshipped in Britain before its conversion to Christianity.[1]

The Saracen Argon explains to Joseph that they do not believe that the pagan images they worship have power in themselves; rather, the power of the god works through its image.[2] When Argon is killed in Joseph's company, the Saracens take his body to their idol of Mahom, in the hope that their god will revive him. But this miracle is only achieved when Joseph prays to the Father, the Son and the Holy Spirit, explaining that they are only one God, who is so powerful that He can raise the dead. The pagan idols are all destroyed by lightning.[3]

Notes

1. In the Forest of Broceliande, when Joseph talks to Argon about God, the pagan wants to know *which* god he is referring to, telling Joseph: *Ja n'avons nous ke .IIII. dieus: Mahom, Tiervagant, Jupiter et Apolin* (*LDL* V, 636). The pagan religion is referred to as *la mahoumerie* (622), suggesting that Mahom is the chief god of the pantheon. The same word is also used to refer to a mosque or pagan temple (644)—before Joseph converts it to Christianity, the Castle of the Dolorous Garde is considered to be *la mahomerie as paiens* (*LM* II, 253)—and *les mahomés* can mean pagan idols in general (*LDG* I, 493).

2. ...*l'ymage de Mahom poet par celui valoir en cui forme il est fait, aussi puet cascune ymage par son dieu* (*LDL* V, 638).

3. *LG* I, 140-2; III, 88-90.

* * *

It is clear that the romance writers (composing their stories at the time of the Crusades) are confusing an ancient British pagan god with the Prophet of Islam, as well as confusing the astral cult of the Saracens (whose spiritual center is the holy city of Sarras) with what they disparagingly call *mahoumerie*.[1]

The extent of the ignorance of medieval Christian romancers about Islam is revealed by this passage, found in both the *Estoire del Saint Graal* and the Vulgate *Lancelot*, in which the Saracens are depicted as revering images of Mahom and other pagan deities: Joseph of Arimathea asks the Saracen if he is saying that the images men make out of wood and other materials are gods which have more power over men than men do over the idols. The author shows a more sophisticated understanding of pagan religion than he does of Islam, when the Saracen explains that "graven images" do not themselves have power, but that they channel the power of the divinity they represent.

Interestingly, when Joseph later explains to Argon's brother Matagran his own faith in the Trinity, Matagran accuses him of worshipping three gods[2]: reflecting a common criticism of Christianity by Moslems, who are strictly monotheistic.

Notes

1. The assimilation of Moslems with pagans and monotheistic Islam with the ancient polytheistic religions is common in the Middle Ages and is found particularly in the *chansons de geste* (*LDG* II, 1952).
2. *LG* I, 142.

The MAIDEN OF THE SILVER TRENCHER

Arriving for the first time at the court of the Fisher King, the young hero Perceval witnesses an astonishing procession of talismans. These are, notably: a boy carrying a Bleeding Lance; after him a girl, carrying a bejeweled, golden Grail; and, after her, another girl, holding a silver trencher, from which roast venison is served to the assembled guests.[1]

When Gawain comes to the same court, he is struck by how beautiful the girl carrying the trencher is[2]; but then, Gawain always has a keen eye for a fair lady. By contrast, when Perceval makes his third visit to the Grail Castle, determining to ask about the trencher and the other things he sees there,[3] it is the beauty of the silver trencher itself, rather than she who carries it, that strikes him.

In answer to his questions, he is told that it was used to cover the Holy Grail, the vessel in which Joseph of Arimathea had caught the Holy Blood at the crucifixion. The silver trencher is now carried by the daughter of Gon of the Land Laid Waste, the Fisher King's murdered brother.[4] After Perceval has avenged her father's murder, he arranges a noble marriage for her. But the trencher stays with Perceval when he retires to a hermitage, finally ascending to Heaven with him when he dies.[5]

Notes

1. *CSG* 29.
2. *CSG* 108.
3. *CSG* 473: In fact, Perceval has already learnt that the trencher, which shines "brighter than the moon," was brought to Britain from the Holy Land by Perceval's long-lived mother Philosofine (422).
4. *CSG* 478: The Maiden of the Silver Trencher is, therefore, the Grail Bearer's cousin. But, as the niece of the Fisher King, she may be identical to the Fair-Haired Girl who sends him a sword destined for Perceval, and who later seeks vengeance for the murder of her brother Silimac.
5. *CSG* 555.

The MAIMED KING

The young hero Perceval's first meeting with the Maimed King is shrouded in mystery. Encountering him fishing on a river, Perceval does not know that he is maimed, that he is a king, or that he is Perceval's cousin. But when the fisherman invites him to spend the night at his "house," Perceval discovers that it is a castle; his host is now a richly-dressed nobleman who is unable to stand.

Perceval witnesses a mysterious procession involving a Bleeding Lance and a golden, bejeweled Grail, but is too polite to ask how the Lance bleeds or who is served from the Vessel.[1] Had he done so, as another cousin later tells him, the king— who has been wounded through the thighs in battle by a javelin and consequently

The MAIMED KING

maimed[2]—would have regained the use of his limbs and the governance of his realm; while the consequence of Perceval's silence is that many ills will befall him and others.[3]

An Ugly Maiden who comes to King Arthur's court spells out these dire consequences: Women will be widowed, lands laid waste,[4] girls orphaned, knights killed.[5] So it is that Gawain, the next knight to come to the castle and meet the Maimed King, makes sure he asks about what he sees there. Unfortunately, he falls asleep before he can hear the answers![6]

Eventually, Perceval returns at last to the house of the Maimed King and asks the questions that he should have asked the first time. He learns that the Bleeding Lance is the one with which Longinus pierced the side of Christ on the Cross, and that the Grail is the Vessel in which Joseph of Arimathea caught the Holy Blood. The king is a relative of Joseph,[7] who brought the Grail and the Lance to Britain, while the weapon which maimed him is not in fact a javelin but a sword once wielded with murderous intent by Partinal the Wild.

Apparently, the sword broke in two when Partinal treacherously killed the king's brother with it. The corpse and the broken pieces of the sword were brought to the king by one of his nieces, who assured him that whoever could repair the sword would be the one to avenge his brother's death. But so distraught was the king that he used the shards of the sword to cut through the nerves of his thighs,[8] rendering himself helpless.[9]

It is Perceval who repairs the sword. After many other adventures have been achieved, and a year and a summer have passed, Perceval returns to the Grail Castle, having killed the treacherous Partinal; only to find that the Maimed King is now healed, his pain and sorrow turned to happiness.[10]

The Vengeance of the Lance

It is also said that after the Fisher King Lambor is killed by a Dolorous Blow, which wastes his Kingdom of Listenois as well as adjacent parts of Wales, both his son Pellehan and his grandson Pellinor are injured by thigh wounds which lead them to be called Maimed Kings.

Thus, some say that Lambor's son Pellehan is struck through both his thighs during a battle in Rome.[11] But others say that he is attacked in his own castle by the Knight with Two Swords wielding the Avenging Lance, a relic of Christ's Passion with which the Fisher Kings have been entrusted.[12]

Pellehan's son Pellinor is also struck through both thighs by the Lance when he attempts to draw from its scabbard the Sword with the Strange Straps, which he finds aboard the Ship of Solomon.[13] As a result he is also known as the Maimed King,[14] and it is prophesied that he will never be cured until he meets the one who will bring to an end the adventures of the Holy Grail.[15]

Unfortunately, Pellinor dies before this can happen. But several Knights of the Round Table arrive by chance at the Grail Castle and meet his brother Pelles and Pelles' father Pellehan, the Maimed King: First, Bors meets Pelles and hears about the Maimed King[16]; then Pellinor's son Perceval meets Pellehan fishing[17]; then, finally, Bors, Perceval, and nine other knights arrive at Corbenic to witness Galahad heal the Maimed King.[18]

Seated at the Table of the Grail, the twelve attend a Mass performed by the spirit of Josephus,[19] descended from the sky. This is watched by the Maimed King on a wooden bed, who welcomes the one who will deliver him from almost unendurable anguish.[20] After the knights receive the sacrament from the very same platter from which Jesus ate the paschal lamb with His disciples, Christ Himself instructs Galahad to take the Lance which an angel had brought into the room and to anoint the Maimed King's legs with the blood that flows from it[21]; whereupon the king rises from his bed in full health.[22]

Thus, King Pellehan is healed by the same Lance with which he had once been maimed.

* * *

From the medieval Grail legends to scholarly speculations about Celtic mythology and into the high modernism of early twentieth century poetry, the image of a king, whose maiming creates a Waste Land, haunts western consciousness. But the poets and scribes who developed the legend are unable to agree about the identity of the king or the nature of his maiming.

The earliest appearance of this theme in the Matter of Britain is probably in the Second Branch of the *Mabinogi*, where we are told that Brân the Blessed, King of Britain, is wounded in the foot with a poisoned spear during his invasion of Ireland. This, however, appears to be a euphemism, for he is also known as Pierced Thighs. As a result of the war, two kingdoms are devastated, and the head of Brân continues to speak to his followers.[23]

Chrétien de Troyes, who wrote the earliest known account of the Grail, may have been drawing on this Welsh tradition when he tells us that the Lord of the Grail Castle has been wounded through the thighs in battle by a javelin. But we enter *terra incognita* with the idea, promoted by Perceval's cousin, that the good king who is now maimed would regain the use of his limbs and be able to manage his lands,[24] if only Perceval had asked about the mysterious procession that he sees in the Grail Castle. When Manessier brings the story that Chrétien started to a much-delayed close, what is needed to heal the Maimed King (whose wounds are now described by the king himself as self-inflicted) is vengeance on the man who murdered the king's brother.

For Jessie L. Weston, who saw at the root of the Grail legend the confused memory of the rituals of a mystery cult, the Maimed King is a literary version of "the god, in whose honor the rites were performed"[25]: a Dying-and-Resurrected God, like Adonis or Attis. In her reconstruction of the rituals of the Grail cult, Weston sees the Maimed King as one of three guardians of the different stages of initiation, each of which has its own Vessel. In contrast to the higher spiritual or "philosophic" and the lower "underworld" initiations, the Maimed King (the god's "activities restrained and hampered by the Flesh in which he is now clothed") initiates the quester into "the middle plane, that of Humanity, or Actuality," where the Grail is not *holy* but *rich*, the feeding Vessel of the ritual feast.[26]

In her last (and most famous) book on the Grail legend, *From Ritual to Romance*, Weston writes: "The Exoteric side of the cult gives us the Human, the Folk-lore, elements—the Suffering King; the Waste Land; the effect upon the Folk; the task that lies before the hero; the group of Grail symbols."[27] These symbols include the Tarot cards, whose four suits of Cups, Wands, Swords and Dishes correspond to the "group of symbols found in the Grail romances"[28]; and some of them recur in T.S. Eliot's *The Waste Land*, a poem first published two years after Weston's book. Here the Suffering King, in an "unreal" Waste City where death has "undone so many," can be seen as one who is "neither/ Living nor dead" and hence emblematic of the psychological maiming of twentieth century humanity, suspended between two worlds like the Hanged Man of the Tarot. Thus, the Grail Question becomes one about whether or not you are truly alive.[29]

Notes

1. *CSG* 27-9.
2. ...*il fu en une bataille/ Navrez et mehaigniez sanz faille,//...il fu ferus d'un gavelot/ Parmi les quisses ambesdeus* (RP ll.3509-10, 3512-13); *Parmi les hanches* (PCG l.3513). Perceval's mother also describes her husband as having been *parmi la jambe navrez/ Si que il mehaigna del cors* (RP ll.436-7). Other manuscripts say that he was *par mi les anches navrez* (CGM l.408), the same variation that is found in the description of the Maimed King's injury—and indeed, in the Vulgate Cycle,

the Maimed King Pellinor is named as Perceval's father.

3. *CSG* 31-2.

4. *Terres an seront essilliees* (*PCG* l.4679): Thus, the Ugly Maiden announces the theme of the Waste Land, which will be developed by later writers.

5. *CSG* 41.

6. *CSG* 108-9.

7. *Je suis ici de son lignaige* (*MTC* l.32764): In the Vulgate Cycle the Maimed Kings Pellehan and Pellinor (the grandfather and father of Perceval respectively) are direct descendants of Bron, Joseph's brother-in-law. In Manessier's Continuation to the Story of the Grail, the Maimed King is Perceval's uncle, his mother's brother (*CSG* 551); and, in the German version of the Grail story developed by Wolfram von Eschenbach, the Maimed King is similarly Perceval's mother's brother (see ANFORTAS).

8. *Parmi les cuises an travers/ M'an feri, si que toz les ners/ An tranchai* (*MTC* ll.32913-5).

9. *CSG* 478-9.

10. *CSG* 549-50.

11. *LG* I, 160: *Aprés lo roi Lambor regna Pellehan, ses filz, qui fu mehaigniez des dous cuisses en une bataille de Rome, et por celui mehaing ... l'apelerent lo Roi Mehaignié* (*ESG* 566). A Portuguese translation of the *Estoire del Saint Graal* tells us that the son of King Lambor is known as the Maimed King (*el Rei Tolheito*) because he is wounded through both thighs by a blow which the Knight with Two Swords struck with the Avenging Lance (*Lamça Vimgador*), thus inaugurating the adventures of Logres (Bogdanow 2003, 45-6).

12. *LG* IV, 212.

13. *...li rois Pelinor que l'en apele lo Roi Mehaignié* (*QSG* 512): In other manuscripts this mishap is attributed to a certain King Parlan (*LG* IV, 66; *QP* 209)—an otherwise unknown Maimed King—while Pellinor's brother Pelles can also be called the Maimed King: *roi mehaignié, ce fu li rois Pellés* (*LDL* I, 122; *LG* II, 16). Malory confuses things even further by calling the king maimed on the Ship of Solomon Pelles, Pelleaus (*MV* 583) or Pelleans (*MD* 756)—again, depending on the manuscript—while the king maimed by Balin the Savage is called *Kynge Pellam off Lystenoyse* (66).

14. *LG* I, 254: *Icel estoit malades et plaïés de la lanche vengeresse ... et apelés Mehaingniés et estoit navrés par ambes .II. les quisses, et fu apelés par son droit non li rois Pellinor de Lystenoys* (*LDG* I, 939).

15. *LG* I, 235.

16. Although he does not actually see the Maimed King, Bors is told by Pelles that the latter's father is *li rois mehaingniez que l'an apela le Roi Pescheor*; that he was struck through the thighs by the sword which must only be drawn by he who is destined to achieve the Grail Quest (*qui les aventures dou Saint Graal doit achever*); and that he will only be healed when that Good Knight anoints his wounds with the blood from the Lance (*LM* V, 273; *LG* III, 272).

17. According to the Post-Vulgate *Suite du Merlin*, Perceval first meets him fishing on a river, despite being richly dressed and wearing a crown. The king tells the knight: "My baptismal name is Pellehan, but others call me the Rich Fisherman. Since I can't make use of my limbs at will or at need, others call me the Maimed King" (*LG* V, 109). This encounter is in striking contrast to Chrétien's original account of the meeting, where the maimed Fisher King is Perceval's cousin (see above).

18. Galahad is born and brought up in the Kingdom of Listenois, thus fulfilling Merlin's prophecy that the one who will bring to an end the "perilous wonders" of the adventures of Britain will emerge "out of the chamber of the Maimed King"; although a further reference to "the adventure-filled Waste Forest" (*LG* II, 253) would apply as well, if not better, to Perceval—perhaps reflecting different traditions as to which of the two heroes was the true Grail winner.

19. Joseph of Arimathea's son who, in his lifetime, was also struck through the thighs by the Lance.

20. *QHG* 274; *MD* 782.

21. *Also I woll that ye take with you off the bloode of thys speare for to anoynte the Maymed Kynge, both his legges and hys body, and he shall have hys heale.... And Sir Galahad went anone to the speare which lay uppon the table, and towched the bloode with hys fyngirs, and cam aftir to the Maymed Kynge and anoynted his legges and hys body* (*MD* 784): *Et Galaad vient a la lance qui ert couchiee sus la table et toucha au sanc, puis vient au Roi Mehaignié et li en oinst les jambes par la ou il avoit esté feruz* (*QP* 271-2). In the Post-Vulgate version, Galahad is led to the chamber where the Maimed King lies and left alone there to perform the healing. King Pellehan makes it clear that his maiming is the result of the Dolorous Blow struck by the Knight with Two Swords (*LG* V, 279).

22. *LG* IV, 84-5; *QHG* 277.

23. *M* 78-81: If the disembodied head of the giant king is seen as oracular, it might shed some light on a curious episode in one manuscript of the Prose *Tristan*: Here Bademagu reminds Arthur of a prophecy made by the Maimed King: that Arthur would hold a *court aventureuse* which would be unexcelled in joyousness, but that it would lead to unsurpassed sorrow: *et cele seroit la daireniere joie del reaume de Logres*. But Arthur responds that they should not treat the prophecies of the Maimed King as infallible, in the way they did those of Merlin (*PV* IV.1, 12-13).

24. *Que tant eüsses amendé/ Le buen roi qui est mehaigniez/ Que toz eüst regaaigniez/ Ses membres et terre tenist* (*RP* ll.3586-9).

25. Weston 1907, 67.

26. Weston 1909, 257-9.

27. Weston 1920, 158.

28. Weston 1920, 77.

29. *WL* ll.39-40, 55, 60, 63, 126.

MANIBEL

A resident of the Palace of Adventures in Corbenic, where he is encountered by Sir Bors,[1] the aged Manibel was originally one of Joseph of Arimathea's followers,[2] who came with him to Britain. But while in the Welsh city of Cleodice, Manibel refuses to venerate the Holy Grail, disbelieving what Joseph has told them about it.[3]

Thanks to the intercession of Joseph, Manibel, like the other apostates (Moses, Simeon and twelve women) is punished physically, but not by the eternal damnation of his soul. Rather, he must live on in torment, awaiting the coming to Corbenic of Galahad, who will free him and the women from their punishment.[4]

In the course of the Grail Quest, Galahad removes two serpents which have been placed around Manibel's neck as punishment for his blasphemy. Manibel dies soon afterwards.[5]

Notes

1. *LG* III, 270–1.
2. *And than the olde man had an harpe, and there he sange an olde lay of Joseph of Aramathy, how he cam into this londe* (*MD* 629). According to the Vulgate *Lancelot*, this lay (*le Lai de Plor*) recounts a magical battle between Joseph and Orpheus the Enchanter, whose influence stretches as far north as the Scottish border (*LM* V, 265–7).
3. The *mescreance* of Manibel and the other apostates consists of treating Joseph's Grail teaching as fictitious: *tenoient a fable ce que Joseph faisoit del Saint Graal* (*TPM* IX, 256–7).
4. *Et seront el Palais Aventureus, et la demoueront em penitance dusc'a la venue del boin cevalier Galaad* (*TPM* IX, 258).
5. *TPM* IX, 253: This conclusion to the mystery of the harpist with two serpents round his neck is found only in the Prose *Tristan* (Barber 2005, 201–3).

MARS

When Joseph of Arimathea leads the Company of the Grail to the pagan holy city of Sarras, the center of an astral cult that stretches as far as Britain, he challenges the demons that live inside the pagan statues to test their power against that of Christ. It is the demon of Mars who takes up the challenge; whereupon Josephus, the first Christian bishop, compels it to smash all the idols in the temple.[1]

Note

1. *LG* I, 30–1: During the Quest of the Holy Grail, when most of the Knights of the Round Table leave Arthur's court and many are killed, King Mark—who is named after the day (Tuesday) and the month (March) of Mars (*RTC* 4)—besieges Camelot but, with the aid of Galahad, the invaders are routed. Consequently, Mark makes an unsuccessful attempt to murder Galahad, an act typical of a king who, in the French prose romances, is increasingly seen as cowardly, treacherous and murderous—qualities that he might have inherited from the demon of Sarras who possesses the idol of Mars.

MARY MAGDALEN

After Jesus casts seven demons out of her, Mary Magdalen becomes his devoted disciple and is the first person to see him after the Resurrection.[1]

* * *

The references to the Magdalen in the orthodox Gospels are supplemented by the Gnostic Gospels, which make of her his closest female companion[2]; while the medieval Cathars, who shared the anti-cosmic dualism of the early Gnostic heretics, considered her to be his wife or concubine.[3]

In the Thirties Otto Rahn, a German student of medieval poetry, searched for the origins of the Grail legend in Languedoc, once Cathar country. Rahn refers to a Provençal tradition that the Magdalen brought the Holy Grail to the south of France.[4] More recently, this idea has been developed by other researchers, who claim that she is herself the Grail insofar as she is the vessel carrying the Royal Blood (Sangreal), for she bears a child to Jesus and mothers a dynasty, the bloodline of the Messiah.[5]

Note

1. Haskins, 3–10.
2. *GS* 335; *NHL* 145; Haskins, 40–1.
3. Stoyanov, 222.
4. Rahn, 111.
5. Baigent *et al.*, 344.

MELIAGANT of Denmark

The Danish prince Meliagant[1] is acting as squire for King Bademagu when his lord is severely injured in combat with a mysterious White Knight, after taking a Red Cross Shield from an abbey. The White Knight gives the shield to Meliagant, bidding him take it to Galahad, to whom it rightfully belongs. After hearing how the cross on the shield was made with the blood of Josephus, the first Christian bishop, Meliagant asks Galahad to make him a knight and ride with him on the Grail Quest.[2]

Meliagant of Denmark is subsequently one of the twelve knights who arrive at Corbenic to witness the accomplishing of the adventure of the Holy Grail.[3]

Notes
1. Also called Meliant, or Melias.
2. *LG* IV, 11–15; V, 126–30; *MD* 679–83; *QHG* 55–66: We are not told if the sword with which Galahad knights the squire is the ill-fated Sword of Avalon (which Galahad inherited from Balin, in Malory's version), but it seems likely, as the first adventure that Meliagant undertakes nearly kills him: When he steals a crown of gold from a deserted lodge, he is severely wounded by the knight who guards it (*LG* IV, 15–16; V, 131–3; *MD* 684–6; *QHG* 67–71).
3. *LG* V, 278–80.

MEMORY OF BLOOD

When Galahad, Bors and Perceval are joined on the Ship of Faith by Perceval's sister, she reveals to them many of its mysteries. The sword that they find on the ship is partly enclosed in a scabbard of rose-red snakeskin. On it is a long inscription, explaining that the tatty baldric attached to the scabbard must only be replaced by a princess who is a life-long virgin in thought and deed, using whatever about her person is most precious to her; it is she alone who can reveal the true name of the sword and the scabbard.

After revealing to her brother and his companions the sacred history of the sword, which was once borne by King David and which was set adrift on the ocean by King Solomon at the behest of his wife, the royal maiden (for she is the daughter of the King of the Land Beyond) replaces the tatty baldric with one woven herself from her own hair—for she had cut it off on the day that Galahad was knighted, in expectation of the great adventure that awaited her. She then reveals to the knights that the true name of the ship's sword is the Sword with the Strange Straps; moreover, the name of the scabbard is Blood Memory, for it was partly made from the Tree of Life, which turned red when Abel was murdered beneath it.[1]

* * *

Miguel Serrano, who recuperated the Grail Quest for his doctrine of Esoteric Hitlerism, understands Blood Memory as the memory of the primordial land of Hyperborea, which is carried in the blood of all true Aryans and which emerges in the Middle Ages as the cult of courtly love (*Minne*). The Scabbard appears personified as the Absolute Woman who declares: "The memory of the love lost at the beginning of time flows through the blood. Seek me in your blood, keep it pure. When you remember what your blood tells you, sing it. You will be a warrior-troubadour, a *Minnesänger*, who will have sung our dream of resurrection and eternal love for all eternity."[2]

Note
1. *LG* IV, 65, 71–2; V, 231–2; *QHG* 216–7, 236–7: In Malory's version, Sir Percivale's sister calls the scabbard Mover of Blood: *the name of the swerde ys the Swerde with the Straunge Gurdyls, and the sheeth, Mevear of Blood. For no man that hath blood in hym ne shall never see that one party of the sheth whych was made of the Tree of Lyff* (*MD* 761).
2. Serrano 1984, 43.

MERLIN

The son of a demon who confers on him all knowledge of the past, including the sacred history of the Holy Grail, Merlin also has knowledge of what is to come conferred on him by Our Lord,[1] because of the goodness of his mother. While still a child, he instructs his mother's confessor Blaise to write down, at Merlin's dictation, the story of Joseph of Arimathea and the dynasty of Grail Keepers; Blaise must take the book he thus produces with him to the place where the Holy Vessel is guarded.[2]

It is Merlin who instructs Uther Pendragon to build the famous Round Table, using as its model the Table of the Grail, which was in turn based on the Table of the Last Supper: The three tables will symbolize the Trinity. There must be a place kept empty at the Round Table, representing the place vacated by Judas when he betrayed Jesus. This empty seat, Merlin prophesies, will only be taken by the one who is destined to fulfill the adventures of the Grail. All this will happen not in Uther's time, but in the days of his successor as King of Britain[3]; God has given Merlin all his wisdom in order for him to help in fulfilling these adventures.[4]

Merlin first talks to Arthur about the Holy Vessel when the king encounters the Questing Beast, which Merlin explains is one of the adventures of the Grail: The beast's full significance will only be known to the king when he learns it from a knight who is not yet born: Perceval of Wales.[5] Merlin later informs the king that Balin will strike the Dolorous Blow: As a result of this, there will be great troubles lasting twenty-two stormy years throughout Great Britain, but especially in the Kingdom of Logres.[6]

Merlin has already forewarned Balin of what will happen.[7] But this does not stop the knight from riding on to fulfill his ill-fated destiny at the Grail Castle, which is ruined when he strikes the Fisher King with the Avenging Lance. Merlin arrives on the scene, lamenting Balin's foolish actions and predicting that many marvelous adventures, involving great peril, are yet to come amid the misery[8]; some of them will be cruel and ugly.[9]

The Fulfillment of the Prophecy

It is said[10] that, after instructing Blaise to write the Book of the Grail and Uther to construct the Round Table, Merlin stresses that the one who is destined to fill the empty seat at the Round Table should only do so after being in the presence of the Grail.[11] The importance of this only becomes evident when Perceval comes to Arthur's court and sits in the place destined only for the finest knight in the world. The Earth groans, the Seat cracks and a voice rings out, declaring that, by allowing this to happen, Arthur has disobeyed Merlin's command.[12]

Merlin had also prophesied that the destined knight, having achieved sufficient renown, will come to the court of the Fisher King and ask the purpose of the Grail. By doing so, he will heal the king, who will pass on to him the Secret Words which the risen Christ spoke to Joseph of Arimathea in prison. After this, the aged king will die and the knight will have the keeping of the Holy Blood, thus bringing to an end the enchantments of Britain.[13] The fulfillment of this prophecy is the goal of the Grail Quest. Merlin consequently intervenes to point Perceval on the true path to the court of the Fisher King, but the knight fails to ask the required question.[14]

A further seven years pass before Merlin confronts Perceval with his failure and, showing him the way once more to the house of the Fisher King, reminds him to ask about the things he sees there. This time the prophecy is fulfilled and the empty seat joined together once more. Merlin finds the aged Blaise and takes him to the house of the Fisher King, to be in the company of the Grail and finish writing his book.[15]

Merlin is never seen again, although he lives until the end of the world.[16]

Note

1. *MG* 55; *LG* I, 172.
2. *MG* 61–2; *LG* I, 176: *iceles parties ou ces gens sont qui ont le saint vaissel del Saint Graal* (*LDG* I, 612).
3. *MG* 92; *LG* I, 196–7: *Et il couvenra qu'il acomplisse les aventures del Saint Graal et ce ne sera mie a ton tans, ains iert au tans le roi qui aprés toi regnera* (*LDG* I, 697).

4. *LG* I, 280: *Nostre Sires m'a donné tant de sens et de discrecion com je ai pour aïdier a complir les aventures del Saint Graal qui doivent estre acomplies et traites a fin au tans le roi Artu* (*LDG* I, 1051).

5. *LG* IV, 171.

6. *LG* IV, 199: *pour coi les aventures dou Saint Graal averront* (*SRM* 118).

7. *LG* IV, 190–1.

8. *LG* IV, 213.

9. *LG* IV, 232.

10. In the version of the Grail story with which most people are familiar (that of Malory, itself based on the prose Vulgate and Post-Vulgate Cycles), Merlin dies before the beginning of the Quest. But, in the earlier and less well-known De Boron Cycle, he takes an active role in its unfolding.

11. *MG* 94: *Et covenra celui qui emplir le doit qu'il ait esté la u li Graaus sert* (*RG* 161). In Micha's edition it is specified that the knight must sit in the empty seat at the Table of the Grail before attempting the Perilous Seat at the Round Table: *et covendra a celui qui doit acomplir cest leu acomplir avant celui dou vaissel dou graal* (*RBM* 190).

12. *MG* 119.

13. *MG* 113: *Et cil, quant il s'ara si essaucié que il pora venir a la cort le rice Roi Pescheor, et que il ara demandé de quoi li Graaus a servi et de quoi il sert, et tant tost sera garis. Et lors il acontera les secrées paroles de nostre Segnor, si trespassera de vie a mort. Et cil cevaliers ara le sanc Jhesucrist en garde. Et lors charront li encantement par le terre de Bretagne, et adont si sera la prophesie toute paracomplie* (*RG* 194–5).

14. *MG* 139–43.

15. *MG* 153–6.

16. *MG* 171.

MESSIOS

Messios the Fisher King, who is the uncle of Perlesvaus, has fallen into a grievous languor and even the valor of King Arthur is waning, as a result of the hero's failure to ask the Grail Question.[1] Nevertheless, the court of the Fisher King remains a blessed place—as Gawain discovers, when a hermit tells him that all who serve him experience his grace, retaining the appearance of youth.[2]

Gawain determines to find the court and ask the healing question; on the way, he frequently hears about the damage Perlesvaus has done by his failure. But when after many adventures he approaches the entrance to the land of the rich Fisher King, where the Mass of the Holy Grail is about to begin, Gawain is told that he cannot approach any closer until he brings the sword with which John the Baptist was beheaded.[3]

This he accomplishes and at last meets the king, to whom he presents the sword. The Fisher King is not surprised by his arrival, having known he was coming with the sword: Neither Gawain nor anyone else could have entered the castle without it. He kisses the sword tenderly and then apologizes to Gawain for the paucity of his welcome, which he attributes to having succumbed to languor ever since Perlesvaus' unsuccessful visit.

Sadly, Perlesvaus will not be the only visitor to neglect the one important thing that could cure the king: When Gawain witnesses the Grail Procession, he is caught up in mystical visions and is unable to speak.[4] Later, when Lancelot—who has been told that the Fisher King's name is Messios—comes to what he calls the Castle of Souls,[5] he cannot see the Grail because of his adulterous affair with Guenevere.[6]

As a result, the Fisher King, worn out by the attacks of his evil brother, the King of Castle Mortal, eventually dies unhealed, with the quest unfulfilled.[7]

Note

1. *HBG* 34–5.
2. *HBG* 42.
3. *HBG* 61.
4. *HBG* 77–80.
5. *HBG* 88: *al Chastel des Armes ... li rois a nun Messyos et gist en langor par .II. chevaliers qui ont esté el chastel qui ne fisent la bone demande* (*HLG* 382).
6. *HBG* 112.
7. *HBG* 146: The fate of Messios—a type of the Messiah who dies for the sins of others?—constitutes a unique variation on the myth of the Fisher King.

MONTESCLAIRE

On the peak of Montesclaire in Ireland sits the Castle of the Circle of Gold where, once a year, the Crown of Thorns that Jesus wore on His head when He was crucified is displayed. The Lady of Montesclaire has had the relic set in gold and precious stones. It is prophesied that only the knight who first sees the Grail in the court of the Fisher King, can win possession of it.[1]

The Queen of the Circle of Gold, as she became known, loved Alan of Escavalon, but he was killed by the Knight of the Dragon, who invaded Logres seeking revenge for the death of his brother. The demonic knight then occupied the Isle of the Elephants, a once beautiful island beneath the peak of Montesclaire. As a consequence, the lady is obliged to look down on its ruins and watch the Dragon Knight killing and dismembering everyone he finds.[2]

Meanwhile, Montesclaire itself is besieged by the three black knights of the desolate Waste Land.[3] The Ugly Maiden, who is the Grail Messenger, comes to Arthur's court when both Perceval and Gawain are there. She tells the court that whoever can raise the siege of Montesclaire and free its lady, will carry off the prize over the whole world; moreover, he will be able to gird on the Sword of the Strange Belt.

Gawain determines to take up this quest,[4] but events overtake him. It is nine months later before he arrives at Montesclaire, raises the siege by defeating the three knights, and wins the sword.[5] But it is Perceval who eventually comes to the Isle of the Elephants and kills the Dragon Knight.[6] The queen crowns him with the Circle of Gold and presents him with the sword with which he killed the knight, urging him to use it to kill all those who will not embrace the New Law of Christ. She herself is the first in her land to be baptized, taking the Christian name Elyza; her body is honored for many centuries afterwards in Ireland.[7]

Note

1. *HBG* 131.
2. *HBG* 158–9.
3. ...*li troi chevalier noir/ De la lande gaste anermie* (*CP* II, ll.4198–9).
4. *CSG* 41.
5. *CSG* 110–6.
6. Gerbert's Continuation gives an account of the defeat of the Dragon Knight (*CSG* 413–9) which differs in significant details from the one in the Romance of Perlesvaus.
7. *HBG* 162–4.

MONTSALVAT

Situated in the mountains of Northern Spain, Montsalvat is the place where two sacred relics (the Cup of the Last Supper and the Spear that pierced the side of Jesus on the Cross) are guarded in a temple by the Order of Grail Knights, led by their king, Amfortas.[1]

Built by Amfortas' grandfather Titurel on the instructions of the Holy Vessel itself, the Temple of the Grail is dedicated to the Holy Spirit and took thirty years to complete.[2] It has a threefold structure: the upper zone is a sapphire-covered dome; the lower, a "sea" of crystal; and, in the intermediary zone, are the choirs or chancels[3] with, at the center, the Holy of Holies where the Grail hovers. The Vessel remains untouched by human hands, until it names Amfortas' sister as its rightful bearer.[4]

Eventually Titurel (who has been kept alive by the presence of the Grail) and his great-grandson Parsifal take the Holy Vessel to the East, lest it fall into the hands of the evil-doers who surround Montsalvat.[5] On their way to India, they pass through a certain city where they leave the inhabitants with an image of Montsalvat, from which the citizens start building their own temple.[6]

* * *

Wolfram von Eschenbach calls the mountain atop which stands the Temple of the Grail *Munsalvæsche*, which he translates as Wildenberg, or Mount Savage (q.v.). But, for Wagner, it is Montsalvat, the Mount of Salvation or Healing, reflecting the intense Christian mysticism of his opera *Parsifal*.[7]

By the early twentieth century, Wagner's symbolic Montsalvat was being identified with Montségur, a mountain in the Pyrenees which has become famous as a place of refuge for the beleaguered sect of dualist Christian heretics known as the Cathars. This identification was promoted by a group who called themselves the Polaires, indicating their belief that the Primordial Tradition of perennial wisdom originated in the Arctic prehistoric spiritual center at the back of the North Wind, Hyperborea (q.v.). One of their associates was the young German student of medieval poetry Otto Rahn, who did much to popularize the idea that Montségur was the Grail Castle and that the sacred Vessel was guarded there by the Cathars.[8]

Rahn visited the region in the early Thirties and spent a winter searching caves for relics of the Cathars who, he believed, hid there after the fall of Montségur to French forces in 1244. He published the results of his researches, amid much speculation about the relationship between Wolfram's *Parzival* and the Cathars, in his first book, *Kreuzzug gegen den Gral* (*Crusade Against the Grail*), which was published in Germany in 1933.

Here he argued, somewhat implausibly, that key figures in Wolfram's poem were based on contemporaneous figures active in the Languedoc. He also claimed that the Grail Stone, which Wolfram calls *lapsit exillis*, should be understood as "a stone that fell from the stars" which "illumines and consoles the world"—a symbol, that is, of the "pure doctrine" of Catharism: "The Grail was a heretical symbol. Those who venerated the Christian cross cursed it and a crusade pursued it. The Cross undertook a holy war against the Grail."[9]

Rahn also refers to the legend that, on the eve of the fall of Montségur, four Cathars escaped the doomed fortress, carrying with them a mysterious treasure, whose true nature has never been identified. For Rahn, this treasure was not earthly wealth but an invaluable belief system: the Desire for Paradise,[10] itself symbolized by the Grail, which Wolfram calls "paradisal, transcending all earthly perfection."[11]

Rahn's identification of Montségur with Montsalvat was taken up by the Chilean esotericist Miguel Serrano, who also located the myth of the Grail within the Hyperborean tradition. In a poetic fable of magic love, Serrano's hero is transported back to Montségur before its fall, where a female troubadour tells him that the Grail was once part of the crown of Lucifer, which broke into a thousand fragments, scattered throughout the firmament. The Grail, "like frozen fire with its green and white light," is the part of the crown that fell to Earth. But it alone can unite the dispersed fragments and return them to their source: "It is a talisman that links the individual with the morning star." It was brought to Montségur from the Orient and, when the citadel falls, it will be sent to a distant land; but Montségur will always be a special place, "for its story will pass down through the ages, transforming the lives of all who know it."[12] He later learns from a Perfect One that "the fall of Montségur is always taking place, each time with a different luminosity."[13]

In the Eighties, other researchers put forward a rather more literal (and a distinctly more sensational) explanation of the Grail treasure that the Cathars were believed to possess. According to this hypothesis, Jesus did not die on the Cross and was moreover married to Mary Magdalen—something the Cathars themselves believed[14]—and she bore Him a son. The Magdalen's womb is therefore the Grail as container of the Holy Blood (or Sangreal). According to this hypothesis, the treasure of Montségur could have included documents relating to her marriage to Jesus or to their children—or even the mummified body of Christ Himself![15]

Note

1. Weston 1896, 176.
2. Barber 2005, 193–4.
3. There is some confusion as to whether the number of chancels is twenty-two or seventy-two but, as Henry Corbin points out, both numbers have an "arithmosophical significance" (1986, 359). Twenty-two is the number of days that Josephus

bleeds after being wounded by the Avenging Lance, and the number of years that the adventures of Logres were predicted to last (*LG* I, 51). Seventy-two is a precessional number, being equivalent to one degree in the circle of 25,920 years that completes the Precession of the Equinoxes: that is, the time that it takes for the Sun to return to the same place in the heavens where it appears to rise at the Spring Equinox, as viewed from Earth—a phenomenon caused by the Earth's wobbling on its axis (Campbell, *The Masks of God* II, 117–8, 129, 200).

4. Barber 2005, 195: For Corbin, the Temple's three zones evoke Sky, Earth and Sea and thus link "the celestial, the terrestrial and the sub-terrestrial. As such, the Temple of the Grail is a sanctuary situated at the center of the world, and Montsalvat is the mountain at the center of the world" (1986, 360).

5. Barber 2005, 196.

6. For Corbin, this episode illustrates his philosophy of the imagination, in which the visionary image must be restored to its central place, mediating between sensory perception and the abstract intellect, in order to resist succumbing to the extremes of materialism and religious fundamentalism: "This *Image* is also what remains to us. No more; but no less. No less, because ... this Image is imperishable, to the extent that we see it rise triumphant in the 'waste land,' from an earth that is spiritually more devastated than the domain of the Grail ever was before the coming of Parsifal" (1986, 389).

7. Weston 1896, 180.
8. Godwin 1993a, 89–91.
9. Rahn, 115.
10. Rahn, 176–7.
11. *WP* 125.
12. Serrano 1972, 44.
13. Serrano 1972, 45.
14. Stoyanov, 222–3.
15. Baigent *et al.*, 400–2.

MORDRAIN

The baptismal name of Evalach, the pagan King of Sarras, who is converted to Christianity by Joseph of Arimathea, Mordrain apparently means "late to believe" in the Chaldean language.[1]

When Joseph and much of the Company of the Grail are imprisoned by Crudel, the pagan King of North Wales, King Mordrain has a vision of their fate in a dream, and sets out with an army to rescue them. Having killed King Crudel, the badly wounded Mordrain tries to get a close look at the Holy Grail, but is blinded.[2]

A voice from a cloud tells him that he will live on until Galahad, the ninth descendant of his brother-in-law Nascien, fulfils the Grail Quest; it is only then and not before that his wounds will be healed and his sight restored, so that he can see his Savior clearly.

Mordrain now retires to a hermitage of white monks, which flourishes thanks to his presence.[3] He lives on there for hundreds of years after the death of Nascien. It is here that he is seen by Perceval, whose mother Philosofine was one of the companions who came to Britain with Joseph.

Mordrain is given the Eucharist in the chapel by a priest attended by an angel, both of whom disappear immediately afterwards.[4] One of the monks tells Perceval that Mordrain will never be healed of his wounds until the arrival of the sinless True Knight, in whose arms he will die. Perceval longs to enter the chapel to attempt to heal the king, but he can find no entrance.[5]

Consequently, it is Galahad, he who alone will be able to see the wonders of the Holy Grail clearly,[6] who arrives at the white abbey and goes to the chapel where the king is lodged. The mere presence of the True Knight restores both the sight and the bodily strength of the incredibly aged king.[7]

Raising himself up, he praises his Savior who has restored to youth and strength his withered body. He prays that the Lord will take him now that he has achieved his heart's desire. At last, he dies, in Galahad's arms.[8]

Note

1. *LG* I, 47–8: If the people of Sarras speak a Chaldean language, this would suggest that the city is in Mesopotamia.

2. *Li rois Mordrains vit le Graal,/ La sainte chose esperital,/ Avant ala sanz plus atendre,/ Qu'a l'esgarder voloit entendre / Por les grans merveilles savoir,/ Mais il ne fist mie savoir/ De che qu'il volt avant passer,/ Car nus cuers ne porroit penser,/ Langue dire, ne oeus veoir / Les grans merveilles, por pooir / Du saint Graal* (GCP ll.10519–29).

3. *LG* I, 135–6: These "white monks" are presumably intended to make us think of the later Cistercian Order, who may have been responsible for the composition of the Vulgate Grail romances. Their abbey is presumably that of Glastonbury, which was identified with Avalon.

4. According to the *Livre d'Artus*, Mordrain is sustained solely by the daily ingestion of a sacred Host—*Mordrains li rois de Sarraz qui ne vivoit mais solement de l'oiste sacrée que li angle li metoit chascun jor en la bouche et ne vivoit d'autre chose* (VS VII, 146)—rather like the old Grail King in Chrétien's poem.
5. *CSG* 420–3; *LG* IV, 28–9; *QHG* 103–8.
6. *… cil qui doit les merveilles dou Saint Graal veoir apertement* (QP 85).
7. Similarly, in the De Boron Cycle, Bron lives for hundreds of years awaiting the arrival of his grandson Perceval in order to be restored to strength and health, but then dies peacefully.
8. *LG* IV, 82; *QHG* 269–70: *il fina entre les braz au glorieus chevalier qui acompli le siege perilleus de la Table Roonde et mena a fin les Saintes Aventures du Graal* (VS VII, 241–2).

MORHOLT

A knight of Ireland and a member of its royal family, Morholt travels with Yvain and Gawain, leading figures in the royal family of Britain, in search of adventure. In the Forest of Aroie on the road to the Kingdom of North Wales, Morholt leads his companions to a spring where adventure is always found. There they meet three maidens of different ages who invite the knights to choose one of them each, to lead them through the adventures of the country for a year. Morholt chooses the one of middle age.[1]

After various adventures, Morholt, his squire and the maiden come to a large, deep forest.

That evening they reach a crossroads where four paths separate and, at the heart of the intersection, they behold a cross of ancient wood standing behind a huge block of newly-dressed marble. On the marble stone an inscription has been cut in red letters, reading that this is the site where many of the marvels of the Holy Grail will happen[2]; but anyone who stays to see them will be killed or wounded, unless it is the Good Knight who is destined to end the adventures.

The maiden tells Morholt that it is known as the Stone of the Stag, although she doesn't know the reason why. Morholt determines to stay there until he has seen for himself some of the alleged marvels.[3]

They sit down under two elms that are nearby and watch until nightfall. In the moonlight they see two knights arrive, fight, make up and leave. A stag then lies down on the stone, only to be killed by four beagles, which are, in turn, swallowed up by a dragon. The dragon heals the stag and vomits up the beagles, which set off in pursuit of the flying stag. The dragon flies away.

Morholt doesn't know whether he's under a spell or dreaming, but falls asleep anyway. During the night he is stricken through the thighs by a spear; his squire and the maiden are killed. He is then attacked by a passing knight who has a grudge against him, and left for dead. Fortunately, Gawain comes that way and takes Morholt to a nearby tower to be healed[4]; but he will die in battle in Cornwall before the Grail Quest begins.

Note

1. *LG* IV, 274–5; *MD* 127.
2. *Sur cest perron puet l'en veoir avenir des merveilles du Saint Graal grant partie* (SRM 438).
3. *…aucune des aventures du Saint Graal que l'en tient a si merveilleuses* (SRM 439).
4. *LG* V, 15–18.

MOSES

When the Christian followers of Joseph of Arimathea leave Judaea, many of them fall into lustful ways, causing their crops to fail. Those most worthy are fed by the Grail, but the sinners go hungry and all drift away, apart from one: Moses, son of Simeon. He attempts to persuade Joseph that he is penitent and should be allowed to sit at the Table of the Grail.

Accordingly, Moses sits in the vacant place next to Joseph himself, a place that is kept empty to symbolize the seat that Judas vacated when he left the Table of the Last Supper to betray Christ.[1] But immediately Moses does so, seven fiery hands carry his burning body off to the Forest of Darnant[2]; it is here that the Company of the Grail will later find him in a ruined castle.

His demonic abduction, we learn, was interrupted by the intervention of a pious hermit, who prayed that he burn-off his lustfulness until the arrival of the Good Knight who will bring to an end the adventures of Britain.[3]

So it is that the Grail Company find Moses in the Perilous Palace engulphed by a huge fire; but thanks to their prayers his torments are halved. Moses tells his father Simeon (another sinner) that his punishment will only end with the coming of Galahad, who will fulfill the adventures of the Holy Grail.[4]

Hundreds of years later, it is in fact Simeon (who is also in need of redemption) who points Galahad in the direction of the Perilous Palace, where his son still burns.[5] Galahad frees the son from torment, just as he has the father.[6]

Notes

1. In the Vulgate version, the empty place is between the son and brother-in-law of Joseph—Josephus and Bron—and symbolizes the place of Jesus, which must remain empty until He returns or sends someone in His place (*ESG* 484–5).
2. *LG* I, 137–8; *MG* 36–9: Robert de Boron tells us that he is swallowed up by the abyss—*si fu fonduz maintenant en terre* (*EG* 96)—and will never be heard of again until he is found once more by the one who is destined to sit in the empty place (ll.2813–9).
3. ...*li buens chevaliers, cil qui menra a fin les aventures de la Grant Bretaigne* (*ESG* 510).
4. ...*Galaaz, le buen chevalier, celui qui menra a fin les aventures del Seint Graal et qui achevera les aventures de la Grant Bretaigne* (*ESG* 512–3; *LG* I, 145).
5. *LG* V, 243.
6. *LG* V, 276.

MOUNT DOLOROUS

The appearance of the Grail Messenger in the form of an Ugly Maiden at the court of King Arthur prompts several heroes to make vows to achieve difficult quests. Perhaps inspired by their example, a Round Table Knight called Kahendin takes up a quest that she has not even mentioned: He swears that he will climb Mount Dolorous and won't stop till he gets there.[1]

Unfortunately, we never learn whether Kahendin reached this mountain, or what he found if he climbed it; but we get an inkling of his fate from the misadventures of his fellows. It is while Perceval is searching for the truth about the Grail and the Lance that he discovers that there is a marvelous pillar on the great peak of Mount Dolorous, where only a very fine knight can tether his horse. Perceval determines to find that pillar in order to know for certain whether he is a good knight.[2]

After many adventures, a villainous knight attempts to trap him in a tomb. When he fails, the knight tells Perceval that, if he goes to the peak of Mount Dolorous, he will surpass the whole world in arms.[3] Later, on his way to the court of the Fisher King, Perceval is once more diverted by finding a knight hanging from an oak tree by his feet. He had been put there by Kay and three other knights who had nearly become deranged by their failure to tether their horses to the pillar on the Mount.[4]

It is nearly a fortnight later when Perceval encounters a child sitting high up in a huge tree, holding an apple, who tells him that, if he goes tomorrow to the pillar on Mount Dolorous, he will hear news that will delight him. The child then vanishes.

The next day Perceval reaches the foot of the mountain, the most beautiful in all the world, where he meets a girl coming down from the peak. She advises him not to try to reach the top, for none go there without encountering the gravest difficulty. Her lover did so and has gone mad.

Undeterred, Perceval rides to the top of Mount Dolorous. There he sees an enormous copper pillar with a ring attached to it. The pillar is surrounded by fifteen stone crosses and, around it, there is a Latin inscription warning that no-one should tether his horse to the pillar unless he were the equal of the finest knight in the world. Perceval does just this and waits.

There then appears, riding a white mule, a girl[5] who invites him to her pavilion, saying that the whole world should honor him. She tells him that she is the Lady of the High Peak of Mount Dolorous and that her mother was the mistress of Merlin, who had used his willpower to make her submit to him. He had made the pillar and the crosses by the art of necromancy,[6] at the request of Uther Pendragon, to enable the king to identify the finest knight in the land. The king was greatly pleased when he heard what Merlin had done, she tells Perceval; consequently, the enchanter led several worthy knights to the pillar. But an ill fate awaited them there.

Following the lady's instructions, Perceval sets off once more for the court of the Fisher King.[7] There he learns that the child in the tree is a divine messenger who was reminding him to always look heavenwards.[8] But what the lady did not tell Perceval—and what he only learns later—is that her father set a demon within the pillar and kept it imprisoned by the crosses.[9] If anyone apart from the finest knight asks who is in there, the demon will instantly drive him mad. This is the fate of Sagremor and Agravain, whom Perceval, who is illiterate, cures of their rage by placing on their heads a sacred letter given to him by the gatekeeper of the Earthly Paradise.[10]

Notes

1. *CSG* 41.
2. *CSG* 239.
3. *CSG* 299: see THE CHESSBOARD CASTLE.
4. *CSG* 305–6.
5. She is called a *damoiselle esperitable* (*CP* IV, l.31654; *DC* l.12263), which Bryant translates as "of otherworldly beauty" (*CSG* 330).
6. ...*Par sens, par art de nigromance* (*DC* l.12490).
7. *CSG* 328–33.
8. *CSG* 336.
9. ...*sor le Mont Dolerous/ A un piler maleürous/ Que Merlins par enchantement/ Fist jadis anciienement,/ Et si l'asist desor cel mont.// Quinze crois trestout entor a,/ Un anemi i estora/ Qu'il a enmuré la dedens* (*GCP* ll.963–7, 971–3).
10. *CSG* 346–7.

MOUNT SAVAGE

After his first, unsuccessful visit to the Grail Castle, Parzival encounters his cousin who tells him that the stronghold he has just been to, is situated in the Savage Land: It cannot be found by anyone who seeks it, unless they are destined to do so, in which case they will come across it unwittingly.

The castle is situated atop Mount Savage. Ancient Titurel bequeathed it to his son Frimutel who, dying young, passed it on to his son Anfortas, who is now its lord.[1]

Note

1. *WP* 132–3; *PT* 106. Mount Savage is A.T. Hatto's translation of Wolfram's *Munsalvæsche* or *Wildenberg*. And so, by analogy, Wolfram's *Terre de Salvæsche*, the "broad realm" in which it is situated, can be rendered as the Savage Land, a strife-torn kingdom (*WP* 218; *PT* 180). Mount Savage is transformed by Wagner, in his opera *Parsifal*, into the Mount of Salvation (Montsalvat). This ambiguity in the name of the location of the Grail may reflect the Christian metamorphosis of originally pagan material.

N

NASCIEN, Duke of Orberica

At the time that the Company of the Grail, led by Joseph of Arimathea, first comes to the Middle Eastern city of Sarras, its ruler King Evalach the Unknown and his brother-in-law Seraph become converts to Christianity. Seraph takes the baptismal name Nascien, which appears miraculously on his forehead; he immediately begins prophesying.[1]

Eventually Nascien asks to see the holy object in the ark brought by the Company of the Grail. He at once realizes it is what he has always desired, beyond anything earthly in his life. His mind is cast back to a time when, on a stag hunt, he had fallen into a reverie and heard an invisible voice telling him that the fulfillment of all his searching would only come about on the day that the wonders of the Grail were revealed to him. This day has now arrived.

Not satisfied with what he has seen, however, he raises the flat plate that covers the vessel to look inside—and is immediately blinded. The king asks him whether he can say anything about what he has seen and Nascien replies that he will tell him as much as mortal tongue can: He has seen, he says, the beginning of the greatest of all endeavors, the most wondrous of all marvels; moreover, the vision of the holy dish is worth the loss of his sight.

At that moment the Angel of the Bleeding Lance emerges from the ark and restores Nascien's sight with the divine blood. The angel announces the beginning of the marvelous adventures that will take place in Logres—the land to which God intends to lead the company of the Grail—and prophesies that, just as Nascien is the first to witness the marvels of the Grail, so the last man in his lineage will be the last to witness them, in accordance with the words spoken by the True Crucified One.[2]

Shortly thereafter Evalach, who has taken the baptismal name of Mordrain, is carried away by the Holy Spirit, whereupon Nascien is accused of murdering him. Nascien and his seven-year-old son Celidoine are imprisoned, but rescued after seventeen days: Nascien, by a fiery hand in a cloud,[3] which carries him to an island in the Western Sea, thirteen days distant from Sarras, between Oragrine Island and the Port of the Tigers.

This is the Turning Island, created at the beginning of the world when God separated the four elements, a barren island where no vegetation grows, nor creatures live. It turns with the rotation of the firmament, hence its name. Nascien arrives on this waste island on the ninth of June. The next day he encounters for the first time the Ship of Solomon, which has been floating on the seas for a thousand years, awaiting the Chosen Knight, the end of the lineage of King David, who will surpass in goodness and chivalry all those who come before and after him. Boarding the Ship, Nascien sees there the Sword of David[4] and three colored spindles made from the Tree of Life. Because he doubts whether the colors are natural, his lack of faith causes him to be plunged back into the sea; he is forced to swim back to shore.

The next day a very old man arrives on a small vessel and explains to him that the Ship is really a symbol, going on to elucidate the allegorical meaning of the things that he saw there: The Ship is Holy Church, protected by faith from the world (= the sea); and the three colored spindles represent the three virtues of virginity (white), charity (red) and patience (green). But while he is listening to all this Nascien, perhaps unsurprisingly, falls asleep.[5]

Over two years will pass before he is eventually rescued by his son Celidoine in the Ship. They come to an island ruled by a giant, who attacks them. Having nothing else with which to defend them, Nascien draws the Sword of David from its scabbard, only to have it break in two near the hilt. He finds a sword lying on the ground and with it kills the giant, then returns to the Ship, which immediately departs from the island.

Looking at David's sword, Nascien says to himself that it was the thing he prized most apart from the Grail itself; but that it had failed him, in his hour of most need.

They soon encounter another ship bearing King Mordrain, who boards the Ship of Solomon and joins the hilt and the blade of the Sword of David back together as easily as they were broken. Then they hear a noise as loud as thunder and a voice telling them to leave the Ship. But, as Nascien does so, he is struck in the left shoulder by a flaming sword and hears the voice again, telling him that he was unworthy to draw the sword and had suffered the vengeance of his Creator.[6]

Nascien is later healed by the ghost of Hermoine, a hermit in whose honor he had founded a church in his capital city of Orberica. The ghost also sends Celidoine off in a small boat, reassuring Nascien that he will be reunited with his son in the land God has promised to him and his lineage.

Nascien returns with Mordrain to Sarras where he is reunited with his sister Sarrasinte and his wife Flegetine, who has been searching for him.[7]

To the Promised Land

Nascien and his wife send far and wide for news of Joseph of Arimathea and his companions (who have long since left Sarras), believing Celidoine may be with them; but they hear nothing. Eventually the duke hears a voice in a dream telling him to go straight to the seashore and enter the first ship he finds there. This, it turns out, is the Ship of Solomon, which he had earlier been forced to leave.

Aboard ship he falls asleep and sees, in a dream vision, a man in a red robe who tells him that his son, along with Joseph and the Company of the Grail, are in the land that was promised both to him and to them and their descendants. Nascien then asks him if he will ever return to his own country. The man replies that neither he nor the Ship will ever be seen in his native country again, except in dreams; Nascien will remain in the land he has been told about and the Ship will remain nearby, until such time as the last man in his lineage boards it in order to travel to Sarras with the Holy Grail.

The man then gives him a letter, which Nascien finds in his hands when he awakens. It tells him the names of the nine men—all kings but one[8]—who will descend from Celidoine, the last of whom will bear the name Galahad.[9]

Later, Nascien is obliged to leave the Ship of Solomon for the last time. He boards another ship that takes him to Britain, where he is reunited with the Company of the Grail. Fed by the Holy Vessel, they travel across country until, on the seventh day, they arrive at the pagan city of Galafort. Here Nascien finds his son Celidoine, safe and sound as foretold, arguing with the clerks about the merits of Christianity.[10]

The Duke of Galafort, Ganor, becomes a Christian. He and Nascien lead their army against the pagan King of Northumberland, who has attacked Galafort, believing the duke to have dishonored himself by abandoning the pagan faith. Nascien himself defeats the king in battle, beheading him when he refuses to surrender.[11]

Nascien and Ganor then set off with an army to rescue Joseph and Josephus, who have been imprisoned by the pagan King of North Wales, Crudel, in whose land they have been proselytizing. On the way they meet up with King Mordrain, who has travelled from Sarras after being warned in a dream about the fate of the Grail Keepers. Mordrain is accompanied by Nascien's wife and sister as well as the daughter of the King of Persia; thus, Flegetine is at last reunited with her husband and son. In the ensuing battle all the pagans are slaughtered.

The victors return to Galafort with the Grail, but Mordrain is blinded and maimed by trying to look too closely at it. On that same day Celidoine is married to the Persian princess and invested by his father with the kingdom of North Wales.[12]

Several years pass. After the death of Josephus, Nascien remains with Mordrain in Galafort Castle to keep him company, until eventually he dies. His wife and King Mordrain's wife both die on the same day as Nascien but, whereas the two ladies are buried in the abbey where King Mordrain now lives, Nascien chose another one. After his father's death, Celidoine takes his son Narpus to the land of North Wales.[13]

Narpus is the first of the kings who will descend from Celidoine: The last is Galahad, who will bring to an end the lineage of Seraph and who, before his death, will become King of Sarras. On the fifth day after he has been made a knight, Galahad comes to the abbey where Nascien lies buried and finds there the Shield of Evalach, on which Josephus had drawn a red cross with his own blood, saying that none but the best knight in the world was destined to bear it.[14]

The sacred memory of Duke Nascien is preserved by the hermits of Logres for hundreds of years, as an example to us all. For, as one of the hermits Lancelot encounters during the Grail Quest tells him, to Nascien had been vouchsafed a vision of the highest secrets and the greatest mysteries of the Holy Grail.[15] Apart from Joseph of Arimathea, no other knight of that time was able to see them with more than a fleeting glimpse. Since that time, no knight has seen them fully except (as Lancelot himself did) in dreams[16]; or, as Galahad would, before dying.

Notes

1. *LG* I, 47.
2. *LG* I, 50–1: *Au premier home du precieus lignaige et au daerrain ai jou devisé a demoustrer mes mervelles* (*ESG* 168). These words of Jesus on the Cross are not supported by the canonical gospels.
3. *LG* I, 69–70.
4. *LG* I, 74–8.
5. *LG* I, 84–7.
6. *LG* I, 96–7; IV, 66; *MD* 755–6; *QHG* 218–20.
7. *LG* I, 112.
8. The line of kings descends from Celidoine to King Lancelot whose grandson, Sir Lancelot of the Lake, is the only one of that line who would never be crowned a king.
9. *LG* I, 113–6.
10. *LG* I, 121–3.
11. *LG* I, 128–9.
12. *LG* I, 132–5.
13. *LG* I, 160.
14. *LG* IV, 11–3; V, 128; *QHG* 59–60; Malory (*MD* 682) confuses Duke Nascien with Nascien the Hermit (see below).

15. ...*les granz secrez et les granz repostailles del Saint Graal* (*QP* 134).
16. *LG* IV, 44; *QHG* 151.

NASCIEN the Hermit

Towards the middle of the eighth century, a hermit living in a remote area of Britain is granted an immense honor: He is given the true story of how the Holy Grail came to Britain. We know that this is the definitive version of the story, because it is given to him by Christ Himself, written by the divine hand in the language of Heaven. The hermit translates it into Latin and it is his version that Robert de Boron, more than four hundred years later, will translate into French, so that it becomes the basis of what we now know about the origins and ultimate destiny of the Holy Vessel.

The hermit never names himself in his own account of the circumstances that led him to translate the Book of the Grail (an autobiographical account which functions as a Prologue to his translation of the heavenly scripture). But clues to his identity found elsewhere enable us to identify him with Nascien, a knight turned hermit with an extraordinarily long life—a longevity that is also attributed to his father Bron.

Nascien's mother is the sister of Joseph of Arimathea. She bears to Bron seventeen sons in all[1] and Britain shines with their light. Nascien is made a knight during the reign of Uther Pendragon (some three hundred years after Bron and his wife came to Britain!) and he is still a young lord at the time of the rebellion of the British kings against Arthur.[2] Sir Nascien performs great deeds in the wars and is made a Knight of the Round Table. He attends the mid–August court at which Arthur establishes an important custom: that he will not sit down to eat until he hears news of some adventure at which his knights can win honor and glory.[3]

It is at this time that news first comes to the Kingdom of Logres of the Holy Grail and Lance which Joseph of Arimathea had brought there, as well as of the prophecy that only the best knight in the world would find them.⁴ In time to come Nascien, whose parents were part of the company that brought the Grail Hallows to Logres, will himself be a crucial agent in their finding. But first he must give up his knightly armor for clerical vestments and remain a chaste virgin for the rest of his life.⁵

It is in this new role as a saintly hermit that Nascien brings spiritual succor to King Arthur when Logres is menaced by the Lord of the Distant Isles.⁶ But as the Hermit of the Grail he will be a stern critic of worldly, as opposed to spiritual, chivalry. Moreover, he takes on the role of mentoring the young Galahad, who will become the paragon of spiritual knighthood.

The Hermit of the Grail

Nascien comes to see Galahad shortly after Easter in the year that the boy reaches the age of knighthood. He then meets up with King Arthur, who is hearing Mass after hunting, to tell him that he should summon all his lords to come to Camelot at Pentecost. At that feast a new-made knight will sit upon the Perilous Seat; it is he who will bring to an end the adventures of the Holy Grail.⁷

We next hear from Nascien on the day that Galahad comes to court, sits in the Perilous Seat and draws a sword reserved for the best knight in the world from a floating stone of red marble. As the king and his courtiers stand looking, a maiden, on a white palfrey, approaches at full gallop, with a message from Nascien the Hermit. She tells King Arthur that he will, that very day, receive the great honor of an appearance of the Holy Grail in his court; furthermore, his knights will be fed by the Holy Vessel. The maiden leaves as abruptly as she arrived, but this is not the last that the court will hear from the hermit.

After the knights have a vision of the Grail and vow to find it, the women who love them offer to go with them on the Quest. However, an old and venerable man wearing a religious habit enters the hall and declares that Nascien the Hermit sends word that no women can be companions on the Quest. This is because its goal is not the fulfillment of earthly desires but the revelation by the Almighty of heavenly secrets and mysteries, the wonders of the Holy Grail, to His chosen servant.⁸

During the course of the Quest, Gawain and Hector arrive at Nascien's hermitage and ask him to interpret troubling dreams that they have had. Nascien explains that Gawain's dream is in part about those who, unlike Gawain himself, are destined to be successful in the Quest: They are the three stainless ones, one of whom will return from the Quest to tell the court what they will lose by living in sin; while the other two will never return because, having tasted the sweetness of the Holy Grail, they will never leave it.

Hector meanwhile, who had dreamt of a beautiful spring, is told that it symbolizes the inexhaustible grace of the Holy Spirit, which manifests in the form of the Grail. The grace of the Grail⁹ is that its abundance is never diminished, like a spring which never runs dry.

But Gawain and Hector are too sinful to be successful in the Quest, whose adventures are spiritual lessons, the signs and wonders of the Holy Grail.¹⁰ Nascien advises them to return to Camelot.¹¹

The Hermit of the Wild

We hear no more about Nascien during King Arthur's reign but, miraculously, he is still alive and living in a wild and remote part of Britain, hundreds of years later; but we now find him struggling with the doctrine of the Trinity. Seven hundred and seventeen years after the death of Jesus, Christ himself appears to the hermit and gives him a book, written in His own hand in a heavenly language: the Book of the Holy Grail.¹² Then an angel takes the hermit up to the Third Heaven, where he openly beholds the Father, the Son and the Holy Spirit.¹³

His doubts about the Trinity thus allayed, the hermit returns to this earthly plane; but he is soon disconcerted to find that the book has disappeared. A celestial voice sends him off to find it, on a quest that resembles those of the Round Table knights to whose company he once belonged: He must first go past the Stone of the Capture to the Valley of the Dead. Leaving the valley, he will come to the Crossing of the Seven Ways in the Plain of Valestoc. A cross marks the site where there was once much killing, by the Fountain of Tears. Here he will see a bizarre animal, which he must follow; but it is only when he has lost it that he will enter the land he seeks: Norwegia.[14]

Nascien sets off, following the angelic instructions, until he sees the animal—part sheep, part dog, part fox and part lion—lying at the foot of the cross. It leads him to a hermit's lodge, where he spends the night, then on to a very beautiful heath, in the middle of which is the Pine of Adventures, beside a wondrous spring.[15] When the Bizarre Beast reaches the pine it rests there awhile and the hermit does the same. As he sits there, he sees a young man ride up, declaring that his lady—she whom the Knight of the Golden Circle rescued from those who would take her land, on the day that he who is known to Nascien witnessed a great wonder[16]—sends him food.

After eating, Nascien sets off with the animal, but soon meets a knight who claims to have known him in the past and who invites him to his house; but Nascien is reluctant to reveal anything about himself for reasons he does not disclose.[17] When he finally arrives in the north, the Bizarre Beast leaves him. But, continuing his quest, he finds the Book of the Holy Grail in a chapel haunted by a demon, which he expels through the power of the Book itself. The beast returns to guide him back to his dwelling, but we hear no more about it.

On his first night back in the remote hermitage, Nascien has a dream in which the Great Master appears to him and instructs him to begin copying the book after celebrating Mass on the second Monday after Easter; he must finish doing so before Ascension Sunday, for the Book will no longer be seen on Earth after that day.[18] Having been entrusted with the Holy Story, Nascien translates it into Latin and then combines it with the book of the Master Blaise,[19] who was given his version of the Grail story by Merlin.[20]

And that is all we know of the career of Nascien son of Bron, Round Table Knight and Hermit of the Grail, from the reigns of Uther Pendragon and Arthur to the middle of the eighth century. We have no idea when, if ever, he died! But we may perhaps attribute his extraordinary longevity to the grace of the Grail, a veritable fountain of youth. In any case, his writings live on after him: For the book of Nascien (the Latin version of the combined books of Christ and Merlin) is later translated into French by Robert de Boron[21] at the command of Holy Church[22]; and this is the History of the Holy Grail that has come down to us.[23]

Notes

1. Bron is usually described as having twelve sons in the Holy Land, so we must assume that the remaining five are born on the way to, or in, Britain. Nascien's mother is named variously Enygeus (*EG* I.2308) or Havingues (*VS* II, 221); or is described as *la bele Damoisele de la Blanche Nue*, who is a relative of Joseph of Arimathea (VII, 241, 246).

2. *LG* I, 288.

3. *LG* I, 345.

4. *LG* I, 352.

5. Nascien's last act as a knight will be to rescue Perceval's older brother Agloval from the uncle of King Rion, who is menacing the lands of the Widow Lady (*VS* VII, 241–2, 261). Shortly afterwards, Nascien sees the Grail for the first time and, unlike his sinful companions, immediately recognizes it. The *saintismes vaissiaus*, covered in a silk cloth, is carried on the back of a white deer (244–5). In the *Tristano Panciatichiano*, the Grail is carried on the horns of a white deer when it appears at Camelot (*TP* 39).

6. The story is told in full in the Vulgate *Lancelot* (*LG* II, 117–124), but it is only in the *Estoire de Merlin* (I, 289) that it is established clearly that the wise man who advises the king is, in fact, Nascien the son of Bron.

7. *LG* III, 338: the identification of this hermit as

Nascien is only found in the *Livre d'Artus* (*VS* VII, 261).

8. *LG* IV, 7–8; V, 122; *MD* 672–5; *QHG* 42–7: *Car ceste Queste n'est mie queste de terriennes choses, ainz doit estre li encerchemenz des grans secrez et des privetez Nostre Seignor et des grans repostailles que li Hauz Mestres mostrera apertement au boneuré chevalier qu'il a esleu a son serjant entre les autres chevaliers terriens, a qui il mostrera les granz merveilles dou Saint Graal, et fera veoir ce que cuers mortex ne porroit penser ne langue d'ome terrien deviser* (*QP* 19).

9. ...*ce est li Sainz Graax, ce est la grace del Saint Esperit ... ce est la grace del Saint Graal* (*QP* 159); *Esta he a graça do Spiritu Santo e do Graal* (*PV* II, 216).

10. ...*les senefiances et les demostrances ... li signe dou Saint Graal* (*QP* 160–1); *As grandes aventuras ... sam demostranças e os grandes signaaes ... e as significanças do Santo Graal* (*PV* II, 218).

11. *LG* IV, 50–2; V, 156–8; *MD* 727–30; *QHG* 169–75.

12. Later we are told: "you will never find a clerk bold enough to say that He ever wrote anything after the Resurrection other than the high writing of the Grail" (*LG* I, 76). In fact, the attribution of heretofore-unknown scripture to Christ Himself is certainly heterodox, if not actually heretical, although the Church seems never to have condemned the Grail texts.

13. The identification of the un-named narrator of the Grail Prologue with the son of Bron and Havingues is confirmed in the Vulgate *Estoire de Merlin* where we are told that the Holy Spirit raises Nascien up to the Third Heaven, where he openly beholds the Trinity. Afterwards he is entrusted with the Holy Story, which he writes down at the behest of the Holy Master (*LG* I, 288–9). In other words, his story is identical to that of the eighth century hermit in the *Estoire del Saint Graal*.

14. Norwegia (*Norvvage*) most likely indicates those parts of northern Scotland that were occupied by the pagan Norsemen from the eighth century onwards (*LG* I, 6n29).

15. "It was unlike any other spring I had ever heard of," the hermit relates, "for the gravel was red like blood and hot like fire, while the water was as cold as ice; and three times a day it turned as green as an emerald and as bitter as the sea, the bitterness lasting as long as the green" (*LG* I, 7). The spring is elsewhere associated with a miracle performed by Josephus (*ESG* 580).

16. ...*chele qui li Chevaliers au Cercle d'Or rescoust de sa terre perdre le jor ke la grans merveille fu veüe de chelui ke vos savés* (*ESG* 15). This can only be a reference to an episode found in both the verse continuation of Gerbert de Montreuil and in the prose Romance of Perlesvaus, where the title of the Knight of the Golden Circle is won by Perceval (who would certainly be known to Nascien as a fellow Round Table Knight), when he rescues the besieged Lady of Montesclaire in Ireland from a fire-breathing demon—a great wonder indeed. He is rewarded by the gift of a sacred relic, the Circle of Gold, which is in fact the Crown of Thorns. As a result of these events the Lady of Montesclaire is baptized, becoming the first person in her territory to do so; she takes the Christian name of Elyza. Her remains are honored in Ireland for many centuries after her death (*HBG* 161–4), surviving until at least the thirteenth century when *Perlesvaus* was written. It would appear that it is the spirit of Elyza who has performed a miracle, sending food to the hermit to strengthen him on his journey; perhaps recalling that, at the lifting of the siege, her own first thought was of food (*CSG* 419). But Nascien, apparently not knowing who the lady is—and that she is deceased—tells the young man who has brought the food to thank her and that God will reward her (*LG* I, 7).

17. "But one thing went wrong for me: he recognized me because of a mark I had, and said he had seen me in the past and named the place. Nevertheless, no matter how much he questioned me, I never admitted anything, and when he saw that it displeased me to be asked, he let things be" (*LG* I, 7). For an attempt at a psychological explanation of this curious, dream-like passage, see Dixon 2017, 101–8.

18. *LG* I, 3–7.

19. The Book of Blaise, dictated by Merlin, is called the *Livre du Graal*. The early part, dealing with the love between Christ and Joseph of Arimathea, is superseded by Christ's own, autobiographical, account; the latter part, the autobiography of Merlin and the prophet's account of the acts of the House of Constantine in Britain, functions as a secular sequel to the sacred autobiography. The *Estoire de Merlin*, attributed to Robert de Boron, is considered by its author to be a branch of the History of the Holy Grail (*ESG* 577).

20. *LG* I, 288–9.
21. *LG* I, 112.
22. *LG* I, 136.
23. *LG* I, 163.

NICODEMUS

A Jew who recognizes that Jesus comes from God,[1] Nicodemus is ordered by Pilate to help Joseph of Arimathea, who is being obstructed by unbelievers, to take the body of Jesus down from the Cross. Nicodemus goes to a local smithy to get a hammer and pincers to remove the nails from the Crucified One.[2] Over-riding the objections of those who believe that Christ will come back to life,[3] he removes the still-bleeding body from the Cross and hands it over to Joseph. Taking the Grail, the vessel with which Jesus had made the sacrament at the

Last Supper, Joseph catches the Holy Blood which had restored his sight to the centurion Longinus.[4]

The angry Jews pursue those responsible for the Deposition and Joseph is imprisoned; but Nicodemus is forewarned and escapes.[5] Many years later, after Joseph is freed from prison by divine intervention, both he and Nicodemus are forced into exile. But Nicodemus has fashioned an image of the face of Jesus, sculpting it so that it exactly captures Him as He was on the Cross. Realizing that they must leave, he places it in a casket and confides it to the sea; the Holy Face can still be seen in the Italian city of Lucca to this day.

Joseph, Nicodemus and their followers embark with the Holy Grail for the land that God has promised them, allowing Divine Providence to guide them.[6] They arrive at the White Island, a part of what is now England, where they settle. In times of hardship, they are fed by the Holy Vessel. The descendants of Joseph and Nicodemus constitute the Grail Dynasty, the guardians of the sacred Vessel and the Holy Blood it contains.[7]

The burial place of Nicodemus remains a mystery until it is uncovered by Perceval, his great-grandson: Between the forest and the castle of Kamaalot (the domain of the Widow Lady, the niece of Joseph of Arimathea, in the "wild west" of Wales) there is an un-walled chapel standing on four marble columns. Within the chapel, open to view, is a beautiful tomb that can only be opened by the finest knight in the world.[8]

Accordingly, when Perceval, having proved his worth by defeating the wicked King of Castle Mortal, returns to his mother's domain, she is eager to see if her son can open it. Miraculously, it breaks open as soon as he touches it, proving to the Widow Lady that Perceval is the finest knight in the world, for only such a one could have caused it to open. Never before has anyone known who lay there.

When her chaplain reads the letters sealed in gold which lie in the tomb, he declares that he who is buried there was one of those who had helped to take Our Lord down from the Cross. Inside the tomb, next to the body, they find the blood-stained pincers with which Nicodemus the Smith had pulled out the nails; but they cannot remove them from beside the body. As soon as Perceval leaves, the tomb seals itself up once more.[9]

Later, when Perceval inherits the Grail Castle, his mother goes to live there. She moves the body of Nicodemus from the tomb to a rich chapel that she has installed there. The body of Joseph of Arimathea, which had been entombed in a cemetery outside the castle, is also moved there; both the Fisher King and the Widow Lady, when they die, are buried in the same chapel. Eventually all the bodies are loaded onto a ship with a white sail emblazoned with a red cross, bound for the Island of Plenty. Perceval embarks, the ship sets sail and they disappear into legend.[10]

Notes

1. *Maistre, nous savons ke vous estes venus de Dieu* (*ESG* 4): The Gospel of John tells us that Jesus is approached at night by a Jewish leader called Nicodemus, who acknowledges Him as a teacher with divine authority. Jesus announces to him one of his most famous sayings: "Except a man be born again, he cannot see the Kingdom of God." Nicodemus takes this literally at first, but Jesus explains that the second birth is of a different order to the first: "Except a man be born of water and of the spirit, he cannot enter into the Kingdom of God" (Jn. 3.1–21), This spiritual rebirth makes us like the wind that blows where it wills: just as we hear the wind, but we do not know whence it comes or whither it is going, so those who are reborn in spirit find a new home in an unseen, unknown divine source and are led by the spirit to an unknown destination (*GJ* 54). Nicodemus later speaks up for Jesus in front of the Pharisees (Jn. 7.50–2) and he accompanies Joseph of Arimathea to the scene of the Crucifixion, bringing with him spices to embalm Jesus' body. Together, they take Him down from the Cross and lay Him in the tomb (19.39–42).

2. As we learn from the Third Continuation, Nicodemus himself was a fine smith (*CSG* 478). It is these details which enable us to identify the un-named body in the Romance of Perlesvaus, buried with his pincers in the tomb at Kamaalot, as that of Nicodemus.

3. *MG* 18-9.
4. *CSG* 569: *Nichodemus le despendi/ Et a Joseph si le rendi./ Ses plaies prisent a saignier./ Cest vaissial fist apareillier,/ Ens degouterent sans mentir;/ Vos le porés ja bien veïr./ Et sacrement fist ens Jhesu* (*DC* ll.13238-44).
5. *MG* 20: Robert de Boron amplifies the role of Nicodemus, drawing on the apocryphal gospels.
6. Joseph and Nicodemus allow themselves to be led by the wind that *bloweth where it listeth*, for their faith in Jesus has meant they are reborn in the spirit.
7. *CSG* 218-9.
8. *HBG* 30.
9. *HBG* 147-8.
10. *HBG* 263-4.

O

ORPHEUS

When Joseph of Arimathea leads his evangelical mission to Britain, his attempt to bring Grail Christianity to the north of the island encounters a magical obstacle, in the form of the enchanter Orpheus. The philosophical debate that follows, in the Castle of Enchantments on the border of what is now Scotland, is the subject of the Lay of Tears, which will be sung to Sir Bors by the apostate Manibel in the castle of Corbenic.[1]

* * *

As with King Arthur, scholars argue about whether Orpheus is a historical or purely mythical figure.[2] Like that of King Arthur, the myth of Orpheus involves a journey to the Otherworld (the Welsh Annwfn) or Underworld (the Greek Hades), a Harrowing of Hell from which not everyone returns. But the most obvious candidate for a British Orpheus is Taliesin, the bard who accompanies Arthur to Annwfn on the ship Prydwen, as Orpheus does Jason on the Argo.[3]

In the *Orphic Argonautica*, a version of the myth of the Argonauts ostensibly narrated by Orpheus himself, the voyagers travel northwest from the Black Sea, bypassing the lands of the Hyperboreans and Cimmerians and circumnavigating Ireland.[4] It would presumably be at this point that they could have stopped off at the Caledonian marches and Orpheus could have built his castle.[5] If what Joseph of Arimathea encountered there, more than a millennium later, was, not Orpheus himself, but adherents of his Mysteries, then we may have found in Orphism another strand of mystical paganism[6] to add to the syncretistic mix that Jessie Weston saw at the root of the Grail cult.[7]

Although we are not told the outcome of his debate with Joseph of Arimathea, Orpheus was claimed by Christian apologists as a convert who rejected the many gods of paganism in favor of the one true deity.[8]

Notes

1. *LG* III, 270: Bors' cousin Sir Lancelot also finds King Bademagu listening to a harpist play a lay of Orpheus on the feast of Mary Magdalen (66-7).
2. The ancient historian W.K.C. Guthrie considers the appeal of Orpheus, as both musician and religious reformer, to be "more universal" than that of Arthur, who appeals "to the imagination of poets and artists" (25).
3. In both cases a cauldron is one of the prizes brought back by the survivors of the expedition: In the classical myth, it is Medea's cauldron of regeneration; in the Welsh poem "The Spoils of Annwfn," it is the cauldron of the Lord of the Otherworld, which some have seen as one of the pagan prototypes of the Grail Vessel.
4. As Ann Wroe points out, in this version Orpheus has already made his journey to the Underworld and, as he guides his companions through the ice-bound seas of the "boreal Ocean" beyond Britain, it is also "a voyage to the unseen places, to dream-realms beyond Earth and life" (75-7).

5. In the Middle English Lay of Sir Orfeo, the poet is King of Winchester and his wife is carried off by the King of Faerie.

6. "His worship," writes Carl Kerényi (1959, 279), "was maintained by a great community which believed itself to be in possession of books containing revelations of Orpheus, accounts of his journey to the underworld and all that he had learned there and afterwards taught and originated." Orphic mosaics have been found from Roman Britain (Guthrie, 21).

7. Weston considers it possible that the rise of Orphic doctrines contributed to the tendency of nature cults with their attendant fertility rituals (such as the Rites of Adonis) to develop into esoteric Mysteries (1913, 86).

8. Guthrie, 255–6.

P

The PALACE OF ADVENTURES

When the pagan King of the Land Beyond is converted to Christianity by the Company of the Grail, he takes the baptismal name Alphasan. He then has the castle of Corbenic built to house the Holy Vessel, which is kept in a chamber adjacent to the main palace.

On the first Sunday after the Grail is brought to the castle, Alphasan gives his only daughter in marriage to Joshua, son of Bron. That night his bed is made up in the palace. Around midnight he is awakened by what sounds like a thousand voices giving praise amid the beating of wings. But he can see no-one, apart from a man dressed like a priest standing before a silver table, atop which is the Holy Vessel.

When the Grail is carried back by unseen hands into the side chamber, a man completely enveloped in flames and carrying a Lance reproaches Alphasan for remaining in the room where the Holy Vessel is so honored; no-one is yet worthy to do so; moreover, the Lord will have His vengeance on those who are foolhardy enough to spend the night there. The flaming man then strikes Alphasan through both thighs with the Lance, warning him that anyone who stays in the Palace of Adventures[1] will know death or ignominy, unless he is the best of knights.

And so it is that, of the many knights who dare the adventure, all are found dead in the morning; until the arrival of Sir Gawain, who survives but is seriously injured and shamed.[2] Sir Bors is also shamed when he spends the night at Corbenic but is not told about the Palace of Adventures; he is consequently accused of cowardice.[3] He makes up for this at the next opportunity, asking King Pelles directly to allow him to spend the night there, but accepting the king's advice to confess his sins before doing so.[4] Consequently he fares much better than Gawain but, although he is the purest knight from King Arthur's court to try the perils of the palace so far, he is not worthy enough to bring the adventures to an end. This will only be achieved by the Good Knight who is to come.[5]

During one of his periodic fits of madness, following the birth of a son who will grow up to become that very Good Knight, Lancelot is cured by being tied up and left all night in the Palace of Adventures, where angels pay honor to the Grail. When the Holy Vessel manifests there, the demon which possesses Lancelot is driven out, for nothing evil can remain in the presence of the Grail; so violent is its expulsion that it takes a large section of the palace roof with it.[6]

Later however, when Lancelot tries to enter the side chamber of the Palace where the Holy Vessel is kept, he is struck down.

Also, when anyone unworthy approaches the Palace, the doors and windows lock themselves against him. This is precisely what happens to Gaheriet, Gawain and Hector[7]; whereas the doors open of their own accord to admit Galahad, Palamedes and Perceval, who are true Knights of the Holy Grail.[8]

Notes

1. So-called, as Alphasan explains to his noblemen, because greater wonders (*aventures et merveilles*) will be seen there than anywhere else in the world (*ESG* 564). Alphasan survives for only ten more days and is buried in the Church of Our Lady in Corbenic; which will, as a result, become known as the Castle of the Perilous Palace (*LG* IV, 210): *Chastiel del Pallés Perilleus* (*SRM* 154).
2. *LG* I, 159: Gawain will later recount to the court how he came to the Fisher King's castle, saw there the most beautiful girl in the world carrying the Holy Grail uncovered, and experienced the wonders of the Palace of Adventures (III, 206): *comment il vint chiés le Roi Pescheor et comment il vit le Saint Graal tout apertement porter devant lui a la plus bele pucele qu'il onques veist et les merveilles qu'il vit el Palais Aventureux* (*LM* IV, 397).
3. *LG* III, 181.
4. *LG* III, 268-9: The king also explains that not all the "adventures" are perilous: Not the least wondrous of them is the daily feeding of his people by the Holy Vessel: *car aventure est ce merveilleuse, quant li Saint Graal nos donne chascun jor viande tele com nos demandons* (*LM* V, 256). All who eat in the Palace need only pray for what they want and it is provided in abundance (*LG* V, 224): *Touz cels sanz faille qui demoroient el Paleis Aventureus en estoient repeu et replein por qu'il l'aorassent en sa venue* (*PV* II, 524-5).
5. *LG* III, 271.
6. *LG* V, 76-7.
7. *LG* V, 266-8.
8. *LG* V, 278: As Galahad says: *Se nos sumes chevaliers del Saint Grahal, les portes nos aouvreront* (*PV* III, 317).

PALAMEDES

Palamedes is a pagan knight who takes up the search for the Questing Beast and is embroiled in an equally fruitless quest to win the love of Iseut, Queen of Cornwall.

It is only when he finally accepts baptism that he is able, at last, to kill the Beast. He then accompanies Galahad and Perceval to Corbenic, where he is one of the twelve knights who witness the accomplishment of the adventure of the Holy Grail. He is, shortly thereafter, killed by Gawain; his father, Esclabor, committing suicide when he hears of his son's death.[1]

Note

1. *LG* V, 278-83.

PARLAN

For as long as he is able to ride a horse, King Parlan is a stalwart champion of Christianity. One day, while out hunting, he penetrates deep into the forest beyond the familiar paths and eventually follows a track which takes him to the sea-shore facing Ireland. There he sees the Ship of Faith, dispatched by King Solomon over two thousand years earlier; a ship whose arrival on British shores had recently cost the life of Lambor, the fifth Fisher King.

Boarding the Ship, he discovers thereon the Sword of King David. On the reverse of the scabbard, which is blood-red, he reads an inscription, stating that the sword will inflict great cruelty on him to whom it should rather be helpful. Feeling no apprehension, for he believes himself to have served his Lord as best he could, Parlan starts to withdraw the sword from the scabbard, only to be struck through the thighs by a lance which appears out of nowhere.

So it is that the sword is cruel when it should be kind; and that the most valiant of knights is henceforth known as the Maimed King.[1]

Note

1. *QHG* 220-1; *LG* IV, 65-6: Parlan appears to be a variant of Pellehan, who has earlier been named as the father of Perceval and his sister (64); although other texts will give them alternative genealogies, as well as providing us with different explanations for Pellehan's maiming. Confusingly, Parlan's misadventure is also attributed to Pellinor (*QSG* 512) and, in the Bonn manuscript of the Vulgate *Queste* (*LDG* III, 1092-3) and Vinaver's edition of Malory, to Pelles—Galahad's grandfather, *maymed for hys hardynes* (*MV* 583).

PARSIFAL

Brought up in the woods by his mother, who dies when he deserts her, Parsifal makes his way to the mountainous Grail Castle, Montsalvat, where he is dismissed as a fool by the sorceress Kundry. But the wounded Grail King Amfortas knows that he can only be healed by a Pure Fool who is made wise by compassion; he therefore allows the lad to participate in the miraculous feast that sustains the Order of Grail Knights. But Parsifal appears oblivious to what he witnesses there and leaves in disgrace.

Kundry, who is being controlled by the evil enchanter Klingsor, lures him seductively to a magic garden to meet his end. But when Klingsor hurls a spear at the lad, it remains suspended in the air above the boy's head. Parsifal seizes the spear and makes the sign of the Cross with it; Klingsor's garden is withered and his castle ruined.[1] Taking with him what is really the Holy Spear that pierced the side of Christ on the Cross, Parsifal carries it to Montsalvat and uses it to heal Amfortas of a festering wound caused by that very weapon; his compassion for the plight of the king and his Order has made him wise. As Grail King he absolves Kundry of her sins and she dies redeemed.[2]

Notes

1. Weston (1896, 210) points out that Wagner is accentuating his presentation of Parsifal as a type of Christ when he has him being tempted, but ultimately conquering temptation, in a garden.
2. Weston 1896, 176–8: Parsifal is the hero of Wagner's eponymous music drama, based on Wolfram von Eschenbach's *Parzival*.

PARZIVAL

Brought up in the Lonely Waste Forest by his widowed mother Herzeloyde, Parzival will later discover that she is the grand-daughter of Titurel, the first Grail King; that her brother, Anfortas, who is the Grail King at the time Parzival first meets him, has no son; and that therefore Anfortas' sister's son is the heir to the Kingdom of the Grail, also known as the Savage Land.

Before he does so, however, Parzival is taught the essence of knighthood by Gurnemanz and marries the Queen of Belrepaire. After a year he requests his wife's leave to go off in search of his mother, not realizing that she died of grief when he first left home. Meanwhile, his wife bears him two sons.

As Parzival rides on, he comes to a lake where he meets a man whom he takes to be a fisherman, but who invites him to lodge at his castle. There Parzival witnesses a ritual procession in the course of which he sees the Bleeding Lance and something that transcends earthly perfection, the Grail Stone, which feeds the company. The man whom he saw fishing is revealed as a Maimed King; he gives Parzival his sword, telling him that it is the one that he wielded himself before he was wounded. He hopes thereby to prompt Parzival into asking a question about his (the king's) infirmity, but the young knight follows the advice drummed into him by Gurnemanz and refrains from doing so out of courtesy.

He stays the night at the castle, but the next morning he finds it deserted; he has missed his opportunity to ask the Grail Question. For this he is duly upbraided by his cousin, who tells him off for his lack of compassion.[1]

Later on, at King Arthur's court, he is cursed by Cundrie the Sorceress for not speaking in the presence of the sorrowful king who welcomed him to his castle: He should have had compassion for the king's suffering; his silence was sinful.[2] But Cundrie's harsh words have the desired effect: Parzival swears he will not rest until he has once more found the Grail; moreover, he abandons his loyalty to God, who has ill repaid his service by bringing him such shame.[3]

But after years of travelling and many battles, Parzival's faith is restored when he comes on Good Friday to the hermitage of his maternal uncle Trevrizent, who tells him about the celestial origin of the Grail and about the Templars who serve it. He discovers that Herzeloyde, his mother, died of grief because of him and, furthermore, that the Maimed King is his uncle Anfortas (the brother of Herzeloyde, Trevrizent and the Grail Bearer).[4]

Parzival is eventually united with his half-brother Feirefiz and the two set out together for Mount Savage, after Cundrie informs Parzival that an inscription has appeared on the Grail, announcing that he is to be its new lord.[5]

Arriving at Mount Savage, Parzival asks his uncle Anfortas what troubles him. Through this compassionate question, Anfortas is instantly restored to health. Parzival, now recognized as the new King of the Savage Land, sends for his wife and children. The company are fed by the Grail.[6]

But when his kingdom is threatened by hostile forces, Parzival wishes to prevent the Grail from falling into the wrong hands. Accompanied by his grandfather Titurel, Parzival takes the Grail with him to India, the land of his nephew Prester John (the son of Feirefiz and the Grail Bearer). There, near the Earthly Paradise, a fitting home is found for the Holy Vessel.[7]

Notes

1. WP 120–35; PT 95–108.
2. WP 164–6; PT 133–5.
3. WP 171–2; PT 139–40.
4. WP 231–43; PT 192–201.
5. WP 387; PT 327.
6. WP 394–402; PT 333–9.
7. Barber 2005, 196.

PELLEHAN

A descendant of Bron and Enygeus (Joseph of Arimathea's sister)—whose son Joshua was the first Fisher King and who founded a royal dynasty that ruled in the sacred city of Corbenic in the land of Listenois—Pellehan is the first of his line to be known as the Maimed King. It is his destiny to be healed by his great-grandson Galahad.

Pellehan is the son of Lambor, the fifth Fisher King. When his father is killed by his neighbor King Varlan wielding the Sword of David, both their kingdoms are laid waste. Pellehan accedes to the throne of Listenois and becomes the sixth Fisher King, guarding the Holy Grail and the Avenging Lance.

Pellehan, who will become known as the Maimed King,[1] fathers three sons—Alan of the Isle, Pelles and Pellinor[2]—before being struck down thanks to the evil deeds of his brother Garlon the Red. Under the cover of his powers of invisibility, Garlon has been murdering innocent knights errant but, in doing so, he incurs the wrath of the ill-fated Northumbrian knight Balin the Savage. Balin pursues the killer to Corbenic, the Castle of the Perilous Palace, where Pellehan is presiding over a feast.

When Balin slays Garlon, King Pellehan is incensed. He pursues his brother's killer through the castle, until he corners him in the very room where the sacred relics are kept. It is at this point that Balin grabs hold of the Holy Lance and strikes Pellehan with it through both thighs: This is the Dolorous Blow, which maims the king and devastates his land.[3]

It is one of Pellehan's descendants, the Welsh hero Perceval,[4] who is the first to encounter the old king: He sees him in a boat on a river between two mountains, wearing a gold crown but looking very sick. The king amuses himself by fishing which, he explains to Perceval, he does because he no longer has the strength for riding and fighting. As a result, some call him the Rich Fisherman but, since he has lost the use of his limbs, others call him the Maimed King.[5]

Perceval will be with Galahad when he comes to Corbenic to accomplish the Quest. But it is Galahad alone who must enter the chamber where the Maimed King lies, not having left it for years—unable to get up, and sustained only by the grace of the Holy Vessel. A voice instructs Galahad to take the blood dripping from the Holy Lance and spread it on Pellehan's wounds, which are as fresh as the day that Balin struck him; the king is immediately healed. In joyous relief he embraces Galahad, but then immediately takes himself off to a hermitage, where he lives for another half-a-year.[6]

During this period, he is visited for the last time by the Grail Knights, who consult him about the meaning of various marvels they have seen, including the mysterious Questing Beast. Having explained all, the king tells them regretfully that he will no longer be the custodian of divine secrets, for the Holy Voice that came to him in the chamber of the Grail does so no longer.[7]

Notes

1. The *Estoire del Saint Graal* specifies that Pellehan is wounded in a battle in Rome (*LG* I, 160). But the Vulgate *Lancelot* and *Queste* agree that he is maimed because he attempts to draw the Sword of David from its scabbard, being struck either by the sword itself (III, 272) or by a flying lance (IV, 66).
2. *LG* I, 254.
3. *LG* IV, 211–4: *And Kynge Pellam lay so many yerys sore wounded, and myght never be hole tylle that Galaad the Hawte Prynce heled hym in the queste of the Sankgreall. For in that place was parte of the bloode of Oure Lorde Jesu Cryste, which Joseph of Aramathy brought into thys londe.... And Kynge Pellam was nyghe of Joseph his kynne, and that was the moste worshipfullist man on lyve in tho dayes, and grete pité hit was of hys hurte, for thorow that stroke hit turned to grete dole, tray, and tene* (*MD* 68).
4. According to some manuscripts of the Vulgate *Queste*, Perceval is the son of Pellehan (*QP* 201). But in the Post-Vulgate and in Malory he is the youngest son of Pellinor and therefore Pellehan's grandson.
5. *LG* V, 109.
6. *LG* V, 279.
7. *LG* V, 283–6: *Tant com je fui en la chambre dou Saint Vessel soi je la verité des greignors merveilles del roiaumme de Logres, car iluec les me descouvroit la divine voiz, mes puis que je m'en sui partiz n'en soi je plus q'un autre home* (*PV* III, 373).

PELLES

A descendant of Bron, a leading light of the Company of the Grail during the evangelization of Britain, Pelles is one of the three sons of Pellehan, the Maimed King.[1] His elder brother, Alan of the Isle, holds the title of Fisher King[2] while his younger brother, Pellinor, is stricken with sickness; Pelles is obliged to watch over him.[3]

Pelles also has a daughter (who bears the Grail in his Castle of Corbenic) and a son, Eliezer. When Eliezer tells his father that he will only allow the best knight in the world to confer on him that order, Pelles prophesies that such a knight will come to Listenois to ask about the Holy Grail, which Pelles' daughter has in her keeping: Although she is only seven years old as yet, when she is grown, a child will be fathered on her by the best knight of the time. Moreover, says the king, the adventures of the Holy Grail must be fulfilled by three knights, of whom two will be life-long virgins while the third leads a chaste life.[4]

Pelles himself holds the title of Fisher King[5] at the time of the visit to the Grail Castle by Lancelot. Pelles arranges with an enchantress, the Lady Brisane, to trick Lancelot into sleeping with his daughter, in order to engender the Knight of the Prophecy. As a result, Galahad is conceived.[6]

When he is fifteen years of age, Galahad is knighted by his father and sets out on the Quest of the Holy Grail. The first time that he meets his grandfather as a battle-hardened knight, Pelles does not recognize him. But, after expelling a demon from an enchanter who has inveigled himself into the royal court, Galahad reveals his true identity, before leaving to pursue further adventures.[7] It is only after he wins the Sword with the Strange Straps,[8] whereby Galahad has proved that he is the best knight in the world, that a dying man, speaking on behalf of the Almighty, tells Galahad that he must return to the Grail Castle to heal the Maimed King, Pelles' father.

When after five years of wandering and adventures Galahad arrives at last at Corbenic, Pelles weeps to see his grandson once again; but he is not permitted to witness the achieving of the Quest.[9] Pelles never sees Galahad again, for the knight departs forthwith for Sarras and, ultimately, Heaven.

The Hermit King

Others say that Pelles is the brother of the good Fisher King and the evil King of Castle Mortal; their sister is Yglais, the mother of Perlesvaus (Perceval).[10]

Pelles has a son called Joseus who murders his mother because she wishes him to give up his rights to the throne in favor of his younger brother and dedicate himself to the religious life. As a result, Pelles gives up his earthly kingdom for one not of this Earth, becoming known as the Hermit King[11]; while Joseus also retires to a hermitage, as his mother had always wished.[12]

Pelles is killed, one day after Mass, by a knight who has abducted his niece Dandrane; he is buried in his hermitage.[13] The castle where his wife was murdered by their son has been burning ever since: It is from this castle and from *one other*, we are told, that the fire which will bring an end to *this* world will be kindled.[14]

Notes

1. According to the Bonn manuscript of the Vulgate *Queste* (*LDG* III, 1092–3) and Vinaver's edition of Malory (*MV* 583), Pelles is maimed, like his father, by the Avenging Lance, when the Ship of Solomon, which has been traversing the seas for two thousand years, arrives on the coast facing Ireland. Pelles is out hunting with his knights when he comes upon the ship, partially draws the sword that he finds therein and is immediately smitten through both thighs by a spear.

In one French manuscript that arguably represents a non-cyclic (that is, pre–Vulgate) Prose *Lancelot*, Pelles is also called the Maimed King, although the nature of his injury is not specified. Here, moreover, he is described as the father of Perlesvaus or Perceval (*LDL* I, 122); and is later described by the Lady of the Lake as having already died before Lancelot's knighthood (408). This curious detail can perhaps be explained by the fact that, in Chrétien's *Conte del Graal*, Perceval's father is believed to have died; but the similarity of his apparently fatal wound to that which maimed the Fisher King leads to the possibility that the report of his death is an exaggeration. Can it be that he lives on, lame and occupying himself with fishing, in the hard-to-find Grail Castle, while the rest of the world, including the Lady of the Lake, believes him deceased?

2. *LG* I, 254.
3. *LG* I, 235.
4. *LG* I, 359.
5. It is presumably after the death of his brother Alan that Pelles' son Eliezer describes himself to Gawain as son of the rich Fisher King, the Grail Keeper (*LG* III, 91). Eliezer's sister later describes herself to Lancelot as daughter of Pelles, King of the Land Beyond: *fille au roi Pellés de la Terre Foreinne* (*LM* IV, 212).
6. *LG* III, 163–5.
7. *LG* V, 224–6.
8. This is the very sword that, according to Malory, Pelles (or Pellehan) found in the Ship of Solomon and which he tried prematurely to draw, leading to his maiming.
9. *LG* IV, 83–4.
10. *HBG* 46: Apart from making Pelles the (maternal) uncle of Perceval, the account of this figure in the Romance of Perlesvaus bears little relationship to that in the Vulgate Cycle. There Pelles is Perceval's *paternal* uncle; and his grandson Galahad completes the Quest in the palace of a still-living Pelles.
11. The idea of Perceval's maternal uncle being a hermit is found in Chrétien (*CSG* 56).
12. *HBG* 60.
13. *HBG* 229–30.
14. *HBG* 256

PELLINOR

When the Ship of Faith, built by King Solomon to bear witness to his foreknowledge of the coming of Sir Galahad, arrives on the shores of Britain after voyaging unmanned for over a thousand years, it bears a sword, originally owned by King David, which will cause untold harm to those it might be expected to protect: the guardians of the Holy Grail and their family.

So it is that Lambor, the fifth Fisher King, is killed by an enemy wielding the sword. An equally tragic fate also awaits Lambor's grandson Pellinor who, at the beginning of Arthur's wars against the Saxons, has twelve sons who are knights, while his wife is pregnant with the thirteenth.[1]

A protector of the poor who does much to enhance the glory of Holy Church, King Pellinor is hunting in one of his woods that stretch as far as the Irish Sea when he comes across the Ship of Solomon. He boards it, despite dire warnings written on its side, because he never doubts his faith in Jesus Christ. He finds inside the Ship a bed and on the bed a sword, which he unsheathes by a hand's-breadth. He would have drawn it out completely, were it not that a Lance, as if from nowhere, suddenly transfixes him through the thighs with such violence that he is disabled as a result. He is destined to remain so until Galahad comes to him.[2]

As a result of this wound inflicted by the Avenging Lance, Pellinor is known as the Maimed King[3] and his kingdom, the Waste Land.[4] He is watched over by his brother Pelles, but he will only be cured with the coming of he who will put to an end the adventures of the Holy Grail.[5] Pellinor is also known as the King of the High Wild Forest, which is where his youngest son, Perceval, is brought up.[6]

The Knight with the Strange Beast

But others say that it is his father Pellehan who is the Maimed King and that Pellinor himself is hale and whole until such time as he meets his end at the hands of Gawain, thus concluding a protracted family feud. It is also said that, despite being born into the dynasty of Grail Guardians, Pellinor devotes much of his life to a futile hunt for the Questing Beast.

King Arthur first meets Pellinor shortly after his incestuous union with his sister, the Queen of Orkney, which is followed by a nightmare involving dragons and griffins. But it is a different sort of strange beast that he encounters while hunting the next day, a bizarre creature from which exudes the sound of thirty barking hounds. It is now that he also meets for the first time the man who is pursuing it.

Pellinor tells Arthur that it is prophesied that only a man of the Grail lineage can kill the Beast. As he is the best knight of his kindred to date, Pellinor assumes that it is he who will achieve the quest.[7]

In the event, Pellinor does not live long enough to do so. In the civil war that follows Arthur's accession to the throne of Logres, the Knight with the Strange Beast, as Pellinor is sometimes known,[8] kills the rebel King Loth of Orkney.[9] He is rewarded with a place of honor at the Round Table, next to the Perilous Seat; much to the chagrin of Gawain, Loth's son. Gawain swears that he will take vengeance on his father's killer[10]— and he will do just that, during the Grail Quest.[11]

In the event the Questing Beast will be killed by Palamedes, who is not of Pellinor's lineage, though observed by Perceval, who is.[12] The strange origin of the beast (born out of brother-sister incest, in a curious echo of the event that preceded its first appearance) will be explained to Perceval by his grandfather, King Pellehan.[13]

Notes

1. *LG* I, 366.
2. *QSG* 512-5: This is an amplification of the information Chrétien de Troyes gives us about the hero's unnamed father who *Fu parmi les janbes navrez/ Si que il maheigna del cors* (*PCG* ll. 436-7). The *Livre d'Artus* calls Pellinor the king wounded in the thigh by the Avenging Lance: *roi Pellinor le roi mahaignié de la cuisse de la lance vencheresse* (*VS* VII, 146). But in this little-known and confused (and confusing) text there appear to be two Pellinors—one, the father of Perceval; the other (his cousin), the Maimed King—which its editor, Oskar Sommer, puts down to a scribal misunderstanding (VIII, 69*n*8).
3. *LG* I, 254: Pellinor's nephew Eliezer, the son of Pelles, tells his father that he longs to see the accomplishing of the adventures of Logres and that he will be very annoyed if he doesn't witness the healing of his uncle's wounds: *Car molt seroie coureciés se je mon oncle ne veoie gari des plaies qu'il a parmi ses quisses* (*LDG* I, 1379). It is not clear whether the uncle he is referring to here is Alan of the Isle or Pellinor, but in the *Livre d'Artus* it is said that neither of them will be healed of their wounds until a knight comes to their dwelling and asks who is served by the Grail (*VS* VII, 147). This also seems to be the only text in which Pellinor (as Alan elsewhere) is also called the Fisher King: *le riche roi pescheor* (146); *li rois peschierres* (243).
4. ...*roi Pellynor de la Terre Gaste* (*LDG* I, 1472); *du chastel de Corbenic* (*VS* VII, 237).
5. *LG* I, 235: *le roi Pellinor ... qui gist malades d'un mal dont ja n'aura garison tant que cil verra laiens qui les aventures du Saint Graal metra a fin* (*LDG* I, 861).
6. The wild woods where Perceval is brought up are called *la gaste forest soutainne* by Chrétien

(*PCG* l. 75) and *la Sauvage Forest Souvrainne* in the *Estoire de Merlin* (*LDG* I, 1410).
  7. *LG* IV, 167–8; *MD* 34–5.
  8. *MD* 61.
  9. *LG* IV, 198.
  10. *LG* IV, 226–7; *MD* 80–1.
  11. *LG* IV, 244.
  12. *LG* V, 278.
  13. *LG* V, 283–5.

PERCEVAL

As one of the knights who is destined to achieve the Grail Quest, Perceval has a suitably illustrious pedigree: His father is of the lineage of Joseph of Arimathea[1]; while his mother Philosofine is one of those who came to Britain with Joseph as part of the Company of the Grail.[2]

After Perceval's father is maimed by a leg wound, the impoverished couple come to live in the lonely Waste Forest during the upheavals that follow the death of Uther Pendragon and the withdrawal of royal protection. When their two eldest sons are killed in battle and her husband dies of grief, Philosofine brings her youngest son up in complete ignorance of the world of chivalry, hoping thereby to spare him the same fate. Chivalry, however, it would appear, is in the blood: For as soon as Perceval encounters knights for the first time (mistaking them, first for devils and then for angels) he determines to become a knight himself, setting off for the court of the king who makes knights.[3]

At King Arthur's court in Carduel it is prophesied that Perceval will become the finest knight in the world.[4] He is consequently taught chivalry by Gornemant of Gohort, one of the Knights of the Round Table. Having learned from Gornemant not to talk too much or ask unnecessary questions,[5] Perceval rides on to Belrepaire, the castle of Gornemant's niece Blancheflor, who is being besieged by an unwanted suitor.

Perceval and Blancheflor sleep together and declare their love for each other.[6] He then defeats her oppressor but, despite her pleas, he will not stay with her. He is concerned about his mother, whom he had seen faint from sorrow when he first left home; he wishes to return to find out whether she is alive or dead. Only then will he return to take his place as Lord of Belrepaire.

On the way, however, he meets a man fishing on a swift-flowing river and is invited to stay in his castle. There he is given a sword that is destined for him. He now witnesses an astonishing procession, in which a boy carrying a white Lance from which blood is dripping is followed by two more carrying candles. After them come a girl carrying a golden, bejeweled Vessel (a "grail" or serving dish), whose light eclipses that of the candles in the hall. She in turn is followed by another carrying a silver carving dish or trencher. They pass into another chamber but Perceval, amazed as he is, is too polite to ask about it all. He stays the night in the castle but, when he wakes up the next morning, finds it deserted.

He rides off, wearing the sword he has been given, only to encounter his cousin, who tells him that the fisherman he encountered is a king who was maimed in battle. Had he asked why the Lance bled and where the procession was going, he would have healed the king, she says; his failure to do so results from the fact that he left his mother to die of sorrow. The cousin also tells him that the sword he was given will break in battle and that only he who made it can ever repair it.[7]

Perceval returns to Arthur's court at Caerleon, where he is upbraided by an Ugly Maiden, who tells him that many evils will befall because he failed to ask the Grail Question. Perceval vows that he will not rest until he finds out who is served from the Grail and why the Lance bleeds.[8]

He spends the next five years in search of adventure but forgetful of God until, on Good Friday, he encounters some pilgrims who demand to know why he is bearing arms on such a holy day. They direct him to the home of a hermit, to whom he confesses.

Perceval learns that the hermit is his uncle, brother to both his mother Philosofine and to the very spiritual man (the father of the Fisher King) who lives in the chamber into which he had seen the Grail Procession pass. The Grail, the Vessel of light carried by the girl, is such a holy thing that the old king who is served from it has been sustained with a single consecrated wafer each day for the last twelve years.

After giving him the standard admonition to honor the worthy men and succor the needy, the hermit asks Perceval to stay with him until Easter Sunday. He then whispers in his ear a prayer containing many of the names of Our Lord, including the greatest ones, which should never be uttered except in fear of death. Having taught him the names, the hermit gets Perceval to agree that he will only use them at the time of his greatest peril.[9]

The Quest for the House of the Fisher King

After many adventures Perceval makes his way back to Belrepaire, but he scarcely recognizes it, as it has been rebuilt by the Lady Blancheflor. Perceval stays three nights, but once more he refuses to marry the lady: This time, although he now knows that his mother is dead, his excuse is that he will not be diverted from his quest to find out about the Grail and the Lance.[10]

He returns at last to the Waste Forest and has an emotional reunion with his younger sister, who was only a little girl when he left home ten years earlier. Together, they visit their uncle, their father's brother, the Hermit of the Holy Spirit, who is served by an angel. Perceval tells him about his visit to the house of the Fisher King and how he had left it without finding an explanation for the Lance that bleeds or the sword that will break, or discovering the truth about the Grail.[11] The hermit in turn tells him about the Passion and Resurrection of Christ and the Harrowing of Hell, whereby the Devil's prisoners were set free.[12]

Continuing his quest, Perceval encounters a lovely lady glowing with such radiance that she seems to be a spiritual being come down from Paradise. Night falls but the lady, who rides a white mule, warns him against staying with her. Then he notices in the distance a supernatural light emanating from five candles, whose flame reaches up to the clouds and lights up the dense forest. He calls to the girl to ask her where the light is coming from, but she has disappeared. He tries to reach the light, but a violent wind rises up and rain pelts down so that he is obliged to seek shelter. The storm does not subside until daybreak.

Around noon, he meets again the Lady of the Mule, who tells him that she experienced no storm the previous night. Moreover, she explains, the light that he has seen came from the Grail, in which the Holy Blood of Christ was gathered when He was on the Cross; it had been brought into the forest by the Fisher King, who lives nearby, as a protection against the Devil.

This is the first time that Perceval has been told that the Grail contains the Holy Blood and, astonished, he begs the lady to tell him who had given it to the Fisher King.[13] But she replies that it is a most sacred thing about which no woman can speak, nor any man unless he leads a holy life. She agrees, however, to his request to show him the way to the court of the Fisher King[14]: He has only to wear a ring she gives him and mount her mule, which will lead him to the ivory bridge over the River Marsonde; he must return both the ring and the mule as soon as they meet again.[15]

Perceval sets off but, once he has crossed the river, he is diverted from his destination by quests to prove his worth. The next day he once more meets the Lady of the Mule, who asks him if he had found what he was looking for: the secret of the obscure adventures about which no one could ever know until the coming of one who is endowed with all knightly qualities.[16] Perceval confesses that he has not yet done so, but he will do so soon; he determines not be so easily diverted next time. He returns the lady's gifts and she rides off, speechless at his inconstancy. Perceval is left bewildered, not knowing how to find the court of the Fisher King.[17]

Riding through a huge forest, Perceval sees a young child so high up a tree that a lance could not reach him. Perceval suggests he climb down, which he refuses to do. Perceval then asks him if he knows the way to the house of the Fisher King. The child refuses to divulge any information about himself or the Fisher King, but instead tells Perceval to make his way to Mount Dolorous, where he will hear news that will delight him.[18]

Accordingly, after Perceval has accomplished the adventure of Mount Dolorous, in which he drives out a demonic presence, Merlin's daughter shows him a broad path through a forest which, she says, will take him straight to the house of the Fisher King there. Perceval swears to himself that if he ever finds it, he will learn about what he saw there. Firstly, however, during the night he encounters a mysterious Tree of Lights and sees the body of a dead knight in the Chapel of the Black Hand.

The next day he comes across four hunters who are in the Fisher King's service and who direct him to his destination. Delighted at this news, Perceval rides on until he encounters a girl on a dappled palfrey who tells him that the things which he had seen in the forest the previous night, are signs that he will soon discover the holy secret of the Lance and the Grail.[19]

He arrives at last at the castle of the Fisher King, where he sees once more a girl carrying the Grail and another girl carrying the Bleeding Lance, those objects he so longed to see again and which had caused him so much trouble.[20] He also sees, for the first time, an unsheathed sword, broken in the middle.[21] Mindful about the consequences of his previous reticence, he asks about this and the other objects in the procession.[22] Perceval also asks about the slain knight in the chapel, the child in the tree and the Tree of Lights.

The king replies that he will first tell him about the child in the tree: The child is a divine being who would not answer any of Perceval's questions because of the knight's many sins; the reason the child was so high up was to remind Perceval to think always of Heaven.

The Fisher King will not reveal anything more until they have eaten, but he invites Perceval to set the pieces of the sword together so that it becomes whole, apart from a small notch. The king says that this means that he surpasses all others in skills of combat, but not necessarily in all of the highest qualities.[23] If at a later date he returns to the castle and is able to repair the notch, he will be able to ask about the Grail and the Lance; only then will he find out the real truth, the secrets of God's working.[24]

He has failed the test because he has not yet atoned for his abandonment of his mother, the king tells him, but this is not his only sin: Perceval later learns from Gornemant that he must fulfill his promise to marry Blancheflor if he is to repair the notched sword and learn all the secrets of the house of the Fisher King.[25]

Perceval, as before, spends the night at the castle, but when he wakes up there is no sign of it. Instead, he finds himself, in a state of confusion,[26] in a meadow near the gates of the Earthly Paradise. When he hammers on the gates to gain entrance, the sword that the king gave him on his first visit to the Grail Castle breaks in two. Placing the pieces in his scabbard, Perceval rides on to Scotswater, which was once a Waste Land, but is now a country of plenty due to his asking about the Grail.[27] There his sword is repaired by the smith who made it, who promptly dies.[28]

The Marriage of Perceval

Perceval eventually finds the court of King Arthur at Caerleon, where he recounts the failures and partial success of his Grail Quest.[29]

While they are at dinner, Perceval can't help noticing, at the head of one of the tables, a striking-looking chair which is strangely empty. It is made of gold, inlaid with precious stones and looks worthy of a king, but no one dares sit in it. It was sent to the king by the Fay of Menor Rock who required it to be placed at the head of the table at every high feast day. The only man who would be able to sit on it without fear would be the one who was destined to learn what no-one else would ever discover: the secrets of the Grail and the Lance.[30]

Six knights of the court had sat in it, but they had each been swallowed up by the earth. Despite the pleas and tears of the king, queen and barons, Perceval sits on the chair, which lets out such a loud groan that it is heard throughout the hall. Everyone shakes with terror as the ground beneath the seat splits wide open, leaving the chair suspended motionless in the air. Out of the abyss which has opened beneath it, there emerge the knights who had been swallowed up previously.

When the crack in the ground closes up again, the rescued knights tell everyone that they had suffered much pain and hardship in the pit, but nothing compared with what awaits those wicked souls who prefer young men to girls![31] It may be this warning which reminds Perceval that it really is time he got married….

As if to reinforce the point, when Perceval spends the night beneath a thorn bush outside a ruined church, dedicated to the Holy Virgin, he is tempted by a demon in the form of the Grail Bearer, the daughter of the Fisher King. She tells him that she is dying for his love and that, if he lies with her and does whatever she wants, she will tell him all the secrets of the Grail, the Lance and the notched sword. Perceval, however, replies that her conduct is foolish and unbecoming in one so beautiful. He makes the sign of the Cross and the demon flies off.[32]

After praying for forgiveness at his mother's tomb and escorting his sister to the Castle of Maidens, Perceval rides on to the castle of his old tutor Gornemant. But he is shocked to find the land about it laid waste and desolate. Gornemant and his four sons are in the midst of a desperate battle against an army of the undead sent by the tyrannical King of the Waste City.[33] No matter how often they are killed in battle, the king's warriors are fighting fit the next day!

After destroying many of their enemies in battle, Perceval determines to watch over their corpses during the night, to see what is going on. In the moonlight he sees a door open in the side of a hill; a light appears and a tremendous groan shakes the ground. A hideously deformed old hag appears, who starts coating the dead warriors with a potion from a cask she keeps round her neck: They are instantly hale and whole. When challenged by Perceval, she says that he will never learn about the Grail as long as she lives—so he cuts her head off, kills the knights she has restored, and uses the potion to heal his allies.[34]

The next day, they all go to the castle of Blancheflor, and Perceval asks for her hand in marriage. That night Perceval sleeps in his own room under an enchanted coverlet[35] and Blancheflor comes in to him, naked beneath her mantle. They spend the night kissing and cuddling, but no more, until dawn, when Blancheflor creeps back to her own bed. The next day they are married in the church by the archbishop.

Blancheflor is a loving and sensual girl, who has long been eager to marry her hero. On their wedding night, however, when she and her husband are lying in each other's arms, she becomes afraid that bodily pleasure will lead her to Hell. She suggests that they aim for the "double crown" of chastity and virginity. Perceval readily agrees, saying that whoever possesses both will win Paradise. After praying, they lie back down together without experiencing carnal love.

During the night Perceval awakens

and hears a voice from God telling him that there are only two reasons why a man should have sex with his wife: firstly, to beget children; secondly, to avoid sin. Carnal pleasure for its own sake is definitely sinful. But as long as he preserves his virginity for the time being while he searches for the Grail and the Lance, he will eventually sire a line[36] which will include a man who turns into a bird. The birdman's niece will have three sons who will conquer Jerusalem, win the Holy Sepulcher and find the True Cross.[37]

After mass the next day, accordingly, Perceval sets off once more on his quest, leaving his wife and the realm he now rules in the hands of his father-in-law Gornemant.[38]

The Adventurous Path

When, in the course of his quest, Perceval comes to a fork in the road, he takes the Adventurous Path. This leads him to a deserted land where he encounters, for the first time, the Questing Beast. Pursuing it until it collapses from exhaustion, he watches as the monstrous creature is devoured by the hounds in its belly; whereupon they go mad and massacre each other.[39]

He comes to a house of thirteen hermits where he wins a shield made by two Chaldeans who had converted to Christianity—a white shield with a red cross on it, with a fragment of the True Cross embedded in it. The shield bears an inscription stating that only he who can take it from the neck of the girl who bears it will win the Grail and Lance; if any but the boldest man in the world attempts it, he will be crushed to death by a thousand stones.

Undeterred, Perceval takes the shield,[40] which serves him in good stead when he encounters the Knight of the Dragon, who is besieging the Queen of the Circle of Gold in her fortress on the peak of Montesclaire.[41] Fortunately, the Red Cross Shield protects Perceval from the flames that come from the dragon's head on the knight's shield. After a ferocious battle, Perceval kills his opponent, despite the fact that at the last moment a girl steals his shield and rides away.

In pursuit of her, Perceval comes to the abbey where King Mordrain, one of the original Grail Companions, has lain for three hundred years, awaiting the True Knight who can heal him of the wounds he sustained in a battle against pagans. Mordrain tells Perceval how the Grail was brought from Sarras to Britain and how Perceval's mother Philosofine carried the silver trencher. Despite Perceval's desire to heal the king, he can find no way to get in so, praying that the means might present itself, he sets off to get back his shield.[42]

After more adventures, praying for guidance to complete his quest,[43] Perceval comes to a place marked by a tall cross, where the path splits into three. Atop the cross is a wondrous wooden hand, which moves of its own accord to indicate which path a traveler should take. Putting his faith in the hand, which he sees as the hand of God, he takes the path it indicates (the middle one) and his faith is rewarded when he sees a castle in a valley beside a broad running river. He knows in his heart that this is the court of the Fisher King.

For the third time, Perceval witnesses the Grail Procession—a girl carrying the Holy Vessel, another carrying the Bleeding Lance, followed by a boy carrying the notched sword—but this time (having made amends to both his mother and his lover) he is able to fully repair the sword. The king is delighted and throws his arms around Perceval, saying that he will bestow upon him everything he owns.[44] Perceval takes the opportunity to ask about all the mysterious things that he has seen.

The king, despite frequent exhortations to his guest to go to bed and sleep, at last reveals all he wants to know: The Lance is the one with which Longinus pierced the side of Jesus on the Cross; the blood which ran from the wound was collected in the Grail by Joseph of Arimathea; and the silver trencher was used to cover it so that the Holy Blood would not be left exposed.

The king further explains that Joseph brought the Grail Hallows to Britain and built the castle to house them. The Fisher King is descended from Joseph,[45] who died in the castle; the Grail Bearer is the king's daughter. The Maiden of the Silver Trencher is her cousin, the daughter of the Fisher King's brother, Gon of the Land Laid Waste, who was treacherously slain by Espinogris' nephew Partinal the Wild, the Lord of the Red Tower.

The sword that Partinal used to kill Gon shattered and its broken shards were used by Gon's brother to maim himself in his grief; he will not be healed until his brother's death is avenged. This can only be done by the man who can make the sword whole again; Perceval is sure he can accomplish this quest.

But he won't sleep until he has found out about the Tree of Lights he saw, which looked as though it was covered with a thousand candles, but which vanished as he approached it. The king explains that it is a tree of enchantment where fairy women gather: The lights, which look like candles to those who view them from afar, are really fays who seek to lead astray all those who do not believe in God. The fact that, when he drew close to the tree, he saw nothing more, is a sign that he is the one who will be successful in the wondrous adventures of the land.

There remains one last mystery to be elucidated: the dead knight in the Chapel of the Black Hand. The king explains that the hand belongs to a demonic creature that appeared when Espinogris killed his own mother and buried her beneath the altar. Since that day the Black Hand has killed a knight every day; it was its latest victim that Perceval saw laid out in the chapel. It would take a very brave knight to confront the demon and exorcise it from the chapel, by dipping the white veil that is kept there in holy water and sprinkling it over everything.[46]

Perceval spends the night at the castle but, the next day, despite the king's entreaties, he rides on to the chapel. There he drives away the demon by making the sign of the cross over his face with the pommel of his sword. Having exorcised the chapel with holy water as the king prescribed, Perceval finds that the demon is still determined to destroy him: It first of all takes the form of a horse that tries to drown him when he mounts it; then it appears to him as Blancheflor, who tries to seduce him. Once again, the sign of the Cross saves him.[47]

The Achieving of the Quest

After battling with a fellow Knight of the Round Table, Hector of the Fens, Perceval is healed of his wounds by a vision of an angel of light carrying the Holy Grail. The angel turns three times around them and then he and the light that envelops him go back up to Heaven.[48] Both of the knights find themselves completely healed of their injuries. When Hector asks Perceval what the sacred Vessel was that the angel was carrying, Perceval replies that it was the Holy Grail, of which Hector had heard so much talk.[49]

This is the prelude to the completion of Perceval's quest. He arrives, in answer to his prayers, at the Red Tower, an impregnable fortress with five turrets, which fears no assault unless it comes from Heaven—and Perceval, who recognizes it as the home of the man who caused so much pain for the Fisher King, does indeed seem to be a messenger of divine justice.

At the gate to the castle is a pine tree with a shield hanging on it. Perceval smashes the shield, a horn blows and Partinal sallies forth to meet him in combat. The fight is bitter but short. It ends with Perceval striking off Partinal's head and hanging it behind his saddle-bow, saying he will take it to the Fisher King. He leaves the body where it lies, but picks up the broken shield, which he hangs round his neck.

Perceval rides on, passing through the Waste Forest, where he was born, until he comes, once more by chance, upon the Grail Castle. As soon as he hears that a knight has arrived with a severed head hanging from his saddle, the Fisher King feels himself completely cured; he easily descends the stairs to greet Perceval. Recognizing Partinal's shield, the king tells Perceval that all his sorrow has turned to joy. He orders the head of his enemy to be stuck on a stake on the tower of the castle and invites Perceval to join him at table.

The Grail Procession passes three times before them and the tables are filled with delicious food, but Perceval is so intent on the hallows (consisting now of the Lance, Grail and silver trencher) that he forgets to eat. On the third occasion that the Grail passes them, it comes right up to him, so that all can see it plainly. Perceval is filled with joy, for now his long quest is ended.

It is only at this point that the king asks the name of the man who has delivered him from suffering and discovers that it is his own nephew who has saved him.[50] He confirms what he said when Perceval mended the broken sword: that he would give him lordship of all his lands, adding that he himself would step down with immediate effect. But Perceval says that he will not wear the crown until the king is dead. He does, however, agree to wear the king's armor.

Perceval travels on to Arthur's court at Carduel,[51] where he recounts his adventures[52] and joins the feasting. On the eighth day, a maiden arrives with a letter from Corbenic: The Fisher King, his uncle, has died, and Perceval is to rule the Kingdom of the Grail. Arthur and his company travel with Perceval to Corbenic, where fourteen kings attend his coronation on the feast of All Hallows.

Afterwards they see the Grail Procession pass three times in front of them and the tables are filled with delectable foods. Unlike Perceval, when he first arrived there, King Arthur asks immediately about what he has seen and is delighted to hear the truth about the hallows. The plenary court stays for a month at Corbenic, fed every day by the Grail, but at the end of that time Arthur returns to his own lands, leaving Perceval to rule his kingdom in peace for seven years.

After this, Perceval gives up his crown to become a hermit.[53] For five years Perceval lives an ascetic life in the forest with a holy man, accompanied by the hallows. He then is received into the priesthood, celebrating his first Mass on the Feast of St. John. For ten years he is fed only by the Holy Grail, which he sees night and day. He dies on Candlemas Eve.

On the joyous day that God takes his soul, the Holy Grail, the Lance and the beautiful silver trencher are also swept up into Heaven, in the sight of all. Since the death of Perceval, no-one has ever seen the Grail on this Earth, no matter how much they search; no-one will ever again see it so openly.[54] Perceval is buried in the Palace of Adventures in Corbenic, next to the Fisher King. On his grave stone is written: "Here lies Perceval the Welshman, who brought to completion the adventures of the Holy Grail."[55]

The Third Keeper of the Grail

Others say that the name of Perceval's father is Alan the Fat, whose father Bron is the Fisher King and whose uncle is Joseph of Arimathea, who becomes the first Grail Keeper.

Joseph is imprisoned by the Jews after the Resurrection because he will not tell them where the body of Jesus has gone. While in prison he is visited by the risen Christ, who speaks to him Secret Words which constitute the Credo of the consecration of the Grail.[56] Christ makes Joseph the first of three keepers of the Holy Vessel. The second keeper is Joseph's brother-in-law Bron and the third keeper is to be Bron's grandson, Perceval.

After leaving prison Joseph is instructed by the Holy Spirit to make a table for the Grail in commemoration of the Table of the Last Supper and to leave an empty place between his and Bron's seats: This empty place at the Table of the Grail looks backwards, to the seat of Judas at the right hand of Jesus, which was made empty when Judas left to betray his Lord; and forwards, to the Perilous Seat at Arthur's Round Table, an empty place that can only be filled by Bron's grandson.[57]

The voice of the Holy Spirit further instructs Joseph to inform Bron's youngest son Alan the Fat, that from him will be born a son to whom His Vessel is to come. As for Bron himself, he is to travel into the West, wherever his heart directs him. Wherever he rests, the Voice tells Joseph, there Bron must wait for the arrival of his grandson. When his hour has come, Bron must pass on to his grandson the Holy Vessel and the grace that he will have received in turn from Joseph. Thus, there will be three keepers, symbolizing the Holy Trinity; the destiny of the third will be in the hands of Jesus Christ.[58] Before he dies, Joseph accordingly entrusts the Grail to Bron and also gives to him, in writing, the Secret Words that the risen Christ spoke to him in prison.[59]

Centuries later the prophet Merlin tells Uther Pendragon, King of Britain, that he must establish a table in the name of the Trinity, but leave one seat empty to correspond to the empty place at the Table of the Grail. Uther naturally asks if the prophet knows who is to fill that place. Merlin replies that it will be the as-yet-unborn child of Alan the Fat, but that he must first have been in the presence of the Grail and sat in the empty place at its table—something which the guardians of the Holy Vessel have not yet witnessed.[60]

All this will happen during the reign of Uther's son, whose conception Merlin now engineers. When Arthur succeeds his father as king, Merlin tells him that when one of the Knights of the Round Table has become the finest knight in the world, found the court of the Fisher King and asked what purpose the Grail has served and now serves, the aged and sick Bron will be healed. When this happens the Fisher King, before he passes from life to death, will tell that knight the Secret Words of Our Lord. Finally, when the knight has the Holy Blood in his keeping, the enchanting of the land of Britain will cease and the prophecy will be fulfilled.[61]

And so it is that Perceval, the son of Alan the Fat, goes to King Arthur's court after his father's death and is made a Knight of the Round Table. At the Feast of Pentecost, Perceval outshines all the Knights of the Round Table at a tournament, whereupon they declare that he should fill the empty seat. Arthur is reluctant, knowing what happened to anyone who has tried to sit there before, but gives in when Perceval threatens to leave his household.

Perceval is overjoyed and, crossing himself in the name of the Holy Spirit, sits in the empty seat; whereupon the stone beneath it, emitting an anguished groan, splits beneath him. A great darkness falls all around. Although he is in fact the knight prophesied by Merlin, Perceval's action is premature, for he has not yet been in the presence of the Grail.

A voice rings out, crying that only the goodness of his father and grandfather have prevented Perceval from paying a terrible price for his audacity. Whoever asks the Grail Question will heal the Fisher King, says the voice: The stone will be mended and the enchantments of Britain, which have now begun, will be brought to an end.[62]

The knights embark on the quest of the Holy Vessel.[63]

Returning to the Waste Forest where he was brought up, in order to be re-united with his sister, Perceval travels with her to visit the Hermit of the Holy Spirit, their father's brother, who had long ago travelled with the Company of the Grail from Jerusalem. He asks his nephew if he has yet been to the house of the Fisher King, his grandfather. Perceval replies that he has not yet found it, although he has been searching for it for a long time.

The hermit tells him that, while their family was still in the Holy Land, the voice of the Holy Spirit had commanded Perceval's grandfather Bron to travel towards the setting sun. Moreover, the voice had prophesied that, in these faraway lands of the West, Alan would father a son who would visit the court of the ailing Fisher King and receive from him his grace and his Vessel. Only then would the aged man be able to die; while Perceval would become the guardian of the Holy Blood.[64]

Riding on for days without reaching his goal, Perceval comes at last to a cross at the meeting of four roads, standing beside a tree in which two children are climbing. They say that they have been sent from the Earthly Paradise by the Holy Spirit to guide him, directing him to take the path to his right. Fearing that he may be misled by phantoms, he hesitates on the path, but is then alarmed to see an immense shadow pass four times in front of him. Perceval crosses himself and a voice comes to him from out of the shadow, with a message from Merlin that, if he is worthy and follows the path, he will fulfill the prophecy Our Lord made to Joseph of Arimathea.

Convinced, Perceval follows the ordained path but, unfortunately, when he comes to the court of Bron and sees the Grail Procession,[65] including the Bleeding Lance, for the first time, he fails to ask what the Holy Vessel was for; had he done so, the prophecy would have been fulfilled and the ailing king restored to health. When Perceval leaves the castle the next morning, finding it deserted, a weeping damsel he meets in the heart of the forest tells him that he is not yet wise or worthy enough to have the blood of Christ in his keeping.[66]

Seven years pass, during which he loses all faith in God. By the time he comes again to the house of his hermit uncle, he finds out that his sister has died. His uncle suggests that he return to take possession of the family home, but Perceval says that he will never rest until he once more finds the court of his grandfather.[67]

Eventually, Perceval meets Merlin in the guise of an old reaper. The prophet says that he knew Perceval's name before he was born and that, when he reaches the court of the Fisher King, Perceval must be sure to ask about what he sees.

Accordingly, within the year and on the very day Merlin specified, Perceval finds himself in the hall where his grandfather lies. This time, he asks the purpose of the things he sees and Bron is instantly cured of his sickness. He explains to his grandson that the Lance is the one with which Longinus struck Jesus on the Cross; the Grail is the Vessel with which Joseph gathered the blood that flowed from His wounds.[68] Then, in obedience to the voice of the Holy Spirit, Bron teaches Perceval the sacred words of Christ that Joseph had taught him in turn, but which cannot be revealed to anyone else. He hands over to his grandson the Vessel containing the Holy Blood, which he had guarded so long. With that, all the enchantments that have so long beset the world are ended.[69]

When Bron dies three days later, Merlin brings his master Blaise to the court of the new Fisher King and they stay together in the company of the Grail. The prophet later goes to Arthur's court in Carduel, where he is told that the stone which split when Perceval sat in the Perilous Seat has now mended. The king asks him the significance of this, to which Merlin replies that Arthur's reign has seen the greatest of all prophecies fulfilled: For the Fisher King has been healed; the enchantments of Britain have been overthrown; and God has made Perceval the new Lord of the Grail.[70]

The Virgin Knight

It is also said, however, that Perceval will be one of three who achieve the Grail Quest and that he will take second place to Galahad, ultimately succeeding him as King of Sarras.

The coming of Perceval is prophesied

by Merlin, who says that his father will be the Maimed King of the Waste Forest[71] on the borders of Logres.[72] To be born in Wales, Perceval will return to the earth as virginal as when he emerges from his mother's womb. Moreover, he alone will be able to explain to King Arthur the meaning of the adventure of the Questing Beast.[73]

After the death of his father and two of his brothers, Perceval is brought up in lonely isolation in the Waste Forest with his mother, his older brother Agloval having already joined the Round Table. One day Agloval returns home for a visit, which ends with his bringing Perceval to Carduel to be made a knight.

After the ceremony, Perceval sits at one of the lower tables in the hall, but the Maiden Who Never Lies (a silk-worker who has never been known to speak) breaks her silence, to the astonishment of all. After staring at the new-made knight for a while, she bursts into tears and then exclaims that this pure, virginal servant of Christ should take his place at the Round Table, next to the Perilous Seat. Leading him to the place once occupied by his father,[74] she explains that the Good Knight will occupy the Perilous Seat, while Perceval will sit at his right hand and Sir Bors on his left, for reasons whose significance will later become apparent. The maiden asks him to pray for her soul on the day that he comes before the Holy Grail. She never speaks again, and dies a few days later.

Embarrassed that he has not yet accomplished any knightly deeds, Perceval spends a year adventuring.[75] After rescuing the impoverished Lady of Belrepaire,[76] Perceval comes across a man wearing a crown of gold fishing in a little river between two mountains. They introduce themselves to each other and, when Perceval says that his father was King Pellinor, the Rich Fisherman recognizes his grandson; for he is King Pellehan, Pellinor's father. Because he cannot make use of his limbs to ride, Pellehan amuses himself by fishing; whence some call him the Maimed King. Before they part, Pellehan exhorts Perceval to strive to be as courageous a knight as his late father.[77]

Perceval (along with Lancelot's brother Hector) is in fact the first of the Knights of the Round Table to see the Grail anywhere other than in the court of the Fisher King. The two knights, not recognizing each other, fight themselves to a standstill; both are near death when a chalice surrounded by light appears to them, borne by an unknown hand.[78] They bow down before it, recognizing its holiness, whereupon their injuries are miraculously healed. Hector explains that the Holy Vessel is that in which Jesus ate the paschal lamb at the Last Supper and that it was brought to Logres by Joseph of Arimathea, where it feeds the court of the Fisher King. Perceval declares that he will nevermore rest easy until he has seen it plainly.[79]

When a sword, stuck fast in a stone through the magic of Merlin, floats down river to Camelot, an inscription on it reads that none but the best knight in the world can draw it out. Perceval tries, but fails[80]; it is Galahad who succeeds. It is Galahad also who alone can sit on the Perilous Seat. When the Grail appears in Arthur's court, Perceval is one of the many Knights of the Round Table who vows that he will not return there until he has learnt the truth about the Holy Vessel.[81]

After saving a hermit from killing himself, Perceval receives a message from on high in the form of a mysterious letter, which informs him that he will follow the Quest to its end. He is nearly diverted from it, however, by the sight of the Questing Beast, which his father Pellinor had pursued for so long. But Palamedes the Saracen, who considers the beast to be his quarry alone, dissuades Perceval from doing so, at the end of a lance.[82]

In the course of his subsequent adventures, Perceval learns from his aunt, the Queen of the Waste Land, that Merlin, after establishing the Round Table in the image of the Table of the Grail and the Table of the Last Supper, had prophesied that two of the knights who complete the Quest would be virgins. It is she, also, who tells him that his mother died of heartbreak as soon as he left for King Arthur's court. Before he leaves his aunt, Perceval is told that he must maintain his virginity so that he can come before the Holy Grail unstained by the sin of debauchery.[83] This, despite demonic temptations, he succeeds in doing.

Eventually he meets up with his fellow questers Galahad (whose sword he inherits[84]) and Bors, as well as with his sister, who sacrifices herself in order to cure a lady of leprosy. As she lies dying, Perceval's sister asks him to place her body in a boat and allow chance to take it. He will find her again in the holy city of Sarras and he should bury her there in the Spiritual Palace, where both he and Galahad will be laid beside her.[85]

After teaming up with the newly-baptized Palamedes to pursue the Questing Beast, Perceval is joined by Galahad to witness the death at the hands of their companion of the bizarre creature which his father King Pellinor had followed for so long.[86] The three knights then journey on together to Corbenic where Galahad heals the Maimed King (Pellehan, who is his great-grandfather and Perceval's grandfather).

After visiting the newly-healed king in the hermitage where he now dwells and hearing the astounding story of the origin of the Questing Beast among other mysteries,[87] Perceval accompanies Galahad and Bors on the Ship of Faith to Sarras. There, they bury Perceval's sister as she requested. Imprisoned by pagans, they are sustained by the Holy Vessel, like the first Grail companions, until eventually freed.

When Galahad dies and the Grail is taken up to Heaven, Perceval lives as a hermit, until he in turn dies. Bors buries him next to his sister and Galahad in the Spiritual Palace.[88]

* * *

The development of the story of the Grail from verse to prose romance entails a development in the character of Perceval from, as Jessie L. Weston puts it, "a genuine, faulty, but loving and lovable human being, true man and faithful husband, into an aggressively proselytizing and persecuting celibate"; a conversion, she argues, that is essential if he is to retain a place, albeit no longer the first one, in the Grail Quest: "he could act as second to Galahad, and, like him, disappear, the quest once achieved."[89]

At the heart of the transition is the question of Perceval's sexuality. Chrétien de Troyes depicts the young Perceval as a lusty but inexperienced heterosexual: His first act after leaving home is to steal a kiss from a maiden. On the first night that he spends in the castle of Blancheflor, his hostess, weeping and half-naked, comes into his bedroom to ask for his assistance against her tormentors. Perceval, who knows nothing of the pleasure women can give to a man, kindly takes her in his arms and, after listening to her woes, invites her to spend the night with him, since the bed is big enough for both of them. They lie together all night, body to body, mouth to mouth, until dawn.[90] We are not told that they did anything more than kiss and cuddle the following night either, even though Blancheflor has put the key of love into the lock of his heart.[91]

It is Perceval's concern for his mother that prevents him from staying with Blancheflor after he has defeated her enemies, but he promises to return and rule the land, whether his mother is alive or dead. Perceval's first return is described in the Second Continuation: Once again, Perceval lies down alone in his own bed, only to experience a nocturnal visitation. This time things appear to go a bit further.[92] But Perceval still will not stay more than three nights because he is now in search of the Grail Castle after his abortive first visit. The later Continuations perceive Perceval as chaste even when he eventually marries Blancheflor[93] and, in this, it is likely that the authors have been influenced by the prose romances.

Thus, in the Romance of Perlesvaus, the

hero is depicted as a very attractive young man who has offers, but is unwilling to pursue them.[94] In the Vulgate and Post-Vulgate Cycles, all references to amorous adventures (except for demonic temptations) are expunged from the story of Perceval to make him, like Galahad, a virgin knight. In fact, it is his life-long chastity that is the key to his success in these versions of the Quest. Although, here, his role is secondary to that of the son of his cousin the Grail Bearer, it is superior to that of Bors, who has fathered a child.

Noticeably, it is Bors alone who returns to Logres, to material reality, after the spiritual Grail Quest has ended; while Perceval will, like Galahad, "disappear," as Weston puts it. In the Vulgate and Post-Vulgate, this disappearance is, initially, from Logres, to which they will nevermore return; then, from the Middle Eastern city of Sarras, whence they are taken up to Heaven. In the Prose *Perceval* the hero ends his days in the Grail Castle, as does Wolfram's Parzival; but Albrecht sends him to India with the Grail.[95] In Manessier's Third Continuation, Perceval leaves the Grail Castle for a hermitage. In the Romance of Perlesvaus, he sails off from the castle in a ship with a white sail bearing a red cross, none know whither; but we have been told that the ship will take him to the Isle of Plenty, where he will reign as king.[96] This island of abundance, full of all good things, could not be further from the lonely Waste Forest where he was brought up: Like Malory's Arthur in Avalon, we can say of him that *here in this world he changed his life.*

Notes

1. *CSG* 219; *PCP* ll.7666–72.
2. *CSG* 422.
3. *CSG* 5.
4. *CSG* 10.
5. *CSG* 16.
6. *CSG* 19.
7. *CSG* 26–33.
8. *CSG* 41–2.
9. *CSG* 55–6: Richard Barber (2005, 358–61) sees these divine names as possibly pointing to a non-apostolic tradition of ritual magic "known to a select few"—"a body of secret lore within the Church" which he links to the Secret Tradition of spiritual alchemy which A.E. Waite proposed as the secret of the Grail.
10. *CSG* 265: He swears that, while there is still life in his body, he will never stop to wander, through forest, land and sea, until he hears the truth about the Grail and the iron-headed Lance—why it bleeds and what precisely it could be—from the rich Fisher King who has honored him so highly: *Et avec ce an covant met/ Que ja ne cessera d'errer/ Par bois et par terre et par mer,/ Tant com ou cors li soit la vie,/ Jusqu'atant qu'il avra oïe/ Dou saint Graal la verité,/ Et de la lance au fer quarré/ Por qu'elle saine et que puet estre./ Trestout an vorra savoir l'estre/ Au bon riche Roi Pescheor/ Qui li porta si grant honor* (*DC* ll.3587–97).
11. He tells the hermit how he lodged at the house of the valorous Fisher King where the Lance and the precious, beautiful Grail are kept, but asked nothing about them and so learnt nothing, leaving before he could find out the truth of these things: *Conmant il ala herbergier/ A l'ostel au Roi Pescheor/ Qui tant estoit de grant valor,/ Ou la lance iert et li graaulx/ Qui tant estoit et genz et biaux, / Et conmant riens ne demanda / Et conmant il s'an desevra,/ Qu'il n'an sot reson ne verté* (*DC* ll.4409–16). He prays that with God's help he could find an explanation for the Bleeding Lance and the Grail—not to mention the sword, which only one knight is able to mend, although he hasn't been able to find out who he is, or what is his destiny. It is as yet unknown to him, but he will learn it eventually: *Se je savoie l'achoison/ De la lance qui saine anson,/ Et dou graal et de l'espee/ Qui ne puet estre resodee,/ Se n'est par .I. seul chevalier!/ Mais ne vos sai mie acointier/ Quex il est ne qui il puet estre,/ Car je n'ai pas si apris l'estre/ Come j'ancore l'aprandai* (*DC* ll.4472–80). The sword to which Perceval refers is the one given to him by the Fisher King; and the unknown knight he refers to will eventually be revealed as the smith Trebuchet or Triboet.
12. *CSG* 272–3.
13. He begs the girl in God's name to conceal nothing of the truth, to tell him about the Grail and reveal the secret of how the rich king came to have it, who gave it to him along with the Lance which bleeds from its iron tip: *La damoiselle ancor pria/ Que dou graal li acontast,/ Et que por Dieu ne li celast/ La verité et lou secroi/ Et l'achoison dou riche roi,/ Com il l'ot et qui li dona,/ Et qui la lance li bailla/ Dont li fer saine par la pointe* (*DC* ll. 6316–23).
14. He asks the girl to tell him if she knows the splendid court of the well-favored king who guards the rich Grail and the Lance which sheds crimson blood from its tip: *Se vos la riche cort savez/ Ou li rois est bons eürez/ Qui garde lou riche graal/ Et la lance qui au pointal/ Rant la goute de sanc vermoil* (*DC* ll.6447–51).
15. *CSG* 284–7.
16. She asks him if he's been to the court of the

Fisher King and what he has uncovered there: if he knows about the Lance now, or what the Grail is; and whether he enquired about the sword which will not be able to be remade; and whether he asked about the obscure adventures which will never be known to any knight until the coming of he who will be endowed with all qualities: *S'a la cort au Roi Pescheor/ Avoit esté, et que li die/ Quelle novelle avoit oïe/ Et se de la lance savoit,/ Et dou graal que ce estoit,/ Et s'anquis avoit de l'espee/ Qui ne puet estre resodee,/ Et demandé des avantures/ Qui a oïr sont molt oscures,/ Que ja chevalier ne savra/ Dusqu'atant que cil i vandra/ Qui avra toutes les bontez* (DC ll.8142–53).

17. CSG 299–300.
18. CSG 328–9.
19. What all this signifies she says to him, is that he will hear the truth about the Grail and the Lance soon, for the things Perceval has told her about are the signs of the holy mysteries, which he will hear about in good time: *ce est senefience/ Que dou graal et de la lance/ Savroiz par tens la verité.// Car quanque vos m'avez conté/ Senefie lou saint secré,/ Don vos orroiz par tens novelle* (DC ll.12844–6, 12864–6).
20. ...*Perceval,/ Qui molt covoite lou graal/ A veoir, donc a eü peine;/ Et la lance donc li fer saine/ Verroit il molt tres volantiers* (DC ll.12918–22).
21. This is not the sword that the Fisher King presented to him and which is destined to break (see THE BROKEN SWORD), but the Sword of Partinal (q.v.), earlier brought to the Fisher King by Gawain, who was also unable to repair it.
22. What he would really like to know, Perceval says to the king, is the truth about the Grail which has passed by them twice now; about the Lance which bleeds; and, with regard to the sword which is broken in the middle, whether it will ever be remade and drawn again in the field of battle: *j'orroie volantiers/ De ce graal la verité,/ Qui par ci a .II. foiz passé/ Et de la lance ausint qui seine//Si me redites de l'espee/ Qui par mileu est trançonee,/ Et se jamés sera refete,/ An champ ne am bataille traite* (DC ll.13039–42, 13046–9).
23. CSG 334–7.
24. CSG 339.
25. CSG 380.
26. He asks himself what's going on. He remembers taking lodging the previous night at the house of the rich Fisher King, seeing the Grail and the Lance that bleeds constantly, despite having no veins or joints—and joining together the sword that is broken, leaving only a small notch that must still be repaired: This much is yet to do: *Je fui ersoir, bien m'en sovint,/ Hebergiez.../ Chiés le riche Roi Pescheor,/ Et vi le Graal et la Lance/ Qui onques de sainier n'estanche/ Et si n'i a vainne ne jointe,/Et l'espee que j'ai ajointe/ Fors l'osque qui est a sauder,/ De tant i a a amender* (GCP ll.122–30).
27. CSG 340–1: How marvelous, he tells himself; no wonder he's astonished: The country was a waste desert the previous night when he came there; now he sees it covered with growth: *Par foi, fait il, je voi merveille/ Dont je doi bien estre esbahis:/ Hersoir quant ving en cest païs/ Vi cest païs gaste et desert./ Or le voi de tout bien covert* (GCP ll.320–4).
28. CSG 346.
29. The king makes him recount all the troubles, the difficulties and the set-backs that he has so far endured on the quest for the Grail, which he has now seen twice in the house of the Fisher King. But he was denied knowledge of who is served by the Grail and told quite openly that he wasn't worthy of knowing its secrets; nor was there anything he could do to find out why the Lance bleeds, no matter how often he asked. But he had more luck repairing a sword which is broken in two, although he left a notch in it. He will not learn anything about the Grail until he has finished the job: *Car li rois li faisoit retraire/ L'anui, le mal et le contraire/ Qu'il avoit en la queste eü/ Del Graal qu'il avoit veü/ Chiés le Roi Pescheor deus fois./ Mais bien li fu mis en defois/ Li raconters cui on en sert,/ Et bien li fu dit en apert/ Qu'il n'ert pas dignes del savoir/Des secrez du Graal le voir,/ Ne de la Lance por coi saine/ Ne puet savoir por nule paine:/ Neporquant molt en demanda./ Mais une espee rasauda/ Qui brisiee est en deus moitiez,/ Mais ne fu pas si rafaitiez/ C'une osque n'eüst en l'espee./ Devant ce qu'ele ert rasaldee / Ne savra nus rien du Graal* (GCP ll.1269–87).
30. A messenger from the fay has told the king that *dignes esteroit/ De seoir cil qui conquerroit/ Del monde le los et le pris/ Et ce que ne puet estre apris/ Par home ne ja ne sera/ Fors par celui qui i serra,/ C'est del Graal et de la Lance,/Mais chil i serra sanz doutance* (GCP ll.1447–54). This golden chair is a variation on the theme of the Feared Seat at the Table of the Grail and the Perilous Seat at the Round Table. "The motif of the vacant seat awaiting a worthy occupant" may have its origins in Irish medieval stories, as Loomis argues (1963, 259), but it has here degenerated into propaganda.
31. CSG 350–2.
32. CSG 358–9.
33. To make matters worse, the *Roi de la Gaste Chité* is a *tyrans soudomites* (GCP ll.5693, 5716). Gerbert de Montreuil thus reinforces the association between the Grail and heterosexual marriage already suggested by the episode of the Fairy's Seat. He adds to this theme the equation of homosexuality with the sterility of the Waste Land.
34. CSG 378–88.
35. Made by the fay Blanchemal, one of Gawain's fairy lovers, on her otherworldly island, this enchanted coverlet will prevent any one who sleeps beneath it from experiencing madness or physical illness, or wanting to cause harm to others (GCP ll.6504–14). Perceval's Christian marriage, it seems, will have the blessing of Faerie.
36. As Louise D. Stephens has pointed out, this prediction does not accord with Gerbert's "emphasis on virginity and the text leaves it left unclear how this problem is to be resolved. This is a distant prophecy and ... it is hard to imagine an ending in which Perceval wins the Grail and then consummates his marriage" (67). But in the De Boron Cycle,

Perceval's father Alan the Fat is also reluctant to marry until a divine voice over-rules him. Where the desire to keep one's virginity as long as possible is a requirement of the Grail hero in the poems centered on Perceval, nothing short of life-long virginity will suit the chosen one of the prose cycles, which may be why Perceval is superseded by Galahad as the principal Grail winner.

37. Here Gerbert makes Perceval the ancestor of the Swan Knight (as Wolfram's Parzival is the father of Loherangrin) and of Godfrey of Bouillon, the hero of the First Crusade.

38. *CSG* 389–95.

39. This is the only occasion in which King Pellinor's prophecy, that the Beast would be hunted after his death by one of his line, comes true. Elsewhere it is killed by Palamedes, though observed by Perceval.

40. *CSG* 405–7.

41. The relief of the siege of Montesclaire is elsewhere attributed to Gawain, while a different version of the defeat of the Dragon Knight is found in the Romance of Perlesvaus.

42. *CSG* 417–23: In the context of the verse Continuation of Gerbert de Montreuil, from which the episode of the meeting with Mordrain is here summarized, the True Knight whose coming Mordrain awaits is surely none other than Perceval himself: He it is of whom the monks speak, when they say that the one who is destined to seek the Grail and Bleeding Lance and heal the old king's wounds is already in the land; may God guide him to the chapel: *Que cil est ja en ceste terre/ Qui s'entremet du Graal querre/ Et la Lance dont li fers saine;/ Chascune plaie seroit saine/ Que li rois a, s'il venoit chi,/ Et Dieus l'amaint par sa merchi!* (*GCP* ll.10561–6). Perceval has indeed been led there, but too soon. He vows to return when he has found the Lance and Grail to heal of all his ills the king who lies wounded in the chapel: *Et la Lance et le saint Graal,/ Et le roi garir de son mal/ Qui gist navrez en la chapele* (ll.10587–9). Unfortunately, we hear nothing more of Mordrain in the verse Continuations; while the healing of Mordrain will become the task of Galahad in the Vulgate *Queste*.

43. Perceval prays to the Creator to guide him to the court of the good Fisher King for, if he finds it, he will want to know who is served from the Grail which he has seen so openly; as well as about the silver trencher, the Lance and the Sword, which he has repaired with his two hands, apart from the notch: *La ou li Rois Peschiere maint;/ Et dist que, s'il trove la cort,/ Que tant tenra le bon roi cort,/ Del Graal, qu'il vit descovert,/ Volra savoir cui on en sert,/ Du tailleoir, et de la Lance,/Et de l'espee l'assamblance/ Que entre ses .II. mains rajoint/ Fors l'osque* [*GCP* ll.16844–52].

44. *CSG* 473–5.

45. The Fisher Kings are usually considered to be direct descendants of Bron, Joseph's brother-in-law, rather than of Joseph himself.

46. *CSG* 477–80.

47. *CSG* 513–21.

48. At midnight a great light appears between them, the like of which they have never seen; but its brightness makes them open their eyes and see within it a "royal angel"—that is to say, a messenger from the Kingdom of Heaven—bearing the Grail. Thrice he turns around them before returning to the light from which he manifested, so that they do not know what has become of him, unless the holy angel has borne the Grail up to Heaven: *Endroit la mïenuit avint/ Qu'entre eus deus une clarté vint/ Si grant c'onques de lor veüe/ N'orent si grant clarté veüe./ Por la clarté les iauz ovrirent/ Et enmi cele clarté virent/ Trestot seul un ange roial/ Qui en ses mains tint le Graal./ Trois torz tot entor eus torna/ Et puis arrieres retorna/ En la clarté o cui il vint,/ Que nus ne sot que il devint;/ Ne mes que vers le ciel monta/ Li sainz anges qui en porta/ Entre ses mains le Saint Graal* (*MTC* ll.41531–45).

49. *Saichiez que c'est le Saint Graal,/ Dont tant avez parler oï* (*MTC* ll.41572–3).

50. This contradicts what his other uncle (the hermit who taught him the secret names of God) told him on Good Friday: that the Fisher King is Perceval's cousin and that it is the old king in the chamber, the one who is served by the Grail, who is the brother of Perceval's mother.

51. *CSG* 547–51.

52. Perceval recounts how the Holy Grail, the Lance from which red blood flows and the beautiful silver trencher were all carried in plain sight, and how he repaired the shattered sword: *Puis lor a conté Perceval/ Conment il vit le Saint Graal/ Et la lance que l'en portoit,/ Dont le vermeil sanc degotoit/ Apertement devant la gent,/ Et dou bel tailleoir d'argent/ Et de l'espee tronçonee/ Qu'il out rejointe et resoudee* (*MTC* ll.42355–62). Continuing with his account of the Chapel of the Black Hand, the Tree of Lights and other demonic temptations, Perceval goes on to tell them how he and Sir Hector fought but were healed by the Holy Grail, which God revealed to them: *Et conment il furent gari/ Par le Saint Graal sanz dotance,/ Dont Diex lor fist la demonstrance* (ll.42402–4). He further reveals how his cutting off the head of Partinal caused the healing of the Fisher King: *Et conment out sa garison/ Li rois por icele acoison* (ll.42413–4).

53. The hallows follow him to the hermitage: *Le Graal et la sainte lance/ Vint aprés lui sanz demorance,/ Et le saint tailleor d'argent* (*MTC* ll.42561–3).

54. *Le jor que Dex l'ame en porta,/ Dont a joie se deporta,/ Fu el ciel ravi sanz doutance/ Et le Saint Graal et la lance/ Et le bel tailleor d'argent,/ Tout en apert, voiant la gent./ Onc puis ne fu, tant seüst querre,/ Nus hom qui le veïst en terre/ Puis que Perceval fu finnez;/ Ne jamés hom qui soit nez/ Nel verra si apertement* (*MTC* ll.42615–25).

55. *CSG* 553–5.

56. *EG* ll.935–6; *RG* 31; *MG* 22.

57. *MG* 35: *Cil lius ne pora estre aemplis devant ce que li fils qui istra del fil Bron l'emplisse* (*RG* 55).

The Prose *Joseph* corrects a confusion found in the metrical *Estoire dou Graal*, whereby it appears to be the son of Bron and Enygeus (that is, Alan the Fat) rather than their grandchild (Perceval) who is destined to fill the Perilous Seat (*EG* ll.2531–6).

58. *EG* ll.3361–76: *...la senefiance de la Trinité, qui est par trois. Lors sera del tierç au plaisir Jhesucrist* (*RG* 69).

59. *MG* 42–3: See THE SECRET WORDS OF CHRIST.

60. *MG* 92–4: *Et cil qui emplir le doit naistra de Alain le gros.... Et covenra celui qui emplir le doit qu'il ait esté la u li Graaus sert. Ne cil qui le gardent ne le virent onques acomplir* (*RG* 161); *et covendra a celui qui doit acomplir cest leu acomplir avant celui dou vaissel dou graal: car cil qui le gardent nou virent onques acomplir* (*MM* 190).

61. *MG* 113: *Et li Rois Peschiere ... ne puet morir desci adont que uns cevaliers qui serra a la Table Reonde ait tant fait d'armes et de cevalerie ... que il sera li plus aloiés del monde. Et cil, quant il s'ara si essaucié qu'il pora venir a la cort le rice Roi Pescheor et que il ara demandé de quoi li Graaus a servi et de quoi il sert, et tant tost sera garis. Et lors li acontera les secrees paroles de Nostre Segneur; si trespassera de vie a mort; et cil cevaliers ara le sanc Jhesu Crist en garde. Et lors charront li encantement par la terre de Bretagne et adont si sera la prophesie toute paracomplie* (*MM* 296–7).

62. *Et lors quant il avra demandé que on en fait et cui on en sert de cel Graal, lors quant il ara çou demandé, si sera li Rois Peschiere garis, et sera li piere rasoldée del liu de le Table Reonde, et charont li encantement qui hui cest jor sont en le terre de Bretagne* (*RG* 205–6).

63. *MG* 119–20.

64. *MG* 128–30: *Et si dist la vois que de Alain le Gros naisteroit uns oirs qui le Graal aroit en se baillie, et dist que li Rois Pesciere ne poroit morir dusqu'atant que vos ariés esté a se cort, et quant vous i ariés esté il seroit garis et vous bailleroit sa grasse et son vaissel, et seriés sire del sanc nostre Segnor Jhesucrist* (*RG* 226).

65. Perceval sees a girl carrying two carving dishes (*tailleors d'argent*) followed by a boy carrying a Lance from the iron tip of which fall three drops of blood; and, after him, another boy carrying the Vessel which Our Lord gave to Joseph in prison: *Aprés vint uns vallés qui aporta une lance, et sannoit par le fer trois goutes de sanc.... Et aprés si vint uns vallés et portoit entre ses mains le vaissel que nostre Sire douna a Joseph en le prison* (*RG* 245).

66. *MG* 139–43.

67. *MG* 146–7.

68. *Et cil vaissiaus que on apele Graal, saciés que çou est li sans que Joseph recuelli de ses plaies qui decouroient a le terre* (*RG* 270).

69. Perceval listens to Bron most willingly and is straightaway filled with the grace of the Holy Spirit. Then the aged Bron hands over to Perceval the Vessel, from which comes such sweet melody and perfume that they seem to be in Paradise with the angels: *et Percevaus l'a oïe molt volentiers, et tant tost fu raplenis de la grasse del saint Esperit. Et Bron li viels bailla Perceval le vaissel entre ses mains, et del vaissel issi une melodie et un flairors issi precieuse que il lor sambla que il fussent en paradis o les angles.... Et chaïrent li encantement et derompirent par tot le mont* (*RG* 271).

70. *MG* 153–6.

71. From the *chambre* of the *roi mahaignié devers la Gaste Forest*, says Merlin, will come one who will be *dès sa nativité jusqu'a sa mort virges et chastes si enterinement qu'il n'ait amor a dame n'a damoisele* (*LDL* III, 138). The *Estoire de Merlin* tells us that King Pellinor is called *mahaigniés et estoit navrés par ans .II. les cuisses* (*VS* II, 159) and that his realm is the *salvage forest* (359) or the *terre gaste* (384). So, we can be sure that we are meant to identify Pellinor with the un-named father of Perceval who Chrétien, in the opening scene of the *Conte del Graal*, describes as being *par mi les anches navrez/ Si que il mehaigna do cors* (*CGM* ll.408–9); while the wild wood where Perceval is brought up is called *la gaste forest* (l.73).

72. Merlin says that the Waste Forest is on the furthest edge of the Kingdom of Lists—*la fin del roiaume de Litee* (*LDL* III, 138)—which is presumably a way of describing Logres as a place of secular tournaments in contrast to the spiritual Grail Kingdom. From it will come a marvelous, lion-like knight who will have no more speech than a thoughtful lady—*po emparlez, dès qu'il resamble de parolle dame pensive* (140)—which, as the text's editor François Mosès points out, can only refer to Perceval's silence on his first visit to the Grail Castle, when asking the Question would have healed the Fisher King (141n1).

73. *SRM* 14: The English translation by Martha Asher, based on a different edition, reads: "he will keep his virginity surely and marvelously, because he will be conceived of a virgin mother and born of a virgin woman." In an age when it was not particularly unusual for a woman to be a virgin until conceiving her first child, this "miracle," as Asher refers to it, which is not mentioned elsewhere (*LG* IV, 171&n6), does seem to suggest that Perceval is a type of Christ and his mother of the Virgin Mary.

74. Merlin sat King Pellinor next to the Perilous Seat on the day that Arthur and Guenevere were wed (*LG* IV, 226).

75. *LG* III, 323–7.

76. *LG* V, 105–7: This is a Post-Vulgate rewrite of Chrétien's account of Perceval's rescuing of Blancheflor, but with any hint of sexual feelings between the knight and lady completely absent.

77. *LG* V, 109.

78. In Malory's version of this episode, based on the Prose *Tristan*, Sir Percivale sees a damsel *all in whyght, with a vessell in bothe her hondys*; and this *glemerynge of the vessell and of the mayden* is only vouchsafed to him because he is also *a perfyte mayden* (*MD* 643).

79. *LG* III, 328: This episode is a variant of that in the Third Continuation (recounted above in The

Achieving of the Quest) where it is Perceval, who is already an experienced Grail Quester in the verse romances, who has to explain to Hector what it is they have seen.

80. *LG* IV, 4; *QHG* 36: *and therewith he sette to hys honde on the swerde and drew at hit strongely, but he myght nat meve hytte* (*MD* 669).

81. *LG* IV, 10; *QHG* 50.

82. *LG* V, 167–9.

83. *LG* IV, 25–7; V, 178–80; *MD* 699–701; *QHG* 94–103: Perceval's aunt warns him against taking on Galahad in battle. In the Post-Vulgate version, she makes it clear that it is not Perceval but Galahad who will bring to an end the adventures of Logres, and who alone has the inner goodness to see the Holy Vessel in all its wonder and purity: *as maravilhas e as puridades do Santo Vaso* (*PV* II, 315).

84. *LG* IV, 74; V, 236; *QHG* 245: This is the sword which Merlin set in the Floating Stone; which Galahad drew out at Camelot; and which the latter discarded when he drew forth the Sword with the Strange Straps on the Ship of Faith. The prose cycles thus thrice demonstrate Galahad's spiritual superiority: Firstly, by showing him sitting in the Perilous Seat at the Round Table; secondly, by his drawing forth the Sword in the Floating Stone, when Perceval failed to do so; and thirdly, by his drawing the Sword with the Strange Straps, which Perceval also attempted unsuccessfully: *So he sette hys honde to the swerde, but he myght nat begrype hit* (*MD* 753). Perceval's inheriting the discarded sword, but not winning it, makes a sharp contrast with the verse Continuations, where he proves worthy of both the sword made by Trebuchet and the one borne by Silimac.

85. *LG* IV, 76; V, 238; *QHG* 249: *Than Sir Percivale made a lettir of all that she had holpe them as in strange aventures* (*MD* 768).

86. *LG* V, 278: This is the nearest that Perceval gets in the prose cycles to fulfilling his father Pellinor's prophecy that the Questing Beast is destined to die at the hands of the best knight of his kindred (*SRM* 5). In Gerbert's verse Continuation to the Story of the Grail, Perceval chases the beast until it bursts (638).

87. It is also a mystery how Perceval would have had the opportunity to pass this information on to King Arthur, as Merlin had predicted he would (*LG* IV, 171).

88. *LG* IV, 83–7; V, 278–80, 283–8; *QHG* 271–84: *Thus a yere and too monethis lyved Sir Percivale in the ermytayge a full holy lyff, and than passed oute of the worlde. Than Sir Bors let bury hym by hys syster and by Sir Galahad in the spiritualités* (*MD* 788).

89. Weston 1901, 142.

90. *CSG* 19–20.

91. *CSG* 23–4.

92. *CSG* 262–3: If Perceval doesn't fail to do more than smother her with kisses, Blancheflor is too *plainne de cortoisie* to deny him anything (*DC* ll.3282–93); just as, on their first night together, it was *cortoisie* which prompted him to take her in his arms (*RP* ll.1977–8). It seems as if a little courtesy could get you a long way in the Middle Ages!

93. In both the German and Welsh versions of this tale the hero is happily wed: Parzival fathers two sons on Condwiramurs, She Who Leads to Love; Peredur, after falling in love several times, finally marries the Empress of Constantinople. In the Long Redaction of the First Continuation, Perceval marries the sister of an enchanter (*CSG* 154), which Weston considers to be "a survival of the original tradition which bestowed on him a fairy mistress" (1906, 125).

94. Here Perceval wishes to preserve his chastity until he dies, to the frustration of any woman who desires him (*HBG* 117)—and he does so (240). See PERLESVAUS.

95. The journey to the East, whether it be Perceval's to Sarras or Parzival's to India, is a re-orientation of the soul of the hero of western chivalry, as Henry Corbin sees it: To be buried in the Spiritual Palace is a form of *occultation mystique*, for Sarras is not a city of *this* world (1971, 177) any more than Albrecht's India is a kingdom of *this* Earth (184–5).

96. *HBG* 251–2.

PERCEVAL'S SISTER

Arriving at a hermitage where Galahad is staying, a mysterious maiden declares that, if he follows her, she will show him the highest of all chivalric adventures. Stopping only to collect a casket of exquisite workmanship from her castle, she leads Galahad[1] to the shore, where they meet up with his relatives Bors and Perceval—who is her brother, but who does not recognize his sister.

All four embark on a ship that instantly takes them out of sight of land. Galahad tells his companions that the maiden must take credit for bringing them together. She soon shows remarkable knowledge of even more ancient events that underlie their quest,[2] as well as of things that are to unfold in the future.

So it is that, when they come to a lonely islet and spot, in a hidden creek, another ship that can only be reached on foot, she reveals that there lies the adventure which they are seeking. Accordingly, they disembark and make their way to the other vessel, which is deserted; but which has on its side an inscription, written in Chaldean, warning any who would board it that their faith must be impeccable.

Revealing for the first time that she is Perceval's sister,[3] she counsels her brother to step on board only if he has perfect faith in Christ. All four embark safely and find on board the Sword of David, which can only be drawn without the risk of injury or death by the man who excels all others. The maiden then tells them the story of King Varlan, who used the sword to kill her great-grandfather Lambor, but who dropped dead as soon as he returned the sword to its sheath. She also recounts the story of King Parlan,[4] who was maimed by the Avenging Lance when he partially drew the sword.

The sword's scabbard is attached to a cheap and flimsy belt of hempen tow, which does not look as if it could support the weight of the magnificent weapon. On it are written letters which reveal that the belt can only be replaced by a virgin princess, who must make a new one from what is most precious to her.[5] Perceval's sister, who is indeed both virginal and a princess, thereupon opens the casket that she brought with her, to reveal a belt made from her own hair: This is the most precious thing she had, which she cut off on the day that Galahad was knighted.[6]

Removing the hempen belt and affixing the new one, she tells them that the name of the weapon is now the Sword with the Strange Straps. Galahad draws it from its scabbard and she girds it on him,[7] saying that it is only now that he is by rights a knight. Having made the noblest man in the world a knight, she holds herself the most blessed maiden of all. She no longer cares when Death will take her.[8]

Death does not wait long. The companions come to a castle, whose custom it is that all virgins who pass by must give their blood to heal the lady of the castle, who is a leper. The three knights fight in her defense but Perceval's sister, to save much bloodshed, agrees to shed her own. She is a virgin both in thought and deed, so that the blood she gives restores the lady to perfect health, but at the cost of her own.

As she lies dying, she begs her brother to place her body in a boat and let it go where chance will take it. They must make their way to the city of Sarras, where they will find her boat below the tower. She prays that they will bury her within the Spiritual Palace.[9]

The boat containing her embalmed body floats down the river that divides in two the Waste Forest, and there it is found by Lancelot. Later he is joined by Galahad, who has separated from his companions. The two live together for half a year on the boat. When father and son separate, the miraculous boat takes Lancelot to Corbenic, then makes its way to Sarras, where it is found by Galahad, Bors and Perceval, who have arrived at the end of their journeying. They bury Perceval's sister, as she requested, in the Spiritual Palace[10]; both Galahad and Perceval, as she prophesied, are buried next to her.[11]

* * *

In the earliest Grail poem, Perceval has brothers and a female cousin, but no sister. It is only in the later prose romances that a sister is introduced; and it is probably their influence that leads to a sister appearing in the Second Continuation to the Story of the Grail. Here, Perceval's (unnamed) sister is only a little girl when he first leaves home, causing their mother to die of grief; when he returns after ten years, they have an emotional reunion. He later escorts her to the Castle of Maidens, where he leaves her in the care of the holy lady Ysabel, who travelled to Britain with their mother as part of the Company of the Grail[12] and who still has visions of the Holy Vessel.[13]

We cannot necessarily identify this anonymous sister of Perceval with the named one who features in the Romance of Perlesvaus,[14] nor can she be the same as the mysteriously knowledgeable, prophetic figure who emerges at a crucial juncture in the Vulgate *Queste* (since Perceval doesn't recognize her when he meets her on the Ship of Faith). Moreover, as the sole woman deemed holy enough to travel at least part of the way with the Grail companions on their quest, the figure of Perceval's unnamed sister inevitably provokes difficult questions: Whence, for example, come her prophetic powers? And why can she only reach Sarras when she is dead?

On the night that she dies, the Castle of the Basin of Blood and its inhabitants are destroyed by a violent thunderstorm. Amid the ruins, Galahad and Perceval find the tombs of twelve highborn ladies who died for "the custom of the castle" and on whose behalf, a voice tells them, divine punishment has been inflicted.[15]

Andrea Williams has suggested that the sister's sacrifice is an imitation of that of Christ, who also cures lepers. Perceval's sister's blood is collected in a silver dish,[16] as Christ's is collected in the Grail; "and the maiden dies for the healing (albeit physical rather than spiritual) of another."

Recognizing the "boldly original," in fact "problematic," nature of this identification,[17] Williams adds: "The appearance of a female Christ-figure in a text of this period is unusual, to say the least."[18] But so is the image of a maiden bearing in procession a dish containing the Holy Blood of Christ. Thus, for R.S. Loomis, the Grail Bearer and Perceval's sister and their stories "may be regarded as differing aspects and activities of the same mythological figure" whom he identifies as "a vegetation goddess known centuries before in Wales and Ireland."[19]

Caitlín and John Matthews see her as the "priestess of the new dispensation"[20] which can reconcile Christianity with the earlier paganism. Just as Christ taught his disciples not to resist evil and forbade them to use violence in His defense when soldiers came to capture Him, so Perceval's sister allows herself to be captured in order to prevent further bloodshed. Instead, she sheds her own; but her Christ-like healing of the leper lady can also be seen as healing the "wasteland face"[21] of the territorial "vegetation goddess," Lady Sovereignty, the Goddess of the Land itself.[22]

Notes

1. In the Post-Vulgate version she first of all takes Galahad to meet a madwoman, a victim of demonic possession—*une dame endyablee* (*PV* III, 11)—who can only be freed from *l'ennemy*, the *mal compaignon*, by seeing the knight who will bring to an end the adventures of Logres: *le chevalier qui doit mener a fin les aventures du royaume de Logres* (15–6).

2. In the Prose *Perceval*, the hero's sister has learnt the history of the Grail from their father's brother, who travelled to Britain from Judaea with Joseph of Arimathea (*MG* 130).

3. Their father is here named as King Pellehan (*QP* 201) but, in the Post-Vulgate version, as King Pellinor (*PV* III, 43): *I am thy syster*, she tells Perceval in Malory's version, *whych was doughter unto Kynge Pellynor* (*MD* 752). In the non-cyclic Prose *Lancelot*, the sister of Perceval (who is here seen as the Grail Winner) is the daughter of the Maimed King Pelles (*LDL* I, 122); while the Bonn manuscript of the Vulgate *Queste* also names their father as Pelles (*LDG* III, 1625). In the Vulgate *Lancelot* the daughter of Pelles (Helizabel/Amite) is Perceval's cousin, rather than his sister, and it is her son Galahad who is the Grail Winner (*LG* II, 16).

4. …*li rois Parlan, que len apele le Roi Mehaignié* (*QP* 209): Parlan is called Pellehan or Pellinor (also the name of Perceval's father in the Post-Vulgate) in some manuscripts (288). In Malory's version, Perceval's sister tells Galahad that *there was a kynge that hyght Pelleans, which men called the Maymed Kynge*; and who was *maymed for hys hardynes* (*MD* 756); but Vinaver's edition gives *Pelleaus* and *Pelles* (*MV* 583). The Bonn manuscript of the Vulgate *Queste* also gives Pelles as the name of the king *mehaigniés par le hardement qu'il fist* (*LDG* III, 1092–3).

5. *LG* IV, 63–6; V, 226–32; *QHG* 209–21.

6. She cut off her hair as soon as she realized what awaited her—*si tost come je soi que ceste aventure m'estoit apareilliee* (*QP* 227); *as sone as I wyste that thys adventure was ordayned me* (*MD* 760)—but we are told neither how she discovered her role in this adventure, nor how she learned the fate of her ancestors. Her knowledge of the Chaldean language is equally mysterious.

7. In the Post-Vulgate version, she tells Galahad that the sword with which she has armed him is the best there is and is endowed with the greatest powers: *Je vos ai, feit ele, garni de l'Espee aus Estranges Renges, la meilleur et la plus vertueuse que onques chevaliers ceinsist* (*PV* III, 43). For Caitlín and John Matthews, her bestowing the sword on Galahad means that they have entered into a spiritual rather than a physical union, leading to a "sacred marriage" after they are both dead (1992, 199).

8. *LG* IV, 71–2; *QHG* 236–7.

9. *LG* IV, 75–6; V, 237–8; *QHG* 245–50: *And as sone as ye thre com to the cité of Sarras, there to enchyeve the Holy Grayle, ye shall fynde me undir a towre aryved. And there bury me in the spirituall*

palyse. For I shall telle you for trouthe, there Sir Galahad shall be buryed and ye bothe, in the same place (MD 768).

10. *LG* IV, 86; V, 287; *QHG* 281: *the thre knyghtes wente to the watir and brought up into the paleyse Sir Percivallis syster, and buryed her as rychely as them oughte a kynges doughter* (MD 786).

11. *LG* IV, 87; V, 288; *MD* 788; *QHG* 284.

12. *CSG* 364.

13. *CSG* 409.

14. See DANDRANE.

15. *LG* IV, 77; V, 239; *MD* 769; *QHG* 252–3: The twelve dead virgin princesses can be seen as inverse reflections of the twelve, *living*, noble Round Table Knights who will sit at the Table of the Grail at Corbenic to share the eucharistic feast. These knights are themselves types of the twelve apostles seated at the Table of the Last Supper.

16. Galahad's seeing this *escuele d'argent* (QP 237) containing healing blood foreshadows his seeing at Corbenic the *escuele* from which Christ ate the Paschal lamb (270) and into which His blood (which will heal the Maimed King) pours at the Table of the Grail (269). In the Post-Vulgate version, the Holy Blood from the Adventurous Lance runs into *un riche veissel d'argent*, which nevertheless appears to be empty. But from it, Galahad is able to pour three drops of blood onto the thighs of Pellehan, the Maimed King, before it escapes his hands and flies off to Heaven (PV III, 320–2). This vessel appears to be the same as the *orçuel d'argent et d'or* in which the Lance is standing (but not dripping blood) when Balin sees it in the castle of King Pellehan before the Dolorous Blow is struck (SRM 160). It contrasts with the *escuiiele d'argent* which a maiden accompanying Balin was earlier obliged to fill with her blood (148). Balin's maiden failed to heal the leprous lady and survived (151). So, *la coustume del chastiel* continued for a long time, with the lady neither dying nor getting better, until the valiant sister of Perceval came there and resolved the adventure of the castle: *Et dura puis cele doleureuse coustume moult lonc tans, que onques la dame del chastiel n'en morut ne n'en gari dusques a tant que la vaillans damoisiele, la serour Percheval le Galois, i vint, qui acompli l'aventure dou chastiel* (152).

17. Williams 2001, 172–3.

18. Williams 2001, 173n12.

19. Loomis 1926, 281–3: From this perspective the capture and death of Perceval's sister can be seen as a variation on the myth of Persephone, whose abduction by Hades causes the crops to fail—a Waste Land motif: "She is the lost Feminine Principle," writes Caitlín Matthews (1984, 4), "who has withdrawn from the world and left behind a wound."

20. Matthews 1992, 195.

21. As a type of Ugly Maiden, the leprous lady contrasts with the unparalleled beauty of Perceval's sister, as described in the Prose *Lancelot*: *si fu de si grant biauté que nus des contes ne dit que nule qui a son tens fust se poïst de biauté a li apareillier* (LDL I, 122). While, in the Second Continuation, Perceval's sister is so beautiful that she resembles nothing less than a fay: *Qui de biauté resambloit fee/ Miauz que nule autre creature* (DC ll.4213–4). Scholars have also noted that Perceval's sister "displays many of the characteristics of the Arthurian fairy female" (Traxler, 267).

22. Matthews 1992, 193: Perceval's sister personifies the Goddess as Empowerer, Initiator and Measurer (*xxxii*). Through her celestial "sacred marriage" with Galahad she "opens the ways of grace, for the healing powers of the Grail to come into the world" (199), pointing to "the resacralization of life" (195). This redemption of the self-sacrifice of Perceval's sister, which some commentators have seen as singularly pointless, contrasts with the view of Janine P. Traxler that, in the world of the Vulgate *Queste*, the best woman is a dead virgin (Traxler, 273–4).

PEREDUR

Raised by his widowed mother in the seclusion of a forest, Peredur sets off for King Arthur's court after encountering three knights from there. His arrival is acclaimed by two dwarfs, who prophesy greatness for the hero. After avenging an insult to Gwenhwyfar (Guenevere), he travels to the court of his mother's brother, who is lame. Peredur's uncle prophesies that the boy will be the best swordsman in the island, but cautions him against asking about things he sees, no matter how strange.

Travelling on the next day, Peredur comes to the court of a second uncle, who tests his ability with a sword by asking him to strike an iron column with one. The sword breaks, but Peredur makes it whole again. When he strikes the column again, both it and the sword break, but he makes both whole. When he strikes the column for a third time, both it and the sword break, but this time he cannot mend them. This means, says his uncle, that he has only come into two-thirds of his strength.[1]

At this point two youths come into the hall bearing an enormous spear from which three streams of blood flow to the floor. At the sight of the youths, loud lamentation breaks out. Barely has the hall gone silent when two maidens come in, carrying between them a large dish containing a man's head floating in blood. The lamentation starts all over again, but his uncle ventures no explanation and Peredur asks no questions.[2]

He is later trained in arms by the Hag of Gloucester (one of nine witches), despite his being destined to harm her.[3] Ultimately, he wins the love of the Empress of Constantinople, with whom he lives and rules.

Fourteen years pass. Peredur, now back at Arthur's court in Caerleon, is berated by the hideous Black Maiden of Proud Castle for not having asked about the spear and other marvels at the court of the Lame King.[4] Peredur swears he will not rest until he discovers their meaning.[5]

After a year Peredur comes again to the Castle of Wonders, where the Black Maiden leads him to undertake further adventures, in order to be reunited with the Empress. After overcoming two oppressors who have laid waste to the realm of the Empress,[6] Peredur returns to the court of the Lame King, where he learns that the head on the dish belonged to his cousin, who was killed by the witches at the time they maimed his father (Peredur's uncle), the Lord of the Castle of Wonders. With the aid of King Arthur, Peredur destroys the witches, thus fulfilling his destiny: as the hag who trained him proclaims, just before her death.[7]

* * *

The Romance of Peredur as it has come down to us is somewhat rambling, confused and often inconsistent; it is clear that at some point the story has become contaminated by Chrétien's *Perceval*. Nevertheless, it is the French name which the Welsh scholar Rachel Bromwich regards as "a loose approximation" of the Welsh name, rather than the other way round.[8] Peredur's story also contains seemingly archaic elements that may derive from Celtic paganism.[9]

An attempt to reconstruct this archaic Celtic story has been attempted by Glenys Goetinck, who sees it as originating in a pre–Indo-European myth of "the search for the ultimate secret of creation." The "inner search" takes the "outer form" of a story involving the testing of the destined ruler who, if he is deemed worthy, is initiated into the "highest mysteries." He finally performs a "sacred marriage"[10] with the Goddess of the Land, who presents him with the Vessel of Sovereignty, symbolizing both "spiritual enlightenment and earthly royalty."[11] The Vessel, a wide and fairly deep lunar dish or platter, supports a solar, phallic head, possibly originally symbolizing "the fire in the water, the ultimate moment of creation."[12]

With the political and religious transition to an Indo-European, patriarchal culture, the head in the platter—"the godhead, source of life"—becomes the severed head of the maimed god Brân,[13] a victim of the champions of mother-right (the nine witches), who are trying to take back control of the land. As the sister's son of the Lame King of the Castle of Wonders, Peredur is the rightful heir under the older, matrilinear system (hence his training by the witches).[14] But he becomes neglectful and allows the land to become waste, reflecting the loss of the primordial balance between old and new.

Confronted by Sovereignty in her ugly aspect,[15] he must set out again to prove himself worthy of her love, which he does by freeing her land from its oppressors. In what Goetinck suggests may have been an earlier ending to the story, the Empress would have appeared to Peredur in the Castle of Wonders, revealing her true identity and explaining that she appeared to him disguised as both the bearer of the platter and the Black Maiden, in order to inspire him to fulfill his destiny. It is Peredur's own father whose head was on the platter; he must now avenge the killing in order to be worthy of Sovereignty.[16]

With the Christianization of the myth, the Mass wafer is substituted for the head (the godhead), Goetinck suggests: The blood in the platter becomes that of Christ; while the platter itself becomes the serving dish of the Last Supper, the Holy Grail.[17] Although the theme of the Vengeance Quest disappears completely in the Galahad Grail cycles, it survives in Welsh literature, perhaps because of the loss of sovereignty the indigenous Britons experienced.[18]

Notes

1. The three attempts to mend a broken sword find echoes in the verse Continuations to the Story of the Grail, where first Gawain, then Perceval attempt to mend the Sword of Partinal which killed Perceval's uncle: Gawain fails; Perceval is only partially successful the first time; but is wholly successful at the second attempt.
2. *MJ* 157–60; *M* 224–6: This is as close as the Welsh romance gets to the procession of Bleeding Lance, Grail Dish and silver trencher described by Chrétien.
3. *MJ* 164–5; *M* 232.
4. Here the two uncles and the two courts have been conflated. Glenys Goetinck considers that the two brothers are "manifestations of the same figure," an enchanter who is in origin a god, the Lord of the Otherworld (1975, 206). Similarly, the Black Maiden and the Empress are "two guises" of Sovereignty, the Goddess of the Land (257).
5. *MJ* 180–1; *M* 248–9.
6. Thus, in the Welsh romance, the theme of the Waste Land is interwoven with, but not directly connected to, the vengeance motif—which was also Manessier's way of resolving the Grail Mysteries.
7. *MJ* 185–8; *M* 254–7: Rhŷs points out that the true ending of the story should have been "the reconciliation of the hero with his wife the Empress" (109). Caitlín Matthews concurs: The royal blood (Sangreal) must "become one with the holy earth of the land" in order for the enchantments upon it to be lifted (2002, 220).
8. *TYP* 478–9: "*Perceval* may have been an unfamiliar name to the French redactors of the romances, judging from their clumsy attempts to analyze it."
9. Loomis equates Peredur with the "mythological figure" of Pryderi (1926, 153). Appearing in the Four Branches of the Mabinogi, one of the seven heroes who survive Brân's ill-fated expedition to Ireland, Pryderi son of Pwyll may be the Welsh original of Perlesvaus son of Pelles, who is described as the Grail winner in the Prose *Lancelot* (*LDL* I, 122).
10. Goetinck 2014, 138.
11. Goetinck 2014, 139.
12. Goetinck 2014, 137.
13. Goetinck 2014, 130.
14. Goetinck 2014, 136.
15. "The Black Maiden and the Empress represent the two guises of Sovereignty. Peredur marries Sovereignty in her fair guise, fails her, and is rebuked by her in her hideous guise" (Goetinck 1975, 257).
16. Goetinck 1975, 272–3.
17. As Caitlín Matthews puts it: "Peredur's Grail is a woman" (2002, 217).
18. "The British Celts had been pushed back by Roman, Saxon, and finally Norman conquerors, creating a powerful and enduring theme of loss in Welsh literature" and "keeping the idea of vengeance very much alive" (Goetinck 2014, 139).

THE PERILOUS SEAT

The renowned Round Table in the court of King Arthur, at which only the worthiest are permitted to sit, has an empty place which is perilous even to those who perform the greatest feats of earthly chivalry, leaving those who attempt it either dead or maimed.[1] The only one who is destined to escape this fate is the True Knight who will bring to an end the adventures of the Holy Grail; he alone can sit in the Perilous Seat without dying, it is said.[2]

The origin of this prophecy can be traced to the events following the Passion of Christ, when Joseph of Arimathea is instructed by Our Lord to build a table in the name of the Table of the Last Supper: a table on which will be served the Feast of the Grail. Joseph is to sit in the place once occupied by Jesus, but the place to his right is to remain empty as it represents the seat once occupied by Judas. However, a similar empty seat in a third table, made in the name of the Table of the Grail, will await occupation by the grandson of Joseph's brother-in-law Bron.[3]

This third table is made hundreds of years later by the prophet Merlin on behalf of King Uther Pendragon. He has it made in Carduel in Wales in the name of the Trinity, which the three tables signify. Mysteriously, Merlin instructs the king to keep a place empty when the first knights are appointed to sit at what will be known as the Round Table. Merlin chooses the fifty worthiest men of the land to sit at the feast; but, although they notice one seat has been left empty, they do not understand why.

After the crowds have gone, Uther asks the prophet who will fill the empty seat. Merlin, who has already explained to him the significance of the empty seat at the Table of the Grail, replies that it is the as-yet-unborn son of Alan the Fat (one of those who sat at the second table with Joseph of Arimathea). But Alan's son must first have been in the presence of the Grail, the vessel which fulfilled the desires of the heart of all who sat at the second table. Although Alan is now in Britain, having travelled here from the Holy Land, he has not yet taken a wife. This means that the prophecy will not be fulfilled during Uther's reign, but in the lifetime of his successor—and that it is the prophesied knight who will then achieve the adventures of the Grail.[4]

The seat remains empty in the reign of Uther's son King Arthur, until he calls a feast at Pentecost where the twelve peers of the realm sit at the Round Table. Perceval the Welshman, the son of Alan the Fat, who has come to Arthur's court in fulfillment of his deceased father's dearest wish, gains the greatest honor at the tournament they hold then. As a result, the king invites him to join the Fellowship of the Round Table; but the honor goes to the young man's head.

Despite being told that only the finest knight in the world can sit in the empty place at the table, Perceval insists on trying it out.[5] But when he does so, the stone beneath it splits and the Earth is plunged into darkness, so that the knights cannot see each other. The Perilous Seat utters an anguished groan as if the world is ending.[6]

A voice then rings out, saying that, if it were not for the goodness of his father and grandfather, Perceval would have suffered, for his audacity, the same fate as Moses, who was swallowed up by the abyss when he sat on the Feared Seat at the Table of the Grail. The stone will not be mended until the finest knight in the world heals the infirm Fisher King, who guards the Grail.

When the Knights of the Round Table hear this, they are filled with wonder and, to a man, declare that they will never rest until they have found the house of the Fisher King.[7] Nevertheless, in accordance with the prophecy, it is Perceval alone who, after many years, finally comes to the Grail Castle and asks the purpose of all he sees there, thus curing the Fisher King of his sickness.

At that very moment, miles away in Carduel, Arthur and his nobles, who are seated at the Round Table founded by Merlin, hear a terrifying grinding noise. The stone beneath the Perilous Seat, which shattered when Perceval sat in it, is miraculously made whole again. The court is awe-struck, not understanding the meaning of what they have witnessed.[8]

Fortunately, Merlin arrives at that point and the king asks him the significance of what had occurred. Merlin replies that Arthur's reign has seen the fulfilling of the greatest prophecy of all time: the healing of the Fisher King; the ending of the enchantments of Britain; and the entrusting to Perceval, the new Grail Lord, of Our Lord's Holy Blood. That is why the split stone beneath the Perilous Seat is now mended.[9]

The Knight Without Fellow

Others say that after Merlin, acting on behalf of Uther Pendragon, has the Round Table built in the name of the Trinity, the king asks the prophet who will fill the empty seat. Merlin will only tell him that the place will not be taken in Uther's time, but in the time of the king who will reign after him; the one who will sit there has not yet been conceived, but it is he who will achieve the adventures of the Grail.[10]

Despite this prophecy, while Merlin is away from the court, one of the nobles persuades Uther to let him try the seat. But barely has he sat down when he melts away until he is lost to sight; no-one ever finds out what has become of him.[11]

In the chaos that follows the death of Uther, the Round Table is transferred from Carduel to the land of Cameliard; its king later makes the table part of the dowry for his daughter Guenevere. When she marries

Uther's son Arthur, he becomes the new Lord of the Round Table Knights, increasing their number to one hundred and fifty. Two seats remain unfilled, however: the Perilous Seat and one next to it. Merlin says that, just as the table begins with a king, so it should end with one. King Arthur, of course, has the first place; so, Merlin gives the last place, the one next to the Perilous Seat, to King Pellinor.[12]

The prophesied knight, who is not yet conceived, it transpires, is Galahad, the grandson of the last Fisher King, fathered by a bewitched Lancelot on Pellinor's niece at the Grail Castle. Galahad is brought up in a nunnery by the abbess, who is Pellinor's sister. Many years later, long after the disappearance of Merlin, his prophecy is fulfilled.

It is the feast of Pentecost and the knights are about to sit at their places at the Round Table, when they see that newly-traced letters have appeared on the Perilous Seat, announcing that on this day, four hundred and fifty-four years after the Passion of Christ, the seat will find its master.[13] The leading Knight of the Round Table, Lancelot, calculates that the seat is to be occupied on this very day. He suggests that no one else should see the prophecy until the coming of him who is destined to fulfill it, so his cousins drape a silk cloth over the seat to hide the writing.[14] It remains hidden until the arrival shortly thereafter of the Desired Knight, Lancelot's fifteen-year-old son Galahad, accompanied by a hermit, a venerable old man robed in white.

The hermit raises the cloth on the Seat and uncovers a new inscription, which claims that the place is Galahad's. He bids the youth sit down, which Galahad does with impunity; much to the astonishment of the assembled knights, who take this as proof that Galahad, through God's will, has been granted the grace to bring to an end the marvels of the Holy Grail.[15] For, as the queen puts it, everyone else who has tried to accomplish this adventure has ended up dead or maimed. For her ladies, it proves that he is destined to bring to an end the adventures of Britain and heal the Maimed King.[16]

For Galahad, the Quest of the Holy Grail is only just beginning.

* * *

The Perilous Seat is a symbolic image which is found in the two great prose cycles of Grail romance, the early De Boron Cycle and the later Vulgate Cycle, as well as in the Post-Vulgate and Malory (the Siege Perilous). In the De Boron Cycle, the Seat is closely tied to the life and fate of Bron, the brother-in-law of Joseph of Arimathea. It is during Joseph's lifetime that an equally dangerous, "feared" seat was established at the Table of the Grail, precisely between the places reserved for Joseph and Bron.

Miraculously, Bron lives on for hundreds of years, awaiting the coming of his grandson Perceval in order to pass on the Secret Words of Christ that he received from Joseph. His dying synchronizes with the repairing of the shattered stone beneath the Seat at the Round Table, which broke when Perceval sat in it prematurely (because he had never been in the presence of the Grail nor sat in the Feared Seat at its silver table).

The breaking and repairing of this stone mark the beginning and ending of Perceval's Grail Quest. But whatever connections early scholars may have found between it and the Irish Stone of Destiny or with the figure of Brân the Blessed as a precursor of Bron, it is clearly a symbol of spiritual election and selection. This is confirmed when the knight who can safely sit in the Seat is Galahad rather than Perceval, a knight whose connections with Bron are distanced in time. For Galahad, the adventure of the Perilous Seat is only the beginning of a quest to fulfill the role he has inherited from his family, the dynasty of Fisher Kings who have descended from (a presumably long-dead) Bron.

The symbolism of the Seat is also transformed significantly in the transition between the two heroes. The empty seat at the Table of the Grail, next to the place of Joseph, corresponds to the seat of Judas at the Last Supper, next to Christ; while the empty place at the Round Table, which has been established in the name of the two earlier tables, we can assume shares their significance (at least in the De Boron Cycle), although this is not spelt out.

An attempt to spell out the significance was, however, made by Emma Jung and Marie-Louise von Franz, following the theories of the depth psychologist C.G. Jung (Emma's husband and Franz's mentor). Carl Jung saw the medieval stories as an attempt of the creative imagination to confront the spiritual problem of Western Europe in the second millennium of the Christian era, a problem which he characterized as the inability of the mainstream image of Christ to adequately embody archetypal wholeness, since it excludes darkness and earthiness.[17] This problematic, wounded god-image appears in the Grail legend as the Maimed King.[18]

For Jung, a four-sided structure (such as the Table of the Grail) evokes the four elements of nature and what he identified as the four functions of human consciousness; these must be assimilated and integrated[19] in order to provide a basis for the realization of the Self, the god-image in man.[20] Consequently what appears on the Table is itself fourfold: The Grail containing the Holy Blood signifies the Trinity and the Vessel itself, the mother of God.[21]

The Grail Table corresponds to the time following the death and resurrection of Jesus and the first two generations of His disciples: The first generation is represented by Joseph and Bron; the second, by their sons Josephus and Alan the Fat. The Round Table, on the other hand, corresponds not to the time of the pseudo-historical Arthur (fifth to sixth centuries) but to the time of the writing of the romances (twelfth to thirteenth)—and to the third generation, that of Perceval son of Alan. But more broadly, the two tables signify the first and second Christian millennia.

The roundness of King Arthur's table presents us with an image of that totality for which the square table provides the foundation.[22] But, because the Feared Seat at the Grail Table remains empty, a spiritual problem from the first millennium is carried over into the second, exemplified in the Grail legend by Judas' betrayal of Jesus.[23]

For Emma Jung and Marie-Louise von Franz, to sit in the Perilous Seat at the Round Table is to confront the problem of human evil (personified by Judas) by recognizing its shadow within our own souls and, by acknowledging it, redeem it.[24] This must be done consciously, hence Perceval should have been in the presence of the Grail before attempting it[25]; but instead, he sits in Judas' place *unwittingly*. As a result, the split in the Christian West between what we believe we should be (the *imitatio Christi*) and what we all too often are, becomes externalized as a shattered stone,[26] recalling the one beneath the Cross.[27]

This split is embodied in the old Grail King, representative of an outmoded consciousness in need of renewal.[28] It is therefore Merlin, a Trickster figure who transcends in his own person the metaphysical dualism of light and dark, *who has the new totality in mind and who tries to lead Perceval towards it*.[29] But although Perceval replaces the old ruler and restores the spiritual Grail Kingdom, externalized as the restoration to wholeness of the shattered stone beneath the Perilous Seat, he does not actually occupy the empty place. For he never returns to Britain, to complete the Round Table.[30] As a result, that noble institution must fall.[31]

Merlin's prophecy, announced in the De Boron Cycle, that the Perilous Seat will be occupied by one who has been in the presence of the Grail, is only completed in the Vulgate Cycle. Even then, it is not by Perceval, but by Galahad, who must have been often in its presence, since he was brought up in Corbenic, where the Holy Vessel appears regularly at meal times for the royal family.

His mother was once the Grail Bearer and the Seat has been destined for him since his conception. It can therefore hold no perils for him.

Notes

1. ...*el Siege Perillous de la Table Reonde ou onques chevaliers ne s'asist qu'il ne fust mors ou mehaigniés* (*LDG* III, 239).

2. ...*li verais chevaliers par cui les aventures dou Saint Graal seront menees a chief et qui serra el siege perilleus de la Table Reonde: onques nus ne s'i asist qu'il ne moreust* (*LM* V, 256).

3. *MG* 38: The voice of the Holy Spirit announces that the third man of Bron's lineage (that is, Perceval) will sit in the Feared Seat at the Table of the Grail (thus symbolically redeeming the betrayal of Judas), or in another seat at another table established in its name: *u un autre qui el non de cestui sera fondés* (*RG* 61).

4. *MG* 92-4: *cil qui l'aconplira n'est encore mie engendrés, et il convendra que cil qui aconplira cel lieu, qu'il aconplisse les aventures del Graal* (*RMP* 312). We read in Micha's edition of the Prose *Merlin* that he who would safely sit in the Perilous Seat must first have sat in the empty place at the Table of the Grail (*MM* 190). In the Vulgate *Queste*, Galahad sits in the Perilous Seat safely but does not sit at the Table of the Grail until he returns for the last time to Corbenic, where he was born.

5. The king is reluctant to let him do so, since a false disciple had once done so and was instantly swallowed up by the Earth: *car el liu vuit s'asist ja uns faus deciples, qui maintenant que il fu assis fu fondus en terre* (*RG* 204). Here Arthur seems to be confusing the Round Table with the Table of the Grail, insofar as this *faus deciples* can only be Moses, a false disciple of Joseph of Arimathea, who was also *fondus* when he sat in the Feared Seat between Bron and Joseph (60). Fortunately, a supernatural voice is about to clarify matters.

6. *Et tant tost com il fu assis li piere fendi desous lui et braist si angoisseusement que il sambla a tous çaus qui la estoient que li siecles fondist en abisme. Et del brait que li terre jeta si issi une si grans tenebrors que il ne se porent entreveïr* (*RG* 204-5). Loomis sees in this an echo of the Irish myth of the Stone of Destiny, which cries out when the rightful king sits on it (1926, 218-9). Perceval is the rightful successor of the Grail King, but his sitting in the Perilous Seat is premature (Walter 2014, 351).

7. *MG* 119-20.

8. *Et estoit a cel jor meïsme li rois Artus a le Table Reonde que Merlins fonda, et oïrent un escrois issi grant que il s'en esfreerent molt durement, et li piere rasolda qui fendi desos Perceval quant il s'assit el liu vuit. Si lor vint a grant mervelle, car il ne savoient que ce senefioit* (*RG* 271).

9. *MG* 156: *Et Percevaus est sire del Graal ... nostre Sire li a baillié son digne sanc a garder, et por çou solda li piere qui fendue estoit desos lui* (*RG* 272). The connection implied here between the *digne sanc* and the *piere qui fendue estoit* takes on added significance when we recall that, in the Prose *Joseph*, a stone beneath the Cross is split when Jesus' blood falls on it: *la piere qui ot esté fendue au pié de la crois por la goute del sanc* (24).

10. *Tant te puis je bien dire qu'il ne sera mie acomplis a ton tans ne cil qui l'acomplira n'est encore mie engendrés. Et il couvenra qu'il acomplisse les aventures del Saint Graal* (*LDG* I, 697).

11. *LG* I, 196-8: His fate almost exactly replicates that of the false disciple Moses, who sat in the Feared Seat at the Table of the Grail.

12. *LG* IV, 226: At the Table of the Grail, the place next to the Feared Seat is occupied by Bron; It is appropriate that the equivalent place at the Round Table should be occupied by King Pellinor, as Bron's direct descendent. In the Post-Vulgate Cycle and Malory, Pellinor is the father of Perceval, who was, of course, the original Grail winner in the earlier De Boron Cycle. In Malory's version, Merlin adds: *But in the Sege Perelous there shall nevir man sitte but one, and yf there be ony so hardy to do hit he shall be destroyed, and he that shall sitte therein shall have no felowe* (*MD* 80). This Knight without Fellow is now Galahad rather than Perceval.

13. *QP* 4: *Foure hundred wyntir and foure and fyffty acomplyvysshed aftir the Passion of Oure Lorde Jesu Cryst oughte thys syege to be fulfylled* (*MD* 667).

14. *LG* IV, 4; V, 115; *QHG* 33-4.

15. ...*car bien pensent que ce soit cil par cui les merveilles dou Saint Graal doivent faillir, et bien lou conoissent par l'espruefe del Siege* (*QP* 9). When Arthur sees in the Perilous Seat the one of whom Merlin and the other prophets in Britain have spoken, he knows that this is the knight who will fulfill the Adventures of Logres: *El rei, tanto que vio na Seeda Perigosa o cavalleyro de que Merlim e todollos outros profetas fallarom na Gram Bretanha, entam bem soube elle que aquelle era o cavalleyro per que seriam acabadas as aventuras do regno de Logres* (*PV* II, 29).

16. *LG* IV, 5-6; V, 117; *QHG* 37-9; *MD* 670-1.

17. Based upon his "empirical" psychological observations, Jung argues that in the archetype of wholeness, which he calls the Self, "light and shadow form a paradoxical unity. In the Christian concept, on the other hand, the archetype is hopelessly split into two irreconcilable halves, leading ultimately to a metaphysical dualism" (Jung 1968, 42) in which the dark half of the archetype is embodied in the Antichrist (44). The figure of Merlin, the son of a nun and a devil, with demonic knowledge of the past and God-given knowledge of the future, is a medieval attempt to embody that "paradoxical unity" or totality.

18. "The ailing Grail King corresponds to an *imago Dei* that is suspended, suffering, on the problem of the opposites; he is thus essentially the image of the Christian age and more especially of its second half" (Jung & Franz, 298).

19. Jung 1970, 202-3.

20. "A symbol of the incarnate deity ... the wondrous vessel which constitutes a feminine analogy to the Son of Man, then appears on the table for the first time" (Jung & Franz, 169).

21. Jung & Franz, 339.

22. Jung & Franz, 386.

23. Jung & Franz, 380.

24. Jung & Franz, 387–8.

25. The authors see this "astounding motif" as reflecting the medieval attempt to achieve something beyond its "intellectual horizon," reconciling the moral dualism of mainstream Christianity: "The motif of the Grail becoming invisible and being finally carried away into the Beyond is probably also connected with this unsolved problem" (Jung & Franz, 343).

26. Jung & Franz, 380–1.

27. Jung & Franz, 304.

28. Jung & Franz, 192: "the ruler is no longer able to hold the opposites together. From this originates the complete devastation of the land, the stagnation of psychic life" (194). It is this psychic stagnation which is so powerfully evoked in the poetry of T.S. Eliot.

29. Jung & Franz, 381: Merlin, representing that "inner wholeness" for which Perceval strives, instigates his quest: "Thus Merlin *is* the mystery of the Grail" (373).

30. The Perilous Seat remains empty while Perceval stays in the Grail Castle, abandoning chivalry for divine grace: "Because Perceval turns entirely to the spiritual, the Round Table now becomes altogether worldly" (Jung & Franz, 384–5).

31. Perceval, "by choosing holiness instead of humanity," allows evil to constellate anew in the person of Mordred, who betrays his lord as Judas did his and brings about the downfall of Arthur's kingdom (Jung & Franz, 387).

PERLESVAUS

The Good Knight who is destined to conquer the Grail, the Holy Vessel in which the Savior's precious blood was collected on the day when He was crucified, is of the highest lineage: Not only is he closely related to Joseph of Arimathea on his mother's side,[1] but he is also a direct descendent of Nicodemus, who assisted Joseph at the Deposition, on his father's side.[2]

Perlesvaus's father Alan the Fat, the grandson of Nicodemus,[3] is the Lord of the Vales of Kamaalot, but he has lost most of his land to his enemy, the Lord of the Fens. Consequently, when his son is born, Alan names him Perlesvaus, meaning He Who Has Lost the Vales.[4] When Alan is killed in battle with the Lord of the Fens, his wife Yglais becomes the Widow Lady of Kamaalot, and her son, her main defender against her enemies.

The Conquest of the Grail Castle

After his unsuccessful visit to the court of the Fisher King,[5] Perlesvaus meets the Queen of the Maidens at her Castle of Galleys and drives off an attack by his wicked uncle, the King of Castle Mortal[6]; then sails around the Isles of the Sea, vanquishing the proud pagan kings. He sails on to Pennevoiseuse in Wales, where Arthur is holding court, to collect the shield of Joseph of Arimathea,[7] which had been left for him there by the Grail Bearer; she prophesied that he would conquer the Grail with it.[8]

His sister, who has been searching for him for some time, eventually catches up with him and beseeches him to return to the Vales of Kamaalot: Of fifteen castles once belonging to the family, only one remains; they have all been seized by the Lord of the Fens. Returning home, Perlesvaus proves that he is the best knight in the world by succeeding in opening the tomb of Nicodemus, his great-grandfather, who was buried with the pincers that he used to take the nails out of Jesus' body. After kissing a piece of the shroud of Jesus, which his sister had won from the Perilous Cemetery, Perlesvaus goes out to destroy the evil lord. He defeats him in battle and then drowns him in the blood of his own followers!

It is now that he learns of the death of his uncle, the Fisher King, who had languished ever since Perlesvaus failed to ask the Grail Question. He also learns about the conquest of the Grail Castle by the King of Castle Mortal, who is attempting to restore the pagan religion.[9]

Perlesvaus rides to the Turning Castle (built by the magician Virgil while he was searching for the Earthly Paradise) and overcomes its enchanted guardians. He converts its inhabitants to Christianity, but discovers that they cannot leave the castle, which is one of the gateways to Hell, as long as a demonic knight, who bears a flaming dragon's head in his shield, is alive. Perlesvaus rides on to the Isle of Elephants, where he battles the Dragon Knight.

When Perlesvaus, protected by the shield of Joseph of Arimathea, strikes the center of his opponent's shield with his sword, the demonic head that the Devil has placed there causes his sword to turn red and flaming. With it Perlesvaus cuts off the Dragon Knight's sword arm and then thrusts his blazing sword into the mouth of the dragon, which roars and angrily consumes its lord in flame, burning him to ashes.[10] The Queen of the Circle of Gold takes Perlesvaus up to her castle and cures his wounds with the ashes of his enemy. She then crowns him with the Circle of Gold and presents him with his sword, urging him to kill with it all those who will not be baptized.

Reborn as a soldier of Christ,[11] Perlesvaus comes to a castle where the inhabitants worship an oracular copper bull.[12] At the gateway to the castle there are two artificial men made by sorcery, wielding iron hammers which they crash together so furiously that anything trying to pass between them would be utterly destroyed. Nevertheless, when Perlesvaus approaches the castle, the copper men stop their hammering and he enters unscathed, only to find the inhabitants unarmed, gathered around the object of their worship. At the point of his sword, Perlesvaus forces them to walk through the gate. Those who can be saved (only thirteen out of fifteen hundred) survive the experience and convert to Christianity; those who are beyond salvation have their brains beaten out by the hammers! The copper bull collapses in a heap when the evil spirit that animated it flies out, as if struck by lightning.[13]

Perlesvaus now sets out to re-conquer the Grail Castle. As he nears it, he comes to the tomb of Joseph of Arimathea, which opens spontaneously at his approach; for he bears his great-uncle Joseph's shield, indicating that he is the prophesied conqueror of the Grail.[14] The King of Castle Mortal has built nine bridges, each guarded by three knights, over the three rivers that surround the castle; but Perlesvaus overcomes them all. His uncle commits suicide in desperation. The Grail Hallows, which had disappeared when the Fisher King died, now return to the castle's chapel.[15] Miraculously, two suns appear over the sky at Carduel, where Arthur is holding court, as a sign of divine joy.[16]

Consequently, Arthur and Gawain make a pilgrimage to the Grail Castle, where Arthur presents its new king with the crown of his wife Guenevere; for she has died, to Perlesvaus' great sorrow.[17]

The Castle of the Four Horns

Perlesvaus's joy at finding himself the Lord of the Grail is marred by the news that his sister has been abducted by Aristor of Amorave, the cousin of the Lord of the Fens, whom Perlesvaus had drowned in the blood of his followers. He sets off to rescue her, only to find that Aristor has also murdered his uncle Pelles, the Hermit King.[18]

When he eventually catches up with the Lord of Amorave, Perlesvaus's vengeance is merciless. Cutting off Aristor's head, he carries it with him until he reaches the castle where his sister is being held captive. Finding his sister in deep distress, he grasps the severed head of her oppressor by the hair and throws it at her feet, exclaiming that her marriage is now officially cancelled![19]

After travelling to the Kingdom of Oriande and converting its queen Jandree to Christianity,[20] Perlesvaus fights his way onto a ship. They sail so far that the steersman now recognizes neither the sea they are in nor the stars above it, until they catch sight of a castle on an island.

Pulling in to the harbor, the ship

immediately finds itself on dry land, as the sea retreats. They see a fountain beneath a spreading tree and two men sitting beside it, with white hair but youthful faces. They recognize the shield Perlesvaus is wearing as having once belonged to Joseph of Arimathea. After he has placed it against the tree, they lead him past a glass cask which contains a mute, living knight, into a hall where the Savior of the World is depicted in his majesty, with His apostles round him.

One of the white-haired men sounds a gong which summons thirty-three men,[21] each dressed in white with a red cross on his chest, appearing to be no more than thirty-two years old.

They sit down at table, with Perlesvaus at the head and he watches as a crown, attached to a golden chain, descends into a wide pit in the middle of the hall. The chain itself is attached to nothing and from the pit rise up cries of lamentation.

After the meal the masters cover up the pit and tell Perlesvaus that he can never leave the island unless he promises to return as soon as a ship bearing a sail with a red cross comes for him; when he does so, he will wear the crown he has seen and sit on the throne of the Isle of Plenty. The rulers of this island must prove their worthiness by enriching it, so that they are chosen to go to a greater kingdom. Those who fail to do so are placed on the Isle of Need, whose people he heard crying from the pit. The Black Hermit (from whose castle Gawain has won the shield of Judas Maccabaeus) has sent a great number of his people there.

Perlesvaus asks one of the ageless masters about the knight in the glass cask, but is told that he cannot learn anything about the mysterious figure until he returns. Having established that the Grail is still in the late Fisher King's chapel, the master reveals that he had seen the Holy Vessel, even before the Fisher King did: He had been with Joseph of Arimathea when he gathered the blood of the World Savior which flowed from His wounds.[22]

The conquest of the Grail Castle, it now appears, was but the prelude to an even greater quest: to win the crown of the Isle of Plenty.

The next day Perlesvaus is given a pure white shield by the masters and asked to leave his own Red Cross Shield there, as a pledge of his return.[23] He travels to the Wild Forest of the Black Hermit, whom he defeats in battle; his own men throw the Black Hermit into a pit in the middle of his castle.[24] Returning to the Grail Castle, where his mother and sister are now installed, he has the body of Joseph of Arimathea placed in the chapel beside those of his uncle the Fisher King and his great-grandfather Nicodemus, which his mother had brought with her from Kamaalot.

Perlesvaus stays at the castle until his mother and his sister die. One day he hears a voice telling him that he cannot stay there much longer, so he should divide the holy relics amongst the hermits of the forest; for the Holy Grail would appear there no more, though he would soon know where it would be found.

At last, Perlesvaus is in the Holy Chapel when he hears a horn blast coming from the sea beyond the castle. Looking out of the window, he sees a ship bearing a white sail with a red cross. Disembarking, the people on board come up to the Chapel of the Grail and place the bodies of Joseph of Arimathea, Nicodemus, Yglais and her brother the Fisher King in coffins of gold and silver, which they carry to the ship. Perlesvaus goes with them, and no one ever knows what becomes of him from that time forth.[25]

* * *

It is de Boron's Christian version of the Grail story that appears to be the main influence on the early thirteenth century prose Romance of Perlesvaus, which nevertheless switches the emphasis from a spiritual quest to a military conquest of holy sites and relics: Perlesvaus becomes a crusader, and the Grail Kingdom, the Holy Land that he must rescue from the infidels.

According to this version, Perlesvaus is not just closely related to Joseph of Arimathea but also a direct descendent of Nicodemus, who assisted Joseph at the Deposition. As with the De Boron Cycle—where the life of Perceval's father Alan bridges the generations between the time of Jesus and that of Merlin and Uther Pendragon—the Romance of Perlesvaus requires us to accept that, although several hundred years must have elapsed between the events of the Passion and the reign of King Arthur (traditionally fifth/sixth centuries), Perlesvaus, the great-nephew of Joseph of Arimathea and the great-grandson of Nicodemus, can entertain Arthur at the Grail Castle and wear the crown of Guenevere.

This chronological telescoping, as if the Grail Castle were an Otherworld nexus where time stands still, would also explain how Josephus, the celebrant of the first Mass (an act attributed in the Vulgate Cycle to the eldest son of Joseph of Arimathea), can be seen as the chronicler of the life of Perlesvaus.[26]

Notes

1. Joseph here is Perlesvaus' mother's uncle (*HBG* 19). This is interesting insofar as there is a tradition—reported by, among others, the nineteenth-century Celtic Revivalist Richard W. Morgan, in his speculative bestseller *St. Paul in Britain* (p.138np)—that Joseph was the younger brother of the Virgin Mary's father, thus making him Mary's uncle and Jesus' great-uncle. Following these genealogies, Perlesvaus would be Jesus' second cousin!
2. According to the Romance of Perlesvaus, the hero has three maternal uncles: the Fisher King, the King of Castle Mortal and the Hermit King, Pelles (*HBG* 20). But in one manuscript that arguably represents a non-cyclic (that is, pre–Vulgate) version of the Prose *Lancelot*, Pelles is Perlesvaus' father and is called the Maimed King, although the nature of his injury is not specified. Here Perlesvaus is called he who sees openly the great wonders of the Grail, succeeds in the test of the Perilous Seat at the Round Table and brings to an end the adventures of the perilous realm that is the Kingdom of Logres: *roi mehaignié, ce fu li rois Pellés qui fu peres Perlesvax … celui qui vit apertement les granz mervoilles del Graal et acompli lo Siege Perilleus de la Table Reonde et mena a fin les aventures del Reiaume Perilleus Aventureus, ce fu li regnes de Logres* (*LDL* I, 122). Pelles is later depicted as having already died before Lancelot's knighthood (408). The story of the adventure of the Perilous Seat is told, not in the Romance of Perlesvaus, but in the Prose *Perceval*: The hero's first attempt to sit on the Seat is catastrophic, as the stone beneath it shatters; but when he heals the Fisher King by asking the Grail Question, it is miraculously restored to wholeness.
3. Whereas, in the De Boron Cycle, Perceval is the grandson of Bron (Joseph of Arimathea's brother-in-law), Perlesvaus' father Alan is here not the son of Bron but of Gais the Fat of the Hermit's Cross, the son of Nicodemus (*HLG* 130). Perlesvaus' mother Yglais, as the niece of Joseph of Arimathea could therefore, by implication, be the daughter of Bron.
4. *HBG* 30.
5. A good knight—as he should be, being of Joseph of Arimathea's lineage (*Buens chevaliere fu il par droit, car il fu du lignage Joseph d'Arimacie. Cil Joseph fu oncles sa mere*)—Perlesvaus has no way with words. In fact, through his neglecting to speak a few words, great misfortunes befell Britain: The lands and islands fell into great sorrow: *Mes, par molt poi de parole qu'il delaia a dire, avindrent si granz meschaances a la Grant Breteingne que totes les illes et totes les terres en chaïrent en grant doleur*…. Perlesvaus will restore to Britain its *joie*, not by asking the Grail Question, but through his knightly valor (*HLG* 128).
6. *HBG* 117–8.
7. *HBG* 121.
8. *HBG* 34.
9. *HBG* 146–52: The pre-Christian pagan religion of Britain is identified symbolically in this romance with the Old Covenant, just as in the Vulgate Cycle it is with Islam.
10. *HBG* 159–63: A somewhat different account of this battle is given by Gerbert de Montreuil: see THE KNIGHT OF THE DRAGON.
11. …*soudoier Nostre Seignor* (*HLG* 666).
12. *HLG* 660–7: This *Tor de Keuvre* can also be understood as a Tower of Copper (*HBG* 164–5). However, an image of a bull is more obviously the likely object of pagan worship, evoking as it does the Biblical Golden Calf (*HLG* 661n1). Copper is the metal of Venus, who rules the cardinal sign of Taurus.
13. *Li malvais esperit qui estoit el tor de keuvre s'en issi fors autresi conme fust esfoudré et li tors de keuvre fondi toz en un mont: onques rien n'i demora* (*HLG*, 664). Alternatively, for those who follow Waite and Weston in associating the Grail with the Tarot, this passage can be understood to describe a Lightning-Struck Tower: an image familiar to students of the cards, where it constitutes the Sixteenth Arcanum (Waite 1971, 132–5).
14. …*il estoit profetissié pieça que cil qui tel escu porteroit conquerroit le Graal* (*HLG* 680).
15. *Li sains Graaus se representa la dedens en la chapele et la lance de coi la pointe saine et l'espee de coi saint Jehan fu decoleis … et les autres saintes reliques* (*HLG* 694).

16. *HBG* 167–73.
17. *HBG* 194–5: Guenevere dies of grief during a civil war that erupts following the murder of her son Loholt. By wearing the Queen's crown, the symbol of Sovereignty, Perlesvaus can be seen as becoming Arthur's spiritual heir in place of the son whom the king has lost. It is as if the Kingdom of the Grail has become joined to the Kingdom of Logres in a symbolic sacred marriage.
18. *HBG* 229–30.
19. *HBG* 234.
20. *HBG* 241–3: Before being baptized, Queen Jandree has a visionary dream of the Incarnation, Passion and Crucifixion of Christ, including seeing Him pierced in the side with a Lance and people collecting His blood in a Holy Vessel: *Il i avoit unes autres genz qui recoilloient son sanc en un saintisme vaissel que il tenoient* (*HLG* 970).
21. Thirty-three is conventionally the age of Jesus when He died. The ever-youthful men appear to be Templars, like those that guard the Grail on Mount Savage in Wolfram's *Parzival*.
22. *Je vi le Graal, fait li maistres, avant que le Roi Pescheor: Josep, qui ses oncles fu, en recoilli le sanc del Sauveor del monde qui decoroit de ses plaies* (*HLG* 1008).
23. *HBG* 250–2.
24. *HBG* 259–60.
25. *HBG* 263–4: We can surmise, however, that he goes to the Isle of Plenty with the bodies of his kin and that the Holy Grail will appear there. We never discover the identity of the knight in the glass cask.
26. *HBG* 98: See JOSEPHUS THE CLERK.

PETER of Orkney

A disciple (and relative) of Joseph of Arimathea who is born in Jerusalem,[1] Peter is sent from the Holy Land to Avalon, but ends up in Orkney, playing a key role in the conversion of Britain to Christianity.

While Joseph is in the Holy Land, a voice tells him that a light will appear to him, bringing with it a letter. He is to give the letter to Peter, one of those who sit at the Table of the Grail,[2] bidding him to go wherever his heart directs; whereupon Peter will say that he intends to go into the West, to the vales of Avalon.[3] Once there he should await the arrival of the son of Alan the Fat, who will read to him the contents of the letter, teach him the power of the Vessel and tell him what happened to the false disciple Moses, lost (seemingly) forever.[4] Moreover, Peter must be told that he cannot die until all this comes about; but his reward will be eternal glory.

The next day the light indeed appears, bringing them the letter. Joseph gives it to Peter, who says that it is safe in his hands and that he will go to the Vales of Avalon, in the lonely West, there to await his Savior's mercy.[5]

Peter learns all he can of Joseph's communications with the Holy Spirit and witnesses Joseph's bequeathing of the Grail to Bron, the Fisher King, before departing for the West.[6] But when the Grail Company is in Britain, near the sea, Peter is stabbed with a poisoned knife by his cousin Simeon, who is jealous of all those who, unlike himself, are worthy to sit at the Table of the Grail.[7] When a small boat is found by the shore, with sail set, the seriously ill Peter believes it is an omen: The Lord has work for him still and will guide him to where he can get well.

Consequently, he is washed up on the shores of Orkney, whose king he converts to Christianity, along with the king's daughter, whom he marries. Peter goes on to convert Lucius,[8] King of Britain, whose close companion he becomes. He also founds the Orcadian dynasty which will produce Gawain and his brothers. When he dies, Peter is buried in a church on Orkney he founded, dedicated to St. Philip,[9] the apostle who baptized Joseph of Arimathea.

Notes

1. *ESG* 540–1; *LG* I, 153.
2. According to the *Estoire del Saint Graal*, Peter is the cousin of Josephus and is vouchsafed a special honor: He is not just a participant at the Grail Feast, rather, once the others are sat down to eat, he is uniquely chosen to carry the Holy Vessel (*LG* I, 139): *Celui jor, qant il se furent einsi apareillié a meingier, porta Perron, un parent Josephés, le saint Graal* (*ESG* 491). Once it is housed in Corbenic, the Grail can only be carried by a maiden; outside the castle, it apparently floats unsupported or is carried by an angel.
3. *...es vaus d'Avaron s'en ira/ Et en ce païs demourra* (*EG* ll.3124–5); *il s'en ira es Vaus d'Avaron: et iceles terres traient vers Occident* (*RG* 65–6).
4. *Enseignera li le pouoir/ Que cist veissiaus ci puet avoir,/ Dira li que est devenuz/ Moysés qui estoit perduz* (*EG* ll.3133–6). Moses was apparently

swallowed up by the Earth when he sat on the Feared Seat at the Table of the Grail, but in the Vulgate Cycle we discover that he was carried off to the Forest of Darnant, awaiting redemption—not by Perceval, but by Galahad. According to the Prose *Joseph*, Peter must learn about *la force* of the Vessel and hear news of Joseph of Arimathea (*RG* 66), who will have died by then.

5. We are never in fact told whether Peter made it to Avalon, but the chronology of the later Vulgate version makes it seem unlikely that he ever met Perceval.

6. *MG* 41-3: Robert de Boron, in the metrical *Estoire dou Graal*, claims that he will go on to tell us what would later become of Peter, what kind of life he leads and how he ends up in a place difficult to find (*EG* ll.3469-72). But this promise is missing from the prose version and we hear nothing more about him in the De Boron Cycle. Instead, his story is taken up by the Vulgate *Estoire del Saint Graal*.

7. *LG* I, 146.

8. This is the *good Lucius/ That*, as Edmund Spenser (*Faerie Queene* II.x.54) puts it, *first received Christianity,/ The sacred pledge of Christes Evangely*. Spenser, however, considers that Joseph of Arimathea must have brought the Holy Grail to Britain *long before that day* since, according to Geoffrey of Monmouth and the other chroniclers, Lucius' conversion would not have taken place until around the first half of the second century. The author of the *Estoire* is also aware of this alternative tradition (which he would probably have known from the French version of Wace, presumably *cil qui la translata en romanz*). But he claims to have a more authentic source: For he relies on the testimony (*la veraie estoire*) of Robert de Boron, who translated into French the Latin chronicle (*ESG* 546) of the hermit Nascien—and Nascien received his version from Christ Himself.

9. *LG* I, 148-54.

PHILIP the Apostle

One of the twelve apostles of Jesus, Philip is Bishop of Jerusalem when he baptizes Joseph of Arimathea.[1] Known as the Apostle of Gaul because of his role in the conversion of what is now France, it is from there that he dispatches Joseph of Arimathea and Josephus, Joseph's son, to evangelize Britain[2]; although some say that Philip himself came here with twelve apostles of his own.[3]

Philip's importance to the conversion of Britain is recognized by Peter (one of the Grail Companions who travel with Joseph from Judaea to the Promised Land in the West) when Peter, having converted the King of Orkney to the Christian faith, founds a church on the island dedicated to Saint Philip and has himself buried there.[4]

Notes

1. Joseph, we are told in the Vulgate *Estoire del Saint Graal, rechut crestienté de la main saint Philippe, ki dont estoit evesques de Jherusalem* (*ESG* 38). Joseph's baptism occurs shortly after his liberation from prison by Vespasian. Historically, this event must be dated just before the general departed for Rome, that is, in 69 CE. However, the fourth century Church historian Eusebius records that Simon, son of Cleophas, was the Bishop of Jerusalem at this time. Ponceau considers that the reference is to the deacon Philip mentioned in Acts 6.5-6, rather than the apostle; moreover, he may have become confused with another, later Philip, who was bishop until his death in 124 (*ESG* 585-6). By contrast, Philip the Apostle is believed to have died in 80 CE in Hierapolis in Asia Minor.

2. The story is told in a sixteenth century verse Life of Joseph of Arimathea, summarized in Lupack, 248.

3. Nitze 1903, 248n2.

4. *LG* I, 154: *Qant Perron dut trespasser de cest siecle, il comanda que l'en le meïst en terre dedenz Orcanie, en une yglise qu'il avoit faite fonder en l'enor de monseignor seint Phelippe* (*ESG* 546-7).

PHILOSOFINE

Philosofine and her cousin Ysabel are part of the Company of the Grail, sixty holy people who carry the hallows across the sea to Logres. Philosofine carries the silver trencher, which shines brighter than the moon[1]; Ysabel, the Holy Lance; while Joseph of Arimathea brings the sacred Vessel itself.[2] The Grail Hallows are kept initially in the Castle of Maidens, where Ysabel rules, but because the land thereabouts becomes waste, they are carried by angels to the court of the Fisher King.[3]

Philosofine marries Gales the Bald[4] and bears him three sons and a daughter. But, when her husband is maimed through a battle injury, Philosofine escapes the chaos that follows the death of Uther Pendragon by setting up home in the Waste Forest. The two eldest sons become knights and die in combat; their father dies of grief as a result.[5] In consequence of this, Philosofine, now known as the Widow Lady of the Waste Forest,[6] keeps her youngest son, Perceval, at home and in ignorance of chivalry. Nevertheless, one day he encounters a group of knights in the forest and determines to become a knight himself. On the day he leaves home his mother dies of a broken heart,[7] although he will only discover this later, after his first visit to the Grail Castle.[8]

His hermit uncle (his mother's brother) tells him that it is this sinful disregard of his mother's feelings that cut off his tongue and prevented him from asking the reason for the endless flow of blood from the head of the Lance which he saw there. It is the same sin that caused folly to seize him when he failed to learn who the Grail serves and that has led to all his subsequent misfortunes.[9] Later, when Perceval returns to the Grail Castle, he is told by the Fisher King that the secrets of the Grail will never be fully revealed to him until he has atoned for the sin he committed against his mother.[10]

It is only after weeping over his mother's grave and begging for God's pity[11] that Perceval even learns her name and her part in bringing the Grail Hallows to Britain.[12] Only now is Perceval ready to learn the secrets of the Grail.

Notes

1. *Philosofine …/ Un tailleoir plus cler que lune/ Aporta* (GCP ll.10411–3).
2. CSG 422.
3. CSG 364.
4. CSG 363: Perceval tells Ysabel that the name of his father was told to him by the Fisher King, but a record of this conversation has not survived. However, in the First Continuation, Gawain is told by the Grail King that Perceval's father is called Guellans Guenelaus (PCP ll.7671–2).
5. In the Post-Vulgate Cycle the two brothers (Lamorat and Driant) and their father Pellinor (the Maimed King of the Waste Forest) are all killed by Gawain and his brothers. In the Romance of Perlesvaus, by contrast, Gawain protects Perceval's mother against her oppressor, the Lord of the Fens.
6. *…la veve dame/ De la gaste forest soutainne* (PCG ll.74–5).
7. CSG 5–6.
8. CSG 32: Perceval's cousin, who was brought up in his mother's house, tells him that she grieves no less for his failure to find out what is done with the Grail, or where it is taken, than she does for his mother's death: *Que tu n'as del graal seü/ Qu'an an fet et cui an le porte/ Que de ta mere qui est morte* (PCG ll.3604–6).
9. CSG 55–6: *Por le pechié que tu en as/ T'avint que tu ne demandas/ De la lance ne del graal,/ Si t'an sont avenu maint mal,//Pechiez la langue te trancha/ Quant le fer qui ainz n'estancha/ De seignier devant toi veïs,/ Ne la reison n'an anqueïs./ Et quant del graal ne seüs/ Cui l'an an sert, fol san eüs* (PCG ll.6399–402, 6409–14).
10. CSG 339: *Et dist devant ce qu'il avra/ Cel pechié et autre amendé/ Ne li seront tot li secré/ Del Graal dit et descovert* (GCP ll.52–5).
11. CSG 360.
12. CSG 364.

PRYDERI

After the death of Pwyll, Head of Annwfn, his wife Rhiannon marries the brother of Brân the Blessed.

One day they are feasting at the court of Pryderi (the son of Pwyll[1] and Rhiannon), who is now Lord of Dyfed. After eating, the family climb up and sit on the nearby Mound of Arberth, an uncanny place of which it is said that any nobleman who sits there will either receive an injury or witness wonders.[2] And so it is that while they are sitting there, a mist descends. When the mist clears, the surrounding countryside has become a wasteland, bereft of people and animals.[3]

Forced to hunt further afield, Pryderi and Manawydan follow a bright white boar to a fortress which has appeared where heretofore no building ever stood. Ignoring a warning that whoever placed the enchantment on the land must also have caused the fortress to appear, Pryderi is unable to resist going inside: There he sees a marble fountain and slab with, over it, a golden basin attached to four chains which reach up to the sky.[4] But when he takes hold of the basin his hands stick to it, and his feet to the slab on which he stands; moreover, his speech is taken from him so that he cannot utter a word.[5]

Notes

1. Given that in one manuscript of the Prose *Lancelot*, Pelles is named as the father of Perlesvaus

(*LDL* I, 122), scholars have consequently seen in Pwyll and his son Pryderi (= Peredur) the originals of Pelles and his son Perlesvaus/Perceval (Carey 2007, 230–40).

2. *M* 52; *MJ* 8.

3. *M* 86; *MJ* 36–7: Loomis (1956, 35–6) sees Pryderi as "the original of Perceval" who brings enchantment upon Logres when he sits prematurely in the Perilous Seat at the Round Table, just as Pryderi brings enchantment upon his kingdom when he sits upon the Gorsedd Arberth, an equally dangerous seat.

4. Loomis (1956, 37) points out that these Otherworldly features are all encountered by Perceval when he visits a mysterious castle in the Romance of Perlesvaus.

5. *M* 89; *MJ* 39–40: Carey (2007, 106–8) considers that the "closest counterparts" to important features of Perceval's first visit to the Grail Castle are found in this tale of Pryderi, including "a vessel of gold whose beauty entraps him into immobility and silence." At the end of the tale, which is found in the Third Branch of the Mabinogi, the Waste Land is restored, as it is in the First Continuation to the *Conte del Graal*.

Q

The QUEEN OF THE WASTE LAND

During the course of his Grail Quest, Perceval discovers that his late mother has a sister who was once the Queen of the Waste Land, one of the richest ladies in the world. But when her husband was killed, fearing that she would fall into his enemy's hands, she fled to the Waste Forest where she built a hermitage; she lives there now as a recluse. From her marriage, however, she has a son who serves his uncle King Pelles at Corbenic.

When Perceval comes to his aunt's hermitage, she tells him about the death of his mother. Insisting that he must maintain his virginity in order to be one of the three who will achieve the Grail Quest, she goes on to explain to him about the three renowned tables: The first of these is the Table of the Last Supper at which Jesus presided. The second is the Table of the Grail, at which Joseph of Arimathea miraculously fed four thousand of his followers. It has a place reserved for whomever God chooses, corresponding to the place of Jesus at the first table; this is known as the Feared Seat. The third table is the one created by Merlin; it is round like the world and Perceval has experienced the brotherhood that exists among its company. But it also has a Perilous Seat reserved for the Good Knight[1] who Perceval witnessed arrive at court clothed in red armor, signifying Pentecostal fire, on the very day that the Quest for the Grail and Lance was inaugurated.[2]

Fittingly, she dies in the same year that the Quest of the Holy Grail comes to an end, when Perceval and his companions have learnt as much of the truth about this as they ever will on this Earth.

At the very hour of her death, she appears to Arthur as he lies sleeping in his room at Camelot. She is wearing her crown, and such is her beauty and such the joy she radiates, that anyone would have been delighted to see her. In fact, Arthur had long desired her and had asked her for her love, but she always refused it, being vowed to chastity. Now, as she stands before him exuding heavenly joy, she exclaims that she is going to that Paradise from which he would have excluded her through his sensuality, which can only bring him suffering.

In token of her goodness, Arthur moves her body from its cell in the Waste Forest and has it buried in St. Stephen's Church in Camelot.[3]

Notes

1. In the Post-Vulgate version, the recluse reveals that Galahad is the knight who at Pentecost accomplished the adventure of the Perilous Seat; that he is the one who will bring to an end the adventures of Logres; and that he will see the wonders and the secrets of the Holy Vessel: *ca este he Guallaz, o quall cavaleyro em dia de Pinticoste acabou a aventuyra da Seeda Perigosa; esto mesmo he o que dara ffim aas aventuyras do reyno de Llogres; este he o que veera ... as maravilhas e as puridades do Santo Vaso* (PV II, 315).

2. *LG* IV, 25–7; *MD* 699–701; *QHG* 95–103: This quest, she concludes, can never be abandoned until the truth about the many adventures that have taken place in the land is uncovered: *Et le jor meismes fu emprise la Queste dou Saint Graal, qui ja mes ne sera lessiee devant que len en sache la verité, et de la Lance, et por quoi tantes aventures en sont avenues en cest païs* (QP 78).

3. *LG* V, 180.

The QUEST FOR THE HOLY GRAIL

After coming across the house of the Maimed King apparently by chance and witnessing a mysterious procession that includes the Grail and a Bleeding Lance—and keeping silent throughout—Perceval is upbraided by an Ugly Maiden for failing to ask the Question that would have healed his host. He thereupon vows that he will never give up until he finds out who is served by the Grail and why the Lance bleeds.[1] But it is only when Sir Galahad comes to King Arthur's court, clothed in armor the color of Pentecostal flame, that the Round Table Knights' Quest for the Holy Grail and Lance is inaugurated—a Quest which, as Perceval's aunt explains to him, will only end when the truth about the adventures of Logres is learnt.[2]

The Quest can only begin when the Round Table is complete. But a problem arises just before Galahad's arrival, when an Irish knight throws himself out of a window and breaks his neck. When his fellows run to him, they find flames coming out of his mouth and nose, and a letter clutched in his hand; it explains that he had raped and murdered his mother and sister, then killed his father and brother when they condemned his action!

Fortunately, the name of Erec, the son of King Lac, appears on the place at the Round Table previously reserved for the suicidal Irishman. Erec in fact takes his seat at the same time as Helain the White, the son of Bors of Ganis. Helain in turn takes a place previously occupied by a knight recently killed by Tristan. Indeed, the arrival of Tristan himself is eagerly awaited, for it will mean that (with the notable exception of the Perilous Seat, which has remained empty since the inauguration of the Round Table) all one hundred and fifty seats will be filled.

At last Galahad, the long-desired knight, arrives and, in fulfillment of all the prophecies, takes his place in the Perilous Seat and then draws a sword from a floating stone in the river that flows through Camelot. These accomplishments indicate that he is the one who will bring to an end the marvels of the adventurous kingdom. Meanwhile, having learned by mysterious means that these things would be accomplished, Tristan also arrives at court. So it is that, for the first and last time since its inauguration, the Round Table is complete.[3]

Towards night, when the fellowship is at table in the palace, a storm breaks and the knights, filled with the grace of the Holy Spirit, see each other as more beautiful than ever before. The Holy Grail, covered with white silk, comes into the palace, bringing with it a fragrance of spices; the tables are filled with every food a man can wish for.

Then the Grail departs as mysteriously as it arrived; none know where it has gone or whose hands bore it. Sir Gawain swears that he will never return to court until he has seen more clearly what he has till now seen only veiled. The Knights of the Round Table follow him in making a similar vow.

That night, a messenger arrives from Nascien the Hermit to tell the knights that no woman can accompany them on the

Quest and that they must be confessed of their sins before setting off; for they are searching for the secrets of Our Lord, who will show the wonders of the Holy Grail to His chosen one. But the king is angry with Gawain for breaking up the fellowship, especially when it is prophesied that his nephew will kill more knights on the Quest than anyone else. Accordingly, he forbids Gawain to go; but the impetuous knight sneaks off just after dawn, before anyone can stop him.

The others take an oath that they will not return to court until they have learnt the truth about the Holy Grail. Galahad is the first to swear, followed by Tristan, then Lancelot and the knights of his kindred: notably his half-brother Hector of the Fens; their cousins Bleoberis, Lionel and Bors, along with Bors' son Helain the White; and others of their famous lineage. Of the lineage of Orkney are Gaheriet, Agravain, Guerrehet and Mordred, all Gawain's brothers; but they are followed by their mortal enemies, the sons of Pellinor, Agloval and Perceval. The oath is also taken by Erec, son of Lac; Kay the Seneschal; Sagremor the Unruly; Girflet, son of Doon; Lucan the Wine Steward; Dodinel the Wild; Calogrenant; Yvain, son of King Urien; Mador of the Gate; King Bademagu and his nephew Patrides; Lambegus of Benoic; Pinabel of the Island; and many more.

And so, they set off. The king accompanies them as far as the edge of the Forest of Camelot; then returns, weeping, to his palace.[4] After an overnight stay at a nearby castle, the knights go their separate ways, lest sticking together might be deemed dishonorable. Weeping piteously, each finds for himself the thickest part of the forest, where there is neither path nor trail to follow.[5]

They will have good cause to weep: For, in the course of a Quest that will last far longer than the year and a day that many have dedicated to this cause, several of their number will die at the hands of their fellows. The deaths will include that of Calogrenant, at the hands of Lionel—and no less than eighteen at the hands of Gawain: most notably, Yvain the Bastard, Patrides and his uncle Bademagu, Erec and Palamedes.

Nevertheless, twelve knights will reach Corbenic for the fulfilling of the Quest. These are: Galahad, Perceval (whose sister has also died in the course of the Quest, unable to take part herself but prepared to shed her blood to assist her brother) and Bors of Ganis; Meliagant of Denmark, who had been made a knight by Galahad; Helain the White, the bastard son of Bors; Arthur the Less, the bastard son of King Arthur; Meraugis of Portlegues; Claudin, son of King Claudas of the Land Laid Waste; Lambegus of Benoic; Pinabel of the Island and Persidos of Calaz. Last, but not least, is Palamedes, who had abandoned his Saracenic heritage and his hopeless love for Iseut in order to take part in the Grail Quest and who would, before being treacherously murdered by Gawain, witness the accomplishing of the adventure.

Galahad goes alone into the chamber of the Holy Vessel to heal the Maimed King, anointing his wounded legs with the blood from the Holy Lance, which is carried off to Heaven. The other eleven knights, who have been waiting outside, then join him at the Table of the Grail, where they each receive from Christ Himself a Host (or consecrated wafer) resembling a living man,[6] which fills them with the celestial nourishment that is the grace of the Grail. They remain in prayer until midnight, when they hear a voice telling them to go where chance leads them. Now they know that they have partaken of the last Grail Feast of the Kingdom of Logres.[7]

At last Galahad, Perceval and Bors depart in the Ship of Solomon for the city of Sarras, from which only Bors will return. They take with them the Holy Vessel, which will never again be seen in Logres, for its people have become too sinful. In fact, as soon as the Grail leaves the kingdom, Logres is devastated by a famine which lasts three years and is so severe that people are nearly driven to eating each other! King Arthur recognizes that through the goodness of Joseph of Arimathea and the Company of the Grail, the Holy Vessel had been brought to Britain; but through the evil deeds of their heirs, it had been lost forever.[8]

Indeed, when Bors, who has witnessed the rapture of the Grail to Heaven, returns to Logres, he finds a kingdom on the brink of civil war.[9] His account of the adventures of the Holy Grail is recorded by clerks and kept in the archive at Salisbury, where several hundred years later King Henry II will have them translated from Latin into French.[10]

Notes

1. *CSG* 42.
2. *LG* IV, 27; *QHG* 100–1.
3. But Arthur fears the worst: *I am sure at this quest of the Sankegreall shall all ye of the Rownde Table departe, and nevyr shall I se you agayne holé togydirs* (*MD* 672).
4. *LG* V, 115–124.
5. *LG* IV, 8–10; *MD* 674–7; *QHG* 44–53.
6. In both the Vulgate and Post-Vulgate versions of the Grail Liturgy celebrated at Corbenic, it is stressed that the Host is *literally* (not *symbolically*) the body of Christ. This gives support to the argument that the Grail legend is the "literary embodiment" of the late twelfth century preoccupation with the doctrine of transubstantiation (Hutton 1991, 319).
7. *LG* V, 278–80.
8. *LG* V, 286.
9. *LG* V, 288.
10. *LG* IV, 87; *MD* 788; *QHG* 284.

The QUESTING BEAST

After the conception of his son Mordred through an incestuous union with his half-sister, King Arthur has a fearful dream in which his land is devastated by griffins and a dragon, which ultimately kills him.

To try to take his mind off this nightmare, he goes hunting. But he chases a stag so long that his horse dies of exhaustion; so, he sits himself down by a fountain and falls into reverie. At that moment he hears what sounds like dozens of barking dogs; but he soon sees that the noise is coming from the strangest creature he has ever seen, a bizarre beast which stops to drink from a well. While it drinks, the dogs inside it fall silent, but they start up again as soon as it moves on.

While he is still sat there, an unknown knight (who we later learn is King Pellinor) appears, who explains that the beast is fated to die at the hands of the best man of his lineage; he therefore dismisses Arthur's suggestion that he take up the pursuit in Pellinor's place.[1] Even Merlin will only tell him that the grotesque, strangely-formed beast[2] is one of the adventures of the Holy Grail. Arthur can only learn the truth about the creature if he is told about it by Pellinor's son Perceval[3]; while Perceval, although he witnesses the destruction of the bizarre beast[4] and hears of its origin from his grandfather King Pellehan, will die in Sarras before he has an opportunity to explain anything to Arthur.

It is Palamedes, a newly-baptized Saracen who was previously involved in a fruitless quest to win the love of Iseut, who finally brings matters to a conclusion, spearing the beast with his lance when it is drinking from a lake. Flames shoot out of the beast as it dies and, as a result, the water of the lake boils; it is believed that it will do so until the Last Judgment. Henceforth it is called the Lake of the Beast.[5]

It is Pellehan, the father of Pellinor, who eventually reveals the origin of the beast: It is the offspring of a demon and a sorceress who, when her brother refuses to satisfy her incestuous passion, has him fed to dogs. The dogs inside the beast bark constantly as a reminder of her sin.[6] Its appearance to Arthur, just after he has unknowingly committed the sin of incest, is a prophetic reminder of his future destiny (known only to Merlin), that he will be killed by the product of that union.[7]

Notes

1. *LG* IV, 167–8: *Whos name was Kynge Pellynor that that tyme folowed the questynge beste, and afftir hys dethe Sir Palomydes folowed hit* (*MD* 35).

2. Malory describes it as having *a hede in shap lyke a serpentis hede and a body lyke a lybard, buttokked lyke a lyon and footed lyke an harte* (*MD* 378).
3. *LG* IV, 171.
4. In the Romance of Perlesvaus, Perceval watches a beautiful white beast give birth to twelve dogs which tear her to pieces (*HBG* 154). Perceval's uncle the Hermit King explains to him that the Yelping Beast signifies Our Lord; the dogs signify those Jews who killed Him who made them in His image (166). In Gerbert's Continuation, the beast is devoured by its own brood (*CSG* 406)—explained as an allegory of people who chatter in church and don't listen to the sermon (408–9).
5. *LG* V, 277–8.
6. *LG* V, 283–5.
7. In that sense, the quest for the beast can be seen as an oedipal quest to avoid one's fate. Arthur, like Oedipus, is ignorant of the incest he is committing; but, like Oedipus' father Laius, he tries to kill the child who is destined to kill him (Mordred), in a shocking echo of the Biblical Massacre of the Innocents (*MD* 46). In doing so, Arthur ironically makes parricide the inevitable outcome. Palamedes the Saracen, who has made the quest his own, becomes a Christian, thus rejecting the "necessity" (*anangké*) of the pagan gods and trusting in divine providence.

R

The RICH FISHERMAN

When Perceval first comes to the Grail Castle, he is guided there by a man whom he sees fishing in the river that surrounds it; this fisherman turns out to be his host, the Maimed King. It transpires that the reason for his fishing is that a javelin-thrust to the thighs has robbed him of the use of his legs and taken away from him the possibility of engaging in other sports.[1]

But it is said that the king that Perceval encounters is not the first Rich Fisher, which turns out to be a hereditary title whose mysterious origins are rooted in the acts of the first Christians: For it is conferred on one of his companions when Joseph of Arimathea and his followers leave Jerusalem, carrying with them the Vessel that contains the Holy Blood.

Initially, they live by working the land; at a certain point, however, the harvest fails them and the people are close to eating their own children. Joseph prays before the precious Vessel and, in response, he hears the voice of the Holy Spirit. The voice instructs him to create a table in the name of the Table of the Last Supper and, when he has done so, to instruct his brother-in-law Bron to go fishing on a nearby lake; Bron is to bring back the first thing he catches. When this is done, those who sit at the table to eat of the fish sense that their hearts are filled with grace.[2] Bron is henceforth to be known as the Rich Fisher.[3]

Others say, however, that it is not Bron but his youngest son Alan the Fat who catches the miraculous fish. Moreover, it happens not in the Holy Land but in Britain, whither the Company of the Grail have brought the Holy Vessel, converting people to Christianity everywhere they go and adding daily to their number. At last, they come to an uncultivated and barren land where it is not easy to find food; but in the middle of a valley in this wasteland they find a large pond and a small fishing boat.

The company sit down to rest by the pond and the Grail is brought before them; all who are worthy are fed through the grace of the Holy Vessel, but those who are weak in faith have nothing to eat. Josephus, the son of Joseph of Arimathea, then calls Alan and tells him to take the boat into the pond and cast the net into the water. This Alan does and, although he brings back only one large fish, Josephus commands him to divide it into three parts and set them out on the Table of the Grail; whereupon, miraculously, the fish feeds the multitude abundantly. Because of this, everyone calls Alan the Rich Fisherman.[4]

Later, when he knows that he is dying, Josephus entrusts the Grail to Alan, who takes it to the Land Beyond, where a stronghold is built to house the Holy Vessel. When Alan dies, he appoints as his successor as guardian of the Grail his brother Joshua, who inherits from Alan the title of Rich Fisherman as well as being made King of the Land Beyond: becoming, in effect, the first Fisher King.

Joshua's descendants form the dynasty that continues to rule the land and guard the Grail until the coming of Sir Galahad, the Good Knight. Galahad takes the Holy Vessel to the Middle-Eastern city of Sarras and there brings the adventures of Logres to an end. But, until that day, in Alan's honor and because of the divine grace that was bestowed on his fishing expedition, all of the kings who are entrusted with the Holy Grail are called Rich Fishermen.[5]

Notes

1. CSG 31.
2. MG 34–5.
3. Those who want to call him by his true name, will know him as the Rich Fisher; he will always grow in honor because of the fish he caught and the grace which was received: *Et cil qui nummer le vourront,/ Par son droit non l'apelerunt/ Adés le Riche Pescheeur./ A touz jours croistera s'onneur/ Pour le poisson qu'il peescha/ Quant cele grace commença* (EG ll.3343–8). In the prose version he is called *le rice Roi Pescheor por le pisson que il pescha* (RG 68–9); even though, at this stage, he has no kingdom to rule.
4. LG I, 139–40: In his honor and because of the grace received that day, all those who are entrusted with the Holy Grail will be called Rich Fishers: *et en henor de lui et por la grace de cele jornee furent tuit cil apelé Riche Pescheor qui puis furent saisi del seint Graal* (ESG 493).
5. LG I, 159: *Tuit cil furent rois et tindrent terre et furent apelé en sornon Riche Pescheor* (ESG 565).

ROBERT DE BORON

In the eighth century of the Christian era, seven hundred and seventeen years after the Passion, Our Lord gives to the hermit Nascien a book in which is written, in His own hand, the high history of the Holy Grail.[1] Some four hundred and fifty years later, Robert de Boron translates this text from the hermit's Latin into French[2] at the command of Holy Church.[3] It is the Story of Stories,[4] but one largely unknown to the writers of the Gospels.[5]

* * *

The Burgundian poet Robert de Boron is widely credited with having definitively Christianized the Grail (which is rather vaguely described as "spiritual" in Chrétien de Troyes' original poem) by linking it to the Passion of Christ. In doing so, he drew on apocryphal texts such as the Gospel of Nicodemus, which recount the trials Joseph of Arimathea underwent in the name of Jesus. But he seems to have invented the idea that the Grail was the sacramental Vessel of the Last Supper, in which was collected the Holy Blood; that there are three Grail Guardians; and that the three symbolic tables of the legend—the Table of the Last Supper, the Table of the Grail and the Round Table—signify the Holy Trinity.

In fact, Nigel Bryant has suggested that Robert's "insistent" use of trinitarian symbolism is an indicator of his religious agenda: to counter the anti-trinitarian beliefs of heretics such as the contemporary Cathars (see MONTSALVAT); and, more generally, to reclaim the ambiguous images of Chrétien's story for orthodoxy.[6] Bryant's interpretation here, it must be said, is the polar opposite of that of Jessie Weston, whose belief that Robert was an initiate of a Grail Cult was once famous but is "now the object of much scepticism."[7]

For Weston, Robert was consciously attempting to translate a pagan "triple Mystery tradition" into the language of Christian mysticism.[8] He "certainly understood the real character of the material he was handling"⁹; knew it, in fact, "from the *in*side," insofar as he had himself been initiated into the cult.¹⁰ For him, the Secret Words passed from Christ to Joseph, from Joseph to Bron and, finally, from Bron to Perceval—words only written down in a book in Robert's possession¹¹—were not "a mere figure of speech!"¹²

According to Weston, Robert took what had survived as an occult, secret tradition within Christianity and translated its symbolism into something more spiritual and ecclesiastical, using as his vehicle a series of poems handed down by the original Grail bard, Bleheris. Although the stories had already assimilated Christian imagery, it was a superficial *rapprochement*: By contrast, it was Robert, "influenced by his own knowledge of the true character of the Grail," Robert, who "knew what the story meant," who "grappled boldly with the central and underlying truths conveyed" and, possibly with the aid of a broad-minded cleric "himself tinged with Mysticism," achieved "a translation of the whole spirit and formulae of the secret teaching into Orthodox terms."¹³

Emma Jung and Marie-Louise von Franz, on the other hand, approaching the Grail legend from the standpoint of depth psychology, consider the esoteric or heterodox elements in de Boron's writings—such as what they see as his presentation of the Vessel as a fourth element that complements the Trinity—to be unconscious.¹⁴ The Celticist John Carey also sees Robert's conscious intentions—to reclaim the "enigmatic" elements of the story to "orthodox holiness"—as being undermined by his exposure to "narrative material" that is non–Biblical—in this case Welsh and, ultimately, Irish.¹⁵

Notes

1. This is not the *grant Estoire dou Graal* (*EG* l.3493), the metrical romance which is generally credited to Robert, but the *haute Estoire del Saint Graal* (*ESG* 2), which substantially rewrites Robert's account of the early history of the Grail in order better to fit it to the Vulgate *Queste*.

2. The *Estoire del Saint Graal* becomes the foundational narrative for the Vulgate and Post-Vulgate Cycles, both of which invoke Robert as authority for the reliability of their version of events: *et einsi le dit messires Roberz de Borron, qui ceste estoire translata de latin en romanz aprés celui saint hermite a cui Nostre Sires la livra premierement* (*ESG* 391).

3. *Et messires Roberz de Borron, qui ceste estoire translata del latin en françois par le comandement de Sainte Yglise, aferme que* (*ESG* 478) or *s'i acorde bien, car la veraie estoire tesmoigne que einsint fu il* (546). When Robert "affirms" or "agrees with" the Vulgate version, we can be sure that we have the real story: for the True History attests that it is so. This True History includes the *Estoire de Merlin*, which is *une autre branche* of the *Estoire del Graal* (577). Yet another branch is the Tale of the Cry (*li Contes del Brait*) in which the Master Helyas takes over the translation of part of Nascien's Latin in order to help out his comrade-in-arms Robert (*SRM* 194).

4. *LG* I, 3: *si haute estoire com est cele du Graal, ki est estoire de toutes les estoires* (*ESG* 1). It is this tale which reveals the truth for, whenever the words appear to take a doubtful turn, it makes everything known completely clearly, so that it is fitting that it should be called the story of stories: *chis contes en demostranche la verité ... car il n'entrait onques avant nule parole ou il puisse doutanche aperchevoir ke il ne le fache de tout en tout apertement counoistre; et pour chou est il a droit apielés* L'Estoire des estoires (249).

5. *MG* 23.
6. *MG* 6–7.
7. *MG* 4n10.
8. Weston 1920, 206.
9. Weston 1909, 224.
10. Weston 1909, 279.
11. With regard to these words, Robert addresses the reader or listener directly, saying that he dare not reveal these words, nor could he even if he wanted to, if he did not have access to that high book in which wise clerks have written down the great secrets that we call the Grail (*RG* 30–1); *Se je le grant livre n'avoie/ Ou les estoires sunt escrites,/Par les granz clers feites et dites./ La sunt li grant secré escrit/ Qu'en numme le Graal et dit* (*EG* ll.932–6). One of these *granz clers* must be the Master Blaise who, in the Prose *Merlin* (attributed to Robert), writes down the Grail story at Merlin's dictation; the other, possibly the author of the Book of Joseph with which Blaise's account was eventually combined; but of course, Christ's own version must take precedence.

12. Weston 1909, 280.
13. Weston 1909, 331–2: "He knew, and that from the inside, the material with which he was dealing" as one "familiar with Christian esoteric teaching" (1913, 120–1); which is to say, "the Christian 'mystery' tradition, in its relation to the pre–Christian, and understood perfectly how the symbolism and

terminology of the one could be translated into the symbolism and terminology of the other" (126). He "was certainly aware of the real character of his material; he knew the Grail cult as Christianized Mystery" (1920, 161). It was he therefore who achieved the conversion of the Grail story into "a definitely Christian romance" when he "radically remodeled the whole on the basis of the triple Mystery tradition translated into terms of high Christian Mysticism" (205–6).

14. "Consciously, de Boron wished only to make the Christian doctrine more comprehensible to the simple understanding of the laity, but thoughts and questions that were not quite in accord with the teachings of orthodoxy arose within him, clearly unintentionally" (Jung & Franz, 346).

15. Carey 2007, 147–9: "With his eyes turned eastward to the Holy Places, Robert nevertheless provides us with further evidence of the legend's western roots."

The ROUND TABLE

The world-renowned Round Table is constructed for Uther Pendragon at Carduel in Wales at the behest of Merlin. It is a replica of the Table of the Grail, which in turn was made by Joseph of Arimathea in commemoration of the Table of the Last Supper. The Round Table is thus the third of the three great tables of Christendom, which are an image of the Trinity.[1]

At the Table of the Grail, Merlin explains to the king, a place was kept empty to signify the place abandoned by Judas when he betrayed the Lord[2]; similarly, Uther must leave one seat empty at the Round Table until the arrival of the hero who is destined to fill it, he who will achieve the adventures of the Grail.[3]

On Whitsunday,[4] Merlin chooses fifty knights to sit at the Table[5]; having done so, he announces that it would be to knights of this very fellowship that the secrets of the Holy Grail would be revealed.[6] As prophesied, it is three Round Table Knights—Galahad (the Destined Knight), Perceval and Bors—who travel to the sacred city of Corbenic to achieve the Grail Quest. They then follow the Holy Vessel to Sarras in the Middle East, whence only Bors returns to tell the tale.

But many Knights of the Round Table are killed on the Grail Quest[7] and the fellowship never really regains its former glory.[8] The Table itself, with its Perilous Seat still bearing the name of Sir Galahad, is destroyed by King Mark after Arthur passes to Avalon.[9]

Notes

1. Although the symbolism is never spelt out, we can see the third table as representing the third person of the Trinity, the Holy Ghost—the spirit of love between the Father (whose mercy the Passover feast honors) and the Son (the archetype of the Maimed King, pierced with a spear)—whose grace is channeled through the Grail Vessel.

2. The creation of a third table has already been revealed indirectly to Joseph by the Holy Spirit, who tells him that the empty place at the Table of the Grail, or *another which will be established in its name*, will be filled by a man of Bron's lineage (*MG* 38). This other place can only be the Perilous Seat at the Round Table which will, in the De Boron Cycle, be occupied by Bron's grandson Perceval; but, in the Vulgate Cycle, by Galahad, a more distant descendant of Bron.

3. MG 94: According to the Prose *Merlin*, the second part of the De Boron Cycle, the Destined Knight will be the son of Alan the Fat. He will need to have been in the presence of the Grail before he takes his seat at the Round Table; none of this will happen in Uther's time, but during the reign of the king who will succeed him. Accordingly, it is Perceval, the son of Alan, who arrives at Carduel in the time of Arthur. But he attempts to fill the Perilous Seat prematurely so that, when he comes into the presence of the Grail, he fails to ask the Question. He thus betrays the Fisher King, in a distant echo of the betrayal of Jesus by Judas. In the Vulgate version, the Seat awaits the arrival of Galahad, while Perceval is only worthy to sit on his right hand.

4. The Pentecostal setting of the foundation of the Fellowship of the Round Table reminds us that it is not just a chivalric institution, but an agency for the working of the Holy Spirit in the world; a working which will be fulfilled when Galahad, at a later Pentecost, arrives to take his seat.

5. *LG* I, 196–7.

6. *LG* IV, 26; *QHG* 99: *By them whych sholde be felowys of the Rounde Table the trouth of the Sankegreall sholde be well knowyn* (*MD* 700).

7. Principal among the casualties are Agloval, Bademagu, Calogrenant, Erec and Palamedes.

8. This tragic eventuality is predicted by King Arthur: *I am sure at this quest of the Sankegreall shall all ye of the Rownde Table departe, and nevyr shall I see you agayne holé togydirs* (*MD* 672).

9. *LG* V, 311.

S

SADOR

The eleventh son of Joseph of Arimathea's brother-in-law Bron, Sador and his younger brother Alan the Fat decline Joseph's offer to choose brides for them: Alan, because he wishes to remain a virgin all his life[1]; but Sador, because he wants to choose his own wife.

Accordingly, when Sador rescues Chelinde, the beautiful pagan Princess of Babylonia, from a shipwreck, he has her baptized and marries her; only for her to be raped by his brother Naburzadan, whom Sador kills when he finds out. Fearing the vengeance of his other brothers, Sador escapes with his wife on a ship sailing for Cornwall. But, when a storm threatens to wreck the vessel, an old fortune-teller among the mariners divines[2] that a criminal on board is putting them all in danger; he identifies the guilty party as Sador.

The sailors throw Sador overboard, while agreeing to take care of his pregnant wife; she is brought safely to the pagan King of Cornwall, Canor. A sworn enemy of Christianity, Canor forces Chelinde to undergo a pagan marriage ceremony.[3] But he is disturbed by a dream in which he hunts a leopard, only for both pursued and pursuer to be devoured by a lion. In order to interpret the dream, he turns to a pagan philosopher of great age, one of the line of Virgil, who knows much about the stars and the obscure things of this world.[4]

The philosopher tells Canor that the leopard signifies Chelinde's Christian husband, who is not dead as assumed, having clung to life on a rock in the sea; while the lion is the as-yet-unborn son of Chelinde who, if he lives long enough, will kill Canor. On hearing this the king determines to dispatch the child as soon as he is born.

When it comes to the crunch, however, Canor is not able to do the deed himself. Instead, he abandons the boy in a forest, where he is rescued by a Cornish knight and his wife. They name the child Apollo the Adventurous, because his beauty is like that of the god Apollo and his survival was a beautiful adventure.

Meanwhile, Sador has, as the philosopher foresaw, washed up on a rock, inhabited only by a hermit. The holy man was one of King Mordrain's men who was converted to Christianity by Joseph of Arimathea.[5] When he prayed to be taken away from the temptations of his former life, he found himself instantly transported from Sarras to this lonely rock.

Sador shares the life of the hermit for three years[6] before being rescued, on the advice of the pagan philosopher; but he dies eventually at the hands of Apollo, who does not recognize his father. Apollo then goes on to kill Canor, thus fulfilling the prophecy.[7]

Offered the throne of Lyonesse on the death of its king, and now a convert to Christianity, Apollo marries the eldest daughter of the King of Ireland[8]; from them are descended the royal families of both Cornwall and Lyonesse.[9] Thus both King Mark of Cornwall and his nephew Tristan of Lyonesse can trace their descent from Sador and, ultimately, from Bron of the Company of the Grail.

* * *

The story of Sador is recounted at the beginning of the vast Prose *Tristan*, which is presented as a translation into French from a Latin text in which is told openly the history of the Holy Grail. The translator of this *estoire vraie del Saint Graal* identifies himself as Sir Luces, Lord of the Castle of Gat near Salisbury.[10]

Whereas Robert de Boron's *Estoire dou Graal* presents Alan's refusal to marry as occurring in the Holy Land (although he then has his wish over-ridden so that he can father Perceval), the Prose *Tristan* follows the Vulgate *Estoire del Saint Graal* in moving these events to Britain. Where the Vulgate Cycle incorporates the Prose *Lancelot* into the Grail story, the Post-Vulgate does the same for the Prose *Tristan*.

Notes

1. Alan says that he wants to serve at the Table of the Grail and that Our Lord will keep his virginity; this proof of his worthiness inspires Joseph to place the Holy Vessel in Alan's keeping at his death: *enz dist qu'il seroit virges tot son aage, et serviroit a la table del Saint Graal, et garderoit a Nostre Seignor sa virginité.... Et Joseph le revest de la garde del saint vessel aprés sa mort* (*TPC* I, 40). By contrast, Robert de Boron has Joseph entrust the Grail to Alan's father Bron; while, in the Vulgate version, it is Joseph's son Josephus who entrusts it to Alan.
2. *Leanz avoit un marinier sortiseor qui ... fist ses charaies et ses conjuremenz* (*TPC* I, 44).
3. *...il la prist a feme a la loi paiene* (*TPC* I, 46).
4. *...un paien ... qui assez savoit d'astronomie et des oscures choses dou monde ... et phylosophe l'apeloient. Et il estoit sanz faille del linaige Virgile* (*TPC* I, 47). The Roman poet Virgil had a reputation in the Middle Ages as a prophet and magician, in which context he is also referred to in Wolfram von Eschenbach's *Parzival* as an ancestor of the sorcerer Clinschor (*WP* 328, 447; *PT* 275, 390).
5. Joseph is also responsible for the conversion of Ireland (*TPC* I, 110).
6. Löseth, 3–5.
7. Löseth, 11: Like Oedipus, who was also abandoned by his father because of a prophecy but ended up killing him, Apollo marries his own mother. He finds out what he has done through the intervention of St. Augustine, in what is but one of many anachronisms in this text. Chelinde dies when she is struck by lightning (12).
8. Löseth, 13.
9. Löseth, 16.
10. *...le grant livre del latin, celui meïsmes qui devise apertement l'estoire del Saint Graal* (*TPC* I, 39).

The SANGREAL

It is shortly after the death of his brother-in-law King Loth at the hands of Pellinor that King Arthur first hears about the adventures of the Sangreal[1] from Merlin,[2] who further discusses it with him after warning him that the woman he wants to marry will betray him.[3]

It is Sir Bagdemagus who is the first of Arthur's knights to come across a sign of the Sangreal, in the form of a holy herb, which he finds just before discovering the fate of Merlin.[4] But the Round Table knights learn more when a hermit comes to the court one Whitsunday and tells them that this same year shall be begotten he who shall sit in the Siege Perilous (Seat of Danger) and win the Sangreal.[5] This is precisely what comes to pass when Sir Launcelot arrives at the castle of King Pelles, whose daughter he is tricked into sleeping with after he sees the holy Sangreal.[6] The child of that deceitful union is first met, not by his father, but by Launcelot's cousin Bors, who also witnesses the Sangreal in Pelles' castle.[7]

Launcelot's half-brother Sir Ector also encounters the Holy Vessel after he and Sir Percivale (one of the four who will achieve the Sangreal[8]) nearly kill each other in battle. It is only Percivale who can see the maiden who carries it, for he also has preserved his maidenhead; but they are both healed of their wounds.[9] Sir Launcelot is also healed of wounds—but of psychic rather than physical ones, when a spell of madness leads him once more to the castle of King Pelles, where he is laid before the Holy Vessel of the Sangreal.[10]

When Launcelot's son Galahad comes to the court for the first time, his father predicts that this same day the adventure of the Sangreal shall begin.[11] Moreover, when Galahad sits in the Siege Perilous, King Arthur recognizes that the one who will achieve what so many others cannot—to bring to an end the Quest of the Sangreal—is at last among them.[12]

During the Quest, the Sangreal appears first to Sir Launcelot in a vision, when he is half-asleep, by a chapel in the Waste Forest; he recognizes the Holy Vessel as the one he saw previously in the house of the Fisher King. He also sees a sick knight, borne on a litter, pray that the Lord who is *within* the Vessel will heal him.[13] Launcelot sees the knight made whole by kissing the Vessel; but he has no power to awaken, because he is in a state of sin.[14]

After meeting his son Galahad on the Ship of Faith, Lancelot makes his way to Corbenic, praying that he might see some tidings of the Sangreal. He is privileged to witness, through an open chamber door, the Mass of the Sangreal but, when he tries to enter, he is struck blind and deaf and helpless. For twenty-four days (corresponding to the number of years that he has indulged his sinful love for the queen) he lies between life and death; when at last he recovers, the people of the castle tell him that he will never see more of the Sangreal. He replies that it suffices him.[15]

Launcelot's cousin Sir Bors, however, sees something of good omen: a bird giving up its life-blood to feed its young. He realizes he has seen something of great significance.[16] But it is not until he comes to an abbey, that a holy man there explains to him that what he has seen is an image of the Sangreal.[17]

Bors later meets up with Galahad and Percivale and, when the three companions arrive at Corbenic, after Launcelot's departure for Camelot, King Pelles recognizes his grandson. There is great rejoicing in the castle for they know that the Quest of the Sangreal is fulfilled.[18] But, after Galahad heals his ancestor the Maimed King with the Holy Blood, the Vessel of the Sangreal on its silver table, covered in red samite, travels with the three companions to Sarras; they are glad to have it in their fellowship.[19]

The pagan King of Sarras imprisons them as soon as he finds out what they have brought with them; but the Vessel sustains them[20] until the king frees them on his death-bed. Galahad dies after seeing the marvels of the Sangreal, whereupon a disembodied hand bears the Vessel up to Heaven.[21] Percivale also passes out of the world while in the far country of Sarras. But Bors makes his way back to Camelot, where he and Launcelot recount the high adventures of the Sangreal.[22]

* * *

According to the Gospel of John (19.34), a soldier (later identified as Longinus) pierced the side of Jesus, after He died on the cross; "and forthwith came there out blood and water." Hence in his First Epistle (5.6), John writes: "This is he that came by water and blood, even Jesus Christ; not by water only, but by water and blood. And it is the Spirit that beareth witness, because the Spirit is truth."[23]

For some this spiritual quality of the Royal Blood is understood more literally. Thus, for the occultist Gareth Knight, Arthur's mother Igraine[24] was a representative of "the line of ancient Atlantean priestly aristocracy" which "was based upon principles of inherited clairvoyance through a particular quality of the blood. This is the basis of the *sang real*."[25]

In other modern manifestations of Grail mythology, the Holy Blood takes on a greater significance than the original Vessel in which it was carried (the cup or dish of the Last Supper); or, rather, the Vessel becomes human, as Mary Magdalen is transformed from the "apostle of the apostles" to the (literal) bride of Jesus and the mother of his child.[26] The Sangreal thus becomes the Royal Bloodline of the House of David, descending through the Merovingian kings of France into the aristocratic families of Europe: a messianic legacy whose import has been the subject of much speculation, but little illumination.

Notes

1. The Vessel in which the blood of the crucified Jesus was collected at the Deposition is known in French as the *saint graal* but becomes, in medieval English transliteration, the *Sankegreall* or Sangreal; this is then interpreted to mean *sang réal* or Royal Blood. Thus, Malory calls his translation of the

thirteenth century Vulgate *Queste del Saint Graal*: *the noble tale off the Sankegreall, whyche called ys the holy vessell and the sygnyfycacion of the Blyssed Bloode off Oure Lorde Jesu Cryste, whyche was brought into thys londe by Joseph off Aramathye* (*MD* 664).

2. *...the adventures of the Sankgreall shall com amonge you and be encheved* (*MD* 62). Merlin also tells Arthur how Balin shall strike the Dolorous Blow, resulting in the maiming of King Pellam (Pellehan) in an inner chamber of his castle: *For in that place was parte of the bloode of Oure Lorde Jesu Cryste, which Joseph off Aramathy brought into thys londe* (68).

3. *MD* 76.
4. *MD* 106.
5. *MD* 620.
6. *And anone there cam in a dove at a wyndow, and in her mowthe there semed a lytyll sensar of golde, and therewythall there was suche a savour as all the spycery of the worlde had bene there. And furthwythall there was uppon the table all maner of meates and drynkes that they coude thynke uppon.*

So there came in a damesell passynge fayre and yonge, and she bare a vessell of golde betwyxt her hondis: When Launcelot asks Pelles what all this means, the king replies that *this is the rychyst thynge that any man hath lyvynge, and whan this thynge gothe abrode the Rounde Table shall be brokyn for a season. And ... this is the holy Sankgreall that ye have here seyne* (*MD* 622). Malory's *holy Sankgreall* is not a tautology, for the *sang réal* ("royal blood") of Jesus, whose kingdom is not of this Earth, is indeed holy. In modern "magdalenian" mythologizing, the Vessel that contains the Royal Blood is the wife of Jesus, the mother of his child; while, in the Tale of the Sangreal, it is the flesh-and-blood damsel, rather than the symbolic Vessel, who will seduce our hero and bear him a son.

7. *And so there cam in a whyght dowve, and she bare a lytyll sensar of golde in her mowthe, and there was all maner of metys and drynkis, and a mayden bare that Sankgreall.... And than they kneled adowne and made there devocions, and there was suche a savoure as all the spycery in the worlde had bene there. And as the dowve had takyn her flyght the mayden vanysshed wyth the Sankgreall as she cam* (*MD* 626–7).

8. The others are Galahad and Bors but the fourth, in a variation unique to Malory, is Sir Pelleas, the husband of the Damsel of the Lake (*MD* 143).

9. *Ryght so there cam by the holy vessell, the Sankegreall, wyth all maner of swetnesse and savoure* (*MD* 643).

10. *MD* 648–50.
11. *MD* 668.
12. *MD* 671.
13. *Fayre swete Lorde whych ys here within the holy vessell....* Here the Holy Blood *is* the Lord contained in *the holy vessell of the Sankgreall* (*MD* 693), as the wine *is* the Lord in the chalice of the Mass, through the miracle of transubstantiation.

14. *MD* 694: For the same reason Gawain and Ector will never find the Sangreal (728–9).
15. *MD* 772–5.
16. *MD* 732.
17. *Than Oure Lorde shewed Hym unto you in the lyknesse of a fowle, that suffirde grete anguysshe for us whan He was putte upon the Crosse, and bledde hys herte blood for mankynde; there was the tokyn and the lyknesse of the Sankgreall* (*MD* 741).
18. *MD* 781.
19. *MD* 785.
20. *And they told hym the truth of the Sankgreall, and the power whych God hath sette there. Than thys kynge was a grete tirraunte, and was com of the lyne of paynymes, and toke hem and put hem in preson in a depe hole. But as sone as they were there Our Lorde sente them the Sankgreall, thorow whos grace they were allwey fullfylled whyle they were in preson* (*MD* 786).
21. *MD* 787–8: *And sythen was there never man so hardy to sey that he hadde seyne the Sankgreal.*
22. *And all thys was made in grete bookes and put up in almeryes at Salysbury.... Thus endith the Tale of the Sankgreal ... which ys a tale cronycled for one of the trewyst and of the holyest that ys in this worlde* (*MD* 788–9).
23. For some early Christian Gnostics, the flesh is the Logos and the blood, the Holy Spirit (*GS* 333).
24. According to the Glastonbury Tablets, Igraine (Ygerna) is the grand-daughter of the Fisher King Lambor (*MTG* 142), and therefore of the Grail family.
25. Knight 1984, 164.
26. For the authors of the "shocking international bestseller" *Holy Blood, Holy Grail*, it is "likely" that Sangreal (Royal Blood) is the "original" name for the Grail (Baigent *et al.*, 306). They refer to "certain accounts" whereby Joseph of Arimathea brought the Grail to Glastonbury; but say that there are "other accounts" whereby Mary Magdalen brought the Holy Grail—but not a cup, this being a "facile association" perpetuated by Malory, which has become a "truism"—to Marseilles in what is now France (286). These "medieval traditions" (308) or "legends" of the Magdalen carrying the Blood Royal to Gaul, where she would have been able to find refuge within pre-existing Jewish communities, support the authors' hypothesis that there might have been "a hereditary bloodline descended directly from Jesus" (313). But unfortunately for this hypothesis, more diligent researchers have not been able to trace any such medieval accounts, traditions or legends.

SARACENS

When the Company of the Grail first arrive in Britain they discover a land of pagans; or, more specifically, of Saracens,[1] that is, followers of the astral cult whose sacred center, before its conversion to

Christianity, was in the Temple of the Sun[2] in the Middle Eastern city of Sarras.[3] The defeat of the Saracen kings by Joseph of Arimathea and his followers leads to the almost total eradication of their pagan cult during the reign of good King Lucius, the first Christian king of Britain, whose daughter marries one of the Fisher Kings, the guardians of the Holy Grail.

The most famous Saracen during the reign of Arthur is Palamedes, who follows the Questing Beast until he is baptised[4]; at which point he kills the Beast and travels to Corbenic with Galahad and Perceval to witness the achieving of the Grail Quest.[5]

Notes

1. The etymology is disputed: The *Estoire del Saint Graal* is dismissive of the suggestion that the Saracens take their name from Sarah, Abraham's first wife, since she was Jewish (*LG* I, 15).
2. Stonehenge, with its *sarsen* stones, has also been identified as a Temple of the Sun (Graves 1997, 53); while John Darrah (1981, 101) has suggested that the Giants' Dance was constructed to honor the dead of the Saracen cult.
3. The name of the sacred city of the star worshippers, Sarras, appears to be a back-formation from "Saracen."
4. *LG* V, 273.
5. *LG* V, 278: Feirefiz, the pagan half-brother of Parzival, also converts to Christianity for love of the Grail Bearer; it is only then that he can see the Grail.

SARRAS

The Holy City of the Grail in Britain is Corbenic, where the Fisher Kings rule. But, hundreds of years before the founding of Corbenic, a city in the Middle East was also prepared to be the home of the sacred Vessel; in fact, its last home on Earth.

The exact location of Sarras is unknown. But it is a coastal city near Jerusalem, situated between Babylon and Salamander,[1] the capital of a realm that borders Egypt. More importantly, it is the place whence came the first Saracens, a sect that worships the heavenly bodies and who are named after the city where their faith was first established.[2] From this city their astral cult spreads as far afield as to Britain, where its principal center is Camelot.

When the prophet Daniel is captured during the first Babylonian attack on Jerusalem (around the beginning of the seventh century before Christ), he passes through Sarras on his way to captivity. Approaching the main palace of the city, he sees Hebrew letters written on the door in charcoal: They declare that it is a spiritual place. From then on it is known as the Spiritual Palace, although no one knows why until Joseph of Arimathea comes there nearly seven hundred years later.[3]

In the Distant Lands of Babylon

Joseph arrives in Sarras eleven days after leaving Jerusalem, where he had been imprisoned since the death of Jesus.[4] He bears with him, in an ark, the Vessel containing the blood of the crucified Christ.

He and his followers, the Company of the Grail, enter the Temple of the Sun. The Saracens consider the Sun to be the noblest of all the heavenly bodies and therefore it is only fitting that its most beautiful building is the solar temple.[5] It is here that Joseph meets the King of Sarras, Evalach the Unknown, who is at war with the neighboring Egyptians; Joseph promises Evalach victory if he will convert to Christianity. The next morning, Joseph's son Josephus is invested as High Priest of the Grail in the Spiritual Palace and establishes the sacrament of the Eucharist.[6]

When Evalach is victorious against his enemies, he and his brother-in-law Seraph, Duke of Orberica, convert—taking the baptismal names of Mordrain and Nascien—and their people are converted with them. Josephus has the pagan statues knocked down and the altars broken in pieces, purifying the temples with holy water.[7]

Before leaving Sarras, Josephus obliges Mordrain to burn the wooden statue of a woman that he keeps in a secret underground chamber and with which he has been having sexual intercourse for the previous fifteen years![8] The burning of the statue restores Mordrain to the love of his true wife, Queen Sarrasinte, who throughout the period of her husband's secret passion has been nurturing her own secret faith: Unbeknownst to her husband, she had inherited the Christian faith from her mother and never returned to idol-worship.[9]

Sarrasinte and her more recently converted relatives travel to Britain and, as part of the Company of the Grail, take part in the conversion of indigenous pagans and the eradication of those Saracens who oppose them, with missionary zeal. They have left the first Christian city in the care of a loyal knight called Aganor.[10] But when, over four hundred years later, Sir Galahad, a direct descendant of Duke Nascien, arrives in Sarras with his companions Perceval and Bors, bringing with them the Grail and Holy Lance, they find that the city has fallen back into its old pagan ways, and they are thrown into prison.

However, the cruel King of Sarras repents on his death bed and frees the companions; a divine voice instructs the people of the city to elect Galahad as their king. With Galahad's death, the Grail and Holy Lance are assumed into Heaven. Perceval dies a year later and Bors, not wishing to remain alone in far-off Babylon,[11] returns to Logres.[12]

As for the city of Sarras, it remains pagan until the Moslem conquest.

* * *

Although no geographical location can be found for Sarras with any certainty, it is possible that the descriptions of the city were inspired by stories about the medieval city of Harran (modern Carrhae, on the border between Syria and Turkey). During the early Middle Ages, Harran was the home of a group calling themselves "Sabians," one of the cults, along with Judaism and Christianity, mentioned in the Koran as worthy of toleration under Islam.[13]

In the mid-tenth century the Arab traveler and historian al-Mas'udi passed through and saw the last remaining Sabian temple. There had originally been seven, each dedicated to one of the planetary gods. Al-Mas'udi goes on to quote from an Harranian poem describing one of the temples, asserting "that it had underground chambers in which were placed idols of the planetary deities. Hidden human guardians made their voices seem to proceed from these during the initiation ceremonies of children, terrifying the latter and so confirming them in their faith."[14]

This quotation might remind us of the passage from the *Estoire del Saint Graal*, referred to above, in which the king is discovered to be having sex with a heathen idol, presumably an image of Venus, in an underground chamber; as well as of an earlier passage, in which an idol of Mars speaks, until the demon that is in it is driven out by exorcism.[15] The Christian author of the *Estoire*, unlike the Moslem historian, felt no necessity to rationalize the story as a trick perpetrated by human agency.

From the ninth to the fourteenth century, Arab scholars took a considerable interest in the Sabians of Harran, a city which became of great strategic importance during the Crusades.[16] It is therefore possible that legends and speculations about the astral cult of Harran, brought to the west by Crusaders, influenced the creation of the fictional Sarras in the early thirteenth century.

For Henry Corbin, on the other hand, although he recognizes its affinity with Harran, Sarras is a city not found on any maps. To say that the land of its king borders on Egypt (the Land of Exile and hence of the material world) is to say that Sarras is one of the cities of the intermediate realm between this world and the next, which Corbin has named the *mundus imaginalis*; and which has many affinities with the Celtic Otherworld. If the inhabitants are described as pagan star-worshippers, he argues, this is precisely because we are in the

World of the Soul; a world which includes all the diverse faiths that battle for it. The Grail passes this way twice: once, on its way to Britain, the Promised Land of the West; and once, on its return journey to the East, whence it will disappear. Josephus appears to the three Grail Knights here, even though he long ago quit this Earth; but this is precisely because we are in Sarras and no longer on this Earth.[17]

Notes

1. Salamander is described as a city in Greece (*LG* I, 121), while Babylon was the medieval name for Cairo; hence, according to Ponceau, it is this city rather than the one on the Euphrates that is meant, because the Kingdom of Sarras borders on Egypt (*ESG* 587). However, references to the language of the Saracens (or Sarrasins) as "Chaldean" (155, 562) suggest a Mesopotamian homeland.
2. *LG* I, 15: Before they became star-worshippers, the people of Sarras had no fixed faith, the object of their worship changing from day to day. But then, they took to worshipping the Sun, Moon and planets; although they would later convert to Islam, when the Prophet Mohammed was sent to save them.
3. *LG* I, 23.
4. Given that Joseph is released from prison by Vespasian, who left the Holy Land in July 69 CE, this gives us an approximate date for his arrival in Sarras; the Company leave the city later the same year.
5. *LG* I, 15–6.
6. *LG* I, 23–9.
7. *LG* I, 47–8.
8. *LG* I, 52–3.
9. *LG* I, 46.
10. *LG* I, 131.
11. ...*en si estrange terre* (*PV* III, 384); *en si loingteinnes terres come es parties de Babiloine* (*QP* 279): *So whan Sir Bors saw that he was in so farre contreyes as in the partis of Babilonye, he departed frome the cité of Sarras* (*MD* 788).
12. *LG* IV, 86–7; V, 286–8; *QHG* 280–4.
13. The survival of the pagan astral cult in Sarras, despite the missionary activities of the Company of the Grail, until the Moslem conquest, would correspond with the survival in Harran of the Sabian religion of the stars, despite the Byzantine persecutions; and on, under Koranic protection, until the eleventh century.
14. Hutton 2003, 147.
15. *LG* I, 30–1.
16. Hutton 2003, 140–1.
17. For Corbin, the westward voyage of the Grail is an Exile followed by an Exodus, corresponding to the descent into incarnation of the soul followed by its re-ascent (and re-orientation) to its spiritual home: *Ce double "voyage" du Graal correspond au double mouvement bien connu de toute la gnose théosophique en Islam, et que dessinent les deux arcs de la descente et de la remontée de l'âme* (1971, 183).

SARRASINTE

The wife of Evalach, pagan King of Sarras, Sarrasinte is a secret Christian, having embraced the new faith as a child, seventeen years before the arrival of the Company of the Grail. Sarrasinte's mother, the Duchess of Orberica, was converted by the hermit Salustes after a miraculous cure. Her daughter was baptized at the same time, after having a vision of Christ in the hermit's chapel[1]; but she keeps her given name at the hermit's suggestion, since it means Full of Faith.[2] She travels with her husband to Britain to aid Joseph of Arimathea in his evangelical mission.

Queen Sarrasinte will never see her homeland again, dying in an abbey built by her husband, on the same day as her brother Duke Nascien and his wife also pass away.[3] By this time, Sarrasinte's nephew Celidoine has married the daughter of the King of Persia who, when she was baptized, also took the Christian name Sarrasinte in honor of the Queen of Sarras.[4] On the occasion of their marriage, Celidoine and his wife are both invested with the rule of the Kingdom of North Wales.[5]

Notes

1. *LG* I, 42–3.
2. *LG* I, 48.
3. *LG* I, 160.
4. *LG* I, 112: The Princess of Persia is baptized in Sarras by Peter (a relative of Joseph of Arimathea who will later found the Christian dynasty of Orkney). From her are descended nine knights, the last of whom, the end of the lineage, is Galahad who, before he leaves this mortal realm, will be crowned King of Sarras.
5. *LG* I, 135: John Darrah sees in this sequence of events the remnants of a pagan myth: "To have continuity in the name of the queen whose marriage conveys kingship, and for her name to incorporate the name of her city, Sarras, suggests that she may have represented the sovereignty of her domains" (1994, 74). Sarrasinte was therefore originally "the

name-giving goddess of sovereignty at the holy city of Sarras" (142). Darrah sees sovereignty as "a common motif in the native paganism" (246–7).

SATURN

The planetary body of the highest of the seven heavens,[1] Saturn's movements along with the moon's changes have a direct effect upon the un-healing wound suffered by the Maimed King, worsening the pain that he feels.[2]

* * *

For Emma Jung and Marie-Louise von Franz, Saturn personifies "the demon of sexuality" which is responsible for the suffering of the Maimed King. Saturn's world is one of "chthonic sexuality, of ecstasy and its wisdom," which has been "very largely repressed by Christian man and for that reason, has turned into a dangerous opponent." They consider that the Grail King represents Christian man and Saturn, the "dark aspect of divinity"; so, it is therefore "significant and obvious" that Saturn, "the malefic spirit opposed to Christianity," should be the cause of the king's injury.[3]

Notes

1. WP 387; PT 327: The Titan Saturn is the King of Heaven in the Golden Age; his eponymous planet is the ruler of the Seventh Heaven; and he gives his name to the seventh day of the week (Saturday).
2. WP 249–50; PT 206–7.
3. Jung & Franz, 206–7.

The SECRET WORDS OF CHRIST

Joseph of Arimathea, having brought the body of Jesus down from the Cross and buried him, is imprisoned by the Jews when the body vanishes from the tomb. Locked in the dungeon of a tower, its entrance sealed with a stone as that of Jesus had been, Joseph is rewarded for his faith by visits from the risen Christ, who brings with Him the Vessel containing His Most Holy Blood.

Christ tells Joseph that he has been chosen to be the first keeper of the Vessel and that he must choose his successor; but that there must only be three keepers in all, in honor of the Trinity. Christ goes on to speak *other* words to Joseph: words which cannot be repeated, the author explains, even if he wanted to; words which the author only knows because they are written in the High Book which contains the great secrets which we call the Grail.[1] He gives the Holy Vessel to Joseph, saying that whenever he calls on the Trinity and that blessed lady who gave birth to God the Son, he will hear the voice of the Holy Spirit.[2]

Later, after Joseph has been freed from prison by Vespasian and wishes to send his followers into the West with the Grail, he entrusts to the Rich Fisher, his brother-in-law Bron, the words which Christ spoke to him in the dungeon. But He does this privately, speaking the Secret Words out loud initially, then putting them in writing, for Bron alone to read and keep safe.[3]

Once Bron has taken the Vessel to the West, Merlin tells King Arthur that, if the knight of most renown in the world comes to Bron's castle in Ireland and asks him what purpose the Grail serves, then Bron will tell him in turn Our Lord's Secret Words.[4] The aged Fisher King will finally pass from life to death and the Grail will have its third and final keeper.[5]

Bron's grandson Perceval, who is indeed that knight of renown, returns to Bron's castle after an unsuccessful first visit and, this time, asks the purpose of what he sees. The voice of the Holy Spirit tells Bron that the prophecy which Our Lord made to Joseph in prison must now be fulfilled: The Fisher King must entrust to Perceval's keeping the sacred words which He taught to Joseph when He gave him the Grail.[6] The Voice departs and Bron does as instructed, teaching Perceval the words which Joseph had taught him in turn—words which the author cannot and must not reveal.[7]

* * *

In the writings in prose and verse attributed to Robert de Boron we find the first known attempt in literature to clearly define the Grail as a Christian Vessel; as well as the combination of orthodox, apocryphal and possibly heretical themes which have so intrigued readers of the Grail literature—readers to whom references to secrets withheld are addressed directly by the author.

De Boron, a Burgundian knight, is particularly insistent on the importance of the doctrine of the Holy Trinity: a doctrine which, at the time he was writing, was being denied by the Cathars in the Languedoc (the Albigensian heresy).[8] However, as Jung and Franz have pointed out, it seems as if de Boron could not help adding a fourth, feminine figure to the powers that must be invoked through the Grail so that it really forms a quaternity. The Grail, as the container of the blood of the Triune God, becomes a symbol of the mother of God herself.[9]

Christ Himself, when he appears on Earth, is a quaternity, according to the heretical writings of those early Christians associated with the second-century teacher Valentinus. Here, as the Catholic polemicist Irenaeus points out, the earthly Jesus is compounded of four elements: The powers from whom Jesus derives three of these elements can be seen to correspond to the orthodox (male) Trinity; but there is a fourth, untouchable element ("the spiritual seed") which derives from a feminine power, Wisdom. In this Gnostic myth, the role of Mary, the mother of God who gives a physical body to her son, is inverted and replaced by that of Wisdom, who gives Jesus His spiritual essence.

Because the Gnostic Jesus does not have a physical body, He, according to the Valentinians, passed through His mother Mary as water through a pipe.[10] The French medieval historian Michel Roquebert has commented that this image is not dissimilar to that used by the equally heretical Cathars a thousand years later to explain their doctrine of *adombration*, "adumbration," as opposed to incarnation.[11]

According to this doctrine, Jesus was contained within the Virgin Mary, living in the shadow of her womb, as it were, without taking anything from her; Mary was, for the Cathars, in any case, an angel. It is a curious coincidence, therefore, that de Boron specifically says that Our Lord "adumbrated" himself inside the Virgin Mary when he came to earth.[12] The Cathar doctrine of adumbration is a form of Docetism, the belief, widespread among the early Gnostic Christians, that Jesus only *appeared* to have a mortal body and die on the Cross.[13]

To be clear, Roquebert does not believe that this use of the term "adumbration" necessarily means that de Boron himself was a Docetist: In fact, he states, everything else that Robert wrote gives the lie to the idea that he would have had in his mind the heretical sense of "adumbration." There is no doubting the reality of the Incarnation and the Passion for the poet who, before all others, made of the Grail the Vessel that received the blood of Christ.[14]

There nevertheless remain the references to Secret Words of Christ, which cannot be revealed apart from to those who are specially chosen; words which have been written down in the High Book of the Grail. Here the historian is unequivocal: This tradition of an esoteric teaching of Christ, he writes, is certainly of Gnostic origin, is found again in the apocrypha and was known to the Church Fathers. In this respect, the Grail romances are shown to be more "gnostic" than Catharism,[15] which, he argues, had no secret teachings, only the prudence dictated by persecution.[16]

By contrast, as in the Grail legends, the earthly Jesus "is the revealer and proclaimer of gnostic wisdom, usually in the form of secret traditions which he imparts to his elect, often through the mediation of privileged disciples ... or in response to their questions.[17] Several documents ... affirm that the heavenly Christ appeared to one of the disciples in a vision and imparted to him the content of the document in question."[18]

This in fact is precisely how the story of the Grail is made known, according to the Vulgate *Estoire del Saint Graal*, to the hermit Nascien, who is struggling with doubts about the doctrine of the Trinity. Christ, in the form of a man of indescribable beauty, appears to him amid unearthly light and gives him a Book which will set straight all his doubts: Inside are His secrets, which He put there with His own hand, He says, secrets which cannot be spoken by any mortal tongue.[19]

Having made a Latin copy of the Book, the hermit tells the history of the Grail, beginning with the story of Joseph of Arimathea. This version corresponds very closely to that of Robert de Boron at first, but with some retrospective corrections; we are led to infer that the hermit's copy must be the original of the High Book which de Boron later possesses.

Notes

1. Robert de Boron here addresses the reader or listener directly: *Lors aprent Jhesucris tes paroles a Joseph que je ne vous os dire ne retraire—ne ne poroie, si je le voloie faire, se je n'avoie le haut livre u eles sont escrites* (RG 30–1); *Ge n'ose conter ne retreire,/Ne je ne le pourroie feire,/ Neis si je feire le voloie,/ Si je le grant livre n'avoie// La sunt li grant secré escrit/ Qu'en numme le Graal et dit* (EG ll.929-32, 935-6). An angel later reminds Joseph of the holy words which Christ spoke to him in prison: precious words of consolation, full of grace and compassion, which are rightly called the secrets of the Grail: *Les seintes paroles dist t'a,/ Ki sunt douces et precïeuses/ Et gracïeuses et piteuses,/ Ki sunt proprement apelees/ Secrez dou Graal et nummees* (EG ll.3332-6).
2. *MG* 22.
3. *...la parole Jhesu Crist/ Qu'en la chartre li avoit dist./ Cele parole sanz faleur/ Aprist au Riche Pescheeur./ Et quant ces choses li eut dites,/ Si li bailla aprés escrites./ Il li ha feit demoustrement/ Des secrez tout priveement* (EG ll.3413-20); *les paroles que Jhesucris li aprist en le cartre, et iceles paroles aprist il au Rice Pesceor en tel maniere qu'il les avoit escrites* (RG 70).
4. *...les secrées paroles de nostre Segnor* (RG 194).
5. *MG* 113.
6. *Nostre Sire te mande que iceles sacrées paroles que il aprist a Joseph en le prison quant il te bailla le Graal, apren a cestui et met en garde de par nostre Segnor* (RG 270).
7. *Et Bron ... li aprist les sacrées paroles que Joseph li avoit aprises, que je ne vous puis dire ne ne doi* (RG 270; *MG* 155).
8. *MG* 4-7.
9. Jung & Franz, 339: In contemporary Grail legend it is Mary Magdalen, the bearer of the child of Jesus, who becomes the Holy Vessel.
10. *GS* 295.
11. Roquebert, 116-7.
12. In the verse *Estoire dou Graal*, de Boron says that it pleased Our Lord to "adumbrate": *Dedenz la Virge s'aümbra* (EG l.31); and, in the prose version, *que il s'aombrast en la virgne Marie* (RG 17; Roquebert, 113-4). Nigel Bryant's translation of the prose version from the Modena manuscript simply reads: "And our Lord came, choosing to come to Earth incarnate of the Virgin Mary" (*MG*, 15).
13. Thus, for the Valentinians, Christ was enveloped in an "animate" (as opposed to physical) body, which "was constructed in some ineffable way so as to be visible, touchable, and capable of experiencing passion" (*GS* 293).
14. *En fait, tout le reste de l'œuvre de Robert dément qu'il ait pu avoir présente à l'esprit une adombration au sens hérétique.... La réalité de l'Incarnation et de la Passion ne fait aucun doute pour le poète qui, le premier, fait du Graal le vase qui reçut le sang du Christ* (Roquebert, 117). Equally, Jung and Franz conclude that insofar as heterodox ideas "arose within him," it was in spite of his conscious intentions (346).
15. *Cette tradition d'un enseignement ésotérique du Christ ... est certainement d'origine gnostique, se retrouve dans les apocryphes, et était connue des Pères de l'Église. Sur ce point, les romans du Graal se révèlent plus "gnostiques" que le catharisme* (Roquebert, 111n17).
16. Roquebert, 113.
17. Thus the Gospel of Thomas begins: "These are the secret sayings which the living Jesus spoke" (*NHL* 126). This secrecy also applies to the Gnostic teachers who came after Jesus. Bentley Layton, who prefers to talk of "obscure" or "hidden" sayings of Jesus (*GS* 380), points out that, in expounding their esoteric philosophy, "Valentinian writers claimed to speak *on the authority* of a secretly transmitted academic tradition, whose origin they traced back to St. Paul" (273-4). Irenaeus tells us, with regard to the followers of Basilides: "One is wholly forbidden to reveal their mysteries; rather, one must keep them secret in silence" (425).
18. Rudolph, 151: According to Robert de Boron a light appears to the Company of the Grail, bringing with it a letter. The Holy Spirit tells Joseph to give it to his relative Peter, who will bear it to the Vales of Avalon and there await the third Grail Keeper, Perceval, who will read the letter to him and explain the power of the Grail (*MG* 41). This letter is the equivalent of a lost Gnostic Gospel; unfortunately, de Boron never reveals its contents to us.

19. *...si i sont mi secré ke je meïsmes escris de ma main ... il n'i puent estre noumé par nule langue mortel* (ESG 4; LG I, 4). Later we are told that "all the adventures of the Grail will not be known by any mortal man. Many must be left in silence" (76).

SELAPHAS

A demon worshipped as a god by the pagans of the Middle Eastern city of Orcaut, Selaphas appears in human form to Tholomer the Fugitive, the Egyptian king who has been imprisoned by the newly-baptized King of Sarras. Selaphas warns Tholomer that his captors intend to have him dragged through the streets by horses before hanging him; but that, if he swears to serve the Devil all the days of his life, Selaphas will release him from prison. Tholomer readily agrees, whereupon the demon transforms himself into a griffin and flies the king out of the prison; only to drop him from a great height, so that Tholomer breaks his neck.

When Josephus arrives in Orcaut on an evangelizing mission, he goes to the temple of the gods. Holding his belt before the main altar, making the sign of the Cross and pronouncing the words of exorcism, he binds Selaphas and drags him through the streets of Orcaut, exposing the reality of a demon which was charged with spreading fear. As the people flock to be baptized in the new faith, Josephus lets Selaphas go, on condition that he causes no harm to the Christian faithful.

But even as Josephus continues to baptize people, there are some diehard pagans who would prefer to leave the city rather than convert. But, as they pass through the main gate, they are struck dead by Selaphas, bearing a bloody sword. When Josephus attempts to remonstrate with the demon, he is himself wounded in the leg by the Angel of the Avenging Lance and will, as a result, walk with a limp till the end of his days.[1]

Note

1. *LG* I, 48–9.

SERAPH

The pagan Duke of Orberica, Seraph's land borders on the Middle-Eastern realm of Sarras and his sister Sarrasinte is its queen. He is converted to Christianity by Joseph of Arimathea, who brings the dish containing the Holy Blood from Jerusalem to Sarras in an ark. When Seraph is baptized, a great light descends upon him, his clothes appear to be on fire and a flaming brand enters his mouth.

Seraph takes the baptismal name of Nascien[1]; and this is the name by which he is known when he comes to Britain. It is on his way there that he learns he will have nine descendants, all of whom will be kings[2]: the last being Galahad, who will become King of Sarras.

Notes

1. *LG* I, 47.
2. *LG* I, 116–8.

SILIMAC

The Lord of the Castle of the Rock,[1] Silimac's destiny is to become mysteriously entwined with that of Gawain. It all starts innocently enough, when Gawain is watching Queen Guenevere playing backgammon while encamped at a crossroads. As darkness is falling, an armed knight rides past them on a warhorse without saying a word to anyone.

Feeling insulted by this, the queen sends Kay the Seneschal to bring him back. Confronted by Sir Kay, the knight apologizes for his unintentional insult but explains that he can't turn back because he has a most urgent task and still has a long way to ride. When Kay tries to force the knight to return by force, he is unseated in combat and loses his horse. The queen then asks Gawain to try; he takes a wand of peace to try to achieve a better result by negotiation.

The knight (who does not reveal his identity, but who we later learn is called

Silimac) explains to Gawain that he can't give up the journey he has undertaken for anyone. No-one apart from him can complete the task, unless it is Gawain himself, Silimac says, although even Gawain would have the utmost difficulty. He is willing to return to the queen for Gawain's sake, but it would mean abandoning his mission unless Gawain is willing to take it up on his behalf. Gawain swears to do so and they set off for the queen's pavilion but, just as they approach it, the knight is struck through the body by a javelin, hurled by an invisible hand.

The dying knight beseeches Gawain to keep his promise: He is to bear Silimac's arms and let Silimac's horse lead him, to accomplish the great mission which Silimac himself was supposed to have carried out. Laying the knight's body in the queen's pavilion, Gawain takes the dead man's arms, including the sword that he bore, even though it is broken.[2] He then mounts Silimac's horse, telling the queen that he is bound to fulfill the mission in order to keep his promise. He will do this even if it leads him to his death and even though he doesn't know what the mission is, or to what land he will be taken.

Led by Silimac's horse, Gawain rides for two days until, at nightfall, he reaches the seashore; he travels along the coast until he reaches a narrow causeway, at the end of which he sees a glowing light. The sea is so rough that Gawain wants to wait until daylight to investigate, but the horse starts leaping about and rearing up and cannot be calmed. Taking the bit between its teeth, it wrenches the reins from Gawain's hands and leaps forward onto the causeway.

Gawain now gives the horse free rein to go where it wants and spurs it on, but it is past midnight when they come to a great hall full of people who receive him with great honor. They tell him his coming is blest, for they have been yearning for it; but, when they disarm him (taking the hilt, the remnant of Silimac's broken sword, in the process) and see his face more clearly, they realize that he isn't the one!

The crowd vanish away and Gawain is left alone, feeling alarmed and dismayed, having heard the crowd whispering to themselves. In the middle of the hall, he sees an immensely long bier, on which lies a dead man covered in a samite cloth, the upper half of a broken sword lying on his breast. After a vigil for the dead is performed and the people have expressed their grief for the dead man, the Fisher King enters, carrying what is left of Silimac's sword. He begins to weep bitterly over the body that lies on the bier and asks God to avenge the ruin brought upon the kingdom by the sword. He places Silimac's half against the other half on the dead knight's breast; it is a perfect match.

The king then asks Gawain to attempt to join the two pieces, assuring him that, if they fuse together, it will mean that he is the finest knight in the world. The king is upset when Gawain fails to do so, but suggests that he might be successful in the future: The mission of vengeance, which had been begun by someone whose arrival they have been awaiting for a long time, can only be achieved by the one who can repair Silimac's broken sword.[3]

But Gawain falls asleep before he can learn more; in the morning he finds himself in a marsh.[4]

The Golden-Haired Maiden

Back at King Arthur's court in Caerleon, Gawain recounts his mysterious adventures after disarming. But he is dismayed to see an unknown knight enter his uncle's hall and take the arms and horse which had been Silimac's. Having left Silimac's sword in the hall at the end of the causeway, he now had nothing left of the knight who died under his protection.[5]

It is sometime later that Silimac's sister arrives at King Arthur's court, where she finds Gawain greatly distressed about the death of the knight whose identity he is determined to discover. He is also upset about the fact that he failed to learn the truth about either the knight's broken sword or the dead man on the bier. Silimac's sister upbraids him for falling asleep at the castle and enjoins him to complete the mission he began on her brother's behalf.[6]

Obeying her injunction to take up Silimac's arms[7] once more, Gawain sets off with the girl to her castle, where she is being besieged by Margon, the King with the Hundred Knights, who wanted to force her to marry his son. Silimac would have championed his sister, if he had not been treacherously killed; she accordingly asks Gawain to take up this mission on Silimac's behalf, as he had agreed to do.

Gawain defeats Margon in single combat and then agrees to avenge the girl's brother, whose death, she convinces him (through her command of astral magic), was at the hands of Kay.[8] She gives Gawain a red silk scarf to dip in Kay's blood and he sets off for Carduel.[9]

On the way, Gawain is falsely accused of being responsible for Silimac's death. He defeats his accuser in battle, but is prevented from killing him by the arrival of Silimac's sister, who now reveals that she is called the Golden-haired Maiden.[10]

Arriving at Arthur's court in disguise, Gawain demands that Kay surrender to the girl, or die. In the ensuing combat Gawain vanquishes Kay, who nevertheless does not admit his guilt and refuses to surrender. Gawain would have been obliged to kill him were it not for the intervention of Silimac's sister who, acceding to the pleas of the king, queen and knights, acquits Kay.[11]

Gawain has avenged the death of Silimac. But Silimac's original mission was to demonstrate that he was worthy to act as an instrument of God's vengeance by re-soldering the broken sword, half of which he was carrying. This will eventually be achieved by Perceval, who discovers that the dead knight on the bier is his uncle,[12] killed by a blow of the sword, the broken pieces of which both Silimac and Gawain had failed, for different reasons, to mend. It is Perceval who will kill the man who struck that blow[13] and thus fulfill the aborted mission of Silimac.

Notes

1. *CSG* 508: This castle is also the one where Eliezer finds the sword which wounded Joseph of Arimathea: see THE BLEEDING SWORD.
2. See THE SWORD OF PARTINAL.
3. *CSG* 211-7.
4. *CSG* 219: The king considers that Silimac chose Gawain to be his messenger and complete his mission because he recognized him as the foremost Arthurian knight.
5. *CSG* 224.
6. *CSG* 496-7: She blames certain unspecified sins with which Gawain is stained for preventing him from finding out who lay dead on the bier and how he died, thus breaking his pledge to Silimac. Similarly, Perceval's sins are often blamed for preventing him from asking the Grail Question.
7. *MTC* l.35257: Although it is not spelt out, we must assume that the unknown knight who took Silimac's arms and horse from Arthur's court was acting on behalf of Silimac's sister.
8. *CSG* 502: She identifies Sir Kay as her brother's killer *par astrenomie* (*MTC* ll.35880-1), which Gawain considers to be magic (*par art*: l.36586). This access to preternatural knowledge may help to identify Silimac's sister with one of the nieces of the Fisher King, whom he describes as *bien aparceüe* (l.32899); which Marie-Noëlle Toury translates as *clairvoyante* and Nigel Bryant as "all-seeing" (*CSG* 479).
9. *CSG* 504.
10. *CSG* 506-8: This *Sore Pucelle* (*MTC* l.36562) may be the same charming and beautiful golden-haired girl—*la Sore Pucelle/ Qui molt est avenanz et belle* (*CP* II, ll.5469-70)—who has earlier appeared at one of King Arthur's Pentecostal courts at Escavalon. Moreover, they may both be identical to the *sore pucele* who is the Fisher King's niece (*RP* ll.3145-6); although there Bryant translates her name as the "fair-haired girl" (*CSG* 28). If this niece is also the one who brings to her uncle the shards of the sword with which the Fisher King's brother, Gon of the Land Laid Waste, was killed by Partinal (479), then the backstory becomes clearer: Her father is murdered; her brother Silimac sets out to avenge him, carrying one half of the Sword of Partinal; Silimac is heading for the court of his uncle the Fisher King, where he hopes to prove his worthiness to avenge his father by joining the two halves of the sword back together; but he is murdered in his turn and Gawain, who takes up his mission, proves unworthy.
11. *CSG* 509-10.
12. *CSG* 551: For Chrétien, the Fisher King (and

therefore by implication his brother Gon also) is Perceval's cousin rather than his uncle.

13. *CSG* 549.

SIMEON

The nephew of Joseph of Arimathea, Simeon is one of the earliest Companions of the Grail, who bring the Holy Vessel out of Jerusalem; but he proves unworthy of that august company. When he and his brother Canaan are deprived of the grace of the Grail because of their sinfulness, Simeon incites Canaan to kill their more worthy brothers and their cousin Peter (the latter, nevertheless, surviving and escaping to Britain, where he converts the king to Christianity). For his role in the crime, Simeon is condemned by the Company. But what is worse, demons carry him off to a cemetery in the Land Beyond, where his body is condemned to burn until the Good Knight can free him from his torment.[1]

Hundreds of years later, Lancelot arrives at the Tomb of the Black Chamber and reads letters on it stating that whoever can raise the lid will dispel the enchantments of the Adventurous Kingdom and bring to an end the adventures of Logres; he is the one who will sit in the Perilous Seat at the Round Table and achieve the high Quest of the Holy Grail.[2] Lancelot tries but fails to raise the lid of Simeon's tomb,[3] thus proving that he is not the long-awaited Good Knight who will end both Simeon's suffering and the marvels which beset the kingdom.

Simeon is eventually saved from hellfire, after burning for three hundred and fifty-four years, by Lancelot's son Galahad.[4]

Notes

1. *LG* I, 146-7: Just as the Biblical Simeon will not die until he beholds Jesus, so this Simeon will not die until he beholds Galahad, his savior.
2. ...*letres qui disoient que cil qui la leveroit abatroit les enchantemens del Roialme Aventureus et metroit fin as aventures et acompliroit le siege de la Table Reonde* (*LM* II, 32); *achievera le Siege Perillous de la Table reonde et metera a fin la haute queste del saint Graal* (*LDG* II, 1351).
3. *LG* III, 12-14.
4. *LG* IV, 83; V, 243-4; *QHG* 270-1: Galahad is told that it is *a mervalous aventure that may nat be brought to an ende but by hym that passith of bounté and of knyghthode all them of the Rounde Table* (*MD* 780). In the Post-Vulgate version, Simeon tells Galahad where he will find his son Moses, who was similarly carried off by demons when he attempted to sit in the Feared Seat at the Table of the Grail.

SOLOMON

Solomon, the son of King David who rules Israel after him, knows all about precious stones, virtuous herbs and the movements of the stars, but he is powerless against the wiles of his wife. But while he is pondering the enigma of woman, the Holy Spirit reveals to him that a woman of his line will redeem the faults of all others; while the last man of his lineage will surpass all others.[1]

Solomon determines that his distant descendant should somehow know that he had foreknowledge of him. But it is his wife, an exceedingly cunning woman,[2] who suggests the means to do so: He must build a ship equipped with a magnificent bed and, at the head of it, set three posts made, one from the red wood of the Tree of Life, the others from the green and white wood of trees made from its saplings. On the bed, Solomon places his crown and his father's sword, fitted with a new hilt and pommel of precious stones.[3] But his wife insists on putting a cheap hempen belt on it, saying that a maiden will one day equip it with one more fitting such a glorious sword[4]; adding that he will soon have further news about the ship.[5]

That night King Solomon dreams that a man borne by angels writes inscriptions on the sword, on its scabbard and on the side of the ship itself—warnings to the unworthy to neither set foot in it, nor attempt to unsheathe the sword. The next morning, the ship leaves shore and Solomon hears a voice saying that it will be found by the last man in his line, who will learn from it about his ancestor. The king tells everyone how it was his wife who solved the problem for him.[6]

Notes

1. The woman of his line (*lignage*) is the Blessed Virgin Mary, although it is rather her husband Joseph who is described in the New Testament as a descendant of Solomon (Matt I.6–16); while the last man of that line is Galahad, who is descended from Solomon through his paternal grandmother Elaine of Benoic.
2. Not all Solomon's fabled wisdom can protect him against *l'engin de sa fame* (QP 220): *So thys Salamon was wyse, and knew all the vertues of stonys and treys; also he knew the course of the stirres, and of many other dyvers thynges. So this Salamon had an evyl wyff* (MD 757); but out of evil will come good.
3. See THE SWORD OF DAVID.
4. See THE SWORD WITH THE STRANGE STRAPS.
5. Philippe Walter (2014, 332-3) considers that the preternatural knowledge displayed by Solomon's wife reveals that she is the Queen of Sheba.
6. *LG* I, 82-5; IV, 69-71; *QHG* 230-5.

The SWORD IN THE FLOATING STONE

At the time when Arthur is at war against the giant King Rion, a maiden is sent by the Lady of the Isle of Avalon to the court at Camelot. She bears a sword that causes her much grief and from which she would be delivered, but it can only be drawn out of its sheath by the best knight of Logres, one who is free from treachery.

To set an example to his barons, rather than because he presumes that he is the best knight there, the king himself is the first to attempt it, but the sword will not budge for all his efforts. Most of the Knights of the Round Table who are at the court at that time attempt to draw it out, but none are successful. Just as the maiden is about to leave, however, a poor knight who has only just been released from prison enters the court and, overcoming the doubts of the maiden, is also allowed to try; he unsheathes it easily.

The poor knight, Balin, admires the sword greatly and consequently, when the maiden asks him to return the sword to her, he refuses, despite the maiden's warning that the first man he kills with it, will be the one he loves most in the world; she adds that he himself will be killed by that very same sword. In the event, the first *person* he kills with it will be a woman, the Lady of the Lake of Fays, who arrives in court demanding from Arthur either the head of Balin or that of the maiden who brought the sword. Balin's response is short and sharp: he beheads the Lady with one stroke.[1]

Merlin later explains that the sword was enchanted by the Lady of the Isle of Avalon, at the request of the maiden, who wished to be avenged on her brother.[2]

Balin, who is now known as the Knight with Two Swords, does not in fact wield the Sword of the Maid of Avalon in combat, until after he has struck the Dolorous Blow which destroys three countries. Later he comes into conflict with an unknown Red Knight who is defending the custom of a castle on an island. They are both thrown off their horses in the first joust and then the Red Knight draws his sword and advances on foot. Balin now takes the Ill-fated Sword[3] and dazes the Red Knight with his first stroke. The battle continues until they are both so injured that they are forced to rest. It is only at this point, when the Red Knight reveals that his name is Balan, that the two opponents realize that they are brothers and that they have slain each other with the same sword.[4]

They are buried, at their request, in the same tomb on the island. Merlin comes there and performs many wonders on what will later be known as Merlin's Island or the Island of Marvels.[5] He leaves Balin's scabbard on the shore (where it will later be found by Galahad), but he fixes Balin's sword into an upright marble stone which he floats on the water.

For many years it remains afloat, until at last it moves downstream to Camelot on the very day that Galahad arrives there,[6] bearing the scabbard by his side,[7] but without a sword. On that day, the feast of Pentecost, King Arthur and his knights have already experienced two marvels. Firstly, an inscription has appeared on the Perilous Seat at the Round Table, saying that its mystery is about to be fulfilled. They are about to eat when Kay the Seneschal reminds the king that it is his custom not to sit at table until he has seen some adventure.

At that moment a squire comes into the hall, announcing marvelous tidings: He has seen a great stone floating in the river that runs beneath the castle; in the stone a sword is stuck. The king and his knights set off at once to see this second marvel. At the river, they read on the pommel of the sword an inscription, stating that only the world's best knight will be able to draw it out.[8]

The king suggests that Lancelot should take the sword, but the knight of Benoic declines the honor and further prophesies that whosoever tries and fails to draw the sword will be grievously wounded by it. He adds that this is the day that the adventures of the Holy Grail begin. Nevertheless, Gawain tries, at the command of the king; Lancelot warns him that he will live to regret doing so.[9]

Perceval is also unsuccessful. It is at this moment that Galahad arrives, without a sword but bearing the scabbard. The king shows him the marvelous Sword in the Floating Stone, which so many great knights have tried but failed to draw out. Galahad says he should not be surprised at that, for it is his adventure, not theirs; because he knew that he would gain the sword, he did not bring one with him.

Laying his hand on the sword, he easily draws it out of the stone and places it in its scabbard. He recognizes it as the sword with which Balin slew his own brother, a tragedy which came about because of the Dolorous Blow[10] by which Balin maimed Galahad's great-grandfather, King Pellehan.[11] Now that he has both Balin's sword and scabbard, Galahad lacks only a shield to be fully equipped as a knight; this God will soon send him, says Arthur, as He did the sword.[12]

Galahad bears the sword throughout his early adventures in search of the Grail. At a tournament he fights Gawain and deals him a serious injury with the sword, leading the injured knight to exclaim that he has now received, from the sword which he tried to draw from the Floating Stone, a blow which he would give a castle not to have received. All is as predicted: Lancelot's words at Pentecost have proved true.[13]

Galahad only relinquishes Balin's sword when Perceval's sister takes it from him in order the gird on him the Sword with the Strange Straps on the Ship of Solomon. Balin's sword he would have left at a hermitage, but Perceval takes it up and swears to carry it always.[14]

Notes

1. He draws the sword, leaps towards the Lake Maiden (who is trying to beat a hasty retreat) and strikes her so hard that her head goes flying to the floor: *Lors traist l'espee du fuerre.... Lors fait un saut tresqu'a la damoisiele et la fiert de l'espee si durement qu'il li fait la teste voler a terre* (*SRM* 72). Although it is not specified which of the two swords which he now carries is the one that he draws from its scabbard, given the enmity that we are told exists between the Lady of the Lake on one hand, and Balin and the maiden who brought the sword to court on the other, it seems fitting that it would be the sword of the Lady of the Isle of Avalon which was used. Malory simply says that Balin smote off the Lake Lady's head *with hys swerde* (*MD* 51), thus retaining the ambiguity of his source.

2. *LG* IV, 185–8: *MD* 46–53: We are left to conclude that, because he would not return the sword that was meant to kill the maiden's brother, Balin is fated to kill his own brother Balan (this being the man he loves most in the world) with it.

3. Malory, whose French source, bizarrely, does not specify which of his two swords Balin is using, calls it *that unhappy swerd*, and says that he nearly kills Balan with the first blow (*MD* 72).

4. It is only in the Spanish version of this tale that it is specified that the brothers accidentally exchange swords, so that the Ill-Fated Sword of the Maid of Avalon ends up killing both of them, as she prophesied (*SRM* 648–9).

5. *LG* IV, 219–22.

6. *Also the scawberd off Balyns swerde Merlion lefte hit on thys syde the ilonde, that Galaad sholde fynde hit. Also Merlion lette make by hys suttelyté that Balynes swerde was put into a marbil stone stondynge upryght, as grete as a mylstone, and the stone hoved allwayes above the watir, and dud many yeres. And so by adventure hit swamme downe by the streme unto the cité of Camelot, that ys in Englysh called Wynchester, and that same day Galahad*

the Haute Prynce com within Kynge Arthure, and so Galaad brought with hym the scawberde and encheved the swerde that was in the marble stone hovynge uppon the watir. And on Whytsonday he enchevyd the swerde, as hit ys rehersed in the Booke of the Sankgreall (MD 74).

Malory is here conflating two different swords that he finds in his source, the Post-Vulgate *Merlin Continuation*: Balin's Ill-Fated Sword, with which Lancelot will kill both Gareth and, later, Gareth's brother Gawain, the knight Lancelot has loved most in the world; and another sword, which Merlin fixes by magic in a block of marble. Merlin makes it look as if it would be easy to draw it out, but in fact it can only be lifted by the Best Knight in the world (Galahad); it is destined to injure the first person who tries to lift it (Gawain). Merlin places enchantments on the stone so that it floats through many countries until it comes to Camelot on the first day that Galahad arrives at court (*SRM* 195–6).

7. *…a scawberd hangynge by hys syde* (MD 669) which, presumably, he found where Merlin left it. According to the Post-Vulgate version, the scabbard is floating in the air above the stone (*PV* II, 21).

8. *And whan they cam unto the ryver they founde there a stone fletynge, as hit were of rede marbyll, and therein stake a fayre ryche swerde, and the pommel thereof was of precious stonys wrought with lettirs of golde subtylé. Than the barownes redde the lettirs, whych seyde in thys wyse: "Never shall man take me hense but only he by whos syde I ought to honge, and he shall be the best knyght of the worlde"* (MD 668).

9. *…thys swerde shall touch you so sore that ye wolde nat ye had sette youre honde thereto for the beste castell of thys realme* (MD 669).

10. As Balin approached the castle where he and his brother would fight to the death, Merlin sent him a message that his imminent ill fortune was God's vengeance for what Balin did in the hall of King Pellehan: *ceste mesqueance vous envoie Diex pour le fait que vous fesistes chiés le roi Pellehan en lieu de venganche* (*SRM* 183).

11. In Malory's version, the king says to Sir Galahad, *here ys a grete mervayle as ever y sawe, and ryght good knyghtes have assayde and fayled.* To which Galahad replies, *hit is no mervayle, for thys adventure ys nat theyrs but myne. And for the sureté of thys swerde I brought none with me, but here by my syde hangith the scawberte.* Drawing the sword from the Floating Stone, Galahad continues: *Now have I the swerde that somtyme was the good knyghtes Balyns le Saveaige … and with thys swerde he slew hys brother Balan…. And eythir slew othir thorow a dolerous stroke that Balyn gaff unto my grauntefadir Kynge Pelleans, the whych ys nat yett hole, nor naught shall be tyll that I hele hym* (MD 671).

Apart from his momentary confusion of Galahad's *grauntesyre*, Kynge Pelles, with the Maimed King Pellehan—*my lorde Kynge Pecchere*, as he has earlier called him (670)—Malory has here skillfully interwoven two sources: the Vulgate *Queste* (which gives him the account of Galahad's arrival at Camelot) and the Post-Vulgate *Merlin Continuation* (which gives him the Tale of Balin, a prequel to the Grail Quest).

12. *LG* IV, 4–6; V, 115–6, 118; *QHG* 34–6, 40–1.

13. *LG* IV, 62–3; V, 189; *QHG* 208: *now ar the wondirs trew that was seyd of Sir Launcelot, that the swerde which stake in the stone shulde gyff me such a buffette that I wold nat have hit for the beste castell in the worlde. And sothely now hit ys preved trew, for never ar had I such a stroke of mannys honde* (MD 750).

14. *LG* IV, 74; V, 236; *QHG* 245.

The SWORD OF DAVID

After his death, the sword of the Biblical King David is sent around the world in a ship by order of his son Solomon, who also has the blade recast with a pommel made from a multicolored stone, adding a hilt made from the ribs of a serpent and a fish with miraculous powers.[1]

King Solomon's wife has a belt made for it using poor hempen cord. But an inscription on the scabbard warns that it can only be replaced by a virginal princess, using the thing on her person that she values most.[2] This same maiden will give both the sword and the scabbard their rightful names. A further warning is inscribed on the blade, to the effect that if anyone apart from the greatest knight in the world should attempt to draw it from its scabbard, the foolhardy one would suffer injury or death; that he who most prizes it will find it blameworthy at a time of need; and that it will be most cruel to him to whom it should be most gracious.[3]

And so it comes to pass, when first Duke Nascien, then King Varlan and finally King Parlan, come across the ship at different times and make the mistake of unsheathing it: Nascien is only wounded,[4] but Varlan uses it to kill his neighbor Lambor (whose death turns the Grail Kingdom into a wasteland), only to drop dead as a punishment for his transgression. This is the first blow ever struck by the sword in Britain.[5]

Later Parlan, the most pious of Christians, partially unsheathes the sword and is in turn punished for his presumption by being maimed by a flying lance. He is thus being treated cruelly by the sword, when it should have been kind to one who furthered the faith by honoring the poor.[6]

It is Perceval's sister who will give up her hair, the thing she values most, to make a belt for the sword, which she now names the Sword with the Strange Straps; she names the scabbard, Memory of Blood.[7]

Notes

1. *LG* I, 77; IV, 64; *QHG* 214: The serpent protects the bearer from heat: an allegorical reference, perhaps, to the fires of Hell. The fish prevents one from being distracted from one's purpose by the memory of sorrow and joy: a single-mindedness that might appeal to religious fundamentalists.
2. *LG* I, 83–5; V, 232.
3. *LG* I, 77–8.
4. *LG* I, 96–7: He draws the sword to defend himself against a monstrous giant, but it breaks in two and must be repaired by King Mordrain. Nascien is then wounded by a flaming sword for having drawn the Sword of David (the thing he most values after the Grail) illicitly.
5. *LG* I, 159–60: *Thus was the swerde preved that never man drew hit but he were dede or maimed* (*MD* 754).
6. *LG* IV, 65–6; *MD* 752–6; *QHG* 215–21: On his second visit to the Grail Castle, Bors is told that it was the sword itself which struck the Fisher King through the thighs, because of "the misdeed he committed when he drew from its scabbard the sword which was not to be drawn except by him who was to accomplish the adventures of the Holy Grail. But because he drew it despite the interdiction placed upon it ... he was maimed, and will never be healed until the Good Knight comes and anoints his wounds with the blood of the lance" (*LG* III, 272). This would constitute the second blow struck by the sword in Britain.
7. *LG* IV, 71–2; *MD* 760–1; *QHG* 236–7.

The SWORD OF PARTINAL

One of the most mysterious adventures to befall Gawain begins when Silimac of the Rock, a knight who is under Gawain's protection, is treacherously slain by an unknown hand outside the queen's pavilion. It will be years before Gawain can avenge the murder; while the quest that Silimac has undertaken will be completed, not by Gawain, but by Perceval.

An Astounding Story

Silimac is on an urgent mission and, when he realizes that he is dying, asks Gawain to complete his quest, although he doesn't explain what it is. Gawain takes Silimac's sword (which is broken below the hilt) and his horse, which is able to lead Gawain to the White Island in order to complete the mission. The hall of the Fisher King is found at the end of a narrow causeway on the sea. Gawain arrives after midnight and is helped to dismount, while the broken half of the sword is taken away. A crowd has gathered to greet Silimac, but they quickly disappear when they realize that his horse bears Gawain instead.

In the hall, Gawain sees a bier on which lies a dead man and, across his breast, the pointed half of the sword. After he has watched the Grail Procession, Gawain is joined by the king, who is holding the hilt of the sword in its sheath and who says that it and the death it has caused have brought about the ruin of his kingdom.[1]

The king takes the two halves of the sword and asks Gawain to join them together, but he is unable to do so.[2] Filled with grief, the king places the point of the sword back on the dead man's breast and replaces the hilt in its sheath. He explains that they had been waiting a long time for the knight, whose horse Gawain is riding, to arrive and to achieve his mission, which can only be accomplished by whoever can repair the shattered sword.

Gawain then asks the king why the Lance bleeds, who the dead man on the bier is, how his death is to be avenged and how the sword can be repaired. The king explains that the Lance is the one with which Longinus struck Jesus on the Cross. The blood that flowed from His side is our ransom; this is the joyous blow. By contrast, the blow struck by the sword has robbed us of all the joy that the blow of the Lance brought. This is the worst blow ever struck by a sword: It has ruined the Kingdom of Logres.[3] The king will now explain to him the astounding story of who it is who has lost his life, and who it was who struck him.

However, just as he is about to explain, amid his tears, the whole truth of the matter, the king notices that Gawain has fallen asleep. When he awakens, Gawain finds himself on a towering cliff beside the sea; the castle has vanished.[4]

The Lord of the Red Tower

In the event, it is Perceval, rather than Gawain, who is destined to avenge the blow that ruined Logres; it is Perceval who will discover who it was who lost his life and who killed him.

Perceval first attempts to repair the sword when (several years after his first, unsuccessful visit and after many adventures) he returns to the Grail Castle. He once more witnesses the Grail Procession; but, this time, unlike on his first visit, it includes a boy carrying a naked sword broken in half. Perceval asks the king to explain to him about the Grail and the Lance, as well as whether the sword will ever be repaired and become battle-worthy. The king replies that a chivalric man who loves God and Holy Church could make the sword whole again.

Perceval accordingly takes the pieces of the sword and joins them together, but there remains a small notch by the join. The king says this indicates that, although none can surpass him in combat, Perceval has not yet demonstrated that he is the man most endowed with all the high qualities of chivalry.

The boy who was carrying the sword in the procession now wraps it in a silken cloth and carries it away. The king says that if he can come back one day and repair the notch in future—and he is the only one who can—then Perceval will have earnt the right to learn the whole truth, even the secrets of the divine workings of the Grail Castle.[5]

These secrets are finally revealed when Perceval comes to the court of the Fisher King for the third time. He watches the Grail Procession, at the end of which he sees the notched sword carried by a boy who lays it on the king's table. The king asks Perceval to take hold of the sword and he does so, brandishing it four times. He has joined it so perfectly that the king is delighted and bestows everything he has on Perceval.

The boy who brought the sword wraps it in a silken cloth and carries it away, while the king explains to Perceval, as he had done to Gawain earlier, about the Holy Lance. He furthermore reveals that the Grail is the Vessel in which Joseph of Arimathea, who was of the Fisher King's family, caught the blood that flowed from the Lance wound in Jesus' side; while the silver trencher carried by a girl in the procession is used to cover the Grail so that the Holy Blood is not left exposed.

Perceval now wants to know how the sword he has twice attempted to repair was originally broken. The Fisher King exclaims that the sword, whose mending should bring him great joy, was responsible for delivering the mortal blow[6] which killed the dead knight on the bier. This was the cruelest blow that could ever strike the kingdom, which is still grieving.

The king goes on to explain that his brother, Gon of the Land Laid Waste, is the dead knight on the bier. In the course of a war with his enemy Espinogris,[7] Gon was treacherously killed by Espinogris' nephew Partinal the Wild, the Lord of the Red Tower. Partinal had taken the arms and weapon of one of Gon's dead knights; but the stolen sword that struck the fatal blow shattered in the killer's hands.[8] Partinal threw down the hilt (which was all that remained in his hand) and fled; Gon's men carried the shattered sword, along with the corpse of their lord, back to the castle.

Gon's daughter, who carries the silver trencher in the Grail Procession, brought the pieces to her uncle, assuring him that any knight who could repair the sword would be the one to avenge her father's death. But the Fisher King was so grief-stricken that he cut every nerve in his thighs with the broken shards, thus laming himself; he will only be healed when he is avenged on the treacherous wretch who killed his brother.[9]

This was originally the quest of Silimac, the son of Gon, but he also died treacherously before he could complete his mission. It is eventually achieved by Perceval, when he comes to the Red Tower and defeats Partinal in battle. When the traitor lord refuses to yield, Perceval beheads him[10] and carries the severed head to the Fisher King, who sets it on a stake atop the main tower of the Grail Castle. The king's wounds are now healed, his grief forgotten.[11]

Notes

1. The account in the First Continuation of the destruction of Logres caused by the blow of Silimac's sword may shed light on a curious passage in the *Estoire del Saint Graal*, in which Josephus prophesies that in the time of King Arthur there will occur such marvelous adventures, caused by the blow of a single sword, that they will provoke wonder among those who hear of them: *Et a celui tens avendra en ceste terre, par le coup d'une seule espee, aventures et si granz merveilles que maintes genz qui puis en orront parler le tendront a fantosme* (ESG 444).

2. According to the longer version of the First Continuation, Gawain has earlier failed to mend the sword of Trebuchet (see THE BROKEN SWORD). Moreover, according to the Vulgate *Lancelot*, Gawain will also fail to join together the two halves of the sword that wounded Joseph of Arimathea (see THE BLEEDING SWORD).

3. *Mais li autres nous ra tolu/ Tant que le tout avons perdu,/ Cil qui fu fais de ceste espee,/ Qui mal fu faite ne tempree./ C'ainc nus si mals cops ne fu fais/ De cop d'espee, ne si lais/ Li roialmes de Logres fu/ Destruis, et toute la contree,/ Par le cop que fist ceste espee* (CP I, ll.13493–8, 13506–8); *Li roiaumes de Logres fu/ Destruis, et tote la contree,/ Par seul le cop de ceste espee* (PCP ll.7476–8).

4. PSG 126–32; CSG 213–9.

5. CSG 336–9: *Et sachiez bien tot sanz doutance/ Que, se cha poez revenir,/ Assez tost porroit avenir/ Que l'osque porriez asalder,/ Et lors si porriez demander/ Et del Graal et de la Lance* (GCP ll.34–9).

6. *L'espee que soudee avez,/ Dont molt grant joie avoir devez,/ C'est celle dont li cox mortex/ Fu faiz* (MTC ll.32819–22).

7. Espinogris appears in the Prose *Tristan* and Malory as the son of the King of Northumberland, the wild country where Blaise retires to compose his Book of the Grail at Merlin's dictation.

8. Manessier calls it *la bone espee* (MTC l.32874) as if to suggest that the virtuous steel shattered in response to the treacherous act it was used to perform.

9. CSG 474–9: It is not clear why either the killing of Gon by the sword or the maiming of the Fisher King by its shards should bring about the destruction of Logres, which is ruled by King Arthur.

10. There would be a pleasing symmetry if Perceval killed Partinal with the same sword that Partinal used to kill Gon, but Manessier does not specify this. His translator Marie-Noëlle Toury (MTC 28) considers that he uses the sword made and repaired by the smith Triboet or Trebuchet (see THE BROKEN SWORD). This is equally fitting, insofar as it was sent to the Fisher King by his niece, Gon's daughter.

11. CSG 547–50.

The SWORD OF THE STRANGE BELT

After Perceval's failure to ask the Grail Question at the court of the Fisher King, an Ugly Maiden arrives at King Arthur's court at Caerleon. She condemns Perceval for his disastrous silence, but goes on to announce that if anyone wants to gain the prize above all the world, he should go to the castle of Montesclaire. Whoever can raise the siege there and free its mistress, would win great praise and prove himself to be worthy to gird on the Sword of the Strange Belt.[1] Gawain declares that he will do this,[2] but many other adventures intervene before he finds himself close to the goal of his quest.[3]

The castle is situated atop a precipice, the ascent to which is guarded by three brothers, who are besieging the Lady because she has refused them her love. After slaying two of the brothers, Gawain receives the submission of the third; whereupon the Lady agrees to show him the sword.

She leads the hero into a garden where the door to a vault, which has been closed for a hundred years, opens spontaneously at his approach. Descending a staircase which leads into the depths, he encounters the dazzling light of innumerable precious stones filling a chamber with golden walls and a ceiling of silver. Hanging on a golden pillar is the marvelous sword, surmounted by an inscription stating that the knight errant who has faith in his own prowess should take it unhindered.

Gawain is delighted when he is able to take the sword and hang it by his left side.[4] Returning to the garden, he is met by a celebrating crowd. The Lady tells him that the sword once belonged to Judas Maccabaeus, but had been brought to Britain by Joseph of Arimathea. It can only be worn by a knight who surpasses all others in honor, courtesy and chivalry; all who have attempted the adventure in the past have ended up in a bad way, both physically and mentally. The sword will, on the other hand, confer invincibility on whoever wields it in a just cause; but cowardice, on whoever handles it unworthily.

Gawain, of course, suffers no ill effects and continues his adventures.[5]

Notes

1. To avoid confusion, I am consistently referring to this remarkable sword by the name given to it by Nigel Bryant in his translation of the *Conte del Graal* and the Long Redaction of the First Continuation in *The Complete Story of the Grail*; in his earlier translation of Chrétien's *Perceval*, Bryant calls it the Sword with the Strange Straps (*PSG* 51), as does William W. Kibler (*SGP* 439). But I have reserved this name for the weapon found by Galahad on the Ship of Solomon; despite their similar names, the two swords have nothing in common apart from their unusual "hangings." What Chrétien de Troyes calls *l'Espee as Estranges Renges* (*RP* l.4712) is also translated by D.D.R. Owen as the Sword with the Strange Baldric (*CTO* 436).
2. *CSG* 41.
3. In his Continuation, Gerbert de Montreuil, who was evidently unfamiliar with Gawain's adventure, says that it is Perceval who comes to Montesclaire and frees its Lady.
4. In the Romance of Meraugis of Portlesguez, the hero hears about the marvelous sword—*L'Espeë as estranges renges,/ La merveille* (*MP* ll.1274-5)—and finds Gawain in search of it, avowing that his honor would be lost if he returned home without girding it on: *L'aventure que j'ai emprise/ De l'espee me covient querre./ Se ge retornoie en ma terre/ Sanz li, m'onor seroit estainte./ Ja mes n'irai ainz l'avrai ceinte,/ L'espee as renges des mervelles* (ll.3457-62).
5. *CSG* 110-115: The story is only found in one manuscript of the Long Redaction of the First Continuation to the Story of the Grail. It has been summarized by Jessie L. Weston, who points out that the name of the sword "is nowhere satisfactorily accounted for. I think we are in all probability dealing with the remains of an old story, the true form of which has not been preserved" (1906, 225). Gawain's winning of the sword is referred to somewhat laconically in the Romance of Meraugis of Portlesguez: *Il la trova e en la terre/ La ceint. Aprés quant ill ot ceintel/ L'espee e sa vertu ataintë,/ Si s'en retorna* (*MP* ll. 5023-7)—the *vertu* of the sword being that whoever uses it for good cannot be defeated.

The SWORD WITH THE STRANGE STRAPS

In the course of their Quest for the Holy Grail, Perceval is travelling with his sister and his fellow Knights of the Round Table, Bors and Galahad, when, in a hidden creek in a lonely islet in the sea far from Logres, they come across the Ship of Solomon, which has been traversing the seas for over two thousand years. On board the ship they find a bed and, on the bed, a sword.

This sword is truly remarkable: Its pommel is made from a stone combining all earthly colors. Its hilt is made from the ribs of two remarkable creatures: The first is a Caledonian serpent whose bones protects the holder from heat. The second is a Mesopotamian fish which takes away, from whoever holds its ribs, all memory of former joy or sorrow, thus enabling him to concentrate his will solely on the purpose in hand.[1] The hilt is covered with a red cloth on which are embroidered letters saying that only he who surpasses all others before or after will be able to grasp it. Perceval attempts to do so, but is unsuccessful; Bors, too, cannot grasp it; Galahad won't even try until he learns more.

The blade of the sword, they notice, is drawn out a hand's-breadth from the scabbard and on it, in letters as red as blood, is written a warning: Anyone who attempts to unsheathe it, unless he is the bravest and boldest, will suffer injury or death. The truth of this is affirmed by Perceval's sister, who tells them how the Welsh king Varlan, who had only recently converted from paganism to Christianity when the ship first arrived on the shores of Britain, used the sword to kill Lambor, the King of the Land Beyond. Thus was struck the Dolorous Blow, which turned the kingdoms of both men into a wasteland. Varlan himself dropped dead as soon as he put the sword back in its scabbard, thus confirming the warning on the wondrous weapon.

Inspecting now the scabbard, they conclude that it is made of red snakeskin; but the belt is made of cheap and flimsy hempen tow, quite unsuited to the splendor of the weapon. On the scabbard are letters in blue and gold stating that the belt can only be removed by a virgin princess, who will replace it with one fashioned by what is most precious to her; from then on, no harm will befall the man who is worthy to hang it by his side. It is this same maiden, the inscription continues, who will first name the sword and its sheath.

Turning the sword over, they find a further message stating that only once in its history will he who most prizes the sword find it worthy of reproach; furthermore, only once will it act cruelly towards the man to whom it should be most kind. Perceval's sister explains that both these prophecies have already been fulfilled.

The first occurred when, more than forty years after the Passion of Christ, the ship came to the Turning Isle, far out in the western sea. There it was found by Nascien, the Duke of Orberica, who had been converted to Christianity by the Company of the Grail and who had been transported far from his pagan enemies by a cloud of angels.

Embarking on the boat, Nascien saw the sword and longed to have it for himself. But he was not brave enough to draw it out of its sheath until, on the ninth day, the ship took him to the island of a giant, far to the east. As the giant attacked, Nascien drew the sword, which he prized above anything the Earth could offer; but, as he brandished it aloft, the blade snapped in half. Nascien then bitterly reproached the sword that he prized so highly for failing him in his time of need. Nascien replaced the pieces of the sword on the bed but, even without it, was able to slay the giant. Later he met his brother-in-law King Mordrain who, through the power of Christ, was enabled to make the sword whole once more.[2] As he left the Ship of Solomon, Nascien was punished for his presumption by a sword wound.

The second prophecy, Perceval's sister reveals, was fulfilled more recently, when King Parlan,[3] who did much for the Church and the poor, came across the ship while out hunting in a forest near the Irish Sea. Since his faith in Christ was unsullied, he ignored the warnings written on the side of the ship, went on board and, when he saw the sword, started to draw it out of its sheath. He had barely drawn it out a hand's-breadth, however, when the Avenging Lance struck him through both his thighs. As a result, he, who was once the most valiant knight of his day, is now known as the Maimed King; while the sword, which should have been kind to such a virtuous man, for once behaved cruelly, in punishing him for his presumption.[4]

A letter that they find inside the ship reveals that the sword had once belonged to King David and that the scabbard was made from the wood of the tree beneath which Abel had been murdered. David's son Solomon had placed them in the ship and sent it off to voyage the seas, for however long it took to find the best knight in the world. Solomon's wife, moreover, had insisted that the sword should have only a hempen belt, until such time as a maiden will provide it with a more appropriate one. The knights declare that they must now seek this maiden, although they have no idea where to find her.

At this moment, Perceval's sister

opens a casket she has brought with her, to reveal a belt made with human hair, interwoven with threads of gold and silk and encrusted with priceless gems. She has, she explains, made the belt out of what was most precious to her, her own hair, having had it shorn on the very day that Galahad was knighted. The sword, she says, will now be known as the Sword with the Strange Straps, while the name of the scabbard is Memory of Blood.[5]

His companions now urge Galahad to gird on the sword, which has been awaited by the Kingdom of Logres more urgently than the coming of Our Lord was awaited by the apostles. It is the means, they are convinced, by which the perilous adventures of the Holy Grail will be brought to an end.[6] Galahad accordingly draws the sword and sees his face reflected in its brilliant blade. He returns it to his scabbard and Perceval's sister, ungirding the sword that he drew from the Floating Stone, hangs the Sword with the Strange Straps on him.

She claims that she is now content to die[7]—and, indeed, shortly after, she gives her life to save a leper. Her companions send her embalmed body off in a boat that finds its way eventually to the Median River, which divides the Waste Forest. Here it is found by Lancelot, who also discovers a letter underneath the head of the dead maiden, explaining who she is, how she died, and how she was responsible for changing the straps on the Sword of David. Lancelot is now joined by an aged hermit, who also reads the letter, exclaiming when he has done so that he had never thought he would learn the name of the sword.

Explaining to Lancelot that his failure to take part in this adventure means that he can no longer be considered the best knight in the world, the hermit departs. Lancelot spends a month on his own in the boat until his son finds him there. After they catch up on all that has happened since they last met, Lancelot asks Galahad whether he has been successful in the adventure of the sword.

In reply, Galahad shows his father the Sword with the Strange Straps. Lancelot kisses it, declaring that this is the most sublime adventure to ever befall a knight.[8]

Notes

1. *...the bonys be of such maner of kynde that who that handelyth hem shall have so muche wyll that he shall never be wery, and he shall nat thynke on joy nother sorow that he hath had, but only that thynge that he beholdith before hym* (MD 753). For Jessie L. Weston "the Sword-test" forms part of the initiation of the Grail hero: The ability to focus without emotional distraction conferred by the sword-hilt corresponds to what Weston calls *holding the consciousness*, an indicator of the hero's worthiness to pass on to the next stage, the vision of the Holy Grail, while retaining full awareness of the earlier stages of initiation. This is why the scabbard of the sword in the Vulgate *Queste* is sometimes called *Memoire de Sens*, meaning The Sense Memory. However, Weston acknowledges that this interpretation might be deemed to be of "too mystical and abstract a character to be available for critical purposes" (1909, 262).

2. The leitmotif of the Broken Sword is also familiar from Nordic mythology and from Tolkien. According to Chrétien's continuators, the sword that Perceval is given in the Grail Castle breaks on the gates of the Earthly Paradise and must be re-forged by him who first made it (see TRIBOET); while the sword that breaks when it is used to kill the Fisher King's brother is mended by Perceval, who uses it to avenge his murder (see THE SWORD OF PARTINAL).

3. This (mis)adventure is also attributed to Pellehan, Pelles or Pellinor, depending on the manuscript (QP 228).

4. *LG* IV, 64–6; *MD* 752–6; *QHG* 214–21.

5. *...ceste espee a non l'Espee as estranges renges, et li fuerres a non Memoire de sanc* (QP 227). Pauline Matarasso in her translation of the Vulgate *Queste* calls it the Sword of the Strange Belt, but I have reserved this name for the sword that Gawain wins at Montesclaire, to avoid confusion. Malory calls it *the Swerde with the Straunge Gurdyls* (*MD* 761).

6. *Car par ceste espee cuident il bien que les merveilles dou Saint Graal remaignent et les aventures perilleuses qui lor avienent chascun jor* (QP 228).

7. *LG* IV, 71–2; V, 231–2; *QHG* 235–7.

8. *LG* IV, 78–9; V, 259; *QHG* 255–8: According to Malory, when Sir Launcelot learns the origin of *the mervayles swerde*, he declares that never until then had he known *of so hyghe adventures done, and so mervalous stronge* (*MD* 771).

T

The TABLE OF THE GRAIL

When, at the end of the Grail Quest, Galahad and his companions set sail for the holy city of Sarras in the East, the sacred Vessel goes with them, resting on a silver table—a table that has a history almost as illustrious as the Grail itself: For it was made in order for a feast to be served on it, a feast in which all are fed by the grace of the Grail.

Joseph of Arimathea and a group of early Christian disciples have left Jerusalem during the destruction wrought by Titus and have escaped to the purity of the desert; but they find that their crops fail, due to the sinfulness of some among them. The Holy Spirit instructs Joseph to send his brother-in-law Bron off to catch a fish, while he himself has a table made in imitation of the Table of the Last Supper[1]; he is to leave an empty seat to the right of his own, to signify the place abandoned by Judas when he betrayed Jesus.[2] This is the Table of the Grail, where the faithful are fed by the Holy Vessel which contains the blood of Jesus, but which excludes the unrepentant sinners. When an unworthy member of the company called Moses rashly sits in the empty seat, he is swallowed up by the Abyss.[3] The empty place at the table is thereafter known as the Feared Seat, or Seat of Dread.

The Table of the Grail accompanies the sacred Vessel on its peregrinations throughout the land of Britain, until a permanent home is found in the Castle of Corbenic.[4] Hundreds of years then pass until the coming of the Good Knight to Corbenic, where the silver table is used as an altar for the celebration of the Mass of the Grail. This mass is officiated by the spirit of the long-dead Josephus, the eldest son of Joseph of Arimathea. Twelve knights are present for this mass and, after the spirit disappears, they take their seats at the table.[5]

The twelve are fed from the Holy Grail with the Host[6] by Christ Himself; He then tells Galahad that he and his companions Bors and Perceval are to escort the Holy Vessel to the eastern city of Sarras, since Corbenic is no longer a worthy home for it. The three ride on to the sea, where they find the Ship of Solomon and, already ensconced within it, the table and the Grail.[7]

The ship takes them to Sarras. They carry the heavy silver table ashore (with the aid of a man who has been disabled for ten years, but who is miraculously healed by Galahad) and establish it in the Spiritual Palace. It was here that the Grail had once been set up in an ark by Joseph of Arimathea, when he first came to Sarras. Galahad symbolically repeats this event, by having an ark of gold and precious stones built over the table to house the Grail. When Galahad dies, the Holy Vessel is taken up to Heaven, never again to be seen on Earth; but the silver table remains in front of a throne that Our Lord once made for Josephus, His first bishop, in the Spiritual Palace.[8]

Notes

1. Perceval's aunt, the Queen of the Waste Land, will later tell him that the second table "resembled the first and preserved its memory"; that it saw the enacting of great miracles, such as the feeding of four thousand with twelve loaves in a waste forest; and that the Feared Seat was originally the place reserved for Josephus at the table (*LG* IV, 25–6; *QHG* 97–9).

2. According to Robert de Boron, this seat (or another established in its name) can only be filled by the grandson of Bron (*MG* 38). This is precisely what happens when—at the beginning of the Prose *Perceval*, which is also attributed to Robert—the eponymous hero sits in the empty place at the Round Table, which has been established in the

name of the Table of the Grail (119). In the Vulgate *Queste*, Perceval's role is usurped by Galahad.

3. *MG* 35-8: According to the *Estoire del Saint Graal*, in which the table is introduced without explanation, Moses is carried off to the Forest of Darnant (*LG* I, 138); his suffering will eventually be ended by Galahad.

4. The Table of the Grail, though here made of ivory rather than silver, features in an episode of the Romance of Perlesvaus, where Gawain comes to the castle of the Fisher King and is invited to share the feast. He is seated at an ivory table next to twelve knights—who are each at least a hundred years old, though they look no more than forty—and witnesses the Grail and the Bleeding Lance carried by two maidens (*HBG* 79). Lancelot sees the silver table in the Waste Forest; a sick knight gains great relief by kissing it and touching it with his eyes (*LG* IV, 20-1; *QHG* 83).

5. Although it is not made explicit, we must assume that Galahad sits in the Feared Seat at the Table of the Grail, just as he sits in the Perilous Seat at the Round Table.

6. Here the prose cycles reconnect with the imagery of Chrétien's *Conte del Graal*, where we learn that the life of the Fisher King's father is sustained by a single Host served from the Holy Vessel.

7. *And whan they com to the bourde they founde in the myddys of the bedde the table of sylver, whych they had lefft with the Maymed Kynge, and the Sankgreall.... Than were they glad to have such thyngis in theire felyship* (*MD* 785).

8. *LG* IV, 84-7; V, 279-80, 287-8; *QHG* 279-83.

TANABOS the Enchanter

One of the characteristics of the castle of the Fisher Kings is that it can only be found by chance. This is due to an enchantment put on it by Tanabos (who lived before the time of Uther Pendragon and who, apart from Merlin, was the wisest necromancer that ever lived in the Kingdom of Logres[1]) to prevent his wife's lover from finding her.[2]

Notes

1. ...*Thanabus, uns enchanteor qui avoit esté devant le roi Uterpandragon et qui avoit esté le plus sage home de nigromance qui onques eust esté el roiaumme de Logres, fors seulement Merlin, cil avoit fondé en tel maniere le chastel estrange qui le queist ne le trouvast, se aventure ne l'i amenast et cheance* (*PV* III, 243).

2. *LG* V, 266: This misuse of magic may have been one of the reasons why the Holy Grail was removed from Corbenic to the holy city of Sarras, never to return.

TITUREL

The founder of the Grail Dynasty, Titurel, the Lord of Mount Savage, is entrusted with the Holy Vessel by an angel, after it is brought down to Earth by those who stood on neither side when Lucifer contended with the Trinity.[1]

A descendant of the Trojans and of the Emperor Vespasian, Titurel's grandfather converts to Christianity.[2] Titurel himself takes a vow of chastity, which causes him to be chosen by the angel for his sacred task.[3] He is fifty years old when angels carry him to Mount Savage, surrounded by impenetrable forest; they instruct him to build a temple there to house the Grail, following the instructions of the Holy Vessel itself.[4]

Grown old, Titurel entrusts the Grail to his son Frimutel. After Frimutel's death, it passes to his son Anfortas, but he proves unworthy and becomes maimed.[5] After Anfortas' nephew Parzival heals his uncle, Parzival travels with his aged great-grandfather to the East. They take with them the Grail, which guides them to Marseilles, from where they embark for India. Here, in the kingdom of Prester John, near to the Earthly Paradise, they settle. Titurel is now five hundred years old, but the presence of the Grail prevents him from dying until Prester John, having heard the story, agrees to conceal it from him.[6]

Notes

1. *WP* 240; *PT* 199: According to the late thirteenth century German poet Albrecht, the Grail is a jasper stone from which is fashioned the dish used by Christ at the Last Supper; the dish is preserved by Joseph of Arimathea before being brought by an angel to Titurel (Barber 2005, 195).

2. As indeed did Vespasian himself, before becoming emperor, according to the Vulgate *Estoire del Saint Graal* (*LG* I, 14).

3. *PT* 349-50.

4. Barber 2005, 193.

5. We can see that the aged Titurel corresponds to the old king in the chamber, fed by a host from the Grail, in Chrétien de Troyes' *Conte del Graal*; and to the equally ancient Bron, in the Prose *Perceval*.

6. Barber 2005, 196.

TREBUCHET the Smith

A forger of enchanted weapons, Trebuchet knows that his own fate is intimately tied up with that of his third and greatest creation: It is destined to break, only he knows when; and, though only he can repair it, he must die shortly after.

When Perceval first comes to the Grail Castle, he is welcomed by its lord, the Fisher King. While they are talking, a messenger enters the hall, carrying a sword[1] round his neck, which he gives to the king. Drawing it half out of its scabbard, the king can see its place of origin inscribed on it. Reading further, the inscription reveals that it is made of such good steel that it will never break, except in one unique moment of danger known only to the one who first forged and tempered it.[2]

The messenger has come from the king's niece, who says that he should give it to whomsoever he pleases, as long as it will be put to good use: For, he adds, he who forged the sword has made no more than three; moreover, he will die before he has the chance to make another sword after this one.[3] The king gives the sword to Perceval, saying that it was destined for him.[4] But later on, Perceval's cousin, after criticizing him for failing to ask about the Grail and Lance that he saw in the castle, tells him that the sword, which has never spilt human blood nor been drawn in need, will betray him, by flying in pieces when he draws it in battle. It can be repaired, but at great cost. Whoever knows how to make his way to the lake below Scotswater will be able to have it beaten, tempered and made whole again there by the smith who made it, Trebuchet: Only he can remake it; no one else who tries will ever succeed.[5]

The Smith of Scotswater

It is only after his second visit to the Grail castle, when he finally asks about the Grail and the Lance, that Perceval shatters the sword when he strikes three blows on the gates of the Earthly Paradise; he is therefore obliged to seek out the smith who made it. Soon enough, Perceval comes to Scotswater, where he marvels that the land thereabouts which, only the evening before, had been waste and deserted was now, thanks to his asking the Grail Question, teeming with wealth of all kinds.

In the middle of a lake at the base of a cliff he sees a great house; atop the cliff is a castle, and it is there that he meets its lady. She entertains him before supper and, as he looks out of the window at the house on the lake, he sees a blue flame rising from its chimney. When he asks the lady how a fire could give forth such a colored flame, she tells him that a very aged smith dwells in the house on the lake. It had once belonged to a king, who gave the smith the house in exchange for three swords that he forged.[6] The last one took him a year to make: He alone knew what hazard would cause the sword to break; he alone can fix it; and, although no fire burns there, the strange blue flame has never gone out. The smith will never forge another sword, because he will die soon after repairing the one that will break. But, to delay the inevitable, he has two chained dragons guarding the bridge to his house.

Undaunted, the very next day, armed with an axe, Perceval kills both the crested serpents and confronts the old man, who is furious. But Trebuchet trembles and turns pale when he sees the sword hanging at Perceval's side, saying that the knight sinned greatly in breaking it at the gate of Paradise. Nevertheless, once repaired, the sword will never break again.[7]

Blowing on the ever-burning fire with a great pair of bellows, Trebuchet re-forges the sword and repairs the inscription so perfectly that there is no sign that it was ever broken. He tells the knight that he doesn't have much longer to live and, with that, he hands the sword to Perceval. But as the knight leaves, he hears bells ringing in all the churches; he knows that the smith who made and repaired his sword is dead.[8]

Notes

1. See THE BROKEN SWORD.
2. *Et avuec ce ancore i vit/ Qu'ele estoit de si bon acier/ Que ja ne porroit depecier/ Fors que par un tot seul peril/ Que nus ne savoit fors que cil/ Qui l'avoit forgiee et tanpree* (PCG ll.3138–43).
3. *Onques cil qui forja l'espee/ N'an fist que trois, et si morra/ Que ja mes forgier ne porra/ Espee nule aprés cesti* (PCG ll.3154–7).
4. CTO 415–6.
5. CTO 421–3: *Qui la voie tenir savroit/ Au lac qui est sor Cotoatre,/ La la porroit feire rebatre/ Et retanprer et feire sainne./ Se avanture la vos mainne,/ N'alez se chiés Trebuchet non,/Un fevre qui einsi a non,/ Que cil la fist et refera,/ Ou ja mes feite ne sera/ Par home qui s'an antremete* (PCG ll. 3674–83). *Cotoatre* has been "plausibly identified" with the medieval *Scottewatre*, which I have modernized as Scotswater, that is, the Firth of Forth. In an interpolation to Chrétien's *Conte del Graal*, Perceval breaks the sword in battle with the Haughty Knight of the Heath (CTO 523).
6. One of the three swords may once have belonged to the Grail Lord Frimutel, since Wolfram von Eschenbach tells us that it was Trebuchet who inscribed the wondrous weapon (WP 322; PT 270). This may or may not be the same as the Sword of Anfortas, the son of Frimutel, which was made by Trebuchet. Anfortas, the Maimed King of the German Grail legends, presents it to Parzival (PT 101; WP 127). It shatters in a battle and must be taken to a spring near Karnant in order to be made whole (PT 183; WP 223) by wetting it with spring-water before daylight, while reciting a magic charm (PT 107; WP 134).
7. Philippe Walter reminds us that Trebuchet's knowledge of the past and future derives from his being in origin a smith god: His name (*trebucher* means "to stumble") reveals that he is lame, like divine smiths such as Vulcan and Wayland: lameness, in this context, being less an infirmity than a sign of election, giving access to Otherworld places and the forbidden secrets of the Beyond: *Cette boiterie est moins une infirmité qu'une signe d'élection. Elle est pour lui un moyen d'accéder plus facilement aux territoires et aux secrets interdits de l'au-delà* (2013, 186). The smith is a master of initiation; but his role as guide to the young hero will be replaced by that of the hermit, whose knowledge is of spiritual rather than earthly secrets (2004b, 170–1).
8. CSG 340–6.

The TREE OF ENCHANTMENT

It is while searching for the court of the Fisher King, after his first unfortunate experience there, that Perceval sees a great leafy oak tree blocking his path. At first the tree seems to be ablaze with more than a thousand candles of miraculous size but, as Perceval rides closer, the light fades away to nothing.

When he eventually reaches the tree, he finds no candles on it; but a light further on leads him to a mysterious chapel containing the dead body of a knight.[1] It is after midnight when he encounters some hunters in the forest who are in the service of the Fisher King. They give him directions for the Grail Castle but, before he gets there, he meets a girl who tells him that his coming upon the tree and the chapel are signs that he will at last discover the truth about the Grail and the Bleeding Lance—the hallows which he saw on his first visit but which he disastrously failed to ask about.

When he reaches the castle, Perceval, having learnt the lesson about his reticence, asks the king about various marvels he has encountered,[2] including the tree of candles and the dead body in the chapel; but for answers he must wait until they have eaten. After dinner, the Grail Procession passes before them, as it did on his first visit.

This time, Perceval asks the king to explain the various mysteries he has encountered. But he is told that he will learn nothing more until he is able fully to mend a shattered sword[3] which formed part of the Procession.[4] This he does not in fact accomplish until his third visit to the castle.

It is only now, having passed the Test of the Sword, that Perceval learns all the secrets of the Grail. As for the tree of lights which he saw, the king explains that it is the Tree of Enchantment where fays gather[5]; they look like candles from afar, but they lead astray all who have put their faith in God. The fact that they vanished as Perceval approached is a sign that he is to accomplish the wondrous adventures of the land[6]: He drove the Ladies (or fairy women) away[7] and they will never be heard of again.[8]

Notes

1. See THE BLACK HAND.
2. See MOUNT DOLOROUS.

3. See THE SWORD OF PARTINAL.
4. *CSG* 333-9: The sword did not form part of the Grail Procession on Perceval's first visit: One half of it was brought to the Grail King by Gawain, acting on behalf of the king's deceased nephew, Silimac (q.v.).
5. *C'est li arbres d'anchantemant,/ Illueques les fees s'asamblent* (*MTC* ll.33000-1).
6. *Les mervoilles de ceste terre* (*MTC* l.33011).
7. *Car vos les dames an chaçastes/ Par ce que de l'arbre aproichastes* (*MTC* ll.33017-8); similarly, Galahad drives out a demon by his mere proximity to a possessed man (see DAGON).
8. *CSG* 480.

TREVRIZENT

After his first, unsuccessful visit to the Grail Castle, Parzival travels over land and sea, hoping to find again Mount Savage, where dwells the Maimed King Anfortas. After being criticized by his cousin for failing to ask any questions when he was there, Parzival defeats in battle one of the Grail Templars. Parzival takes the warrior's horse, but is upbraided by pilgrims he meets for travelling fully armed on Good Friday.

They tell him about a holy man who lives nearby. Parzival, who has lost all sense of time, as well as of God, allows his war-horse to lead him where it will. It takes him to the Wild Fountain, where dwells the hermit Trevrizent,[1] his mother's brother; he retired from knighthood after their other brother Anfortas was wounded.

Trevrizent includes in his religious teaching the story of the Grail: He has seen it himself and he knows it can only be found by he who is destined by Heaven to find it. Guarded by Templars, this *lapsit exillis*[2] is a Stone, by the power of which the phoenix is burnt and reborn from its own ashes. No-one who has been in its presence will age for a week afterwards; moreover, it restores youth to flesh and bones.

The Grail was brought to Earth by those angels who would not take sides in the war between Lucifer and the Trinity; but one of God's angels entrusted it to the family of Anfortas, who became its guardian after the death in battle of his father Frimutel. The Stone itself reveals the names of all those who are destined to serve it; it also feeds them through the power of a small white wafer brought by a dove from Heaven every Good Friday.[3]

Trevrizent also tells Parzival about his uncle Anfortas, who fought for love without the approval of the Grail; he was punished for his hubris by being wounded by a pagan's spear. None of the remedies they tried were successful: The Grail itself has told them that the king can only be healed when a knight, unprompted, asks him what ails him.[4]

Parzival has now learnt what he must do to remedy his earlier mistake. After the healing of his brother Anfortas, Trevrizent is delighted to learn that the asking of the Grail Question has brought him peace.[5]

Notes

1. *WP* 226-31; *PT* 186-91.
2. See THE GRAIL STONE.
3. *WP* 239-41; *PT* 197-9.
4. *WP* 243-7; *PT* 201-4.
5. Finding the origins of Wolfram's Grail story in hermetic gnosis, Henry and Renée Kahane derive the name Trevrizent from Trismegistus, via OFr. *Treble Escient* (Kahane, 62-3). But if the hermit of the Wild Forest is indeed related to thrice-wise Hermes, the initiator of the Emerald Tablet, Trevrizent seems also to have retained his mercurial trickery. For, after telling Parzival that the neutral angels who brought the Grail Stone to Earth could have earnt salvation (*WP* 232, 240; *PT* 192, 199), he later retracts this statement, claiming that God is constant in His judgments. Trevrizent explains, somewhat unconvincingly, that he lied in order to distract Parzival from his quest, knowing that it could not be achieved by fighting (*WP* 396; *PT* 334).

TRIBOET

When Perceval meets his cousin after his first visit to the Grail Castle, she warns him that the sword which the Fisher King gave him there will break when he is locked in mortal battle. In order to repair it, he must find the smith Triboet who made the Sword. Triboet alone can mend it; no one else who sets his hand to it will be successful.[1]

And so it is that when Perceval is in great peril, fighting ten knights who have abducted a lady, the sword breaks as predicted, much to his distress.² After defeating the knights, he recovers from his wounds at the castle of the lady he saved and afterwards he sets off on his adventures. He takes with him the Broken Sword, very much wishing and hoping that he will somewhere find a smith who can remake and solder it; this matter is much on his mind.³

Later, when he is on his way to visit his ladylove, Blancheflor, who is being besieged by a villainous knight called Aridés, he stops at a forge to get a stone out of his horse's shoe. His mission accomplished, Perceval asks the smith his name. The latter responds without anger,⁴ stating, for whoever wishes to know it, the name by which he is known in many parts.⁵

The smith continues by saying that he made the sword that hangs at Perceval's side; the knight thus realizes that he has found the only man who can repair it. This Triboet does with alacrity, enjoining Perceval to use the sword only when necessary, since he will never again see the like; moreover, he will have great need of it the following evening. The smith hopes that he himself will live to see the morrow.⁶

Perceval commends Triboet to God, thanks him for the service he has rendered him and promises to repay it if he ever has the opportunity.⁷ Later, when he has defeated Aridés, Perceval says he will spare his life if he puts himself at the mercy of the renowned Triboet. Aridés replies that he knows the smith and that he would end up going to prison like a common criminal if he were sent to Triboet.⁸ Perceval relents and sends him to the court of King Arthur instead.⁹

Notes

1. *N'alez se chiés Triboët non,/Un fevre qui ensi a non,/ Car cil le fist et refera,/ Ou jamais faite ne sera/ Por home qui s'en entremete./ Gardez que autres main n'i mete,/ Qu'il n'en saroit venir a chief* (*RP* ll.3679–85; *PSG* 40). In some manuscripts of the Story of the Grail, the smith who makes and is destined to repair the Broken Sword of Perceval is called Trebuchet (q.v.); the circumstances in which the sword breaks and is repaired also vary.

2. *...an deus brisa/ L'espee, don molt s'angoissa* (*MTC* ll.33493–4; *CSG* 484).

3. *L'espee brisiee am porta;/ Molt desirre, molt convoita/ Que an aucun leu fevre truisse/ Qui refaire et soder li puisse;/ De ce fu an molt grant balance* (*MTC* ll.37185–9; *CSG* 513).

4. *Et celui li respont sanz ire* (*MTC* l.38975): Triboet's lack of anger contrasts with the fury of Trebuchet (in Gerbert's Continuation), who knows that he will die once he has repaired the Broken Sword.

5. *L'an m'apelle Tribüet, sire,/ Par mon non, qui le viaut anquerre,/ Suis conneüz an mainte terre* (*MTC* ll.38976–8). This interchange might suggest that Triboet, like other smiths, is a magician, for whom names are power.

6. This is a reference to the prophecy in Chrétien's poem that he would not live to make another such weapon, the niece of the Fisher King sending Perceval word that he who forged the sword would soon die (*CSG* 28).

7. *CSG* 526–7.

8. Triboet's reputation obviously precedes him, but we do not know if Aridés' fear is justified, or if it is merely an example of the superstitious awe in which smiths were traditionally held: "The 'mastery of fire,' common both to magician ... and smith, was, in Christian folklore, looked upon as the work of the devil" (Eliade 1978, 106).

9. *CSG* 528–9.

TRISTAN

Although he is best known for the adulterous affair that he carries on with his uncle's wife, Tristan is connected through his family with that Holy Vessel which is the object of the highest spiritual quest in the Kingdom of Adventures; for he is descended from Sador,¹ who was one of the twelve sons of Bron born in the Holy Land and therefore a nephew of Joseph of Arimathea.²

Tristan is thus a member of that exalted lineage which first came to Britain when it was a pagan country and converted it to Christianity in the time of good King Lucius. Tristan first hears something of this sacred history when he is escorting the Irish princess Iseut to Cornwall to marry his uncle King Mark. As they are passing the Distant Isles, a violent storm blows them into apparently safe harboring, near the ominously named Castle of Tears, on an island of giants.

They quickly learn the evil custom of the castle, which has earnt its name: Any knight found there will be killed unless he can overcome its lord in battle; any woman will be killed if she proves less beautiful than the lady of the castle. This custom had apparently arisen when Joseph of Arimathea came to the island and started converting its people, including its lord's twelve sons; whereupon the giant had them and all the other Christians who would not abandon their new faith beheaded.[3] Fortunately, on this occasion, Tristan proves to be stronger than the island's current lord, and Iseut, more beautiful than its current lady.[4]

When Tristan hears that the Very Good Knight who is to put an end to the adventures of Logres[5] has arrived at Arthur's court, he makes his way immediately to Camelot to greet Galahad, who now sits in the Perilous Seat[6]; so that, when Tristan also takes his place, the Round Table is complete.[7] To celebrate such a special occasion, the king proclaims what he believes will be the fellowship's last tournament. At this, Galahad overcomes all opposition, including that of Tristan; for, although Tristan is the noblest, gentlest and most courteous of *worldly* knights, Galahad has been elected to be the best knight in the world through the grace of God.

After being defeated in the tournament, Tristan and the other Knights of the Round Table return to the royal palace to eat; but, before anyone can bring food to them, they feel the palace shaking and they are plunged into darkness. Then the hall is pervaded with a paradisiacal perfume. The knights witness a Vessel, covered in vermilion samite and carried by unknown hands,[8] pass through the hall. As it does so, they are filled with every food imaginable, but the Holy Vessel, passing through the hall, vanishes. As the knights praise God for such sweet food, there is fulfilled the prophecy of Joseph of Arimathea,[9] who proclaimed that God's grace would be spread among His congregation; but that, though all would receive it, few would observe it.[10]

Tristan is among those knights errant who swear to pursue the quest for the Grail. One day, he and Lancelot arrive at the castle of the Felon Knight, a pagan enchanter whose strength is magically enhanced to make him five times more powerful than any opponent. Tristan is knocked out and Lancelot made prisoner at their first encounter. A penitent who lives in the nearby forest and who announces that she is Lancelot's daughter tells Tristan the secret of overcoming the felon: He must swear before the crucifix that is in the ruined chapel by the castle gate that he will sin no more with Queen Iseut. Then, if he calls on Jesus Christ for help, every time he does so, the felon will lose the strength of one man.

Tristan follows the maiden's advice and defeats the felon, freeing the prisoners.[11] But it is not so easy for him to free himself from his attachment to his uncle's wife, an attachment that eventually leads to his murder at the hands of his jealous uncle.[12]

Notes

1. Sador's son Apollo is the first Christian King of Lyonesse; his descendant Felix is the father of Tristan's mother Heliabel (Walter 2014, 370).
2. Sador's brothers include Alan the Fat (the Rich Fisher) and Joshua, the first of the Fisher Kings who guard the Grail in Corbenic.
3. According to the French Prose *Tristan*, the Castle of Tears is erected on ground soaked in the blood of the missionaries (*TPC* II, 71–2), the fourteenth century Italian Arthurian cyclical text *La Tavola Ritonda* adding that the victims numbered nearly eighty thousand. The lord of the island at this time was "a mad Jewish giant called Dialantes" who must have been disconcerted to find apostate Jews (that is, Christians) evangelizing so far from home. Unusually, Joseph of Arimathea is numbered among his victims (*TRT* 82). According to another fourteenth century Italian text, the compilation called *Tristano Panciatichiano*, the foundations of the Castle of Tears are built on the bones of the Christian dead (*TP* 191).
4. *RTC* 89–90.
5. Tristan has already encountered some of these adventures: He first meets Pellehan the Maimed King when a marvelous boat (*la Nef de Joie*) leads him up the river that encircles Corbenic. King Pellehan criticizes him for his adultery with Iseut

(*RTP* 306–9). Nevertheless, Tristan vows to join the Grail Quest (387–8). Later he meets the Maiden of the Bloody Sword on her way to Camelot (396–8), where she will reveal the many deaths which will be caused by Gawain.

6. *Gallaaz, o mui boõ cavalleyro ... aquelle que ha de acabar a Seeda Perigosa e ha de dar fim aas aventuras do regno de Logres* (*PV* II, 36).

7. *LG* V, 119.

8. The *Tristano Panciatichiano* provides us with a unique variation in which a ray of sunlight suddenly lights up the hall and the knights are filled with the grace of the Holy Spirit. Struck dumb, the knights can only stare as a white deer enters, tied with golden chains held by four men in white robes; on its horns, a Vessel covered with cloth of white samite which contains the *Santo Gradale* or Holy Grail (*TP* 39).

9. To Joseph's table, modelled on that of the apostles, God sent "the holy vessel or true ampulla" made from the earth soaked in the blood of Christ. It contains the wine in which the wounds of Christ were washed, but the Holy Blood itself has rejoined the body of Christ since His Resurrection. Merlin made the Round Table "in reverent memory" of Joseph (*TRT* 277–8).

10. *TRT* 227.

11. *TRT* 285–8.

12. Tristan's death from a lance wound *par mi la quisse* (*TPM* IX, 188) is described as a *caus dolereus* (193), like the Dolorous Blow which struck the Fisher King (311).

U

The UGLY MAIDEN

When the knight Perceval is at King Arthur's court in Caerleon (following his first, unsuccessful visit to the Grail Castle), a hellishly ugly, bestially-deformed, goat-bearded maiden with black hands and neck arrives on a mule, holding a whip.

She curses Perceval for failing to grasp the hand of Fortune—who has beautiful hair in front, but is bald behind—when he met her.[1] Perceval is wretched because, when he came to the castle of the Maimed King and witnessed the wonders there, he failed to ask why the Lance bleeds and who is served by the Grail. Had he done so, she continues, the Fisher King would have been healed of his wounds; many evils will result from the fact that he stayed silent.

After daring the assembled knights to raise the siege of Montesclaire and win the Sword of the Strange Belt, she departs, to spend the night at Proud Castle,[2] which was built by the Knights of the Waste Land.[3] Perceval vows to search for the truth about the Grail and the Bleeding Lance.

* * *

Chrétien de Troyes, who introduces this intriguing figure, did not live to complete the story but, although an anonymous continuator concludes the adventure of Proud Castle, we hear no more about the Ugly Maiden in the Grail poems. A Hideous Damsel[4] arrives at Camelot at the beginning of the prose Post-Vulgate Quest, carrying a sword which will turn bloody when handled by the knight who will kill more of his fellows than anyone else[5]; but we do not know the nature of her ugliness, nor whether she has any connection with Proud Castle.

For Wolfram she is Cundrie, the Grail Messenger, who appears in Wagner's *Parsifal* as Kundry, a seductress seeking redemption. In the Welsh Romance of Peredur she is the Black Maiden, whom Glenys Goetinck considers to be the angry face of Lady Sovereignty—the Goddess of the Land, whom the hero has neglected.[6]

For Caitlín Matthews, the Ugly Maiden or Hideous Damsel and the beautiful Grail Bearer are reflections of "a once potent image of the Divine Feminine,"[7] which is both immanent and transcendent: on Earth she is Sovereignty, in Heaven she is Sophia, Divine Wisdom. In Gnostic mythology, Sophia falls from closeness to God and, as she does so, she creates a world in which she is condemned to wander, sad and confused, seeking "a way of return." The ugliness of the Hideous Damsel is that of her "dark, exiled face"[8]; we must embrace her and listen to her voice, however harsh her words, in order to restore both her and the land she personifies to the beauty they once possessed: Only thus can the Waste Land become once more the Earthly Paradise, symbolized by the Grail.[9]

Notes

1. This may have inspired the author of the Romance of Perlesvaus to depict the Grail Bearer as losing her hair as a result of Perceval's "unfortunate" failure to ask the Grail Question.
2. *CSG* 41.
3. *CSG* 561.
4. *Donzella Laida* (*PV* II, 42).
5. *LG* V, 120–1.
6. Goetinck 1975, 257–8.
7. Matthews 1984, 117.
8. Matthews 1984, 122.
9. Matthews 1984, 127: "The Grail is … the cup of sovereignty, of wisdom: a draft from that cup is a remembrance of paradise" (124).

V

VARLAN

A former Saracen (that is, a worshipper of the heavenly bodies), the newly christened King Varlan[1] is waging war against his neighbor, King Lambor, when the Ship of Faith arrives on the shore. Having the worst of the battle, Varlan runs into the ship and grabs the sword he finds there,[2] using it to cleave Lambor to the earth with one stroke. The consequences are disastrous for both their realms: Great pestilence befalls; neither corn nor grass nor fruit increase; no fish are found in the waters. Thus, the Dolorous Blow creates the Waste Land.

Seeing how well the sword carves flesh, Varlan goes back aboard ship to find the scabbard; but as soon as he puts the sword back in its sheath, he drops down dead. He lays there until a maiden comes aboard to cast his body out, thus proving that any man who draws the sword will be killed or maimed.[3]

Notes

1. Malory calls him King Hurlaine.
2. See THE SWORD OF DAVID.
3. *LG* I, 159–60; IV, 65; *MD* 754; *QHG* 215–6.

VESPASIAN

When the Roman general Vespasian falls ill with leprosy, a knight from Capernaum tells him about the life and death of the Prophet Jesus, assuring him that anything Christ had touched would cure him.

At Vespasian's request the knight returns to the Holy Land and finds the Veil of Veronica, the cloth with which she had wiped Jesus' brow on the day of His crucifixion and on which the image of His face was miraculously preserved.[1] The knight brings the Veil to Rome but, on the eve of his arrival, Vespasian dreams that a man descends from Heaven and scratches him all over with his nails; Vespasian has to look in a mirror to see if he still recognizes himself. But at that moment everyone on Earth starts running after him, crying that he should come to see the dead man who lives once more.

As soon as he sees the imprint of the Prophet's face on the cloth, Vespasian is cured. In gratitude, he vows to avenge the death of Jesus on those responsible. The general immediately sets off for Jerusalem. As soon as he arrives, he rounds up all those still alive who were implicated in the death of the Holy Prophet.

At this time Elyab, the wife of Joseph of Arimathea, comes to see Vespasian, asking for justice for her husband, who has been imprisoned by the High Priest Caiaphas for taking the body of Jesus down from the cross and placing it in the sepulcher. Vespasian has the other Jews burnt, but promises Caiaphas he will die neither by fire nor by the sword, as long as he shows him where he imprisoned Joseph.

Caiaphas takes Vespasian to his stronghold in the marshes, about seven leagues from Jerusalem, where Joseph was imprisoned in a dungeon beneath a pillar. Not knowing whether Joseph is alive or dead, but believing that the God who healed an unbeliever like himself is powerful enough to keep His servant alive, Vespasian has himself lowered into the underground cell. Here he encounters a brilliant light and finds the disciple, well and unaged, despite the fact that forty-two years have passed and several emperors have died,[2] since Joseph was imprisoned. He has, we discover, been fed by the Holy Grail and has no concept of the time that has passed. Reuniting Joseph with his family, Vespasian sentences Caiaphas to be set adrift at sea in a rowboat, thus keeping his promise to the High Priest while allowing God to determine his fate.[3]

On the morning that he leaves the Holy Land, Vespasian is secretly baptized by the Apostle Philip. Joseph, who has also been baptized by the apostle's hand,[4] begins the long odyssey that will take him at last to Britain, the Promised Land of the Grail.

* * *

The hero of the Roman invasion of Britain, General Vespasian was sent by the Emperor Nero to crush the Great Jewish Revolt which broke out in 66 CE. Vespasian, accompanied by his eldest son Titus, took control of the campaign against the Jews, laying siege to Jerusalem and destroying other centers of revolt.[5] Following the assassination of Nero, Vespasian was declared emperor by his troops in July 69. It is shortly before this date, therefore, that we must place the legendary events recounted in the De Boron and Vulgate Cycles—beginning with the imprisonment of Joseph, shortly after the death of Jesus, in 27 CE.[6]

Vespasian left the Holy Land in August 69, placing the Siege of Jerusalem in the hands of his son Titus. He travelled first to Egypt, where he experienced a vision in the Temple of Serapis[7] in December, finally arriving in Rome in the middle of the following year. History, sadly, does not remember him as the first Christian Emperor; but Christian legend remembers him as a "good" pagan who avenged the death of Jesus on the Jews.

Notes

1. *EG* ll.1593–1614; *RG* 41.
2. ...*et si poés conter .XLII. ans del cruchefiement Jhesucrist jusc'au delivrement de Joseph* (*ESG* 28). According to the *Estoire del Saint Graal*, Tiberius Caesar ruled in Rome when Jesus was crucified and three emperors reigned after him: Gaius (better known as Caligula), then Claudius; and Nero, during whose reign St. Peter was also crucified and St. Paul beheaded. Vespasian later says that his father was the fourth emperor to reign after Tiberius (35); whereas Vespasian in fact became the fourth emperor to reign in 69 CE (583). Our authors consistently refer to Vespasian's father as the Emperor Titus, whereas Titus was actually his son and only became emperor after Vespasian's death.
3. Caiaphas will be encountered alive, hundreds of years later, by Galahad and his companions (*ESG* 585); his fate bearing witness to the perfidy (*desloiauté*) of those whom Christ called His sons, the Jews showing Him less honor than those He called Gods: For the Jews crucified Him but the pagans avenged Him: *car li Juif l'avoient cruchefiiet et li paien le vengoient* (37). This example of medieval antisemitism is not untypical: When Chrétien's Perceval encounters penitents who guide him to the Grail Hermit, they tell him that the *faus juïf* should be killed like dogs, although the result of their actions in crucifying Christ would be to bring about their ruin and "our" salvation (*RP* ll.6292–6).
4. *LG* I, 11–14; *MG* 23–34.
5. *STC* 276–7.
6. This date for the Crucifixion can be established if we accept the authority of Robert de Boron for Joseph's being imprisoned three days

afterwards—*Au tierç jor aprés que li prophete fu mis en crois* (*RG* 46; *MG* 30)—and the authority of the Vulgate *Estoire del Saint Graal* for his being in prison for forty-two years (*LG* I, 11). Manessier makes it forty years (*MTC* l.32745).

7. *STC* 279: According to Manessier, before settling in Britain, Joseph accompanied Vespasian to Rome, carrying the Holy Lance, with the Grail following after (*MTC* ll.32753–9; *CSG* 478).

W

The WASTE CITY

While Perceval is staying at the house of his uncle the Hermit King, having failed to ask the Grail Question at the court of the Fisher King, Lancelot is among those Knights of the Round Table who set off to find the Grail Castle and achieve the sacred quest.

He comes to a wasteland whose soil is so dry and poor that it cannot sustain bird or animal life.[1] Gazing afar, he sees an enormous ruined city with crumbling walls and leaning gates; riding into it, he sees derelict churches and palaces, deserted market places, and a crowd of lamenting knights and ladies huddled in one of the least ruined buildings. What a shame, they cry, that he must go to his death; hated be he who has condemned Lancelot to this fate.

At this, there emerges from the great hall a knight, bearing a huge axe. He confronts Lancelot and offers him a stark ultimatum: Unless Lancelot strikes off his head, he will kill him on the spot; but if he decapitates the knight, Lancelot must return in a year's time to submit to the same ritual, this time as victim. Faced with a choice between instant death and a year's deferment, Lancelot chooses to delay the inevitable. He strikes off the knight's head and swiftly takes his leave.[2]

Returning as promised at the appointed time, Lancelot's life is spared by the intervention of the sisters of the Poor Knight of the Waste Castle, who remind Lancelot how he had helped them on a previous occasion, adding that twenty knights had previously tried this adventure, but none of them had returned to fulfill their promise. If Lancelot had also failed to return, they would have lost the city forever.

The city now fills with people, rejoicing that they can return to their homes and churches. The spell has been broken.[3]

It is also said that the King of the Waste City is a tyrannical pagan who not only refuses to believe in the true spiritual God,[4] but also controls an army of the undead! He sets the army onto one of the Knights of the Round Table, Gornemant of Gohort. In this, he is served by a deformed old hag who restores the warriors to life whenever Gornemant and his sons kill them. Perceval comes to the aid of his former mentor, only to discover that the conflict is seemingly endless.

However, he determines to discover how the dead are brought back to life and, waiting up until midnight on a moonlit night, he captures the hideous hag[5] responsible. Before he cuts off her head, Perceval learns from the ugly old woman that the demonic king wanted to punish Gornemant for making Perceval a knight and to stop Perceval from finding out anything about the Grail.[6] With her death, as she herself foretold, nothing can now prevent him from achieving his quest.[7]

* * *

There are two quite distinct accounts of the Waste City in thirteenth century Grail romances; if we put them together, we have an image of a city placed under an enchantment by pagan magic, a curse that can only be broken by the willingness of a Christian knight to sacrifice himself to save others.

Gerbert, in his Continuation to the Story of the Grail, does not explain specifically why the king and the hag who serves him are so determined to keep Perceval ignorant of the Grail; but it may be that since, as is often stated, the Grail winner will bring to an end the enchantments of Britain, they fear that their magical powers will then die. They appear to embody a spiritual evil determined to thwart the will of God.[8]

Like the hag of Gloucester in the Romance of Peredur, the *vieille laide* recognizes Perceval as the one who will bring about her death[9]; with her out of the way, nothing can prevent him from achieving his quest for the Grail. At the moment, he does not know who is served from the Holy Vessel, what is done with it, or why the Lance bleeds; but he will learn all this at last,[10] though not from her.[11]

Unfortunately, we learn nothing more about the Waste City in the Continuations; but the Romance of Perlesvaus fills in some of the details. Perceval's uncle Aliban (the eleventh and youngest of the brothers of Alan the Fat, Perceval's father) was once King of the Waste City but, like all his brothers, Aliban was killed by a pagan red giant and buried on the giant's island.[12] It is then, we must assume, that the demonic tyrant took control of the city with his undead army and placed its human inhabitants under an enchantment: For, when Lancelot returns there, the living can only be heard and not seen,[13] as if they are gradually becoming less substantial with every failure of a knight to be true to his word. But Lancelot's willingness to make the ultimate sacrifice breaks the power of the demonic king; the city and its surrounding lands are restored to the dispossessed.

Notes

1. ...*une tere gaste et un païs grant et large ou n'avoit ne beste ne oisiaus, car la tere estoit si seche et si povre qu'il n'i troverent point de peuture* (HLG 388).
2. HBG 90–1.
3. HBG 181–4: The theme of the Beheading Game can be traced back to Irish mythology (391n1), but it has its most famous incarnation in the Middle English alliterative poem *Sir Gawain and the Green Knight*, on which David Lowery's 2021 film *The Green Knight* was based.
4. The attack on Gornemant was *dit et comandé/ Du roi de la Gaste Chité,/ Qui n'a pooir ne volenté/ De croire en Dieu l'esperitable* (GCP ll.5692–5).
5. Gerbert's description of the hag (GCP ll.5528–77) seems designed to outdo Chrétien's Ugly Maiden; Perceval wonders if she got so misshapen as the result of a charm or a magic spell—*Est che par charm ou par arture/ Qu'ele est si laidement formee?* (ll.5582–3)—but no answer is forthcoming. He witnesses her place the head back on a decapitated body and bring it back to life with the help of a balm. This *poison* is the very one with which Jesus was anointed when He was laid in the sepulcher; that is why it has been given the power to bring the dead back to life (ll.5628–33). How the hag got hold of the precious relic is never explained.
6. *Por che qu'il voloit destorner/ Que du Graal rien ne seüsses* (GCP ll.5718–19).
7. CSG 378–88.
8. GCP ll.5705–10.
9. GCP ll.5653–57.
10. *De che que vous empris avez/ Du Greal, que vous ne savez/ Cui on en sert ne c'on en fait,/ Mais encore vous ert tot retrait,/ Et de la Lance por coi saine* (GCP ll.5661–65).
11. GCP ll.5680–83.
12. HBG 257.
13. HLG 738.

The WASTE LAND

When the Company of the Grail comes to Britain and begins the process of evangelization, one of their number, Peter of Orkney, converts King Lucius to Christianity; while the king's daughter marries Aminadap, the second of the Fisher Kings who guard the Grail in Corbenic in the Land Beyond.

Their great-grandson is Lambor, who is struck down by his neighbor Varlan, one of the Welsh kings, with disastrous consequences: For it is not just that the Grail Keeper has been slain by one who had only recently converted, but the weapon used is the Sword of David. Varlan found it on the Ship of Faith, a vessel dispatched over a thousand years earlier by King Solomon and which had only recently washed up on British shores. Moreover, there is a divine prohibition on the sword's being drawn by any but the Best Knight. As a result, Varlan, being far from being that knight, drops dead shortly after killing Lambor.

But the effect on the lands of the two kings is even more disastrous: The earth, when cultivated, bears no produce; no wheat, oats nor any other grain will grow; trees will not bear fruit; and few fish can be found in the waters, apart from the very smallest ones. For this reason, as divine vengeance for the death of a king much loved by God, the two kingdoms that border each other—Wales and the Land Beyond—are utterly devastated.[1] They are henceforth known together as the Waste Land.[2]

The Kingdom of the Land Beyond remains waste until the time of King Arthur: Its wretched appearance is a sign that it has been placed under a curse, but it also protects it from being conquered by Rion, the giant King of Ireland.[3] After defeating King Rion on behalf of Arthur, the ill-fated knight Balin the Savage goes on to strike another grievous blow against the ruler of the Grail Kingdom. But this time the victim will be Lambor's son King Pellehan and the weapon used will be a Lance rather than a sword.

It is not as if Balin is not forewarned: Merlin prophesies to Balin that he is destined to strike a blow against the most valiant knight in the world, a Dolorous Blow that will cause three kingdoms to lie waste for twenty-two years.[4] And so it comes to pass: Arriving at the Kingdom of Listenois, Balin smites the Grail Keeper Pellehan with the Avenging Lance. The king is maimed, his castle destroyed and the countryside devastated, as if struck by lightning everywhere. The region has become so unfamiliar as a result of its ruination that it is henceforth known as the Waste Land or the Strange Country.[5]

The wasting of the Grail Kingdom can only be reversed by the Best Knight in the world, the pinnacle of spiritual as well as earthly chivalry, in the next generation. Thus, when the daughter of Pellehan's son Pelles, King of the Land Beyond, seduces Lancelot, with the connivance of her father, their deceit is justified by the fact that God did not want the kingdom to remain a wasteland forever: It is the divine will that the land should be restored to the beauty it had, before it was devastated by the blow from the Sword of David. The fruit of their union will be Galahad, who will replenish many lands and achieve the adventures of the Holy Grail.[6]

Yet Had That Land Been Waste

Some say that Sir Gawain is responsible for the partial restoration of the Waste Land, when he comes to the White Island and witnesses the Grail Procession—including the Bleeding Lance and a broken sword lying athwart the dead body of a knight on a bier—in the hall of its king, who bids Gawain ask anything he likes about the things he has seen. The knight asks whence comes the blood which springs from the point of the Lance and who the knight is who lies dead on the bier.

The king is happy to explain to Gawain that the Bleeding Lance is the one with which Jesus was pierced on the Cross; for which we should rejoice because His blood will be our ransom. *That* blow won us great joy; but the foul blow struck by the sword has brought nothing but ruin to the Kingdom of Logres and the whole country, as Gawain has no doubt heard long ago. That is why the king and his people have come to the island[7]: As a result of that blow, the land which was so highly valued, the entire kingdom, has been laid waste.[8]

The king is about to tell Gawain who struck the blow which killed the dead knight on the bier, but unfortunately the hero, who has had a very long journey, falls asleep, waking up the next morning on a lofty cliff by the sea, with no sign of the hall of the Grail King. But as he sets off across the countryside, he is struck by something quite remarkable: What had only the day before been a devastated kingdom, utterly bereft of life, was now better provided with water, woods and pastures than anywhere that had ever been seen.

At the stroke of midnight, God had set the waters to flow once more through their channels and restored to the woods their former verdure; this had all happened the previous night, as soon as Gawain asked why the Lance bled so profusely. If the land was not fully re-populated, it was because he did not ask anything more.[9] As he rides through the newly green landscape, the people condemn him for not also asking about the service of the Grail: Had he done so, their joy would have been beyond words.[10]

Gawain is able to complete his healing of the Waste Land when he returns to the hall of the king and at last asks about the miraculous Grail. He is reminded that his relative Perceval had been there before him, but had failed to learn the secret of the Grail, not daring to ask[11]; yet, as Gawain now learns, the fatal blow which has caused so much distress is the one by which Perceval's father was killed by his own brother. It is for this treachery that God cursed the land: The living had all been driven away and the dead alone populated the castle, kept in a state of "undead" animation. Once the truth has been revealed, they can rest in peace—and the kingdom can be peopled again by the living.[12]

* * *

A metaphor for the spiritual sickness of the twentieth century, after its scholarly popularization by Jessie L. Weston[13] inspired T.S. Eliot's eponymous poem, the literary theme of the Waste Land developed through the blossoming Grail legends of the twelfth and thirteenth centuries; but it can be traced back, like so much of Arthurian romance, to medieval Celtic literature.

Thus, in the Third Branch of the Mabinogi, the hero Pryderi causes an enchantment to fall upon the land of Dyfed, in south-west Wales, leaving it bereft of people and animals; hence the fourteenth century bard Dafydd ap Gwilym refers to the region as the Land of Illusion and the Realm of Glamour.[14] Several Grail texts refer to the achieving of the Quest as bringing to an end the adventures or the enchantments of Britain, or of Logres (what is now England).[15]

If the wasting of Logres (like that of Wales and the Land Beyond) can be the result of a fatal sword-stroke,[16] it can also be attributed to other causes: Thus, the Grail poem known as the *Elucidation* blames it on the violation of the Maidens of the Wells who serve the Fisher King.[17] As a result, the wells are lost, the land becomes sterile and the court of the Fisher King disappears[18]; only when it is found again will the Waste Land be restored.[19]

For Chrétien and some of his continuators, the wasting of the land and its restoration are intimately related to the Grail Question—the failure to ask it, or the inability to hear the answer. Gerbert's Continuation to the Story of the Grail shows Perceval, after his unsuccessful first visit to the castle of the Fisher King, getting a second chance to put things right. This time he asks about the Grail and the Bleeding Lance, but is too burdened with sin to learn their secrets. Awakening the next morning to find himself not in a castle but in a lush meadow near the gates to the Earthly Paradise, he rides on through a fertile land, rich with rivers and populous towns. He marvels at this, for only the previous evening when he passed this way, he had found the country waste and deserted; now it is flourishing.[20] Arriving at a nearby castle, he is hailed by its lady as her savior and as the restorer of the lonely Waste Land, in which every river and spring had been dried up, but which were now overflowing. All that they were lacking has now been restored to them[21]; all this has come about because he finally asked about the Grail and the Lance.[22]

But Jessie Weston sees the focus on the Grail Question as a later deviation from the original Waste Land theme, which is, as in the First Continuation and the Vulgate Cycle, the result of the killing of the king or of his maiming, which must be understood as a sexual wound. Weston invokes, in support of her thesis, the late thirteenth century Romance of Sone, in which Joseph of Arimathea is stricken through the loins as divine punishment for his marrying a pagan princess; as a result, the Kingdom of Logres is laid waste.[23]

Transmuted into the modernist poetry of T.S. Eliot, Weston's interpretation of the Waste Land evokes images of sexual "indifference" as a reflection of spiritual anomie.[24] Eliot's setting of his lands in order led him in the late Twenties to embrace royalism in politics; while in the Thirties, the Italian esotericist Julius Evola evoked the paralysis of the wounded king as an image of the decline of the West. The "indifference" which is the most grievous fault of the Grail hero is that which he displays when faced with the tragedy of one who can no longer wield the power he is supposed to represent; to ask the Grail Question is to transcend that indifference.

In Wolfram's poem, before asking the king what ails him (indifference giving way to compassion), Parzival asks where the Grail is: meaning, according to Evola, where is the royal power symbolized by the Grail, which also confers spiritual authority? To ask the Question is to initiate "the absolute action that brings about a restoration. The miraculously redeeming power" is unleashed.[25]

The central importance of asking the right question was also taken up in the Fifties by Mircea Eliade, for whom the Waste Land is the result of that "metaphysical and religious indifference" which is "our indifference to immortality." The most important question for Eliade, as for Evola, is to ask where the Grail can now be found: Where is the sacred center of our being, "the supreme reality ... and the source of immortality" symbolized by the Holy Grail? To ask the Question is to initiate the process of salvation: "In that very instant, everything is transformed: the King rises from his bed of suffering, the rivers and fountains flow once more, vegetation grows again, and the castle is miraculously restored." The only thing that prevents us from asking the Question is "lack of imagination."[26]

The transformative power of the imagination is precisely what we need to (re)discover, according to Henry Corbin, if we are to restore the Waste Land that our world has become. We too must penetrate to the heart of the Kingdom and ask the whereabouts of the Grail[27]; but we cannot remedy our state of exile[28] if we refuse to recognize that we are in it. We must refuse the refusal in order to re-sacralize the world.[29]

Notes

1. In medieval Welsh literature, the devastation of two neighboring kingdoms is also the consequence of a war, but here it is between Ireland and the Island of the Mighty (Britain), whose king, Brân the Blessed, the possessor of a magic cauldron, is wounded in the foot (or the thighs) by a poisoned spear: "The presence of Brân (the sexually incapacitated Fisher King of later Arthurian tales) and the cauldron, and the destruction of both Ireland and Britain," writes Jeffrey Gantz, the translator of the tale, "may also suggest that this is an early and primitive version of the Grail legend" (*M* 66).

2. *LG* I, 160; IV, 64; *QHG* 215–6: *Si en avint si grant persecucion a ambedous les roiaumes, el roiaume de Terre Foreine et el roiaume de Gales, por le vengement del roi Lambor qe Dex amoit tant, qe de grant tens les terres as laboreors ne furent gaaigniees.... Et par ce fu puis apelee la terre des dous roiaumes la Terre Gaste.... Par ceste aventure ... furent essilié et deserté li dui roiaume qui marchissoient li uns a l'autre* (*ESG* 566); *and so befelle there grete pestilence, and grete harme to bothe reallmys; for sythen encresed nother corne, ne grasse, nother well-nye no fruyte, ne in the watir was founde no fyssh. Therefore men calle hit—the londys of the too marchys—the Waste Londe, for that dolerous stroke* (*MD* 754).

3. This at least is the most plausible explanation of a somewhat enigmatic episode in the *Estoire de*

Merlin: Here Rion is boasting of his territorial conquests, when he tells King Arthur that his domains extend to the country of good grazing (*la terre de pastures*). They would reach even further (*outre*) if he could only persuade his people to venture that far; but they are put off by the sheer ugliness (*laide samblance*) of the territory beyond the grasslands. The ancients say that as soon as that appearance is transformed, the beginning of the end of the adventures of Logres will be in sight: *et li anchien dient que ja si tost ne sera cele figure ostee que les aventures del roialme de Logres ne commencheront a finer* (*VS* II, 231; *LG* I, 294).

The *figure ostee* suggests a curse lifted from the face of the land; but, in the late thirteenth century Bonn MS., the *laide samblance* is understood as a hideous idol which wards off potential invaders (*LDG* I, 1109–10). It was put there by Judas Maccabeus to mark the boundary of his conquests in Britain (!); whoever removes it must throw it into the Gulf of Satalia, in Asia Minor—or else it was put there by Judas Iscariot and must be thrown into the Abyss of Satan (1859).

4. *LG* IV, 190–1: Merlin compares the sin Balin will commit with that of Eve: Just as through her actions we all suffer *la grant dolour et la grant misere*, so thanks to Balin's deeds *seront cil de trois roiames en povreté et en escil* (*SRM* 85); *thorow that stroke thre kyngdomys shall be brought into grete poverté, miseri and wrecchednesse* (*MD* 57). Caitlín Matthews also equates the destruction of the Grail Kingdom with the loss of Eden: "The Waste Land is our state of exile: the place that is not paradise" (1984, 124).

5. ...*toutes les choses si degastees comme se effoudres fust courus en chascun lieu.... Il trova si dou tout destruit le roiame de Listinois qu'il fu puis de tous apielés li roiames de Terre Gastee et li roiames de Terre Forainne pour chou que si estraigne et si agastie estoit devenue trestoute la terre* (*SRM* 167). Martha Asher translates *Terre Forainne* as the Strange Land (*LG* IV, 214), but Carol J. Chase translates the same name as the Land Beyond when it appears in the *Estoire del Saint Graal* (*ESG* 288; *LG* I, 84) as the place where the Grail missionaries will house their sacred Vessel. If Listenois is *forainne* in the sense of *étrangère* when Alan the Fat and the Company of the Grail first arrive there, a place previously unknown to them and perhaps deemed mysterious by others, it will become even more strange and unfamiliar when twice devastated by dolorous blows: the first killing the king, the second maiming his son.

6. ...*le fruit ... dont tos li païs doit estre retenus en sa premiere biauté qui par le dolerous cop de l'espee avoit esté desertés et essiliés.... Et nonpourquant li Sires ... ne voloit mie qu'il fuissent tous jours en essill, si l'ordonna tel fruit a engendrer ... de qui terre fu raplenie ... cil qui les aventures del Saint Graal mist a fin* (*LDG* III, 238–9).

7. *CSG* 217: *Bien avés oï longuement/ Parler del grant destruiement/ Par coi nos somes chi venu./ Li roialmes de Logres fu/ Destruis, et toute la contree,/ Par le cop que fist ceste espee* (*CP* I, ll.13503–8): "Ye shall have heard tell of the great destruction through which we came hither, how that the kingdom of Logres was destroyed, and the country laid waste by the stroke of this sword" (*GGC* 27).

8. *Ce fu damages et pechiez,/ Quar por ce cop fu essilliee/ La terre qui tant est prisiee* (*CP* II, ll.17770–2). This account of the wasting of Logres, taken from the First Continuation to the Story of the Grail, has clear resonances with the story of the wasting of Wales and the Land Beyond, since in both cases the devastation results from a king's being killed by a sword. But, when the storyline is concluded in the Third Continuation, the dead king is not Lambor but Gon of the Land Laid Waste and the sword is not that of David but of Partinal.

9. *Mais ainc d'iex ne fu esgardee/ Nule terre si bien garnie/ De bois, d'iaue, de praeries;/ Ce fu li roialmes destruis./ N'estoit pas plus que mïenuis/ Le soir devant que Diex avoit/ Rendu, issi come il veoit,/ As iaues lor cors el païs./ Et tuit li bos ...*/ *En verdure furent torné/ Si tost come il ot demandé/ Por coi si durement sainnoit/ La lance qui puepler devoit/ Le regne, mais plus ne puepla/ Por che que plus ne demanda* (*CP* I, ll.13560–74): "and never might one behold a land so fairly garnished with wood, with water, and with fair pastures. Yet 'twas the Waste Kingdom, but at midnight had God made it even as he saw it; for so soon as Sir Gawain asked of the Lance, wherefore it bled thus freshly the waters flowed again through their channels, and all the woods were turned to verdure. So was the land in part repeopled, but more it might not be, since he had asked no more" (*GGC* 28–9).

10. *CSG* 219–30; *PSG* 132–3.

11. The reference is to Chrétien de Troyes' *Conte del Graal*, in which the consequence of Perceval's failure to ask the Grail Question is that lands will be laid waste: *Terres en seront escillies* (*RP* l.4679).

12. *HTC* 328–30: "Yet had that land been waste, but God had hearkened to their prayer, and by his coming had folk and land alike been delivered, and for that were they joyful" (*GGC* 46).

13. "As a matter of fact I believe that the 'Waste Land' is really the very heart of our problem; a rightful appreciation of its position and significance will place us in possession of the clue which will lead us safely through the most bewildering mazes of the fully developed tale" (Weston 1920, 63–4).

14. Rhŷs, 291: Carey comments that in the story of Gawain's visit to the White Island in the First Continuation, "as in the Third Branch, the lifting of a curse transforms a wilderness into a prosperous and populous land" (108).

15. Malory says that the Waste Land *was in the realme of Logris* (*MD* 754).

16. See THE DOLOROUS BLOW.

17. See AMANGON.

18. You have never heard the true story, we are told, of how the wealthy land of Logres was destroyed: *Coment et por coi fu destruis/ De Logres li rices païs// Li roiaumes torna a perte,/ La tiere fu morte et deserte* (*EB* ll.26–7, 29–30): "The land

turned to waste: no tree ever bore leaf again; the meadows and the flowers withered; the rivers dried to a trickle. And from that time forth no one could ever find the court of the wondrous Fisher King, which had made the land resplendent" (*CSG* 557–8).

19. *CSG* 559–60: The *Elucidation* refers to seven adventures—the last of which leads to "repopulation after the great destruction"—through which the court of the Grail is found again and the kingdom is restored.

20. *Hersoir quant ving en cest païs/ Vi cest païs gaste et desert,/ Or le voi de tout bien covert* (*GCP* ll.322–4).

21. *...en ceste regne n'avoit riviere/ Qui ne fust gaste ne fontaine/ Et la terre gaste et soutaine,/ Or ont lor cors, chascune est saine.// Et de toz biens i a assez/ Dont devant estiens soffraitoz* (*GCP* ll.492–5, 500–1).

22. *CSG* 341–3.

23. *Es rains et desous l'afola/ De coi grant dolor endura.// Lorgres est uns nons de dolour// Tant que li rois fu mehaigniés* (*SN* ll.4775–6, 4843, 4853): "Now there can be no possible doubt here, the condition of the King is sympathetically reflected on the land, the loss of virility in the one brings about a suspension of the reproductive processes of Nature on the other. The same effect would naturally be the result of the death of the sovereign upon whose vitality these processes depended ... the land becomes Waste, and the task of the hero is that of restoration" (Weston 1920, 22–3).

24. *WL* ll.235–42, 47–52.

25. Evola 1997, 122–3.

26. Eliade 1991, 56: Although Eliade references Weston as his scholarly source, it is clearly to Evola that he is indebted for the idea that the Question (Where is the Grail?) offers salvation from cosmic indifference. Eliade continues: "Those few words of Parsifal had been enough to regenerate the whole of Nature." But this salvific moment is not found in Wagner's *Parsifal*, nor in his German source where, as Weston points out, "of a Land laid Waste, either through drought, or war, there is no mention.... The punishment falls on the hero who has failed to put the question, rather than on the land, which, indeed, appears to be in no way affected, either by the wound of the King, or the silence of the hero" (1920, 18–9).

27. *...pour Parsifal, pénétrant dans le domaine du Graal, une seule question importe, parce que de cette question va dépendre la réjuvénation du monde, cette question: Où est le Graal?* (Corbin 1983, 260).

28. *Essillié*, the Old French word used in both prose and verse to describe the Waste Land, can mean both "exiled" and "devastated" or "ravaged" (*CGL* II, 139).

29. Corbin 1986, 276–7.

The WHITE ISLAND

The White Island, off the coast of Britain, is only one of the places where the Holy Grail dwells on Earth; and the only hero who reaches it is Gawain, when he takes up the quest of the murdered Silimac, riding by night along a causeway until he reaches a regal hall.

Seated at supper with the king of the island, Gawain sees the Grail going unsupported from table to table, serving the assembled knights with whatever food they desire. The king tells Gawain that he should not be surprised that the Vessel has such power, since it was so loved by Our Lord that He honored it with His Holy Blood on the day of His Crucifixion.[1]

The king goes on to recount how Joseph of Arimathea created the Grail from pure gold, as a Vessel in which to catch the blood that ran from the feet of Our Lord as He hanged on the Cross. After burying Jesus Christ, Joseph places the Grail in his house where he prays every day before the true blood of Our Lord,[2] until his people report him to the Jewish authorities.

Joseph is imprisoned in a high-walled tower but God, responding to Joseph's prayer that the Grail should be kept safe from the Jews, raises the walls up so that Joseph can escape. This time, the Jews force him into exile; before leaving, he has a vision in which God tells him that he will be given a land in which he can live in safety.

Joseph leads a company including Nicodemus, who assisted him at the Deposition and who has carved an image of Christ on the Cross; they make ready their ships and set off without delay, sailing without stop until they came to the land which God promised to Joseph: Known as the White Island, it is a part of what is now England entirely surrounded by sea.[3]

The Company of the Grail builds dwellings there and lives in peace for two years. But in the third year, the local inhabitants take up arms against the incomers and Joseph's people, after suffering reverses in battle, find themselves short of food. Joseph, when he was in the tower, had prayed the Lord to lend him the powers of the Grail in time of need; this was certainly such a time. So, he prays to God the Creator in His mercy to provide him with the Vessel in which he had collected the Holy Blood, following which the company sit down at table.

The Grail appears straightaway, giving out wine and food in abundance to everyone according to their desire[4]; it is thus that the first Feast of the Grail is celebrated on British soil. Thanks to the power of the Holy Vessel, Joseph can keep his enemies at bay.

When he is nearing the end of his life, Joseph prays that his lineage be made guardians of the Grail: The Fisher King is of Joseph's family and so is Perceval.[5]

Gawain falls asleep while listening to the tale; when he awakens, he is no longer on the island.[6] When Gawain returns to King Arthur's court, he recounts his adventures there[7]; but no Knight of the Round Table ever again finds the White Island.

Notes

1. *Bien en puet avoir grant pooir,/ Que c'est icel Graal por voir/ Que nostre Sires tant ama/ Que de son saint sanc l'anora/ Au jor que il fu en croiz mis* (CP II, ll.17567–71).
2. *...por l'anor/ Du verai sanc nostre Seignor* (CP II, ll.17623–4).
3. *...le païs/ Que Diex ot a Josep promis./ Ille Blanche ot non la contree,// Une partie est d'Engleterre/ Que la mer clot entor et serre* (CP II, ll.17695–7, 17699–700).
4. *Et li Graaus manois venoit/ Et le vin par trestot metoit* (PCP ll.7653–4); *Et li Graaux par tot aloit/ Et pain et vin par tot portoit,/ Et autres mes a grant planté,/ Ce que chascun venoit a gre* (CP II, ll.17723–6).
5. The Short Redaction of the First Continuation names Perceval's father Guellans Guenelaus as one of that lineage: *Li Rices Peschieres por voir/ En fu estrais et tuit si oir,/ Et dïent Guellans Guenelaus,/ Et il et ses fius Percevaus* (PCP ll.7669–72). The Long Redaction gives the name as Greloguevaus, Galozgrenax or Grelogrenaus, but does not say he is Perceval's father (CP II, 529).
6. CSG 217–9.
7. CSG 224.

Y

YGLAIS

The niece of Joseph of Arimathea, Yglais has three brothers: Pelles, the Hermit King; Messios, the Fisher King, who guards the Grail and other sacred relics; and the evil King of Castle Mortal, who will die trying to win the relics. Yglais has two children: Perceval the Good Knight and his sister Dandrane. Her husband is Alan the Fat, the grandson of Nicodemus.[1]

Alan is the Lord of the Vales of Kamaalot, but he is attacked by the Lord of the Fens and, after his death in battle, all his fifteen castles are lost, apart from Kamaalot itself. Yglais, the Widow Lady, is eventually restored to her lands by her son, although her joy is tempered by the news of the death of her brother the Fisher King and the usurpation of his realm by the King of Castle Mortal, whose relationship to her grieves her greatly.[2] She ends her days with her daughter in the Grail Castle, which was once ruled by her brother the Fisher King, thanks to its reconquest by her son; she has the body of Nicodemus brought there.[3]

Notes

1. *HBG* 19–20: Perceval's mother is elsewhere called Philosofine and her family connections vary greatly within the romances.
2. *HBG* 152.
3. *HBG* 263–4.

YSABEL

The cousin of Perceval's mother Philosofine, Ysabel travels with her in the Company of the Grail from the Holy Land to

Britain. They settle in a land where four maidens build a castle for them but, because the land is waste and full of sinners, the Grail itself is carried away from there by angels, who take it to the realm of the Fisher King. Ysabel has brought with her from the Holy Land the ointment used by the three Marys upon Jesus; she uses it to treat Perceval for wounds he has suffered in battle.[1]

Perceval's sister comes to live with the holy Lady Ysabel who is, by now, hundreds of years old, her life sustained by the frequent sight of legions of angels winging towards the Fisher King's castle, bearing the Holy Grail with the Host that sustains the life of his father.[2]

Note
1. CSG 364.
2. CSG 409.

YVAIN

The son of the infamous Morgan the Fay, King Arthur's half-sister, Yvain's father is Urien, King of Gorre, a descendant of the first Christian King of Wales.[1]

Travelling with his cousin Gawain and the Irish knight Morholt, he enters the Forest of Aroie in the Country of Strange Adventures. There, by a fountain at the head of a stream in a deep valley, they come across three maidens who offer to lead them to adventures. Yvain, who is the youngest of the three knights, chooses the eldest maiden, a white-haired sixty year old, agreeing to keep her safely in his company for a year.[2]

Unfortunately, this is not how things turn out. Riding west together, after several adventures, they arrive at the Rock of the Stag, where Yvain sees an inscription saying that one can see many of the marvels of the Holy Grail there, at the risk of being killed or maimed. The old lady wants to leave but Yvain persuades her to stay the night with him under his protection.

He would have done well to heed the wisdom of age: During the night they hear two knights fighting but can see nothing because the sky is so black and overcast. They fall asleep but, when they awaken, Yvain discovers that he has been pierced through the left shoulder by a sword; both the lady and his squire are dying of loss of blood after a blade wound through the chest. Yvain can find no sign that a mortal man has been there; he therefore concludes that it must have been a demon who killed them.[3]

Lamenting his dishonor, Yvain vows that he will never stop wandering in search of adventure until he has learnt how they were killed, if it is possible for a knight to do so: He would, he says, prefer to die rather than remain in ignorance of an adventure that could lead to people being killed without warning.[4] But in the end he takes the advice of two other Knights of the Round Table, Kay and Girflet, to accept that the wonders of the land—even those of the Holy Grail[5]—are the will of God, whose vengeance falls on the just and unjust alike.

Yvain finally returns to the fountain where he originally met the murdered maiden and where he agreed to meet up with his companions at the end of a year; but they are not there. He waits until evening, when a maiden clad in scarlet arrives from the Forest of Aroie. She brings him news of Gawain and Morholt, who have been ensorcelled.

The scarlet maiden then goes on to explain as much as she can to Yvain about what befell him at the Rock of the Stag, which is one of the adventures of the Holy Grail: Their manifestation is more wondrous in some places than in others; they will not stop happening to Yvain or anyone else until the arrival of the Good Knight who will bring the wonders of the Kingdom of Logres to an end.[6] The Good Knight will achieve all those perilous adventures which no other Round Table Knights will be able to accomplish.

She goes on to tell him that the Good Knight is not yet conceived but that, if she is still alive when he is baptized, she will know his name as soon as he receives it; Yvain will see him when the knight comes to Arthur's court one Pentecost and sits in the Perilous Seat.[7]

Yvain now attempts but fails to free his former companions from their enchantment (it will be left to Gahariet, Gawain's youngest brother, to rescue them); he returns to Arthur's court alone.[8]

Notes

1. *LG* I, 156: According to the Vulgate *Estoire del Saint Graal*, Galahad, the youngest son of Joseph of Arimathea, marries the daughter of the King of the Distant Isles and fathers Lyanor, who rules Wales after Galahad. From Lyanor descends King Urien, from whom issues Yvain: *Cil Galaaz prist a feme la fille au roi des Lointaignes illes et engendra en li un filz qui fu apelez Lyanor, qui puis fu rois, enprés Galaaz, de Gales. Et de celui Lianor fu puis ... li rois Uriens, dont Yveins oissi* (*ESG* 552). Urien also has an illegitimate son, also called Yvain; this Yvain, known as the Bastard, will have a son called Cahus who will meet his end because of a mysterious nightmare while acting as King Arthur's squire. Yvain the Bastard himself will die at the hands of Gawain in the course of the Grail Quest (*QP* 153; *LG* IV, 49).

2. *LG* IV, 274-5.

3. Morholt, who had preceded them with his maiden, had a vision of a dragon rescuing a stag from a pack of hounds; his maiden and squire were also killed (*LG* V, 16-7).

4. He will never do so. But Balin has also encountered a knight who killed people invisibly; he turned out to be Garlon, the brother of King Pellehan. Although Balin has killed Garlon, could it be the same *deables ou ennemis* (*SRM* 472) at work?

5. *...les merveilles de cest terre, mesmement celles du Saint Graal* (*SRM* 472).

6. *Ce sont ... des aventures du Saint Graal, qui ainsi aviennent plus merveilleusement en ung lieu que en autre. Si ne remaindront ja qu'elles n'aviengnent ainsi ne pour vous ne pour autre jusqu'a tant que le Bon Chevalier qui les merveilles du royaume de Logres devra mener a fin viendra* (*SRM* 476).

7. *LG* V, 23-6.

8. *LG* V, 28-30.

Afterword

Higher Mysteries: Grail Initiation as Twentieth Century Mythology

> "What form precisely the parallel to the 'higher mysteries' of pre–Christian faiths assumed in the primitive Church is now difficult to ascertain; but there is no doubt that what we now know as Gnosticism enshrines in its few and fragmentary remains the tradition of a great system of early Christian esoteric teaching and practice."
> —Jessie L. Weston (1913, 105–6)

Although much mainstream scholarship finds the origin of elements of the Grail legend (insofar as it is necessary to seek beyond the personal creativity of the poets) in Celtic literature and mythology, there is a minority view that it lies in heterodox, if not actually heretical, forms of Christianity. It was the English scholar Jessie L. Weston (1850–1928) who most famously argued for a golden chain leading from the pagan mystery religions, through Gnostic Christianity, to the exalted mysticism of the later Grail romances.

Early in the twentieth century Weston argued that in the rites of the Mysteries (such as those of the Babylonian Tammuz, the Egyptian Osiris, the Phrygian Attis and the Syrian Adonis) we find the best explanation of certain curious features of the romances: "In these rites the death of the god was annually commemorated with weeping and lamentation; a figure of the deity was carried by weeping women to the sea-shore, where it was committed to the waves. With the death of the god, vegetation was held to die, and revive with his revival, after a certain period, sometimes three days."

Weston finds a survival of these rites in the details found particularly in the visit of Gawain to the White Island in the First Continuation to the Story of the Grail, where we find a dead body on a bier, wailing women and a wasted land by the sea (1906, 330).

But Weston's conclusion—that the Grail Castle must be considered to be a Temple of Initiation—is weakened in the eyes of more mainstream scholars by its association with late nineteenth century and early twentieth century occultism, in some streams of which she saw a continuity with ancient initiation rituals: "The difficulty of these investigations," as she herself puts it (1906, 331n2), "lies in the fact that those who know the details accurately, and from the inside, have always been pledged to secrecy. We are thus obliged to rely, more or less, on outside testimony, and therefore cannot be certain that we have either the full description of the rites, or of the symbolism involved."

Of the testimony that she does rely on, some of "those who know" remain anonymous. But she does name as sources the scholar of esoteric traditions G.R.S. Mead (1863–1933), the poet and occultist W.B. Yeats (1865–1939) and the Christian mystic A.E. Waite, with whom Weston would have a scholarly feud which continued after her lifetime—on Waite's part, at least!

Both Mead and Yeats were at one time members of the Theosophical Society, which had been founded in 1875 in order to revive western esotericism through an encounter with the wisdom of the East. Mead contributed important scholarly studies on Gnosticism, Neo-Platonism and Vedantic philosophy to the school of "divine wisdom" (Goodrick-Clarke 2005, 4–7), but resigned from the Society in 1909 after it was riven by internal disputes. He then founded the Quest Society "to promote investigation and comparative study of religion, philosophy, and science, on the basis of experience."

Waite and Weston would both contribute articles on the Holy Grail to its quarterly review,[1] which also received contributions from Waite's friend Arthur Machen (1863–1947), a noted writer of supernatural fiction[2]; as well as from the Anglo-Ceylonese scholar Ananda K. Coomaraswamy (1877–1947), an adherent of the Traditionalist school associated with the French metaphysician René Guénon (Goodrick-Clarke 2005, 19–24). Coomaraswamy would declare himself an adherent of Weston's Ritual Theory (Goetinck 2014, 120). Mead's Gnostic studies were an important influence on C.G. Jung's theory of archetypal images; while the Quest Society can be seen as a fore-runner of the Eranos conferences (26–31), to which we will return.

Yeats, by contrast, pursued his esoteric quest from Theosophy to the Hermetic Order of the Golden Dawn, a magical and initiatory organization of "unbounded eclecticism," in Kathleen Raine's phrase, whose membership would include well-known writers such as Waite, Machen, Algernon Blackwood and Charles Williams[3]—as well as the infamous Aleister Crowley, whom Yeats was instrumental in ejecting from the Order (Raine, 2–6). Crowley would go on to become the head of the British lodge of another initiatory order, the O.T.O. (Ordo Templi Orientis); a position earlier held (briefly and perhaps surprisingly) by the Austrian philosopher Rudolf Steiner (Lachman, 154–6).

Best known today as the founder of the Waldorf School movement and inventor of "bio-dynamic" farming techniques (which use astrology as well as more conventional organic methods), Rudolf Steiner (1861–1925) was an influential teacher of "occult" or "spiritual" science who, in the first two decades of the twentieth century, lectured and wrote extensively on the pagan mystery religions and their relationship to Gnosticism and Christianity. Independently of Weston, using methods of super-sensory perception that were alien to mainstream Arthurian scholarship, Steiner outlined a path of initiation that would lead to the science or knowledge of the Grail, in which the essence of the ancient Mysteries is renewed in the post–Christian age (Steiner 2001b, 11).

A Brotherhood of Initiates

After becoming disillusioned with the Theosophists, Steiner, like Mead, would found his own society, one based on the principles of "anthroposophy," which he defined as "a path of knowledge to guide the spiritual in the human being to the spiritual in the universe."[4] The path to this universal spirituality is found in what is sometimes called Johannine Christianity, the mystical wing of the mainstream Church, rooted in the

Gospel of John rather than the three Synoptic Gospels, which appealed to unorthodox Christians such as Waite and Steiner.

For Johannine Christians, Steiner wrote, "the mystery of the higher ego"—which is "what had been reborn for all humanity" at Golgotha—was symbolized by the Vessel of the Last Supper in which Joseph of Arimathea caught the blood that poured from the wound in the side of Jesus Christ (2001b, 22-3). Steiner promulgated the idea that the essence of the ancient pagan Mysteries had been refined in early Christianity[5] by the Gnostics,[6] preserved by angelic beings "while human beings were diligently eradicating exoteric Gnostic knowledge" (32) and entrusted to a "brotherhood of initiates" who guard it in "a holy place" (23-4).

These initiates—who included the Knights Templar (2007, 43)—are known as the Brotherhood of the Holy Grail because in that symbol, "if understood in its true character," is embraced everything which characterizes "the secrets of the human soul" (2001b, 45) in its evolution from (bodily) sentience, through mind or intellect to spiritual consciousness. Modern Grail initiates, by contemplating the chalice containing the blood of the Redeemer, may receive the higher or Christ ego "into their being."[7]

Steiner's writings about the Grail, scattered throughout his lectures and books, were systematized and developed after his death by his disciple Walter Johannes Stein (1891-1957), who published his own book on the legend in 1928. Stein follows Steiner in relating characters and events in Wolfram von Eschenbach's *Parzival* to historical figures in the ninth century (just as Otto Rahn would later attempt to do with figures from the Albigensian persecution, as we will see below). But the heart of his book is a detailed summary of the poem (the English-language version using Weston's 1912 verse translation), accompanied by a spiritual exegesis.

Here he develops at length Steiner's insight that the story of Parzival is a path of initiation, leading us beyond the "intellectual soul" (personified by the wounded Amfortas) into the contemporary "consciousness soul,"[8] on the basis of which can be kindled "the development in our age of a new and full understanding of the Mystery of Golgotha" (Steiner 2001b, 33). The "historical" events of the New Testament are "recapitulated" in the Grail legends because the Christian initiate beholds taking place in "the sense-perceptible world" what, in the pre-Christian Mysteries, was experienced purely "on a supersensory level."[9]

A New Testament event that takes on a particular "occult" significance in Steiner's writings is the piercing of the side of Jesus on the Cross and the flowing of blood therefrom, an event depicted only in the Gospel of John (19.34). Adding to this verse, Robert de Boron, in his *Estoire dou Graal*, describes the blood falling on a stone at the foot of the Cross and splitting it; the blood is later collected by Joseph of Arimathea in the Vessel in which Jesus made the sacrament at the Last Supper (*EG* ll.393-4, 555-572; *MG* 18-9).

For Steiner, the Grail story of the flowing of the Holy Blood onto the Earth is an image of a cosmic event that changes human evolution on the planet: The Holy Spirit or solar Logos enters into Jesus at His baptism, so that He becomes the Christ. When His blood flows onto the ground, the Holy Spirit unites with the Earth; the solar Logos becomes the Spirit of the Earth. This is both a "spiritual process" *and* a historical event (2001a, 57-8). So it is that Walter Stein asks: "When will mankind awaken to the knowledge that with the gift of the poem of the Grail, *the age of the Holy Ghost has begun*? When will it recognize that … in the story of the Grail, faintly dawned the Mysteries of the *Spirit*. When will mankind recognize that the *earth is the Temple of the Grail*, the Body of the Christ?" (256).

But while such questions about the spiritual evolution of humankind continue to resonate among Steinerians and other adherents of Christian esotericism, it was an extended footnote, exploring the history of the weapon which caused the Holy Blood to flow, which would have the greatest afterlife in popular culture, linking in with a contemporary obsession with Nazi occultism.

Drug-Induced Pilfering

In the First Continuation to the Story of the Grail, the Bleeding Lance (which Chrétien de Troyes says is destined to destroy Logres and which Wolfram says is wielded by a heathen to maim the Grail King) is identified with the Lance with which a soldier pierces the Son of God to the heart (*CP* II, ll.17513–8; *CSG* 217).

For Stein, what is portrayed in the poems "as an imaginative picture within Parzival's vision, is also an historical and physical object." He explores some of the most important legendary associations of this Lance, such as that it was possessed by Constantine the Great, Charles Martel and Charlemagne (great conquerors all) and that it may be identified with the so-called Maurice Lance currently in the Vienna Treasure Chamber, concluding: "The lance is an object which appears in inner vision for Parzival. For the symbolism of the Empire what was inner vision has become externalized" (323–4).

This externalization of an imaginative vision was continued in a very literal fashion by an author who claimed to have been friends with Stein. Trevor Ravenscroft (1921–1989), stated that he wished to present further researches of Stein's to a wider public; researches which the professor himself had not lived to publish. If Stein's was "a curious and learned book," the same can perhaps be said of Ravenscroft's sensationalist *The Spear of Destiny* (1973), which adapted the spiritual science of Steiner and Stein to "the mythology of occult Nazism"[10]—but critics would add that it is more curious and less learned.

Ravenscroft recounts that, in his meetings with Stein, they discussed how their own personal explorations of "higher levels of consciousness" had revealed to them that Wolfram was an Occult Initiate. They also learned that *Parzival* was an Initiation Document based on a tale which Wolfram's teacher Kyot had found in the Chronicle of Anschau—which is "not a physical place at all but a state of transcendent consciousness … in which past, present and future were united in a higher dimension of time" (Ravenscroft 1982a, xvii-xviii). But their fascination with the poem was shared by a "dark genius" who saw the Grail Stone as an alchemical symbol for the Third Eye which, if activated, would vouchsafe "a vision of the hidden secrets of Time and the meaning of human destiny!" (50).

Stein is alleged to have first met Adolf Hitler in 1912 after discovering the future Führer's own tattered copy of the German poem, complete with annotations, in a pawn shop run by a black magician. But whereas Stein understood the adventures of Parzival "as initiation trials on a prescribed path to the heights of transcendent awareness," Hitler's jottings revealed the "racial fanaticism" of "a dark and brooding genius" (48–9). The sevenfold path of initiation that he followed was one that would lead him to become the vessel of the Folk Spirit of the Aryan race by "reawakening the latent powers in the blood" (70).

But Hitler had not submitted to the traditional disciplines of the spiritual path to "occult initiation"; on the contrary, like "countless adventurous members of the younger generation of the present psychedelic age,"[11] he had taken an entheogenic shortcut: a mescaline trip, prepared for him (from peyote supplied by the black magician) by an "herbalist who retained in his peasant's blood the last traces of the atavistic clairvoyance of the ancient Germanic tribes." In the course of his mushroom trip, Hitler was vouchsafed a vision that is usually only available to those who have attained "the highest virtues" of the Grail Quest: a tapestry of images from history that revealed "the spiritual biography" of his past lives.

But what he learned in the course of this "drug-induced pilfering" from the Cosmic Chronicle was that he was the re-incarnation of the monstrous historical figure on whom Wagner had based his fictional Klingsor. Like Klingsor in the music drama, he must gain possession of the Lance which pierced the side of Christ: the Spear of Destiny, a "talisman of power" which would transform him into a "chalice for the Spirit of the Anti-Christ" (77–88).

Hitler was therefore well-advanced on "a path of self-initiation" when, after the First World War, he encountered the magicians of the inner circle of the Thule Society. Named after a mythical Hyperborean paradise, a sort of northern Atlantis, the Thule Gesellschaft was founded in 1918; over a hundred years later, it lives on as a channel for "black initiation" in the fantasies of crypto-historians (Goodrick-Clarke 1992, 218), and in the virtual afterlife of the Internet.[12]

The ideology of Thule begins, like Mead's Quest Society and Steiner's Anthroposophy, with Theosophy; from which, in the years before the First World War, there developed a virulently racist and antisemitic offshoot called Ariosophy (100–2), evoking the occult wisdom of Aryan Man rather than Steiner's broader concept of the Human Being (Anthropos). The term Ariosophy was first coined in 1915 by Jörg Lanz von Liebenfels (aka Adolf Lanz, 1874–1954), a former Cistercian monk who had become obsessed with the idea that the Templars, who were themselves closely associated with the Cistercian order, were the medieval champions of a "racist gnosis" symbolized by the Grail of Holy (Aryan) Blood.

According to Lanz, the *templeisen* of Wolfram's *Parzival* who guarded the Grail were the historical Knights Templar, who preserved the purity of the blood of the Aryan race, with its "pan-psychic" powers, through "strict eugenic practices" which were "designed to breed god-men." Lanz decided to found anew the suppressed Order in order to continue its work by launching an "ario-heroic" crusade to reverse "the triumph of the racial inferiors"; to this end he bought a ruined medieval castle above the River Danube in Upper Austria to serve as the Order's Montsalvat (107–8).

But while Lanz's Order of the New Temple appealed only to an esoteric elite, his Ariosophical message was spread through a popular magazine called *Ostara* which was probably read by the young Adolf Hitler.[13] Ariosophy was also one of the influences on the fledgling Germanenorden, or German Order, which attempted to unite esoteric racists into pseudo-masonic lodges, where novices were led into a Wagnerian "grove of the Grail" to be consecrated as "brothers"; but which soon fell prey to a schism out of which emerged, in 1916, the Germanenorden Walvater[14] of the Holy Grail (129–31). It was the Bavarian lodge of the Germanenorden Walvater which took the cover name of

Thule and adopted as its emblem "a long dagger superimposed on a shining swastika sun-wheel" (144).

Historians have now begun to untangle the web of interconnections between the Thule Society and the nascent NSDAP or Nazi Party. What history does not tell us, but Trevor Ravenscroft does, is that the Thule also developed astrological rituals which were designed to open communication with "non-human Intelligences" (161–4); it would now facilitate the next step on Hitler's path to become the Chalice of the Anti-Christ. For it was in the presence of several Thulists that Hitler was initiated by a Master-Adept, the violently antisemitic journalist and playwright Dietrich Eckart (1868–1923), "in a monstrous sadistic magic ritual" which opened Hitler's "occult centers" to the evil Intelligences for whom he would now become a channel (155).

Hitler is here seen to have undergone a perversion of the authentic Grail Initiation which Stein is considered by Ravenscroft to have achieved. This threefold process begins with the acquiring of Imaginative Cognition by emptying the consciousness of "thought images," leading to the attainment of that "vision of the celestial hierarchies, which has inspired a hidden thread of Grail Initiates since the days of Joseph of Arimathea." This in turn leads the initiate to develop the faculty of Inspiration whereby, "through the purification of the life of feeling," he can directly communicate with these "sublime spirits." Only now can the initiate, by strengthening "the moral powers of the will," take the third and final step "to the ultimate realization of the Grail," attaining "intuitive identification" with the spirits of super-sensory worlds: a stage which is signaled by seeing, with the Third Eye, one's name and those of one's previous incarnations inscribed on the Grail Stone (198–201).

But it would be wrong to think that Hitler achieved the same results simply by dropping mushrooms and indulging in obscene rituals. Ravenscroft reveals that the final stage of Hitler's anti-Grail Initiation was presided over by another occult *eminence grise*, none other than Professor Karl Haushofer (1869–1946), who taught the Thulist Rudolf Hess political geography or "geopolitics" at Munich University.

It was in the presence of Hess that Haushofer, in the summer of 1924 (shortly after Eckart's death), allegedly initiated Hitler into the Secret Doctrine which underlay geopolitics. Hitler was at this time in Landsberg Prison in Bavaria, serving a year's imprisonment for an attempted coup; but four walls do not a prison make when you can have the "time consciousness" of your etheric body expanded and metamorphosed, as Hitler apparently did.[15]

This Ancient Talisman of Power

It was nearly thirty years after he first saw the Lance of Longinus in the Hofburg in Vienna that Hitler was at last able to take possession of the relic that he believed would confer on him the destiny of the world; although, in reality, it would pass to the Americans after seven years (Ravenscroft 1982a, 316–8). According to Ravenscroft, Hitler first became aware of the "illusive message" of "this ancient talisman of power" in 1909: "The Spear," he later recounted, "appeared to be some sort of magical medium of revelation for it brought the world of ideas into such close and living perspective that human imagination became more real than the world of sense" (7–9).

It was in that same year, 1909, that Jessie Weston published the second volume of her *Legend of Sir Perceval*. It was here that she developed the suggestion (first made three years earlier in a paper she presented to the Folk-Lore Society of London, at which W.B. Yeats was present) that the Lance was a phallic symbol; it was precisely the sexual nature of the Rites of Adonis—which, she had concluded, were what lay behind "the scene enacted in the presence of the chance visitor to the Grail Castle" (Grayson, 61)—which resulted in those pagan fertility rites, "Christianity once in possession," falling "under the ban of the Church" (Weston 1909, 254).

For those of us living in a post–Freudian world in which anything longer than it is wide is capable of being interpreted as a phallic symbol, Weston's suggestion seems singularly uncontroversial; but in her lifetime, as an unmarried woman, she had to deal with snide remarks such as that of Waite about "her Fertility complex." Moreover, assumptions about "suppressed sexual urges in the spinster's life" were "a point of humor not reserved to Waite and his circle" (Grayson, 40).

When we consider the personal (masquerading as intellectual) flak that "Miss" Weston took for daring to suggest that the Lance was a phallic symbol, we can see (without consulting the Cosmic Chronicle) how far we have travelled in the nearly sixty years separating Ravenscroft's unrelentingly sensationalistic *The Spear of Destiny* from Weston's first boldly speculative but deeply researched Grail studies. What spans this half century is what I would describe as decades of scholarly myth-making: mythography morphing into mythopoeia. The scholars, we might say, had interpreted the Grail; their present task became to refashion it in their own image.

Despite Weston's early disclaimers—"I would here guard against being supposed in any way to advocate the view that the mediaeval minstrels were the conscious guardians, and transmitters, of an occult tradition" (1906, 332*n*1)—she later became convinced that authors such as Kyot (1909, 202) and Robert de Boron (279–80) were themselves initiates. This changing perspective she herself attributes to her contact with individuals who were contemporary practitioners of similar cultic rituals, one of whom commented, on being presented with a copy of her translation of Gawain's adventures on the White Island: "This is the story of an Initiation told from the outside" (253).

The American scholar William A. Nitze (1876–1957), working contemporaneously, also put forward a theory of the origin of the Grail legend in the ancient Mysteries. For him, the Fisher King symbolizes the creative forces of Nature: "And his weakness or infirmity agrees with Nature's declining strength; thus, his land lays waste or is under the ban of enchantment." The Lance is "the instrument of sacrifice." The Grail Knight is the initiate, guided to the Otherworld by the Fisher King, who presides over the repast at which the mortal hero partakes of the divine food, for which the Grail is the receptacle. By so doing, he "establishes a blood-bond with the god," who is symbolized by the Fisher King's aged father (Nitze 1909, 396–404). The initiate who passes the tests "is thereby made immortal and becomes the Fisher King's successor" (380). Such a mystery cult, Nitze argued, could have been brought to Britain from the Mediterranean, where the myth that accompanied the ritual would have been transformed by indigenous beliefs, thus explaining the presence of Celtic elements in the stories (411–18).

But, while agreeing with Nitze that the story of the Grail is an "initiation story," Weston stresses that it is an initiation *manqué*: For the Grail Quest only begins when the hero, having failed his first test at the Temple of the Grail, sets out to find it again (1913, 95). Although the development of the romance cycle owes much to imaginative literary invention, "the groundwork of the story, the 'kernel' of the cycle, is not invention, but tradition; it is the legendary record of something that really happened, of an experience at once terrifying and exalting, which left an indelible impression upon the mind of him who underwent it" (97). Such an experience, she argued, was preserved in the story of the squire Cahus, whose death results from a horrific encounter on the astral plane during a failed test of fitness for initiation (1920, 182).

The pagan Mystery, already altered by being transplanted from the eastern Mediterranean to Britain, would have been further transformed by its encounter with Gnostic Christianity, in which the saving knowledge (*gnosis*) that comes from a personal revelation of the divine is more important than mere faith.[16] Weston points specifically to the second century Gnostic sect known as the Naassenes (or Snake People, so called because they revered the serpent of Genesis as the bringer of gnosis), for whom Adonis, Attis and Osiris were identified with Jesus the Blessed as the True Gate to the accomplishment of the Mysteries.[17]

Such a syncretistic Gnostic Mystery cult could have survived the imposition of orthodoxy in Roman Britain in the late fourth century by being "secretly practiced in lonely and inaccessible districts in Wales; the mountain glens and fastnesses of that country offering a shelter to the worshippers of a dying faith." The text known as the *Elucidation*, which many scholars would argue elucidates nothing at all, takes on a "peculiar interest and significance" when read in the light of the Ritual Theory: For it tells of a king committing an outrage against the Maidens of the Golden Cups, bestowers of plenty; as a result of which the court of the Fisher King disappears and the land is laid waste.

Weston suggests that we have here "an account of the disappearance of a once-popular form of worship" which nevertheless survives as an underground cult, preserved in secret by certain families who were the hereditary guardians of this tradition. A member of such a family would have been the storyteller known as Bleheris in the First Continuation and Blihos Bliheris in the *Elucidation* (a knight who ended up as Malory's Sir Bleoberis), whom Weston considered to be responsible for passing on "the traditional record of a genuine experience" in the form of an Arthurian romance to the French (1913, 109–115).

Strange Currents

The Grail romances, preserving fragments of a faith forgotten, were part of the "strange currents" that Weston saw as "stirring in those days," which also included the symbolic writings of the troubadours and the alchemists, as well as the heretical beliefs of the Albigenses (or Cathars). To these, she suggested could be added the alleged heresy of the Knights Templar: "There is a stream of tradition, running as it were underground, which from time to time rises to the surface, only to be relentlessly suppressed" (136–8)—as were, indeed, both the Cathars and the Templars.[18]

In a later work—in what is indeed her most famous book, in which she sums up her theories of the evolution of the Grail story (*From Ritual to Romance*)—Weston further suggests that the Templars might have encountered in the East the survival of a sect such as the Naassenes (1920, 187). Moreover, she finds in the Tarot cards another survival, preserved in images brought from the East, of "a very ancient ritual, of which fragmentary survivals alone have been preserved to us" (80).

The four suits of modern playing cards—Spades and Clubs (black), Hearts and Diamonds (red)—appear in the earliest known packs in the Italian Renaissance as Swords, Batons or Staves, Cups and Coins—to which are added twenty-two Trump cards in order to produce the Tarot pack, now widely used for divination. In the late nineteenth century, it was adopted by the magicians of the Hermetic Order of the Golden Dawn as a symbol system which they could incorporate into an eclectic body of correspondences to use in their ceremonies; Yeats, who was initiated into the Order in 1890, would also use it for his writing (Raine, 5).

Yeats also linked the symbolism of the four suits with that of the four treasures of the gods of pagan Ireland (28)—cauldron, stone, spear and sword.[19] In a prose story, Yeats' dreaming protagonist Red Hanrahan is offered the sacred objects by four women sitting in high chairs. But he fails to choose one, as Perceval fails to ask concerning the Grail and Lance—"and presently is overcome once more with the irresistible sleep of forgetfulness" (33), as Gawain is, after seeing the Grail, Lance and Sword on the White Island. Weston, who corresponded with Yeats on the subject (1920, 79), considered that the four treasures of the Irish god-kings and the Grail symbols share a "common original" (74) and that, along with the analogous Tarot symbols, they are all "connected with a very ancient ritual, of which fragmentary survivals alone have been preserved to us" (80).

It is these fragmentary survivals which feature so powerfully in a work better known today than Weston's, but partly inspired by it, an influence openly admitted by the author: T.S. Eliot's modernist poem, *The Waste Land* (1922). *From Ritual to Romance*, he states in the Notes to the poem, suggested "the plan and a good deal of the incidental symbolism" as well as the title; thus, we find references to the Tarot pack, notably the twelfth arcanum (The Hanged Man) and The Man with Three Staves (or Three of Wands), whom Eliot associated with the Fisher King (*WL* 76).

It is the Fisher King who speaks in the fifth and final section of Eliot's poem, sitting between the sea and an "arid plain," of the need to order his lands (74). Here we see the Fisher King as Weston saw him, as "the essential center" of a fertility cult, "a being semi-divine, semi-human, standing between his people and his land, and the unseen forces which control their destiny" (1920, 136). Whether or not it is the Fisher King who speaks the evocative line—"These fragments I have shored against my ruins" (*WL* 75)—we seem to be pointed to what Weston called "the *disjecta membra* of a vanished civilization" (1920, 7), in whose ruins we can only create a wasteland unless the god who dies is also resurrected. But can the fragments be re-assembled in the modern world in anything like a meaningful whole?

Weston's writings hint that she was not merely concerned to establish the origin of the symbols of a medieval literary cycle, but was attracted to the idea of a prehistoric perennial wisdom at the root of human culture.[20] Eliot was concerned to show how the image of the Waste Land revealed the spiritual emptiness of the modern world; but his solution was to involve a return to mainstream Christianity.[21]

A Mystifying Compound

While the Initiation Theory of Grail origins put forward by Weston and Nitze was criticized in some quarters, it also had powerful adherents. Notable among these was the American scholar Roger Sherman Loomis (1887–1966) who, in 1926, published *Celtic Myth and Arthurian Romance*, the first of a series of major studies of the Arthurian and Grail legends, which remained highly influential among the wider reading public in the late twentieth century. In this early work he attempts a hypothetical reconstruction of an ancient British initiation ceremony, but he considers the ritual to be devoid of any mystical significance (1926, 269n3). Where Weston looked to the Rites of Adonis and the Mysteries of Attis (and later Mithras) for the origins of her Grail cult, and Nitze favored the Eleusinian Mysteries, Loomis postulated that the ritual had its origins in the Mysteries of Samothrace, which would have been brought to Britain from the Mediterranean.

"The scenes in the Grail Castle," writes Loomis, "are a mystifying compound of mythological tests of the power of the young god and ritual tests of a human initiate into a fertility cult." These tests, of a virginal youth of noble blood, "introduced at night to an island sanctuary or a strange palace hall" would involve his encounter with an aged, suffering man, wailing women, a maiden bearing a cauldron and a youth bearing a lance which bleeds into it. If the initiate asks: "For what do these things serve?" the aged king declares that his infirmity is healed and that the fertility of the land is assured. The youth is then obliged "to exercise his generative energies" in a ritual marriage with the maiden of the cauldron (269–70).

Although "Miss Weston" (as she was always known) had argued, to the bemusement of some of her male colleagues, that the Grail and the Lance were sexual symbols, she did not consider it possible that the "coarsely pagan ritual" described by Loomis could have generated the Grail romances (Grayson, 18). As her biographer Janet Grayson has pointed out, Loomis' support for Weston did not long outlive her death in 1928: within two years he was retreating from positions stated in his first book (7). By the late Forties, when he published his second great work on Arthurian Tradition, Loomis had abandoned all ties with the ritual theory of origins.[22] Moreover, in an essay published in the Fifties, he wrote that while Weston's "theory of the Waste Land as illustrating a sympathetic nexus between the vitality of a divine king and the life-forces of his kingdom" has the support of several medieval texts, "her speculations about a primitive vegetation cult, partly Christianized and transmitted from the Orient to Britain, lacked solid foundations" (1956, 53). In the Preface to his last book (*The Grail: From Celtic Myth to Christian Symbol*), he states that he retracted his adherence to "Weston's ingenious hypothesis concerning the Grail and Lance, for lack of valid and clearly pertinent evidence" (1963, *ix*).

Nevertheless, Loomis paid tribute to Weston as one of those who "advanced the limits of our knowledge in a large way and into obscure regions" (1949, 6). Although Nitze had by this time also abandoned the Initiation Theory (Grayson, 32), its influence (however indirect) is apparent in the work of creative writers from the Twenties onwards, notably George Moore, John Cowper Powys and Naomi Mitchison (Marino, 47–58); as well as in fantasy novels from the Sixties and Seventies by writers such as Susan Cooper and Tim Powers (59–61).

The most popular and successful reworking of the Arthurian legend and its Grail mythology in the late twentieth century is undoubtedly Marion Zimmer Bradley's *The Mists of Avalon* (1982), which spawned a TV miniseries as well as several prequels linking the Arthurian period with the fall of Atlantis. The central figure of the book is Morgan the Fay, here called Morgaine, who is initiated as a priestess of the Mother Goddess but is forced to come to terms with the encroaching Christian religion. The priestesses (for whom all the Gods are one God and all the Goddesses, one Goddess) are entrusted with guarding the Four Treasures of the Mysteries (sword, spear, cup and platter, analogous to the Tarot suits) which are also known as the Druidic Holy Regalia of Avalon; they fear that the regalia will be profaned by the priests of a God who will have no others before Him (Marino, 61–4). The ensuing struggle, between the old ways and the new, makes for a powerful narrative; while providing an imaginative and plausible reworking of many familiar characters and themes from Arthurian literature.

Chrétien's Symbols	Tarot Suit	Modern Playing Cards	Yeatsian Symbolism	Irish Treasure	Bradley's Avalonian Regalia
Sword of Triboet	Swords	Spades	Courage	Sword of Nuadu	Sword
Bleeding Lance	Wands	Diamonds	Power	Spear of Lugh	Spear
Bejeweled, golden Grail	Cups	Hearts	Pleasure	Cauldron of Muirias	Cup
Silver Trencher	Pentacles	Clubs	Knowledge	Stone of Fál	Platter

It is easy to see the Avalonian religion as the heir to Weston's fertility cult, with its "higher mysteries" making a bridge to Christian mysticism.[23] But at the same time Bradley introduces a feminist dimension to the novel lacking, or at least underplayed, in Weston's theories. It is this aspect which is taken up by the medieval scholar Prudence Jones who, unlike Weston, is herself a practicing neo-Pagan.[24]

Jones presents us with a clear summary of what Weston herself always presented as a work-in-progress, revealing what the initiation into the Grail Mystery would have been like. The initiate first encounters the Cup and the Lance in the court of the King of Castle Mortal, associated with the colors black and green. He must then brave the Perilous Chapel, in order to be proved worthy of reaching the court of the Maimed King, "the spirit encased in flesh," ruler of the "rich" Grail as feeding vessel in the Red Land. Having seen the wonders in the Grail Castle, the initiate must re-solder the Sword, "symbol of conscious awareness," and/or ask the significance of "this earthly richness." If he is able to do this, he wins to the *Holy* Grail, which is the "highest level" of the symbol ("invisible to mortal eyes, source of spiritual life and blessedness"), in the court of the Fisher King, who rules over the White Land (Jones, 145).

But Jones laments the fact that, although Weston acknowledges that the Grail Cup symbolizes female sexuality, this principle is otherwise "as invisible in her commentaries as it was at the time in the culture at large." Weston's failure to emphasize "the female aspect of deity" meant that her researches remained unfinished. But the task of healing the modern Waste Land has fallen to those who re-invoke "the ancient power" of the Great Mother as Earth Goddess: "The Goddess *is* the Grail, both the feminine principle symbolized by the Cup, and the mystical principle of fulfilment" (Jones, 148).

Constantly Recurring Triads

In Prudence Jones' summary of the process of initiation into the Grail Mystery, above, she draws attention to the three kings who preside over its rituals and to the colors associated with them. This requires further elaboration, since these colors and a series of analogous triads were, in fact, central not only to Weston's concept of Grail Initiation, but also to the intellectual journey she went on, from studying the origins of the Arthurian legends to developing a theory that would explain the evolution of their most sacred symbol from ritual to romance.

Weston's first two Arthurian books were studies of the Legend of Sir Gawain (whom she saw as essentially a pagan, mythic hero) and of Sir Lancelot, whose involvement with the Grail Quest she dismissed as full of "false and wholly sickly pseudo-morality" (1901, 113). But in an Appendix to the latter work, published as a separate volume, she explores the significance of the fact that Lancelot is on three separate occasions described as changing the color of his armor from white to red to black (or green), the order of the sequence changing with the context (1902, 9–11). While most of her study is concerned with parallel episodes in folklore and romance, Weston adds in a footnote a reference to a subject that will become increasingly important in her later work: "A friend, learned in such matters, has informed me that these sets of colors represent certain alchemical processes…. It seems possible that there may have been some hidden and mystical significance attached to their earliest use; we have not fathomed all the secrets of folk-lore" (37*n*1).

In her later study of the Legend of Sir Perceval, Weston notes that, in alchemy, black and green, being Earth colors, are interchangeable (1909, 257&*n*1); so that we have a triadic structure analogous to those found in other branches of occult philosophy, as communicated to her by "a Mystic of experience" (257). Thus, there are three planes or worlds: that of God or Spirit, whose color is white; that of Humanity, or Actuality, in which Spirit and Matter are combined, and whose color is red; and the realm of pure Matter, whose color is black or green. These three worlds also correspond to the three aspects of the forgotten faith that Weston argues underlies the Grail romances.

Grail Kings	*Symbols*	*Wagnerian Drama*	*Colors*	*Three Planes*	*Three Levels*
King of Castle Mortal	Cup and Lance	Klingsor	Black or Green	Matter	Phallic Initiation
Maimed King	Rich Grail	Amfortas	Red	Humanity	Exoteric Rites
Fisher King	Holy Grail	Titurel	White	Spirit	Philosophic Initiation

The "external" or exoteric aspect of this faith is a religious practice analogous to the Rites of Adonis: Thus, we have a god who dies (corresponding to the dead body on a bier in the Grail romances), mourned by weeping women; a communal feast with a mysterious food-providing Vessel (corresponding to the "rich" Grail); and a question regarding the significance and use of the Vessel which, when asked, appears to bring about the restoration of the land, laid waste by the death of the god-king.

The esoteric aspect of this faith is an initiatory practice which has two levels, which Weston characterizes as Phallic and Philosophic; these being the Lesser and the Higher Mysteries, concerning physical generation and spiritual regeneration. The phallic initiation involves an encounter with the mysteries of sex and death, the lesser secrets; the test of worthiness to undergo initiation may have proved fatal in some instances, as exemplified by the story of the death of the squire Cahus in the Perilous Chapel. To be proved worthy of progressing to the philosophic initiation, into the higher Secrets of the

Mysteries, the aspirant must achieve the test of the Sword, which symbolizes will-power, as Gawain discovers on the White Island.

This test involves *holding his consciousness* (which, Weston explains in a footnote, means "retaining the memory of what has been seen on more than one plane") so that he may attain the highest stage of initiation. At this point Gawain would behold the *Holy* Grail, the spiritual Vessel, "wrought of no material substance"; he must then ask what it is and what purpose it serves: "But this he cannot do, he loses consciousness, falls into a trance or slumber and misses the Vision" (1909, 262).

If there are three aspects to the Grail faith (the exoteric rites and the two stages of initiation), there are three kings or guardians,[25] one of which presides over each aspect or plane: The Fisher King presides over the highest, "white" plane, that of the philosophic initiation, symbolized by the Holy Grail; but on the lower, "red" plane of Actuality, "his activities restrained and hampered by the Flesh in which he is now clothed," he becomes the Maimed King, guardian of the *Rich* Grail, the Feeding Vessel; while the lowest, "black" plane, that of phallic initiation, symbolized by the Cup and Lance, is presided over by the King of Castle Mortal (257–9).

Such threefold groupings are just some among the many triads whose "constant recurrence," Weston considers, may betray an affinity with the symbol systems of the Gnostics: "The correspondence of certain of their speculations with ideas preserved in the Grail romances is curious" (256n1). While writing *The Legend of Sir Perceval*, Weston was particularly interested in the "speculations" of the early second century Alexandrian Gnostic Basilides, whose system had been partially reconstructed by G.R.S. Mead, the pioneering scholar of the western esoteric tradition to whom Weston frequently defers as an authority on such matters. Weston went so far as to find in the system of Basilides analogies with the three Grail questers of the Vulgate Cycle.[26]

If there are three knights who achieve the Quest in the later prose romances, there are also three earthly guardians of the Grail (Joseph of Arimathea, his brother-in-law Bron and Bron's grandson Perceval) in the *Estoire dou Graal* of Robert de Boron, and the prose cycle derived from it. It is there also that we learn of three tables (the Table of the Last Supper, the Table of the Grail and the Round Table) symbolizing the Trinity. This Trinitarian emphasis, Weston construes as indicating that de Boron was an initiate of the Grail faith "and was treating his subject from the *in*side, and not from the *out*side" (279).

At the same time there is a strong emphasis in the De Boron Cycle on the Secret Words which Christ spoke to Joseph, and which are passed down to Bron and finally to Perceval. These words, which are never revealed in the romances, Weston takes to be: "There be Three which bear witness—And these Three are One" (273). It is de Boron whom she credits with being the first to translate "the symbolism and terminology" of a pagan faith into a Christian one[27] and to transform Mystery into romance.[28]

Other Words

It is the sacred words which Christ spoke to Joseph of Arimathea in prison—words that de Boron claims that he read in the High Book that is "the creed of the great mystery of the Grail" (*MG* 22), but which he dares not tell to us—that lie at the heart of a rival initiatory interpretation of the Grail legend. It is one that was inaugurated by the Christian mystic A.E. Waite, but developed in the second half of the twentieth century by the French scholar Henry Corbin (1903–1978) in his philosophy of the Imagination.

Brought up as a Catholic, Arthur Edward Waite was drawn to the occult in his youth, progressing from an early interest in spiritualism and Theosophy to a serious study of what he preferred to call the Secret Tradition within Christianity. He had already published books on magic and alchemy by the time he joined the Golden Dawn; he would encourage his friend, the Welsh writer of supernatural fiction Arthur Machen, to do the same, when he became concerned that Machen was dabbling in Black Magic as a way of coping with the death of his wife. By comparison, the Order's rituals seemed "relatively harmless"; but Machen only lasted a year (Gilbert, 66). The reality was that the two friends had quite different attitudes to magic, as Waites's biographer points out: "Machen was fascinated but condemned it all—he was rooted firmly in the Church of England and never really deviated from his traditional Christian faith—whereas Waite sought a common reality behind both occultism *and* the Church" (62).

A frequent subject of discussion between the two friends was the Grail legend, on which they also profoundly disagreed (97–8). Machen would go on to express his Grail vision in fiction; while Waite published his first book on the subject in 1909—*The Hidden Church of the Holy Graal* (retaining its French spelling)—and delivered a lecture to Mead's Quest Society that same year on "The Romance of the Holy Graal" (103).

At the outset of his book, Waite states that he considers that within the Grail legend can be found an ecstatic initiation into a "mystery of illumination" (1909, *xi*). While not denying the antecedents of the story in pre–Christian traditions—"If the hand of God is in history, it is also in folk-lore" (5)—he considered that their symbolism had been converted into a Christian form, as the alchemists converted lead into gold. Lead (like the pagan folktales) is the indispensable antecedent, "but the great fact is the conversion" (139). The Grail legend therefore represents the otherwise "worthless" motifs (122) of Celtic mythology passed through the "alembic of transmutation" to reveal a new manifestation of the Mystery of Faith (178), symbolized by a Secret Church possessing "a super-valid formula of Eucharistic consecration" and a "super-apostolic succession" (*viii*). By this he means: firstly, the Grail Mass celebrated in the Vulgate *Queste*; and secondly, the consecration at Sarras of Josephus as the first minister of Christ, whose successors as Grail Guardians are Alan, the Rich Fisher, and, after him, the Fisher Kings of Corbenic.[29]

Thus, although acknowledging that the Sword and the Lance (two of the four sacred objects in the Grail Castle which he refers to as Hallows) may preserve traces of folklore, he insists that we will see, either that "the people" preserved something more than folklore, or else that folklore itself had other than the usually recognized meanings, when we rediscover the Hallows "under a very slight modification in the most unexpected of all places" (127): that is, in what he considers to be the antecedent to the modern pack of playing cards, the Tarot.

The Four Hallows have been hiding in plain sight, as it were, in the four suits of cards which we know as Hearts, Diamonds, Spades and Clubs but which are also the Talismans of the Tarot (Cups, Wands, Swords and Pentacles), as modified in accordance with the symbol system of "certain secret schools." These Talismans are in turn identical to the Grail Hallows: Cup, Lance, Sword and Dish (600–4).

Grail Hallows	Waite/Smith Tarot Suit	Modern Playing Cards
Cup of the Precious Blood	Cups	Hearts
Lance of Longinus	Wands	Diamonds
Sword of David	Swords	Spades
Dish of the Last Supper	Pentacles	Clubs

Two years later Waite, who had been promoting within the Golden Dawn the idea that Tarot cards were, as he put it, "gates which opened on realms of vision beyond occult dreams," published his *Pictorial Key* in conjunction with the artist Pamela Colman Smith; having, probably with the help of Yeats, re-designed the cards in order to show that they represent aspects of the Secret Tradition (Gilbert, 138). But in 1933 he would sum up his theories on the Tarot and other initiatory aspects of the Grail legend in what would become his *magnum opus* on the subject: *The Holy Grail: Its Legends and Symbolism. An Explanatory Survey of their Embodiment in Romance Literature and a Critical Study of the Interpretations Placed Thereon.*[30]

As the length of the title would suggest, Waite gives us an exhaustive survey of the medieval literature and the principal critical theses up to 1930; in the process, disassociating himself not just from the Celticists, but also from the initiation theories of Nitze and Weston. Waite finds himself in agreement with Weston about the inadequacy of Celtic theories of origins,[31] and of Nitze's analogy with the Rites of Eleusis,[32] but is equally critical of Weston's own theories. Although he accepts that the ancient Mysteries can be understood as portraying, through the symbolism of "seed-time and harvest," the Birth, Death and Resurrection of the God, he cannot affirm that their rituals were portrayed at the time as "the story of the soul which dies to earthly things, that it may rise into the knowledge and attainment of those things that are eternal" (2006, 424). In other words, Waite cannot find evidence of the "higher or deeper intention" in the Mysteries that Weston, who had died five years before his book was published, characterized as the philosophic initiation.[33]

Moreover, Weston's claim to have knowledge of the survival to the present day of the initiation rituals which lay behind the Grail stories only indicates that she was being "spoon-fed" by the kind of occultists that Waite himself had devoted a "considerable part" of his life to exposing.[34] While he concurred with her view that the royal path could not lead to the Celtic Twilight, he considered that "regions of occult practice and their dubious lights amidst Cimmerian darkness are still less an adequate goal for a life's research" (432). The Mystery behind the Holy Grail is only intelligible as "a Mystery of Christian Religion prolonged into the unknown"; the Temple approached by the aspirant to Grail Initiation is only intelligible as "the place of a Secret Church."[35]

The prolongation of the Grail Mystery, Waite finds in Christian Kabbalism, spiritual alchemy, the higher grades of Freemasonry and the mysticism of the German Catholic Karl von Eckartshausen (1752–1803). But, if their connection with the legend of the Holy Vessel seems tangential, this is because Waite admits "that in so far as there is mystic purpose or Hidden Doctrine in the Grail literature it is often like an echo from afar—a rumor, a legend which had fallen into the hands of romancers" (466).

For some contemporaries of Waite, however, both the Christian mysticism which he applauds and the Celtic paganism which he undervalues are themselves echoes of a pre-Christian, in fact primordial, tradition.

The Sense of Eternity

In an article first published in 1934,[36] Waite's book on the Holy Grail was discussed by the French metaphysician René Guénon who had, since the Twenties, been developing a trenchant critique of the modern world, a civilization that he saw as fast approaching its nadir. Guénon and the writers who came after him—most notably Julius Evola and Frithjof Schuon (1907–1998)—were attempting to restore a sense of the perennial wisdom (*sophia perennis*), which they believed underlay all "traditional" cultures, to those living in what they considered to be our anti-traditional world—not so much to delay the inevitable catastrophe, as to try to ensure that at least something of that wisdom would survive among those who crawl from the wreckage.

Unfortunately, the genuine insights brought to bear upon modern society and modernist ideology by this group have been tainted by the association of some of them with extremist political views.[37] It would be a mistake, however, to identify their anti-modernist and anti-secular views too closely with those of contemporary "spiritual terrorists": the constant theme of the Traditionalists was the underlying unity of spiritual truth, not the violent enforcement of one spiritual path at the expense of others. The Traditionalists share the fundamentalists' hatred of a secular society with no spiritual values; but the fundamentalists have no truck with the Traditionalist gnosis that sees all spiritual traditions as facets of the one primordial wisdom.

For Guénon, the Grail symbolizes both the "primordial state" of humankind (which he characterizes as possessing the "sense of eternity") and the tradition which connects us to that state.[38] As humankind becomes increasingly alienated from the Primordial Tradition—a degeneration symbolized by the loss of Paradise (the supreme spiritual center) in the Myth of the Fall—it fragments into the various faith traditions of the world. These are each sustained by their contact with one of the "lesser spiritual centers" which have been established as images of Paradise Lost. To be in possession of the Grail "represents the integral preservation of the primordial tradition in a spiritual center"; while the loss of the Grail represents a spiritual center's losing direct contact with the supreme or World Center.[39]

At the core of Guénon's presentation of the Grail is a myth whose origin is obscure—Guénon rarely reveals his sources, giving the impression of speaking *ex cathedra*—but which reads like a variation on the medieval legend of the Tree of Life:

> The Grail is a chalice fashioned by angels from an emerald which drops from the forehead of Lucifer (the Third Eye) when he falls from Heaven.[40] It is entrusted to Adam in Paradise but left behind when he is expelled from Eden. Adam's son Seth is enabled to return there and rescue the Grail, which is thenceforth protected by a succession of guardians (including the Druids) until the time of Christ, who uses it as the cup of the Last Supper. After collecting the blood and water that flow from Christ's side in the Grail, Joseph of Arimathea brings it to Britain, where Merlin designs the Round Table[41] to receive the Holy Vessel (Guénon 1983, 25–9).

We know from the medieval stories, however, that the Chosen Knight, whether Galahad or Perceval, never brings the Grail to the Round Table. Rather, it lures the knights on a quest from which many of them never return; ultimately it leaves Britain forever, abandoning the West for the East. For Guénon, this means that European "orthodox organizations" no longer have any "consciously established link" with the spiritual center—a break which began with the suppression of the Knights Templar, one of whose principal roles was to connect East and West (47). It is therefore significant that the Grail is described as journeying to the East or as being assumed into Heaven, which is symbolically the same thing (1962, 41).

Guénon agrees with both Weston and Waite that the key to the Grail legend lies in initiation; but for him, initiation is the esoteric aspect of all traditions, just as religion is the exoteric aspect. He can therefore not follow Weston and Waite in their denigration of the importance of what they call Celtic "folklore." On the contrary, the Celtic element in the legend reveals the fact that the Druids had been the guardians of the initiatory aspects of the Primordial Tradition since prehistoric times and that, through them, it was transmitted into Christian esotericism (36). The Primordial Tradition is expressed in an essential doctrinal unity on the esoteric level that underlies the apparently conflicting dogmas of the various religions, whether monotheistic like Christianity or polytheistic like Celtic paganism. This inner unity explains the commonality of traditional symbols in cultures so diverse in time and space that there is no question of "diffusion" or deliberate "borrowings."

Whatever contacts aboriginal Britons and Iron Age Celtic peoples may have had with the civilization of the eastern Mediterranean since prehistoric times—and whatever external influences there might have been on the development of a native mystery religion (about which both Nitze and Weston speculated)—it is Guénon's assertion that no culture is more "privileged" than another in its inheritance of the Primordial Tradition. From this point of view, the Celtic tradition (that is to say, the Primordial Tradition as it was filtered through Celtic culture) would have had its own esoteric as well as its exoteric aspects, its own forms of initiation as well as of religious belief and practice. The Grail legends themselves could be much older than is usually thought, states Guénon, not because early texts have been lost, but because the stories could have been the object of an oral transmission lasting several centuries; at a place and time that it is now difficult to determine, they would have been modified (but only in their outer forms, not their inner meaning) by what he calls the *jonction* between two traditional forms,[42] the ancient Celtic and the new Christian traditions (31–2).

Guénon also agrees with Weston and Waite that Robert de Boron's poem shows more understanding of the "higher aspects" of the legends than does Chrétien's. But he does not consider it important to establish whether either de Boron or Chrétien were initiates, since even "profane" poets could be chosen by an initiatory organization to "exteriorize" esoteric teachings (35–6). Such an organization, Guénon maintains, could have existed within the so-called Celtic Church, the anchorites known as the Culdees representing the public face of a Celtic tradition that was still very much alive when the Grail legends developed (31–2).

Insofar as the Grail literature emanates from an initiatory organization, this is still a far cry from believing that the stories reveal an initiatory *ritual—comme certains l'ont supposé*, Guénon adds, in what is presumably a swipe at Weston, *assez bizarrement* (38)—but he is equally critical of Waite's concept of a Hidden Church, which Guénon believes confuses religious mysticism with the exact knowledge and precise technique required by an initiatory order (40). That such an order lay behind the Knights Templar is indicated by their role as guardians of the Holy Land, this being another name for the primordial spiritual center (84–5); it is in that sense that they were indeed keepers of the Holy Grail (89). As warrior-monks, they combined in one order the spiritual authority and temporal power which are as one in the World Center. With their destruction in the early fourteenth century begins the rupture of the Christian world with the primordial spiritual center, as a result of which the path to the Holy Land is now closed (92). The Grail is lost to the West.

The Mystery of Warrior Initiation

The importance of the Order of the Knights Templar to Grail Initiation is also explored by the Italian Traditionalist, Julius Evola, who believed he could discern "an analogical tie between the ideal model of the Grail's chivalry and the inner dimension of historical Templarism" (1997, 135).

A Dadaist and experimenter with mind-altering substances in his youth, Evola pursued what he called the path of the Absolute Individual—"the lawless destroyer of all bonds" (2010, 97)—in oriental spirituality and western magic, before encountering, in the late Twenties, the writings of René Guénon. Evola would champion Guénon's exposition of the Primordial Tradition, but he would also adapt it to his own world-view. Evola now saw that the true Absolute Individual is not he who rejects all "supra-human" constraints, but precisely he who, having achieved transcendence, identifies himself with the Lord of the World, the "non-human" axis and legislator of traditional civilization (98). It is this position which places the Absolute Individual in revolt against the modern world.[43]

Like Guénon, Evola sees modernity, not as progress, but as degeneration from the primordial Hyperborean civilization which existed at the North Pole in distant prehistory, but which froze over when the Earth tilted on its axis, bringing to an end the paradisiacal Golden Age (1995, 188–9). One consequence of this "fall" is the separation of spiritual authority and temporal power, which are united in the Lord of the World; so, that priesthood becomes distinct from kingship and is sometimes opposed to it. Where Guénon favored the "priestly" qualities of contemplation and knowledge as the means to re-integrate the primordial condition of humanity, Evola believed that it was the quest for sovereignty through heroic action that would restore the Absolute Individual (2010, 103).

But both Guénon and Evola agreed that the Grail is a symbol of the Primordial Tradition[44] and that the Templars are considered to be its guardians because, as warrior-monks, they unite in themselves the spiritual and temporal aspects of the pre-lapsarian world. Evola even sees "a sort of occult syntony" between the "mysterious exhaustion of the sources of inspiration of the Grail romances" and the "tragic end" of the Templars, as if the one foreshadowed the other (1997, 135).

The Order was an attempt to realize the spiritual chivalry of the Grail through "the mystery of warrior initiation" (2010, 144); therefore, its suppression by the same combined forces of Church and State which had already destroyed the Cathars was more deserving of the term "crusade against the Grail" (1997, 129). Evola is here distancing himself from the thesis of the German medievalist Otto Rahn (1904–1939), whose *Kreuzzug gegen den Gral* was published in Germany in 1933, some four years before Evola's own book on the Grail.[45]

Immersing himself in the poetry of Wolfram von Eschenbach, Rahn came to believe that the Grail, the Stone that Fell from Heaven, is a symbol of the Desire for Paradise (2006, 56&*n*4). The Cathars of Languedoc may have inherited the Grail Tradition from the Druids of the south of France, who had embraced a form of Gnostic dualism (66); it is therefore a heretical symbol, having nothing to do with a relic of the Last Supper (115).

In order to write his book, Rahn conducted extensive excavations in the caves of the mountainous region around Montségur, the Cathars' last refuge in the French Pyrenees; for it was here, legend has it, that the Grail Stone fell to Earth when it was broken off from the crown of Lucifer during the War in Heaven (47). All this has led some in recent years to see Rahn as a Nazi Indiana Jones (the fictional hero of a series of Hollywood films by Steven Spielberg about an adventurous archaeologist).[46]

Rahn's relationship with the Nazis was actually quite complex. Impressed by his first book, Heinrich Himmler made him an offer he couldn't refuse: to join the SS and research another book on the Grail under the auspices of the Ahnenerbe, a scholarly institute promoting German Ancestral Heritage, which would fund his travels.[47] The result was a somewhat disjointed travelogue, in which Rahn meditates on the Luciferian impulse towards enlightenment; it was almost certainly tampered with by the publishers to make it better conform to National Socialist ideology. Rahn himself had become increasingly disillusioned with the direction his country was heading and, amid rumors of homosexuality and Jewish ancestry, he apparently committed suicide in the Alps (xi-xiii).

Rather poignantly, Rahn speaks about the Cathar attitude towards suicide (the "endura") in a chapter of his first book entitled "The 'Pure Ones' and their Doctrine." The Cathars, he claimed, would voluntarily relinquish all Earthly ties, including physical life itself, when they had gone beyond "sadness and lies"; two always died together. Sadly, this was not the case with Rahn; but he might have felt, as he believed the Cathars did, that "the supreme definitive act of death requires heroism," even when what is being left behind is Hell on Earth (89–91).

The Stone of Exile

Himmler was not the only Nazi to interest himself in Rahn's theories about the Cathars and the Grail.

The Chilean diplomat Miguel Serrano (1917–2009) was a Marxist in his youth, but he abandoned the radical Left for the radical Right, exchanging an *internationalist* for a *nationalist* variety of socialism in the late Thirties. In February 1942 he was initiated into a "mystico-martial order" which venerated Hitler as an enlightened being who had voluntarily incarnated on Earth in order to bring to an end the Kali Yuga, the last and darkest of the four ages of traditional cosmology (Goodrick-Clarke 2003, 174–6).

In waging this Holy War, Hitler was (and *is*, for he lives on in the warm oases of Antarctica) acting as the agent of—and was frequently possessed by—the Hyperborean gods, the divine ancestors of the Aryan race (180). His enemies were and are the Jews, agents of the Demiurge, the false creator who seeks to trap pure-blooded Aryans in his material prison by making them forget their polar origins (182); but the Grail Hallows hold the key to their remembering who they truly are and whence they come.

Underpinning Serrano's doctrine of Esoteric Hitlerism is a variation of the Traditionalist story of the Grail: During the War in Heaven, Lucifer is struck by the sword of the Enemy (the satanic Demiurge) and his crown breaks; a jewel falls from it, which

Lucifer carries to the North Pole where he founds Ultima Thule, the capital of Hyperborea. When that island is destroyed, the White Gods, the followers of Lucifer, preserve the pieces of his broken crown "in the form of a stone on which is inscribed the Law and the Great Secret." This is the Grail, or the Stone of Exile (Serrano 1984, 17); it is carried by the White Gods, along with the Sword, the Lance and the Cauldron, to their new home in the West, which we call America but whose alchemical name is Albania,[48] the White Land (26–7). From there the Hallows are transported to "the icy wastes of the south of the world, with Parsifal, in a Templars' ship"; thence to the Inner Earth, whose entry is at the South Pole, where the Golden Age lives on (40–1).

Whereas for Evola (1997, 138), the Cathar spirit has little in common with that of the Grail Templars, for Serrano the Cathars, the Templars and the Grail Lords were the revealers in the Middle Ages of the Hyperborean Initiation of A-Mor, meaning both "not death" and the chaste love of the warrior: "Only with the memory of his beloved in his heart can the initiate achieve the Grail" (1984, 11). The archetype of the Beloved appears in Hyperborea as Morgana, the priestess of "magic love" (72) who offers to the hero the Emerald Chalice, formed from the Stone of Light, in which the liquor of Eternity is drunk; but if he takes possession of her physical body, he risks losing his soul (42). Rather, their spiritual union is symbolized by the warrior's sword sheathed in the scabbard: a "symbolic possession" which enables the Grail Knight to maintain his "sacred chastity" (147).

This scabbard is called Blood Memory (meaning the memory of the Hyperborean Golden Age, which is dormant in the blood of all true Aryans[49]) and is "made of wood from the apple trees of Avalon, from the Tree of Paradise, from the Hyperborean oaks, from the tree whose silken threads join the earth to the sky." It breaks if sheathed carelessly. But if the lovers can put the broken pieces back together again, they will have an opportunity to "break down the walls of the great circle and end the turnings of the wheel"; in other words, to escape the material prison of the Demiurge. By drinking from "the cup of immortality" they will discover "the stone of change" and thus complete "this most ancient Hyperborean Initiation of A-Mor, revealed in the mystery of the Grail" (40).

That Dream of Totality

Between 1960 and 1984, Miguel Serrano wrote a series of books which were translated into English and published by mainstream scholarly houses. Most were poetic fables steeped in mythological symbolism of considerable obscurity, in which no political message could be easily discerned. The earliest of these, *The Visits of the Queen of Sheba*, was furnished with a brief Foreword by C.G. Jung, written a year before his death.

Serrano had first read Jung during a trip to the Antarctic, and came to see analytical psychology as a "path of initiation" into "a new sense of reality or of the Self" (1997, 59–61). The archetype of wholeness, the Self—"that dream of totality" (65)—manifests as the image of God in the psyche when the dualism of conscious and unconscious is transcended; this "transcendent function" can be symbolized by the Grail "as the vessel in which the 'soul substance' of the god is preserved" (Jung & Franz, 156–7)

But according to Serrano, who met Jung in 1959 and both visited him and corresponded with him over the next two years, the Master of the Sphinx (as he called Jung) was wary of "psychologizing" the sacred mystery of the Grail.[50] Identifying himself as a Hyperborean and therefore a stranger in the world of the Demiurge, the Master declares himself to be one of the losers of the war of the Kali Yuga whose work can only be truly appreciated by poets (Serrano 1984, 65). The Grail Quest is what he calls the path of individuation which leads to the Self, "an oasis of warm water in the midst of the ices," the lost continent of the Golden Age: "There lies the gate through which one can enter and leave Ultima Thule" (68), the way into and out of incarnation.

For the Master of the Sphinx, as for Evola's Templars, the Grail Quest is a warrior initiation: Parsifal will require "fury" in order to achieve "the ultimate solitude of the Superman," resisting "the way of sainthood," which is the way of Galahad. But the Quest is also, as for Rahn's Cathars, an initiation into a chaste or "loveless" love,[51] which is "the mystery of the Grail." According to the Master, the "miraculous Hyperborean initiation" is "individual" and "aristocratic"; it has been "vulgarized" and its symbolism "adulterated" by the "exotericism" of the Roman Church, which "destroyed" the Hyperborean Grail Lords, guardians of the Blood Memory, with consequences which we can see in contemporary culture: "The initiatory poem has deteriorated into the novel, the popular literature and the unhealthy sexualism of our day" (70–3).

It is very hard to know what Jung would have made of this attempt to recuperate his psychology of archetypal images and alchemical imagination in support of the "divine myth" of Hyperborean Blood Memory (72). Serrano's own account of what Jung said to him at their meetings, published within five years of the latter's death, reads very differently to the fictionalized expositions of esoteric doctrine attributed to the Master of the Sphinx in *Nos*, fifteen years later.

First appearing in Spanish in 1980, *Nos* was translated into English and published in 1984 by Routledge & Kegan Paul, a scholarly house which also had the British rights for Jung's Collected Works. But that same year Serrano published in Chile a book with the unambiguous title: *Adolf Hitler, el Último Avatāra*. Not surprisingly, neither this nor any of his later books, interweaving his doctrines of Esoteric Hitlerism and white racial supremacy with Jungian archetypes, would ever be published in English outside of the microcosm of the radical Right small-press and the Internet.[52]

Jung has also in recent years been criticized for wanting to create a cult of the Aryan Christ, with himself as Redeemer. Richard Noll has argued,[53] controversially, that Jung underwent a Mithraic initiation, albeit as an inner, psychic experience—on what Jessie Weston would call the astral plane—and it is interesting in this regard that Weston saw Mithraism as an intermediate stage, between the Mysteries of Adonis and Gnostic Christianity, in the development of the Grail legend in Britain. While accepting that the issue of whether or not Jung was personally antisemitic remains a matter of dispute (Noll, 273–7), he argues that Jung saw Mithraism as an Aryan cult in contradistinction to the Judaic monotheism that is the historical ground of mainstream (as opposed to Gnostic) Christianity (142–3). Further, Noll claims that Jung identified himself with the Parsifal of Wagner's opera who, after much inner turmoil, finds his way to the Gralsburg or Grail Castle, Montsalvat: "Jung found the Gralsburg when he became the Aryan Christ" (Noll, 155).

But although it was through the inner image of Mithras that Jung had achieved his own personal transformation, Noll argues, it was a different archetypal pagan figure who engaged his attention in the Thirties, the decade of Hitlerism triumphant. In 1936 Jung published an essay on the re-emergence of Wotan (corresponding to the Norse

Odin), whom, according to Noll, he considered to be "the true god of the German peoples." The rise of Nazism meant that they had become possessed by this archetypal figure because they were unconscious of it: "If only they would become conscious of their god, then the Germans would find their way to a true spiritual rebirth" (274–5).

Odin-Wotan also figures in Serrano's Hyperborean Mythos as a northern Lucifer, the Gnostic Light Bringer (1984, 182); he is equated with Parsifal, whose "fury" is Odinic (*Wodan, id est furor*). At the Twilight of the Gods, Odin whispers the answer to the Grail Question into the ears of the wounded Balder (1984, 174)—a type of the God who Dies and is Reborn, like Adonis and Christ—before leading his followers into exile under the sign of the Swastika of Exodus, "the one that turns according to the present earth's time and descends to the lowest depths of Kaliyuga."

But it is prophesied that the Twilight will not last forever (125): The descendants of the exiled Hyperboreans, the heroic Wild Hordes, led by Odin and Parsifal, will fight the Last Battle against "the animal-men who caused the cataclysm and who will bring about its repetition through their rebelliousness and their ignorant pride" (130). The contemporary reader, aware of the massacres that continue to be perpetrated by "sacred warriors" rebelling against the modern world, may think it is precisely "ignorant pride," albeit of a highly educated and sophisticated variety, that could lead a cultured, international figure such as Miguel Serrano—"a man in full command of the esoteric field and familiar with the corridors of worldly power"—to ignore or excuse the crimes of (exoteric) Hitlerism, including what he dismisses as the Myth of the Six Million (Godwin 1993a, 73).

Fishing for the Redeemer

In contrast to the martial fury of Serrano's Quest—"Only the Wild Hordes of Odin and Parsifal will achieve the Grail" (1984, 149)—Emma Jung (Carl Gustav's wife, also an analyst) and Marie-Louise von Franz (one of Jung's leading disciples and collaborators), who took on the task of "psychologizing" the "sacred mystery," present the legend as an inner struggle against the archetypal shadow[54] rather than an outer struggle against "animal-men."

Perceval's first visit to the Grail Castle—in which he sees a procession of mysterious objects, fails to ask a redemptive question and finds himself summarily excluded the next day, on awakening—can be seen, they suggest, as an "initiation dream."[55] In tribal initiations the young novice is enabled to separate himself from the "realm of the mothers" (the unconscious) by his male relatives, especially his mother's brother, who is considered to be his "spiritual father" and who establishes his relationship with the ancestors (Jung & Franz, 75).

But the only male relative that Perceval encounters directly is his cousin, the maimed Fisher King: his mother's brother, the old Grail King, remains hidden in an inner chamber, where, so spiritual is he, that his life is sustained by a single Host from the Grail Vessel. Had Perceval asked who is served by the Grail, he would have learnt about his family. Because he failed to do so, he must go through many hardships and a spiritual crisis before he learns, from another maternal uncle (a hermit), of the existence of a family beyond the widowed mother who brought him up; as well as, later, of a kingdom which he is destined to inherit.

However, these later stages of his journey only come about when Perceval is confronted by the Loathly Damsel (or Ugly Maiden), a monstrous figure who reproaches Perceval for his failure to ask the Grail Question and goads him into committing himself to the task of redeeming his earlier failure (175–7). For Jung and Franz, this indicates that he has achieved a level of consciousness which "could be considered as an essential result of his initiation, his first visit to the Grail Castle" (186).

The process of initiation moves to a higher level when Perceval meets his hermit uncle, who succeeds, where the old Grail King failed, in fulfilling the role of spiritual father or "godfather" to the knight, who is older but not yet wiser: He has, after all, spent the intervening five years in killing other knights at the rate of about a dozen per annum! It is his hermit uncle who explains to Perceval his family relationship to the Grail Lords, and reveals the answer to the question that the young man failed to ask: that the old King, the hermit's—and Perceval's mother's—brother, is he who is served by the Grail.

What is more, the old man is fed, not with the fish that Perceval's cousin the Maimed King catches, but with the sacred wafer, the Host: "Thus, the Grail is presented as a purely symbolic vessel, providing spiritual, not physical, sustenance." For Jung and Franz, the process of symbolizing requires a higher level of consciousness than the egocentric, goal-oriented stage Perceval reached earlier, thanks to the intervention of the Loathly Damsel; for the symbolic life potentially leads to the mystical experience in which the ego is dissolved (222–3).

However, Jung and Franz argue that it is precisely this overly spiritual, world-denying attitude that is the soul-sickness of the second Christian millennium.[56] The old Grail King is "the archetypal image of Christian man"; but, "viewed from the perspective of the unconscious," he personifies an outmoded spirituality that is "in need of renewal or of redemption by a successor" (196). But this successor cannot be his son, who is himself maimed by his father's shadow, in the form of a "pagan adversary."[57] Hence what the Maimed King is really doing in a boat on the river is *fishing for the redeemer* (198).

To what extent Perceval is able to be the longed-for redeemer varies with the different attempts to finish Chrétien's story. In Manessier's Continuation, which completes the verse Story of the Grail, Perceval heals the Maimed King, who grants him the rule of the Grail Kingdom after his death; when his soul is taken up to Heaven, the Hallows ascend with him.

In the cycle attributed to Robert de Boron, Merlin prophesies that Perceval is destined to sit in the Perilous Seat at the Round Table, the one that corresponds to Judas' place at the Table of the Last Supper; but that, before he does so, he will need to have been in the presence of the Grail (*MG* 92–4). Perceval sits in the seat prematurely (119), as a result of which Merlin's prophecy can only partly be fulfilled: Perceval heals the Fisher King in the presence of the Grail, but he does not return to Arthur's court to take his place in the Perilous Seat.

In the final quarter of *The Grail Legend*, which Marie-Louise von Franz completed after the death of Emma Jung in 1955, the focus shifts to Merlin as the Prophet of the Grail who leads Perceval to his destination, taking over from the Fisher King and the hermit uncle as the "spiritual godfather" or initiator of the young hero.[58] Franz stresses the similarities between Merlin and the spirit Mercurius of the alchemists, whose "efflorescence" in the West coincided with that of the Merlin legends[59]; so that we can now see to what extent Perceval's journey in the De Boron Cycle corresponds to the three stages of initiation and the alchemical colors associated with them, as outlined by Weston.

In the Prose *Perceval*, the final part of the cycle, as also in Chrétien's and Wolfram's poems, the eponymous hero starts off his chivalric career in red armor (*MG* 117–8). Red, as we have seen, corresponds to what Weston calls the middle realm of Humanity or Actuality, situated between the realms of Matter and Spirit; it is the sphere of *exoteric* religion. His encounter with the Grail and Lance in the court of the Fisher King (141) corresponds to the "blackening" (the alchemical *nigredo*), which is the first phase of transmutation. This is what Weston calls the Phallic Initiation, into the mysteries of sex and death: the lower sphere of the *esoteric* faith.

It is Merlin who sets Perceval (who has just won a tournament at the White Castle) on the path to complete the next stage of his quest: the return to the Grail Castle, the asking of the Question, the healing of the Fisher King and, finally, at the prompting of the Holy Spirit, the passing on of the sacred words. These are "the holy words of the sacrament of the Grail" (42) that Christ spoke to Joseph of Arimathea in prison and that Joseph in turn passed on to Bron, the Fisher King. Perceval sees angels carry off the soul of Bron and becomes, at Our Lord's decree, Fisher King in his turn (155–6). Heralded by his victory at the White Castle, this is Perceval's "whitening" (the alchemical *albedo*); it corresponds to what Weston calls the Philosophic Initiation, the "higher mysteries" of the esoteric faith.

But if Perceval has succeeded where Gawain (falling into the sleep of unconsciousness on the White Island) failed, his victory is, in alchemical terms, incomplete: For, in the Hermetic Art, the process that begins with the *nigredo* and is followed by the *albedo* must be fulfilled by the *rubedo*, the "reddening." The end of the Great Work is not the spiritualization (whitening) of the body but rather the embodiment (reddening) of the spirit; the emphasis being not on transcendence but on immanence, the manifestation of the spirit in Earth-bound existence (Burckhardt, 182–3).

Now Perceval began as the Red Knight; so, the reddening would be, for him (to paraphrase T.S. Eliot) to arrive where he started *And know the place for the first time* (*TSE* 197). But, in defiance of Merlin's prophecy, having been in the presence of the Grail, he does not return to take his place in the Perilous Seat, corresponding to the place of Judas at the Last Supper; to have done so would have been, symbolically at least, to have redeemed Christ's shadow.[60] Instead he remains in the Grail Kingdom, renouncing the life of *this* world: but "he should have brought the Grail to the Round Table, so that instead of the Spirit being divorced from the world, the world would have been impregnated with the Spirit" (Jung & Franz, 389).

Perceval's failure to reconcile the Grail with the world means that its suffering King continues to cast his shadow over the post-medieval epoch. As the personification of an overly spiritual attitude to life—*il, qui est esperitax* (*RP* l.6426)—his shadow is "a dark heathen god-image that has not been taken into account by the prevailing attitude of consciousness." It is, in fact, none other than the furious Wotan, the Germanic figure of the archetypal Sleeping Lord, who has long been "waiting to reappear in this world" (Jung & Franz, 197); a god who, having been pierced by a spear, like Christ and the Grail King, is both "the wounded and the wounder." For his re-emergence in the Thirties constitutes another "devastating spear-thrust that Wotan has inflicted on the Christian humanity of today" (208).

But if the Grail King has been maimed by a "dark spirit of nature, standing in opposition to the one-sidedness of Christianity" (211)—for Wotan, like Merlin, symbolizes aspects of "an image of inner wholeness which presses its still unfulfilled claims on man" (375)—then Perceval's failure (his initiation *manqué*) opens the floodgates to that Odinic fury which, unleashed in twentieth century Europe, would lead to the persecution and extermination of all those that Serrano's "avatar" would condemn as "animal-men," *untermenschen*. And if the redeemer for whom the Maimed King was fishing has failed his initiation at the last hurdle—unable to symbolically redden the Waste Land into life, thus necessitating a more literal reddening through a world-wide bloodletting—then who will redeem the redeemer?

For Franz, who wrote a major study of C.G. Jung (first published twelve years after the German edition of her and Emma Jung's Grail book), that redeemer is the prophet of the soul whom she saw as the twentieth century Merlin. She recounts a dream he had in which he found that the task had fallen to him alone of bringing the hidden Grail from its secret location to the castle where it must be celebrated (Franz, 272–3). She interprets the dream as saying: "Seek the Self within, and then you will find both the secret of the Grail and the answer to the spiritual problem of our cultural tradition" (279).

Franz follows Jung himself in seeing Merlin as the dark brother of Perceval or Parsifal, whose secret is carried on, first by alchemy, and latterly by the psychology of the unconscious (280–1). She describes Jung as undergoing a "journey to the beyond" in the years leading up to the First World War (102–7) which, like a shamanic initiation, enabled him not only to heal others through the individuation process (262–3), but also to anticipate a "rebirth of our world" (110–1). If this encounter with the spirit-world was at least in part prompted by his break-up with Freud (105), he would, from the Thirties onwards, find other allies on his initiatory journey.

Still Vaster Symbolism

In 1933, the year that Hitler came to power in Germany, there was held on the shores of Lake Maggiore in Switzerland the first of what would be a series of conferences which would continue almost without interruption to the present day; their story has been said to constitute "an alternative intellectual history of the twentieth century."[61] In the name of Eranos, meaning a symposium in which all the participants bring a gift of the spirit, have gathered and spoken leading figures in the humanities and (to a lesser extent) the sciences, braving the reputation of the conferences for mysticism.

From the beginning, the guiding spirit or godfather of Eranos was Jung, although it later attracted figures such as the French philosopher of the imagination and scholar of Islamic esotericism Henry Corbin and the Romanian historian of religion Mircea Eliade, who engaged in a constructive dialogue with the psychology of the unconscious within their respective disciplines. Corbin spoke at nearly every conference from 1949 to within a couple of years of his death; while Eliade's first lecture was given in the year after Corbin's, at the 1950 gathering.

Speaking on the theme of the sacred center, Eliade ended by placing it in the context of the "still vaster symbolism" of the Grail myth (1991, 55), focusing on the hero's return to the castle of the Maimed King in Wolfram von Eschenbach's *Parzival*. Here we read that the wounded Anfortas is despairing of his pain-filled life and wishes only for his nephew Parzival to remove him from its presence, in order that he can die. Hearing this, Parzival asks him where the Grail is, adding: "Uncle, what troubles you?" But on hearing these questions, Anfortas is restored to health and youth (*PT* 333; *WP* 394–5).

In his study of the Grail legend, Evola drew out what he considered to be the significance of the first of these questions to the King: "Where is the power of which you should be the representative?" It is this question, according to Evola, which brings about a miracle (1997, 123); presumably because it reconnects the sacred king with the Hyperborean Tradition which is the source of both his spiritual authority and his temporal power.

Similarly, Eliade, for whom Evola was an early influence,[62] describes the question which will heal both the King and the Waste Land (Where is the Holy Grail?) as "the one question" which can forever renew the cosmos.[63] But it is not until his Haskell Lectures of 1956 that Eliade specifically identified the Grail Quest as an initiation, although he remained agnostic on the controversial issue of whether the stories contain memories of rituals actually practiced.

The important point for Eliade is that there is a "proliferation of initiatory symbols and motifs" in the romances[64]; indicating that, once their "ritual reality" is lost, patterns of initiation re-emerge in popular literature: "This is as much as to say that they now deliver their spiritual message on a different plane of human experience, by addressing themselves directly to the imagination."[65]

It is this imaginative (but not *imaginary*) plane that is at the heart of the writings of Henry Corbin, Eliade's colleague at Eranos. In his 1974 lecture, he sees the Templars who guard the Grail at Montsalvat as an "initiatory knighthood" (1986, 339); the Temple itself is situated in a place where physical laws do not apply, a sacred center linking the three realms of Heaven, Earth and Underworld (359–60). That is why Corbenic "must be sought elsewhere than on the rugged slopes of Wales" (352).

For Corbin, the Grail Kingdom is a region of the Interworld, an intermediate realm of visionary images, situated between the world of sensory perception and that of the intellect; a region of what he calls the *imaginal world* or *mundus imaginalis* (265). It is at the heart of a threefold cosmology that Corbin has attempted to rescue from the triumph of rationalist dualism. In this cosmology there is, firstly, the *sensory* world (the one that can be perceived with our physical faculties); secondly, an *imaginable* world (that can be perceived with the faculty of creative or spiritual imagination); and, thirdly, an *intelligible* world (that can be perceived with the faculty of intellectual intuition).

These three worlds correspond, on the human plane, to a threefold anthropology of body, soul (or psyche) and spirit; a model of the human being that has gradually been supplanted, in the West, by the dualism of body and soul (in religion), or of mind and matter (in science). This development Corbin considers to be a metaphysical tragedy. The importance of this distinction for our understanding of Grail Initiation becomes apparent if we compare Corbin's threefold model with that of Jessie Weston, with its three alchemical colors and its three kings.

What Weston calls the (red) middle realm of Humanity or Actuality, between (black) Matter and (white) Spirit, is, in the traditional cosmology championed by Corbin, the realm of psyche. Whereas for Weston the Grail Initiation was one practiced in time and space, for Corbin it is a soul event; Corbenic can be found, not in Wales, but in the *mundus imaginalis*. And this is Corbin's answer to the question: Where is the Grail?

If we look for the Grail in the sacred center of our being, in the imaginal world that

Corbin describes as on the threshold of the soul, then we do not need to die *physically* (as Cahus does, perishing of literalism after encountering his dream shadow in the Perilous Chapel) but *psychically*, in order to be reborn in spirit. For Eliade, this rebirth enables us "to obtain a definitive and total *renovatio*, a renewal capable of transmuting life"; for the goal of "initiatory renewal" is nothing less than "spiritual transformation" (1958, 135). In this regard the key initiatory text, for Corbin, is Wolfram's *Parzival*; moreover, the initiatory rituals presented are not those of Adonis, but of Hermeticism.

In exploring the Hermetic nature of Wolfram's "initiatory poem," Corbin (1971, 152) draws on the earlier researches of Henry and Renée Kahane, who saw in Trevrizent, Parzival's spiritual father, the figure of Hermes Trismegistus; the Grail itself is the Krater of the Emerald Tablet.[66] But in one important aspect Corbin distances himself from the approach of the Kahanes: Whereas they see Wolfram's poem as illustrating Hermetic doctrines, Corbin sees the poem as a "visionary recital" which expresses a soul-event; not allegorical exposition, but an imaginative doorway into esotericism (1971, 192–200).

The French scholar Pierre Gallais (1929–2001), in a work dedicated to Corbin, explores more specifically Chrétien's *Conte del Graal* in the context of esoteric philosophy. He sees Perceval as having five spiritual fathers: firstly, Arthur, in whose court he gains his first suit of armor; secondly, Gornemant, who knights him and first teaches him about chivalry; thirdly, the Fisher King; fourthly, the hermit uncle; and, finally, the Old King, to whom Perceval would presumably have returned at the end of the romance and into whose presence he would presumably have been admitted if he had asked the Question (1998b, 126–7).

It is precisely because Perceval fails to ask the Grail Question, Gallais argues, that the Lance shows its malefic aspect, threatening the destruction of the Kingdom of Logres (173). But the colors of the Lance—the redness of the blood contrasting with the whiteness of the iron point and shaft—are found again in a visionary reverie that Perceval experiences, when the sight of blood on snow reminds him of the complexion of his ladylove Blancheflor,[67] as if she is the inverted mirror image of the Lance.

And who is to say, asks Gallais, that another such ecstatic experience would not have led him back to the place of the Lance, to find again the Grail (136)? Thus, Blancheflor mediates between Perceval and the sacred object of his quest (166). She is a type of Sophia, Lady Wisdom: the archetypal Beloved, whose beauty will lead him through human to divine love and open his heart to the possibility of a true spiritual initiation (113–5).

But we will leave the last word on a century of scholarly myth-making to another French medievalist, Francis Dubost, who, in a book first published two years before the end of the millennium,[68] suggested that what the scene of the blood on the snow points to is, indeed, an initiation; but one into the *mode symbolique* itself, into the function of symbol-making as a means of self-discovery. For what the image of red on white conjures up for Perceval is something unique to him: the memory of his beloved.

At the same time, its whiteness and redness points back to what he has already witnessed but not yet understood: the scene in the Grail Castle. But whereas what the knights of the Vulgate *Queste* discover in the course of their *initiation mystique* is perfectly explicable by the theology of the time (and is elucidated at great length by the hermits they meet), what Perceval discovers in the *Conte del Graal* through this "chromatic analogy" is the faculty of symbolization itself[69]: at once a fundamental principle of literature and a means of opening up new ways of seeing ourselves and our world (Dubost, 126–30).

For whether we see it as a pagan talisman or a Christian relic, as "rich" or "holy," the Grail is above all a symbol; while the vision of the Grail is always an initiation into a new way of being.

Notes

1. Ezra Pound, who helped T.S. Eliot to edit *The Waste Land* into the form that is known today, wrote an article for the review and lectured to the Quest Society on the troubadours (Goodrick-Clarke, 23). Pound claimed never to have read Weston and to have no intention of doing so (Surette, 76).
2. Machen featured the Grail in a novella (*The Great Return* of 1915) and a novel (*The Secret Glory* of 1922), as well as in essays ("The Secret of the Sangraal," published in 1923 and "The Sangraal," published in 1924), in which he sees the origin of the symbol in Celtic Christianity (Marino, 124–8).
3. Williams, now best known as the Third Inkling (after his more famous friends J.R.R. Tolkien and C.S. Lewis), featured a battle for the Grail in his novel of 1930, *War in Heaven* (Marino, 128–32). He also explored the symbolism of the Vessel in two books of modernist Arthurian poetry and an accompanying essay, with commentary by Lewis, reprinted together in one volume in the Seventies (Marino, 65).
4. Lachman, 171: The Anthroposophical Society was founded in 1912, restructured in 1923 and continues to this day: https://www.goetheanum.org/en/aag/history/overview/.
5. According to Steiner "there were almost always individuals who were capable of lifting themselves up into the higher worlds through Imagination, Inspiration and Intuition. In the Christian era, these people were the successors of the initiates of antiquity who had been leaders and members of the centers of mystery wisdom" (2001b, 34).
6. For Steiner, the Gnostics were early Christians "striving to comprehend Christianity from the viewpoint of the Mysteries. From their perspective, Christ is above all a spiritual being, the Logos" (Steiner 2001b, 27).
7. "And in the Grail lives the ego united with the eternal and immortal, just as the lower ego is bound to the ephemeral and mortal. Those who know the secret of the Holy Grail know that from the wood of the Cross there springs ever new life" (Steiner 2001b, 23).
8. Steiner 2001b, 61: In the Grail stories we are shown "the sufferings and conquests" that the candidate for initiation has to experience in the intellectual soul; but in the figure of Parzival is crystallized "that which has to be enacted in the consciousness soul" in order to "penetrate into the mysteries of the spiritual worlds in modern times" (53).
9. Christian initiation into what Steiner calls the Mystery of Golgotha allows a fully conscious connection to what, for the faithful, is an unconscious connection to the events of Christ's Passion (Steiner 2001b, 22).
10. Goodrick-Clarke 1992, 221–3: Joscelyn Godwin calls Ravenscroft's book "a blood-curdling work of historical reinvention" (Godwin 1993a,.99).
11. Ravenscroft bemoans the "grave error and illusion" into which such adventurers are led by "almost totally unprepared and morally unearned precipitation into the oceans of transcendent awareness" (1982a, 83–4).
12. A more reliably-researched history of the Thule Society and its role in the early development of the NSDAP has been presented by Goodrick-Clarke in Chapter 11 of his *Occult Roots of Nazism* and, more recently, by David Luhrssen in *Hammer of the Gods* (2012).
13. Goodrick-Clarke 1992, 195: The congruence between the ideas of Lanz and Hitler becomes evident in statements attributed to the Führer, such as when he argued for arresting "racial decay" by creating an initiatic Order, a "brotherhood of Templars round the holy grail of pure blood" (197).
14. Walvater is the triune deity of the newly "rediscovered" Aryo-Germanic faith of the Thulists; the first person of this pagan trinity is Wotan (Goodrick-Clarke 1992, 145).
15. If Eckart had opened the centers of Hitler's astral body, "giving him the possibility of vision into the macrocosm and means of communication with the powers of darkness," Haushofer contributed "degrees of initiation of a far higher order," taking on the role of Mephistopheles to Hitler's Faust. Haushofer initiated Hitler "into the occult significance of the blood and the part which blood rites would play in creating a magical mutation in the Aryan Race, a mutation which would bring about a new stage in human evolution, the birth of the 'Superman' … the Man-God who would lead the Aryan race in the conquest of the world and set up a new order which would last for a thousand years" (Ravenscroft 1982a, 230–4).
16. The East German scholar Kurt Rudolph stresses the part played by the pagan Mysteries in the formation of Gnostic Christianity, citing the Naassenes as a community in which ideas propagated in the mystery religions, such as "the common fate of the divinity and the faithful" would have found acceptance (285–6). Rudolf is here referring to the archetype of the Redeemed Redeemer, who both saves and *is* saved; like the

Maimed King, we might add, who must be healed (redeemed) but whose restoration to health restores the fertility of the land and its people (redemption).

17. A Naassene "homily" and other Gnostic writings were preserved by the anti-heretical Church Father Hippolytus, although only in order to refute them! They are available online at: http://www.newadvent.org/fathers/050105.htm.

18. Weston admitted that we cannot tell whether or not the Templars were Gnostics; but she was "strongly inclined to believe" that there is a factual foundation for the connection between them and the Grail indicated in Wolfram's *Parzival* (where "we find the Grail in the care of a body of semi-religious, semi-militant knights, who bear the significant name of Templeisen") and hinted at in the Romance of Perlesvaus ("where we have a body of knightly hermits, bearing the Cross on their robes"). Ultimately, "the same influences which brought about the ruin of the one were responsible for the disappearance of the other" (1913, 136).

19. For Yeats, Spades and Diamonds symbolize Courage and Power; Clubs and Hearts, Knowledge and Pleasure (Raine, 31). These suits in turn correspond to the Grail Sword, Lance, Dish and Cup (Weston 1920, 79).

20. "The more closely one studies pre–Christian Theology, the more strongly one is impressed with the deeply, and daringly, spiritual character of its speculations, and the more doubtful it appears that such teaching can depend upon the unaided processes of human thought.... Certain it is that so far as historical evidence goes our earliest records point to the recognition of a spiritual, not a material, origin of the human race.... Folk practices and ceremonies ... do not represent the material out of which the Adonis-Attis cult was formed, but surviving fragments of a worship from which the higher significance has vanished" (Weston 1920, 7).

21. Leon Surette argues that we need not suppose that Eliot believed in Weston's lost Mystery Religion, only that he saw in her writings "an account of the suppression and loss of a religious faith" (81). In *The Waste Land* there is no resurrection: "In Grail terms the poem stops in the Chapel Perilous" (92). Eliot would later "regret having sent so many enquirers off on a wild goose chase after Tarot cards and the Holy Grail" when, as Jonathan Ullyot argues, Weston's text was mainly inspirational to the poet "as a structural or guiding model." It "may explain some of the incidental symbolism and elucidate some difficulties, but will not reveal a hidden meaning to the poem" (48).

22. "I regard it as impossible to trace certain Celtic sources of Arthurian romance back to a remote origin in the Eastern Mediterranean, though some striking analogies exist" (Loomis 1949, ix).

23. "Weston's syncretism of Christian and Celtic pagan Grail traditions is instrumental to Bradley's New Age relativism. To Bradley, according to the deeper Mysteries of which only the enlightened pagans are aware, Christianity and Celtic paganism are two compatible manifestations of a single source truth.... Christianity and Celtic paganism are presented as two variants of a higher and inclusive belief system centered on fertility and rebirth, the death and revival of a deity" (Marino, 63).

24. http://www.prudencejones.co.uk. Jones writes that "it would seem" that Weston was never an initiate, her loyalty to the Christian faith remaining unquestioned: "Yet clearly she understood the mystical realm of insight where all religions meet and can communicate their different approaches to the truth" (145).

25. Weston considered that these three kings feature in Wagner's *Parsifal* as Titurel (the Fisher King), Amfortas (the Maimed King) and Klingsor (the King of Castle Mortal), leading her to conclude that "here, as so often elsewhere, Wagner's dramatic genius had led him to a reconstruction of the *original* form of the legend" (1909, 259n1).

26. Weston compares Galahad, Perceval and Bors to the Three Rulers of the system of Basilides, by which she presumably means the Triple Filiality or Sonship: "Of this triply divided Sonship, one aspect was the subtlest of the subtle, one less subtle, and one still stood in need of purification." The subtlest Sonship rises up to the transcendent Godhead, the less subtle follows after, with the aid of the Holy Spirit, while the third Sonship remains below in our world (Mead, 260–2). The analogy, however far-fetched, is with Galahad (as the first Sonship), whose soul is carried up to Heaven from the oriental city of Sarras; Perceval (as the second Sonship) who follows a year later; and Bors (as the third Sonship) who, being chaste rather than wholly virginal, is obliged to remain "below," in our world, at the end of the Grail Quest.

27. Weston 1913, 126: "He knew, and that from the inside, the material with which he was dealing.... For him the Grail is equated with the Christian Eucharist. There can, I think, be little doubt that he designed his version from the point of view of one familiar with Christian esoteric teaching, one to whom the threefold aspect of the Grail naturally translated itself into the threefold significance of the Eucharist, as the Feast of Communion, the actual Body and Blood of the Lord, and the Source of Spiritual Life" (120–1).

28. De Boron "was certainly aware of the real character of his material; he knew the Grail cult as Christianized Mystery, and ... handled the theme on distinctively religious lines, preserving the Mystery element in its three-fold development, and equating the Vessel of the Mystic Feast with the Christian Eucharist" (Weston 1920, 161).

29. According to Waite, the reason that the Mass of the Holy Grail is more valid than any other is that the Guardians use the Secret Words (the ones which Christ spoke to Joseph of Arimathea in prison and

which were passed on by him to his "super-apostolic" successors) in the consecration of the Eucharist (1909, 63).

30. The length of the title is reflected by that of the book. It was republished with a new introduction by John C. Wilson in 1961; a third edition was issued by Dover Books in 2006 under the more manageable title: *The Holy Grail: History, Legend and Symbolism*.

31. "We have done nothing to explain the Ascension of the Grail to Heaven and the Assumption of Galahad when we have ascertained that some possible centuries before there were myths about a Cauldron" (Waite 2006, 314).

32. Waite 2006, 418–423. He concludes: "Supposing that the Grail Romances at once conceal and offer intimations concerning a Rite of Initiation, that which will least of all suffer comparison therewith is the ceremonial congeries of Eleusis."

33. Waite 2006, 426: "It would enlist all my own interest had she held one ounce of real evidence in her hands or had even portrayed in adequate outline its supposed measure and term."

34. Waite even wondered whether "she may have been admitted personally before the close of her life" into "one of those very numerous so-called Orders which were mushroom growths of the period but which were paraded invariably among believers who fell into their toils as institutions of remote antiquity" (2006, 432–3).

35. Waite 2006, 441: "It was the place of a Christian Mystery; the place of a Maimed King; the place of a King in his passing; the place of a Secret Hierarchy; the place of Masses said nowhere else on earth; the place of Secret Consecrations; the place of Strange Hallows; the place of reception and the communication of miraculous Eucharists administered by Christ Himself; the place where unknown Candidates or Epopts, coming from far countries, might enter unchallenged and behold the Mystery unveiled."

36. "Le Saint Graal" in the journal *Le Voile d'Isis* (later *Etudes Traditionelles*); reprinted in Guénon 1962, 29–42.

37. See in this regard Sedgwick (2004).

38. Guénon 1983, 26: "Owing to one of those verbal assimilations which play quite a significant part in the field of symbolism, and which carry a more profound meaning than is at first obvious, the Grail is at once a 'vase' (*grasale*), signifying the primordial state, and a 'book' (*gradale* or *graduale*), signifying the tradition." As sacred vase or sacrificial Vessel it restores the "sense of eternity" to whoever drinks from it; as book it conveys the knowledge that effects reintegration into the primordial state (28–9).

39. Guénon 1983, 27: The supreme spiritual center "always keeps the tradition intact, and remains untouched by any changes occurring in the exterior world," but it can remain hidden: "Such is the state of this present epoch, the beginning of which reaches back well beyond what is accessible to ordinary and 'profane' history" (28).

40. Here Guénon is "correcting" the German story that the emerald falls from the *crown* of Lucifer (Barber 2005, 190–1).

41. "The table itself is one of those very ancient symbols always associated with the idea of spiritual centers, guardians of the tradition" (Guénon 1983, 29).

42. We might think here also of what Chrétien calls the *mout bele conjointure* that he makes out of *un conte d'avanture*, which professional story-tellers have a habit of mangling. *Depecier et corronpre* (*EE* ll.13–4, 21–2): Is this not the fate of the Primordial Tradition itself, according to Guénon, in the Kali Yuga or Iron Age?

43. Hence Evola's magnum opus is entitled *Rivolta contro il mondo moderno*. First published in 1934 in Fascist Italy, it had to wait over sixty years for an English translation.

44. "The Grail essentially embodies the source of a transcendent and immortalizing power of primordial origin that has been preserved after the 'Fall,' degeneration and decadence of humanity" (Evola 2010, 144).

45. Rahn's first book had to wait more than seventy years to be translated into English.

46. Flowers & Moynihan, 35: It has also been claimed that the SS found the Grail near Montségur after Rahn's death; commandos apparently concealed it in a glacier in the Austrian mountains at the end of the war, awaiting the rebirth of the Reich (Goodrick-Clarke 2003, 122).

47. Rahn's section head in the SS was Karl Maria Wiligut (1866–1946) aka Weisthor, aka Himmler's Rasputin, who advised the Reichsführer-SS on the development of his Black Camelot, the Wewelsburg Castle in Westphalia; where, it is believed, the Grail was evoked as a symbol of the Holy Blood of Hyperborea (Goodrick-Clarke 2003, 188).

48. America is the Land of the White Gods because it is "the traditional refuge of the descendants of the Luciferan Hyperboreans, the followers of the God of the Losers of the Kaliyuga, the warriors of the Morning Star…. For this reason, in ancient times America-Albania was visited by the Druids, the Celts, the Vikings, the Templars, and Parsifal, who came in a ship with all its lights on, with the emblem of the Lefthanded Cross on its sail and carrying the Grail" (Serrano 1984, 84). The Lefthanded Cross is, of course, the Nazi Swastika, symbolizing the "movement of return, towards the Golden Age" (187).

49. This is Serrano's racialist interpretation of *Memoire de sanc*, the name of the scabbard which sheathes the Sword with the Strange Straps in the Vulgate *Queste*. According to Perceval's sister, the scabbard is so called because it is partly made from the wood of the Tree of Life, which turned red when

Abel was murdered beneath it; it will always remind men of understanding of that bloody deed (*QP* 227; *LG* IV, 72).

50. Serrano gave a fascinating account of his meetings with Jung and Hermann Hesse, who were both living in Switzerland when Serrano visited Europe, in a work published in Spanish in 1965, and which appeared in English translation a year later. His discussions with Jung were dramatized in *Nos*, the last of his books to be accorded mainstream respectability. Here the Master of the Sphinx proclaims: "The mystery of the Grail has preoccupied and moved me deeply since my youth. For this very reason, I did not wish to touch it but passed it by on tiptoe, because I had a presentiment that this was something sacred that should not be 'psychologized.' Unfortunately, I am not sure that others may not do so in my name after I have gone" (Serrano 1984, 70).

51. Because carnal love means the propagation of the human species in a world of death, the "laws of chastity" reigned in Montségur as in Munsalvæsche, where the Grail Templars "are of an immaculate purity" (Rahn, 106–7). Serrano's archetypal Beloved, the Absolute Woman, fulfilling the Myth of Feminine Immortality, announces: "The Grail doesn't tolerate unbridled passions, it loves pious reticence, a reverent attitude," a sentiment with which Nascien and the Grail Hermits would have wholeheartedly agreed. And when She concludes: "With the memory of your beloved in your heart, you will achieve the Grail" (41–2), we know that She can be (spiritual) Muse but not (physical) companion on the Quest.

52. Nevertheless, the association of Serrano with Jung, however limited it might have been in reality, can only add to the troubling questions about the legacy of analytical psychology (its "shadow") already raised by some of Jung's statements in the Thirties. Jung himself famously confessed that he had "slipped up" in his pre-World War II relations with the Third Reich (Franz, 63–5); it is certainly difficult nowadays to read the distinctions he made then between Jewish and Aryan psychology with equanimity. Franz, like other Jungians in the Seventies, had no qualms about quoting Serrano's reminiscences of Jung verbatim.

53. See Noll (1997), esp. Chapter Seven: "The Mystery of Deification."

54. For Jung and Franz, Perceval's initiatory journey involves overcoming personal shadow figures such as the Red Knight (56) and Orguelleus, the Proud One. In one version, it is during his battle with the latter that the sword which Perceval was given by the Fisher King breaks (81–2).

55. Jung & Franz, 73: "In primitive initiation rites the novice is instructed and initiated into the tribal mysteries by the ancestors or the ancestral spirits. In the same way the treasures guarded by the Grail King are brought out for Perceval, rather as if they were the holy relics of the tribe" (75).

56. If King Arthur's circle of Round Table Knights "mirrors the symbol of the Self"—that is, of psychic wholeness—as it manifested in the first Christian millennium (Jung & Franz, 216), the circle of knights seated at the Grail Table mirrors that symbol in the second millennium, which began with the Crusades and ended with the Nazi Holocaust and 9/11. Thus, history bears witness to the "remarkable" shadow which the authors see as being cast by the Grail King (196).

57. The "heathen opponent" is Wolfram's solution to the identity of the man who maimed the Fisher King, left unresolved by Chrétien; this fits the authors' contention that Christian spiritual pride "constellated a negative pagan demonism, leading to a destructive estrangement from instinct and nature" (Jung & Franz, 240).

58. Representing the archetype of the Self, Merlin instigates Perceval's initiatory quest for that "inner wholeness" symbolized by the Vessel: "Thus Merlin *is* the mystery of the Grail" (Jung & Franz, 373).

59. Capping a "remarkable" list of features shared by Merlin and the alchemical Mercurius, "both represent the mystery of a 'divine vessel' which serves as the object of men's search" (Jung & Franz, 368–9).

60. For Jung and Franz, the traditional ecclesiastical figure of Christ cannot fully represent psychic wholeness since His shadow "appears split off into the contrasting figure of the Antichrist." What the authors call "a paradoxical symbol of the Self in which the opposites were reconciled" is provided by the alchemical Mercurius and by his counterpart in the Grail legend, the figure of Merlin, in whom survive certain psychically valuable pagan elements (Jung & Franz, 103). To complete the image of Christ, the Grail authors make use of both Celtic mythological material and early Christian apocrypha (104).

61. Hakl (2013).

62. As Guido Stucco notes, in the Foreword to his English translation of Evola's *Mistero del Graal*, Eliade maintained a correspondence with Evola from the Twenties onwards (Evola 1997, xiv).

63. Eliade 1991, 56: In his 1971 Eranos lecture, Corbin follows Eliade in seeing only one question (*Où est le Graal?*) as mattering, for on it depends the rejuvenation of the world (Corbin 1983, 260).

64. Eliade singles out Perceval's passing the night in the Chapel of the Black Hand as the "very type of the initiatory night watch. The ordeals that the Heroes undergo ... suggest passage to the beyond, the perilous descents to Hell; and when such journeys are undertaken by living beings, they always form part of an initiation." This also applies to Perceval's inheriting the Grail Kingdom, since "it is well known that the function of sovereignty is generally bound up with an initiatory ritual" (Eliade 1958, 125).

65. Eliade 1958, 125–6: "The fact that people listened with delight to romantic tales in which initiatory clichés occurred to satiety proves, I think, that such adventures provided the answer to a profound need in medieval man. It was only his imagination which was fed by these initiatory scenarios; but the life of the imagination, like the life of a dream, is as important for the whole psyche of the human being as is daily life."

66. Corbin's revisiting of the theories of the Kahanes is presented in "La Lumière de Gloire et le Saint Graal," Chapter IV of the second book of his magisterial study, *En Islam Iranien* (1971).

67. *Li vermels sor le blanc assis* (*RP* l.4204). Nor should we forget that the whitening and the reddening represent the two final stages of the threefold alchemical model of transmutation. In the Welsh Romance of Peredur, all three stages (*nigredo, albedo* and *rubedo*) are represented when the hero sees a raven feeding on a dead duck in the snow: "Peredur stood there, comparing the blackness of the raven and whiteness of the snow and redness of the blood to the appearance of the woman he loved best: her hair was black as jet, her skin white as the snow, and the two red spots in her cheeks like the blood in the snow" (*M* 233; *MJ* 165).

68. *Le Conte du Graal ou l'Art de Faire Signe* (1998), esp. Chapter III: "Sous le Signe de l'Initiation."

69. *Par l'intermédiaire de cette analogie chromatique, il ... accède à la lecture des signes, au fonctionnement poétique de la métaphore. Je ne sais si l'on peut parler d'initation au langage des signes, mais il est évident que Perceval apprend ici à déchiffrer le monde* (Dubost, 126).

APPENDIX I

The Grail Chronology

6 BCE: Birth of Jesus of Nazareth.[1]

9 CE: 17 November: *Birth of Vespasian.*[2]

27: Passion, Crucifixion and Deposition of Jesus. Imprisonment of Joseph of Arimathea.[3]

37: 16 March: *Death of Tiberius; Gaius becomes emperor.*[4]

62: Summer: Celidoine is born to the Duke and Duchess of Orberica.[5]

69: 11 July: *Vespasian is declared emperor by his troops in Judaea.*[6] He frees Joseph of Arimathea from prison, is baptized by St. Philip[7] and leaves the Holy Land on his way to Rome via Egypt.[8] Joseph leads the Company of the Grail eastwards and, after eleven days, arrives at the city of Sarras.[9] The next day, in the Spiritual Palace, Josephus is ordained by Christ as the first Christian bishop.

Autumn: The Angel of the Bleeding Lance prophesies the coming of Galahad. The next day, the Company of the Grail leaves Sarras; and the following day Mordrain, King of Sarras, is carried off by the Holy Spirit. Three days later, Celidoine and his father Nascien suffer imprisonment.[10] After seventeen days, Duke Nascien is miraculously liberated[11]; and, on the following day, Celidoine is carried off by nine angelic hands.[12]

70: Summer: Duke Nascien finds himself on the Turning Isle.[13] The next day, he boards the Ship of Faith, built by King Solomon, for the first time.[14]

72: When he is ten years old,[15] Celidoine encounters the King of Persia, whom he converts to Christianity and whose daughter he will later marry.

79: 23 June: *Death of the Emperor Vespasian.*[16]

133: Simeon, a nephew of Joseph of Arimathea, is carried off by two flying men with burning hands.[17]

156: Death of Lucius, first Christian King of the Britons.[18]

465: Balin, the Knight with Two Swords, strikes the Dolorous Blow, maiming the Fisher King Pellehan and inaugurating the adventures of the Holy Grail, which will last for the next twenty-two years. Death of Merlin.[19]

466: Birth of Galahad,[20] son of Lancelot of the Lake and the Grail Bearer.

481: Feast of Pentecost: Galahad draws the Sword from the Floating Stone and takes his place at the Round Table in the Perilous Seat.[21] The Grail Quest begins.

482: Lancelot returns to Logres after a year.[22]

487: Galahad, Perceval and Bors arrive at Corbenic to accomplish the Grail Quest.[23]

489: Death of Galahad in Sarras. The Holy Grail and Lance are taken up to Heaven.[24]

490: Perceval, having become a hermit after Galahad's burial, dies a year and three days later.[25]

744: Nascien the Hermit receives from Christ the Book of the Grail.[26]

c. 1190–1200: *Robert de Boron writes the metrical* Estoire dou Graal, a translation into French of the Latin text of Nascien the Hermit—itself a translation of the heavenly Book of the Grail, given to Nascien by its author, Christ Himself!

Notes

1. This date is arrived at by counting backwards from the year 69, when the historical record shows that Vespasian was in Jerusalem. If, as stated in the Vulgate, Joseph of Arimathea had been in prison for forty-two years (*LG* I, 11) by then, having been imprisoned shortly after the Deposition, then the death of Jesus, traditionally at the age of thirty-three, can be dated to 27 CE. Later dates which are reckoned from the Passion have been adjusted accordingly.

2. *STC* xii, 275. Passages in italics indicate events which can be historically verified.

3. *LG* I, 10–11: *Et Joseph fu en la prison ... tant qu'il i demoura .XLII. ans, et lors l'en geta Vaspasiiens, l'empereres de Rome.* The forty-two years are accounted for thus: Tiberius is Roman Emperor on the day that Jesus Christ is crucified; he rules for another ten years. His nephew Gaius (Caligula) succeeds him, but only reigns for a year. He is followed by Claudius then Nero, who both reign for fourteen years. Next comes Titus; it is in the third year of his reign that Joseph is freed from prison. *Et au tierch an ke Titus reçut l'empire fu Joseph jetés de prison: et si poés conter.XLII. ans del cruchefiement Jhesucrist jusc'au delivrement de Joseph* (*ESG* 28).

4. *STC* xii: *Au jour ke Jhesus fu crucefiés tenoit Tyberius Cesar l'empire de Rome et aprés che le tint il .X. ans. Aprés regna Gaius* (*ESG* 28; *LG* I, 11).

5. Carol J. Chase, in her English translation of the *Estoire del Saint Graal*, gives the date as the second of June (*LG* I, 69). However, the edition of Gérard Gros for the Pléiade Library gives *el jour des kalendes de juingnet*, that is, the first of July (*LDG* I, 214–5).

6. *STC* 279.

7. *LG* I, 13–14.

8. *STC* 279.

9. *En chele cité vint Joseph et sa compaignie a l'onsime jour qu'il issi de Jherusalem* (*ESG* 43; *LG* I, 15).

10. Celidoine is seven years and five months old when he and his father are incarcerated (*ESG* 233; *LDG* I, 214; *LG* I, 69), on the third day after Mordrain's disappearance: *Et che fu au tierch jour aprés chou ke li rois avoit esté pierdus* (*ESG* 184; *LG* I, 56).

11. *Si demoura Nasciens bien .XVII. jours en tel prison* (*ESG* 234; *LG* I, 70).

12. *ESG* 239; *LG* I, 71.

13. Bogdanow's edition of the Vulgate *Queste* says that this occurs a good forty-three years after the Passion—*bien a .XLIII. ans aprés la Passion* (*QSG* 506). The English translation of the *Estoire del Saint Graal* by Carol J. Chase gives the date as the ninth of June (*LG* I, 75). However, the edition of Gérard Gros for the Pléiade Library gives *au noevisme jour des kalendes de juingnet* (*LDG* I, 235)—the twenty-first of June, that is, the summer solstice (1709). Either way, Nascien has spent several months in a timeless limbo.

14. *LG* I, 77.

15. *LG* I, 87: The chronology again becomes doubtful here: In a short time—*en petit d'ore*—after being carried away, Celidoine—*il, qui estoit joenes enfes en l'aage de .X. anz seulement* (*ESG* 299)—has aged over two and a half years!

16. *STC* xiv, 287.

17. *LG* I, 147: The year of Simeon's abduction can be calculated by counting backwards from the last year of the Grail Quest, when Simeon tells his relative Galahad that he has been suffering in great heat for three hundred and fifty-four years, in expiation of a sin he committed against Joseph of Arimathea: *Ge sui Symeu vostre parent, qui en ceste grant chalor que vos veistes ore ai demoré trois cenz anz et cinquante et quatre por espeneir un pechié que je fis jadis envers Joseph d'Arymacie* (*QP* 264).

18. *HKB* 124–6.

19. Merlin prophesies that two marvels will occur on the same day: He will be delivered to death by the tricks of a woman *et si fera li Chevaliers a .II. espees le Doloreus Caup ... pour coi les aventures dou Saint Graal averront ... et duerront sans doutance .XXII. ans* (*SRM* 118; *LG* IV, 199). The year in which these events take place can be calculated by counting backwards from the date of the accomplishment of the Grail Quest, when the adventures associated with the Holy Vessel will no longer take place: *ne des or mes n'en avendra aventure* (*QP* 271; *LG* IV, 85).

20. The year of Galahad's birth can be calculated by counting backwards from the date he sits in the Perilous Seat, which he accomplishes when he is fifteen. According to the Vulgate *Lancelot*, Galahad stays at an abbey of nuns until he is old enough to be knighted: *si i demora tant que il fu granz demoisiaux de l'aage de .XV. anz* (*LM* VI, 243). A hermit who lives near the abbey suggests that he now enter the order of knighthood; the same hermit then tells King Arthur that on the feast of Pentecost a newly-made knight will sit on the Perilous Seat at the Round Table (*LG* III, 338).

21. According to the Vulgate *Queste*, on the day of Pentecost Lancelot knights Galahad then returns to Camelot, where his fellows of the Round Table find letters newly inscribed on the Perilous Seat, saying that it will find its master four hundred and fifty-four years after the Passion: *Et il regardent les lettres qui dient: .CCCC. ANZ ET .LIIII. SONT ACOMPLI EMPRÉS LA PASSION JHESUCRIST; ET AU JOR DE LA PENTECOUSTE DOIT CISTE SIEGES TROVER SON MESTRE* (QP 4). Lancelot calculates that this day is the very one referred to (*LG* IV, 4).

22. After reaching the Grail castle, a month after his last meeting with his son Galahad, Lancelot tells King Pelles that he wants to return to Logres, which he hasn't seen for a year: *il voldra aler au roiaume de Logres, ou il ne fu bien a passé un an* (QP 261; *LG* IV, 82).

23. After his last meeting with his father Lancelot, Galahad, accompanied by Perceval, rides for five years until he has accomplished all the adventures of Logres: *et chevaucha en telle maniere .V. anz toz entiers ainz que il venist en la meson lo Roi Mehaignié. Et en toz les .V. anz li tint Percevax compaignie en quel leu que il onques alast. Et dedenz celui terme orent il si achevees les aventures del roiaume de Logres* (QSG 626). They meet up with Bors and ride together to Corbenic (*LG* IV, 83).

24. Leaving Corbenic, the three companions spend "a long time" at sea in the Ship of Faith, which takes them to Sarras. There, they are imprisoned for a year, nourished by the grace of the Grail. On their release, Galahad is crowned King of Sarras, but dies on the first anniversary of his coronation (*LG* IV, 86-7).

25. *Un an et trois jorz vesqui Perceval en l'ermitage, et lors trespassa del siecle* (QP 279); Bors returns to Britain (*LG* IV, 87).

26. *Il avint aprés la passion Jhesucrist .VII. cens et .XVII. ans* (ESG 2; *LG* I, 3).

Appendix II

The Medieval Grail Literature

The CROWN

A German poem by Heinrich von dem Türlin, *Diu Crône* ("The Crown") was composed about 1230. Uniquely, Gawain is presented as the hero who brings to an end the enchantments of the Grail Kingdom.

It has been translated by J.W. Thomas (*HTC*).

The DE BORON CYCLE

Three continuous texts—the Prose *Joseph*, *Merlin* and *Perceval* (qq.v.)—tell the complete story of the Grail from the Passion of Christ to the destruction of the fellowship of the Round Table.

All three romances are attributed to the Burgundian poet Robert de Boron and have been translated by Nigel Bryant (*MG*).

The ELUCIDATION

Composed as a prologue to the Story of the Grail (q.v.), the *Elucidation* gives a unique account of the wasting of Logres and the loss of the Fisher King's castle.

It has been translated by Nigel Bryant (in *CSG*).

The FIRST CONTINUATION

When Chrétien de Troyes left his Romance of Perceval (q.v.) unfinished, the story was continued by four other poets. The first of these continuations is sometimes known as the Gawain Continuation because it focuses on the adventures of King Arthur's nephew rather than on those of Perceval. Probably composed in the last decade of the twelfth century, the First Continuation is found in three redactions (Short, Long and Mixed). In all three, Gawain partially restores the Waste Land by enquiring about the Bleeding Lance which he sees in the Grail Castle.

The Mixed Redaction has been partially translated by Nigel Bryant (in *PSG*); Bryant has also translated the whole of the Long Redaction (in *CSG*).

GERBERT'S CONTINUATION

The unfinished Second Continuation to the Story of the Grail (qq.v.) was followed and brought to a conclusion by Manessier's Continuation (q.v.) in the thirteenth century. But another attempt was made by a poet usually identified as the northern French

Gerbert de Montreuil. He recounts how Perceval breaks his sword on the gates of the Earthly Paradise and has it repaired by the smith who forged it. At the end of the poem, Perceval returns to the Grail Castle and repairs the sword which was used to kill the Fisher King's brother. Gerbert may have concluded the story but, if so, his ending is lost.

Gerbert's Continuation has been partially translated by Nigel Bryant (in *PSG*); Bryant has also translated the whole poem (in *CSG*).

The HISTORY OF THE HOLY GRAIL

The first part of the narrative of the Vulgate Cycle (q.v.), but not the first to be written, the *Estoire del Saint Graal* ("The History of the Holy Grail") begins with a reworking of Robert de Boron's Prose *Joseph* (q.v.). But it continues with an account of how Joseph of Arimathea, his son Josephus and their family and followers bring the Grail from the Holy Land to the Middle Eastern city of Sarras and thence to Britain, where the dynasty of Fisher Kings is established to guard the Holy Vessel. It thus fills in many details of events which are only recalled retrospectively in the Vulgate *Quest of the Holy Grail* (q.v.).

It has been translated by Carol J. Chase (in *LG* I).

JOSEPH OF ARIMATHEA

Robert de Boron's verse *Estoire dou Graal*, also known as *Joseph d'Arimathie*, was written around the last decade of the twelfth century. It acts as a prequel to Chrétien de Troyes' Romance of Perceval (q.v.), identifying the Grail as a relic of the Last Supper. Drawing on apocryphal sources, it tells of Joseph's imprisonment, but continues with an original account of his sustaining by the Grail and the revelation to him of the Secret Words of Christ. He is liberated by Vespasian and passes the Grail and the Secret Words to his brother-in-law Bron, the Rich Fisher. The poem has been rendered into prose by an unknown hand to form the first part of a prose trilogy which I refer to as the De Boron Cycle (q.v.).

It has been translated by Jean Rogers (*JA*).

LANCELOT

The central part of the Vulgate Cycle, the Prose *Lancelot* tells of visits by Gawain, Bors and Lancelot to the mysterious Grail Castle. During his first visit, Lancelot is tricked into sleeping with the Grail Bearer and, as a result, fathers a son, Galahad, who is destined to bring to an end the adventures of the Holy Grail.

It has been translated by Samuel N. Rosenberg, Carleton W. Carroll, Roberta L. Krueger and William W. Kibler (*LG* II–III).

The LATER TITUREL

The late thirteenth century German poet Albrecht elaborates the information given to us by Wolfram von Eschenbach about the grandfather of the Maimed King, in *Jüngerer Titurel* ("The Later Titurel"). The poem includes an elaborate description of the Grail Temple, which has been translated into English by Barber & Edwards (2003), with a looser version in Matthews & Knight (2019).

The LIVRE D'ARTUS

A variation on the second half of the *Estoire de Merlin*—"The Story of Merlin" (q.v.)—the fragmentary text known to scholars as the *Livre d'Artus* contains several references to the Grail, but they are not always consistent with other romances in the Vulgate Cycle (q.v.). Notable is an account of the first sighting of the Grail by Sir Nascien, who will later become a hermit.

It has been edited by H. Oskar Sommer (*VS* VII); no English translation is currently available.

MANESSIER'S CONTINUATION

Usually known as the Third Continuation—although Gerbert's Continuation (q.v.) is sometimes interpolated between it and the Second—Manessier's poem brings to an end the long-drawn out Story of the Grail (q.v.) begun by Chrétien de Troyes. Perceval finally learns the truth about the Grail, the Lance and the silver trencher; moreover, he heals the maimed Fisher King by avenging the murder of the king's brother.

Manessier's Continuation has been partially translated by Nigel Bryant (in *PSG*); Bryant has also translated the whole poem (in *CSG*).

The MERLIN CONTINUATION

The Post-Vulgate Cycle (q.v.) incorporates the first part of the Vulgate *Estoire de Merlin*—"The Story of Merlin" (q.v.)—but breaks off in an original direction after recounting King Arthur's marriage to Guenevere. We learn that the Fisher King Pellehan is maimed by the Dolorous Blow struck by Balin the Savage and that, as a result, his kingdom is wasted for twenty-two years. The Knights of the Round Table encounter their first Grail adventures.

It has been translated by Martha Asher (in *LG* IV–V).

MORIEN

A medieval Dutch romance which presents Perceval as unsuccessful on the Grail Quest, its eponymous hero Morien is the illegitimate son of Perceval's older brother Agloval. It is notable for a dream Agloval has, in which the Grail is a bridge between Heaven and Earth.

It has been translated by Jessie L. Weston (*MW*).

Le MORTE DARTHUR

In his famous masterpiece of fifteenth-century English literature, Sir Thomas Malory "reduces" into English the Tale of Balin—part of the Post-Vulgate *Merlin* Continuation (q.v.)—and the Tale of the Sangreal, based on the Vulgate *Queste del Saint Graal*—"The Quest of the Holy Grail" (q.v.).

PARZIVAL

The German poet Wolfram von Eschenbach, writing early in the thirteenth century, reworked Chrétien de Troyes' Romance of Perceval (q.v.)—providing a prologue and conclusion to the unfinished French poem. Among other departures from the French original, changes which Wolfram credits to a source called Kyot, the Grail is a stone guarded by Templars.

It has been translated for Penguin Books by A.T. Hatto (*WP*) and, along with the fragments of *Titurel*, by Cyril Edwards for Oxford World's Classics (*PT*).

PEREDUR

The hero of a Welsh romance, the relation of which to Chrétien de Troyes' *Perceval* is uncertain, Peredur sees a decapitated head on a bloody dish in a wondrous castle and must avenge a murder and a maiming.

It has been translated for Everyman's Library by Gwyn and Thomas Jones (in *MJ*), for Penguin Books by Jeffrey Gantz (in *M*), and by Sioned Davies for Oxford World's Classics.

PERLESVAUS

An early thirteenth century prose romance telling of the adventures of Perceval (here called "Perlesvaus," since he has "lost the vales" once ruled by his father) after his first, unsuccessful visit to the Grail Castle. Following the death of the Fisher King, Perlesvaus conquers the castle but, ultimately, sails away with its sacred relics, including the five-formed Grail.

It has been translated for Everyman's Library by Sebastian Evans (*HH*), and by Nigel Bryant (*HBG*).

The POST-VULGATE CYCLE

Adopting the *Estoire del Saint Graal* and the first part of the *Estoire de Merlin* from the Vulgate Cycle, the Post-Vulgate follows on with an original *Suite du Roman de Merlin*—"Merlin Continuation" (q.v.)—a greatly expanded *Queste del Saint Graal* and a truncated *Mort Artu*. The whole cycle ends with the destruction of the Round Table and its Perilous Seat.

It has been translated by Martha Asher (in *LG* IV–V).

The PROSE JOSEPH

The first part of the De Boron Cycle (q.v.), the Prose *Joseph* is an adaptation of the verse *Estoire dou Graal*, also known as the *Joseph d'Arimathie*—"Joseph of Arimathea" (q.v.)—in which, for the first time, the Grail is clearly identified as a relic of the Last Supper.

It has been translated by Nigel Bryant (in *MG*).

The PROSE MERLIN

The second part of the De Boron Cycle (q.v.), the Prose *Merlin* is an adaptation and continuation of a fragmentary metrical version, of which only about five hundred lines have survived. It presents Merlin as the Prophet of the Grail, instructing Uther

Pendragon to create the Round Table with its Perilous Seat and dictating the Book of the Grail to Blaise.

It has been translated by Nigel Bryant (in *MG*).

The PROSE PERCEVAL

The third part of the De Boron Cycle (q.v.), the Prose *Perceval* shows the hero sitting prematurely on the Perilous Seat but eventually being guided by Merlin to achieve the Grail Quest.

It has been translated by Nigel Bryant (in *MG*).

The PROSE TRISTAN

Just as the story of Lancelot was incorporated into the Vulgate Cycle (q.v.), the great medieval love story of Tristan and Iseut was reworked under the influence of the Post-Vulgate *Roman du Graal*. Although, like Galahad, a direct descendant of Bron, the brother-in-law of Joseph of Arimathea, Tristan recognizes that the Grail Quest is not for him; unlike his great rival for the love of Iseut, the pagan Palamedes, who converts to Christianity and becomes one of the twelve knights to sit at the Table of the Grail in Corbenic.

There is a partial translation by Renée L. Curtis for Oxford World's Classics (*RTC*); while several adventures of Tristan on the Grail Quest are translated by Martha Asher (in *LG* V).

The QUEST OF THE HOLY GRAIL

The fourth part of the Vulgate Cycle (q.v.), *La Queste del Saint Graal* recounts the arrival of Galahad at Camelot, the appearance there of the Grail and the beginning of the quest for the Holy Vessel, which culminates in the arrival of twelve knights at Corbenic, the Grail Castle. Three go on to the sacred city of Sarras; only one returns.

It has been translated by Pauline Matarasso for Penguin Books (*QHG*), and by E. Jane Burns (in *LG* IV).

The ROMANCE OF PERCEVAL

The twelfth century poet Chrétien de Troyes began *li contes del graal*—"The Story of the Grail" (q.v.)—but left it unfinished, spawning both prequels and sequels. What remains of his own work is a Romance of Perceval, in which the naive young hero's adventures are juxtaposed with those of the more worldly-wise Gawain. Perceval encounters a maimed Fisher King who presents him with a sword that is destined to break. He witnesses a mysterious candle-lit procession involving a lance that bleeds, a golden, bejeweled serving dish (a *graal*) and a silver trencher; but fails to ask any questions about what he sees. Long-lost members of his family turn up to explain at least some of the mysteries of the Grail Castle, but much remains to discover.

The are several translations available, notably those of D.D.R. Owen for Everyman's Library (in *CTO*), William W. Kibler for Penguin Books (*SGP*) and Nigel Bryant (in *PSG* and *CSG*).

The ROMANCE OF SONE

The late thirteenth century Romance of Sone is not Arthurian, but features a visit by the hero to Norway. Here Sone sees the Grail and the Lance of Longinus, and hears the story of Joseph of Arimathea who, in this version, is the maimed Fisher King.

The Romance of Sone has been partially—and the Grail sections fully—translated into English in Matthews & Knight (2019).

The SECOND CONTINUATION

Following on from Chrétien de Troyes' unfinished Romance of Perceval, the First Continuation (qq.v.) focuses on the adventures of Gawain; but the Second picks up the story of Perceval where Chrétien left him, at the hermitage of his uncle, where he has learnt some, but by no means all, of the mysteries of the Grail Castle. Various distractions, some magical and otherworldly, delay his return to the court of the Fisher King; but, when he eventually finds it, he is told he must mend a broken sword before he can learn the whole truth about the Grail.

The Second Continuation has been partially translated by Nigel Bryant (in *PSG*); Bryant has also translated the whole poem (in *CSG*).

The STORY OF MERLIN

The second part of the narrative of the Vulgate Cycle (q.v.), but arguably the last to be written, the *Estoire de Merlin* ("The Story of Merlin") begins with a reworking of the Prose *Merlin* (q.v.) attributed to Robert de Boron. But it continues with an account of how Merlin aids King Arthur in his wars against the invading Saxons and their native allies until the prophet's beguiling by the Lady of the Lake, which links the cycle to the beginning of the *Lancelot* (q.v.).

It has been translated by Rupert T. Pickens (in *LG* I).

The STORY OF THE GRAIL

Following his ground-breaking series of romances featuring the Knights of the Round Table, Chrétien de Troyes completed only the first nine thousand or so verses of a Romance of Perceval (q.v.). Four continuations by other poets eventually brought the story to its conclusion in which Perceval, having become the new King of the Grail Castle, retires from this world after seven years and becomes a hermit. For ten years he is sustained only by the grace of the Grail until finally he and the other holy relics are taken up to Heaven.

Nigel Bryant has translated Chrétien's poem and sizeable extracts from the continuations (in *PSG*); and the whole of all five texts, along with the *Elucidation* (q.v.) and another prequel entitled *Bliocadran* (in *CSG*).

The VULGATE CYCLE

Robert de Boron's Prose *Joseph* and *Merlin* (qq.v.) were reworked (c.1215–35) as part of a huge cycle of texts which incorporates the *Estoire del Saint Graal*—"The History of the Holy Grail"—the *Estoire de Merlin*—"The Story of Merlin"—the *Lancelot* and the *Queste del Saint Graal*—"The Quest of the Holy Grail" (qq.v.). The whole cycle ends with the breaking up of the fellowship of the Round Table after the Grail Quest.

The first four romances of the cycle have been translated by Carol J. Chase, Rupert T. Pickens, Samuel N. Rosenberg, Carleton W. Carroll, Roberta L. Krueger and William W. Kibler (in *LG* I–IV), under the general editorship of Norris J. Lacy.

APPENDIX III

The Company of the Grail

Some Twentieth Century Writers

Henry Corbin (1903–1978) was best known as a scholar of esoteric Islam, but he also wrote extensively on the Grail, exploring its symbolism in the light of Iranian Zoroastrianism, Hermeticism and Johannine Christianity, but synthesizing these elements within his own philosophy of the imagination.

Thomas Stearns Eliot (1888–1965). Although in later life he would express regret for sending his readers on a wild goose-chase after the Grail, the Anglo-American poet powerfully evoked the spiritual emptiness of the years following the First World War in his modernist poem *The Waste Land* (1922), citing J.L. Weston as a source for his imagery.

René Guénon (1886–1951) was a French metaphysician who combined studies of religious symbolism with a trenchant critique of modernity. He saw the Grail as symbolic of the Hyperborean Tradition, referring to a primordial spiritual center which underlies all authentic faiths and which alone confers true initiation. His belief that the West had lost contact with the spiritual center was developed by the Italian esotericist **Julius Evola** (1898–1974) who, in his book *Mistero del Graal* (1937), argued that the Grail Question was as much about the loss of spiritual sovereignty as it was about compassion. Evola in turn influenced the young Romanian novelist and journalist **Mircea Eliade** (1907–1986), who would in later life become the leading historian of religions in France and the U.S. In a lecture of 1950, Eliade interpreted the Grail legend in the light of the symbolism of the sacred center, whose loss now haunts the West.

Carl Gustav Jung (1875–1961) was a Swiss depth psychologist whose writings about the archetypes of the collective unconscious continue to have a cultural influence far beyond the therapeutic consulting room. For Jung, the path of individuation leading to the encounter with the inner Self is the modern Grail Quest; but it would be his wife **Emma Jung** (born Emma Marie Rauschenbach, 1882–1955) who wrote the definitive detailed study of the medieval literature in the light of Jungian archetypal theory. Left unfinished at her death, the book was completed by **Marie-Louise von Franz** (1915–1998), for whom Carl Jung was a modern Merlin, the Prophet of the Grail.

Roger Sherman Loomis (1887–1966). An American scholar who initially supported a version of J.L. Weston's Ritual Theory of Grail origins, Loomis later became an enthusiastic champion of the idea that the symbol evolved from pagan Celtic mythology to Christian mysticism.

Otto Rahn (1904–1939). A medievalist who searched for the Grail in the ruins of the Cathar stronghold of Montségur, Rahn was recruited by Heinrich Himmler to work for the German Ancestral Heritage section of the SS, leading to his posthumous reputation as a Nazi Indiana Jones. While his doubts about the direction his country was headed may have led him to suicide, Rahn's linking of the Grail with the Albigensian heresy was later absorbed into the Hyperborean mythos of an unapologetic neo–Nazi, **Miguel Serrano** (1917–2009). A former Chilean diplomat, whose account of his friendship with Carl Jung and Hermann Hesse lent him a certain cultural cachet, Serrano's doctrine of esoteric Hitlerism was concealed within mysteriously poetic imagery in those early books which were translated into English in the Sixties and Seventies. But we know from the fates of Simeon and his son Moses that not all who seek to join the Company of the Grail are worthy to sit at the Table of the Holy Vessel.

Rudolf Steiner (1861–1925) was an Austrian philosopher whose lectures and writings on alternative approaches to agriculture, medicine and education have had a lasting impact. He saw the Grail as symbolizing the Mystery of Golgotha (inner, esoteric Christianity), the renewal of which he believed was essential for humanity's spiritual evolution. His scattered references to the Grail Quest were synthesized and developed by his disciple **Walter Johannes Stein** (1891–1957), who followed Steiner in connecting the story of Parzival with events in the ninth century. Stein's researches in turn inspired the more lurid and sensational writings of **Trevor Ravenscroft** (1921–1989), who traced Adolf Hitler's alleged obsession with the Lance of Longinus.

Arthur Edward Waite (1857–1942) was a Christian mystic who wrote prolifically on the Grail legend, being the first to draw attention to the similarities between the Hallows (the sacred objects in the Grail Castle) and the four suits of the Tarot cards. He saw the Grail as a symbol of a secret, Johannine church, but was wary of the occultism which he saw in the writings of Jessie Weston.

Jessie Laidlay Weston (1850–1928) was the leading English Arthurianist of the early twentieth century. In a series of books published between 1909 and 1920, she developed the thesis for which today she is best known—that the Grail is the symbol of a ritualistic cult with its own path of initiation.

Bibliography

Primary Sources: Texts and Translations

AG—Gathercole, Simon, tr. *The Apocryphal Gospels*. London: Penguin, 2021.

BCP—Stevenson, W.H., ed. William Blake, *The Complete Poems*. 3rd ed. Harlow, England: Longman, 2007.

BT—Lewis, Gwyneth, and Rowan Williams, trs. *The Book of Taliesin: Poems of Warfare and Praise in an Enchanted Britain*. London: Penguin, 2019.

CDE—Rockwell, Paul Vincent, ed. and tr. *French Arthurian Romance III: Le Chevalier as Deus Espees*. Cambridge, England: D.S. Brewer, 2006.

CGL—Lecoy, Félix, ed. Chrétien de Troyes, *Le Conte du Graal (Perceval)*. 2 vols. Paris: Honoré Champion, 1998.

CGM—Méla, Charles, ed. and tr. into modern French. Chrétien de Troyes, *Le Conte du Graal ou le Roman de Perceval*. Paris: LGF, 1990.

CSG—Bryant, Nigel, tr. *The Complete Story of the Grail: Chrétien de Troyes'* Perceval *and Its Continuations*. Cambridge, England: D.S. Brewer, 2015.

CP—Roach, William, ed. *The Continuations of the Old French* Perceval *of Chrétien de Troyes*. 5 vols.
_____. Vol. 1. *The First Continuation: Redaction of Mss T, V, D*. Philadelphia: University of Pennsylvania Press, 1949.
_____, and Robert H. Ivy, Jr., eds. Vol. 2. *The First Continuation: Redaction of Mss E, M, Q, U*. Philadelphia: University of Pennsylvania Press, 1950.
_____. Vol 4. *The Second Continuation*. Philadelphia: The American Philosophical Society, 1971.

CTO—Owen, D.D.R., tr. Chrétien de Troyes, *Arthurian Romances*. London: J.M. Dent, 1987.

DC—Gingras, Francis, ed., and Marie-Louise Ollier, tr. into modern French. *La Deuxième Continuation du Conte du Graal*. Paris: Honoré Champion 2021.

EB—"*Elucidation* et *Bliocadran*." In *Les Prologues au* Conte du Graal, ed. Hélène Bouget. 100–36.

EE—Rousse, Michel, ed. and tr. into modern French. Chrétien de Troyes, *Èrec et Ènide*. Paris: GF Flammarion, 1994.

EG—Nitze, William, ed. Robert de Boron, *Le Roman de l'Estoire dou Graal*. 1927. Paris: Honoré Champion, 1971.

ESG—Ponceau, Jean-Paul, ed. *L'Estoire del Saint Graal*. Paris: Honoré Champion, 1997.

GCP—Gerbert de Montreuil. *La Continuation de Perceval*. 3 vols.
_____. Williams, Mary, ed. Vols. 1 and 2. Paris: Honoré Champion, 1922–5.
_____. Oswald, Marguerite, ed. Vol. 3. Paris: Honoré Champion, 1975.

GGC—Weston, Jessie L., tr. *Sir Gawain at the Grail Castle: Arthurian Romances Unrepresented in Malory's* Morte d'Arthur, No.6. London: David Nutt, 1903.

GJ—Fenton, J.C. Introduction and commentary. *The Gospel of John in the Revised Standard Version*. Oxford: Oxford University Press, 1970.

GN—Gathercole, Simon, tr. "The Gospel of Nicodemus." In *The Apocryphal Gospels*. London: Penguin, 2021. 212–239.

GS—Layton, Bentley, tr. *The Gnostic Scriptures*. London: SCM, 1987.

HBG—Bryant, Nigel, tr. *The High Book of the Grail: A Translation of the Thirteenth-Century Romance* Perlesvaus. Cambridge, England: D.S. Brewer, 1978.

HG—Tennyson, Alfred. "The Holy Grail." In *The Major Works*, ed. Adam Roberts. Oxford: Oxford University Press, 2000. 413–36.

HH—Evans, Sebastian, tr. *The High History of the Holy Graal*. 2d ed. London: Dent, 1929.

HKB—Thorpe, Lewis, tr. Geoffrey of Monmouth, *The History of the Kings of Britain*. Harmondsworth, Middx., England: Penguin, 1966.

HLG—Strubel, Armand, ed. and tr. into modern French. *Le Haut Livre du Graal: Perlesvaus*. Paris: LGF, 2007.

HTC—Thomas, J.W., tr. Heinrich von dem Türlin, *The Crown: A Tale of Sir Gawein and King Arthur's Court*. Lincoln: University of Nebraska Press, 1989.

JA—Rogers, Jean, tr. Robert de Boron, *Joseph of Arimathea: A Romance of the Grail*. London: Rudolf Steiner Press, 1990.

LDG—Walter, Philippe, ed. *Le Livre du Graal*. 3 vols. Paris: Gallimard, 2001–9.

LDL—*Lancelot du Lac: Roman français du XIIIe siècle*. 5 vols.

──────. Kennedy, Elspeth, ed., and François Mosès, tr. into modern French. Vol. 1. 2d ed. Paris: LGF, 1991.

──────. Mosès, François, ed. and tr. into modern French. Vol. 3: *La Fausse Guenièvre*. Paris: LGF, 1998.

──────. Lepage, Yvan G., ed., and Marie-Louise Ollier. tr. into modern French. Vol. 5: *L'Enlèvement de Guenièvre*. Paris: LGF, 1999.

LG—Lacy, Norris J., ed. *Lancelot-Grail: The Old French Arthurian Vulgate and Post-Vulgate in Translation.* 5 vols. New York: Garland, 1993–6.

LM—Micha, Alexandre, ed. *Lancelot: Roman en prose du XIIIe siècle*. 9 vols. Geneva: Droz, 1978–83.

M—Gantz, Jeffrey, tr. *The Mabinogion*. Harmondsworth, Middx., England: Penguin, 1976.

MD—Field, P.J.C., ed. Sir Thomas Malory, *Le Morte Darthur*. Cambridge, England: D.S. Brewer, 2017.

MG—Bryant, Nigel, tr. *Merlin and the Grail: Joseph of Arimathea, Merlin, Perceval: The Trilogy of Arthurian Romances Attributed to Robert de Boron.* Cambridge, England: D.S. Brewer, 2001.

MGL—Lachet, Claude, ed. *Les Métamorphoses du Graal: Anthologie*. Paris: GF Flammarion, 2012.

MH—Hult, David, ed. and tr. into modern French. *La Mort du Roi Arthur*. Paris: LGF, 2009.

MJ—Jones, Gwyn, and Thomas Jones, trs. *The Mabinogion*. 1949. New revised ed. London: J.M. Dent, 1993.

MM—Micha, Alexandre, tr. into modern French. Robert de Boron, *Merlin*. Paris: GF Flammarion, 1994.

MO—Innes, Mary, tr. *The Metamorphoses of Ovid*. Harmondsworth, Mddx., England: Penguin, 1955.

MP—Szkilnik, Michelle, ed. and tr. into modern French. *Méraugis de Portlesguez*. Paris: Honoré Champion, 2004.

MTC—Roach, William, ed., and Marie-Noëlle Toury, tr. into modern French. Manessier, *La Troisième Continuation du Conte du Graal*. Paris: Honoré Champion, 2004.

MTG—Krochalis, Jeanne, ed. "Magna Tabula: The Glastonbury Tablets (Part I)." *Arthurian Literature* No. 15, 1997. 93–183.

MV—Vinaver, Eugène, ed. Sir Thomas Malory, *Complete Works*. 2d ed. Oxford: Oxford University Press, 1971.

MW—Weston, Jessie L., tr. *Morien: A Metrical Romance Rendered into English from the Middle Dutch: Arthurian Romances Unrepresented in Malory's Morte d'Arthur*, No. 4. London: David Nutt, 1901.

NHL—Robinson, James M., ed. *The Nag Hammadi Library in English*. 3rd ed. Leiden, The Netherlands: Brill, 1988.

P—Bouget, Hélène, ed. *Les Prologues au* Conte du Graal. Paris: Classiques Garnier, 2018.

PCG—Hilka, Alfons, ed., and Jean Dufournet, tr. into modern French. Chrétien de Troyes, *Perceval ou le Conte du Graal*. Paris: GF Flammarion, 1997.

PCP—Roach, William, ed., and Colette-Anne Van Coolput-Storms, tr. into modern French. *Première Continuation de Perceval (Continuation-Gauvain): Texte du Ms L*. Paris: LGF, 1993.

PKL—Lachmann, Karl, and Bernd Schirok, eds. Wolfram von Eschenbach, *Parzival*. Berlin: De Gruyter, 1998.

PSG—Bryant, Nigel, tr. Chrétien de Troyes, *Perceval: The Story of the Grail*. Cambridge, England: D.S. Brewer, 1982.

PT—Edwards, Cyril, tr. Wolfram von Eschenbach, *Parzival and Titurel*. Oxford: Oxford University Press, 2006.

PV—Bogdanow, Fanni, ed. *La Version Post-Vulgate de la* Queste del Saint Graal *et de la* Mort Artu: *Troisième Partie du* Roman du Graal. 4 vols. Paris: Honoré Champion, 1991–2001.

QHG—Matarasso, Pauline, tr. *The Quest of the Holy Grail*. Harmondsworth, Middx., England: Penguin, 1969.

QP—Pauphilet, Albert, ed. *La Queste del Saint Graal: Roman du XIIIe Siècle*. Paris: Honoré Champion, 2003.

QSG—Bogdanow, Fanni, ed., and Anne Berrie, tr. into modern French. *La Quête du Saint Graal*. Paris: LGF, 2006.

RBM—Micha, Alexandre, ed. Robert de Boron, *Merlin: Roman du XIIIe Siècle*. Geneva: Droz, 2000.

RG—Cerquiglini, Bernard, ed. Robert de Boron, *Le Roman du Graal*. Paris: Union Générale d'Éditions, 1981.

RHG—Micha, Alexandre, tr. into modern French. *Le Roman de l'Histoire du Graal*. 1995. Paris: Honoré Champion, 2007.

RMP—Füg-Pierreville, Corinne, ed. and tr. into modern French. *Le Roman de Merlin en Prose*. Paris: Honoré Champion, 2014.

RP—Roach, William, ed. Chrétien de Troyes, *Le Roman de Perceval ou le Conte du Graal*. 2d ed. Geneva: Droz, 1959.

RTC—Curtis, Renée L., tr. *The Romance of Tristan: The Thirteenth-Century Old French Prose Tristan*. Oxford: Oxford University Press, 1994.

RWP—Robb, Stewart, tr. Richard Wagner, *Parsifal*. Chester, NY: G. Schirmer, 1962.

SGP—Kibler, William W., tr. "The Story of the Grail (Perceval)." In Chrétien de Troyes, *Arthurian Romances*. 2d ed. London: Penguin, 2004. 381–494.

SN—Goldschmidt, Moritz, ed. *Sone von Nausay*. Tübingen, Germany: Literarischer Verein, 1899.

SRM—Roussineau, Gilles. *La Suite du Roman de Merlin*. 2d ed. Geneva: Droz, 2006.

STC—Graves, Robert, and J.B. Rives, trs. Suetonius, *The Twelve Caesars*. 2d ed. London: Penguin, 2007.

TP—Allaire, Gloria, ed. and tr. *Tristano Panciatichiano*. Cambridge, England: D.S. Brewer, 2002.

TPC—Curtis, Renée L., ed. *Le Roman de Tristan*

en Prose. 3 vols. Woodbridge, Suffolk, England: D.S. Brewer, 1985.
TPM—Ménard, Philippe, general ed. *Le Roman de Tristan en Prose.* 9 vols. Geneva: Droz, 1987–97.
_____. Harf-Lancner, Laurence, ed. Vol. 9: *La Fin des Aventures de Tristan et de Galaad.* 1997.
TRT—Shaver, Anne, tr. *Tristan and the Round Table: A Translation of* La Tavola Ritonda. New York: State University of New York: Medieval & Renaissance Texts & Studies, 1983.
TSE—Eliot, T.S. *The Complete Poems and Plays of T.S. Eliot.* London: Faber & Faber, 1969.
TYP—Bromwich, Rachel, ed. and tr. *Trioedd Ynys Prydein: The Triads of the Island of Britain.* 3rd ed. Cardiff: University of Wales Press, 2006.
VS—Sommer, H. Oskar, ed. *The Vulgate Version of the Arthurian Romances.* 8 vols. Washington, D.C.: The Carnegie Institute, 1908–16.
WL—Eliot, T.S. "The Waste Land." In *The Complete Poems and Plays of T.S. Eliot.* 59–80.
WP—Hatto, A.T., tr. Wolfram von Eschenbach, *Parzival.* Harmondsworth, England: Penguin, 1980.
WPW—Hutchinson, Thomas, and Ernest de Selincourt. William Wordsworth, *Poetical Works.* 2d ed. London: Oxford University Press, 1936.

Secondary Sources

Angebert, Jean-Michel. *Hitler et la Tradition Cathare.* 3rd ed. Rosières-en-Haye, France: Camion Noir, 2008.
Ashdown, Paul. *The Lord Was at Glastonbury: Somerset and the Jesus Voyage Story.* Glastonbury, Somerset, England: The Squeeze Press, 2010.
Baigent, Michael, Richard Leigh and Henry Lincoln. *Holy Blood, Holy Grail.* New York: Dell, 1983.
Barber, Malcolm. *The Cathars: Dualist Heretics in Languedoc in the High Middle Ages.* Harlow, Essex, England: Longman, 2000.
Barber, Richard., and Cyril Edwards, trs. "The Grail Temple in *Der Jüngerer Titurel.*" *Arthurian Literature* No.20, 2003. 85–102.
_____. *The Holy Grail: The History of a Legend.* London: Penguin, 2005.
Bernadac, Christian. *Montségur et le Graal: Le Mystère Otto Rahn.* Paris: France-Empire, 1994.
Bogdanow, Fanni. *The Romance of the Grail.* Manchester: Manchester University Press, 1966.
_____. "The *Vulgate Cycle* and the *Post-Vulgate Roman du Graal.*" In *A Companion to the Lancelot-Grail Cycle,* ed. Carol Dover. Cambridge, England: D.S. Brewer, 2003. 33–51.
Brown, Arthur C.L. *The Origin of the Grail Legend.* Cambridge, MA: Harvard University Press, 1943.
Burckhardt, Titus. *Alchemy: Science of the Cosmos, Science of the Soul.* Tr. William Stoddart. Shaftesbury, Dorset, England: Element, 1986.

Campbell, Joseph. *The Masks of God.* 4 Vols. Harmondsworth, Middx., England: Penguin, 1976.
_____. *Romance of the Grail: The Magic and Mystery of Arthurian Myth.* Novato, CA: New World Library, 2015.
Carey, John. "Henry Corbin and the Secret of the Grail." *Temenos Academy Review* No.14, 2011. 159–78.
_____. *Ireland and the Grail.* Aberystwyth, Wales: Celtic Studies Publications, 2007.
Corbin, Henry. *En Islam Iranien: Aspects Spirituels et Philosophiques* Vol. 2: *Sohrawardî et les Platoniciens de Perse.* Paris: Gallimard, 1971.
_____. *L'Homme et son Ange: Initiation et Chevalerie Spirituelle.* Paris: Fayard, 1983.
_____. *Swedenborg and Esoteric Islam.* Tr. Leonard Fox. West Chester, PA: Swedenborg Foundation, 1995.
_____. *Temple and Contemplation.* Tr. Philip Sherrard. New York: KPI, 1986.
D'Arcy, Anne Marie. *Wisdom and the Grail: The Image of the Vessel in the* Queste del Saint Graal *and Malory's* Tale of the Sankgreal. Portland: Four Courts Press, 2000.
Darrah, John. *Paganism in Arthurian Romance.* Woodbridge, Suffolk, England: The Boydell Press, 1994.
_____. *The Real Camelot: Paganism and the Arthurian Romances.* London: Thames & Hudson, 1981.
Dixon, Jeffrey John. *Gawain and the Grail Quest: Healing the Waste Land in Our Time.* Edinburgh: Floris Books, 2012.
_____. *Goddess and Grail: The Battle for King Arthur's Promised Land.* Jefferson, NC: McFarland, 2017.
Dubost, Francis. *Le Conte du Graal ou l'Art de Faire Signe.* Paris: Honoré Champion, 1998.
Duggan, Joseph J. *The Romances of Chrétien de Troyes.* New Haven, CT: Yale University Press, 2001.
Eliade, Mircea. *The Forge and the Crucible: The Origins and Structures of Alchemy.* Tr. Stephen Corrin. 2d ed. Chicago: University of Chicago Press, 1978.
_____. *Images and Symbols: Studies in Religious Symbolism.* Tr. Philip Mairet. Princeton, NJ: Princeton University Press, 1991.
_____. *Rites and Symbols of Initiation: The Mysteries of Birth and Rebirth.* Tr. Willard R. Trask. New York: Harper & Row, 1958.
Evola, Julius. *The Mystery of the Grail: Initiation and Magic in the Quest for the Spirit.* Tr. Guido Stucco. Rochester, VT: Inner Traditions, 1997.
_____. *The Path of Cinnabar.* Tr. Sergio Knipe. 2d ed. London: Arktos, 2010.
_____. *Revolt Against the Modern World.* Tr. Guido Stucco. Rochester, VT: Inner Traditions, 1995.
Flowers, Stephen E., and Michael Moynihan. *The Secret King: The Myth and Reality of Nazi Occultism.* 2d ed. Los Angeles: Feral House, 2007.
Fortune, Dion. *Avalon of the Heart.* 1930. 2d ed. York Beach, ME: Weiser, 2000.

Franz, Marie-Louise von. *C.G. Jung: His Myth in Our Time*. Tr. William H. Kennedy. New York: Putnam, 1975.

Frappier, Jean. *Autour du Graal*. Geneva: Droz, 1977.

Gallais, Pierre. "La 'maison' du Roi-Pêcheur." In *Polyphonie du Graal*, ed. Denis Hüe. 1998a. 45–58.

———. *Perceval et l'Initiation: Essai sur le dernier roman de Chrétien de Troyes, ses correspondances "orientales" et sa signification anthropologique*. 2d ed. Orléans, France: Paradigme, 1998b.

Gilbert, R.A. *A.E. Waite: Magician of Many Parts*. Wellingborough, Northants., England: Aquarian Press, 1987.

Godwin, Joscelyn. *Arktos: The Polar Myth in Science, Symbolism and Nazi Survival*. London: Thames & Hudson, 1993a.

———. "Mentalism and the Cosmological Fallacy." *Alexandria: A Journal of the Western Cosmological Traditions* No.2, 1993b.

Goetinck, Glenys Witchard. *Peredur: A Study of Welsh Tradition in the Grail Legends*. Cardiff: University of Wales Press, 1975.

———. "The Quest for Origins." In *The Grail: A Casebook*, ed. Dhira B. Mahoney, 2014. 117–47.

Goodrick-Clarke, Nicholas. *Black Sun: Aryan Cults, Esoteric Nazism and the Politics of Identity*. New York: New York University Press, 2003.

———. *The Occult Roots of Nazism: Secret Aryan Cults and Their Influence on Nazi Ideology: The Ariosophists of Austria and Germany, 1890–1935*. 2d ed. London: I.B. Tauris, 1992.

Goodrick-Clarke, Clare, and Nicholas Goodrick-Clarke, eds. *G.R.S. Mead and the Gnostic Quest*. Berkeley, CA: North Atlantic Books, 2005.

Graves, Robert. *The Greek Myths*. 2 vols. Rev. ed. Harmondsworth, Middx., England: Penguin, 1960.

———. *The White Goddess: A Historical Grammar of Poetic Myth*. 1948. Ed. Grevel Lindop. Rev. ed. Manchester, England: Carcanet, 1997.

Grayson, Janet. "In Quest of Jessie Weston." *Arthurian Literature* No.11, 1992. 1–80.

Guénon, René. *The Lord of the World*. Trs. Carolyn Shaffer, Olga de Nottbeck et al. North Yorkshire, England: Coombe Springs, 1983.

———. *Symboles de la Science Sacrée*. Paris: Gallimard, 1962.

Guthrie, W.K.C. *Orpheus and Greek Religion: A Study of the Orphic Movement*. 1952. Princeton, NJ: Princeton University Press, 1993.

Hakl, Hans Thomas. *Eranos: An Alternative Intellectual History of the Twentieth Century*. Tr. Christopher McIntosh. Bristol, CT: Equinox, 2013.

Haskins, Susan. *Mary Magdalen: Myth and Metaphor*. London: HarperCollins, 1993.

Hüe, Denis. *Polyphonie du Graal*. Orléans, France: Paradigme, 1998.

Hutton, Ronald. *The Pagan Religions of the Ancient British Isles: Their Nature and Legacy*. Malden, MA: Blackwell, 1991.

———. *Witches, Druids and King Arthur*. New York: Hambledon & London, 2003.

Jones, Prudence. "The Grail Quest as Initiation: Jessie Weston and the Vegetation Theory." In *The Household of the Grail*, ed. John Matthews, 1990. 137–151

Jung, Carl. *Aion: Researches into the Phenomenology of the Self*. Tr. R.F.C. Hull. 2d ed. Princeton, NJ: Princeton University Press, 1968.

———. *Mysterium Coniunctionis: An Enquiry into the Separation and Synthesis of Psychic Opposites in Alchemy*. Tr. R.F.C. Hull. 2d ed. Princeton, NJ: Princeton University Press, 1970.

Jung, Emma, and Marie-Louise von Franz. *The Grail Legend*. Tr. Andrea Dykes. 2d ed. London: Coventure, 1986.

Kafton-Minkel, Walter. *Subterranean Worlds: 100,000 Years of Dragons, Dwarfs, the Dead, Lost Races and UFOs from Inside the Earth*. Port Townsend, WA: Loompanics Unlimited, 1989.

Kahane, Henry, and Renée Kahane, in collaboration with Angelina Pietrangeli. *The Krater and the Grail: Hermetic Sources of the* Parzival. Urbana: University of Illinois Press, 1965.

Kerényi, Carl. *The Gods of the Greeks*. Tr. Norman Cameron. London: Thames & Hudson, 1951.

———. *The Heroes of the Greeks*. Tr. H.J. Rose. London: Thames & Hudson, 1959.

Knight, Gareth. "Dion Fortune and the Graal." In *The Household of the Grail*, ed. John Matthews, 1990. 104–119.

———. "Merlin and the Grail." In *At the Table of the Grail*, ed. John Matthews, 1984. 159–73.

———. *Merlin and the Grail Tradition*. 2d ed. Cheltenham, Glos., England: Skylight Press, 2011.

———. *The Secret Tradition in Arthurian Legend*. Wellingborough, Northants., England: Aquarian Press, 1983.

Lachman, Gary. *Rudolf Steiner: An Introduction to His Life and Work*. Edinburgh: Floris, 2007.

Loomis, Roger Sherman. *Arthurian Tradition and Chrétien de Troyes*. New York: Columbia University Press, 1949.

———. *Celtic Myth and Arthurian Romance*. 1926. London: Constable, 1993.

———. *The Grail: From Celtic Myth to Christian Symbol*. 1963. Princeton, NJ: Princeton University Press, 1991.

———. *Wales and the Arthurian Legend*. Cardiff: University of Wales Press, 1956.

Löseth, Eilhert. *Le Roman en Prose de Tristan, le Roman de Palamède et la Compilation de Rusticien de Pise: Analyse Critique d'après les Manuscrits de Paris*. Paris: Émile Bouillon, 1891.

Luhrssen, David. *Hammer of the Gods: The Thule Society and the Birth of Nazism*. Washington, D.C.: Potomac, 2012.

Lupack, Alan. *The Oxford Guide to Arthurian Literature and Legend*. Oxford: Oxford University Press, 2005.

Mac Cana, Proinsias. *Celtic Mythology*. 2d ed. Middx, England: Newnes, 1983.

Mahoney, Dhira B., ed. *The Grail: A Casebook.* London: Routledge, 2014.

Marino, John B. *The Grail Legend in Modern Literature.* Cambridge, England: Brewer, 2004.

Markale, Jean. *The Grail: The Celtic Origins of the Sacred Icon.* Tr. Jon Graham. Rochester, VT: Inner Traditions, 1999.

Matthews, Caitlín. *King Arthur and the Goddess of the Land: The Divine Feminine in the Mabinogion.* 2d ed. Rochester, VT: Inner Traditions, 2002.

_____. "Sophia: Companion on the Quest." In *At the Table of the Grail,* ed. John Matthews, 1984. 111–28.

_____. *Sophia: Goddess of Wisdom, Bride of God.* 2d ed. Wheaton, IL: Quest, 2001.

_____, and John Matthews. *Ladies of the Lake.* London: The Aquarian Press, 1992.

_____, and John Matthews. *The Lost Book of the Grail: The Sevenfold Path of the Grail and the Restoration of the Faery Accord.* Rochester, VT: Inner Traditions, 2019.

Matthews, John. *The Elements of the Grail Tradition.* Shaftesbury, Dorset, England: Element, 1990a.

_____. *The Grail: Quest for the Eternal.* London: Thames & Hudson, 1981.

_____, ed. *At the Table of the Grail.* London: RKP, 1984.

_____, ed. *The Household of the Grail.* Wellingborough, Northants., England: Aquarian Press, 1990b.

_____, and Caitlín Matthews. *King Arthur's Raid on the Underworld: The Oldest Grail Quest.* Glastonbury, Somerset, England: Gothic Image, 2008.

_____, and Gareth Knight. *Temples of the Grail: The Search for the World's Greatest Relic.* Woodbury, MN: Llewellyn, 2019.

_____, and Marian Green. *The Grail Seeker's Companion: A Guide to the Grail Quest in the Aquarian Age.* Wellingborough, Northants, England: Aquarian Press, 1986.

Mead, G.R.S. *Fragments of a Faith Forgotten.* London: Theosophical Publishing Society, 1900.

Méla, Charles. *La Reine et le Graal.* Paris: Seuil, 1984.

Morgan, Richard W. *St. Paul in Britain: or, The Origin of British as Opposed to Papal Christianity.* Oxford, England: Parker, 1861.

Nitze, William A. "The Fisher King in the Grail Romances." *PMLA* (Publications of the Modern Language Association) Vol.24, No.3, 1909. 365–418.

_____. "Glastonbury and the Holy Grail." *Modern Philology* Vol.1, No.1, 1903. 247–257.

Noll, Richard. *The Aryan Christ: The Secret Life of Carl Jung.* New York: Random House, 1997.

Nutt, Alfred. *Studies on the Legend of the Holy Grail with Especial Reference to the Hypothesis of Its Celtic Origin.* London: Publications of the Folk-Lore Society, 1888.

Olschki, Leonardo. *The Grail Castle and Its Mysteries.* Tr. J.A. Scott. Manchester: Manchester University Press, 1966.

O'Reilly, Kevin. "The Shop-Soiled Galahad: Raymond Chandler's Knight." *AJAS* Vol.1, No.2, July 1981. 39–52.

Partner, Peter. *The Knights Templar and Their Myth.* 2d ed. Rochester, VT: Destiny Books, 1990.

Paton, Lucy Allen. *Studies in the Fairy Mythology of Arthurian Romance.* Boston: Ginn, 1903.

Pauphilet, Albert. *Études sur la Queste del Saint Graal.* Paris: Honoré Champion, 1921.

Pickens, Rupert T. "Autobiography and History in the Vulgate *Estoire* and in the *Prose Merlin.*" In *The Lancelot-Grail Cycle: Text and Transformations,* ed. William W. Kibler. Austin: University of Texas Press, 1994. 98–116.

Poiron, Daniel. "L'Ombre Mythique de Perceval dans le *Conte du Graal.*" In *Polyphonie du Graal,* ed. Denis Hüe, 1998. 77–88.

Rahn, Otto. *Crusade Against the Grail: The Struggle Between the Cathars, the Templars and the Church of Rome.* Tr. Christopher Jones. Rochester, VT: Inner Traditions, 2006.

Raine, Kathleen. *Yeats, the Tarot and the Golden Dawn.* 2d ed. Dublin: The Dolmen Press, 1976.

Ravenscroft, Trevor. *The Cup of Destiny: The Quest for the Grail.* York Beach, ME: Weiser, 1982b.

_____. *The Spear of Destiny: The Occult Power Behind the Spear Which Pierced the Side of Christ.* 2d ed. Boston: Weiser, 1982a.

_____, and Tim Wallace-Murphy. *The Mark of the Beast: The Continuing Story of the Spear of Destiny.* Boston: Weiser, 1997.

Rhŷs, John. *Studies in the Arthurian Legend.* Oxford, England: Clarendon, 1891.

Roberts, Anthony, ed. *Glastonbury: Ancient Avalon, New Jerusalem.* 3rd ed. London: Rider, 1992.

Roquebert, Michel. *Les Cathares et le Graal.* Toulouse, France: Privat, 1994.

Rudolph, Kurt. *Gnosis: The Nature and History of Gnosticism.* Tr. Robert McLachlan Wilson. Edinburgh: T & T Clark, 1980.

Sansonetti, Paul-Georges. *Graal et Alchimie.* 2d ed. Paris: Berg, 1993.

Schonfield, Hugh J. *The Essene Odyssey.* 2d ed. Dorset, England: Element, 1998.

Sedgwick, Mark. *Against the Modern World: Traditionalism and the Secret Intellectual History of the Twentieth Century.* New York: Oxford University Press, 2004.

Serrano, Miguel. *El/Ella: Book of Magic Love.* Tr. Frank MacShane. New York: Harper & Row, 1972.

_____. *Nos: Book of the Resurrection.* Tr. Gela Jacobson. London: RKP, 1984.

Steiner, Rudolf. *The Goddess: From Natura to the Divine Sophia.* Tr. Christian von Arnim. Ed. Andrew Welburn. East Sussex, England: Rudolf Steiner Press, 2001a.

_____. *The Holy Grail: The Quest for the Renewal of the Mysteries.* Tr. Christian von Arnim. Ed. Andrew Welburn. East Sussex, England: Rudolf Steiner Press, 2001b.

_____. *The Knights Templar: The Mystery of the Warrior Monks*. Tr. Christian von Arnim. Ed. Margaret Jonas. East Sussex, England: Rudolf Steiner Press, 2007.

Stephens, Louise D. "Gerbert and Manessier: The Case for a Connection." *Arthurian Literature* No.14, 1996. 53–68.

Stoyanov, Yuri. *The Hidden Tradition in Europe: The Secret History of Medieval Christian Heresy*. London: Penguin, 1994.

Surette, Leon. "*The Waste Land* and Jessie L. Weston: A Reassessment." In *Literary Modernism and the Occult Tradition*, eds. Leon Surette and Demetres P. Tryphonopoulos. Orono, ME: The National Poetry Foundation, 1996. 73–96.

Thomas, Neil. *Diu Crône and the Medieval Arthurian Cycle*. Cambridge, England: D.S. Brewer, 2002.

Traxler, Janine P. "Dying to Get to Sarras: Perceval's Sister and the Grail Quest." In *The Grail: A Casebook*, ed. Dhira Mahoney, 2014. 261–78.

Ullyot, Jonathan. *The Medieval Presence in Modernist Literature: The Quest to Fail*. New York: Cambridge University Press, 2016.

Waite, Arthur Edward. *The Hidden Church of the Holy Graal: Its Legends and Symbolism*. London: Rebman, 1909.

_____. *The Holy Grail: History, Legend and Symbolism*. 1933. New York: Dover, 2006.

_____. *The Pictorial Key to the Tarot: Being Fragments of a Secret Tradition Under the Veil of Divination*. 1911. London: Rider, 1971.

Walter, Philippe. *Dictionnaire de Mythologie Arthurienne*. Paris: Imago, 2014.

_____. *Galaad: Le Pommier et le Graal*. Paris: Imago, 2004a.

_____. *Gauvain: Le Chevalier Solaire*. Paris: Imago, 2013.

_____. *Perceval: Le Pêcheur et le Graal*. Paris: Imago, 2004b.

Weston, Jessie L. *From Ritual to Romance*. 1920. Rev. ed. 1957. Princeton, NJ: Princeton University Press, 1993.

_____. "The Grail and the Rites of Adonis." 1907. *Arthurian Literature* No.11, 1992. 63–74.

_____. *The Legend of Sir Lancelot du Lac: Studies Upon Its Origin, Development, and Position in the Arthurian Romantic Cycle*. London: David Nutt, 1901.

_____. *The Legend of Sir Perceval: Studies Upon Its Origin, Development, and Position in the Arthurian Cycle*. 2 vols. London, David Nutt, 1906–9.

_____. *The Legends of the Wagner Drama: Studies in Mythology and Romance*. London: David Nutt, 1896.

_____. *The Quest of the Holy Grail*. 1913. New York: Dover, 2001.

_____. *The Romance of Perlesvaus*. Ed. Janet Grayson. Holland, MI: Studies in Medievalism, 1988.

_____. "The Ruined Temple." 1916. *Arthurian Literature* No.11, 1992. 74–7.

_____. *The Three Days' Tournament: A Study in Romance and Folklore*. London: David Nutt, 1902.

Williams, Andrea M.L. *The Adventures of the Holy Grail: A Study of* La Queste del Saint Graal. Oxford, England: Peter Lang, 2001.

Williams, Mark. *Ireland's Immortals: A History of the Gods of Irish Myth*. Princeton, NJ: Princeton University Press, 2016.

Wilson, S.R. "The Grail Utopia in Southern Germany." *Temenos Academy Review* No.14, 2015. 138–158.

Winick, Mimi. "Scholarly Enchantment." *Nineteenth-Century Literature* Vol.73, No.2, September 2018. 187–226.

Wood, Juliette. *The Holy Grail: History and Legend*. Cardiff: University of Wales Press, 2012.

Wroe, Ann. *Orpheus: The Song of Life*. London: Jonathan Cape, 2011.

Zimmer, Heinrich. *The King and the Corpse: Tales of the Soul's Conquest of Evil*. Ed. Joseph Campbell. 2d ed. Princeton, NJ: Princeton University Press, 1956.

Index

alchemy 9, 11, 107, 130, 205
allegory 7, 99, 105, 179, 251, 303
antisemitism 37, 266, 281–2, 297
apocrypha 93, 124, 129, 140–1, 186, 242, 307, 313
archetypal images 64, 71, 93, 113, 115, 131, 150–1, 278, 297–300
archetypal world 9
archetypes 126, 136, 217–8, 233, 296–8, 303–4, 307, 319
Asher, Martha 208, 272
astral cults 15, 55, 60, 66, 74, 144, 147, 164, 169, 237–40
astral plane 52–3, 284, 297
astrology 7, 38, 57, 59, 60, 128, 278, 282

Barber, Richard 205
Bogdanow, Fanni 7, 310
Bouget, Hélène 17
Bradley, Marion Zimmer 286–7, 305
Bromwich, Rachel 213
Brown, A.C.L. 113, 122–3
Bryant, Nigel 5, 24, 43, 109, 141, 146, 178, 231, 243, 246, 254

Campbell, Joseph 71
Carey, John 9, 17, 111, 226, 232, 272
Catharism 9, 92, 123, 169, 174, 231, 242, 284, 294–7, 320; *see also* heresy
Cerquiglini, Bernard 43, 141
Chandler, Raymond 3, 11
Chase, Carol J. 272, 310
Coomaraswamy, Ananda K. 278
Corbin, Henry 2, 43, 64, 92, 94, 123, 128, 131, 136, 141, 174–5, 209, 239–40, 271, 290, 301–3, 307, 319
Crook, Mackenzie 3
Crowley, Aleister 278

Darrah, John 85, 108, 142, 240
demons 20, 23, 30–3, 41, 46, 62–4, 66, 88–9, 97, 137, 143–4, 154, 169, 173, 177–8, 183–4, 187, 191, 196–7, 199, 204–5, 207, 211, 220, 229, 239, 241, 244, 247, 261, 267, 275, 307
the Devil 30–2, 41, 63, 66, 89, 109, 132, 149, 195, 220, 244, 262
devils 25, 66, 160–1, 194, 218
Docetism 242; *see also* heresy

Druidism 66, 108, 110, 116–7, 287, 292–3, 295, 306
dualism 124, 169, 217–9, 295–6, 302
Dubost, Francis 122–4, 303

Eckart, Dietrich 282, 304
Eliade, Mircea 8, 126, 271, 273, 301–3, 307, 319
Eliot, T.S. 1, 167, 219, 270–1, 285, 300, 304–5, 319
enchanters 7, 17, 28, 45, 60, 64–5, 149–50, 169, 178, 186, 189, 191, 209, 214, 258, 263
enchantment 1, 6–8, 9, 11, 45, 47, 60, 62, 78, 85, 93, 95–6, 102, 132, 147–8, 150, 178, 186, 197, 199, 206, 219, 226, 247–8, 250, 259–60, 268, 270, 276, 283, 312; theory 1, 8–10
the enchantments of Britain 22, 79, 171, 201–2, 214–5, 268, 270
esotericism 7, 9, 17, 71, 92, 94, 116–7, 122, 126, 129–30, 136, 170, 174, 187, 232, 242, 271, 277–8, 280–1, 288–9, 293, 295, 297–8, 300–1, 303, 305, 319–20
eternity 7–8, 70, 116, 129, 170, 292, 296, 306
Evans, Sebastian 108
Evola, Julius 7–8, 126, 128, 271, 273, 292, 294, 296–7, 302, 306–7, 319

Faerie 20
Faery 17–8
fairies 29, 55–6, 59, 75, 105, 107, 122–3, 199, 206, 209, 212, 260
fairyland 113
fays 22, 24, 26–7, 30, 58–9, 74–6, 102, 104–5, 151, 160, 197, 199, 206, 212, 248, 260, 275, 286
fertility 8, 13, 17, 141, 145, 187, 270, 283, 285–7, 305
folklore 9, 17, 122, 167, 262, 288, 290, 293; theory 1, 8–10
Franz, Marie-Louise von 217, 232, 241–3, 298–9, 301, 307, 319
Füg-Pierreville, Corinne 43

Gallais, Pierre 106, 113, 122, 303
Gantz, Jeffrey 271
Gingras, Francis 128
gnosis 20, 55, 261, 281, 284, 292
Gnosticism 1, 9, 17–8, 81, 123, 130–1, 169, 237, 242–3, 261, 264, 277–9, 284, 289, 295, 297–8, 304; *see also* heresy
goddesses 13, 31, 47, 55, 65, 105, 107, 111, 122–3, 147, 150, 211, 241, 264, 287
gods 9, 13, 15, 17, 21, 46, 66, 113, 122, 143–4, 147, 164, 213–4, 230, 234, 239, 244, 260, 277, 283, 285–6, 288, 291, 295–6, 298, 300, 306; god-king 288; god-men 281, 304
Godwin, Joscelyn 71, 304
Goetinck, Glenys 31, 111, 213–4, 264
Gooch, Stan 95
Goodrick-Clarke, Nicholas 304
grace 6, 9–10, 21, 24, 41, 45, 50–1, 53, 59, 63, 66, 68, 78, 87, 102, 113, 118, 119, 133, 137, 144, 147, 152, 158, 172, 182–3, 190, 201–2, 216, 219, 227–8, 230–1, 233, 257, 263–4, 311, 317
Grayson, Janet 286
Green, Marian 116
Gros, Gérard 310
Guénon, René 7, 94, 115, 129, 278, 292–4, 306, 319
Guthrie, W.K.C. 186, 303

Hammer-Purgstall, Joseph von 130
Harrison, Jane Ellen 9
Hatto, A.T. 178
Haushofer, Karl 282, 304
heresy 9, 115, 122–4, 130, 169, 174, 184, 231, 242, 277, 284, 295, 305; Albigensian 242, 279, 284, 320; *see also* Catharism
Hermeticism 9, 83, 261, 278, 285, 300, 303, 319
Hitlerism 297, 298; esoteric 170, 295, 297, 320; *see also* Nazism

imagination 2, 8, 9, 14, 64, 66, 92, 113, 136, 217, 271, 280, 282, 290, 297, 301–4, 307, 319
initiation 1, 8, 13, 21, 46, 52–3, 80–1, 82, 94, 107, 110, 117, 122, 129, 131, 149, 151, 163–4, 167, 213, 231–2, 256, 260–1, 277–91, 293–308, 319–20; phallic 149, 288–9, 300; philosophic 81, 149, 167, 288–9, 291, 300

327

Index

Initiation Theory 81, 122, 285–6
Islam 15, 21–2, 55, 132, 164–5, 222, 239–40, 301, 319

Jones, Prudence 287, 305
Jung, Carl 217, 278, 296–8, 301, 307, 319–20
Jung, Emma 217, 232, 241–3, 298–9, 301, 307, 319

Kahane, Henry 18, 83, 261, 303, 308
Kahane, Renée 18, 83, 261, 303, 308
Kerényi, Carl 14, 187
Kibler, William W. 254
Knight, Gareth 46, 236

Lanz, Adolf (Jörg Lanz von Liebenfels) 281, 304
Layton, Bentley 243
Lewis, C.S. 123, 304
literalism 8, 52, 107, 148, 174, 236, 280, 301, 303
Loomis, Roger Sherman 17, 31, 63, 141, 159, 206, 211, 214, 218, 226, 286, 319
Luhrssen, David 304

Mac Cana, Proinsias 111
Machen, Arthur 278, 290, 304
magic 9, 28, 43, 46, 49, 59–60, 65–6, 80, 95, 102, 104–5, 115, 132, 148, 169, 174, 186, 189, 205, 246, 250, 258, 268, 271, 278, 282, 290, 294, 296, 304, 317
magicians 7, 64–66, 88–9, 151, 219, 235, 262, 280–1, 285
Maltwood, Katharine 108
Matarasso, Pauline 75, 256
Matthews, Caitlín 17–8, 55, 60, 65, 92, 122, 150–1, 211, 214, 264, 272
Matthews, John 17, 55, 60, 92, 111, 116, 122, 150–1, 211
Mead, G.R.S. 278, 281, 289–90
metaphor 6, 270
Micha, Alexandre 141, 172, 218
miracles 3, 5, 16, 18, 39–40, 43, 53, 61, 74, 78, 88, 90, 94, 105, 117, 133, 143–4, 160, 179, 184, 189, 208, 210, 220, 222, 237, 265, 270–1, 297, 302, 306, 309
Morgan, Richard W. 222
Mosès, François 208
mundus imaginalis ("imaginal world") 64, 92, 123, 136, 239, 302; *see also* imagination
mystery religions 1, 8–9, 13, 17, 20, 52–3, 80–1, 94, 105–6, 122, 167, 186–7, 231–3, 277–9, 283–4, 286–91, 293, 297, 300, 304–7, 320
mysticism 1, 6–8, 80–1, 121, 123, 132, 151, 172, 186, 231–3, 256, 277–8, 286–8, 290–1, 293, 295, 299, 301, 305, 319–20
mythology 1, 9–10, 25, 65, 82, 93, 105, 115, 123, 135, 151, 160, 236–7, 256, 280, 286, 296; Celtic 8–9, 71, 117, 122, 167, 211, 277, 290, 307, 319; Gnostic 18, 264–5; Irish 24, 56, 268; Welsh 142, 214

myths 8–10, 13, 19, 24, 48, 63, 105–6, 109–10, 117, 135, 151, 167, 173, 186, 213, 218, 240, 281, 283, 288, 292, 297–8, 301, 303, 306–7, 320

Nazism 1, 163, 280
necromancy 151, 178, 258
Nitze, W.A. 43, 80–1, 283, 286, 291, 293
Noll, Richard 297–8
Nutt, Alfred 8, 46, 92, 94, 122, 150

occultism 1, 9, 92, 107, 232, 236, 277–83, 288, 290–1, 294, 304, 320
Olschki, Leonardo 122–3
Otherworld 8, 18, 50, 55, 59, 80–1, 105–6, 178, 186, 206, 214, 222, 226, 239, 260, 283, 317
Owen, D.D.R. 254

paganism 1, 9–10, 15, 17, 33, 45–6, 53–55, 57, 61, 66, 81, 83–4, 90, 92, 105, 112, 115, 122, 139, 141–2, 144–5, 151, 164–5, 169, 178, 180, 186, 211, 213, 219, 222, 231, 234, 238–41, 255, 262, 268, 277–9, 283, 289, 291, 293, 304–5, 307, 319; *see also* mystery religions
Partner, Peter 130
Paton, Lucy 17
Pickens, Rupert T. 32–3
Ponceau, Jean-Paul 119, 224, 240
Pound, Ezra 1, 304

Rahn, Otto 169, 174, 279, 294–5, 297, 306, 320
Raine, Kathleen 278
Ravenscroft, Trevor 21, 163–4, 280, 282–3, 304, 320
Rhŷs, John 55, 74, 214
rites 13, 80–1, 167, 187, 277, 283, 286, 288–9, 291, 304, 307
Ritual Theory 1, 8–9, 122, 278, 284, 286, 319
rituals 81, 107, 122, 151, 167, 187, 189, 205, 277, 282–8, 290–1, 293, 302–3, 307, 320
Roquebert, Michel 242
Rudolph, Kurt 304

Serrano, Miguel 170, 174, 295–8, 301, 306–7, 320
Sommer, H. Oskar 193
sorcery 17–8, 20, 60, 189, 220, 229, 235, 275
sovereignty 6, 9–10, 31, 111, 123, 135, 150, 211, 213–4, 241, 264–5, 294, 307, 319
Stein, Walter Johannes 279–80, 282, 320
Steiner, Rudolf 20, 131, 278–81, 304
Stephens, Louise D. 206
Stevenson, W.H. 66
Strubel, Armand 24, 116
Stucco, Guido 307
Surette, Leon 305
Swinburne, Algernon Charles 7

symbolic images 10, 216
symbolism 9, 71, 94, 112, 116, 126, 216, 231–3, 280, 285, 287, 289–91, 296–7, 301, 304–6, 319
symbols 3, 7, 9, 38, 43, 45, 48, 65, 81, 94, 101, 105, 111, 122–3, 126, 130–1, 151, 156, 167, 174, 179, 216, 219, 223, 242, 279–80, 285, 287–90, 293–5, 302–4, 306–7, 319–20; sexual 283, 286–7

Tarot 123, 167, 222, 284–5, 287, 290–1, 305, 320
Tennyson, Alfred 3, 7, 109, 115, 117
Thomas, Neil 107
Tolkien, J.R.R. 48, 123, 256, 304
Toury, Marie-Noëlle 246, 253
traditionalism 116–7, 135–6, 174, 278, 292–5, 306
transubstantiation 24, 94, 106, 117, 229, 237; *see also* miracles

Ullyot, Jonathan 305

Vinaver, Eugene 188, 192, 211

Wagner, Richard 7, 18, 20, 48, 60, 65, 94, 115, 117, 126, 149–50, 162–3, 173, 178, 189, 264, 273, 281, 288, 297, 305
Waite, Arthur Edward 9, 61, 121–3, 141, 205, 222, 278–9, 283, 290–3, 305–6, 320
Walter, Philippe 93, 109, 111, 160, 248, 260
wastelands 4, 10, 17, 19, 27–8, 35–6, 40, 62, 67, 71, 77, 79–80, 84, 95–6, 98, 104, 109, 125, 132, 152, 156, 159, 161–2, 166–8, 175, 190, 193, 211–4, 224–5, 230, 250, 259, 265, 267, 269–73, 275, 277, 283–8, 301–2, 312, 314
Weisthor (Wiligut), Karl Maria 306
Weston, Jessie L. 1, 8–9, 11, 13–4, 17–8, 20, 52–3, 94, 105–7, 122–3, 131, 149, 151, 167, 186–7, 189, 204–5, 209, 222, 231–2, 254, 256, 270–1, 273, 277–9, 282–9, 291, 293, 297, 300, 302, 304–5, 319–20
Williams, Andrea 211
Williams, Charles 123, 278, 304
Williams, Mark 123
Wilson, John C. 306
Wilson, S.R. 275
Winick, Mimi 8–9, 11
Wisdom (Sophia) 18, 65, 111, 117, 123, 130–1, 242, 264–5, 278, 303
witchcraft 47, 132, 216
witches 213
Wroe, Ann 186

Yeats, W.B. 278, 283, 285, 287, 291, 305

Zimmer, Heinrich 28

www.ingramcontent.com/pod-product-compliance
Ingram Content Group UK Ltd.
Pitfield, Milton Keynes, MK11 3LW, UK
UKHW050543150426
5217IPUK00026B/2047